Counselling Skills

The book professionalises counselling through the scientific application of appropriate knowledge and skills at various stages of the counselling process.

With the aim of equipping readers with fundamental and advanced counselling skills, this book:

- Examines a range of key skills from various theories and models of counselling to enable students and professionals to understand the underlying techniques which need to be applied from the time the client approaches the counsellor until the conclusion of the counselling process;
- Sheds light on the complex psychological state of clients to discuss training for a holistic assessment in terms of emotions, cognition, motivation, and behaviour;
- Presents extensive materials that train the students in skills to provide emotional relief to the client, to help the client change from self-defeating negative thoughts to promising positive thinking, enhancing motivation and self-confidence to initiate action;
- Integrates discussions on case studies, live as well as hypothetical examples, traditional and contemporary theories on counselling with the art of communication.

An invaluable guidebook on developing counselling skills, this volume will be of immense interest to students, researchers, teachers, professionals, and practitioners of psychology, behavioural sciences, mental health, counselling, and education.

Meena Hariharan is the Founder Director of the Centre for Health Psychology, University of Hyderabad, India and retired as Professor in the Centre. She is the founder president of Association of Health Psychologists and Chief Editor of *Indian Journal of Health Studies*. She works in the fields of behavioural cardiology, ICU trauma, coping with non-communicable diseases, and resilience studies. Her 35 years' experience in counselling enabled her to contribute to this book.

Usha Chivukula teaches at the Centre for Health Psychology, University of Hyderabad, India. She works in the areas of psychosocial care in intensive care units, behavioural cardiology, community health psychology, and adolescent health. She serves as an executive member of Association of Health Psychologists and is an assistant editor of *Indian Journal of Health Studies*. She has experience of teaching and practicing counselling for over 20 years.

Meera Padhy teaches at the Centre for Health Psychology, University of Hyderabad, India. She has published extensively in the areas of health psychology, developmental psychology, and occupational health psychology. Her research interests include behavioural diabetology, occupational health, social support, leisure, and well-being. She has standardised several psychological tools.

Counselling Skills

Theory and Practice

Meena Hariharan, Usha Chivukula, and
Meera Padhy

Routledge
Taylor & Francis Group
LONDON AND NEW YORK

Cover design image: © Getty Images

First published 2024
by Routledge
4 Park Square, Milton Park, Abingdon, Oxon OX14 4RN

and by Routledge
605 Third Avenue, New York, NY 10158

Routledge is an imprint of the Taylor & Francis Group, an informa business

British Library Cataloguing-in-Publication Data
A catalogue record for this book is available from the British Library

ISBN: 978-1-032-50092-8 (hbk)
ISBN: 978-1-032-60489-3 (pbk)
ISBN: 978-1-003-45941-5 (ebk)

DOI: 10.4324/9781003459415

Typeset in Sabon
by Newgen Publishing UK

Dedicated to

Our teacher

Prof. Adhikari Srikata Dash

Contents

Figures

Tables

About the Authors

Meena Hariharan is the Founder Director of the Centre for Health Psychology, University of Hyderabad and she superannuated as the Professor of the Centre. She completed her MA and Ph.D. from the Centre for Advanced Studies, Utkal University, Odisha, India. She joined the University of Hyderabad in 1992 and has published about 100 articles in peer reviewed journals. She has authored/edited five books that includes a textbook in Health Psychology, *Coping with Life Stress*, *Health Psychology: Contributions to Indian Health System*, *Trauma and Pain Management*, and *Contextualizing Social Science Research*. Prof. Hariharan has been involved in standardizing a number of psychological tools. Along with her team she has evolved the synergy model of Resilience and standardised the Resilience Test Battery, thus enabling resilience to be measured with one comprehensive score. Her research work in the field of Health Psychology covers Behavioural Cardiology, ICU Trauma, Coping with Non-Communicable Diseases, and Resilience Studies. She has guided ten Ph.D. scholars. She is the Founder President of the Association of Health Psychologists and the Chief editor of the *Indian Journal of Health Studies*. She is on the editorial boards of some peer reviewed journals and a member of the Board of Studies in several Universities. Her 35 years' experience in counselling enabled her to contribute to this book.

Usha Chivukula received her doctorate in Psychology from the Centre for Health Psychology, University of Hyderabad, for her research in the area of Psychosocial Care in Intensive Care Units. She is the first Ph.D. from the Centre for Health Psychology. She worked as a faculty member in St. Francis Degree College for Women, Hyderabad, before joining as the faculty in the Centre for Health Psychology, University of Hyderabad. She has extended her research into the areas of Behavioural Cardiology, Community Health Psychology, and Child and Adolescent Health. She is guiding five research scholars and is the co-editor of the book *Health Psychology: Contributions to Indian Health System* (Routledge, 2023). She has published more than 20 articles in national and international journals. She has contributed substantially in standardizing a number of psychological tools. She is the life and executive member of the Association of Health Psychologists and the assistant editor of the *Indian Journal of Health Studies*. She has experience of teaching and practicing counselling for the past two decades. She was one of the core members of the team from Association of Health psychologists which started the first helpline for Counselling Services in India during COVID-19 pandemic.

Meera Padhy received her Ph.D. degree from Utkal University in 1996. She was a recipient of UGC JRF fellowship during her Ph.D. She has been associated with the

Centre for Health Psychology, University of Hyderabad, India since its inception in 2007. She has published extensively in the area of Health Psychology, Developmental Psychology, and Occupational Psychology in national and international journals of repute and has presented at many conferences. She is a co-editor of the book *Health Psychology: Contributions to Indian Health System* (Routledge, 2023). She, along with her team, has standardised a number of psychological tools that have contributed immensely to the field of research. Three scholars have completed their Ph.D.s under her guidance and many more are still working with her. Her work has been recognised with awards like the best Health Psychologist, IPERA in 2013 and best paper presenter award at the 21st and 52nd International Conference of the Indian Academy of Applied Psychology in 2017. She is the life and executive member of Association of Health Psychologists and one of the associate editors of the *Indian Journal of Health Studies*. Her research interests include Behavioural Diabetology, Occupational Health, Social Support, Leisure, and Well-being.

Foreword

Malavika Kapur

Visiting Professor, National Institute of Advanced Studies, Indian Institute of Science Campus

This book on Counselling Skills is indeed timely, melding ancient Indian and contemporary Western concepts and practices in counselling. In this book, all techniques are empathic. This is an admirable bias as far as I can see. The chapters are organised sequentially to provide the students with the skills to be used from the time the client approaches the counsellor until the termination. The examples and cases cited make it interesting for the students.

The book consists of 11 chapters; the first is an introduction to counselling and the second chapter is an excellent overview of most of the commonly employed theories and approaches to counselling. Chapter 3 is on building the counselling relationship and Chapter 4 focuses on pre-counselling skills. Chapters 5 to 8 segmentally deal with the themes of skills for providing emotional relief, cognitive restructuring, motivation and restructuring behavioural change. Chapter 9 focuses on termination. Chapter 10 deals with counselling in varied settings and the eleventh and final chapter focuses most importantly on assessment and documentation.

Chapter 1: Introduction to Counselling. The first chapter being an introductory one is brief. It starts with the notions of what is counselling and what is not. The authors term commonplace counselling as a 'dirty dozen'. However, they may be considered as 'supportive techniques' by some practitioners. The chapter traces the history of counselling in the West as well as in India. It is brought to our attention that counselling has been the Indian ethos for more than 5,000 years, alluding to the counselling offered to Arjuna by Krishna in the Bhagavad Gita by many Indian thinkers.

Chapter 2: Theories and Approaches in Counselling. This is the longest chapter where the five waves of approaches are illustrated in a simple manner. It starts with psychoanalysis and proceeds to the variants. The chapter diligently covers various theories. The Adlerian approach is explained covering the concept of style of life from early years, adoption of the growth model, social interest, inferiority superiority complex, birth order and relations to siblings. Behaviour therapy is explained on the basis of various learning theories propounded by pioneers like Pavlov, Skinner, and Bandura. The chapter systematically links different theories to techniques such as systematic desensitisation, aversion therapy, exposure therapy using different contingency management, techniques, token economy and other procedures. The chapter elaborates on Cognitive Behaviour Therapy (CBT), Acceptance Commitment Therapy (ACT) by Steven Hayes, Dialectical Behaviour Therapy (DBT) by Marsha Linehan, Gestalt Therapy by Fredrick and Laura Perls and Paul Goodman, Person Centred Counselling, the Humanistic approach of Carl Rogers, Existential therapies and Reality therapy and post-modern approaches. The chapter ends with a section on Buddhism. The reader would find the Western approaches to counselling provide a good overview but the section on Buddhism is riveting, scholarly and saturated with details. It is a must-read section. The chapter ends by offering models of integration of approaches, in short, with 'technical eclecticism' with some models of approaches. The high point is its simplicity which makes it novice reader-friendly.

The next section contains Chapters 3 to 8, which together provide the essentials of the counselling process with illustrations, narratives and dialogues of real-life counselling sessions. This is more essential than any other training in counselling.

Chapter 3: Building a Partnership. Chapter 3 is an attempt to delineate the effective characteristics of a counsellor. Rogers' conditions for therapeutic alliance are succinctly described. Empathy emerges as the most essential characteristic but requires a prerequisite setting up of boundaries with the client. This is highlighted with several pertinent questions to illustrate how to manage it with several supportive techniques. The chapter explains how a counsellor can use Millar's Pyramid Model of Knowledge to enhance performance. The other attributes of the counsellor including psychological flexibility, and non-judgemental acceptance are elaborated. The need for personal counselling for counsellors is a pointed observation that highlights the importance of self-care. In the Indian context of an extraordinary range of diversity of geography, language, social class, caste, religion, gender, ethnicity, mainstream and tribal heritage, and isolation, the counsellor needs to be competent to appreciate and be embedded in the biopsychosocial and cultural contexts of the client. This aspect of the multicultural competence of the counsellor has been beautifully illustrated using the acronym of RESPECTFUL. Obstacles to counselling in the form of Resistance and Reluctance are highlighted. The focus is on the soft skills of counselling and not the rigid guidelines offered by many schools. In addition, adding a component 'empowering with building resiliency' could have been brought in at this juncture.

Chapter 4: Pre-Counselling Skills. These are described under 'attending' and responding skills with physical and psychological presence. Communication skills and non-verbal recognition skills are essential components of Egan's contribution. A comparison of skills by Carkhuff, Ivey, and Egan's models is described. The environmental factors were not overlooked in the models of these schemes which accentuates the universal requirement that there should be no disruptions. 'Distance and touching' between the clients and counsellors need to be nuanced and adhered to the Indian context with cultural properties. Non-verbal communication is well supported by Shakespearian and Mehrabian quotes. To sum up, the emphasis on empathy, and the careful illustrations of a real-life conversation between the client and the counsellor light up the path of novice counsellors.

Chapter 5: Skills for Emotional Relief. There are excellent illustrative narratives of providing emotional relief. Two examples stand out, one of a doctor being falsely accused of molestation where the entire story is narrated, while in the second only the initial emotion released by the woman client is shown. It leaves the reader with a curiosity as to what eventually happens. In illustrative stories, the reader's need for closure needs to be kept in mind. There is yet another complete story of a bereaved COVID widow which is poignantly portrayed demonstrating the complexities of emotional relief. The narratives remain the strength of this chapter. Play therapy and bibliotherapy are recommended. While speaking about music therapy, the authors have a box to show of how different ragas are linked to different emotions. The reader needs such innovative approaches by the authors in their own cultural context. The chapter is a delight to read.

Chapter 6: Cognitive Restructuring. The chapter provides the theoretical background of Gestalt Therapy, Existential approach, and Cognitive Behaviour Therapy (CBT) to explain cognitive restructuring. Cognitive distortions are described with concreteness of cognitive distancing of day-to-day examples. These detailed case studies reveal known techniques such as probing and challenging and other activities such as maintaining a cognitive diary, engaging in dialogue, evidence testing, statement reorganisation, and so on. The chapter though brief is very informative and offers excellent practical guidelines.

Chapter 7: Skills for Motivating the Client. This is often an overlooked ingredient in counselling, though it is very powerful social media influence used by Godmen and motivational speakers. A counsellor works through motivating visualizing a positive future, and formulating goals to enhance motivation. Abundant illustrations are the strength of this chapter.

Chapter 8: Skills for Behaviour Change. This important chapter is indeed a novel way of clustering these core chapters. It discusses the need for behavioural change in three realms that are inefficient, deficient, and pathological behaviour. It highlights that the natural environments, that give 'pleasure' to persist or give 'relief from pain', tend to be self-sustaining. The formats are given in boxes in a clear manner and the detailed presentation in the field of alcohol addiction and childhood problems, makes the process clearly understood by the reader. The interventions are individually tailored to solve the specific problem of a specific person with unique characteristics of the person and his environment. It is not a 'one-size-fits-all' solution.

Chapter 9: Winding up and Termination. The chapter rightly ties up loose ends in the processes of therapy. This should be part of planning in the initial part of the counselling: the checklist of what needs to be examined in the light of what has been achieved. The case illustrations reveal a range of situations encountered in the termination stages. Several issues highlighted as unsatisfactory are client dependency and learned helplessness, not being able to transfer skills learnt to real situations, procrastination, natural decay, entropy, along with relapse and 'rationalisation' an unconscious defense mechanism. The client needs to be prepared for these exigencies. However, a word of caution is that among Indian patients, termination is often an exception due to failures in follow-up in almost all settings.

Chapter 10: Counselling in Different Settings. Counselling settings vary widely, but the very nature of the setting is an important ingredient. These could be in individual or group settings, marital and pre-marital counselling, grief counselling, community, industrial, educational, and healthcare settings, and counselling for special needs populations and counselling during a disaster.

Though there are generic techniques described earlier, each setting needs a unique cluster of approaches, methods, and tools. This section is covered briefly yet with examples which are very helpful. School counselling is the major topic and justifiably so. Theories of career counselling provide important details of the works of pioneer career counsellors. Marriage and family counselling are dealt with briefly but with illustrations. Family therapy and its variants are described. Counselling in the health setting is an important area. The critical issue of modifiable and non-modifiable medical factors is covered in Box 10.1. The use of support groups is highlighted and the role of crisis intervention too has been noted. Heath Psychology should be a major concern of policymakers, administrators, and social welfare agencies, especially in countries where healthcare is beset with problems at the grassroots level. This needs the attention of researchers and practitioners alike.

Chapter 11: Assessment and Documentation. This is the most important aspect of helping processes. In addition to the interview, assessment forms are an essential part and give baseline information about the client to build and carry out strategies and finally to examine if the goals have been achieved.

Though the chapter is covered briefly, it needs to be read diligently by the reader, scholar, and researcher. The second part gives a gamut of assessment tools, developed by the authors and their teams. These are well-standardised, validated, and ready to use. This is a remarkable achievement in the Indian setting. This is a major research contribution of the authors and their teams. All the scales are worth examining in detail and using for their research in child and adolescent areas of development, mental health, and counselling needs for assessment.

To conclude, this is a remarkable, pragmatic, simple instructive compilation anchored to academic and applied counselling. It would be a good textbook in counselling for novice trainee counsellors.

Preface

The question whether counselling is a science or an art may elicit responses that lack convergence. For some, who feel that communication constitutes the core of the skill, it may be construed as an art. Others who see the need for a systematic approach to the whole process, with a strong foundation of theoretical understanding of human psychology, it may appear as a science. However, for the authors of this book, counselling is an essential synergy of science and art. The application of skills in counselling demands scientific precision in perception, interpretation, and diagnostic skills as well as the right communication skills combining verbal and non-verbal messages. The right composition of skills as well as the scientific approach is what makes a counsellor competent and successful. Training novices in these is a challenge. It calls for good resource material. This book is a modest attempt by the authors towards providing a good resource that emphasises the professionalism involved in counselling.

The void of a good resource book in counselling skills was felt by each of us teaching the course at various levels. This came out in one of our casual discussions. The fact that all three of us have been independently and simultaneously documenting the case studies and the experiences was something that helped us team up for this challenging project.

This book is intended for undergraduate and postgraduate students who are in the process of getting inducted into counselling and for those who wish to be thoroughly trained in counselling skills. This book also serves as a good resource for practicing counsellors. One thing certain about this book is that anyone who reads this would understand the professional approach to this serious process called counselling. Years of research by several psychologists across the globe have contributed immensely to the field. Still, we feel that we are yet to be perfect in this profession. This book is an attempt to bring into one volume the contributions of several eminent psychologists and apply it to the context.

The chapters in the book are hierarchically organised to educate the reader systematically on the skills to be applied from the time the client approaches the counsellor till the time of termination of the session. In a way, the training involves a carefully planned expedition into the world of counselling involving a gentle hand-holding of the student. Every chapter has examples at every possible step so that the student understands and visualises the application of the specific skill explained. While discussing the responses of the counsellors in contexts, not only the right responses but the possible wrong responses are also brought in and discussed, so that the students alongside learning 'what is correct' also learn 'what should not be'. We made a special effort to fit in the cases we have handled at appropriate places so that the learners will have exposure to the culture-specific problems of the clients. While planning the book, we decided that it should be of use to a novice as well as a student who has basic knowledge in counselling. Any student or practitioner at the stage of building a relation with the client, applying pre-counselling skills, at the time of the client releasing emotions, at the stage where the counsellor's goal is cognitive restructuring, invoking motivation to act, implementing new behaviour in the real life situation, or trying to end the process of counselling may have doubts about whether he/she is on the right track. Reading through the pages of this book can provide the needed clarification to the counsellor.

The book is divided into 11 chapters. Chapter 1 provides an introduction to counselling skills. The chapter first highlights what is not counselling and then goes to explain what is counselling. It discusses the origin of counselling in the Western world as well as in India. In the Indian context, the origin of counselling is as old as Srimad Bhagavad Gita, with 18 chapters and 700 *shlokas* (verses). This part of the manuscript is the conversation between Lord Sri Krishna and Arjuna in a situation of battlefield when Arjuna in utter distress seeks guidance from Lord Sri Krishna. The chapter also highlights the structure of the Indian family where the counselling process was integrated into the system so that until three decades ago, the need for formal counselling was not felt. Chapter 2 deals extensively with the theoretical foundations of counselling. The chapter provides an intensive analysis of all major theories of counselling starting from the classical theories to the theories developed in contemporary times. The detailed sketch of the theories will be of great use for students who are getting oriented to counselling. Care has been taken to provide a visual representation of every theory so that the students can comprehend the salient features of every theory. Chapter 3 refers to the skills used by the counsellor in building a professional relationship with the client. It emphasises the need to establish a partnership with the client. This is essential in inculcating client responsibility into the process of counselling. The chapter emphasises that counselling is a two-way process where both the counsellor and the client will have to play their parts effectively to optimise the outcome. The role of the counsellor in protecting the rights and the dignity of the client, following the ethical guidelines and understanding the client's sensitive position is highlighted as the skills for building a partnership relationship with the client. Chapter 4 deals with pre-counselling skills. These skills are essential prerequisites for the counsellor. They refer to the counsellor's predisposition; the basic skills of attending, listening, and responding to the client with empathy enable the client to feel 'understood' so that he/she proceeds with further communication. Chapter 5 explains the counselling skills needed to facilitate the client to release emotions. Often the client may not be able to ventilate their emotions either because of inhibition, or due to their psychological condition. Empathy and probing are the two essential skills that help in facilitating the expression of the client. In cases where the client's inhibition is high, therapeutic interventions such as music therapy, play, or art therapy can be applied. The chapter goes deep into the various contexts and degrees of emotions experienced by the client. Chapter 6 refers to the skills used in cognitive restructuring. Probing and challenging are the prominent techniques that are effective in bringing cognitive restructuring. The goals, contexts of challenging, techniques of challenging and the client's possible reactions to challenging are discussed at length. Chapter 7 deals with the skills to motivate the client. The problem of driving the client to action is a huge challenge for a counsellor. The chapter discusses various techniques that guide the client to visualise a better future to help the client chalk out a definite agenda. The chapter lays specific emphasis on techniques like motivational interviewing that functions as an active propeller that nudges the client to action. Chapter 8 describes the need for behaviour change and its sustenance. The chapter discusses three contexts where a client's behaviour change becomes necessary. Skills to be applied under each context vary from the simple application of reinforcement in day-to-day life to the administration of behaviour therapy. Each technique and the context is carefully analysed. The techniques of evaluation through the behavioural balance sheet and application of force-field analysis are described by citing cases. Chapter 9 is devoted to various minute steps while winding up or terminating counselling. All protective, precautionary measures and follow-up principles are touched upon. Chapter 10 describes counselling in various settings. Though the principles and values of counselling are universal, the settings in which counselling has to take place may demand some amount of flexibility in a counsellor. For example, the techniques adopted in group counselling differ from those used for individual counselling or marital counselling. The chapter brings to light the various settings of counselling and the theories supporting those. Examples and case studies relevant to the context enriches the chapter. The eleventh chapter is the last chapter of the book. This is enriched with the description of procedures adopted in the documentation process. Documentation of the case history, assessments, procedures, prognosis and summary constitutes an important element in professionalizing counselling. The chapter extensively explains these processes. In addition, the chapter also provides a variety of general assessment tools developed and standardised by the authors. The assessment tools are provided with manuals for ready reference and use by the students, researchers and practitioners.

As indicated earlier, this book is a modest attempt to provide a comprehensive package of all the skills used in the process of counselling. One may adopt any approach to counselling, such as the Humanistic, Behaviouristic, or Cognitive approach, but the skills to be applied to attain various goals will be the same. This book talks about goal-oriented skills at various stages of counselling. We hope this will be of great use to the students, teachers, practitioners, and researchers.

Meena Hariharan
Usha Chivukula
Meera Padhy

Acknowledgements

A textbook of this type was possible by pooling the experiences of all three authors. The examples and cases cited constitute an important part of this textbook on counselling skills. Every session with the clients and every class with the students has been a learning experience. At the outset, we thank all the clients who have contributed immensely in enriching our experience. Every batch of students that we taught has been a challenging experience. The classroom interactions have triggered many ideas, and helped in organizing our thoughts in such a way that some cases cited in the book are discussed in the classroom. We wish to thank all the students who through their quest for learning sustained our passion for the profession.

This book would not have been possible without the support of the successive Vice-Chancellors of University of Hyderabad. One of them, Prof. Syed E Hasnain was instrumental in starting the Centre for Health Psychology in the University with a course in PG Diploma in Counselling Psychology and provided all support in the growth of the Centre. The others helped immensely by facilitating the much- needed time for the authors to write the book. We owe our gratitude to all of them.

While we could prepare the manuscript of the book, our team of Ph.D. scholars happily volunteered to read the chapters and give critical feedback, proof-read the chapters, and help us with all the technical support. We thank the Ph.D. scholars working with all the three authors.

The illustrations of the book 'add spice' to the content. Anupam Arunachalam, who extended timely support with illustrations deserves a big 'thank you' from us.

There is one institution in India which can either make everything possible or impossible – that is the institution of the family. Needless to mention the understanding and encouragement extended by our families during our year-long engagement in the project of writing this book. They never minded our absence from family gatherings, missing functions and festivals, deferring visits, rushing back home in the middle of a party and many more actions that were inevitable in honouring the timelines. We are grateful to them.

This book is the outcome with the support of all those mentioned in this page and some not mentioned here. We bow down to all with humility.

1 Introduction to Counselling

When you are walking on a busy road, you walk through umpteen number of stimuli. People walking, talking, laughing, working, crying, fighting, shouting, screaming, falling down, etc. Of the human actions mentioned, what is more likely to catch your attention? You may not stop or turn your head to have a second glance at the people engaged in the first four actions, but there is a high possibility of the last five actions of anyone on the road catching your attention. Why so? Because, the first four actions are considered 'natural' for a human being. But, crying, fighting, shouting, screaming, or falling down are viewed as a deviation from the normal. Anything that is not normal is bound to draw our attention. The inference that can be drawn from this is that being unhappy, having conflicts, and being angry are not the natural state of human being. On the other hand, being happy, harmonious, and peaceful are the natural state of a human being. The constant effort of an individual is to attain and sustain this state. This, though it cannot be expected to be a constant state, is something that an individual strives for one's own well-being. This is beautifully and precisely expressed in Hindu scriptures which states that the natural state of human being is *Sat Chit Ananda* (also known as *Satchitananda*) that translates to True, Conscious Bliss. It can be stated that the nature of conscious self is that of *Ananda* or bliss. This is what is the state of equilibrium of the original state of 'self'. All human efforts are driven towards sustaining this state of equilibrium. However, actions of one's own self, perception of actions of others towards one and acts of physical, social, and psychological environment impacts a human being in such a way that this equilibrium is disturbed. When this happens, the individual suffers. The suffering drives one to action that restores the homeostasis. Can the individual be always successful in restoring the homeostasis by mitigating the suffering? How long does the suffering last? What happens when the suffering lasts either because the efforts by self are inadequate or when one undergoes suffering for a prolonged period? When it is physical suffering, one goes for medical intervention so that the treatment regimen restores health. But what if the suffering involves psychological distress manifesting sadness, anger, aggression, frustration, helplessness, hopelessness, or dejection and so on? Such conditions also are considered unnatural and deviation from the original state of blissfulness calling for appropriate intervention to restore the psychological equilibrium to the state of *Sat chit Ananda*. Thus, when the individual fails in one's own personal attempts in restoring the state of happiness and effective life, one needs psychological intervention from a professional. This intervention is Counselling.

DOI: 10.4324/9781003459415-1

What is Counselling and What IS NOT?

In order to have a clear understanding of what counselling is, one must first know what is not counselling. This sieving process helps the new learner discard all the misnomers about counselling. This is considered an essential step forward because the term counselling is one of the most misused and abused in the regular vocabulary, which in a way is responsible for degrading this scientific process to unscientific randomness. Very often when parents want their incorrigible children admonished, they are seen making a statement like 'This guy needs a good counselling'. In educational institutions from schools to universities, teachers are asked to 'counsel' their erring wards meaning that they need good advice. Students qualifying for the common entrance examination for professional courses are found to be put through 'counselling' where they are provided with information on vacant seats in various courses in different institutions and are required to make their decision 'fast' and pay their fees to complete the admission process. Parents sometimes interact with their children explaining to them about moral conduct and family values and choose to label such sessions 'counselling'. The principals in school assemblies spend five to ten minutes sermonising students based on a major or minor undesirable incident in the school or in society wherein they discuss various repercussions of it and document it as a 'counselling' session. A teacher or a parent communicates his/her unhappiness over the child's lack of hygiene by criticising or comparing the child with those who are very hygiene conscious and give it the nomenclature of 'counselling' without hesitation. It is imperative to state that none of the above qualify as counselling.

Since the term 'counselling' is thus misconstrued, people's expectation of counselling has been along these lines. The realisation that this is not what happens in a counselling session gives rise to two reactions – one of awe and a correction in the existing schema and the second is rejection and ridicule of the actual process. Way back in the 1980s an attender at an educational institution decided to admit his only son to the kindergarten of another school rather than the one where he was employed, which was known as a Model Preschool in the whole city and where the middle class and upper class desired to admit their children. When asked why he chose another more expensive school rather than the best where he worked, his reply stunned the management. He said 'what sort of school is this? The teachers never use the cane to correct the child; not even a reprimand; don't make the kids recite the numbers and alphabet......I don't think my son can learn anything where there is no fear....'. This reply originates from the concept of schooling this man has been nurturing either due to his personal experience or because everyone around him believed so. The same can be extrapolated to the outcomes of misnomers about counselling. Continuous misuse of the term is likely to have created a schema that needs correction. Hence, we need to elaborate on what is not counselling to 'clean the slate' and start afresh on the correct definition, meaning and scope of counselling.

For the sake of a deep impression in the minds of students the 'Dirty Dozen' that has no place in the counsellor's interactions with the counselee is listed in Box 1.1.

Figure 1.1 What Is NOT Counselling

Box 1.1 The Dirty Dozen in Counselling

Solving Problems
Advising
Moralising
Passing Judgements
Directing
Blaming/Complaining
Criticising
Admonishing
Explaining
Reassuring
Befriending
Labelling/Branding

One striking characteristic of the dirty dozen mentioned in the box is that they happen as an 'instance' that may be called a 'one time event/occurrence'. For example, advising, moralising, judging, or reassuring can happen as a response that lasts for a short time. Hence, they are onetime occurrences. On the contrary, counselling is a process.

Definition of Counselling

In the year 2010, The American Counselling Association met in Pittsburg and converged on a comprehensive definition of Counselling. It stated 'Counselling is a professional relationship that empowers diverse individuals, families, and groups to accomplish mental health, education, and career goals' (Kaplan et al., 2014). This definition was accepted largely by various professional bodies in America on the ground that the definition is broad and comprehensive bringing every dimension under a single umbrella. While the definition certainly covers all areas of counselling and the dyadic relationship between the counsellor and the client, the definition does not speak about 'what goes into counselling'. The authors in an attempt to fill this gap define counselling thus:

> *Counselling is **a process** where the counsellor helps the **client or a group of clients** to uninhibitedly **express their feelings, experiences, and behaviours,** and facilitate **identification of their strengths, weaknesses, opportunities and resources** so as to obtain a **cognitive reorientation** towards the problem, invoke the **motivation to work on their problems, manage the emotions** effectively and **initiate the behavioural change** that contributes to **cope effectively to minimise the stress, restore equilibrium and optimise productivity in life.***

The above definition brings in the salient features of counselling as a professional service as against the dirty dozens mentioned earlier. The following features need to be highlighted in this definition:

1. Counselling is a process but not a one-time event. Thus, in a single stroke it excludes a number of misconstrued features such as advising, moralising, etc.

2. The process of counselling may involve a single client or a group. This takes care of the individual and group counselling setting.
3. The process of counselling facilitates expression of feelings, experiences,. and behaviour. This part highlights the preliminary outcomes in the 'process' of counselling
4. One of the objectives of the counsellor is to help the client identify the internal strengths, weaknesses, as well as the opportunities and the available resources. The counsellor helps the client to identify them from what the client expressed in terms of feelings, experiences and resources. By delineating this, the popular phrase that the counsellor helps the client help himself/herself is reiterated.
5. A counsellor helps the client have a cognitive reorientation. When the client, after one's own expression of feelings, experience, and behaviour related to the problem is aided by the counsellor to identify one's own strengths, missed opportunities, and unused resources, to which he/she was blind earlier, is doing nothing but restructuring one's own cognition about the problem.
6. The counsellor, during the process of counselling places the facts narrated by the client in such a way that through cognitive restructuring invokes the client motivation to work on the problem in a way different from the earlier methods. The cognitive reorientation helps the client to take an alternative perspective of the problem, which now emanates new hope that invokes his/her motivation to rework on the problem.
7. The counselling process helps the client to manage emotions in an effective way. When the client approaches the counsellor, he/she is likely to be in an emotionally sensitive or fragile state. This is a natural consequence of ambiguity of problem perception, frustration due to failure in handling the problem deftly that add to the emotional turmoil originating from the initial encounter with the problem itself. To enable the client to work on the concrete problem, it is essential to handle the emotional turmoil of the client. This is done through facilitating expression of one's own feelings and experiences, to channel emotions in a meaningful way.
8. Counselling, by rekindling motivation, drives the client to initiate a behaviour towards bringing about a positive change in the stressful situation.
9. The purpose of this new behavioural initiative is to minimise the existing stress and restore the equilibrium.
10. Once the stress is minimised and the equilibrium restored, life's productivity goes up.

Thus, the final goal of counselling is to help the client release the emotions, develop a new perspective of the problem, invoke motivation, and resume action with a new hope to minimise stress and enhance a positive emotional state, and productivity in life. In other words, the final goal of counselling is to help the client minimise life's stress and cope effectively so as to optimise productivity at personal, social, and professional levels. This is true in any professional counselling setting – be it an individual setting for enhancing well-being, school setting to handle the academic performance, context of marital discord, a parental counselling in the context of a child's delayed milestones, or a family in the context of handling a terminally ill patient. Whatever be the context, the final goal of counselling, to optimise the well-being and productivity remains unchanged.

History of Counselling

What is the genesis of counselling? Was counselling conceptualised in the beginning the way it is practiced today? How did it evolve to this form and method? These are the common questions that may be triggered in the minds of students introduced to the subject. We will briefly track the origin and evolution of counselling.

Evolution of Counselling in the West

Counselling as a discipline in the West is the outcome of the contributions of many branches of knowledge that includes philosophy, religion, psychology, education, social work, family studies, and health sciences. Hence, it took some time to establish its identity. It is only in the past 50 years that counselling has been conceptualised as a special branch of study that includes practice and research.

According to Kottler and Shepard (2008), if counselling is equated to 'healing the feelings' then the religious leaders such as Moses, Mohammad, and Buddha should be considered as the first to introduce counselling to the world. A similar purpose was served by philosophers like Lao-tzu, Confucius, Socrates, Plato, and Aristotle. It was Hippocrates about 2,000 years ago who, by advocating diagnostic interviews and understanding the complete life history of the patients prior to initiating treatment process, actually set the path for counselling.

Later in the early 1890s Freud, through the introduction of psychoanalysis popularised the concept of a 'talking cure'. Talking cure referred to sick people sharing their painful experiences, ventilating their feelings, and reaching the point of catharsis that provided them with relief. Freud had a huge following that included Adler, Jung, and Anna Freud. In later years though many of them branched out, the basic foundation of a 'talking cure' was not disputed by any of them. Thus, by giving a scientific fervour to therapeutic counselling, Freud became the pioneer of creating the first generation of counsellors. Later on, contributions of the Gestalt Psychologists on the one hand and Behaviourists on the other strengthened the approach to counselling by providing essential nurturance. However, the basic idea of Freud that was founded on the principle of healing through talking continued to be the central theme in counselling. Even today the concept is popular where it is believed that *Dukh* (Misery) is reduced by sharing. The contributions of William James (1842–1910) who described a human being as a combination of emotions, thought, reason, and action lay the foundation for the counselling from the perspective of what we now describe as emotional ventilation, cognitive functioning, and behavioural change. It is his contributions towards 'pragmatism' that paved the path for assessment techniques in counselling.

Facilitated by the tools of assessment, and coinciding with the industrial revolution, the early 20th Century identified the need for counselling in areas other than health. Frank Parson (1909) deserves the credit of applying counselling in the area of vocational choice. He made a very objective and professional approach in matching the individual's aptitudes, interests, and needs to the needs of human skills in industry through the application of assessments. This can be considered as the second important milestone in the history of counselling that gave rise to the emergence of 'Career Guidance'. This service started to apply in schools where students, based on their aptitude, were given inputs on the type of employment that would fit their abilities and interest. This set in motion the movement for educational and vocational guidance which ascribed 'professionalism' to counselling services. In the course of time the testing process was introduced in defence and other crucial areas of employment. However, the educational and guidance services assumed an important role in counselling for more than half a century in the West.

During the mid-20th Century, when bio-medical approach and mental health needs were significant concerns, Carl Rogers (1902–1987) came with his observation that all individuals who faced emotional turmoil cannot be branded as mentally ill. The majority of them going through emotional problems just need a nudge through creation of a therapeutic relationship that provides a secure environment. He came up with the important concept of unconditional positive regard for the patient (who was called the client), a basic requirement for building a relationship and building a safe environment. This approach advocated that the process of counselling should follow the client's direction, with the client assuming an active role and the counsellor playing a supportive role providing clarifications where needed by the client. Client-Centered Counselling propagated by Carl Rogers was embraced by practitioners and trainers under the banner of 'humanistic approach'. This continued to be practiced till the 1970s.

The limited role of counsellors and many other aspects in Rogerian approach faced scrutiny from the cognitive (Ellis, 1962; Beck, 1967) and behaviour therapists who emphasised on the significance of thinking and later added the behavioural aspect to it that led to the emergence of cognitive behaviour therapy. Carkhuff and Berenson (1977) attempted to standardise the process of counselling and thus bring more order into the role of counsellors. They argued that counsellors like any other professionals must be equipped with the necessary skills to be applied in the counselling process. These skills were to be standardised and applied so as to bring in the reliability factor to counselling process. This movement brought a new found objectivity to the process of counselling. Counselling skills training gained importance and various skills of counselling were identified, defined and techniques to assess these skills were developed. Thus, the need for training in counselling skills gathered prominence in the field. This remained an important land mark in qualifying for the profession of counselling. Counsellors in contemporary times are focused on applying context appropriate skills irrespective of the model adopted. Counsellors now have a wide choice of models to adopt, including Psychodynamic, Cognitive, Cognitive-behavioural, Humanistic, Gestalt, Transactional Analysis, Developmental, Reality, and Ivey models. However, the common factor accepted by counsellors across the models are the skills to be learned, mastered, and applied. There are counsellors who go for an eclectic approach. Box 1.2 summarises the evolution of counselling in the West

Box 1.2 Summary of Major Landmarks in Counselling

1	Hippocrates	Diagnostic interviews preceding treatment
2	Freud	Talking cure
3	William James	Pragmatism and assessment tools
4	Frank Parson	Vocational guidance
5	Carl Rogers	Humanistic approach
6	Albert Ellis, Aaron Beck	Cognitive/behavioural approach
7	Robert Carkhuff	Skill development in counsellors and standardisation of skills

Counselling Services in India

There is a need to explain in detail the Indian origin of counselling, which is Srimad Bhagavad Gita over 5,000 years ago. This is a perfect example of counselling where Krishna, the Counsellor responded only when Arjuna, the counselee sought his intervention. First of all, Krishna allowed Arjuna to express his feelings, experiences, and behaviour completely, paying undivided attention to him. This is the first skill of any counsellor. Second, Krishna neither decided for Arjuna nor did he solve his problem, but he provided a cognitive reorientation to Arjuna by helping him identify the reality which was blinded by Arjuna's emotions. He placed all the options before Arjuna and allowed him to make an informed choice. Krishna played a perfect supportive role without allowing Arjuna to become dependent on him. Arjuna, caught in a value conflict looked to Krishna to extricate him from the dilemma of destruction of his own kin in the battle for upholding his *Dharma* (duty) towards the kingdom and the people. The following paragraph explains the situation when Arjuna, the counselee sought the help of Krishna as the counsellor, just as a client approaching the counsellor expresses one's stressful encounter and the symptoms and the despair and anguish Arjuna did pour out to Sri Krishna.

> A despondent Arjuna on seeing his own cousins and relatives as his opponents in the battlefield expressed his despair to Krishna in so many words that expressed his emotional distraught manifested in physical and mental disequilibrium. He said to Krishna 'seeing these my kinsmen, collected here prompted by war, my limbs fail me, my mouth is parched'.
>
> (Swami Chidbhavananda, 1965, p. 99)

He further said 'My body quivers and my hair stands on end. The bow *Gandiva* slips from my hand and my skin burns all over. I am unable to stand; my mind whirls as it were; and Kesava, I see adverse omens' (Swami Chidbhavananda, 1965, p. 100).

The above lines from Arjuna clearly depict the physical and psychological reactions of his stressful encounter. But only when Arjuna explicitly sought the intervention did Sri Krishna start laying down the options 'My nature is weighed down with the taint of feeble-mindedness; my understanding is confused as to duty. I entreat you, say definitely what is good for me. I am your disciple. Do instruct me who have taken refuge in you'.

Again, it may be observed that this is often the typical characteristic of a counselee, to expect the counsellor to instruct, direct and do things for him/her.

The unblinding process of counselling started when Krishna addressed Arjuna by bringing to his notice that despondence is uncharacteristic of him. He spoke to Arjuna saying

> *Kutasthva Kasmalamidam Vishame Samupasthitam*
> *Anaryajushtam Aswargyam Akeertikaramarjuna*
>
> (Bhagavad Gita, Chapter 2, Verse 2; trans. 'From where did you get this dejection at a time of crisis? This is unworthy, unholy and disreputable')

Further, in verse 3 Krishna said

> *Kshudram Hridayadaurbalyam Tyaktvothishta parantapa*
>
> (Bhagavad Gita, , Chapter b2, Verse 3, Line 2; trans. 'raise above this petty weakness of heart (read weak emotions)')

It may be observed from the responses of Sri Krishna that his approach to unblinding is through challenging with an element of direction. What is to be noted here are the counselling skills used.

It is important to mention here that the approach to counselling has to differ depending on the cultural ethos. Indian culture being highly affiliation oriented, certain liberties with the other person is allowed and appreciated while Western culture values individual privacy and hence any direction is viewed as an intrusion into individual privacy. Until recently directions from the wise has been considered a privilege even among the urban middle class, while it still continues in rural India.

In later pages, while responding to various questions of Arjuna, Krishna placed several options for the way of life for an individual, from which one may adopt the one most suitable. This is where the counselee has the liberty to create one's own agenda to pursue life's goal. What the West advocated in their counselling model in later part of the 20th Century was already being practiced 5,000 years ago in India. However, the variation in this counselling is to suit the cultural context of India, which is essential in serving its purpose.

There have been observations from scholars in the field of psychology who identified the treasure of Bhagavad Gita as a great source of counselling and psychotherapy. Sharma (2014) and Osho (2011a, 2011b) endorsed that Bhagavad Gita has adequate resources to be the text book of counselling.

The second example of the existence of counselling in India is in an educational setting. The ancient Indian education practiced *Gurukula* system (where the disciples resided with the family of the teacher for years until the completion of their education). Here, the teacher and his wife were responsible for the overall development of the student. Effective counselling from the couple helped the students overcome all developmental hurdles in the process of education. Education in the traditional Indian system referred to preparing one for life. One obvious example of successful counselling process in an educational set up is that of *Panchatantra*. This is the process of counselling that used modelling as the approach. This refers to the stories told by Vishnu Sharma, an octogenarian Brahman to the three sons of the king of Amarashakti who were not only low in intellectual abilities but also had an aversion to formal education. Vishnu Sharma by narrating interesting stories of the animal characters communicated the practical ways of life to the three princes in such a way that the princes gained a new insight into life through cognitive reorientation, and evolved as effective and productive progeny of the king. If the purpose of counselling is to optimise life's productivity and efficiency, Vishnu Sharma's interventions to the three princes helped to develop them as effective and productive human beings. Counselling in a school set up which is recognised and practised in the contemporary Western world has thus been an integral part of education in ancient Indian *Gurukula* system.

The structure of schooling in ancient India and the family structure until as recently as a generation ago never felt the need for formal counselling as the support was inbuilt into the social structure. In the Indian joint family system, the presence of family members of different ages, and the wisdom of the elderly that was naturally handed down to the next generation in the family continuously groomed sensitivity towards the others that rendered timely support to those in need in the family even before the person explicitly sought help. This helped in curbing distress before it manifested as emotional turmoil or a mental health problem. However, with the gradual break down in the joint family system giving way to nuclear families, one child norm, urbanisation, globalisation, and changes in the workplace progressively increasing stress among the youth, children, and special groups, the need for formal counselling is being increasingly felt.

In response to the changing situation and the need for regulating education, training, and the practice of counselling, the Government of India established the Rehabilitation Council of India as a statutory body (1993) recognised as the licensing authority for counselling. However, the Mental Health bill and the National Commission for Allied and Healthcare Professions Act, 2021 brought the education, training, and services of counselling under its purview. Since it is a very recent move, the implementation of the same is still awaited. The significant change to note is that counselling services have been brought under the allied healthcare services in the country.

By and large the global effort has been to standardise counselling as a professional service. In this process, what is universally practised is to first build a relationship with the client and help the client ventilate feelings and emotions as a preliminary step. As a progressive process, the endeavour is towards cognitive reorientation that paves the way for change in coping strategies so as to minimise stress, as illustrated in Figure 1.2 below. The efforts of a counsellor as illustrated in Figure 1.3 is to help the client move from negative to positive emotions, thoughts and behaviour, that enhances the productivity in life.

Counselling as a profession thus seems to have started in response to human needs and developed as a non-professional service, later evolving and being shaped as a science with several theoretical foundations. This science, to be successful, requires specific skills in practice which can be learned through training. Thus, counselling as a professional service demands a scientific knowledge base in combination with the art of stimulating, responding, probing, motivating, that culminate in optimising the coping skills of the clients. Thus, it may not be wrong to state that counselling is an applied discipline that brings an unparalleled synergy between science and art.

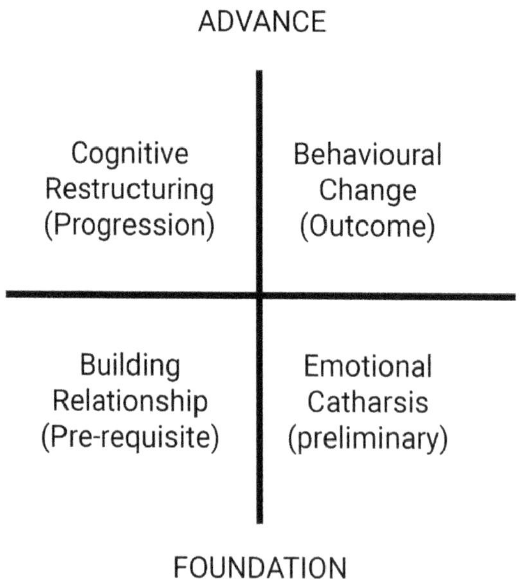

Figure 1.2 Progression of Counselling

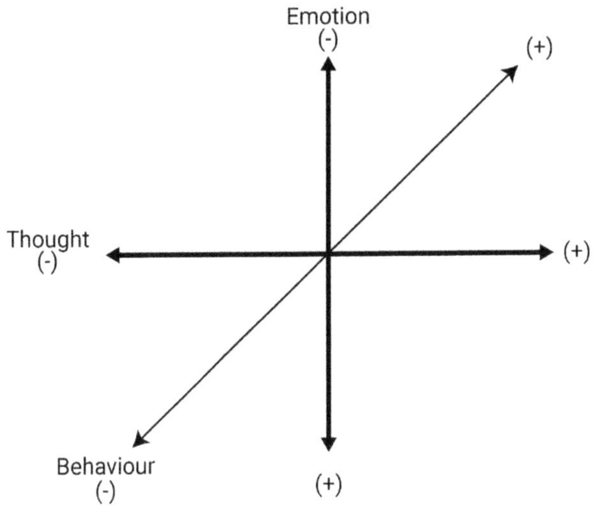

Figure 1.3 Evolution of Counselling

Counselling Needs in the 21st Century

The 21st Century has witnessed significant changes in sociocultural, political, and economic spheres. These changes are bound to impact the interpersonal relationship and the psyche of the individual. The new demands in the educational sector that started laying the emphasis on high cognitive demands in combination with applied skills cannot avoid pressure on children and youth. The workplace demands that have demolished global boundaries requires youth to adapt to various time zones and change the biorhythm at individual levels. The liberal economy opening the plethora of scope on the one hand and widening the divide between social classes on the other influenced the social dynamics and social support system. The extinction of the extended family system and the preference for no children or a single child only among the Indian middle class has resulted in individuals functioning in isolation. Evidence-based diagnosis and treatment in healthcare system has left patients overwhelmed. If there is one common adverse consequence of all this, it is the human relationship. All these have certainly influenced the human relationship in terms of weakening interactions, fading of attachments, lack of bonding, and the lowering of approachability leading to fragility in human relationships. In the face of increasing competitions, piling demands, constant uncertainty, and having to live in an environment that is packed with insecurities, the individual encounters multiple sources of stress. Non-availability of informal helpers within the family, lack of time, distrust of one's peer group (due to cut-throat competition), information overflow and overexposure and premature exposure to the realities of life are found to drive the individuals of different age groups to faulty coping strategies, take to various addictions, or take the extreme step of taking one's own life. India can no longer boast about the strength of informal family resources that functioned as a cushion to absorb life's stress of the family members. Having almost lost that, the only way to ensure the psychological wellbeing of individuals is to strengthen the formal services of counselling through trained professionals. Indian society is seeing an increased prevalence in non-communicable diseases, tobacco and alcohol consumption, and deaths due to cardiac and pulmonary diseases (Hariharan, 2020). While globalisation has brought in a number of positive changes, one of the offshoots is an imbalance between work and family life. There has been a sudden overemphasis on work life at the cost of family time. As a consequence, the role of family as stress absorbent is progressively declining and on the verge of becoming extinct. The cultural invasion, extended time of work life, increasing demands at work, ever increasing stiff competition at work, are constant contributors to stress. While these factors push one towards stress, the factors that counter the stress and pull one out of it are found to work in the reverse direction. Being an agrarian society Indian food has always been region and climate specific. Physical exercise used to be adequate and sleep habits followed the discipline of time, particularly because unlike other nations India as a country follows a single time zone. Socialisation, family gatherings, leisure used to be the major relaxation that protected one from stress. Major life changes that came with globalisation deprived Indians from these naturally integrated cultural norms. Dietary preferences, physical activities, informal socialisation, and leisure having undergone drastic changes seems to have lost their natural therapeutic characteristic to heal stress. The repercussions of these changes are reflected in the incidence of suicides, and non-communicable diseases including mental health. The number of suicides in India shows a progressive trend between 2015 (1.33 lakhs) and 2019 (1.39 lakhs). This, as per the newspaper reports has touched an all-time high in 2020 during the COVID-19 pandemic, which cast severe psychological adversity among the people. People of India are now in dire need of professional counselling services to mitigate, minimise, or soothe their psychological distress arising from multiple sources. There is a severe dearth of professionals from the field of psychiatry and psychology. Counselling as a profession is likely to have a high demand in the next decade. Therefore, it is essential to train and produce qualified counsellors to meet the national demand. In the absence of qualified counsellors, non-professionals tend to occupy the space where the services would be devoid of ethics and values and hence may prove dangerous.

Ethics and Values in Counselling

Before discussing the ethics and values in counselling, it is important to understand these two concepts and the distinction between them. Ethics refers to a branch of philosophy and they are associated with the moral conduct of a group involved in a common engagement. To elaborate, ethics refers to the rights and wrongs related to the conduct of a particular profession. They are laid down to guide and restrain individuals in the profession and bind one by obligations to abide by the stipulated standards. Values refer to the set of principles that trigger human behaviour, by deciding the priorities. They are the behaviour triggers and motivations for the individual to choose a particular action over another. In a professional context, one may say that ethics functions as a restraining force in setting limits to the functioning while values function as a propelling force to prioritise the actions. While ethics lays down a set of 'rights and wrongs' which the counsellor has to comply with, values of a counsellor constitute an important component in building the counsellor-client relationship, and determining the success of a practising counsellor.

Based on the above we shall now identify the ethics and values in counselling.

Ethics in Counselling

Professional bodies of psychologists and counselling are normally responsible in developing the code of conduct for the practitioners. More often than not the code of conduct not only specifies the rights and wrongs but also stipulate the penalty for violation of ethical norms. The American Psychological Association (APA), British Association for Counselling (BAC), American Counselling Association (ACA), and Rehabilitation Council of India (RCI) are some of the associations that developed the ethical codes of counsellors in their respective countries.

For a detailed reading, one may refer to a book on ethics in counselling. But for a broad understanding of the concept, we will discuss ethics under five sub-headings. These five may be called the Panchasutras of Counselling Ethics as shown in Figure 1.4.

Trustworthiness

This is fundamental in the profession of counselling and also the cornerstone in counsellor-client relationship. The foundation of trustworthiness begins with a clarity in communication regarding mutual expectations between the counsellor and the client. Thereafter, the counsellor has to live up to the expectations of the client in discharging professional obligations and responsibilities. First and foremost is to build an understanding about the confidentiality about the client's information. The client should be made to understand that the process of counselling is guided by the principle of confidentiality with the sole purpose of protecting the interest of the client. Confidentiality includes inaccessibility of the case records by anyone other than the counsellor or the authorised person who can view the records after blinding the identity of client, allowing the client to access his/her records on request so that transparency is protected, and anonymity of the client if using the client data for research.

This ethical clause is something that the counsellor never compromises on. In the context of one very reputed university, the counsellor refused the demands of the Dean Students' Welfare (DSW) to have access to the record files of the students who were

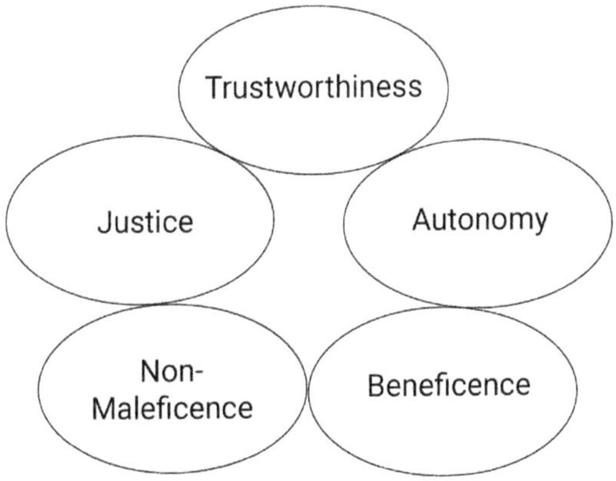

Figure 1.4 Panchasutras of Counselling Ethics

seeking counselling from the counsellor. When the unfair pressure started building upon her and she failed to gain the support of the University administration on this aspect she chose to tender her resignation rather than compromise on this fundamental ethical code.

Educational institutions should respect this ethical guideline of the profession and provide autonomy to the counsellor and avoid subordinating the counselling services to the administrative bureaucracy. Counselling services can function more efficiently under the supervision of the Department of Psychology than under the offices of the registrar or DSW, because in this way counselling in universities can have the advantage of professional guidance and supervision from the senior colleagues who are well versed in the ethical codes.

Autonomy

The guiding force of counselling is to help the client help himself/herself. Counselling is effective when the client views a problematic situation differently and gains the confidence to handle it on his/her own through personal efforts. This is done by helping the client identify their own resources, opportunities, and make decisions. It is very common to have clients who expect the counsellor to solve the problem, make decisions, and at least hint to the client about 'the right direction and decision'. The counsellor has to exercise the utmost restraint to avoid falling into this trap. The client's expectations are understandable because being in a state of exhaustion, helplessness, or hopelessness one may look up to others to solve the problem. However, by doing so, the counsellor would be promoting dependency of the client, and fail to invoke the ability in the client to effectively and optimally utilise their own resources. This would be considered a significant failure on the part of the counsellor in discharging their professional responsibilities. The obligation of the counsellor is to encourage the client to exercise their own thinking from the new perspective after cognitive reorientation, consider and weigh various available options, choose what he/she judges as the best and go with the decision. The job of the counsellor is to facilitate the cognitive restructuring, and the new thinking. By doing so, the counsellor would help the client to feel responsible for their own decisions and actions and also evaluate the repercussions of possible infringements into other people's rights which creates a window for all mid-term corrections. Protecting the autonomy of the client as an ethical code preserves the sanctity of the value of placing the client's agenda first, rather than influencing the client with the counsellor's values or judgements. The counsellor has to continuously self-monitor and guard himself/herself on any inadvertent event of influencing the client with one's own perspectives, values, or opinions.

Beneficence

This clause relates to working in the best interest of the client. Sometimes the autonomy clause may have limitations either because of the extreme distress state of the client, his/her immaturity, minor status, or crisis situation. Under these circumstances, any initiative from the counsellor should be on the consideration of its impact on the client. For example, when a school student referred to the counsellor is found to have suicidal ideation, the counsellor has to choose between protecting the confidentiality by not disclosing the information to anyone, which leaves the client at risk of committing suicide, or alerting the parents/school authorities in the interest of saving the life of the client.

In other situations, such as handling the client with resistance when the counsellor has to choose challenging the client, one has to take into consideration the cognitive, emotional disposition of the client and the possible impact of the challenge on the client's psychological state. The counsellor's decision at every step during the progression of counselling should be based on the consideration of client's interest. Further, in the interest of the client, the counsellor should continuously upgrade his/her knowledge and skills and keep themselves updated with recent developments in the field so as to provide the best benefit of the professional services to the client. For this, the counsellor's endeavours to sustain the quality of services by upgrading the competence levels is of primary importance.

Non-maleficence

This is a term borrowed from medical ethics. The term is derived from the maxim *primum non nocere*, which translates to 'first, do no harm'. The counsellor is bound by this code to refrain from exploiting the client in any way, financially, emotionally, morally, or legally which can cause harm. It implies that the counsellor should not harm the client intentionally or incidentally.

This clause is nothing but the extension of the code of beneficence. The counsellor is directed to refrain from any action that has the potential harm to the client. Here, one has to carefully examine the clause. Many stimuli from the counsellor may place the client at initial discomfort. For example, helping the client towards cognitive restructuring and unblinding the blind spots, or breaking the resistance and reluctance, extricating the client from perpetual procrastination causes an amount of stress and discomfort in the client. Should the counsellor avoid all these based on this clause? The right way to assess and comply with this clause is to weigh the final benefits against the temporary discomfort and proceed. This point implies that the counsellor should continuously evaluate the planned direction of the counselling with reference to its outcome in terms of its impact on the client.

Justice

The principle of justice requires the counsellor to treat the client in a way that protects his/her dignity and human rights. The counsellor may have to deal with clients from various sociocultural backgrounds. Justice here connotes equal treatment to all, it needs to be followed in spirit. In certain cases, perceiving the client with a different sociocultural context, the counsellor may have to deal with the problem differently in the best interest of the client. This discretion has to be exercised by the counsellor. There may be instances where the client may encounter legal obligations while handling a client. In such case the conflict between the ethical and legal obligation has to be sorted out in a way that protects the rights of the client as well as the obligations of the counsellor.

The counsellor has to be very cautious about these *Panchasutras* in the initial phase of the practice. However, as the time progresses one is likely to get well acquainted with this in such a way that it becomes an integral part of the practice.

Values in Counselling

Values are much more than ideals. They are developed with the influence of culture and constitute practical criteria in decision-making process and function as triggers to behaviour. In a counselling context many decisions related to the client are taken by the counsellor on the basis of the set of values they have. These values are neither offered on a platter nor shoved down the throat of the counsellor. They are developed by the individual counsellors and imbibed into the practice. It is these values that distinguish one counsellor from another in the way they are perceived by the client. To take an example from the discipline of medicine, assuming that all cardiologists are same on their knowledge base, the reason that some are highly successful can be traced back to their values. Some of them are preferred because of the empathy expressed to the patients while some are chosen because of their practice of participatory decision making where they explain the problem to the patients with all the pros and cons and help them make a choice of treatment course, yet others gain reputation because they prescribe minimum drugs and prescribe lifestyle changes. These differences in practices are due to the values on which doctors operate. The same is true about counsellors. These values are so developed that they do not contradict the prescribed ethics. Though the values one imbibes is left to the individual counsellor, here we discuss seven general values and call them *Sapthapadi*, meaning the seven steps. In traditional Hindu context, *Sapthapadi* refers to the seven solemn vows taken during the marriage which should guide the couple in their married lives. A counsellor who imbibes these values as a guiding force in their profession is likely

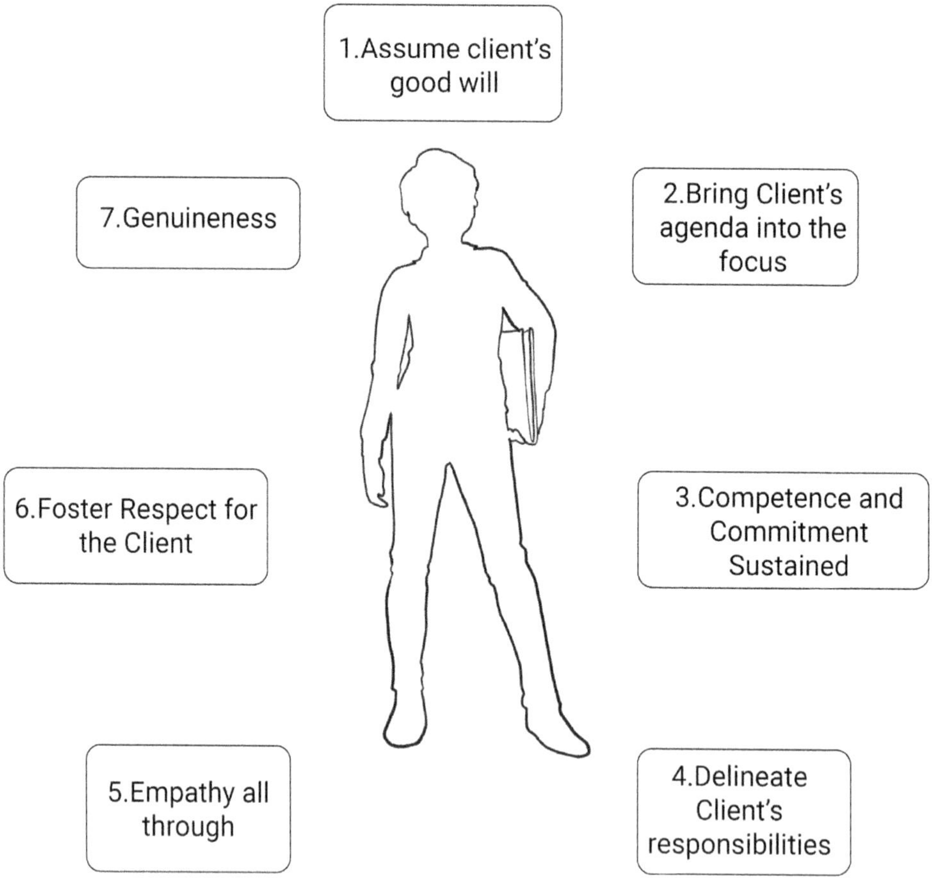

Figure 1.5 Values, the *Sapthapadi* of Counselling

to do well. They are arranged in alphabetical order from A to G for easy remembering for the student. Though we have given the nomenclature *Sapthapadi* to it the seven guidelines mentioned here are different from that of marriage vows.

Assume Client's Good Will

Very often the client may not put forth the problem systematically or may not be able to communicate at all. This may mislead the counsellor that the client is not interested or motivated to work on the problem. However, the very fact that the client has approached the counsellor is testimony for the motivation and good will of the client to work on the problem and minimise stress to opt for quality of life. Manifestations of resistance and reluctance in the client is not the evidence of ill will of the client. Assuming the good will of the client gives the counsellor an advantage of positivity leading to an objective assessment and going forward with the sessions. Otherwise, it casts a negative impact on the relationship building with the client, and also functions as a demotivating factor to work with the unwilling client. Thus, it may disturb the compliance with basic ethical code such as beneficence.

Bring Client's Agenda into Focus

Counsellors who fail to prioritise client's agenda may end up losing the client. There may be occasions when the counsellor finds the client's agenda trivial, but from the client's perspective that may be of prime importance. For example, a client may approach the counsellor after a close friend relocates to another city due to which he/she started feeling lonely. The counsellor may feel that this aspect is not so much of a priority compared to other issues such as the negative reports that he/she has been receiving at work on performance. However, for the client, the close friend's absence that translates to a vacuum in having a shoulder to lean on when distressed due to workplace stress may be the last straw. Any indication of trivialising the stress due to the absence of the friend may lead to the client's dropping out. Prioritising the client's agenda sends an indication to the client that the counsellor has understood and works in the interest of the client which motivates the client to move forward in the counselling process.

Competence and Commitment Sustained

Professional competence and commitment to the profession are two sides of the coin. The combination gives rise to the counsellors who are 'competent and caring'. Care alone cannot bring reputation to the profession because 'incompetent caring' professionals are certainly not preferred. The counsellor should structure the professional obligations in a way where a dedicated time and effort is allocated to learning and updating one's knowledge base. This is likely to happen only when the commitment to the profession is present. Egan (2010) argued that not all trained counsellors are competent and sustain the level of competence during practice. Thus, only those who inculcate it as a value maintain and improve the competence.

Delineate Client's Responsibilities

Counselling is a process that involves two partners – the client and the counsellor. The process will be successful only when both the partners are aware of their roles and responsibilities. By virtue of training the counsellor is aware of his/her responsibilities. Since the client is new to the situation, he/she should be apprised of the responsible role he/she is expected to play. The 21st Century can be labelled as 'The Age of Responsibility' where every individual and group is expected to be aware of the role one needs to play. This awareness is considered as empowerment. The counsellor need not blatantly read out the responsibilities of the client and call it 'empowerment'. Using the professional skills that one is trained in, the counsellor helps the client identify his/her strengths and resources. The client is helped to develop them further so that they are useful both during the session as well as in daily life through transfer of skills. This is real empowerment of the client.

Empathy all Through

Empathy is the characteristic of the counsellor that occupies the front line. It refers to the ability of the counsellor to feel the plight of the client in distress. Whether empathy is a way of 'being' or the way of 'doing' is a matter of debate. Asked whether it is an innate characteristic or an acquired skill, one may be placed in a dilemma. However, the important point to note is that whether it is a part of one's personality or an acquired skill, it needs to be a significant ingredient in the perception and communication of the counsellor. The empathy practised regularly helps the counsellor prioritise attending the distress and the painful aspects in the client with spontaneity and genuineness. A counsellor needs to structure empathy as a part of professional transactions especially in view of the multicultural set up one needs to operate in. Understanding the situation of clients with various cultural backgrounds does not come naturally. One needs to first acquaint oneself with diverse cultures and be trained in perceiving the events and experiences against the relevant background. A lot more about empathy will be explained in the chapters that follow.

Foster Respect for the Client

Respect is reflected in the acceptance of the client with all inherent strengths, weaknesses, fragility, emotions, and behaviour not compliant with social norms. Unconditional positive regard is the underlying principle for respect. The counsellor has to be absolutely non-judgemental in his/her attitude towards the client. Many a time the initial judgements set the tone for further interaction and impact the human relationships. Very often the initial judgements are also proved wrong. Hence the counsellor who views and accepts the clients just for the virtue of their being a human being is the one who upholds the value of respect. A counsellor who respects the client is the one who gives undivided attention to the client during the counselling. Further, respect for the client is also seen when the counsellor underplays all his priorities during the time allocated for the client. Thus, a clear message 'I am here for you' goes to the client which enhances the value of counselling sessions for the client.

Genuineness

Counsellors who are genuine live the professional role effortlessly. Genuineness is also referred to by some authors as 'congruence'. In *Sanskrit*, the oft quoted phrase is '*Manasa vaacha Karmana*' meaning thought, word, and action indicating congruence between the three. Genuineness refers to this aspect of convergence between thought, word and action in the counsellor. A competent counsellor who has a positive attitude towards the client does not have to spend a lot of time deciding on what to say, and how to respond. He/she is spontaneous. He/she responds to the client rather than react, which may violate the ethical code of beneficence. Genuineness includes being non-defensive. In the face of the client expressing negative attitude to the counsellor, it should trigger examining the antecedents of such negative behaviour or understand the client's perspective rather than taking a defensive position. This value of genuineness also includes being consistent in the attitude towards the client. Further, the openness of the counsellor towards the client also helps in the social influence process. A counsellor who is open and spontaneous with the client tends to use self-disclosure appropriately. This in turn helps in the desirable social influence process.

The *Sapthapadi* followed judiciously along with the *Panchasuthras* brings more passion and commitment to the profession than discharging the services mechanically. Counselling is one profession where service can never be extended mechanically. Hence, abiding by ethics and developing a set of values is essential. The counsellor imbibing these and other unique values and complying with the ethical codes is the one who is identified as having the characteristics of a good counsellor.

What does it Take to be a Counsellor?

Counselling is an applied discipline. Studying counselling as a subject relates to knowledge addition. But aspiring to be a counsellor demands a lot more than knowledge and skill acquisition. It would not be wrong to state that a definite way of life is a prerequisite to the profession of counselling. It is essential for a student to know what it calls for before setting a goal to be a counsellor.

There is no doubt that one derives immense satisfaction from the services rendered as a counsellor. The professional satisfaction one feels when a client expresses gratitude for being listened to that relieved him/her of the distress, or when the client is finally successful in his/her new coping behaviour is something precious and unique. The pleasure you derive from successfully applying an innovative approach that is discussed in academic circles and adopted by practitioners is certainly cherished and preserved. The recognition you may enjoy as a competent practitioner is to be reckoned with. However, behind all this glory, the profession also harbours certain realities to be simultaneously handled.

While joy over success is the brighter part of the story, the other side of the coin has certain realities to be aware of before deciding on the career option of a counsellor. The profession of counsellor also includes experiences such as frustration over resistant clients, impatience over reluctant clients, helplessness over the restrictions imposed by institutions and policies, distress over the wrong choices of clients avoiding interventions due to inertia and procrastination. These experiences will not contribute to your happiness index. Choosing the career of a counsellor should be an informed decision based on the realities of professional experiences.

The process of counselling demands the undivided attention of the counsellor. Memories cropping up from a situation similar to what the client is describing at the moment, an urgency to call a family member to handle a crisis situation, discomfort of a rumbling stomach, disapproval of the client's values, discomfort of the loud voice of the client, distraction of the phone ringing in the ante room and above all your own negative affect state arising out of an adverse event the previous day – all these personal needs, interests and priorities will have to be subjugated to the on-going counselling process. Counselling is a process of mindfulness meditation by the counsellor where the focus is the client while the rest of the world, however important, occupies only the periphery (Kabat-Zinn, 2005; Segal et al., 2001). Subjugating all personal interest during the professional services is something that one should be ready before opting for the career.

Professional counsellors will have to subject themselves to continuous self-evaluation that involves identifying strengths and weaknesses in interactions. It is this self-scrutiny that helps the counsellor progress and sustain professional competence. The discipline of counselling is ever advancing. Assessment of one's own competence vis-à-vis recent advances helps the counsellor identify gaps in knowledge and meet the challenges by continuous learning. Thus, aspiring to pursue the profession of counsellor involves commitment to constant learning and upgrading of knowledge and skill. One should be open to this.

The profession of a counsellor involves handling human emotions, feelings, behaviour, and thoughts. As a counsellor, in a professional setting you will be trained to stimulate the person in a certain way to elicit reactions and responses. This skill is likely to become an integral part of your natural interactions with people. It is not far-fetched that your personal interactions with people in close circles would start to be similar to the one's at a professional level, the common factor being human interaction at cognitive-emotional levels. In such a case, there is a possibility of change in the expectations of standards of behaviour from others in your personal life. Just as a doctor spontaneously applies his/her skills in diagnosing the visible discoloured skin, shivering hands, or pot belly of a family member/friend or a relative and advise the person on this though unsolicited, a counsellor is also likely to apply a skill to elicit a response which may not be responded to. This may lead you to interpret the interaction as unsuccessful and superficial which is very dissatisfying in personal life. This is to project the possibility that the choice of career to be a counsellor may impact your way of life and relationship with the world. One should be prepared to handle this aspect so that one does not have to endure the dissatisfaction.

Even if you consciously separate your personal life from your professional life, the responses of others may change because they are conscious of your profession. The authors of this book have invariably and independently come across reactions like 'You are a psychologist; I need to be careful with you'.

Coping with the profession of counselling calls for a different disposition. This is a profession of paradoxical disposition where one has to feel and remain comfortable in the presence of the expressed distress and discomfiture of a fellow human being. The client, in the counselling environment is likely to feel secure, protected and accepted. Hence, it is highly probable for the client to give vent to the expressions uninhibitedly. In that process, the client may cry, scream, or shout at the counsellor, accuse or blame the helper, express hatred and hostility for the counsellor as a process of displacement, be aggressive and stamp the feet, bang the table or even put up an oppressive silence. The counsellor, by virtue of the profession has to absorb this range of emotional energy emitted from the clients, and yet maintain a disposition of comfort and composure. This requires a considerable amount of endurance and practice. A student aspiring to be a counsellor has to assess oneself in terms of these characteristics or at least be open to imbibe these qualities and prepare oneself to practice these skills and acquire the required composure.

The above discussion on the life of a counsellor is certainly not intended to discourage one from choosing the profession, but to encourage students to make an informed decision in choosing the profession. This helps in producing competent professional counsellors. Because counselling is a profession where one would flourish not only due to one's knowledge, skills, and competence but an overriding passion for the profession. One who decides to choose the profession of counsellor with complete knowledge of what it has in store, would do so because of the intense interest and passion for the profession. Society is direly in need of counsellors who are competent and passionate.

References

Beck, A. T. (1967). *Depression: Causes and treatments*. University of Pennsylvania Press.

Carkhuff, R. R., & Berenson, B. G. (1977). *Beyond counselling and therapy*. Holt, Rinehart and Winston.

Chidbhavananda, S. (1965). *The Bhagavad Gita*. Tapovanam Publishing House.

Egan, G. (2010). *The skilled helper: A problem management and opportunity development approach to helping*. Cengage Learning.

Ellis, A. (1962). *Reason and emotion in psychotherapy*. Lyle Stuart.

Hariharan, M. (2020). *Health psychology: Theory, practice, and research*. Sage Publications.

Kabat-Zinn, J. (2005). *Wherever you go, there you are: Mindfulness meditation in everyday life*. Hyperion.

Kaplan, D. M., Tarvydas, V. M., & Gladding, S. T. (2014). 20/20: A vision for the future of counselling: The new consensus definition of counselling. *Journal of Counselling and Development*, 92(3), 366–372. https://doi.org/10.1002/j.1556-6676.2014.00164.x.

Kottler, J. A., & Shepard, D. S. (2008). *Introduction to counselling: Voices from the field*. Thomson Corporation.

Osho. (2011a). *Gita darshan* (Vol. 1). Full Circle Publishing.

Osho. (2011b). *Gita darshan* (Vol. 2). Full Circle Publishing.

Parson, F. (1909). *Choosing a vocation*. Houghton Mifflin.

Segal, Z., Williams, J., & Teasdale, J. (2001). *Mindfulness based cognitive therapy for depression*. Guilford.

Sharma, S. (2014). Cognitive behaviour therapy in perspective of the Bhagwat Gita. *International Journal of Humanities and Social Science Invention*, *31*(1), 19–21.

2 Theories and Approaches in Counselling

A mindful application of counselling is very much needed for a steady, logical approach to helping a client. This leads the counsellor to utilise the knowledge of different theories that have been established with strong evidence over many years. An understanding and assimilation of these theories make the work of counsellors easy. As correctly pointed out by Edwards Deming, the American engineer, professor and author that 'experience teaches nothing without theory'. Without the knowledge of any theory, the work of counsellors will be difficult. According to Immanuel Kant, 'practice without theory is blind'. Practice and theory go hand in hand, each providing incentives to the other. Theory without practice is stale; practice without theory is sterile. Hence, adding theory to practice will show the correct path to follow. Like any other discipline, counselling psychology has several theories. Before explaining these theories, the basic difference between different concepts related to theory needs to be explained.

Key Concepts

Theory

A theory is a broad concept or set of general principles that are accepted by science and are meant to explain an interesting phenomenon. A theory is a well-organised set of presumptions and guidelines that explains certain phenomena and their relationships. Theories enable us to provide a framework for understanding the facts in a particular field. For example, Newton's theory of gravity is a set of ideas that every mass attracts every other mass in the universe. Piaget's theory explains that to achieve the stage of formal operation of cognitive development one has to proceed through the other three stages: sensory motor, preoperational, and concrete operational stages. A theory explains how facts relate to each other with defined terms, has been tested, and is reliable with scientific ideas. According to the definition by the Merriam-Webster online dictionary, a theory is a general principle or set of general principles put forth to explain a phenomenon; a hypothesis put forth for the purpose of discussion or research; a science, or an art, the examination of a group of facts in connection to one another. Theories are a collection of hypotheses that appears to explain empirical facts. The APA Dictionary explains theory as 'a principle or body of interrelated principles that purport or predict several phenomena'. A sound and accurate psychological theory ought to give a practitioner assurance on what to perform and why. Better treatment plans should be the product of a good theory of human behaviour. 'A scientific theory is based on testable hypotheses and makes falsifiable predictions; internally consistent and compatible

DOI: 10.4324/9781003459415-2

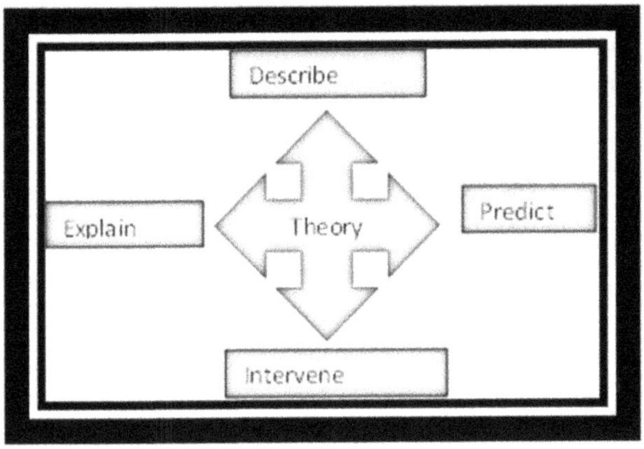

Figure 2.1 Aspects of a Theory

with extant theories; supported by evidence; and modifiable as new evidence is collected' (Goel & Helms, 2013, p. 418).

A theory helps people to do four things: what is happening (describe), why it is happening (explain), what is likely to happen (predict), and how to influence (intervene).

Aspects of a Theory

In the context of counselling and psychotherapy, a theory is a set of concepts used in psychotherapy to describe human cognition and behaviour, such as what leads people to change. In practice, a theory establishes the therapeutic goals and provides the details of achieving them (Craske, 2017). Theories of psychotherapy must be simple for the counsellors to understand as well as inclusive to account for a wide range of possibilities. A theory directs one towards a successful result of action and creates confidence in both the counsellor and the client that there is a good chance of recovery. According to Maddi (1996), a good theory has the following characteristics:

Precision – includes concepts and constructs that are simple, clear, elegant, and precise.
Testability – generates a hypothesis that is testable.
Parsimonious – provides the simplest explanation with an assumption that other qualities are present.
Stimulation – stimulates research to test, validate, confirm, or disconfirm.
Practicability – is practical or applicable.

Characteristics of a Good Theory

> Every genuine test of a theory is an attempt to falsify it or to refute it. Testability is falsifiability; but there are degrees of testability: some theories are more testable, more exposed to refutation than others; they take, as it were, greater risks. One can sum up all this by saying that the criterion of the scientific status of a theory is its falsifiability, or refutability, or testability.
>
> (Popper, 1965, pp. 36–37)

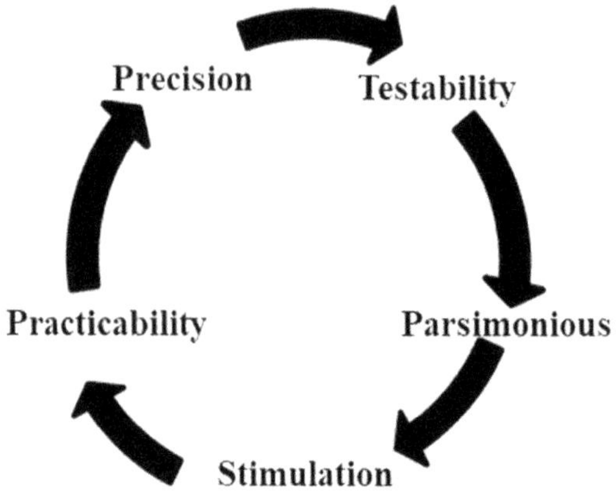

Figure 2.2 Characteristics of a Good Theory

Model: A model is usually a minuscule exemplification of something, a description for the visualisation of something. Goldschmidt (2013, p. 433) defines a model as 'a simplified and schematic representation of the essence/skeleton of a theory', which is 'highly linked to the disciplinary approach within which the theory is embedded'. A model is a specific tool or technique used in practice. 'Models do things while theories explain things' (Sonalkar et al., 2013, p. 69). The difference between a theory and a model can be summarised as a theory is a conceptualised framework while a model is a representation that explains the theory. For example, the theory of classical conditioning conceptualises that by associating a neutral stimulus with an unconditional stimulus (UCS) repeatedly, the neutral stimulus acquires the power of eliciting the same response that the organism gives to the unconditioned stimulus and is called a conditioned stimulus (CS). The model that represents this theory is as follows.

Unconditioned stimulus/UCS (Food)	→	Unconditioned Response/UCR (Saliva)
Neutral stimulus (Bell)	→	No response (No saliva)
Few exposures of Bell + Food	→	Response (Saliva)
CS (Bell)	→	Conditioned Response/CR (Saliva)

Approach: The approach is the direction one takes. It refers to the initial steps towards the achievement of a particular purpose. An approach is a methodology for obtaining the facts. The theory is a prediction or assumption about a particular situation while the approach is a practical way of handling that situation. To solve a certain problem, there are several approaches. It is not necessary that each one must follow the same approach. For example, to get the answer for a particular statistical problem, someone will approach the teacher while others will follow different books. There will be others who search the internet. Put simply, the approach explains an overall way of working. An approach gives rise to methods.

Method: A method is a planned strategy, technique, or manner of investigation that is applied to a particular field of study or an art form (Merriam-Webster online dictionary).

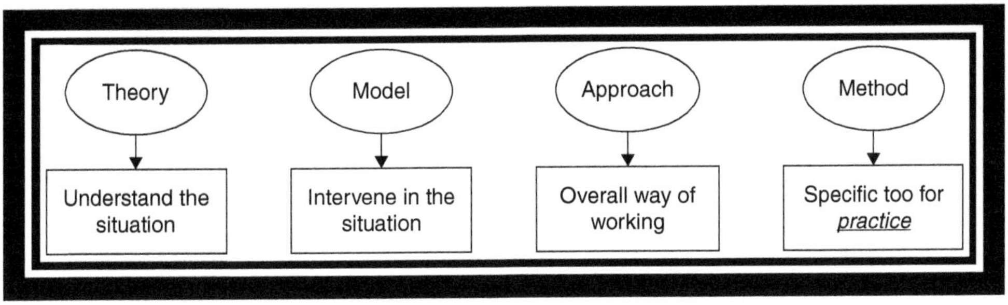

Figure 2.3 Illustration of Theory, Model, Approach, and Method

It generally comes from a model and a way of doing something. By following the model of classical conditioning, one can design the experiments in a laboratory or real-life setting.

In summary, the theory offers a framework for comprehending the situation; the model explains how to intervene in the situation; the approach outlines the general working process; and the method is the specific tool for practising, typically derived from a model.

Illustration of Theory, Model, Approach, and Method

A counselling theory functions at various levels of prediction. For counsellors, the application of any theory depends on which level of prediction they are employing. The job of counsellors is to respond effectively and attentively to multifaceted and perplexing sources of information. Sometimes the counsellors encounter dramatic incongruities in the counselling chamber. Let us understand this with the following example. In the first situation, an adolescent girl comes to the counsellor after fixing an appointment and says nothing. In the second situation a prosperous qualified officer comes for counselling related to burnout but after meeting the counsellor expresses the fear of being a victim of gender discrimination. There are many cases where the clients fail to maintain coherence while explaining the problem. In these situations, the use of a theoretical framework comes in handy for the counsellors to approach the situation. The counsellor can effectively integrate the theoretical foundation with the practice. Theories provide a framework for counsellors to handle the clients' conundrums. Theoretical approaches are an essential aspect of the counselling process. The counsellors should: (1) identify the theory that explains the situation, (2) apply the selected theory to the situation and explain the mechanisms behind it, (3) justify the choice of the theory (4) explain how the theory worked, (5) return to theory when interpreting the progress of the counselling and explain that from a theoretical viewpoint.

Theoretical Approaches to Counselling

In counselling there are many schools of thought that are commonly referred to as waves. Psychodynamic theories (Adlerian, psychoanalytic) are the first wave; learning theories (behavioural, cognitive–behavioural) are the second wave; humanistic theories (person-centred, Gestalt, existential) are the third wave; feminist and multicultural theories are the fourth wave; and postmodern and constructivist theories are the fifth wave (narrative,

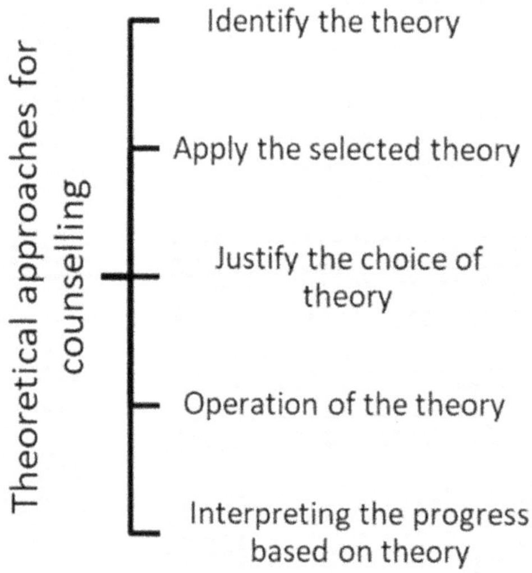

Figure 2.4 Theoretical Approaches to Counselling

solution-focused). These waves depict how psychotherapy and counselling have evolved and changed in response to changes in psychology, culture, and epistemology, as well as changes in psychotherapy itself. Psychotherapy, like the theories that drive it, is fluid and adaptable. The large range of theories demonstrates the various ways in which the same human behaviour can be conceptualised.

Psychoanalytic Therapy

Psychoanalytic therapy is one of the oldest and most familiar psychotherapeutic techniques based on the concepts of Sigmund Freud (1856–1939) the father of modern psychotherapy. This therapy is often referred to as 'the talking cure' because psychoanalysts spend a lot of time listening to clients talk. Psychoanalysis assumes that human nature is deterministic. Freud explained that in the first six years of life, human behaviour as being determined by unconscious motivations, irrational forces, biological, and instinctual drives, and psychosexual activities. Hence psychoanalysts connect the present reactions to situations with the experiences of the past. Therefore, counsellors look for trends and incidents that could be contributing to the clients' current issues. Clients are encouraged and empowered to seek their personal truths through introspection and insight. Counsellors assume the role of guides who accompany clients as they explore and examine their psyche.

Key Theoretical Concepts of Psychoanalysis

Theory of Basic Urges

Freud's approach to personality is biological. Freud developed the theory of basic urges under the biological approach to personality theory. According to him, there are two basic urges: the instinct of Eros and the instinct of Thanatos. The instinct of Eros is the love instinct or life instinct, the source of sexual behaviour. Libido is the force that makes people come into close physical contact with one another as an outlet for their energy. Freud defined sexual life as all the behaviours in which people engage in close physical contact with each other. Physiologically, it helps the individual to grow. Psychologically, it protects the individual from the environment. It is the basis of all innovative intellectual activity. The instinct of Thanatos is also called the death instinct or hate instinct. In a physiological sense, it signifies the energy that tends to extinguish organic life. Psychologically, it gives rise to antagonistic and aggressive behaviour. It manifests itself in destructive intellectual behaviour. Both instincts operate simultaneously. Individuals not only love and hate others, but they can also love and hate the same person. This is called the Freudian principle of Ambivalence.

The Topographical Aspect of Mind/Levels of Consciousness

Freud divided the psyche into the conscious, preconscious, and unconscious parts, with an individual's behaviour predominantly motivated by unconscious drives. According to Freud, the human mind is like an iceberg; the small visible portion represents the conscious experience, while the larger part under the water represents the unconscious experience. The conscious includes sensations and experiences that a person is constantly aware of. The preconscious contains a variety of recoverable memories and experiences. The unconscious aspect of the human mind is the storehouse of impulses, primitive instincts, and passions that influence one's thoughts and behaviour. Freud wanted to explore this unconscious aspect through free association.

The Dynamic Aspect of Personality

Freud postulated that personality comprises three key systems: the id, ego, and superego. The id is the source of personality out of which the ego and superego develops. It is associated with the biological processes and the source of energy (libido) for the three systems to function. The id pursues immediate satisfaction of needs over all other considerations because it functions on the pleasure principle. The ego, on the other hand, follows the reality principle. It operates through realistic and logical thinking and achieves satisfaction. The superego is the internalised exemplification of the morals and values of society and always judges things according to societal norms. The superego includes two aspects: conscience (internalised values) and ego ideals (feeling good about us). While the id searches for pleasure, the ego checks reality, and the superego attempts perfection. The ego always tries to maintain a balance between the id and superego. In a healthy person, these three components of personality coexist amicably.

The Psychosexual Stages of Development

Freud distinguished five stages of personality development, each characterised by a dominant mode of gratifying libidinal pleasure. Freud believed that the childhood stages are related to deriving pleasure associated with different body parts at different ages. This leads to sexual gratification during the adult stage. He named these stages psychosexual stages of development. Children's sexual urges change as they progress from stage to stage, according to Freud. The names of the stages (oral, anal, genital, etc.) reflect where children focus their erotic energy at the time. These developmental stages are characterised by a particular sexual focus and have their mark on adult personalities. The stages are:

i. The oral stage (birth to 1 year): At this stage pleasure is obtained through stimulation of the mouth (thumb sucking).
ii. The anal stage (2–3 years): The gratification in this stage is attained through holding faeces.
iii. The phallic stage (4–5 years): In this stage, pleasure is achieved through fondling the genitals.
iv. The latency stage (6–12 years): This is a stage when the attention is towards skills needed for coping with the environment.
v. The genital stage (adolescence period): In this, the focus of pleasure is on heterosexual relationships. The experiences of the earlier stages are combined into the genital stage. This leads to adult sexual satisfaction and reproduction.

Fixation

Fixation refers to an individual getting stuck at a stage. When the child fails to attain satisfaction at a stage, one gets fixated. It is like a truck getting stuck in muddy water. To get out of the pit, the engine has to invest more energy. Similarly, when the child gets fixated on a stage, considerable libidinal energy is invested in moving forward from the stage, as a result the stage casts an impact on the personality of the child that manifests itself in later stages of life.

Problems faced at any one stage may lead to fixation at that stage. Oral fixation occurs due to unmet oral needs in early childhood. For example, a person fixated on the oral stage may be dependent on other people and may search for oral stimulation through eating, drinking, or smoking. The child-rearing practice at a particular stage cast its influence too. For example, a child in the anal stage is toilet trained by the parent. Some parents do it with strict discipline while others may show some tolerance. With a highly punitive parent, the child may show fixation by becoming anal-retentive and with parents who are permissive, the child may turn anal-expulsive. Anal-retentive in the later stage may manifest characteristics such as being obsessively organised and tidy while anal-expulsive may manifest messy, untidy, and disorganised characteristics. Box 2.1 summarises the psychosexual stages of development.

Anxiety

In psychoanalysis, anxiety is defined as a sense of dread that develops from suppressed emotions, memories, and wants. It results from a conflict between the id, ego, and superego for dominance of the available psychic energy. Anxiety can be classified into three sections, reality, neurotic, and moral. Fear of danger in the outside world is known as reality anxiety, and its intensity is proportionate to the threat level. Threats to a person's 'balance of power' cause neurotic and moral anxiety. When a person feels threatened by their ego or like they are losing control of their lives or themselves, they develop neurotic anxiety. When a person believes that their morals are about to be compromised, moral anxiety sets in. Violations of moral codes are likely to make people feel bad if they have a strong conscience. The balancing act of ego reduces anxiety and restores equilibrium. When logical and obvious methods of reducing anxiety fail, the ego will occasionally turn to indirect strategies like ego-defense mechanisms (Corey, 2017, p. 61).

Box 2.1 Stages of Psychosexual Development

Age (approximately)	*Stage*	*Focus on erotic zones*	*Major developmental tasks linked to the stages*	*Manifestation of fixation at later age*
Birth–1 years	Oral	Mouth	Weaning (from breast or bottle)	Chewing gum, biting nails, smoking, drinking, indulgent talking
2–3 years	Anal	Anus	Toilet training	Obsessed with tidiness/organised or messy and disorganised
4–5 years	Phallic	Genitals	Recognising adult role models	Sexually aggressive
6–12 years	Latency	None	Developing interpersonal relationship	Immaturity, inability to have an interpersonal relationship
Post puberty	Genital	Genitals	Beginning intimate relationships; Working to contribute to society	Well-balanced, warm

Defense Mechanisms

The ego defense mechanism is a psychological operation originating from the unconscious and functions to protect a person from anxiety-provoking thoughts and feelings related to conflicts are internal and stressors that are external (Di Giuseppe et al., 2020) The ego encounters various pressures, both contradictory and insistent: id frustration, superego guilt, and the demands of reality. To ease these pressures, the ego uses defense mechanisms regarded as the unconscious strategies for escaping or decreasing intimidating feelings, such as fear and anxiety. Defense mechanisms are unconscious reactions that protect a person from negative emotions like anxiety and remorse and guilt. The two main characteristics of defense mechanisms are: first, they distort or deny inner or outer reality in some way or second, they operate unconsciously. The following are the various defense mechanisms:

- ***Repression*** is a process where the ego avoids pain by transferring painful experiences to unconsciousness, e.g., a person forgets the details of an automobile accident which happened due to rash driving on his/her own part.
- ***Fantasy*** is the type of defense mechanism where the individual avoids frustration in a relationship with one's spouse, by imagining or fantasising about a romantic relationship with a celebrity.

- ***Rationalisation*** is a process where guilt is minimised by producing a logical explanation for some wrongdoing as an attempt to deny one's true motives (to oneself or others), e.g., not getting good marks in the examination is explained with an argument that examination is only one dimension while life has many other fields to prove one's worth.
- In ***identification***, one adopts the behaviour of another person one perceives as powerful, e.g., a victimised one adopts the behaviour of a victimiser.
- ***Projection*** is a defense mechanism where one attributes the cause of anxiety to others, e.g., the deceitful husband doubts his wife as unfaithful.
- In ***reaction formation***, one expresses the behaviour that is completely opposed to the impulses or feelings that one is repressing, e.g., a male employee harasses a lady colleague because he is attracted to her at a subconscious level.
- In ***fixation***, the guilt of inadequacy is avoided by refusing to progress to the next developmental level of functioning, e.g., refusal to move forward because progress is associated with anxiety in some way.
- ***Regression*** refers to a phenomenon where one returns to the previous mode of functioning to get rid of the current pressures, e.g., in a conflict or anxiety situation, the child shows the behaviour of thumb-sucking to recover the lost sense of safety.
- ***Displacement*** is a defense behaviour wherein frustration is avoided by replacing the desired but unavailable one with a less desirable but available object, e.g., anger related to incompletion of work is displaced on the subordinates.
- In ***compensation***, someone who is unable to perform the desired activity avoids feelings of inadequacy by pursuing alternative interests, e.g., dedicating extra efforts to the publication of articles to overcome feelings of not receiving the Ph.D degree.
- ***Sublimation*** is a redirection of more basic desires into one that is more socially acceptable, e.g., inappropriate sexual impulses can be released in several creative pursuits (a boy who went through a breakup may channel his emotions into writing novels).

Defense mechanisms always hide original motives but do not alleviate them and leave residual of anxiety. Sometimes they create frustration, guilt, and/or actual pain. Everyone, according to Freud, employs defense mechanisms to some degree. They only become problematic when a person is overly reliant on them. When defenses are distorted, psychological disorders are shown. As found by the empirical research, the following aspects related to defense mechanisms should be remembered (Cramer, 2015):

a) People use defense mechanisms more often when facing stress or a threat to their sense of self.
b) Defense mechanisms shield individuals from emotional distress.
c) Overreliance on defense mechanisms can impair one's mental health.

Goals of Psychoanalysis

The goals of psychoanalysis are to 'make the unconscious conscious', since it is essential to identify unconscious thoughts and feelings to cope maturely and realistically with them. Its goal is to improve clients' self-awareness and understanding of their thoughts, feelings, and beliefs in relation to their past experiences, particularly their childhood experiences.

Box 2.2 Psychoanalysis in a Nutshell

The teacher asked some questions about psychoanalysis:

Based on an assumption that children did not know about Freud and dream analysis.

Students remembered their student life and became conscious,

They were taught that 'Dream is Royal Road to unconscious'.

The questions the teacher put forth were What is meant by Id?

Id is the primitive aspect of Personality that wants immediate gratification of needs.

Good! What do you mean by Ego?

Ego maintains the balance between the Id and Superego.
Very good! Describe what you know about the Superego's action?
Id seeks pleasure, Ego tests reality and Superego strives for perfection.
When Unconscious, Preconscious, and Conscious constitute the topographical aspect of the self like an Iceberg,

One-tenth (1/10) of the conscious level is visible, while nine tenths (9/10) is submerged.
Now explain the defense mechanisms in psychoanalysis.

It's unconscious reactions that protect a person from negative feelings.

Please name and explain Freud's five psychosexual stages,

These childhood stages are associated with deriving pleasure from different body parts at different ages.

The first one is oral, then comes anal, phallic, and latency followed by genital.

Oral centred on the mouth, whereas anal is on bladder and bowel.

While phallic focus on genitals, in latency, sexuality is dormant,
The beginning of intimate relationships in the genitals is protuberant.
What is the second Instinct when the first one is the instinct of Eros?

The immediate answer was the instinct of Thanatos.

The Instinct of Eros is the life Instinct as Freud states,
Thanatos is the death instinct that one makes.
Libido is the energy which physiologically helps the individual to grow,

Psychologically, it is the basis of all innovative intellectual activity to flow.

Counselling in Psychoanalysis

Psychoanalytic therapy creates awareness and brings an insight into the clients' behaviour. Hence in the therapeutic sessions, the counsellors try to bring up a change by helping the clients dig their past and early life events that might have influenced the present. The therapeutic sessions vary based on clients' problems. Clients are asked to spend their time talking freely with the counsellors in a non-judgemental conducive environment. The counsellors listen empathetically to the clients and relate the events into a significant pattern. Psychoanalytic therapy emphasises that unconscious feelings and some childhood events play a major part in mental distress. The counsellors use techniques such as free association, projective techniques, therapeutic transference, and interpretation to help the clients in understanding and identifying possible causes of distress.

Free Association

Freud emphasised a 'talking cure', an effective method of treatment where the clients are allowed to narrate traumatic memories and reveal their innermost unconscious desires. In the initial sessions of psychoanalytic therapy, the clients describe the symptoms and narrate relevant facts from their biography. Then they prepare to enter upon free association. In free association, they are asked to share their thoughts, and feelings, that comes to their mind without hesitation. The basic rule of free association is 'say everything that comes to your mind without selecting and editing'. Sometimes the clients fail to tell many things because some thoughts seem to be unimportant, silly, or very private. The clients unconsciously resist recalling certain thoughts because they fear that acknowledging these thoughts will lower their self-image. The role of the counsellors is to help the clients in overcoming the resistance. Sometimes the clients have the free flow of associations until something blocks them. Then the mind goes blank. This blankness is due to the resistance to recalling the repressed incidents.

Resistance

Resistance is a set of mostly unconscious defensive tactics designed to obstruct the therapy progress. It is seen to be an inevitable aspect of psychoanalysis (Samberg & Marcus, 2005). Clients are unwilling to confront the difficult, upsetting conflicts that have been buried in their subconscious. Despite seeking assistance, individuals are hesitant to confront their true problems. Clients' resistance is when a client avoids troubling, painful, or traumatic material in therapy. Counsellors help clients to overcome the resistance and lead them towards the complete understanding of self through interpretation. This is done following two procedures. First, counsellors bring the attention of the clients to their resistances, as a result of which the clients realise the resistance. Second, counsellors infer the nature of resistance from the clients' previous statements and provide a clue to facilitate the session further. Sometimes the clients express something which might appear insignificant. In the actual case, this indicates something important. Hence the interpretation should be properly scheduled for the significant association.

Projective Techniques

Projective techniques are sensitive to unconscious part of the mind. Data obtained in projective settings are used to infer defense mechanisms, latent urges, and anxieties.

Clients are asked to respond to ambiguous images, scenarios, or words using projective techniques. Counsellors would most frequently show their clients an ambiguous image and then ask them to respond with the first thought that comes to their mind, revealing the hidden emotions or conflicts that the clients project onto the image.

Interpretation

Counsellors' attempts to explain the inner significance of the clients' thoughts, feelings, memories, and behaviours are referred to as interpretation. It is the clients, not the counsellors, who must determine what is important. Interpretation has three major areas: **dreams, parapraxia, and humour**. The investigation of repressed emotions that can be expressed in a person's dream is known as dream analysis. The counsellors' search for hidden latent contents (hidden intentions, fears, or wishes) inside the manifest contents (the dream as it appears) of the dream, which usually involves recognising symbolic meanings. The counsellors listen to the narration of the dream and interpret the symbolism of the dream. Freud believed every dream to be a by-product of repressed, anxiety-producing thoughts. For example, being unable to board the train to reach a destination is related to anxiety dreams. Parapraxia is a Freudian slip. The counsellor is to be aware of any slips of the tongue which is unconscious and bring this unconscious to conscious. 'According to Freud, there is a fundamental conflict between the demands of social life and our instinctual urges. Society demands that sexual and aggressive instincts be repressed or pushed from conscious awareness. Freud argued that what is repressed returns to haunt us in disguise. Jokes or humour, like dreams and slips of the tongue, bear the traces of repressed desires' (Billig, 2002, p. 451). In this case, the counsellor must watch for patterns and themes.

Therapeutic Transference

Transference is a psychological phenomenon in which people assign represented features of meaningful and formative connections to other people. Client transference occurs when a client's emotions, expectations, and wishes are transferred to another person, in this case, the counsellor. It is the unconscious rerouting of feelings from one person to another, the transferring of thoughts or feelings connected to influential figures in the life of the clients onto the counsellors. For example, the client sees the characteristics of his mother/father in the counsellor, even though the counsellor is unlike the parent. Transference is not always the manifestation of false perceptions; the clients often express the same emotions towards the counsellors that they used to feel towards others who were earlier important in their lives. The counsellors take the expressed emotions and interpret the nature of the impulses displayed and provide appropriate counselling.

When the counsellor applies the psychoanalytic tools and processes on the client the response of the client is in expected lines. Very often the client reaches what is called 'catharsis'.

Catharsis

This refers to the process of releasing repressed emotion, reaching the climax, and getting relief out of that. Neurosis has its origin in repressed traumatic events of the past. The role of the counsellors is to empower the clients to recall their repressed emotions and bring them into consciousness. Such free expression which brings relief in the clients is known as 'abreaction'.

Psychodynamic Therapies

The psychoanalytic method developed by Freud, a century ago, was aimed at the type of clientele he treated in Vienna. As psychoanalysis spread across Europe and America, some of his followers realised that psychoanalysis needed to be adapted for different cultures, changing times, and new types of clients. They are referred to as psychodynamic approaches to therapy. Based on psychodynamic theory and research, it has been determined that (1) unconscious forces can affect behaviour, (2) internal conflict frequently contributes to psychological distress, (3) early childhood experiences influence adult personality in a substantial way, and (4) people may use defense mechanisms to reduce their experiences of unpleasant emotions (Bornstein et al., 2013). Psychodynamic therapy also includes the following key features, according to Shedler (2010): (1) emphasising emotional experience and (2) exploring the pursuit of avoiding distressing thoughts and feelings, (3) identifying recurring patterns in the client's life, (4) discussing their childhood experiences, (5) evaluating their interpersonal relationships, (6) emphasising the therapeutic relationship, and (7) exploring their dreams and fantasy lives.

The development of psychoanalysis by Sigmund Freud set the foundation for numerous other types of psychotherapy. Some of his early ideas, like the unconscious, are still used in a variety of therapeutic methods. Regardless, psychoanalysis is one of the most divisive approaches to psychotherapy, and it has received a lot of criticisms over the years. The main criticism was its focus on fundamental biological urges as the major motivator of human action, ignoring considerations such as free will, genetics, and the environment. The counsellor often remains detached and there is no egalitarian relationship between the counsellor and client.

Successful psychoanalytic counselling is achieved when the clients cope well with the problems and lead a comfortable life without recurrence of the symptom for which counselling was provided. Psychodynamic approaches are helpful in the treatment of various disorders, including depression, anxiety disorders, personality disorders, and substance abuse (Josephs & Weinberger, 2013; Barber et al., 2013).

Adlerian Theory

Alfred Adler (1870–1937) named his theoretical process 'individual psychology', derived from the Latin word 'individuum' meaning indivisibility or essential unity of the person. Individual psychology, often known as Adlerian psychology, is a theory of human behaviour that emphasises the need for belonging and engaging in constructive actions (Adler, 1956). Individual Psychology is based on a phenomenological, holistic understanding of human behaviour. According to the phenomenological perspective, each person experiences situations from a unique perspective. Each one has their view of the world which they think is right and hence lives life accordingly. Adlerian psychology, also referred to as individual psychology, is a theory of human behaviour that places a strong emphasis on the need for affiliation and taking part in constructive activities (Adler, 1956). The foundation of individual psychology is a phenomenological, comprehensive understanding of human behaviour. Each person views circumstances differently, according to the phenomenological perspective. Everyone has a worldview that they believe is accurate, and as a result, they live their lives in accordance with it. The moment the view becomes distorted, everything gets upset. The thinking becomes defective, emotions become negative, and behaviour becomes improper. A person is indivisible and should be treated holistically. Individuals cannot be understood by examining their parts; rather all aspects of a person must be understood concerning the overall pattern and social structures (Maniacci et al., 2014). The Adlerian theory highlights the importance of contextual circumstances and focuses on a philosophy of human connections based on social equality.

According to Adler, individuals are unique, creative, and responsible for their fate. Unlike Freud, Adler did not emphasise sexual instincts and biological determinism as the source of human behaviour but rather social determinism and the impact of family and environment on an individual's behaviour. Adler argued that the top human drive is a drive for superiority and viewed it as a universal drive to adapt and improve oneself as well as to master life's challenges. He felt that in comparison with older children and adults, young children feel weak and helpless. These early inferiority feelings inspire people to learn new abilities and cultivate new talents.

Individuals are motivated to learn new abilities and acquire new talents because of their early inferiority feelings. He felt that all behaviour is goal oriented. The way people work in social organisations motivates them to seek 'belonging' or significance and purpose in their lives (Adler, 1956). People choose behaviours to get a sense of belongingness and security. His view was that people's understanding grew from knowledge of their goals and drives, family dynamics, logic, social system, and lifestyles.

Key Theoretical Concepts of Adlerian Counselling

Adlerian theory is found on the assumption that humans are socially embedded and have a need to belong. Children develop inferiority feelings and battle against them throughout their entire lives. People are creative and self-determinant, and reality is subjectively perceived (Kottman & Ashby, 2015). They can choose their emotions, behaviours, personality traits, and attitudes (Carlson & Englar-Carlson, 2017). Helping clients how to recognise their choices to perceive and react to situations and relationships is one of the therapeutic goals.

Adler's theory is not based on any medical model but rather on the philosophy that people are accountable for their thoughts, emotions, and behaviour. The key concepts of Adler's theory include lifestyle, social interest, inferiority and superiority complex, family constellation, birth order, and private logic.

Style of Life

According to psychotherapists, a person's cognitive orientation and lifestyle are developed throughout the first few years of life and are influenced by their social environment. In accordance with the family constellation, every behaviour has a reason for existing and takes place in a social setting. Family constellation includes gender lines, family values, family atmosphere, and the family's primary birth order. The way of life is affected by one's position in the family. Each person has a unique lifestyle, which is influenced in part by how the family members react to different behaviours and attitudes. Our lifestyle includes all of the ways we act, think, and perceive the world. It also includes how we live. We select methods for overcoming the challenges and chores in life based on our lifestyle.

Adler was not in favour of personality types. He believed that it could lead to the negligence of each person's distinctiveness. He did, however, identify 'lifestyle' tendencies, which develop in childhood and could be useful in treating those who fall into these categories. Adler asserted that once a counsellor understands a person's lifestyle, 'it is sometimes feasible to predict his future by talking to him and having him answer questions' (Adler, 1956, p. 100). Adler and his supporters compare a person's lifestyle to 'the socially adjusted human being' (Adler, 1956, p. 101).

Adlerian counselling supports the growth model. Individuals are always in the process of 'becoming'; nothing is predetermined. They are in the process of becoming the best version of their lives. Individuals who are experiencing 'psychopathology' are not sick but discouraged (Maniacci et al., 2014; Sperry et al., 2015). Psychopathology occurs if children are overprotected, neglected, or both. Psychopathology is defined as a condition characterised by erroneous beliefs and assumptions, a lack of social interest, discouragement, and a dysfunctional lifestyle (Sperry et al., 2015). The dysfunctional lifestyle is inflexible. Instead of using a more task-oriented and socially helpful 'common sense', which is what problem-solving should be, people choose to use a self-protective 'private sense'. Individuals have trouble seeing or responding to life in different way after this set of incorrect psychological convictions has consolidated and self-protective coping strategies have been created. As a result, they cannot effectively deal with life's challenges or enjoy the rewards of their efforts, let alone maintaining healthy interpersonal connections. On the other hand, the flexible lifestyle is the consequence of a set of psychological beliefs and coping styles that are positively moulded by children's experiences of mastery, creativity, and joyful loving interactions. People with flexible lifestyles can use their creativity to choose alternative approaches to dealing with life. The role of counselling and psychotherapy then shifts to encouraging the clients to acquire more social interest and construct a more successful lifestyle to handle life's demands.

Social Interest

In the Adlerian approach, the desire to belong and cultivate a social interest – a wish to contribute to the welfare of others – is the fundamental human motivation. Adler believed that the ability to move through life with courage and common sense was the defining characteristic of a healthy, nonpathological individual. Adler named this distinguishing feature 'social interest' (Sperry, 2015). With the concept of struggling for superiority or significance in life, he included social interest in his theory. Adler claimed that no one could achieve success unless they had a basic social sense of belonging to their community, and he recognised social interest as the foundation for success in the social, romantic, and vocational realms. Due to the multidimensionality of how it is presented and the distinctiveness of everyone, social interests will differ. According to Adler, people's perceptions of social context can influence their sense of belonging and their knowledge that their actions affect others. Understanding how people struggle for importance and are part of a social environment is necessary to know how social interest is engendered. Humans are driven to increase their growth, competence, and perfection. The pursuit of perfection is moderated by the social interest in a way that serves the community. According to Adler (1956), this desire for social interest must be supported.

Inferiority Complex

According to Adler, the fundamental need of an individual is the need for belonging. With the feeling of belongingness, the desire to do good for others increases. This promotes in the individual a sense of mastery and significance. But when they do not get a chance to fit into the system and contribute then they get discouraged and their chance to contribute diminishes. This leads to feelings of inferiority. Adler claims that all children have feelings of inferiority and inadequacy as soon as they enter the world. Feeling inferior is not abnormal but rather the driving force to achieve one's goal. 'Inferiority feelings are those universal human feelings of incompleteness, smallness, weakness, ignorance, and dependency included in our first experiences of ourselves in infancy and early childhood' (Griffith & Powers, 2007, p. 60). According to Adler, the trademark of an inferiority complex is that individuals are constantly striving to discover a scenario wherein they excel. This drive occurs from their irresistible feelings of inferiority. A healthy reaction to inferiority is to overcome it in either a socially interesting way (e.g., I know I am not the most talented on this team still I will play my best to contribute to this team and the outcome of the match) or a self-focused way (e.g. I know I am not the most talented in this team but I must show my talent or else I am a failure). Inferiority complex becomes pathological only when the individual will have a sense of inadequacy which makes him incapable of development and depressed. The purpose of Adlerian therapy is to support the clients to overcome the feelings of inferiority.

Superiority Complex

Individuals with inferiority complexes believe their behaviour and thinking as the only way to achieve perfection because they feel they must be perfect. All personality disorders, according to Adler, are the result of erroneous ideas that they are better than they are, they develop a superiority complex. Not listening while others are speaking, talking over others, and depreciating persons or things that others value are all examples of a superiority complex. The goal of this behaviour is to hide one's inferiority mentality in the hope that no one notices. This aggravates the issue because other people are likely to respond in an unproductive way, further upsetting the process.

Family Constellation

This refers to the dynamic relationships between siblings and other members of the family where individuals feel a sense of affiliation and self-worth. It represents the action of the family system, comprising of parents, siblings, and any extended family members. Adler suggested that an individual's position in a family constellation is an important factor for development. Each child has a position in the family that is shaped by the family's interactions and transactions.

Birth Order

The order in which people are born to their siblings is referred to as birth order. Adler believed that the birth order of children in a family is a strong predictor of a child's personality and feelings of inferiority.

- *First-born*: First-born children have an advantage since their parents see them as the bigger, stronger, and older ones. So, firstborn children acquire the characteristics of a protector of law and order. Until their sibling arrives, the first-born children enjoy greater attention and a sense of uniqueness. After the birth of siblings, they feel as disadvantaged as problem kids, neurotics, criminals, drinkers, and deviants. Under favourable circumstances, the oldest child tends to develop the tendency to be protective, accountable, and organised. However, he believed that the oldest children were more prone to be troublemakers.
- *Second-born*: Because of the existence of their elder, more dominant brother, second-born youngsters are continuously 'striving for superiority under pressure'. If the second-born are supported, they will be able to rise to power and collaborate with the first-born. Second-born children are motivated to seek power and superiority since their older sibling is constantly just ahead of them, threatening the firstborn's security. Feelings of envy and neglect are supposed to motivate the second-born.
- *Youngest children*: They function in a persistent state of inferiority. They feel helpless; need more attention and warmth from their parents than siblings. They become more competitive and persistently try to prove themselves, to overcome their inferiority perceptions. They will appear cowardly and sluggish and will suffer from feelings of inferiority. Because they lack the audacity to compete in the same field as the rest of their family, the youngest children choose to work in a different field.
- *Only child*: The only child, pampered by everyone in the family and dependent, is not accustomed to difficult situations in life. Constant attention from their parents leads them to a strong sense of feeling valuable and searching for support all the time. Only children, on the other hand, are scared and lack independence due to their parents' cautious treatment of them.

Private Logic

Private logic is the cognitive map that guides individuals' perceptions and actions. Based on private logic, individuals interpret the life events which becomes their lifestyle. It is distinctive to each person and sometimes is not rational. Adlerian treatment aims to help people better understand how their beliefs get in the way of their ability to function, eliminate faulty thinking, and alter their approach so that they can perceive things more healthily. Feelings of superiority or inferiority have their own logic, and they only have significance to the individual. People act according to their private logic, which is generally unknown to them yet influences their actions. Private logic changes when one achieves true self-knowledge.

Goals of Adlerian Counselling

In Adlerian psychotherapy, the goal is to help the clients to overcome feelings of inferiority because it focuses on making the clients feel competent and connected. This process includes lowering the superiority complex, or exaggerated feelings of superiority, to the point where the client aspires to significance without feeling overwhelmed. It also entails removing the inferiority complex, or persistently determined to be superior to others; and fostering feelings of belonging and equality.

Adlerian Counselling

The Adlerian viewpoint is optimistic and emphasises resources, strengths, and protective factors. High levels of social interest influence psychological health and well-being whereas problems occur because of a low sense of belonging, or unhealthy belonging patterns. Clients' incorrect lifestyle views or views against social interest are manifested in psychopathology. Even though some psychopathology is caused by biology, the clients' maladaptation is a sign of being subjected to discouragement. The clients act as though their false views about themselves, other people, and the outside world are true. Clients either give up or become discouraged because of their feelings of inferiority, or they over-compensate by demonstrating a 'lesser degree of social feeling and ability to cooperate' (Adler, 1958, p. 23). Adler believed that a counsellor must analyse both internal and external aspects to properly understand a person.

Counselling is viewed as a learning process to enhance a sense of cooperation and social interest and is based on four stages of counselling (Manaster & Corsini, 1982):

i) *building a therapeutic relationship*: An egalitarian bond between counsellor and client is the first step in building trust. The counsellor must be warm and empathic to establish this. The therapeutic relationship is one of mutual cooperation, and the client is expected to take an active part in the process of change.
ii) *gathering information*: In this stage, information on lifestyle evaluation, present functioning, symptoms, and so on is gathered. To build an effective therapeutic process, the therapist needs to undertake a thorough assessment of the client.
iii) *gaining insight*: The client and counsellor analyse the data to determine the client's perceptions of self, others, and the world – that is, their lifestyle and the elements that impact belief systems (Manaster & Corsini, 1982). Once the client has made some progress and the therapist and client have discussed the significance of the client's movement in relation to his goals, the treatment is ready to start looking at the client's way of living.
iv) *developing new skills*: Finally, the phase of reorientation and re-education begins. Adlerian believes that for change to occur, the client must first understand what is going on and why. By encouraging insight into the suitable aspect(s) of the client's lifestyle, he or she can determine whether they are ready to change (Manaster & Corsini, 1982). The counsellor would next work with the client to change the interfering convictions/misbeliefs and related behaviour so that the client can get what he or she wants more effectively and pro-socially.

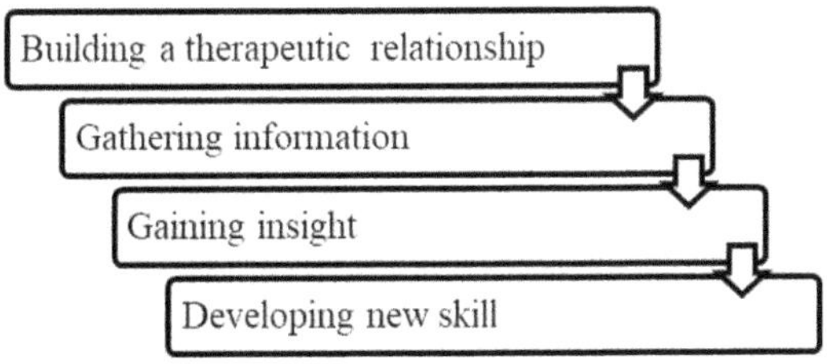

Figure 2.5 Stages of Adlerian Counselling

Like many psychodynamic approaches to human psychology, Adlerian individual psychology is criticised for being unscientific and challenging to objectively verify. Because Adlerian psychology relies on the unconscious objective, it is argued that it cannot be falsified. The present perspective of Adlerian psychotherapy is that, while it is basic and easy to understand for the layperson, it is faulty since it is not empirically based. Adler's method of therapy has been criticised for its shallowness, particularly because it lacks a foundation that addresses issues other than birth order and early childhood development (Capuzzi & Stauffer, 2016, p. 142).

Application

People who suffer from poor self-esteem, loneliness, or negative thinking may benefit from Adlerian treatment. By validating themselves and reviving social contacts, people can gain confidence and empowerment, enabling them to pursue their objectives and make wise decisions. When a child is acting aggressively or refusing to go to school, Adlerian therapy is effective. Adlerian therapy is also more effective at orienting children towards collaboration (rather than competition) and encouraging them to become socially interested (rather than self-oriented).

Behaviour Therapy

Behaviour therapy acknowledges its origin in the works of Russian Physiologist Ivan Pavlov (1849–1936). It was further developed by other behaviourists, namely John B. Watson, Edward L. Thorndike (1874–1949), B. F. Skinner (1904–1990), Albert Bandura (1925–2021), and others. Pavlov discovered the principle of 'classical conditioning' which focuses on the responses of the organism to a specific stimulus in the environment without cognitive interpretation of the stimulus. This process fits in with the views of Watson, the father of behaviourism, who emphasised the objective study of observable behaviours. To investigate human behaviour, Watson was interested in a method that could be used for both prediction and control of human behaviour. Watson disagreed with ideas about concepts including consciousness, thought, and imagery (Spiegler & Guevremont, 2010). Based upon the principle of classical conditioning, Watson conducted the classic experiment with an 11-year-old boy named Little Albert. Initially, Albert was not afraid of a white rat shown to him and played calmly with it. Then the experimenter created a loud noise behind Albert while he was playing with the rat. After repeated exposure to the noise, Albert developed a fear towards the white rat even though no sound was there. The neutral stimulus (the white rat) elicited the fear associated with the noise by being paired repeatedly with the noise.

Key Theoretical Concepts of Behavioural Therapy

Conditioning

When a neutral stimulus is associated with an unconditioned stimulus, the neutral stimulus elicits the same response as the unconditioned stimulus. This is called conditioning.

Classical Conditioning

This was developed by Ivan Pavlov (1906) and is the learning that arises when two stimuli are presented in temporal proximity to each other. It is a form of learning in which a neutral stimulus (conditioned stimulus) elicits the same response that was initially elicited by the unconditioned stimulus. 'The contingency between the neutral stimulus and the unconditioned stimulus typically leads to the conditional stimulus acquiring at least some of the emotional valence of the unconditioned stimulus and the capacity to elicit a response (the conditioned emotional response)' (Zinbarg & Griffith, 2008, p. 8).

Operant Conditioning

This was developed by B. F. Skinner (1953, 1974) and is the type of learning in which voluntary actions are controlled by consequences following them. While classical learning explains the relationship between stimulus and response, instrumental learning explains the effect of response on behaviour. Operant conditioning highlights the effects of environmental contingencies (rewards and punishment) on the occurrence of a behaviour. It operates on the principle that behaviour followed by pleasant consequences will be repeated in future whereas behaviour followed by unpleasant consequences will tend to be discontinued. According to Thorndike's '*Law of Effect*', behaviour that is followed by a 'pleasing condition of things' is more likely to occur. Through the process of shaping, operant conditioning encourages the formation of increasingly complex behaviours. The method of shaping involves motivating repeated approximations of a challenging desired behaviour. For example, the training of a dolphin for different types of play follows this process of reinforcing behaviour. The trainer divides the training process into many steps. Each phase of the process serves as a self-contained reward for the desired behaviour.

Social Learning Theory

During the 1960s social learning theory, developed by Albert Bandura, included the principles of classical conditioning and operant conditioning. The early approach of Bandura's therapy included Skinnerian learning. In addition to that, he emphasised observation, cognitive control, and reciprocal determinism. Bandura added the cognitive components to behaviourism in the 1960s and called the model social cognitive theory. Bandura agreed with behaviourism that personality is mainly shaped by experience. However, he asserted that conditioning is not a mechanical way of doing in which people participate passively. He claimed that individuals search and process information about their environment to get the best outcomes. Bandura postulated that behaviour, environment, and personal factors have a mutual relationship called reciprocal determinism (also known as triadic reciprocity) where a person's behaviour both influences and is influenced by personal elements and the social environment. The term 'personal' denotes the importance of cognitive and affective factors, as well as self-regulatory systems that help people control their behaviour. Social learning theory suggests that new behaviours are learned by observing the behaviours of others. Learning also occurs by observing rewards and punishments given to others which is known as vicarious reinforcement. According to the social cognitive perspective, most maladaptive behaviours result from dysfunctional expectancies. A shy person, for example, may avoid social gatherings for

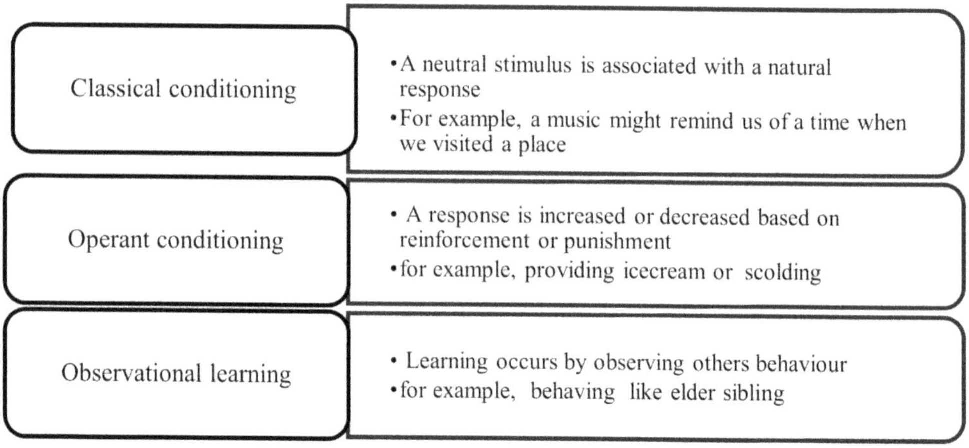

Figure 2.6 Types of Learning

fear of unrecognition, whereas a street-smart person may assume that any situation can be handled easily.

Behaviour therapy assumes that maladaptive behaviour is learned, and the role of counsellors is to help the clients to substitute appropriate responses for this maladaptive behaviour. The target is 'unlearning' problematic behaviour. For example, if the parents have reinforced the children's temper tantrum behaviour by fulfilling the unreasonable demands of the children, they may be asked to choose alternative ways of responding. The behavioural counsellor emphasises changing those factors that are thought to predispose, elicit, reinforce, or sustain problematic behaviours. They work directly on problematic patterns of behaviour by assisting their clients to make changes. Unlike the humanistic approach, behaviour therapy is directive and encourages the clients to follow exercises and assignments to practice new ways of responding.

Types of Learning

Counselling Based on Different Learning Theories

Two main principles underpin behavioural therapy. To begin with, behaviour is the result of learning. Regardless of how self-destructive or disordered a client's behaviour is, behaviourists think it is the outcome of previous conditioning. Second, something that has been learnt can be unlearnt. It is possible to prevent maladaptive behaviour by understanding the learning principles that explain its occurrence in the first place. As a result, behaviour counsellors use the principles of different learning theories to change their clients' behaviour.

Classical Conditioning

Classical conditioning is relevant to behaviour in everyday life and is important in understanding the causes and treatment of clinical illnesses. Classical conditioning can explain complex phenomena in humans. For instance, an individual's emotional response to a scene or tune is based on an experience with which it is associated; the scene or tune is a CS that elicits an unpleasant emotional response because it was previously associated with the death of a close friend. Various behaviour therapy techniques for behaviour change are based on the principle of classical conditioning. It is also implicated in a variety of fears and phobias that might develop due to generalisation. Originally coined as behaviour modification, it is usually referred to as applied behaviour analysis (Pierce & Cheney, 2017). The different techniques of behaviour change include:

Systematic Desensitisation

This was developed by Salter (1949) and Wolpe (1958), based on reciprocal inhibition. It is based on the simple principle that one cannot be relaxed and anxious at the same time. It is based on the idea that people avoid what they are afraid of, and that avoidance might lead to increased anxiety over the feared object. This method involves systematic and continuous exposure to the fear-provoking object or scenario, with early exposures having low-intensity fear, and more intense exposures being added only after the anxiety associated with gentler levels of exposure has subsided. This is done by having the counsellor lead the client through the various degrees of exposure in real-time, utilising encouragement and modelling to encourage a progressive approach to the feared object or circumstance. This technique involves three phases. In the first phase, the counsellor works collaboratively with the client to generate a sequence of events arranged from least to most anxiety-provoking one. These events are again ordered from greatest anxiety-provoking events to least-provoking events. Take the example of a person who is afraid of climbing an escalator. Such a person's anxiety hierarchy may look something like this:

i. *Talking about escalator*
ii. *Seeing the escalator from afar*
iii. *Seeing others using the escalator*
iv. *Being nearby to the escalator*
v. *Climbing the escalator while it is stationary*
vi. *Climbing the escalator while the green signal is on for movement*
vii. *Climbing an escalator while it is moving*

In the second phase, the client is asked to relax. The client is taught progressive muscle relaxation (PMR) or other suitable exercises that make a calm and composed physiological state. In the third phase, the client is asked to relax deeply and imagine the least anxiety-provoking item from the hierarchy. Then the client is again asked to relax. When this is achieved, the client is asked to ponder the next item from the list, and so on till the entire list is covered. If progression from one stage to the next creates anxiety, the client is asked to return to the earlier stage for further exposure. This procedure allows the client to gradually come near to the situation that was too fear-provoking to ponder beforehand. Such an approach should be done gradually by the counsellor with utmost care otherwise the fear will never extinguish. People are trained to replace a fear response to a situation with relaxed responses through this procedure. Relaxation and breathing techniques are taught first. The therapist will gradually expose them to the fear arousing scenarios in gradually intensifying doses while they practice these tactics after they have mastered them.

Aversion Therapy

Aversion therapy is frequently used to address disorders like addiction and alcoholism. It works by having people to associate a pleasurable but unhealthy stimulus with a highly unpleasant sensation. It is possible that the unpleasant sensation is anything that causes discomfort. For example, a counsellor may teach the clients to associate alcohol with an unpleasant memory. Clients who undergo chemotherapy have food aversions because of nausea which makes them difficult to eat a variety of foods later on. Treatment consists of attempting to prevent aversion by lowering the predictable link between the CS and the US, using the classical conditioning process.

> Blocking occurs when clients are given food with a very prominent, novel taste in novel circumstances, and the novel cues overpower the tastes of more familiar items. As a result, the clients develop a strong aversion to cues that will no longer be present once treatment is completed. This is effective and produces no problems because when familiar meals are consumed at home, there is less development of conditioned nausea.
>
> (Ferrandiz, 2004, p. 348)

Exposure Therapy

Exposure therapy is a behavioural treatment approach that is a refinement of a collection of processes known as flooding or implosion. Masserman (1943), who examined anxiety reactions and avoidance behaviours in cats, is credited with developing exposure treatment. Masserman's research involved shock-induced 'neurotic behaviours' in cats under certain environmental conditions. As soon as they were placed in the box, the cats began to exhibit anxiety behaviour. Later, he discovered that the cats' neurosis vanished if they were made to stay in the box and fed there. He interpreted it as 'breaking through the motivational conflict'. The shock delivered in the box established a link between the place and an unpleasant after-effect. The sight of the box induced anxiety establishing a conditional emotion response (CER). Masserman counteracted the CER by feeding the cat in the box. The anxiety vanished as the anticipation of food replaced the shock at the sight of the box. These discoveries were used to produce anxiety remedies for humans. Presenting the conditioned stimulus (CS) alone and intensely is aimed to erase the conditioned fear response. It is mainly applied to phobias and anxiety where individuals are exposed to objects or situations, they are afraid of. For example, a person who is afraid of a lizard will be exposed to a lizard for a prolonged period.

Anxiety-inducing stimuli are often provided in one of two ways during exposure sessions: in fantasy (in imagino) or in real life (in vivo). In vivo is a Latin phrase meaning in life. In imaginal exposure, the counsellor describes a setting that represents the client's lowest level of anxiety in the hierarchy while the client is relaxed. Clients who receive in vivo exposure, on the other hand, are exposed to scary real-world stimuli while participating in a relaxation exercise. Exposing a lizard-phobic person to lizards, or a compulsive hand-washer to dirty hands, is an example of in vivo exposure. Although in vivo exposure is more effective than imaginal exposure at reducing anxiety reactions and avoidance behaviours, imaginal exposure is frequently used because it is simpler to administer. Sometimes in vivo exposure is impractical or potentially harmful. When clients have strong phobias, this sort of therapy must be used with caution. Several clients have panic attacks during flooding procedures. If the panic attack happens in a secure setting in the presence of a therapist, it will subside in 10–20 minutes.

According to Barlow and Cerny (1988), several characteristics must be present in exposure therapy for the clients to receive the maximum benefit: 1. longer exposure is preferable; 2. repeat the exposure until all fear and anxiety are gone; 3. gradually increase the exposure to high-anxiety stimuli/situations from low-anxiety stimuli/situations, 4. clients must pay attention to and interact with the dreaded stimulus as much as feasible; 5. anxiety must be induced by exposure.

Operant Conditioning

The primary determinants of behaviour are consequences that have the power to either strengthen (reinforce) or diminish (penalise) behaviour. These effects are acquired through people's experiences. Skinner identified two types of reinforcement: positive reinforcement and negative reinforcement. A response is enhanced (increases in frequency) when it is followed by a pleasurable consequence. The concept of positive reinforcement is basically equivalent to that of reward. Negative reinforcement happens when an unpleasant stimulus is removed after a response occurs. Negative reinforcement, like positive reinforcement, strengthens a response that can get rid of an unpleasant stimulus. Reinforcement is positive (providing a movie ticket) in response to a behaviour that is acceptable. Reinforcement is negative (removing an aversive object like a snake) in response to an escape behaviour. Punishment is positive when it involves receiving an aversive consequence (caning) after a behaviour that is undesirable, whereas negative punishment involves removing something desirable (no permission to go for a movie) following a counterproductive behaviour.

A stimulus or event that raises or sustains the rate of the dependent response is referred to as a positive reinforcer. The problem is its impact on the response rate, not the stimulus or event itself. The behavioural techniques associated with principles of operant conditioning for behaviour change are:

Contingency Management

Operant conditioning emphasises an organism's response to produce the reinforcing stimulus. The organism must respond to receive reinforcement, which is an example of contingent reinforcement. The use of reward and punishment to improve the frequency

Box 2.3 Four Quadrants of Positive and Negative Reinforcement and Punishment

	Reinforcement Acceptable Behaviour	*Punishment Unacceptable Behaviour*
Positive (+) By providing/adding	Movie ticket	Scolding
Negative (-) By removing	Scary object	Preferred TV channels

of desired and adaptive behaviour is known as contingency management. Simple contingency plans, such as rewarding the individual with an unusual lunch for not smoking, can be used in this method. Contingency management also includes the removal of reinforcement through time-out.

Token Economy

The token economy, which is built on positive reinforcement, is a collection of contingencies based on token (conditioned) reinforcement. Tokens are given contingent on the performance of the appropriate behaviour, which later can be exchanged for reinforcement within a predetermined economy system. The contingencies define when and why a specific behaviour is reinforced with tokens. The word 'economy' signifies the exchange of tokens for goods and services much like money (Pierce & Cheney, 2017). In this technique, the counsellor offers individuals 'tokens' that can be replaced for privileges or preferred items when positive behaviour (adherence to medication) is shown.

Observational Learning

Bandura's explanation of observational learning is his most important theoretical contribution. An organism learns through observing others, known as models, in observational learning. Bandura did not view observational learning as completely different from classical and operant conditioning. On the other hand, he claimed that when one observes another's behaviour, both classical and operant training occur indirectly.

Bandura (1997) viewed self-efficacy as an important aspect of personality. Self-efficacy is considered one's belief about one's capability to perform behaviours that lead to anticipated outcomes. When individuals have high self-efficacy, they feel self-confident in implementing the actions needed to earn reinforcements. Individuals with low self-efficacy worry that the necessary responses may be out of reach. The perception of self-efficacy is subjective and related to specific types of tasks. For example, one may feel confident about his/her ability to handle academic challenges but doubtful about handling difficult social situations. People's perceptions of their self-efficacy can affect what challenges they take on and how well they perform.

Behavioural Rehearsal

A behavioural rehearsal is a set of techniques where a counsellor and a client model a scenario that is problematic to the client. Behavioural rehearsal is also considered as modelling, assertiveness training, role-playing, or social skills training.

Social Skills and Communication Skills Training

Behavioural counsellors point out that human beings are not born with social skills and these skills are acquired through learning. People often lack skills such as being friendly, making conversation, expressing emotions appropriately, etc. Lack of social skills can give rise to anxiety, fear, feelings of inferiority, and different disorders. Considering these findings, counsellors increasingly use social skills training to improve their clients' social skills. Social skills training is used to develop adaptive interpersonal behaviours and make social reinforcement easier to acquire. Social skills and communication training, according to Antony et al. (2020), includes teaching individuals or groups the effective way of communication. Learning basic skills (e.g., listening to others without interrupting) or more complex skills may be part of this process (e.g., performing effectively in interviews). Usually, social skills training includes psychoeducation, modelling, goal setting, behavioural rehearsal or role-plays, and feedback. In role-playing, clients may be videotaped so that they can review their performance. Social skills training is mainly used in the treatment of social anxiety (Beidel et al., 2014), depression (Thase, 2012), emotional and behavioural problems in children (Antshel & Remer, 2003), autism (Otero et al., 2015), and schizophrenia (Mueser et al., 2013).

Role-play

In role-play, clients are asked to participate in role-playing activities during treatment sessions, where the counsellor first models the appropriate skills. Clients are then encouraged to display the same skills. To let the clients use their new abilities in practical situations and receive genuine social reinforcement, some real-world activities that put them to test are essential. For example, eye contact with others during a conversation, greeting others with a smile, demonstrating empathy, and displaying appropriate emotional responses to the circumstance are some of the activities the clients may be encouraged to display in role-playing.

Psychoeducation

Psychoeducation is provided in the early sessions of therapy. At the beginning of psychoeducation, the client and counsellor discuss a model for the problem, the treatment process, and the impact of treatment procedures on problem behaviour. After the finalisation of the model, the client is presented with new evidence and is asked to give feedback on whether the symptoms are dependent or independent of the model. Depending on that new information that is more reliable is provided to the client.

Goal setting

Goal setting is a significant aspect of behaviour therapy. The client and the counsellor together develop initial treatment goals after identifying the client's main problems. While clients choose which goals to be taken, it is the counsellors who help them in making sure that the goals are safe, specific, measurable, and attainable.

Modelling

The APA dictionary of psychology defined modelling as 'a technique used in cognitive behaviour therapy and behaviour therapy in which learning occurs through observation and imitation alone, without comment or reinforcement by the counsellor'. In modelling, the individual learns behaviours and their consequences through observations called vicarious learning. The individuals acquire new behaviour, facilitate behaviour, and decrease behaviour due to the adverse consequences of the model.

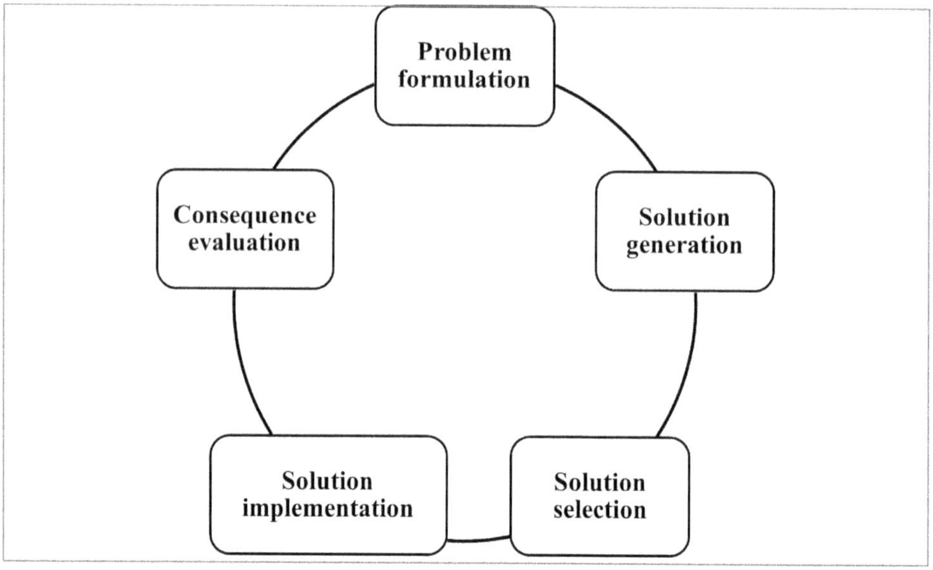

Figure 2.7 Problem-Solving Skills

Problem-Solving Training

In problem-solving training, clients are taught to solve their problems successfully to improve psychological and behavioural functioning. Problem-solving includes:

(a) *Changing one's problem orientation*: The process of assessing how well individuals can deal with problems that arise and their awareness of them is called 'problem orientation'. It consists of strategies to remove the barriers to problem-solving, enhance self-efficacy, recognise problems, consider problems as challenges, and not react impulsively.
(b) *Teaching problem-solving skills*: These training skills help the clients how to solve problems efficiently. The clients use five steps to solve problems: (i) formulation of problem, (ii) generation of probable solutions, (iii) selection of the best solutions, (iv) implementation of solutions, and (v) evaluation of consequence.

Problem-Solving Skills

According to Lazarus (1966), behavioural rehearsal is better than direct advice and reflective listening. Behavioural rehearsal includes four steps (Goldfried & Davidson, 1994):

(a) *Prepare the client*: The counsellor explains the rationale for behavioural rehearsal and asks the clients to try out alternative behaviours in difficult situations. Educating the clients about appropriate social expectations may also be part of the preparation for behaviour rehearsal.
(b) *Identify targets for change*: Like systematic desensitisation; a hierarchy of situations is created. Clients use role-plays to try out different behaviours and the counsellors also role-play and model effective behaviours.

(c) *Behavioural rehearsal (role-play)*: Counsellor and client maintain a situation that resembles as much as possible a real-life situation. To interact with the clients, the counsellor might employ confederates. The clients assume the role of a difficult mother-in-law, a colleague, or an audience member.
(d) *Actual utilisation of newly acquired skills in real-life situations*: Throughout the role-play, the clients can try out different behaviours to decide which ones are effective, with the counsellor stopping at various points to model behaviour or provide feedback. The clients who practiced starting a conversation may try to do so at different settings. Clients who practice how to be assertive with their colleagues will deal similarly with their colleagues in real life.

Behaviour therapy has been widely criticised for its restricted focus on visible human behaviour and lack of attention to thoughts and feelings, which are also important components of a person's functioning. Another critique of behavioural therapy is its mechanistic action-oriented approach, which overlooks the relationship between the counsellor and the client, as well as the necessity of self-awareness in the transformation process.

Application

Counselling and psychotherapy have benefited greatly from behaviour therapy. As patients look for relief from phobias and other anxiety disorders, behavioural treatments are one of the recognised treatment approaches. Behaviour therapy has also served as a foundation for the development of a variety of other approaches, such as reality therapy and multimodal therapy. Behavioural approaches provide the theoretical framework for a wide range of effective procedures that are now used in a behavioural approach to counselling. Bandura and his colleagues concentrated their early empirical tests of social learning theory on modelling for phobic illnesses. Exposure treatments for specific phobias, panic disorder, post-traumatic stress disorder, and obsessive-compulsive disorder have obtained empirical support for their success.

Cognitive Behaviour Therapy

The roots of Cognitive Behaviour Therapy (CBT) can be traced back to different approaches to psychological theories. In the 1970s the approach of behaviour theory was not limited to observable behaviours alone, rather its focus expanded to cognitions and emotions. 'Cognition' is derived from a Latin word meaning 'get to know'. It refers to a mental action or process of obtaining knowledge and understanding through experiences and thoughts. This is key to CBT which is based on the theory that what we think and believe shapes our behaviour. In social learning theory, Bandura (1986) explained that children learn new behaviour by observing, internalising, and replicating the observed behaviours which are the interplay of cognitive activities. During that time two trained psychoanalysts namely, Albert Ellis (1913–2007) and Aaron T. Beck (1921–2021) realised that experience, unconscious process, and personality dynamics alone did not have a significant contribution to psychotherapy. It was people's beliefs that affected how they viewed the world and responded to the situation. Cognitive assessment and cognitive change were considered the focal points for later behavioural adaptation and emotional success. This led to the development of cognitive behavioural therapy which focused

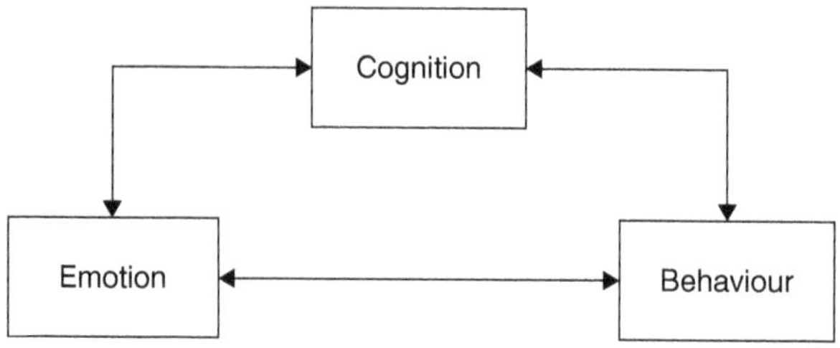

Figure 2.8 CBT Model

on maladaptive behaviour and cognitions. Craske (2017) defines CBT as an amalgamation of cognitive and behavioural interventions, taken from theories of learning and theories of cognition, and directed by principles of pragmatic science. Ellis and Beck both believed that the targets of intervention may be the reason and the clients' underlying assumptions. Their view was an active interaction of counsellors with clients rather than passive listening. The earliest forms of Cognitive behavioural therapy that have been receiving more attention are – Rational Emotive Behaviour Therapy (REBT) (Albert Ellis in the 1950s) and Cognitive Therapy (Aaron T. Beck in the 1960s). The other two popular therapies are – Acceptance and Commitment Therapy (ACT) (Hayes et al.,1999) and Dialectical Behaviour Therapy (DBT) (Linehan, 1993).

CBT is based on the notion that cognition, emotion, and behaviour interrelate with each other. Individuals' feelings and behaviour are determined mainly by their thought processes.

CBT Model

The thoughts (cognition) act as a mediator between the events and ensuing reactions. The reciprocal interplay between thoughts and emotions influences behaviours, which then interact with the environment. This interplay with the environment and its consequences then reciprocally influences the thoughts and emotions. Even though thought plays a primary role in affecting emotions and behaviour, once the process begins, all factors can reciprocate with one another (Volungis, 2019).

The Core Aspects of Cognitive Behaviour Therapy

The basic principles of CBT are: (a) cognition plays the mediating role between an event and the response to the event, (b) cognitions are conscious, and can be modified with training, and (c) systematic changes in cognition have better therapeutic outcomes. Individuals' essential ideas about themselves, others, the world, and the future are described by Beck (2011). These beliefs are rigid, absolute, and generalised, and are established during childhood or periods of stress. The negative, automatic, and impractical thoughts cause distress and create problems. This psychological distress has a negative influence on the behaviour or actions of the individual. Initially, the counsellors help the individuals become aware of what, when, and why they make negative interpretations; the behaviour that facilitates the negative thinking; and to find substitute thinking to reduce distress. Cognitive change can be made through cognitive, behavioural, and emotive strategies (Lorenzo-Luaces et al., 2015). Identifying, analysing, and changing the perception is the first step in reducing distress. The process of challenging distressing automatic thoughts, assumptions, and beliefs; and thereafter, substituting them with better realistic thinking patterns is referred to as the cognitive restructuring technique, one of the most significant tools for properly managing stress.

Goals of Cognitive Behaviour Therapy

Craske (2017) has explained the four different goals of CBT. The first goal of CBT is to replace maladaptive cognitive, emotional, and behavioural reactions with more adaptive responses to increase the quality of life. Cognitive counsellors are of opinion that if problem behaviours, cognitions, and emotions are acquired through experience and learning, then these maladaptive behaviours can be changed through new learning. The second goal is to help the clients in achieving self-sustaining long-term beneficial effects of new experiences. To *achieve* this, clients must practice the new learning experiences in different situations and occasions. This will make clients become less reliant on counsellors and develop their own sets of skills to deal with difficult situations. As rightly pointed out, 'Give a man a fish, and you feed him for a day. Teach a man to fish, and you feed him for a lifetime'. The third goal focuses on individually based functional analysis to find out the causal relations among cognitions, behaviours, emotions, and environmental and cultural factors. This helps in creating tailored intervention procedures for specific problems, instead of providing the same therapeutic interventions to all. The fourth goal is flexibility in implementation. This is facilitated by continuous evaluation and modification of cognitive–behavioural intervention strategies as required. This demands a collaborative approach between counsellor and client.

Rational Emotive Behaviour Therapy (REBT)

REBT developed by Albert Ellis (1955) can be considered the first approach within cognitive behavioural therapy (CBT) practice. According to Ellis individuals formulate different assumptions about self and the world. Ellis emphasised the view of ancient Stoic philosophers that 'people are not disturbed by things, but by the views, they take of them'. The main tenet of REBT, he added, is that people are affected more by their thoughts about situations and events than by the circumstance or event itself. This enables them how to react and handle the situation. While some people's assumptions are rational, it is irrational for others. At its foundation, REBT asserts that both rational and irrational beliefs serve as important cognitive intermediaries between our inferences and our emotional and behavioural consequences. In REBT rational beliefs are logical (compatible with reality), flexible, and non-extreme whereas irrational beliefs are illogical (incompatible with reality), rigid, extreme. These irrational assumptions lead them to behave in ways that jeopardise their happiness. For example, not getting attention from the boss in a meeting, the manager developed irrational thoughts (such as failures) and felt rejected. REBT helps people how to deal with irrational beliefs, manage their emotions, and how to behave more realistically.

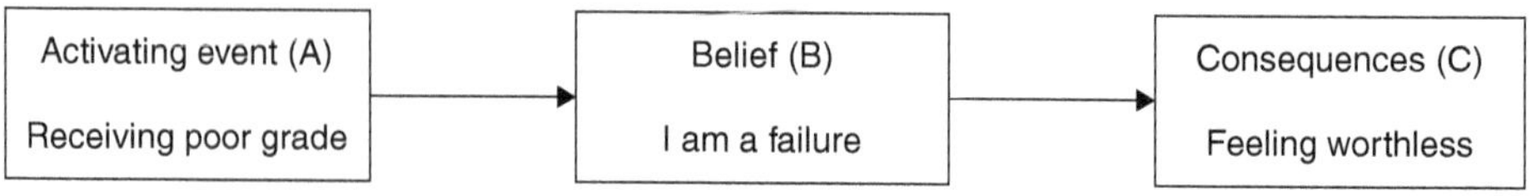

Figure 2.9 The ABC Model

ABC Model of Albert Ellis

The ABC model is a mnemonic that represents the three stages that determine an individual's behaviour.

A – Activating Event: Event that leads to an emotional response or negative thinking
B – Beliefs (negative thoughts)
C – Consequence: Dysfunctional behaviours

The belief acts as a mediator between the events and the maladaptive behaviours. It is not the event (A) that causes the negative feelings and dysfunctional behaviours (C), rather how the person interprets these events (B). In the examples given below, though the situation or event (A) was the same, each person's perception (B) was different which subsequently influenced the emotion and behaviour (C).

Examples of ABC Model

Situation: In an online meeting, a person said Hello to a colleague. Even though the colleague usually responds immediately in all meetings, she did not respond that day. Here are some examples of how one might have thought, felt, and behaved in that situation.

Person 1 thought, 'She deliberately ignored me', felt angry, and repeatedly said hello until got a response.
Person 2 thought, 'I might have done something wrong', felt sad, and remained silent.
Person 3 thought, 'She was not in a good moment', felt anxious, and tried to know the reason.
Person 4 thought, 'Something bad must have happened to her', felt anxious, and tried to help.
Person 5: 'She was probably busy with the meeting', remained normal, and did not react.

As explained above, these examples show that belief 'B' is the significant determining factor of functional and dysfunctional responses 'C' to antecedent events 'A'. The 'C' can be cognitive, emotive, and behavioural.

When an irrational idea is discovered, the counsellor helps the client to reconstruct evidence from his experience to challenge negative views. This helps the client in developing more rational ideas and better workarounds. Take another example: 'the manager was upset because the boss did not interact in the meeting'. Here the Activating event (A) is 'no interaction', Belief (B) is 'he (the manager) is very knowledgeable and capable', and

Consequence (C) is 'the manager is dejected'. The counsellor would be able to help the manager understand that the boss may not be able to interact with everyone, or that he (the manager) is not the only competent person in the group. Seeking attention from the boss is desirable, but feeling dejected is not appreciable. The ABC framework helps clients understand that it is their irrational beliefs (B), not the events (A), that create their dysfunctional behaviours (C). More so, they have control over their beliefs and they can choose how they would respond to adversity.

Therapeutic Approach to Help Clients Produces Rational Beliefs

In response to initiating events, REBT counsellors apply the D–E–F approach in which irrational beliefs are disputed (D) to give rise to effective (E) new thinking that is logical and flexible, which promotes functional (F) emotions and behaviours (David et al., 2004). According to Ellis (2003), irrational beliefs can exist below one's consciousness, and to confront them, they must first be brought into awareness. As a result, as the client relates to a variety of experiences and emotional circumstances, the counsellor listens to the terms that reflect absolutist and dogmatic beliefs. Like the humanistic approach, REBT emphasises the unconditional acceptance of clients.

At the same time, clients are trained how to accept others and themselves unconditionally. Ellis believed that too much warmth should not be shown by counsellors towards their clients because it might lead to over-dependence. The counsellor establishes a rapport with clients by demonstrating that he believes in their ability to change and that he would like to assist them in doing so. Instead of portraying oneself as a secretive authoritative figure, it's crucial to build as many egalitarian relationships as you can. The counsellor must handle transference properly if it occurs and should not be encouraged which is based on irrational beliefs (Ellis, 2002).

Application

REBT has proven to be useful in treating a wide variety of mental health issues such as depression, anxiety disorder, obsessive-compulsive disorder, posttraumatic stress disorder, eating disorders, panic disorder, psychosis, and self-harm.

Cognitive Therapy

Cognitive therapy (CT) developed by Aaron Beck in 1967 is used mostly for depression. Cognitive therapy focuses on automatic thoughts that are learned and fixed during childhood, and then develop dysfunctional patterns over time. CT tries to undo these automatic thoughts. The role of counsellors is to help clients how to recognise themselves and how to interpret real-life events differently. They guide the clients in examining and challenging their dysfunctional thoughts, experimenting with new interpretations, and applying alternative ways of thinking in their daily lives. This enables individuals to confront their negative mental patterns. Beck opined that a person's reaction to specific disturbing thoughts plays a significant role in abnormal behaviour. The myriad of challenges that we encounter, generate both soothing and unpleasant thoughts in our minds. Beck referred to these uninvited thoughts as automatic thoughts.

Depression occurs if someone is bombarded with negative thoughts (I'm unable to publish articles, I'm not keeping well, my professor is not supporting me, I don't have a

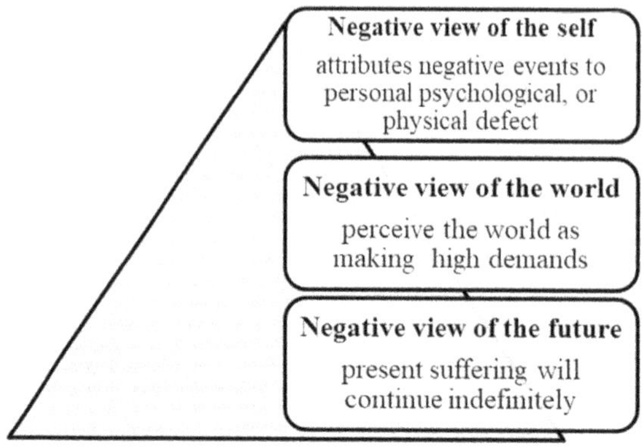

Figure 2.10 Cognitive Triad

supportive peer group, I don't have the chance to get a promotion). Even when confronted with contradictory evidence, these negative thoughts persist. Beck (1967) explained three mechanisms responsible for depression: **the cognitive triad, cognitive distortion, and negative self-schemas.**

Cognitive Triad

The cognitive triad refers to thoughts about oneself, the world, and the future. Depressed individuals have negative views in all three instances: (a) negative opinion of the self-attribute negative events to personal, psychological, or physical defect; (b) negative opinion of the world – perceive the world as presenting obstacles to reach life goals; and (c) negative opinion of the future – anticipating the indefinite continuation of the current problems or suffering. The interaction of these elements obstructs normal cognitive functioning, resulting in difficulties in memory, perception, and problem-solving, as well as the person's obsession with negative thoughts. They think that they are good for nothing, the people in this world are ungrateful and their future is uncertain.

Cognitive Distortions

Cognitive distortions are irrational, rigid, or extreme interpretations of information created by a series of errors in an individual's thinking. Cognitive distortions frequently reveal a negative bias and reinforce a negative belief about self in relation to the world (Beck, 1976).

Beck (1967) identified several irrational thinking processes known as thought distortions. These irrational thoughts are self-defeating and create anxiety or depression in the individual. Beck talked about errors of thought and the patterns of habitual and maladaptive thinking. The counsellor's major focus is to help the clients in recognising the distortions (their content, degree of client belief, style) and their impact on the client's life. These distortions occur in many permutations and combinations. These included the following:

Box 2.4 Types of Cognitive Distortions

	Cognitive Distortions	*Explanation*	*Example*
1	**Arbitrary inference**	The individual quickly comes to a decision based on limited evidence.	That person did not pick up my phone. He does not like me.
2	**Selective abstraction**	The individual draws a conclusion based on the available evidence.	My professor asked me to do the work. He is partial.
3	**Overgeneralisation**	The individual assumes that everything will have the same consequences based on one negative event.	I did not get a good grade in internal. I cannot be successful.
4	**Magnification**	The individual amplifies the undesirable events.	I could not stop the car near the traffic light, I am not a good driver.
5	**Minimisation**	The individual underemphasises the significance of an event.	Though I got an award, I don't think it will make any significant effect on my career.
6	**Personalisation**	The individual attributes the negative feelings of others to himself.	My father is not in good mood, and so he must be angry with me.
7	**All-or-none thinking / dichotomous thinking or black-and-white thinking**	The individual thinks in extremes.	If I am not perfect, then I am a failure.
8	**Jumping to conclusions / Mind reading**	The individual assumes what someone is thinking. It includes the individual's unreasonable attempt to guess about others thinking and its influence on oneself.	My parents think that I am incompetent.
9	**Catastrophising / Mental filter**	The individual sees an unfavourable outcome to an event.	If I travel by car, there will be an accident. Because there are too many accidents nowadays. Better to avoid it.
10	**Comparing**	The individual compares oneself with others.	I am not a good singer like others.

	Cognitive Distortions	Explanation	Example
11	**Perfectionism**	The individual desires to be perfect in every aspect.	If I don't get full marks in the exam, my teacher will think that I am a failure.
12	**Disqualifying the positive**	The individual takes success as a matter of chance.	I have done well in class, but I'm really not that smart.
13	**Always being right**	The individual proves that he is right.	I want to win this argument because I am always right in my argument.
14	**Emotional reasoning**	The individual has confusing feelings for facts.	How do I know I'm useless? Because I feel useless, that's how.
15	**'Should' statements**	The individual develops absolutistic statements.	I should be extrovert. I'm very shy.
16	**Labelling**	The individual uses negative labels about oneself or others rather than describing the event.	If I wasn't such a weak person, I would have answered back nicely to her.
17	**Blame**	The individual internalises or externalises responsibility inappropriately. This thinking style involves blaming others for outcomes the individual is responsible for or blaming himself for outcomes that he had no control over.	If I had received more time, my speech would be nice.

Negative Self-Schemas

Schemas or schemata are somewhat permanent, organising structures that lead to situational information processing. Schemata are the cognitive structures developed early in life from experiences and identification with significant others. Further learning experiences strengthen early conceptualisations, which, in turn, impact the establishment of other beliefs, values, and attitudes. Dysfunctional schemata are negative in nature and are made up of immature, rigid, and absolute attitudes about oneself and the universe. According to Beck (1976), negative self-schemas are developed by people who are prone to depression, and schemas cause a variety of cognitive distortions. They hold a set of negative expectations and beliefs. Schemas may be positive, thereby helping in coping, or maybe negative and dysfunctional. According to Beck, these negative schemas might be acquired because of traumatic events in childhood. Individuals with negative self-schemas are more likely to fall victim to logical fallacies in their thinking and to focus only on certain facets of a situation while ignoring the crucial details.

According to Beck and Weishaar (1989), cognitive therapy is a collective process between client and counsellor that aims to modify inaccurate information processing and change dysfunctional ideas and assumptions that maintain maladaptive behaviours and emotions. It includes the characteristics of rapport building, empathy, trust, active listening, and the maintenance of the therapeutic alliance. The counsellor's goal is to assist clients in making the best use of their present energy while also increasing their energy reserves. During the session, the counsellor collects information to perform a preliminary assessment of the clients and provide direction and goals for treatment. Cognitive therapy focuses on establishing factors contributing to the way of thinking, evidence based on previous evaluation, and hypothesis testing to develop the thoughts and prediction of the rational thoughts that one will have. It uses a combination of behavioural and verbal strategies to assess the clients' beliefs, challenge the dysfunctional ones, and provide skills for adaptive cognitive processing. All these factors make it possible to treat the problems induced by the thoughts.

Cognitive change occurs mainly at several levels: involuntary thoughts or automatic thoughts, voluntary thoughts, and assumptions. Based on the degree of accessibility and stability, these levels of cognition are hierarchically arranged. Voluntary thoughts, under this measure, are the most accessible and least stable sort of cognition because they can be engaged at will and are only temporary. Automatic thoughts on the other hand come spontaneously, and are highly powerful, more stable, and less accessible. They intrude between a stimulus event and one's emotional and behavioural reactions to it. They are accompanied by effect and are plausible, highly prominent, and consistent with that person's thinking at the time they are experienced. Automatic thoughts receive a lot of attention in the early phases of therapy because of their mediating role between stimuli and reactions, as well as the prevalence of cognitive distortions. Clients frequently require training to notice automatic thinking.

Automatic thoughts indicate distortions in information processing as well as the individual's beliefs and underlying assumptions. Automatic thoughts are created when an underlying assumption is aroused by an event or circumstance. As a result, the counsellor's access to the clients' basic assumptions is frequently through automatic thoughts. For example, the individual with a belief, 'Unless my supervisor helps, I cannot progress in my career', would have amplification of negative automatic thoughts following resentment towards the supervisor. Assumptions mainly concern how one thinks about oneself and the outside world. These are the rules that are gained through personal experience or from others. Assumptions are quite stable and unnoticed by the clients. The role of the counsellor is to identify the schemata and counteract their negative effects. Once these core beliefs called schemata or assumptions can be changed, then the individuals will have less chance of vulnerability to future distress (Beck & Weishaar, 1989).

Application

Cognitive therapy has been established to be useful in anxiety disorders and depressive disorders. It can be used in treating eating disorders, personality disorders, marital discord, and phobias.

Box 2.5 Differences Between REBT and Cognitive Therapy

REBT	*Cognitive therapy*
Developed in the 1950s by psychologist and psychotherapist Albert Ellis (1913–2007)	Developed in 1960s by Aaron Beck (1921–2021)
REBT is directive, persuasive and confrontive	Cognitive therapy emphasises the client's discovery of misconceptions for themselves
It contends that negative evaluative demands are at the root of psychological disturbance	It contends that negative representational beliefs are of central relevance
In REBT, Unconditional Self-Acceptance (USA) is the idea that a person should always think well of himself	The goal of cognitive therapy is to reinforce positive attributes about a person in order to counteract negative feelings about that individual
It is not essential for therapists to have a warm relationship with their clients in REBT	The quality of the therapeutic relationship is important for cognitive therapy to be effective
REBT employs a variety of techniques based on the client's personality	Cognitive therapy is based on the disorder

REBT and CT are similar in several ways. Their main argument is that ideas, beliefs, attitudes, and thinking have a greater influence on human emotions and behaviour as opposed to actual events. Hence, changing one's thinking results in emotional and behavioural changes.

Acceptance and Commitment Therapy (ACT)

ACT was developed by psychologist Steven Hayes in 1980s. One of ACT's main teachings is to accept what is beyond your personal control and commit to action that will enhance and enrich your life. Its key message is to accept the things you cannot change and resolve to make decisions that will improve and enrich your life. The purpose of ACT is to assist individuals in realising their full potential and leading rich, fulfilling lives. The philosophy proposed by ACT is functional contextualism which assumes that human actions are always contextualised within their historical and current environments. Thinking and feeling are viewed as forms of human behaviour in this approach (Baer & Huss, 2008). ACT defines a context as a set of circumstances. Human behaviour is always influenced by environmental events. While individual behaviours are influenced by some of these events, the cultural practices or the survival of the species is influenced by others (Hayes, 1987).

The view of ACT is that different sorts of behaviours, such as thinking, feeling, and acting, are often functionally related. When one thinks that 'No one assists me', he or she may feel depressed and isolated. Staying isolated does not always result from the occurrence of such a thought. The apparent causal relationship between thoughts (no one helps me) and behaviours (staying solitary), according to Hayes and colleagues, is dependent on social and verbal circumstances in which thoughts are regarded to be genuine and essential, necessitating specific behaviours. If thoughts are perceived as mere thoughts, their influence on behaviour may be reduced considerably. This would allow for other factors such as important goals and values (e.g., cultivating a more active social life) to have a greater impact. Hayes and colleagues developed a treatment known as comprehensive distancing (Hayes, 1987; Zettle & Hayes, 1986) that challenged assumptions that thoughts must govern behaviour. The primary therapeutic process is distancing, which weakens the influence of thoughts on other behaviours. Using comprehensive distancing, participants identified and recognised their depressive thoughts and engaged in adaptive behaviour while they were experiencing them.

Unwanted emotional experiences are not defined as symptoms or issues in ACT theory. On the other hand, dealing with these unpleasant events without evaluating them necessitates abilities. Unlike cognitive behavioural therapy, it encourages clients to create a fresh and compassionate relationship with their experiences rather than attempting to control or halt undesired thoughts or sensations. This shift can help people overcome problems in trying to control their experiences and become more receptive to taking actions that are compatible with their ideals. It is an action-oriented approach giving importance to value-based mindful action. One needs to be engrossed in action with complete awareness of the surroundings. 'The aim of ACT is to help us create a rich, full, and meaningful life while accepting the pain that life inevitably brings' (Harris, 2009). On the other hand, the fundamental idea of ACT is acquiring acceptance for unwelcome, intimate situations that are beyond one's control as well as activity and dedication to leading a life of value.

The core of ACT is based on **Relational Frame Theory** (RFT; Hayes, et al., 2001). RFT is a behavioural model of human language and cognition that explains how normal cognitive processes can lead to psychological problems. RFT is a behaviour-analytic approach to language that explains how language and behaviour are linked. RFT is founded on the idea that humans can form connections between thoughts, words, and images, which are the foundation of 'higher cognition' – or the ability to connect. The social-verbal community, in which humans are embedded, in particular, promotes cognitive fusion and experience avoidance.

Cognitive fusion describes a time when we become attached to our thoughts and merge with them. Cognitive fusion makes no distinction between what we think and the conditions that make us think that way. When we experience cognitive fusion, we become inseparable from our thoughts. Our thoughts become our reality. We feel removed from the outer world of our minds, our senses, our actions, and even the people around us. We neglect to contrast our thoughts with the reality that gave rise to them. We have 'fused' with them.

Experiential avoidance is defined as a desire to avoid, escape, or remove unpleasant internal occurrences (e.g., feelings, sensations, and cognitions). It is referred to as emotional avoidance, emotional unwillingness, thought suppression, and unwillingness. When individuals try to manage their internal experiences like worry, for example, they may employ unproductive strategies such as suppressing their thoughts, which paradoxically increases their frequency of unwanted thoughts because this type of avoidance provides short-term relief. For instance, thought stopping or stopping one's thoughts can lead to thought rebounding, whereby one is confronted with even more unfavourable thoughts. To deal with internal experiences, people frequently practice various forms of experiential avoidance. For example, we can watch a movie when we're bored. These behaviours become problematic when they get in the way of everyday activities or when they're used harmfully. Although while these avoidance behaviours are an attempt to manage one's inner experiences, they eventually aggravate suffering and frequently have fatal consequences. Many psychopathologies and illnesses are consequently linked to inappropriate and unsuccessful attempts to suppress unpleasant internal feelings.

Mindfulness (described in detail in Buddhist counselling) is an awareness process of paying attention to the present moment. ACT uses acceptance and mindfulness strategies to help people live and behave in ways that are compatible with their values while enhancing psychological flexibility. Psychological flexibility refers to completely engaging in the current moment and adapting or persevering in behaviour at the service of chosen values based on the circumstances. There are six core integrated components of ACT approaches that help in building psychological flexibility. These six components are – being present moment, cognitive defusion, acceptance, self-as-context, values, and committed action.

Being present moment is explained as keeping oneself completely in the present moment, detaching from various thoughts. Contacting the present moment has to do with 'being in the now'. It focuses on an individual's 'observing self' rather than the 'thinking self'. This principle explains that one must focus on the happenings of the present instead of focusing on what has happened in the past and going to happen in the future.

Cognitive defusion is the opposite of cognitive fusion. Detaching a little from our thoughts and taking a step back from what is going on in our minds is known as cognitive defusion. It refers to the recognition of thoughts as just thoughts. It helps people to fuse negative thoughts. According to Harris (2009), cognitive defusion is: looking at thoughts rather than from thoughts. Observe thoughts rather than getting engrossed in them. We can examine our thoughts and other internal processes while in this defusion state without entangled with, trapped by, or fused with them. If we choose to, we can simply be aware of our ideas, watch them, accept them, and let them go. The principle that thoughts are not facts – that just because we think something, it doesn't necessarily imply it's true – can help us defuse our thoughts. The potential for our thoughts to overtake reality occurs when we are in a state of cognitive fusion. We can attain cognitive defusion by understanding that thoughts are really thoughts-just mental events-rather than facts, and we can defuse thinking by simply acknowledging, 'perhaps I'm confused a thought with a fact', to ourselves. In this case instead of thinking, 'if I drive, there will be an accident', say to yourself, 'I'm having the thought that "if I drive, there will be an accident".

Acceptance means allowing the person to be open to unpleasant thoughts, emotions, and occurrences. Instead of initiating a fight to get rid of the unpleasant feelings, it allows the feelings to happen while building the courage for the necessary change. 'Acceptance is based on the notion that, as a rule, trying to get rid of your pain only amplifies it, entangles you further in it, and transforms it into something traumatic. Acceptance, in the sense it is used here, is not nihilistic self-defeat; neither is it tolerating and putting up with your pain' (Hayes & Smith, 2005. p.7).

Self-as-context explains 'the observing self' or the observation of what is happening within. One should be aware of one's thoughts while experiencing bodily or emotional experiences. In simple words, it is thinking about thinking.

Value-based living emphasises people's values. These values provide direction to accomplish behaviour. Values have to do with what people want their life to be about, what they want to stand for, and ultimately what they experience as their genuine motivation, experience as their true drive. Values help people in directing their behaviours towards what is important to them.

Committed action explains taking effective action and behaving in ways that are guided by one's ideals. This enables people to live lives that are both rewarding and satisfying. Value-based actions produce a wide range of ideas and feelings, both pleasurable

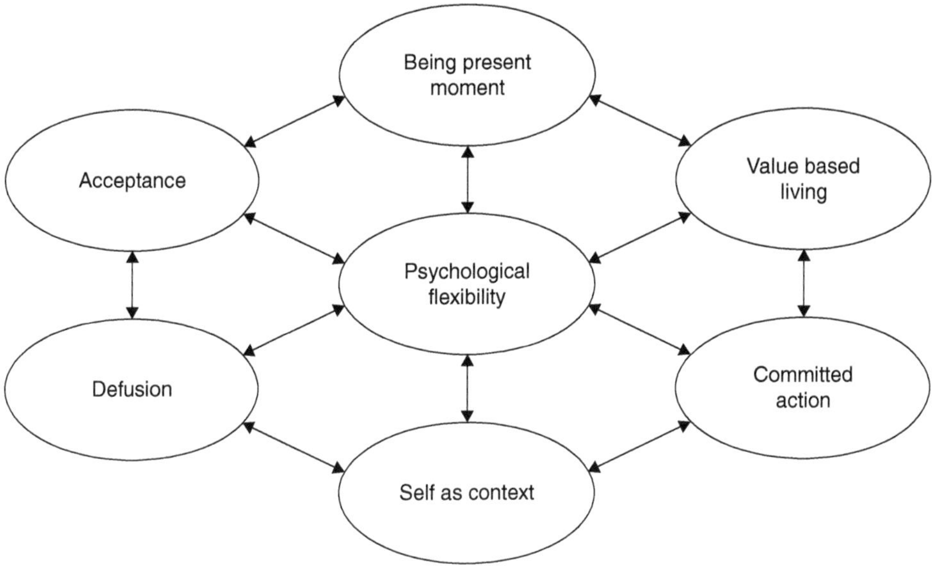

Figure 2.11 Integrated Components of ACT Approach

and painful (Harris, 2009). Ensuring our deeds adhere to our values despite enduring pain and discomfort is the idea of committed action.

Integrated Components of ACT Approach

The approach of ACT is optimistic and explains that in the middle of suffering and pain, an individual can find purpose, meaning, and vitality. ACT does not focus only to reduce human suffering; on the other hand, it helps people handle the suffering and grow out of it. It teaches how to develop vulnerability and become resilient.

In ACT, emphasis is also placed on the counsellor and client's shared subjectivity in that both are subject to the same general 'language traps' of fusion and experiential avoidance (Hayes et al., 1999). ACT counsellors and their clients often form a strong bond. To do so, the therapist needs to be open, accepting, and consistent with ACT principles.

Application

ACT is a versatile method that may be used with a wide range of people and disorders in individual or group settings. Anxiety, psychosis, depression, substance abuse, and a variety of other therapeutic disorders have all been treated with this method. It has also influenced subclinical issues including work productivity, athletic performance, and academic accomplishment.

Dialectical Behaviour Therapy (DBT)

DBT was established by Marsha Linehan in the year 1993. Earlier in her career, Linehan was fascinated by the application of behavioural theories to suicidal behaviour. While treating clients with extreme distress, two core points emerged which gave rise to DBT. First, treatment focused on change-based and acceptance-based methods. Second, 'adapting' to the two conflicting approaches required a structural or philosophical context. Hence the word 'dialectical' was used for this therapy. The word dialectical means 'acting through opposing forces'. Dialectical refers to the use of logic while expressing opinions and ideas and solve difficult problems that are out of one's control. It is based on the idea that combining acceptance and change in therapy is more beneficial than focusing on either one. For example, dialectics between change and acceptance. This dialectic posits that 'change can only occur in the context of acceptance of what is; however, "acceptance of what is" is itself change' (Linehan, 1993a, pp. 98–99). The treatment of DBT focuses more on behaviourism than cognition. She was interested in the relevance and application of Zen principles and the practice of mindfulness in health care. While Kabat- Zinn was the first to integrate mindfulness into intervention in psychological medicine, Linehan brought mindfulness into a psychological intervention (Swales & Heard, 2017). She created a set of techniques that could be taught to clients who were upset and dysregulated by modifying the concepts and application of mindfulness (Linehan, 2015).

Linehan incorporated skills training into DBT because pervasive skills impairments were found as a major concern among adults who fit the criteria for Borderline Personality Disorder (BPD) and participated in suicidal behaviour (Linehan, 2015). Biosocial theory views, behavioural dysfunction associated with BPD is caused by a mismatch between a temperamentally sensitive and reactive person and their environment. Environmental factors and the emotionally vulnerable person help to shape and promote one another's excessive behaviour. Due to insufficient modelling, coaching, and encouragement of expressive behaviours, excessive punishment or intermittent reinforcement of highly expressive behaviours develops (Cowperthwait et al., 2019). This transaction results in impairments in the skills needed to control emotions and endure emotional distress over time, which leads to maladaptive behaviours used to control negative affect and/or inhibit emotional responses. As a result, persons who match the criteria for BPD are seen as having emotion dysregulation because of skill deficits.

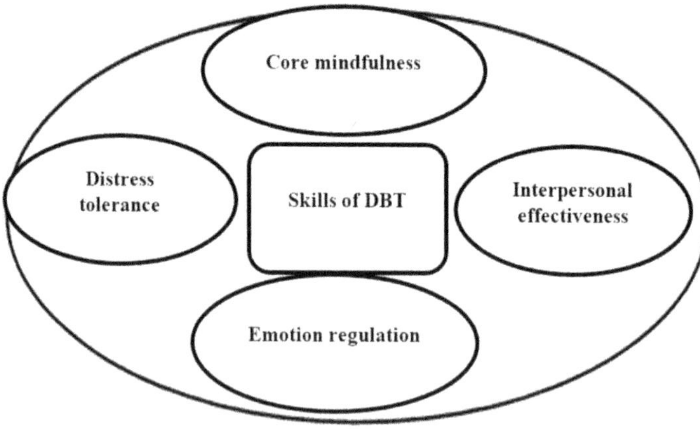

Figure 2.12 Four Skills of Dialectical Behaviour Therapy

Dialectical Behaviour Therapy Skills

DBT aims to train people how to be more in control of their emotions, deal with stress effectively, live in the present now, and maintain a healthy relationship. DBT treatment typically starts with allowing someone to accept themselves and their lives as they are, rather than how they think they should be. They will then be led to understand that to succeed in life, they must make certain changes. DBT skills training is to teach skills and increase their application in everyday circumstances. A skills training group teaches four all-encompassing skill sets: core mindfulness, interpersonal effectiveness, emotion regulation, and distress tolerance. These skills were primarily employed to rectify emotional, behavioural, interpersonal, cognitive, and social dysregulation and skill deficits that are common in those with BPD, as well as those who struggle with emotion regulation.

Four Skills of Dialectical Behaviour Therapy

Core Mindfulness Skills

Based on Eastern spiritual practices of Zen, these skills emphasise participating in the present moment efficiently in an accepting, non-judgemental way. They're at the heart of DBT skills and strategies and are taught at the start of other modules (Linehan, 2015). The main objective of DBT mindfulness skills is to target self-dysregulation (identity disturbance or unstable self-image) and to reduce susceptibility to paranoid thinking, dissociation, and over-personalisation (Lynch et al., 2003).

Interpersonal Effectiveness Skills

These skills were originally developed to combat intense and chaotic interpersonal relationships and interpersonal dysregulation, which often leads to fear of being abandoned. These skills include assertiveness in seeking things or rejecting appeals, establishing relationships with others, and sustaining self-esteem in interpersonal situations.

Emotion Regulation Skills

These skills are used in recognising emotions, understanding emotions, labelling feelings, encouraging pleasant emotional experiences, and limiting vulnerability to negative emotions. Clients with emotional dysregulation who fulfil criteria for a variety of disorders can benefit from these skills.

Distress Tolerance Skills

Crisis survival and reality-acceptance strategies are included in these skills. Crisis survival skills are short-term strategies for coping with difficult life situations without engaging in impulsive behaviours like self-harm or suicide. The purpose of radical acceptance is to alleviate suffering; therefore, acceptance skills focus on radically accepting difficult situations that are unlikely to alter (Linehan 1993, 2015).

The group skills instruction is quite structured for two to two and a half hours. One 'leader', who is in charge of content and learning, and one 'co-leader', who is in charge of process and group dynamics management, teaches the skills training group. The first half of the group consists of mindfulness exercises and a review of the previous week's written homework. The second half of the session includes direct training in new DBT skills as well as a homework assignment. The teaching of all four skills training modules takes about six months, while the amount of time varies on the number of skills to be taught (Neacsiu et al., 2013). Each of the other three modules repeats the core mindfulness module, and new clients are encouraged to join skills training while the group is learning the core mindfulness module (Linehan, 2015).

With Dialectical Behaviour Therapy, clients are encouraged to develop a genuine and egalitarian relationship. In DBT, a strong, supportive relationship is essential and may be the main factor in sustaining clients' treatment or even keeping them alive during challenging times (Linehan, 1993). Relationships are described to an end as well as ends in themselves. Clients' intrinsic potential for healing, learning, and growth is stimulated by a healthy relationship in which the counsellor is caring, sensitive, adaptable, and welcoming. At the same time, the therapeutic connection allows the counsellor to teach new skills to clients and persuade them to apply them, even when they are reluctant. Counsellors that practice DBT are compassionate, affirming, and sincere, as well as irreverent at times. In a constant dialogue with clients, they accept them as they are and then help them change. Counsellors nurture clients while making compassionate yet reasonable demands that they engage in constructive behaviour when they can do so. As a coach and cheerleader, the counsellor teaches the clients any needed skills that are lacking in their repertoire.

Application

DBT is an inclusive treatment approach that was originally established to treat borderline personality disorder (BPD), but it is now being used to treat a variety of other issues. DBT is still the best researched and tested of all the treatments. Its primary goal was to treat impulsive and suicidal behaviours as well as personality problems. In addition to treating personality disorders, it is used in treating eating disorders, depression, substance abuse, and anxiety. DBT is used to help people diagnosed with bipolar disorder, attention deficit hyperactivity disorder (ADHD), eating disorders, post-traumatic stress disorder (PTSD) as well as substance abuse.

REBT is regarded as a pioneer in the field of Cognitive Behavioural Therapy. According to Ellis, people can change but find it difficult to do so because they have become accustomed to their dysfunctional beliefs, feelings, and behaviours. REBT's major goal is for clients to vigorously challenge their irrational beliefs, resulting in more rational and adaptable thinking, as well as healthier attitudes and behaviours. Clients are better equipped to operate successfully despite adversity, to embrace themselves and others more fully, and to experience more self-fulfilment, according to Ellis, if they strive hard to accomplish these deep adjustments in their belief systems. DBT is a research-based treatment for those who have borderline personality disorder (BPD) and suicidal ideation. It is based on the use of validation and problem-solving skills to minimise psychological distress in clients. It focuses on teaching clients' mindfulness, interpersonal effectiveness, emotion control, and distress tolerance among other skills. While DBT is largely used to treat people with BPD and suicidal behaviour, there is growing evidence that it can also be used to address other psychological illnesses like substance abuse, eating disorders and elderly depression. Cognitive Behavioural Therapy is a widely used treatment for psychological illness. There are various specific treatments that fall into the general category of CBT and share similar guiding principles and processes. It is based on training clients in recognising maladaptive cognitions and modifying them to minimise psychological distress. Moreover, it is used to treat a variety of symptoms, illnesses, and subgroups of clients. CBT has a wealth of evidence to support its effectiveness in treating a variety of psychological illnesses in children, adolescents and adults, especially internalising disorders such as anxiety and depression.

Gestalt Therapy

Gestalt therapy was developed in the 1940s by Frederick Perls, Laura Perls, and Paul Goodman. Gestalt is the German word for configuration or pattern. The term gestalt explains that we perceive and experience the world in a meaningful whole and not in isolation. According to Goodman, individuals are perceived as a whole, more than the sum of their behaviours. Gestalt therapy is based on psychoanalysis, Gestalt psychology, and early phenomenological work. It is a relational and process-oriented approach that focuses on individuals' healthy functioning. Gestalt therapy involves basic notions of phenomenology, field theory, existentialism, and dialogue. These are called the four pillars of gestalt therapy.

Phenomenology

Rather than segmenting relevant mental events for later investigation, phenomenologists study them as they occur. The phenomenological perspective methodically analyses clients' current experience, intending to help them be self-aware. Gestalt counsellors focus on the client's subjective experiences and pay as much attention as possible to what is truly understandable through the senses. Therapy involves meeting the clients where they are and describing what the counsellor observes instead of explaining or interpreting. Clients are encouraged to do the same. As a part of the treatment process, the counsellors also share their thoughts, feelings, and awareness with the clients.

Field Theory

Gestalt psychologists apply field theory from physics to psychology. A field theory explains that the field is dynamic and interconnected, nothing stands alone. They held the view that a person's experiences have an impact on every aspect of that person. For example, the world looks different if one has knee pain or a cold. Gestalt psychologists emphasise totality and not isolated parts. For them, 'to dissect is to distort'. Gestalt psychologist Kurt Lewin developed a theory of human motivation around field theory. His view was that human behaviour at any given moment is decided by several psychological facts and a person's life space (field) is the sum of all these psychological facts. These facts will have both positive and negative influences on an individual's behaviour. Facts that are consciously experienced only influence behaviour. A person resides in a constantly shifting field of influences, and any change in one has an impact on the other. The counsellor in gestalt therapy pays attention to the entire field, encompassing substance and subject matter, as well as the current process. This involves both verbal and non-verbal communication with the clients. The clients' communication and engagement style, tone of voice, facial expression, gestures, postures, and affect are all factors to consider. The therapeutic field also encompasses the client's past and present circumstances, the therapeutic connection, the clients' and counsellors' sentiments, and their joint impact.

Existentialism

Existentialism focuses on the truth of the individual's relationships to the environment. Its focus is on understanding people's existence in the world in terms of awareness. By assisting individuals to experience the present, Gestalt psychologists enable greater self-awareness and understanding.

Dialogue

The last one is the dialogue which explains the interaction with other individuals in the environment. This includes inclusion (without being mistaken for another), presence (the counsellor being present with the client), commitment to dialogue (enabling contact to occur), protecting clients' integrity, and experiencing dialogue rather than simply talking about it. Taking a dialogic stance needs the counsellor to be 'present', confirm the clients, and be open to an 'I–Thou' manner of interacting. The counsellor's presence is defined as bringing everything of himself to the meeting in the present moment. Confirmation entails seeing and accepting clients for all that they are and can become. A mutually beneficial 'I–Thou' relationship is characterised by openness, directness, presence, intensity, and cordiality. These characteristics result in a non-hierarchical therapeutic partnership and a healing encounter between the client and the counsellor.

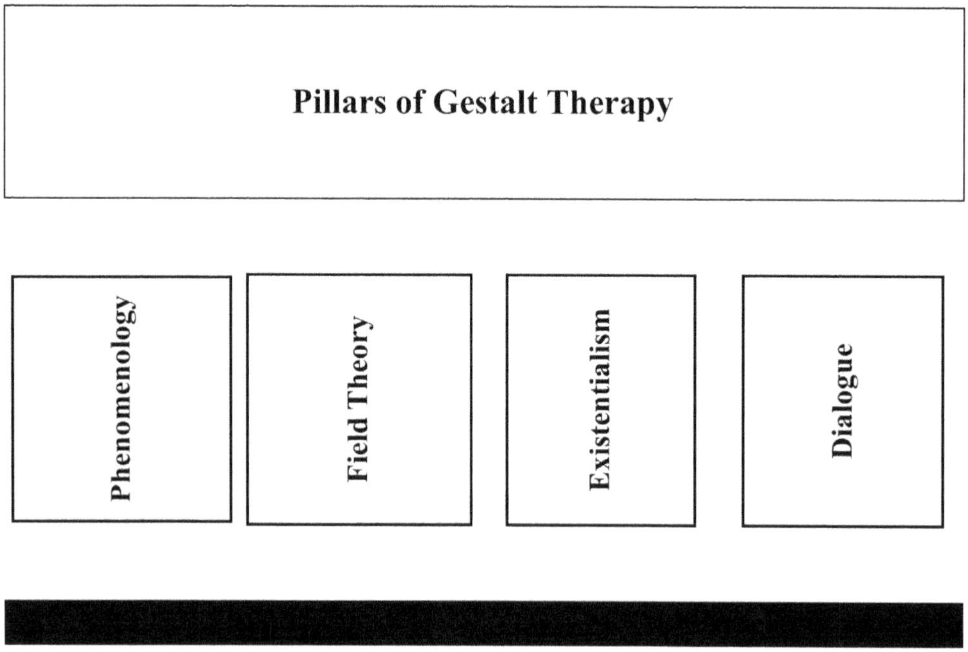

Figure 2.13 Pillars of Gestalt Therapy

Key Theoretical Concepts of Gestalt Therapy

Gestalt therapy differs considerably from existential and person-centred approaches to treatment that employ fewer specific intervention techniques.

View on Humankind

Perls, like other humanists, had a positive and empowering perspective of individuals, emphasising the necessity of self-actualisation: 'Every individual, every plant, every animal has only one inborn goal to actualise itself as it is' (Perls, 1969a, p. 33). He felt that individuals were inherently decent and capable of effectively navigating their lives, while he acknowledged that they occasionally required assistance. Healthy humans, according to Perls, were productive in their survival and maintenance activities and intuitively gravitated towards self-preservation and progress. Gestalt therapy aids in the development of self-awareness, inner power, and independence.

Wholeness, Integration, and Balance

Gestalt therapy highlights the significance of integration and balance in people's lives. People cannot be divided into components (such as body and mind) or removed from their environment (Murdock, 2009). The human organism, according to Perls (1969), is not a summation of parts but a combination of the whole.

Awareness

To Gestalt counsellors, awareness is essential to health: 'Awareness in and of itself-by and large-can be therapeutic; because once you become aware of this organismic self-regulation, you can let the organism take over, to rely on its wisdom' (Perls, 1969, p. 17). The trademark of a healthy individual is awareness, and treatment aims to promote it. Through experimentation, a focus on the here and now, and process statements, Gestalt therapy facilitates awareness. The counsellors do not practice reflective listening because they are unable to simply talk about their feelings. Instead, they pay attention to nonverbal cues – the way their clients sit, or how they speak or tap a ringer. Clients are encouraged to dig deeper as they pay attention to these and other body movements, allowing them to relive their emotions in the present moment of treatment and to comprehend both the physical and verbal significance of what they are projecting.

Goals of Gestalt Therapy

Gestalt therapy aims to improve people's wholeness, integration, and balance by fostering attention, clarity, and awareness, as well as assisting them in living in the present moment (Seligman & Reichenberg, 2014). Gestalt therapy aims to develop awareness like awareness of oneself, others, and the environment, to promote personal growth and integration. Even if the clients exhibit specific symptoms like anxiety, depression, stress-related health concerns, relationship difficulties, or character/personality issues, it does not focus primarily on symptoms or behaviour change. The counsellors adopt a holistic approach, viewing symptoms and problematic behaviours as clients' best efforts to handle conflicting wishes or needs that clash with environmental demands.

Counselling through the Gestalt Approach

The psychological problems, symptoms, and challenges of individuals in relationships are the result of once creative changes that have become rigid, reflexive and imperceptible, limiting their sense of self and options. The counsellor concentrates on the moment-to-moment process in the treatment session to explore the process of establishing the individuals' sense of self, other self-identities, and how these experiences affect their current situation. Gestalt therapy focuses on the clients' capacity for creative solutions rather than directly on problem solving. It teaches a person to get the solution instead of providing the solution. To achieve solutions to the problem behaviours, the counsellor gives importance to clients' present experiences through dialogue and phenomenology. This needs a robust working association between the counsellor and the client. Through direct contact with the counsellor, clients need to develop complete self-awareness and self-regulation of a complete (whole) existence encompassed of essential parts. This involves good gestalt (whole is organised in good form) and creative adjustment (balance between self and the environment). Self-regulation is attained through phenomenology, dialogue with the counsellor, and cognisance of the whole field concept (what, how, and why it is done). Instead of focusing directly on problem-solving, the counsellor focuses on what restricts clients' ability for creative solutions.

Gestalt therapy gains control over the essence of individuals' existential position, which influences all facets of self-experience and social relationships. For example, the client becomes upset but unable to cry, expresses regret without reason, and shifts the topic if it relates to uncontrollable emotions. The role of the counsellor is to understand the blocks to examine how they started initially. The aim of treatment is the re-establishment of awareness, which highlights the experience of reality both in clients and in counsellors. It helps clients focus on the present, instead of perceiving the future based on experience. It is an existential approach in that it emphasises individuals' concern for themselves and their ability to regulate their own current experiences.

Techniques Used in Gestalt Therapy

Gestalt therapy is carried out through exercises and experiments that can be done alone or in groups. Two important gestalt therapy strategies used to help clients in therapy raise their awareness of immediate experiences are the empty chair technique and the exaggeration exercise. The empty chair or two-chair experiment can also be used to draw attention to an internal conflict. Through exercises and spontaneous experimentation, Gestalt therapy enables people to reconnect with aspects of themselves that they may have neglected, rejected, or failed to acknowledge. In the empty chair therapy exercise, the clients sit near an empty chair and are asked to imagine that someone is sitting in the chair (such as a spouse, colleague, or relative). In therapy, the therapist encourages clients to discuss their thoughts, emotions, and behaviours with the empty chair. The roles are sometimes reversed, and the persons in therapy assume the role of the metaphorical person or part of it. People can use the empty chair technique to help themselves become aware of the whole situation and regain a sense of self that has been lost or disengaged. In the exaggeration exercise, the individuals in therapy are asked to repeat and exaggerate an expression or movement, such as grimacing or fist fighting to increase their awareness of their emotional side.

The theory of healthy functioning in Gestalt therapy is based on a biological concept known as **organismic self-regulation**. This explains that an organism takes in what it needs from the environment for survival and discharges what it doesn't need to maintain homeostasis. The same theory is also applied to healthy psychological functioning. People need others to be heard to vent their emotions. Gestalt therapy considers the individual and environment are not separate from each other but rather the individual as a distinct entity of the environment. According to Gestalt therapy, the figure formation/destruction process is responsible for such self-regulation. This is a continuous process. The person is seen as self-regulatory and proficient in motivating oneself to deal with difficulties. Individuals can work towards growth and development as their circumstances permit. A mentally healthy individual is one who can self-regulate through life's changes and has established a sense of 'wholeness' between mind and body (Corsini & Wedding, 2000). The individual forms a figure of interest in order to satisfy the need. Once the need is satisfied, the figure is replaced by other needs. Sometimes the individual makes creative adjustments if there is no match between the needs and what is available in the environment. These creative adaptations gradually lose their usefulness, become rigid, and fade from consciousness, which hinders a person's ability to satisfy their needs. The role of the counsellor is to find out how the self-regulatory process is disrupted. The following five processes explain how disruption of contact happens.

There is a clear-cut boundary between the individuals and others around them and they must realise their functions in the environment. When boundary functions are effective, people switch between connecting and disconnecting with their environment and disengaging from them. Disruption results due to problems demarcating between oneself and others in the environment. These disruptions are – confluence, retroflection, introjection, projection, and deflection.

Confluence refers to the absence of difference between self and others. It is 'dysfunctional closeness, two persons behaving as one'. It is a failure to recognise the differences between oneself and another. In confluence, there is an attempt to deny the existence of a self/environment barrier. Organisms and the environment are interdependent. For example, a wife may harm herself because she is angry at her husband and doesn't want to harm him.

Retroflection is the suppression of behaviour and the redirection back onto the self. It is 'doing to oneself instead of the other'. Retroflection occurs when an action that could be targeted towards the environment is targeted at oneself. 'Do to yourself that you would do to someone else'. There are two types of retroflecting: in the first case, when the person directs feeling or action towards himself that is meant for someone or something else in the environment. For example, the boss who is unable to direct the colleague to do the work might finish doing it himself. The second type entails doing for oneself what another person would have done for him. For example, instead of getting a gift from someone, the person gets satisfaction by buying a gift for him.

Introjection refers to a lack of discrimination or assimilation of new information gained. 'It means taking information in whole without critical examination'. Introjects are 'standards, attitudes, behaviours, and ways of thinking that are not actually ours' yet organise our functioning (Perls, 1973, p. 35). According to Perls, introjects form because of the environment's excessive control due to which the individual is not permitted to act in line with his or her own wants and sense of self. A person who introjects identifies so strongly with a person or object that they cannot separate themselves from them. For example, the employee talks like his employer.

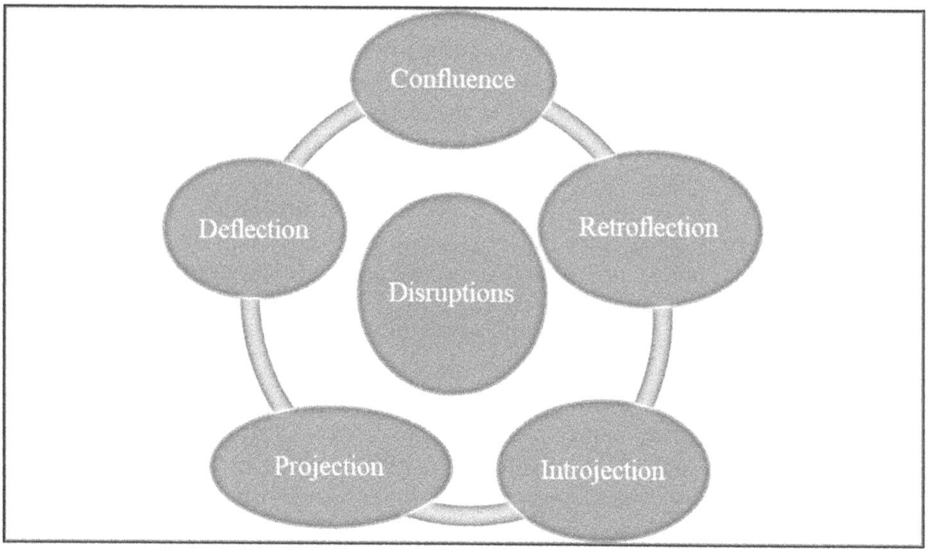

Figure 2.14 Disruption of Contact

Projection is the confusion of self and others. It refers to rejecting the feeling, behaviour, and attitude of one's own and attaching it to another or the environment. 'It is to put one's feelings on to others'. The boundary disturbance of projection occurs when an event that occurs in one's own self is wrongly assigned to another person to evade knowledge of one's own experience. For example, a person who is unable to be annoyed with someone may mistakenly believe that another person is angry with him.

Deflection refers to the avoidance of contact with others. It refers to disregarding or turning aside either internal or external stimuli to avoid full recognition or awareness. 'It is distancing from one's feelings and others'. Deflecting is a technique for reducing or diluting the intensity of contact. For example, not making eye contact, laughing off one's own words, and understating one's genuine feelings.

Field theory, phenomenology, and dialogue are the foundations of Gestalt therapy. Gestalt therapy focuses on the person/environment field and is based on a process-oriented approach. According to this therapy, a healthy person is conscious of their own existence and lives in the present rather than the past or future. The empty chair method is found to be more useful in decreasing anger and building positive attitudes. It is also more effective in creating a greater depth of understanding than empathic reflection or focusing.

Applications

Gestalt therapy is effective for a myriad of problems across the population.

The Gestalt therapist makes no claim to know what is best for the client, and he has no preference for a specific outcome. The main goal is to raise client awareness, which will lead to more options. Gestalt therapy was first used to help persons who were nervous or depressed but did not have any substantial clinical symptoms. It has been demonstrated to be effective in treating clients with a borderline personality disorder. It can be used to solve varied issues (anorexia nervosa, addiction problems, affective and personality disorders, adjustment disorders, grief, and posttraumatic stress disorders). Gestalt therapy can be used to solve issues related to different interpersonal issues of individuals, couples, and families (Corsini & Wedding, 2000).

Person-Centred Counselling

The person-centred approach is based on concepts from humanistic psychology. Humanism comes from the ancient Greek tradition of 'knowing thyself' (Grondin, 1995, p.112). 'Humanism is a theoretical orientation that emphasises the unique qualities of humans, especially their free will and their potential for personal growth' (Weiten, et al., 2018, p. 44). Hence, humanism can be understood as a process of knowing oneself. As a humanistic psychologist, Carl Rogers (1902–1987) emphasised individuals' potential growth for self-direction and freedom of choice. 'Self' here is referred to as an individuals' experiences. While both psychoanalysis and behaviourism portray people as helpless creatures struck by internal instincts or external stimuli, the humanistic approach is more concerned with the individual's self-perception, immediate experiences, and personal views of others. The humanistic approach emphasised 'here and now' instead of early childhood experiences.

The humanistic theory came into existence during the period when psychoanalysis dominated clinical psychology and modernism challenged the traditional education system. Person-centred counselling and psychotherapy coined by Rogers are also known as non-directive or client-centred approaches. It is nondirective because the counsellor does not try to direct the clients' attention to specific topics. It is client-centred because the clients arrive at the insights and make the interpretation instead of the counsellor. The name person-centred emphasises positive views of the individuals, believing that they tend to move towards fully functioning persons. Though Rogers' primary work was influenced by Freud's psychoanalytic notions, the view changed when he realised that 'it is the client who knows what hurts, what directions to go, what problems are crucial, what experiences have been buried' (Rogers, 1961, pp. 11–12). While psychoanalysis attempts to relate clients' problems to their early childhood experiences, the client-centred theory focuses on the client's current attitudes and behaviour. Rogers purposefully used the term 'clients' in place of 'patients'. His view on 'patients' implied sick individuals looking for a cure while 'clients' implied individuals seeking support, controlling their fortune, and overcoming their difficulties. This leads to self-direction, an important aspect of client-centred therapy. Person-centred therapy, as with other humanistic and existential approaches, can be understood as a form of counselling and psychotherapy which puts particular emphasis on 'conceptualising, and engaging with people in a deeply valuing and respectful way' (Cooper, 2007, p. 11).

Humanistic theorists believe that (1) it is in human nature to seek personal growth, (2) individuals are free to decide their own choices, and (3) humans are rational beings, hence unconscious, irrational needs and conflicts cannot dominate their behaviour. Humanistic theorists give importance to one's subjective understanding of the world rather objective reality.

Rogers argued that incongruence between a person's perception of reality and their self-concept creates distress in them. His theory holds that people who experience incongruence often feel helpless by realistic feedback about themselves. In Rogers' view, anxiety over such feedback often results in defense mechanisms, distortions of reality, and stifled personal development. Clients who depend excessively on others to approve and accept them may exhibit excessive incongruence.

Rogers' psychotherapy and counselling arose from his work as a therapist, his interactions with colleagues, and his research into the therapeutic process and practice. According to Rogers (1966), the aim of counselling is not to solve problems, but rather to help clients in their growth process which can help them to cope better with their current and future problems. Rogers believed that each person could change; the counsellor only facilitates the change. Clients are considered the best experts in their lives and masters of their destinies. The counsellor acts as a 'confidential sounding board' while the client explores and analyses the problem. The goals of counselling and therapy according to Rogers are to help individuals to become congruent, self-accepting persons by appraising their talents, competencies, and general worth. Client-centred counsellors promote clients' awareness that they do not have to constantly strive to please others and be accepted. Clients are encouraged to respect their own feelings and values by counsellors. They assist people in reshaping their self-concept to better accord with reality. The goal of the counsellors is to promote self-acceptance and personal development. In the counselling process, assessment of the clients was done by appraising their current awareness and experiences. The counsellor tries to bring psychological changes through genuine and empathic relationships. Rogers focused more on the psychotherapeutic conceptualisation of personality change.

In a client-centred approach, the counsellor builds an atmosphere in which the clients feel self-worth. The ambience atmosphere arises because of the counsellor's belief that every individual is important, and everyone has the competency to deal with the situation productively. The counsellor accepts the clients' outlook, listens to the clients intently, and indicates that he can see things as the clients see without emotional involvement.

In a client-centred approach, the counsellor begins by explaining the nature of the counselling sessions. Then follows the other aspects like the clients having the responsibility for working out their problems; the clients being free to leave at any moment and thinking about whether to return to the session; the session being a confidential one, with the clients free to speak about any confidential matters. Once the counsellor starts the session in a structured manner, clients do most of the talking or explaining. Clients have a considerable degree to express something that has been worrying them and that they have wanted to express. The counsellor is an active and sympathetic listener. When the clients stop sharing, the counsellor acknowledges and accepts the feelings of the clients. For example: If the client talked about how he was misbehaved by his boss, the counsellor might acknowledge by saying, 'you feel that your boss's behaviour is annoying you'. Here the role of the counsellor is to clarify the feelings of the client, neither to provide any judgement nor to elaborate.

The Core Aspect of Client-Centred Counselling

Rogers believes that individuals are reliable, resourceful, capable of making positive changes, and competent to live successfully and productively. The role of the counsellor is to communicate with their support, caring, and non-judgemental understanding which leads to significant changes in the clients. The person-centred approach included six fundamental conditions to accomplish personality or psychotherapeutic changes

(Gillon, 2007; Rogers, 1957). Based on his clinical experience, Rogers thought that if the following six conditions were satisfied, changes would be imminent in the clients. The six fundamental conditions are:

1. **Two persons are in psychological contact (psychological relationship)**: Carl Rogers highlighted the role of the relationship between counsellor and client as of primary significance in counselling practice. The psychological relationship focuses on the relationship between the counsellor and the client having some impression and influence on each other. The counsellor does not force the clients to do something that they do not want to do but encourages the clients to develop their potential.
2. **The client is in a state of incongruence, being vulnerable or anxious (incongruence)**: In incongruence, the feelings of the clients are not aligned with their actions. Incongruence refers to the discrepancy between the self-concept and reality, wearing a mask to hide the true feelings. Clients occasionally are unaware of this incongruence, but as they become more conscious of it, they become more receptive to the therapeutic process.
3. **The counsellor is congruent or integrated into the relationship (congruence and genuineness)**: Congruence implies that counsellors are real; that is, they are authentic during the counselling session. It refers to the counsellors' ability to realise the full extent of their own organismic experience. In counselling, the counsellors must genuinely be of their own self and not be 'pretentious'. They are open to their feelings, thoughts, reactions, and attitudes in their relationship with the clients. Genuineness explains the counsellor's effort to be fully aware of his or her experience with the clients and to provide feedback to the clients openly and honestly. Mearns and Cooper explain 'When two people come together in a wholly genuine, open and engaging way, we can say that they are both fully present' (Mearns & Cooper, 2005, p. 37).

   The following is an example of a counsellor responding genuinely. Sometimes the client only provides information without any emotions that make the counsellor apathetic. In this case, the counsellor must express his/her concern to the client.

   [*Counsellor*] I am feeling diverted by your story. I would like to listen, and I find that I have trouble paying close attention to what is being said.

   In the above example, the counsellor voiced his concern genuinely to the clients. Sitting with the clients, not attending, and not articulating their opinion to the clients in a gentle way, may perhaps signify incongruence on the part of the counsellor. This may lead to discomfort for the clients, and the clients in the end may notice the distraction of the counsellor, and may even challenge the counsellor for not listening to them.
4. **The counsellor shows unconditional positive regard for the client (unconditional positive regard)**: The counsellor without any conditions of acceptance, must accept and appreciate the clients as they are (Rogers, 1957). Both bad and good feelings need to be accepted by the counsellor. Unconditional positive regard is more than acceptance. Acceptance refers to showing concern for the clients as distinct individuals rather than agreement with the clients. Unconditional positive regard is firm respect or regard for the clients devoid of the behaviour demonstrated by the clients. Counsellors do not always show unconditional positive regard for their clients, but it is the goal towards which they strive for a successful counselling process. The positive self-regard of the

clients is enhanced when the clients value the unconditional positive regard of the counsellor.

5. **The counsellor shows an empathic understanding towards the client's feelings and communicates this feeling to the client (empathy):** Empathy is not sympathy or feeling sad for clients. To be empathic means to enter other persons' worlds without being influenced by one's own views and values (Rogers, 1975; Freire, 2007). Empathy involves understanding the meaning and feelings of clients' experiences. In the words of Watson:

> Counsellors need to be able to be responsively attuned to their clients and to understand them emotionally as well as cognitively. When empathy is operating on all three levels- interpersonal, cognitive, and affective- it is one of the most powerful tools counsellors have at their disposal.
>
> (Watson, 2002, pp. 463–464)

Rogers described it, 'to sense the client's private world as if it were your own, but without ever losing the "as if" quality- this is empathy, and this seems essential to therapy' (Rogers, 1957). Based on Fiedler's (1950) research, Rogers listed the following benefits of empathy: a therapist can understand the client's feelings well, the therapist is always certain of what the client means, a therapist's comments fit right in with the client's mood and content, a therapist's voice, tone conveys a complete understanding of the client's emotions.

The following is an example of a counsellor responding empathically:

[*Client*] I'm stressed up, totally stressed up. Don't know what to do and how to handle it.

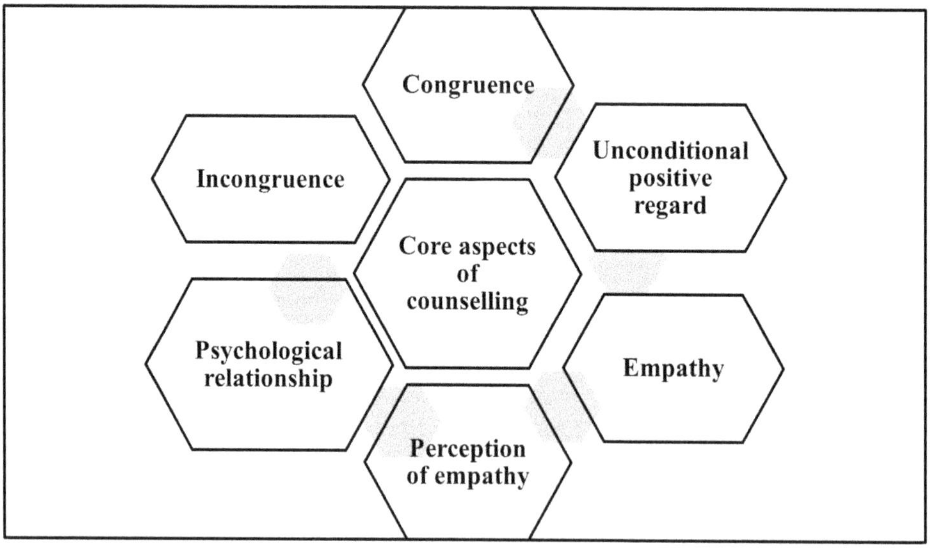

Figure 2.15 Humanistic View of the Core Aspect of Counselling

[*Counsellor*] You're feeling stressed and not sure what to do. I understand your anguish and feel I'm here for you.

The counsellor articulates her feelings openly. She/he genuinely feels for the client and expresses her/his desire to be with the client.

6. **The communication of the counsellor's empathic understanding and unconditional positive regard is perceived by the client (perception of empathy and acceptance):** It is not enough for the counsellor to accept the clients unconditionally and empathise with them. Clients must also believe that they are understood and accepted in some way. Empathy and acceptance can be communicated verbally or non-verbally, but it must be spontaneous and not forced or manufactured.

Humanistic View of Core Aspect of Counselling

Bozarth et al. (2001) concluded the following: At the beginning of the counselling session, the client, not the counsellor, is in charge. This style of person-centred therapy is related to better understanding, more self-discovering, and enhanced self-concepts.

Second, a move from the clarity of feelings to emphasise the client's set of ideas develops. A genuine relationship, and the client's possessions, are the heart of effective counselling.

Third, the attitude of the counsellor-empathy towards the client's world, and the ability to communicate non-judgementally to the client, are the basic to successful counselling outcomes.

Rogers outlined 12 steps in the person-centred counselling process and stressed that these steps are not separate events but rather interwoven. These steps explain the person-centred counselling process in a nutshell.

1. The person comes for assistance.
2. The helping situation is typically described as an opportunity for personal development.
3. The therapist encourages the client to communicate his or her feelings freely regarding the issue.
4. The therapist acknowledges, accepts, and clarifies the negative emotions.
5. The faint and tentative expressions of the positive impulses that foster growth come after the person's negative emotions have been thoroughly acknowledged.
6. The therapist welcomes and recognises the positive feelings that are communicated in the same manner that he has accepted and recognised the negative sensations... giving the person the chance to finally realise who he is as a person for the first time in his life. Self-awareness and insight just flow through naturally.
7. The foundation on which the person can go to greater degrees of integration is provided by this insight, this understanding of the self, and this acceptance of the self.
8. This process of insight is accompanied by a process of clarification of potential decisions and courses of action.
9. The start of modest but important positive acts follows.
10. There is more insight.

11. With less fear and more self-confidence, the client engages in more comprehensive positive action.
12. The partnership must stop because it appears that the client does not need more support.

(Rogers, 1952, pp. 30–45)

The person-centred approach highlights the distinctive role of the group counsellor as a facilitator who can create a harmless and healing environment, a place where the members of the group can have honest and meaningful ways of interaction. With support from a counsellor and group members, participants understand that they do not have to scuffle for the change. As group members become more at ease with each other, they think that it is the group as a united body, is the source of change towards self-direction and empowerment. Rogers (1970) believed that to make the group progress, the facilitator must express a deep sense of faith in the members, and avoid giving interpretive comments, as such types of comments make the group self-conscious and decline the process.

Application of the Person-Centred Approach

The person-centred approach can be applied to individuals, groups, families, schools, organisations, and different types of crisis interventions. In educational settings, the person-centred approach can be applied from primary to graduate classes. Giving importance to 'Freedom to Learn', teachers are considered as 'controlling managers to facilitators of learning' (Rogers & Freiberg, 1994). They believed that learning, problem-solving, and creativity were found to be better in classrooms with a person-centred climate. In crisis interventions, like unwanted pregnancy, illness, and traumatic situations, the application of a person-centred approach is significant. People working both in the medical and paramedical sectors can do much if they follow the basic skills described earlier in this approach. In a crisis, people want to express their problems first. While expressing their problems, they need someone to listen, hear, and understand them. Being heard and understood, helps individuals return to their level of functioning prior to the crisis, and cope with future problems more effectively. The individuals may lose hope of 'returning to normal' and may stop seeking care in the future if they do not feel understood and accepted. Unpretentious support, compassion, and generous warmth can persuade people to resolve the crisis. Communicating a sense of empathy should always come first before providing interventions to the problems of clients.

Reality Therapy

Reality therapy is based on the principles of the choice theory developed by Dr. William Glasser in 1965. Choice theory operates on the simple principle that individuals can control themselves, but they have limited control over others. When one uses choice theory, they can take responsibility for their own lives, while withdrawing from trying to influence other people's decisions and lives. Reality therapy emphasises self-evaluation as counselling intervention. Self-evaluation is described as the basis for change (Glasser, 1972). Individuals are responsible for their decisions and are empowered to help others take responsibility for their decisions. Reality therapy focuses more on a person-centred approach that concentrates on the present rather than previous concerns. For Reality therapy, experience has little importance. It encourages problem-solving and better choice-making to attain specified goals. Glasser believed that changing one's own conduct rather than trying to influence someone else's would lead to greater success in achieving one's own goals.

Similarity and Dissimilarity of Reality Therapy with Other Therapies

Adlerian therapy. The love and need for affiliation in reality therapy supports Adler's view that the need for affiliation is a major goal of the lifelong effort. Both theories are consistent with the phenomenological aspect of understanding, which is the client's subjective view of the world. Reality therapy, on the other hand, contradicts Adler's view of the importance of experience. Reality counsellors do not focus more attention on the past. On the other hand, they believe that past problems are reflected in the current unsatisfying relationships and behaviours (Seligman & Reichenberg, 2014).

Humanistic therapy. Both reality therapy and humanistic therapy believe that all behaviour has a purpose, and that the counsellor-client relationship requires empathy, unconditional positive regard, and genuineness. While humanistic therapists consider that the conditions of relationships are sufficient for change, reality counsellors opine that more is needed. In general, reality therapists are more active, directive, technology-oriented, and educational than human-centred therapists.

Existential therapy. Existential therapy and reality emphasise the need for personal responsibility and constructive client-counsellor relationships. The main similarity lies in the resemblance between the 'needs' of reality therapy and the 'givens of existence' of existential therapy. The existential theory argues that all human beings must deal with the reality of meaninglessness, death, freedom, and isolation. In the same way, reality therapy states that all humans must meet five basic needs. Needs and givens vary from place to place, but they seem to overlap quite a bit.

Counselling in Reality Therapy

Personality Development: *Function of the Psyche.* Reality therapy promotes problem-solving and is based on the notion that people suffer from psychological distress when their basic psychological needs are not addressed. These needs are not mutually exclusive but rather interact through our physiology as well as our feelings, thoughts, and actions. Human problems arise when one or more of the five fundamental psychological needs are not met. To find happiness, one needs to be proactive in responding to those needs without annoying others.

People are not forced to behave in a fixed fashion by the environment. Everyone has their own choice. No doubt that the outside environment significantly influences people's way of living. People may be persuasive. According to choice theory, people produce behaviours for the sake of sustaining five universal needs, such as the need for survival, love and belonging, inner control or power, freedom, and fun. The first basic need is a survival need. Then follows belonging which plays an important role in reality therapy practice. All five needs are different from each other, yet they interact in the same situation. For example, going for dinner with friends can fulfil the needs for survival, belonging, freedom, and fun. The five universal human needs are discussed below.

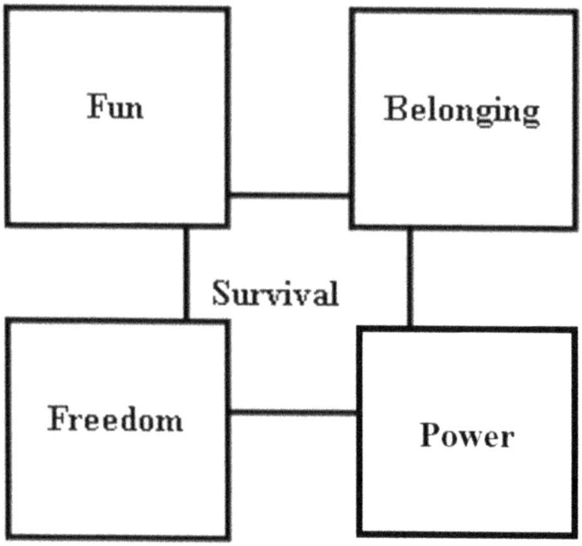

Figure 2.16 Five Universal Human Needs

Five Universal Human Needs

1. *Survival.* It includes the basic needs of shelter, food, and sexual fulfilment. This is about how to protect oneself from danger, damage, and so on. It also covers security and safety. The biological urge of any species on this earth is to live and reproduce to assure survival in the future. The behaviours that improve individuals' chances of survival are eating a healthy diet, physical exercise, and good sleep, as well as behaviours that improve the human species' chances of survival, such as sexual behaviour.
2. *Love and belonging.* Glasser believed that most longstanding psychological problems are the product of relationship problems. This includes connecting to family, friends, colleagues, and neighbours. We must work together, care for one another, share, and participate to belong. Positive human relationships improve mental health and well-being. The need for affiliation can be embodied by recognising three types of affiliations: family affiliation, work affiliation, and social affiliation (Wubbolding, 2017). The need to belong to a family is expressed within the family above all else. Children need to feel safe, raised, and cherished, and as they grow up, they need to feel cherished. Children are born with the need to connect with the people around them. Work belonging needs include what people expect from their occupation. In the work atmosphere, job satisfaction and job commitment increase when employees feel they are well-connected with others and get support from others. Social belonging need emphasises the relationship with friends, neighbours, and others. As Glasser pointed out, 'To satisfy every other need, we must have relationships with other people. This means that satisfying the need for love and belonging is the key to satisfying the other four needs' (Glasser, 2000, p. 23). A significant goal for a reality therapist is to assist clients in satisfying their complex need for belonging. The need for belonging is not fulfilled by negative behaviours like arguing, fault findings, dominating, accusing, and criticising.

3. *Power*. Power here is characterised by the urge to do, not the exercise or exploitation of our control over others. It is a sensation of accomplishment, self-importance, and self-esteem; an exterior sense of being heard and appreciated; as well as feeling competent and receiving recognition. It can involve feelings of success, accomplishment, or self-worth. For example, a sense of achievement or accomplishment occurs after delivering a speech at a conference or after conducting a successful surgery. Gaining power by creating problems for others, such actions as violating rules, unethical means, or bribery, are irresponsible fulfilment of this need.
4. *Freedom*. The need for independence and autonomy is considered freedom. It means the ability to freely determine, create, explore, and express oneself. To be free, individuals must not feel restricted in making choices and must have free will.
5. *Fun*. Fun is a psychological need to enjoy. It refers to the desire to enjoy one's work, to have a good sense of humour, to engage in hobbies, to be interested and to have leisure time. Having fun involves experiencing fun, joy, relaxation, laughter, and learning. Laughter and humour have many benefits, including healing properties.

Glasser (2003) defined the five individual human needs as a set of genetic instructions for human motivation. Human beings, according to this perspective of motivation, have innate drives that determine their behaviour, particularly their decisions. Individual needs are intertwined. For example, individuals cannot survive without the support of anyone. The intensity of the needs varies. For some people, freedom takes precedence above a need to belong. People are sometimes unsure of which needs to satisfy and are unable to control their thoughts and actions which affect their mental health. Reality therapy is intended to address persons' basic needs and help them to become aware of their undesirable beliefs and behaviours and simultaneously to change them. Reality therapy includes a collaborative approach between the therapist and the client. The procedure continues until the client and the therapist are confident that beneficial effects are already occurring or are about to do so. If one plan of action fails, then new ones are planned.

Structure of the Psyche

In choice theory, the brain is the central structure, the control system of living organisms. The five human needs described above provide additional specific motivators. According to Wubbolding (2017), people acquire distinct needs, or pictures, relating to each need while interacting with the outside world. This collection of desires is referred to as their quality world influenced by past experiences. People are born with the ability to form a variety of psychic constructs. One of them is the **quality world**, often known as the inner picture album. The images in this mental album, according to Glasser, falls into three categories: 'the people we most want to be with; the things we most want to own or experience; and the ideas or systems of belief that govern much of our behaviour' (Glasser, 1998, p. 45). There are a lot of individual differences in definite desires associated with the five-need system.

The Interrelationship Between Human Nature and Environment in Personality Development

Though human needs are set from birth and continue, how people behave to achieve them alters over time. For example, a child's belonging need is significantly different from an adolescent or an adult. People's behavioural choices are unique to them, and they might satisfy multiple needs at once. One can go for the morning walk to meet his/her requirements for fun, support, and freedom. For example, some people like fun by watching comedy shows whereas others like to spend time leisurely with friends. Sometimes the person who likes comedy wants to watch a particular show not all. Hence the images in the quality world are exclusive to everyone though human wants are universal and innate. Sometimes these images are not clear to the individual. For example, a person may want to be the boss of an organisation for power but has no confidence to deal with subordinates. The counsellor's role is to assist the clients in clarifying their unclear images.

Glasser (1998) recognised the need for love as the basis for meeting all other wants. Needs or desires, while pleasing to one person, might create dissatisfaction with the wants of another person. These disagreements and conflicts lead to horrendous relationships in the organisation to family life. Healthy functioning according to choice theory is characterised by responsible behaviour: the ability to satisfy one's own needs without disturbing others to fulfil their needs. As a result, this will help people to form and maintain good healthy relationships with others. On the other hand, a healthy relationship cannot be maintained if one tries to fulfil one's needs at the cost of others. The choice theory emphasises healthy adjustment by giving respect to others' needs. In addition to belonging needs, fulfilment of other needs is necessary for healthy functioning.

Mental Illness

Glasser does not accept the disease model related to mental illness. Though he acknowledges that people experience symptoms, he accepts that something is incorrect with their brains. Mental distress is not the product of a mental disorder rather it is the product of a socially universal human state that develops when a person's basic psychological needs are not satisfied.

Mental Health

People who fulfil their five basic needs are considered as healthy. These styles of humans pick their thoughts, feelings, and behaviours accurately and responsibly. Setbacks are considered alerts that people want to look at their behaviour and relationships and make higher choices. People who are emotionally healthy attempt to enhance their own lives and make the world a better place by helping others (Seligman & Reichenberg, 2014).

Wubbolding proposed a staged approach for meeting fundamental requirements in a balanced manner. The model is referred to as 'effective life direction' (Wubbolding, 2000, p. 70), and the stages are as follows:

1. *I Want to Change, and I Want to Grow*: At this stage, one wants a change in the current lifestyle. This change is required before certain concrete behavioural changes occur. The characteristics of a healthy individual are that they make the effort and commitment to effective choices.
2. *Effective Behaviours*: Then follows the action-taking phase based on the articulating or thinking of a commitment to change where the individual put the words into action. According to Wubbolding (1988, p. 71), behaviours that indicate healthier lifestyle choices include:
   i. *Assertive and Altruistic Behaviours*: People are goal-oriented and have ownership of long-term and short-term goals. Selecting behaviours that help individuals

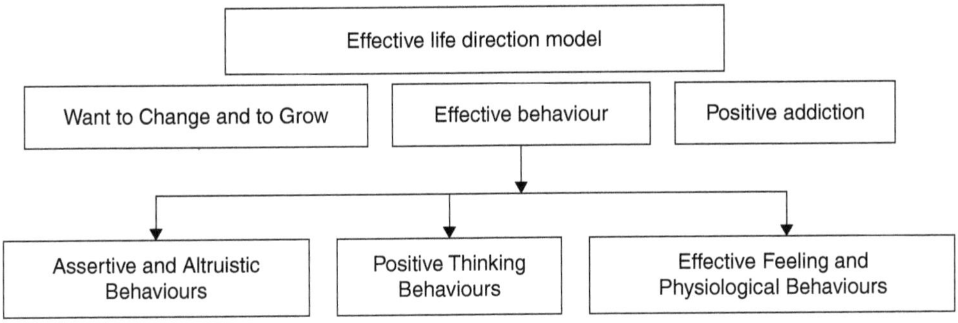

Figure 2.17 Stages of Effective Life Direction Model

connect with others in a positive way is a clear feature of these behaviours. Participating in philanthropic initiatives is characteristic of these people.

ii. *Positive Thinking Behaviours*: Cognitions are vital in the total behaviour model. Healthy individuals utilise positive inner statements for healthy living. For example, 'I am responsible for my health' and 'I can win' are all thoughts that help enhance effective living. It is like giving positive autosuggestions.

iii. *Effective Feeling and Physiological Behaviours*: Healthy people develop emotions that help meet their needs, and these emotions manifest themselves in the rest of their behaviour. For example, having patience, trust, and hope. People engage in behaviours that enhance physiology. Taking meals on time, going for regular exercise, and taking proper rest are a few examples.

3. *Positive Addictions*: According to Wubbolding (2000), only a few reaches this stage. To establish a positive addiction, the individual must engage in behaviour daily with concentration, allowing the mind to be free from stresses of everyday life. For example, chanting 'Aum' or doing 'Yoga'.

Stages of Effective Life Direction Model

Personality Change

Glasser (1992) pointed out that people are ready to change when they realise that they must change their behaviour to achieve success. Reality counsellors do not focus on the past experiences of the clients as discussed earlier rather focus on the present. By experiencing a satisfying healthy relationship with counsellors, clients can learn to improve the problematic relationships that led them to counselling. Therefore, the first phase of the counselling process is called **'making friends'** Wubbolding (1988). Wubbolding and Brickell (2015) shows some of the characteristics of a good therapist.

1. *Continuously Practicing the ABs (Always Be):* Wubbolding (1988) briefed the ABCDEFG approach of a counsellor characteristics.

   AB: always be
   C: courteous to the client even when in anger

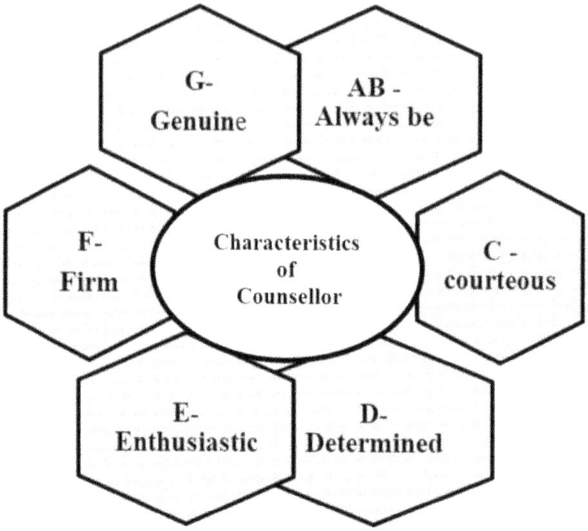

Figure 2.18 ABCDEFG Approach of Counsellor Characteristics

D: determined that the client can change by creating several choices
E: enthusiastic towards the client
F: firm regarding the client's plans and commitments in therapy
G: genuine with the client, client-friendly, and treat all clients honestly

2. *Focusing on the Present*: Reality counsellors use their client-counsellor relationships as it is occurring in the present (now) and spend very little time discussing past issues.
3. *Using Humour*: Counsellors need to demonstrate responsible humour as a means of fostering relationships.
4. *Use of Empathic Confrontation*: The counsellor's primary role is to influence clients and make more effective decisions. The ability to connect with and understand each client is the foundation of influence. As a result of this understanding, counsellors effectively confront clients and encourage more responsible and satisfying behaviour. Therefore, an effective counsellor can connect with and confront the client and is willing to respond.

At the same time the counsellor should not accept excuses from the client, should not argue, should not criticise, and moreover should not give up quickly.

Stages and Techniques

Wubbolding (1988, 1991, 2000) described the 'WDEP' system to pronounce the stages of reality therapy.

Wants: Reality counsellors investigate clients' desires and images in a quality world, focusing on what they get, what they want that they don't get, and what they get that they don't want (Seligman & Reichenberg, 2014). Reality counsellors can help clients

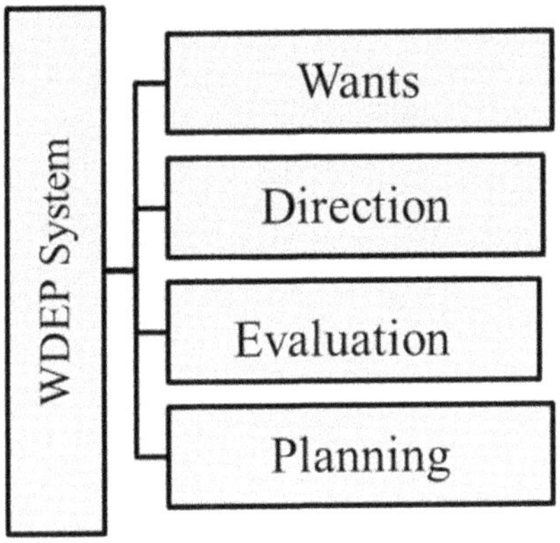

Figure 2.19 WDEP System Describes the Stages of Reality Therapy

identify which desires are unreasonable or irrational, as well as which ones can help with the relationship-building and recovery process.

Direction and Doing: Counsellors dedicate substantial attention to the study of people's overall behaviour, including actions, thoughts, emotions, and physiology. Helping people explain their overall behaviour as accurately as possible, including their goals and the effects of those behaviours, is an integral part of treatment. Reality counsellors focus on what people do, not why they act in a particular way.

Evaluation: The evaluation of clients objectives, behaviours, and perceptions as well as the effects of their actions is encouraged. The purpose of evaluation is to determine whether behaviours and perceptions are reasonable and beneficial to clients and others (Seligman & Reichenberg, 2014).

Planning: Plans encourage people to set long-term plans and goals. These are broken down into a sequence of short-term, realistic plans (Seligman & Reichenberg, 2014). The main goal of the plan is to help people make better decisions and control their lives.

WDEP System of Reality Therapy

Once the plan is started on a regular basis, different problems may be explored and the WDEP process can begin over. Reality counsellors can investigate clients' plans using the SAMI^{2}C^3 system, the acronym for the following aspects of assessment.

Simple: plan must be simple so that the clients may follow it.

Attainable: plans must be attainable or realistic. This will encourage the clients to continue with the plan.

Measurable with regards to outcome and timeline: plans must be measurable. Clients need to know the progress of the plan.

Immediate: The plans must be implemented immediately. Clients will be demotivated if the waiting time is too long to implement a plan.

Involves counsellor: counsellor involvement provides support and objective feedback for the clients. It should be done in an ethical manner to promote the independence of the clients.

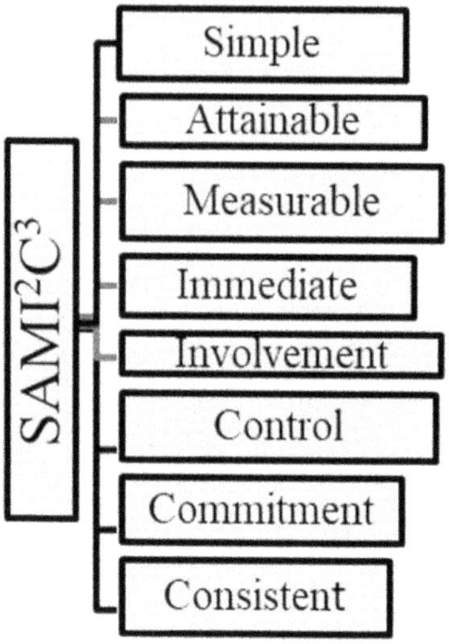

Figure 2.20 Assessment of Client Plans Using the $SAMI^2C^3$ System

Controlled by the client: the clients should be responsible for executing the plan. This idea highlights the importance of personal responsibility for one's actions.

Commitment: clients must commit to their plans. The plan will only work if clients are fully invested in it.

Consistent: the implementation of effective plans is ongoing. The behaviour must establish a pattern in the clients' life for meaningful transformation to occur.

Once the plan has been followed consistently, more issues are investigated, and the WDEP process is restarted. Reality therapy is not a linear model. On the other hand, the counsellors address multiple difficulties that the clients are processing at various stages in the WDEP system. The counsellors help the clients relinquish those behaviours that do not fulfil their needs and replace them with new total behaviour that will help the clients acquire what they want.

Behaviour is viewed as a choice in reality therapy. It's built on accepting responsibility for the behaviours and deciding on more effective ones. This is supposed to aid in the treatment of psychological symptoms and mental illnesses. Reality therapy, on the other hand, has drawn a lot of criticism for its unconventional approach. The psychiatric profession disagrees with Glasser's claim that there is no such thing as mental illness. A reality therapist helps people create new behaviours. Some contend that the therapist can then impose their views and opinions on the patient in this way. According to Glasser, medication is never necessary to treat mental health disorders. Opponents claim that he should have addressed the benefits of conventional therapy rather than completely discarding drugs.

Application of Reality Therapy

Reality therapy is helpful in treating a wide range of issues. It is particularly useful in treating problems children and adolescents face at school and in their societies. The effectiveness of reality therapy in improving overall classroom functioning, teamwork, and reducing challenging behaviour is demonstrated by trained teachers and school counsellors. Reality therapy encourages people to take accountability for their behaviour if they want to change it.

Existential Psychotherapy

Soren Kierkegaard is generally considered the father of existentialism (Dreyfus, 2006). The concept **'existentialism'** is derived from the Latin word 'ex-sistere', which means to 'stand forth' or to 'become'. Existential psychology emphasises the importance of human choices and feelings of admiration towards life. Human existence and the way we live and exist in the world are the focus of existential psychotherapy and counselling.

Existential therapy is a philosophically informed approach that influences a counsellor's therapeutic practice. It includes a varied range of theories and practices and is based on a wide spectrum of insights, values, and principles derivative of phenomenological and existential philosophies. The two traditions that have led to the foundation of existentialism are the ethical philosophy of Soren Kierkegaard (1813–1855) and Friedrich Nietzsche (1844–1900), and the phenomenological method of Husserl (1900–1970).

The practical study of existentialism covers the procedural and situational aspects of human problems. Existential counselling psychology is considered as a practical application of philosophy in daily life. This approach assumes that people have choices and actions according to their existence. They decide their lives and make plans accordingly. Existential philosophy is fundamentally an inquiry into personal meaning. Every human behaviour is underpinned by assumptions about the nature of truth, reality, and the foundation of human meaning (Adams, 2014). The field of vision of the existential perspective comprises biological, psychological, social, and spiritual realms, and it extends beyond the individual to analyse the human situation in a larger philosophical and socio-political framework. It prefers to think about persons' abilities to meet the problems that life will certainly throw at them (Deurzen & Adams, 2011, p. 9).

Martin Heidegger (1962) coined the expression **'being-in-the-world'** to describe how we are both making and being made by the world we live in. We are intimately linked to the world, and we gather knowledge about it by connecting with it rather than simply seeing it.

Goals of Existential Counselling

The goal of an existential counsellor is to make philosophical inquiry practical. Rather than forcing clients to fit into pre-determined interpretation frameworks, they engage with them throughout their lives in their search for truth. A lack of explicit assumptions will influence the conclusions drawn. Assumptions about life must be questioned; it isn't an admission that perception is faulty; but rather, it is the phenomenological principle of becoming aware of life processes through reflexivity (Finlay, 2011). Existential therapy aims to assist clients in understanding their issues as problems in living, clarifying the underlying difficulties, and enabling them to find new ways of living.

Unlike psychoanalysis and behaviourism, existential therapy is more concerned with people in crisis. Counsellors work with clients to find philosophical meaning in their anxiety by helping them think and act in an authentic and responsible way. According to Warnock (1970), existential theories have three key assumptions:

1. *Existence comes before essence* (Sartre, 1973, p. 26). This explains the fact that 'we are – our existence', is more basic than 'what we are – our essence'. We search for our essence out of our established existence. According to Heidegger (1962), we are 'thrown' into our lives existentially. This means that several parts of our existence, including our genetic make-up, familial circumstances, gender, culture, and even our birth, are imposed on us without our choice. We're also thrown out of our lives since we don't know when we're going to die. We are given something that is neither ours nor desired – our existence – and our life task is to make it into something which is personal and owned, and we will lose it when we die (Adams, 2014). Existentialists Jean-Paul Sartre and Albert Camus describe this situation as 'absurd' and the most basic challenge of life. We must find a way to live with this absurdity and find a way to give ourselves what we think we need. One should keep in mind that what one needs will change throughout their life.
2. *Personal responsibility* (Warnock, 1970, p. 12). From an existential point of view, what we consider to be our essence, our 'personality', our 'self' is a matter of interpretation and choice, changing throughout life. Existentialists prefer to use the term 'sense-of-self'. Hyphens here emphasise the superiority of experience and are based on science-based concepts, so there is no 'true' self to live. According to Sartre (2003, p. 129) 'to be free is to be condemned to be free'. This illustrates that, whether we like it or not, we are responsible for our lives. When we admit that we are the product of our choices and actions, then it creates too much anxiety, existential anxiety. When we realise this, we have the option of either becoming an active creator or a passive recipient of our lives. In addition to granting us freedom, letting go of the idea that our identities are shaped by the past also makes us accountable for bringing about change.
3. *How the theory is arrived at.* We must employ a research technique that is appropriate for the data and the research topic if we are to know anything about reliability. According to phenomenology, we can never leave life to witness it, contrary to the scientific idea of an objective spectator. We are always observers. Existentialism and phenomenology are related in that existential thinking is the body of knowledge that results from the application of systematic phenomenological research techniques to the study of human existence. Because phenomenology is the foundation of existential counselling, there is a strong ethical connection between theory and practice. Being phenomenological allows us to express existential queries and worries.

Existential therapy is made possible by the method of phenomenology, which allows the therapists to draw on ideas from existential philosophy. Kierkegaard was fascinated by '**angst**', a Danish and German word that means something between dread and anxiety in English, as well as the role anxiety and uncertainty play in our lives. Existential anxiety is not unhealthy and is linked to making basic decisions about how we wish to live. Kierkegaard (1843) explains three stages in existential development: **the aesthetic, the ethical, and the religious.**

The aesthetic stage is marked by sensual engagement in the world, a desire to escape monotony, as well as an emphasis on possibilities rather than reality. In Kierkegaard's words, this stage is a fantasy way of protecting oneself from aghast, despair, or worry that must be confronted through acknowledgement of the fundamental freedom and responsibility of existence.

The ethical stage is required before the progression of the religious stage, and Kierkegaard views it as a further limited stage of existence in which one thinks and acts unreflectively following current societal norms. Unlike the aesthetic stage, here one shows a commitment to the social world, pushing beyond the individual aesthete's self-serving goals. Because anguish motivates people to act ethically rather than thinking through the significance of their acts for themselves, the norms they follow are arbitrary, hidden behind seemingly rational communication and socio-political discussion.

The religious stage incorporates characteristics of both aesthetic and ethical stages but is transformed with the addition of the possibilities of aesthetic imagination and the ethical sense of social commitment realised through a personal subjective passion. In various ways, freedom of subjectivity causes anguish, as everyone is responsible for making decisions for the rest of their life, creating both dread and elation at the prospect of choice. Individual religion is the result of subjective passion. Faith is the way by which one attains a sense of genuine selfhood, which is then judged by God in eternity. Persuasion or forces are ineffective in moving people through these stages since everyone must make their own decisions about how to spend their life.

The Four Dimensions of Life

In Heidegger's view, individuals are not isolated subjects who inhabit a world, but are interconnected with the world; he called this **'Being-in-the-World'**. Binswanger (1946) emphasised three dimensions of human existence based on Heidegger's Being-in-the-World. Binswanger (1958, 1963), in his early formulation of existential therapy, first outlined the importance of examining life through three dimensions or modes: the physical world (**umwelt**), the social world (**mitwelt**), and the psychological world (**eigenwelt**). Later, Deurzen-Smith (1984, 1988) added the fourth dimension, the spiritual world (**überwelt**). The dimensions overlap but this idea remains a useful one for existential therapy.

The physical world (umwelt) encompasses our physical surroundings, our health and illness capacities, and our attitude towards our mortality. We relate to others and the world around us in the social dimension (mitwelt). It's about other people's presence in the world. They are essential to our survival, and we are weakened without them. The personal world (eigenwelt) is concerned with our relationship with ourselves, our imagination, and our understanding of our previous experiences and future potential. We relate to the unknown in the spiritual realm (überwelt) and develop a personal value system and a picture of an ideal world we would like to live in. The spiritual world is at the heart of existential counselling because life is about generating meaning.

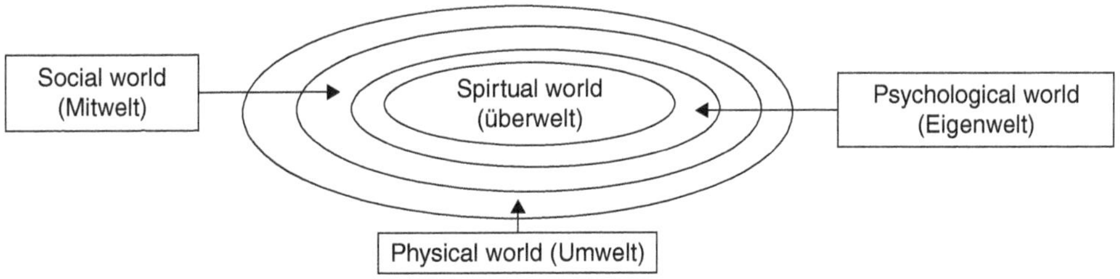

Figure 2.21 Four Modes of Life

The key elements of existential practice are to attend to how clients are engaged with these four dimensions of existence, whether they are in balance or they are neglected.

Personality in Existential Psychology

The core inclination of personality, according to existential psychology, is to achieve an **'authentic being'** (Maddi, 1980, p. 725). 'Being' denotes the distinct quality of human cognition in which life is viewed as a series of choices (Maddi, 1980). In this sense, there are mainly two paths before the individual: i) must choose between one path which leads them to an unknown future or ii) return to the secure and unchanging past. While the path to the future may cause existential anxiety, the path towards the past may cause existential guilt or regret because of a missed opportunity (Cole 2016). Hence, any act of choice might elicit feelings of anxiousness in and of itself (Lucas 2004). As a result, authenticity requires summoning the courage to accept this painful condition of existence and move forward despite existential anxiety. People are essentially accountable for their existence from an existential standpoint, and they can choose not just what they will do but also who they will be (Bugental 1978). Therefore, one's personality might be perceived to emerge from their decisions. Individuals who are overcome by worry or neuroses, for example, can be perceived as choosing to oppose progress and may require the assistance of a therapist to discover and become their true selves (Misiak & Sexton 1973).

The Pursuit of Happiness

From the existential perspective, happiness is the enduring calmness that comes with completeness. People are ever complete at death because death is the end of possibilities, so there is no such thing as permanent happiness as everyone will experience stress at some point in their lives. While the absence of tension and conflict is significant and meaningful, it does not last since we are reminded of the tensions that develop from the challenges of ordinary life sooner or later (Adams, 2014). Existentialism has correlated happiness with meaning and purpose, with ambition, and with overcoming adversity. The role of counsellors should focus on the search for meaning and purpose, rather than the search for symptom relief or happiness (Deurzen 2009).

Phenomenology as the Basis of Existential Counselling

In phenomenological practice, the counsellors respect the clients' existential concerns. In the early 20th Century Edmund Husserl devised phenomenology as more appropriate for the human sciences. According to Husserl, neither natural science nor introspection is appropriate for researching human experience. Phenomenology does not itself operate without assumptions, but its assumptions are closest to what it means to be human. These assumptions include that we actively interpret and shape the world around us, that no observation is ever free from assumptions, and that none of the meanings we make are ever entirely independent of or dependent upon others (Adams, 2014, p. 51).

Husserl's original ideas have been developed for the skills of existential counselling (Deurzen & Adams 2011). According to Husserl, individuals' basic position towards the world is that they always make meaning of it in terms of what they already know. People perceive their views as factual, but in reality, they are merely interpretations based on concealed assumptions. These assumptions reduce the understanding of each person and they should try to reduce their impact by approaching things as though for the first time. The questioning in existential counselling is more of a collaborative 'questioning-with' than an interrogative 'questioning-of'. Counsellors should not interpret what they say or advise them on what to do based on a theory. They should figure out what they don't know that is impacting their decisions, choices, and actions.

The fact that the clients are distressed and have questions about their lives shows that their assumptions are faulty, inconsistent, or unexamined. Rather than focusing on whether or not assumptions are objectively right, the focus should be on what these assumptions mean to the clients and how they influence their life decisions, as well as whether or not these choices are acceptable to them.

The Skills for Existential Counselling

Attention

Phenomenologically, to understand clients, counsellors first need to be attentive. On a skill level, counsellors need to be quiet and encourage the clients to talk without influencing them unduly. When counsellors' attention wanders or searches for an explanation or a theory, it denotes that they are not focused. The existential approach is often called an existential-phenomenological approach to psychotherapy. Heidegger later advocated Husserl's phenomenological method to answer the question of Being, which underlines the importance of Husserl's phenomenological method. The phenomenological method was developed to understand the fundamental nature of experience, to get back to 'the things themselves'. Spinelli (2005) adapted Husserl's phenomenological method for use in psychotherapy. To work phenomenologically, he first proposed 'The Rule of Epoche', then 'The Rule of Description' and finally 'The Rule of Horizontalization'. There are two parts of existential practice that phenomenologists call **epoché** and **verification** and both are sustained by attention.

Epoché (Learning to Clarify)

The ancient Greek term epoché is viewed as 'suspension of judgement', as well as the 'with holding of assent' in Hellenistic philosophy (Ancient Greek philosophy corresponding to the Hellenistic period in Ancient Greece). It is the first step towards knowing things, from seeing things as they appear, from returning to things themselves, free of preconceptions and assumptions. It is the approach to something as if it was new to you, all prejudices and biases are put aside and the phenomenon is then revisited. Epoché is about bracketing our expectations and assumptions temporarily so that the focus is purely on the experience. This can only be partial bracketing as it is impossible to bracket our assumptions and biases. Counsellors must know precisely what their assumptions are and how they affect how they understand and see their clients. Counsellors do this through reflection and self-questioning while listening to the client. *The essence of époché is to learn to see what is before us rather than to decide that we know the answer.* Epoché is concerned with building a rapport, listening, clarifying, and becoming aware of one's assumptions. It can be summed up as 'describe, don't explain'. Just describing is more difficult than it seems. Counsellors need to stay close to their clients' experiences. If counsellors are nervous, they may feel compelled to explain to alleviate their confusion. Unfortunately, it rarely does, and instead increases the clients' confusion. There are two parts to epoché – **description and equalisation.** Counsellors do them simultaneously and the skills they use are those of clarification.

Description

The questions 'what' and 'how' are used more frequently than 'why'. Overuse of 'why' questions will result in defensiveness and a limiting of the conversation. Counsellors must limit themselves to the thoughts, feelings, and acts that the clients have mentioned at the outset of their engagement. The further away from these the counsellors go, the greater will be the risk that their assumptions will underpin their inquiry.

Equalisation

In equalising the counsellors view all of the content and process as equally important until they are told otherwise. Their ability to listen is always affected by their life experiences, and they are always making sense of what they see. If they find themselves judging something to be important before they are told, it may be that they are not equalising well enough and that they are acting on some assumptions they have not examined. Counsellors should remember that clients come to counselling because they are confused and muddled. Thus, they will have a harder time putting into words their experiences, especially the ones they have tried to examine, and this makes the chance that they may distort what is being said that much higher. Furthermore, the clients may be unable to articulate what they need to say at all. However, if they are describing it only to themselves, sooner or later certain elements will begin to stand out.

Horizontalization – Getting Some Perspective

The skills of the first stage of epoché are mainly clarification, and those of the next stage of verification are interpretive. Horizontalisation establishes the link between epoché and verification when the counsellors attempt to contextualise the clients' worldview by placing what is becoming known against a horizon. This prevents the work from becoming purely introspective. Every meaning is context-dependent, but the context is often ignored, evaded, or denied. Simply placing the experience in its context can provide the clients with a new perspective on their own life. This can be freeing: the clients suddenly see themselves as if from the outside instead of feeling trapped from the inside. When clients realise that their conclusions, thoughts, and feelings are context-dependent, personal responses rather than being based on facts or causation, they will be prepared to move from work where clarification is the primary objective to work that can include verification. It is premature to try to verify before this point and will probably lead to intellectualised dialogues and the client being led by the therapist (Deurzen & Adams, 2016, p. 61).

Verification – Challenging and Interpreting

Verification is the process of challenging what has already been clarified – it is when counsellors begin to comprehend the implications of meanings. Verification is the same concept as interpretation and challenge in phenomenology. During verification, the goal is to uncover hidden meanings, link them, as well as to discover common factors and recurrent themes that may be owned and questioned. Verification that is sensitive to the client's experience will give them the impression that their difficulties are being taken seriously and that they can be better understood. When the counsellors confront the clients, they bring to light how they are struggling with the givens of their existence, their paradoxes, and problems, their authenticity, and accountability. It is where the counsellors do something with the questions they accumulated from clarification and where they use their intuitions and knowledge of life. Long interpretations might be confusing and impair the development of the clients' self-analytic capacity. Interpretations should be kept as short as feasible. They should establish a link between a trigger event and its repercussions, reinforcing the clients' sense of control over their life. Challenges should also be stated in a way that encourages rather than discourages dialogue.

Therapeutic Techniques and Procedures

Existential therapists' views about the nature of human existence are philosophical. While existentially oriented practitioners may incorporate several techniques from other models into their practice, they do so in the context of attempting to understand the clients' subjective world. Rather than diagnosis, treatment, and prognosis, they prefer to describe, understand, and explore the clients' subjective reality (Deurzen, 2002). Respect for the therapists' and clients' creativity is at the heart of existential therapy. Counsellors must tailor their interventions to suit their personalities and styles while remaining sensitive to the needs of each client. There is a fundamental guiding principle in existential practice that every client's intervention should be responsive to their uniqueness (Deurzen, 2010).

Deurzen (2012) argues that practitioners should begin existential work by clarifying their perspectives on life and living. The goal of existential work is to help individuals live more comfortably and skilfully. Deurzen identifies how counsellors differentiate themselves from their clients: 'We help them to get better at reflecting on their situation, deal with their dilemma, face their predicament and think for themselves' (Deurzen, 2010, p. 236). Existential therapy, according to Deurzen, is a collaborative journey in which both the client and the therapist are changed if they allow life to touch them. The therapeutic process is at its optimum when the therapist's innermost self meets the client's deepest self. Therapy is a creative and ever-evolving three-stage process of self-discovery.

Phases of Existential Counselling

Initial Phase

In the initial phase of counselling, counsellors help the clients to identify and clarify their assumptions about the world. Clients are asked to define and question how they perceive and understand their existence. Clients may initially see their problems because of external factors, which is a challenging task. They often focus on how others make them feel or how others are responsible for many of their actions or inactions. During counselling, the counsellors help the clients identify their existence and examine their role in causing their problems.

Middle Phase

The middle phase of existential therapy involves helping clients examine their current value system more deeply and examine its sources and authorities. In the process of self-exploration, new insights usually emerge, and attitudes and values are sometimes reformed. Individuals gain a better understanding of the sort of life they consider worthy to live and gain greater insight into their own internal valuing processes.

Final Phase

During the final phase of existential counselling, clients are encouraged to put their newly acquired knowledge into practice. Transformation takes place outside of therapy sessions as well. Therapeutic hours are one way to help someone engage with life again or prepare for life (Deurzen, 2002). A therapeutic process is designed to help clients put their internalised ideals into practice between sessions and after therapy is completed. Clients frequently discover their abilities in therapy and learn how to use them to live a more purposeful life.

Application of Existential Therapy

Several clients, including those with substance addiction issues, members of racial and ethnic minorities, homosexual and lesbian clients, and psychiatric patients have received existential therapy in a variety of contexts (Schneider, 2011). One of the perspective's advantages is its emphasis on practical solutions and ways to advance humankind. Those who are experiencing developmental crises, grieving a loss, approaching mortality, or facing a significant life decision might benefit greatly from existential therapy. These crucial turning points that delineate transitions from one stage of life to the next include dealing with the struggle for identity in adolescence, facing potential disappointments in middle age, adjusting to children moving out of the house, dealing with failures in marriage and the workplace, and managing increased physical demands, to name just a few.

These developmental difficulties present both risks and possibilities. The process includes uncertainty, worry, and difficult decision-making situations. Deurzen (2002) asserts that this kind of therapy works best for those who are determined to cope with their difficulties in life, who feel excluded from the social norms at the time or who are looking for meaning in their lives. It works well with people who are contemplating major life decisions, anxious to challenge the status quo, and at a crossroads in their lives. It can aid those who are contemplating suicide or on the edge of death, as well as those going through developmental or situational crises, feeling as though they don't fit in their current environment, or beginning a new stage of life.

Postmodern Approaches

Encyclopaedia Britannica explains postmodernism as 'a late 20th-century movement characterised by broad skepticism, subjectivism, or relativism'. Some proponents of these approaches questioned the historical assumptions that underpin psychotherapy and proposed new ways of thinking about and practicing therapy. This drive is not based on a single model, approach, or school but rather on the work of various thinkers and experts who provide a philosophical and epistemological foundation. While modernist believes in objective and scientific reality, postmodernist believes in the subjective realities that do not exist without observational processes. As a challenge to scientific explanations of reality, postmodernists challenge the idea of 'objectivity'. It claims that rather than merely perceiving reality as it is, we actively make it in our imaginations. Our ability to build it is largely determined by the tools, habits, and structures we have built. These are, in turn, influenced by our cultural and personal experiences. 'We have entered a postmodern world, and truth and reality are often now understood as representing points of view bounded by history and context rather than being objective, immutable facts' (Corey, 2017, p. 368).

Postmodern, narrative, collaborative, discursive, conversational, post-structuralist, and social constructionism are some of the terms used to describe these therapies. Therapy is considered a discussion and a linguistic process, according to discursive and conversational terms. People who are interested in the narrative have a strong interest in the way stories or narrations of their experiences create meaning in their lives. A social constructionist considers knowledge, meaning, and identity as products of interaction. According to social constructionism, individuals always interpret the world through the lens of their culture, gender, ideologies, and so on (Hoffman, 1990). Social constructionists view that people live in a world of symbols and social reality that looks natural to them but is constructed collaboratively by many individuals. Those who are poststructuralists do not see human difficulties as the manifestation of underlying structures. In collaborative terms, therapy is viewed as a joint effort by the counsellors and the type of relationships they want to develop with their clients. Language affects our conscience and forms our world, according to postmodern therapy, and it is more than a way of transmitting information. Collaborative therapist Harry Goolishian said, 'I never know what I mean until I say it' (Anderson, 2005, p. 4).

Postmodern Era

The industrial age is considered as the modern era, a period in which goods were produced in factories, whereas postmodernity is identified as the era of information technology. The postmodernity era begins in the second part of the 20th Century and until the present day. In the postmodern world, transportation and communication are easier and faster than ever, allowing places, people, and cultures to interact. Our daily lives are filled with numerous models and ways of being, as well as countless descriptions of reality and different truths. Modern technology allows us to keep in touch with an ever-widening range of people. At any time, people from one continent can contact others from another continent. People are unable to feel the distance. 'In many respects, we are reaching what may be viewed as social saturation' (Gergen, 1991, p. 3). According to Gergen, technological advancements and the resulting societal saturation have fundamental implications for our understanding of ourselves. The three main postmodern therapies are (1) **solution-focused therapy** (SFT); (2) **narrative therapy**; and (3) **collaborative therapy**. Although they have significant distinctions, they are sometimes put up together as they share some fundamental assumptions about language, knowledge, interpersonal connections, and identity (Anderson, 2006; Paré & Tarragona, 2006).

Solution-Focused Therapy

In the late 1970s, Milwaukee psycho-counsellors Steve de Shazer (1940–2005) and Insoo Kim Berg (1934–2007) developed solution-focused therapy, which focuses on finding out what works for different sorts of people rather than different types of issues. The main feature of the progress of SFT is that it has been an inductive procedure of 'observing individual interviews and simply paying attention to what was most useful' (De Jong & Kim Berg, 2002, p. 11).

Goals of Solution-Focused Therapy

The most important part of SFT is determining the goals of therapy. Clients are asked to establish their goals and counsellors help the clients to clarify their goals in a number of ways. The general goal of SFT is to build solutions. The counsellors seem to have put aside any preconceived notions about the clients' issues and therapeutic objectives. The therapist tries to empower each client to develop their own solutions based on their distinctive experience and situation.

Assessment in Solution-Focused Therapy

There is no assessment process in SFT and it does not use any psychometric or psychological tests and diagnosis. There is, however, a thorough investigation of what clients would like to see changed in their life, as well as exceptions to difficulties. When the counsellor asks about the problem's exceptions, the attention is on the past and present. The counsellor's questions focus on the future once the goals have been established (Tarragona, 2008).

Process of Solution-Focused Therapy

SFT views empowerment from a strength-based perspective. In working with clients, counsellors must discover the resources and positive aspects the clients may be able to contribute to the situation. During solution building, the counsellors ask the clients what they would like to see a change in their lives, ask them what they would like to change, and inquire if there are exceptions to problems (De Jong & Kim Berg, 2002).

To represent the counsellors' perspective in SFT, Kim Berg employed Harlene Anderson's term 'not knowing'. Listening, framing open-ended questions, receiving details, repeating clients' words, summarising, paraphrasing, admiring, approving clients' perceptions, normalising, noticing clues of possibility, exploring clients' meanings, probing relationship questions, and magnifying solution talk are some of the skills she proposed for not knowing.

Strategies and Interventions in Solution-Focused Therapy

De Jong and Kim Berg (2002) explain the following steps of SFT.

i. *Explaining to the clients how the therapist works.* The therapists participate actively in the discussion, which is a shared investigation of goals and solutions. Accepting that clients as masters of their own lives does not imply that the therapists should take a back seat. The therapists in SFT, according to Kim Berg, 'leads from one step behind', by practicing skills that allow the clients to disclose knowledge about their circumstance and themselves.

ii. *Describing the problem* (emphasising solutions and expectations). The goal of SFT is to find out and apply the solutions. Solution-focused counsellors pay attention to discovering solutions than to examining the problems. Although it is important to know what upsets the clients to better apprehend what changes they wish to make in their lives, they explain that in certain cases it may be easier to jump right to solutions without necessarily going through a problem exploration stage. SFT is about building solutions, not merely solving problems. When the client and counsellor discuss the problems and it is clearly defined, they then move on to discussing exceptions to the problems. Exceptions are times when the problem does not arise, or when it occurs less frequently or less intensely (De Jong & Kim Berg, 2002). Clients are asked to identify these events and describe what is different during these times, including where they are, who they are with, and what they are doing when things are better, even if these occurrences are rare.

iii. *Finding out and amplifying what the clients want* (defining goals). Solution-focused counsellors begin the first session with a few goal development questions. The counsellors may ask the clients in various ways what they hope will be different after coming to therapy; what needs to happen for them to be able to perceive in the future that coming to therapy was not a waste of time; or what they hope to accomplish because of coming to therapy. To help their clients identify a goal, counsellors ask them questions designed to cause them to imagine what their lives will be like after they have achieved the goal.

iv. *Exploring exceptions*. The primary SFT technique is highlighting the exception for any client issue that is currently being presented. The therapist will direct the client to a situation where there is an exception to the problem. The exception is when there was an issue, but things still went smoothly. The three main techniques therapists use to explore exceptions are asking the miracle question and using scales.

a) *Asking Miracle Questions*

A therapist, or counsellor may utilise the miracle question to help the client imagine how things will be different in the future once the problem has been resolved. For the therapist, the intervention has the potential to uncover clients' untapped resources and find solutions for their current issues (Yu, 2019). The client's potential for therapy is unlocked by the miracle question.

The therapists will instruct the clients to pretend that they have gone to a place of worship and that when they came back, their issues have vanished. Following this depiction, they will question the clients about how they know the problems or issues are no longer there, and what specifically has changed. For example, imagine that you go to a place of worship, a miracle occurs, and you came up feeling rejuvenated and your difficulty has vanished. I'd like to hear how you know your problem is resolved. 'What makes this day special? What is it in your life that has vanished or changed?' After visualising what it would be like to come up without it. This question can assist identify and obtain a better knowledge of what the problem is and how it affects the person, as well as providing inspiration to move forward and conquer it (de Shazer et al., 2007).

b) *Scaling*

Instead of being normed scales, solution-focused scales are self-anchored. Clients are asked to score their priorities, goals, hopes, issues, challenges, coping mechanisms, motivation for change, safety, confidence, and satisfaction on a scale of 1 to 10. These questions are quite flexible and can be used to evaluate practically any aspect of the patient's viewpoint (Berg, 1994). They are a crucial tool for measuring a wide range of client concerns and can be posed from a wide range of perspectives.

In a scaling technique, counsellors will ask clients to rate the severity of their problems or issues on a scale of 1 to 10. This aids both the counsellors and the clients in visualising their current situation. 'On a scale of 1 to 10, where would you place yourself to achieve this goal?', 'On a scale of 1 to 10, can you rate your current level of satisfaction?', 'from 1 to 10, how much do you rate your addiction level to be one of the main hindrances in your social relationship?' This can help both the counsellor and the client notice whether anything else needs to be done to get to a 9 or 10, and then begin the process of figuring out what it is. Scaling aids in clarifying the clients' sentiments, giving sessions direction, and highlighting whether something is impeding the clients' ability to tackle the problem.

These procedures can be utilised throughout sessions to match where the clients are currently now to where they were in the first or second session, as well as to rate how far away or close they are from their ideal state of being or from achieving their goal.

c) *Exception Questions*

Clients can use exception questions to identify periods when things were different for them. Identifying moments when the issue was less of an issue. Exception questions include the following: 'Tell me about times when you felt most satisfied'. 'What was it about that day that made it a better day?', 'Can you think of a time when the problem was not present in your life?' A counsellor can enable clients to discover a solution by analysing how these instances occurred.

v. *Formulating and offering feedback to the clients.* Solution-focused brief therapy includes direct and indirect compliments throughout the treatment process based on careful observation of wonderful things clients do or say. Clients are motivated to change when their therapists validate what they are already doing well and admit how difficult their issues are. This indicates that the counsellors have been paying attention (and care). In therapy sessions, compliments are intended to highlight and validate what the clients are doing well. In solution-focused treatment, indirect compliments are frequently given in the form of admiringly toned inquiries such as 'How did you do that?' that allow clients to commend themselves by responding to the inquiry.

vi. *Seeing, amplifying, and measuring client's progress.* After solution-focused counsellors and their clients have found some previous solutions and exceptions to the problem, the counsellors invite the clients to do more of what has previously worked, or to try adjustments that they have advised – this is usually referred to as a 'homework experiment'.

Application

Children, schools, protective services agencies, people with drinking problems, mandated clients, and people in crisis have used solution-focused therapy with great success, among others. Symptoms of addiction and trauma will be reduced, marital issues will be resolved, and classroom behaviour will improve in special education students.

Narrative Therapy (NT)

This was developed by Michael White and David Epston (1990). By separating problems from people, it assumes that people possess a range of skills, proficiencies, beliefs, values, and obligations that can minimise the impact of problems on their lives (Morgan, 2000). Language, discourse, and communication are major components of people's social and cultural identities (Speedy, 2008).

Goals of Narrative Therapy

Clients determine the therapy's objectives. Counsellors seek to help clients rewrite their lives such that a painful or dysfunctional tale no longer defines who they are, and that the creation of new stories brings them closer to their ideal selves. Communities and society are of interest to narrative counsellors. Connecting the clients life to the lives of others is one of the narrative therapy's goals. The role of families, communities, and society in supporting or resolving problems is extensively discussed.

Assessment Procedures in Narrative Therapy

Because narrative therapy is not a normative method, clients are not assessed in terms of diagnosis or evaluation. Nonetheless, the impact of difficulties on clients' lives and the extent to which clients can affect the problems are carefully evaluated. Narratives are made up of events that occur across time. A counsellor seeks to learn about the past, present, and future of a person when they ask about problems and unique outcomes.

Process of Narrative Therapy

Narrative therapists are heavily involved in the clients' interaction. The counsellors usually contribute by asking questions. White (2000) describes the counsellors' role in narrative therapy as 'decentred but influential'. It is decentred because it prioritises the clients' experiences, worries, and agendas. It is influential because the counsellors' questions shape the discourse.

Narrative counsellors do not emphasise intervention; rather, they emphasise practices and therapy as a joint exploration. 'The working style of narrative therapy includes different practices of conversations between clients and counsellors, including, 1) externalising conversations, 2) identifying unique outcomes, and 3) thickening the plot by asking landscape of action and landscape of identity questions' (Tarragona, 2008, p. 184).

Externalising Conversations

Clients frequently come to treatment with the preconceived belief that their issues are tied to their personalities. They think that they or other people are the source of their problems. And because of this belief, they are just further entrenched in the problems they are trying to tackle. By objectifying the problem, externalising conversations might act as a counterbalance to these internal understandings. Because of this, it is possible for people to have an identity that is distinct from their problem; as a result, the problem becomes the problem and not the person. Clients begin to see that problems are different from theirs because of externalising conversations, which allows them to perceive new possibilities for living with problems, or perhaps live without them. Why are problems externalised?

a) Externalising creates a situation in which people perceive themselves as separate from the problems, and the problems cease to communicate to them about their identity or the 'truth' about themselves.
b) The issue is the issue; the person is not the issue.
c) People's own expertise is elevated to the foreground, and they become experts in their own lives.
d) Labelling and pathologising have lessened their impact.
e) Externalising lessens shame and blame while yet allowing for accountability.
f) Externalising allows people to have a point of view or a position on the situation, as well as options for them to act rather than being overwhelmed by it.
g) Externalising allows individuals to come together over challenges and their consequences.

Naming the problem, mapping the problem's consequences across multiple domains of the person's life, and deconstructing or contextualising the problem are some of the strategies used in externalising problems (Morgan, 2000). This allows the problem to be placed into a narrative, demonstrating that the problem is not something that the person has. Instead, it is something that has evolved over time and has been influenced by a variety of causes.

i. *Naming the problem*: This externalised labelling or description of the problem is one that is expressed in the person's own terms. It's also a name that describes the person's unique perspective on the issue. This is referred to as the 'experience-near' explanation of the problem. Externalising brings the context of people's experiences and meaning making to light.
ii. *Mapping the effects of the problem*: This strategy examines the problem's effects on several aspects of the person's life, as well as some of the techniques the problem employs to exert its influence. This is an opportunity to fully understand the impact of the problem on the individual's life. It's critical that this remains an externalised conversation rather than an internalised one.
iii. *Deconstructing the problem in context*: In this case, counsellors look at how dominant discourses and social practices affect their clients' lives.

Identifying Unique Outcomes

The problem and its consequences are part of the prevalent narrative. The counsellors go deeper into these and begin asking about periods or incidents in the client's life that contradict the prevalent narrative. There are some experiences that the dominant or problem-saturated story could not have predicted. In the client's account, the counsellor listens for evidence of other plausible stories about the client's identity. These contradictory details are known as unique outcomes. These are instances when the person has successfully overcome a challenge or dealt well with similar issues. 'Unique outcomes' encourage the clients to recognise and acknowledge behaviours, intentions, and personal characteristics that go counter to the mainstream narrative (Wolter et al., 2006). They also take note of any hopes, ideals, or other good beliefs that the clients have maintained throughout their unpleasant circumstances. When a person shares a 'unique outcome' experience that appears to dispute, contradict, or change her dominant problem-saturated tale, the counsellor welcomes her to elaborate on the nature and circumstances of these unique outcomes, as well as how they differ from the dominant story. This enrichment of the unique results aids in their stabilisation and leads to the deconstruction of the prevailing narrative. The distinctive outcomes provide the foundations for preferred change (Payne, 2006).

Thickening the Plot by Asking Landscape of Action and Landscape of Identity Questions

Narrative therapy is founded on the premise that structuring our experiences as stories or narrations gives them significance. Certain stories begin to dominate our life, and if they are too narrow, they may leave out crucial components of our identity. The first stage in creating alternative stories or plots is to find distinct outcomes that contradict the mainstream story. The prevailing story is likely to be very strong or have a lot of weight at first. Individuals who are insecure can tell numerous examples of how, when, and where insecurity has impacted their lives, yet they may only recall one or two instances when they feel safe and capable. These events may serve as the basis for a new storyline or a different interpretation of their lives, but it is vital to strengthen this alternative story because it appears to be fragile at first. Narrative therapy is a technique for rewriting the stories that shape the identities of people. According to White (1995, 2004), therapeutic dialogues are talks that are re-authored around two types of inquiries: (1) questions about action or behaviour, and (2) questions about the meaning of action and behaviour. Counsellors can ask several questions regarding what the clients did to behave that way or take that step or how they prepared themselves to act in that manner if a distinct outcome has been determined. These are considered landscape action questions (Russell & Carey, 2004; White & Epston, 1989). For example, a diabetic who frequently forgets to take his medication says that he has been taking it consistently for the past two weeks. This is a fantastic result. The therapist inquires as to what he did to ensure that he was able to take the medicine without fail. In this case, the therapist asks the following questions: What did you do to get your medicine? How did you manage to accomplish this? Did someone make a comment about you not taking your medicine? What do you think will happen if you continue to take medicine for the following two weeks? It's also crucial to learn about the significance of unique outcomes, which White and Epston (1989) refer to as landscape identity. Some examples of these kinds of questions in our example are: What do you think it says about you that you decided to take medicine after skipping so many times? What do you believe your relatives think of you? Is there any connection between the decision to take the drug and something interesting?

The narrative counselling process appears relatively unique to the specific client and counsellor working together. The counsellor determines the most effective strategy for overcoming obstacles and facilitating progress depending on the client's issues. Many clients, for example, tend to stay in storytelling while the counsellors try to get them to focus on internal states. The counselling approach with such clients frequently alternates between talking about emotional personal narratives and attempting to discover meaning in those narratives. Other therapists describe the counselling process as assisting clients in staying with and articulating their emotions. This allows crucial narrative aspects to completely emerge while also constraining earlier interpretations. At the beginning of a story, there is usually more emotion present, and clients should not try to interpret their stories but rather let them come out. Later in the process, meaning is discovered in narratives. As a result, it appears that a successful therapy process involves the client completely investigating and experiencing a personal narrative, followed by making meaning of (or extracting lessons from) the events of the narrative.

Application

When a young person's self-efficacy or ability to take positive action is being suppressed by negative self-beliefs, narrative therapy can be useful. Narrative approaches are also particularly beneficial for those who have suffered trauma or abuse and are unable to move on from their experiences. Narrative interventions are more likely to engage young people who are open to talking about their past experiences.

Collaborative Therapy

During the 1980s, Harlene Anderson and her colleague Harold A. Goolishian developed collaborative therapy. Collaborative therapy focuses on developing a collaborative and egalitarian relationship between the client and the counsellor in order to facilitate dialogues that lead to good change. Individuals, families, groups, and even organisations are treated using this strategy. Collaborative therapy can help individuals, couples, or groups develop mutual understanding, improve communication, or resolve conflict by allowing them to explore diverse views.

Goals of Collaborative Therapy

Among the philosophical approaches included in collaborative therapy is scepticism towards knowledge and the belief that knowledge is not a universal truth but a socially constructed concept. There are two key concepts of collaborative therapy. First, knowledge is fluid, and it develops in coordination with the development of language. Hence, growth and learning come about through dialogue. The second one is that there are multiple realities, so there is no one right way to see a situation. The viewpoints of both the counsellor and the client are considered equal in collaborative therapy. Both the counsellor and the client gain new knowledge and insight as meaningful talks take place and numerous views are discussed.

Process: Anderson (2007) defines the collaborative approach as a collection of interconnected notions such as conversational partnerships, therapy as research, the client as an expert, taking a 'not knowing' stance, insecurity, being public as a therapist, and therapy as a part of the day-to-day life.

Conversational partnerships: Collaborative counsellors use techniques such as inviting the clients to tell their stories in their own way and showing sincere interest in their experiences. In therapy, the therapists will listen and respond attentively, pay attention to verbal and non-verbal communication, ask about the client's interpretations of the experience, and pause, allowing space for reflection.

Therapy as research: During the session, the counsellor and the client develop a relationship in which they freely talk with each other. The counsellors actively listen to the stories of the clients and seek to understand their viewpoints. Counsellors can expedite the dialogue by asking questions, making comments, and ensuring that they understand what the clients are saying. Collaboration helps in gaining a new understanding of clients' experiences, allowing them to change.

The client as an expert: In collaborative therapy, counsellors recognise that clients are the masters of their own experience. Counsellors do not assume an authoritative role or act as if they have more knowledge. In therapy, they may offer ideas or perspectives, but they do not impose their own views. The counsellors' expertise is 'in establishing and fostering an environment and condition that naturally invites collaborative relationships and generative conversational processes' (Anderson, 2006, p. 47).

Assuming a 'not knowing' position: As Anderson (2005) notes, this does not imply that the therapists are clueless, a blank slate, or unwilling to express opinions.

Insecurity/Uncertainty: Language is generative, so it's impossible to predict where the conversation will proceed or where it will end. In a discussion between clients and counsellors, the parties get ideas they did not have before the discussion.

Being public as a therapist: Individuals always have exterior dialogues with others and internal dialogues with themselves throughout their lives. In therapy, 'becoming public' is being open to sharing interior conversations rather than keeping them covered or concealed. Counsellors participate fully in the conversation rather than directing it by expressing opinions. Bringing the counsellors' ideas to the table can impede the clients from engaging in the conversation because what isn't spoken can generate problems with the counsellors' request for information or contribution to the dialogue (Anderson, 2006).

Therapy as part of everyday life: Among many of the conversations people engage in, Anderson stresses the importance of therapy as one such system. Collaborative counsellors do not use technical or professional language rather they use colloquial language in therapy that is very similar to the language they use in everyday life.

> In collaborative therapy, each client and each session are viewed as unique. Every relationship and every conversation are different. What is a constant across different situations and problems is the therapist's philosophical stance or position regarding the clients.
>
> (Tarragona, 2008, p. 194)

Postmodern therapies regard language as a tool for constructing (and deconstructing) individuals' identities and understanding of the social environment. The methods used in postmodern therapy avoid diagnostic labelling in favour of focusing on what's working and the client's unique subjective experience.

Postmodernism has faced a barrage of criticism since its inception. Critics contend that Postmodernism is merely confused though seems to be profound. They point out that seeing everything as dialogue and treating every interpretation as equally valid lead to anarchy. Finally, they argue that, in preaching against abstract truth and unique value, Postmodernism is implicitly preaching against its own implicit claim to capture truth and hold worth.

Application

Collaborative therapy is used to treat anxiety, depression, and issues related to marital and family life. It is beneficial for children, families, and couples in gaining a better understanding of the causes and triggers of problems in their life, as well as learn appropriate coping skills. Collaborative therapy, as a philosophy, allows the therapist to help their clients in brainstorming solutions while yet allowing them to take the lead.

Buddhist Counselling

Buddhism is a philosophical tradition that originated in ancient India based on the teachings of Gautama Buddha. Buddhism is an assemblage of philosophical, psychological, and cultural traditions that developed from the original story of Buddha (Gethin, 1998). It is a set of practices and principles to relieve suffering and move towards liberation. Buddhist teaching includes specific beliefs (philosophy), a specific theory regarding the human mind and its behaviour (psychology), and a specific set of ethical guidelines (ethics). A virtuous life and ways of conduct are enshrined in the text, emphasising both ethical and psychological characteristics of behaviour. Buddhist Psychology is a branch of Psychology based on the teachings of Buddha and Buddhist philosophical literature. It is defined as the 'central aspects of a manifold philosophical, psychological, and spiritual tradition of thought and practice that was originally developed and systematised in India during the last 400 years Before the Common Era (BCE)' (Chakkarath, 2014, p. 185).

Buddhism is mainly associated with happiness. Happiness and sadness are our responsibility and are entirely within our control, according to Buddhist thinking. Buddhism focuses on developing positive emotions and personal assets and virtues to enhance well-being and that pleasures and desires are at the centre of human unhappiness. Buddhism has focused on human flourishing than on illness and advocates that mindfulness and compassion can enhance well-being which is now being adopted by positive psychology. In Buddhist psychology, persons' psychological states are determined by how they relate to what happens in their lives, not by the things they do. Buddhism maintains that everything in the world arises from the mind, and if we train our minds properly, happiness will follow. Buddha said, 'Our life is moulded by our mind: we grow into what we think'. Buddhist philosophy does not pathologise any issue. According to Buddhist philosophy, a man can never be free of all desires. Buddhism acknowledges that pain is a part of life and cannot be avoided. Our actions and thoughts, as well as our efforts to control the things around us, can exacerbate our psychological suffering. A human being is stressed and tensed because of social conflicts, which disturb harmony. To maintain harmony and peace, one should strive to resolve conflict by finding its cause, introspecting, self-analysing, and being diligent. Therefore, one should strive for ideal behaviour and control of desires.

Buddhism emphasises the individual, self-cognisant, and personal growth (Stein, 2017). Mental suffering is rooted in the notion of the 'self' in psychology. Buddhism holds that the 'self' is an illusion created by the mind, and the attachment to it is what creates suffering in life (Albahari, 2006). Buddhist counselling is described by Lee and colleagues (2017) as 'a process of reducing individual suffering utilising wisdom and interventions from Buddhism, which attempts to train the human mind to attain a state of calmness, happiness, and liberation'.

Core Concepts in Buddhist Psychology

In Buddhism, psychological qualities that are socially valuable are- dama (self-control), sama (mental control, equilibrium), and niyama (restraining self, discipline). These affect the financial, physiological (e.g., sickness), and psychological aspects. The *Buddha, the*

Dharma, and the Sangha are referred to as the 'Three Jewels' (Three Gems) by Buddhists. A Buddha is a fully enlightened person, the Dharma is Goutama Buddha's teachings on understanding and love, and Sangha is a group of Buddhists who come together to practice the Dharma and seek enlightenment (Suzuki, 1960). Being a part of a Sangha can provide us with the energy and drive we need to develop Bodhicitta (mind of awakening), the altruistic desire to help all people achieve enlightenment. Being permeated with *Bodhicitta* immediately transforms us into a *Bodhisattva* (one whose goal is awakening).

A few of the Buddha's own teachings provide a summary of his philosophy: There is this verse, *Sarva Papasyaakaranam kushalashyopasampada, sva chitta paryopadanam, etad Buddhanam sasanam.* It explains 'avoiding unskilful actions performing skilful actions and purifying the mind' that is the dispensation of the Buddha (Dhammapada, verse 183). The three marks of existence, the four noble truths, and the noble Eightfold Path are the basic tenets of Buddhism. Buddhism affirms that everything, including suffering, is subject to change and impermanence. We need everything permanent in a temporary life. Ultimately, the Three Marks of Existence are the impermanence of all conditioned phenomena (anicca), the pain caused by them (dukkha), and the absence of self (anatta).

Three Marks of Existence

Buddha's focus was on the cause and cure of human suffering. Suffering here includes physical, emotional, and spiritual sufferings that occur at various stages of life. This is explained in the four noble truths (the catvari-arya-satyani) of Buddha: i) The Truth of Suffering (Dukha Satya): Suffering is part of life (dukkha), ii) The Truth of the Root cause of Suffering (Samudaya Satya): Suffering has a cause (dukkha – samudaya), iii) The Truth of the fact that this root can be uprooted or this suffering can cease (Nirodha Satya): Suffering has an end (dukkha – nirodha), and iv) The Truth of the Path to the elimination of Suffering (Dukha Nirodha gamini Marga): For the end of suffering there is a way (dukkha-nirodha-marga). The individual and their individualistic sufferings are at the forefront, and the aim is to realise that there is an end to suffering and to work towards it.

Four Noble Truths of Buddha

This eight-fold path (ashtanga-marga) consists of the right view, right intention, right speech, right action, right livelihood, right effort, right mindfulness, and right concentration. The right view (samma-ditthi) and the right intention (samma-sankalpa) fall under the category of prajna or wisdom. Two of the segments deal with realising nature is impermanent, understanding suffering is the result of our actions and feelings towards others, and having a desire for Nirvana in the form of freedom from attachments. The

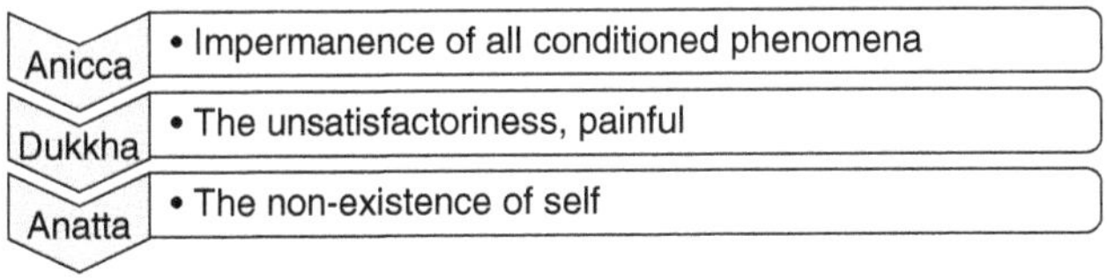

Figure 2.22 Three Marks of Existence

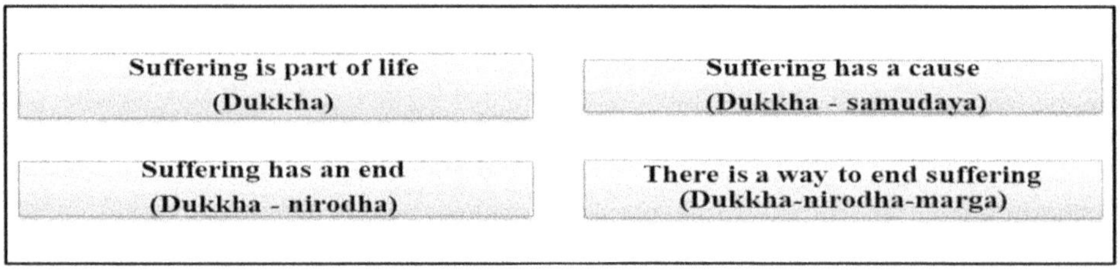

Figure 2.23 Four Noble Truths of Buddha

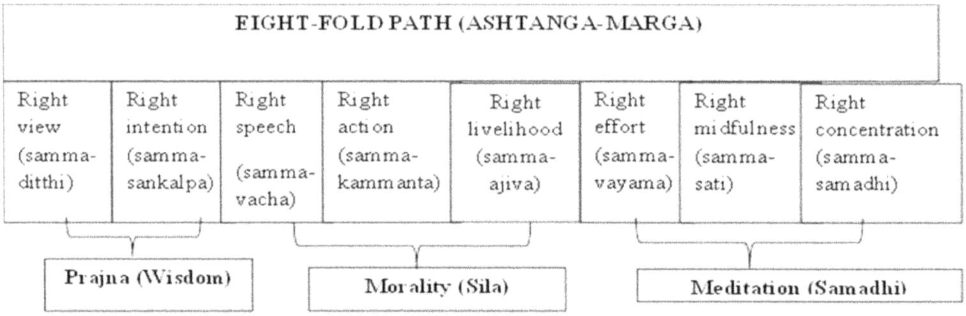

Figure 2.24 Eight-Fold Path

next three segments of the path belong to the category of morality (sila) and include right speech (samma-vacha), right action (samma-kammanta), and right livelihood (samma-ajiva). Abstaining from hateful speech, killing, and making an honest living are included in this. The last three segments of the path are focused on meditation and mindfulness involving the right effort (samma-vayama), right mindfulness (samma-sati), and right concentration (samma-samadhi).

Eight-Fold Path

As a basic code of ethics for lay Buddhist followers, the Five Precepts reinforce the importance of morality in Buddhism. The Five Precepts are: Do not kill, steal, commit sexual misconduct, lie, or get drunk. For those entering monastic life, these precepts are extended (Harvey, 2013). In ancient texts of various Buddhist traditions, the Five Precepts are at the centre of Buddhism and Buddhist morality.

Buddhist Kālāma Sutra emphasises the importance of prudence in searching for truth, wisdom, and knowledge, regardless of religion. As opposed to beliefs born of blind beliefs, doctrines, and flimsy reasoning, Kālāma Sutra encourages people to acquire knowledge based on their direct experience. Overall, Buddhism suggests constantly searching for truths that have been shown to reduce one's stress and misery, rather than passive acceptance. Buddhism advises against relying on information that has been acquired by repeated hearing, tradition, or rumour, as well as on scriptures, assumptions, axioms, fallacious reasoning, bias, or the seeming competence of others. Buddha advises us to accept teaching only if we personally experience it as skilful, blameless, praiseworthy, and conducive to happiness – and only if it is well regarded by the wise. The Kalama Sutta is therefore widely regarded as the Buddha's Charter of Free Inquiry that declares 'war on fanaticism, prejudice, dogmatism and intolerance' (Kalama Sutta: The Buddha's Charter of Free Inquiry, 2013).

Goals of Buddhist Counselling

Buddhist psychology has two therapeutic goals: **Samacariya** following a healthy, virtuous life and **Nirvana** the goal of cessation of dissatisfaction and suffering or dukkha. The inclusion of Buddhist psychology in counselling happened due to the consideration of the four noble truths and 'Chan meditation' as healing techniques to deal with mental challenges. The aims of Buddhist counselling focus on relieving stress, helping the client to reduce their struggles and sufferings, and enabling them to be more productive. Buddhist enlightenment experiences can enable transformation, and healing, as well as help an individual, finds existential meaning (DeAngelis, 2014). Salvation is the ultimate goal of an individual, according to Buddhist philosophy, and this act can be performed by a self-reliant individual – which counselling seeks to achieve. Psychological aspects are important along with physical and environmental aspects for social well-being. To achieve Samacariya and Nirvana, Buddhist psychology focuses on the following:

1) *Alleviation of human suffering*: Buddhist psychology emphasises the role of free will in a human's life to make decisions and act to face the consequences of the actions themselves. Assessment in Buddhist psychology occurs through the diagnosis of suffering (dukkha), which is believed to be a product of desire or craving (tanha). In general terms, an individual who desires more than what is required often becomes the victim of mental suffering. The following shloka in Sanskrit explains the consequences of desire.

लोभात् क्रोधः प्रभवतिलोभात् कामः प्रजायते I लोभात् मोहश्च नाशश्च लोभः पापस्य कारणम् II

'lobhaat krodhaH prabhavati lobhaat kaamaH prajaayate,lobhaat mohashcha naashashcha lobhaH paapasya kaaraNam'

(Greed gives rise to anger; greed also gives rise to desire; attachment and ruin comes from greed; greed is the cause for sin).

2) *Discovering and following the eight-fold path to lead to liberation*: Buddhism sees the eight-fold path for relieving suffering from which humans sometimes become victims. As part of this process, one must take control of the mind, accept new thoughts and perceptions, and reach Nirvana through deeper conversation.
3) *Attaining Nirvana or liberation*: The goal of the eightfold path is to attain Nirvana, the liberation from worldly attachments. One of the ways to attain Nirvana is to detach from worldly pleasures, recognise the true nature of the experience, and focus on the conscious reality. Buddhist psychology gives importance to realising the ultimate truth and meaning of life.

Buddhist Principles in Counselling

As per Buddhist philosophy, intellectual knowledge can only help an individual if it is transformed on the experiential level. The experiential level is the essence of Buddhist counselling teachings. Therefore, a therapeutic component is an accustomed component in counselling. Prior to working with or helping others, Buddhist counsellors encourage clients to understand their own minds (Murgatroyd, 2001). When such an approach fits clients' worldviews, they are more willing to seek counselling and comply with the therapeutic intervention.

Meditative, mindfulness, gratitude, and compassion-informed intervention practices are applied to the counselling context in order to promote being present, uncertainty, acceptance, and softening into discomfort. Practising this allows individuals to quiet the mind as they observe and accept their true nature and present as they observe everyday life experiences.

Compassion

Counselling with compassion includes different components, including wisdom and mindfulness. To be compassionate is to have a balanced and detached mental state of equanimity to help others. Through deep listening and acknowledging the client's emotional suffering, compassion is practised in counselling. Having established trust, clients are introduced to compassion by discussing past experiences of gratitude and assistance during difficult times, sharing stories of compassion, and providing brief readings on compassion. This helps the clients in recalling and experiencing compassion.

Gratitude

Grateful people are more optimistic and are more likely to report higher positive affect, vitality, optimism, motivation, and life satisfaction and are less likely to report depression and stress. According to Buddhist psychology, developing gratitude is a positive state of mind and is encouraged. The clients can be encouraged and given homework to express gratitude explicitly by giving them homework to write one to three things that they are grateful for in their lives. This can change their unhealthy mental state of greed or aversion to love and generosity.

Counsellors adhere to the Buddhist perspective by being less knowing, less leaping, and assuming less in their counselling practice. Buddhist counsellors are trained to appreciate and articulate their clients' experiences. By doing so, they refrain from thinking they are better than clients and leaping to judgement or assuming that their own experience is better to those of the clients. As a result, the counsellor does not diminish or disempower clients but gives them room to grow and change. In counselling training and practices, it is introduced and incorporated before dealing with clients' concerns to facilitate personal growth and development. Counsellors help clients understand the connections between the symptoms that led them to the clinic and their general feelings. In their discussion, the counsellor introduces clients to three Universal Natural Laws (Suffering, Impermanence, and Selflessness) and explains that suffering comes from clients' desire for transient things and unwillingness to accept adverse outcomes. Rather than focusing on previous occurrences, these stresses educating clients to focus on the present and pay attention to their reflective thinking habits. This psychological shift focuses on the 'here and now', reassessing the client's health, balancing mental (or psychological) and physical problems, and achieving a state of awareness. The goal is to assist them in alleviating their misery.

The therapeutic implications of various Buddhist concepts like Zen Buddhism have been realised and these have been increasingly incorporated into psychotherapy, for example, counsellors can listen to their clients with a 'Zen-like attention and non-attachment' to be present for them and read between the lines while not getting carried away with them, preventing bias from personal feelings. The Buddhist concept of **satori** (unsurpassed transformation to wholeness), when looked at through the lens of intellectualism can be seen as sharing goals of self-transformation in psychotherapy. Using Zen meditation can help sharpen focus, gain new insights, increase existing insight, improve creativity, and help overcome negative effects and pessimistic thoughts (Fromm & Suzuki, 1960).

Buddhism recommended two types of meditation: tranquillity (samatha) and insight (vipassana). The goal of insight meditation is to develop introspective insight. Introspection is taken into consideration as a primary method of therapy. Through introspection, one can gain insight, which leads to the abandonment of ignorance and lust. The process of meditation is precisely characterised by four components – forms, objects, attitudes, and behaviours. The form explains what happens to the body during the procedure. Whether it's breath, a sight, a chant, or imaginary beings, the major focus of one's attention is classified as an object. The attitude with which one enters the process is a combination of expectations, associations, moods, and intentions. Concentration and mindfulness are examples of behaviours. Acceptance is a component of the attitude component of meditation, which has a significant impact on attachment. Mindfulness is merely being aware of events without accepting or rejecting them (de Silva, 2014). Meditation can help the client become more self-aware (Tanphaichitr, 2005). Although mindfulness and meditation are employed in the Buddhist tradition to bring about enlightenment, they are also utilised in counselling to educate clients on how to regulate their emotional state and manage their suffering (Kabat-Zinn, 1982, 1994; Robins, 2002).

Mindfulness and Buddhist Meditation

Meditation training is a key component of Buddhist counselling. There are five cardinal virtues proposed by Buddha, they are mindfulness, morality, faith, vigour, and concentration in pursuit of wisdom. The development of human learning processes brings new experiences to connect with their prior experiences resulting in the creation of new knowledge. 'Thinking' (Sammaditthi) knowing the reason and result, solving the cause and effect thinking with wisdom can find sustainable solutions. Buddha stated,

> Mind is luminous, but is being tainted with transitory mental impurities (greed, hatred, and delusion) and requires strength to unveil the sword of compassion, as this is the only cure for suffering. If one can always maintain mindfulness and self-awareness, one's mind will be luminous and serene and will be liberated from the burden of all mental impurities and suffering.
>
> (Tanphaichitr, 2005, p. 15)

'Asaṅga (fourth century), one of the founders of the Yogācarā school of Buddhist thought, defines mindfulness as not mentally losing a familiar object and in effect non-distraction' (Gethin, 2015). Mindfulness explains that thoughts are mere thoughts. They are not 'you' or 'reality'. They are our internal ongoing reflection on ourselves and the world.

The moment we realise this we can liberate ourselves from the fractured reality that we have all created for ourselves through unending worrying, brooding, and ruminating by this straightforward understanding. We can once more see a straight path through life (Williams & Penman, 2010, p. 36).

Note, Know, Choose Model

The Note, Know, and Choose model (Lee & Ong 2019) has three main purposes: (a) *deconstruction*: guiding the clients on how to experientially break down a mental phenomenon into its various supporting factors and components in the body and mind; (b) *discernment*: collaboratively exploring the interdependent nature of the causes, factors, conditions, and effects with the clients; and (c) *detachment*: allows clients to let go of unhealthy and unrealistic psychological ideas and replace them with more informative ones (Lee & Tang 2021). To attain these goals, the model contains three treatment phases: (a) improving the level of concentration to be aware of mental habits and qualities (b) gaining insights to understand how unrealistic expectations of the mind contribute to suffering (c) selecting sound thoughts and actions without being bound by specific judgements and interpretations. In the note stage, clients practice a variety of Buddhist mindfulness techniques, including mindful breathing, paying attention to different areas of the body, and chanting or chanting mantras to build clarity and stability in the mind. Throughout the treatment process, clients engage in regular contemplation practices. The know stage helps clients understand how their emotional engagement with external objects can cause misery, desire, and longing. This identifies and addresses previously overlooked decision points. The choose phase focuses on developing the skills needed to make different decisions using the insights gained from everyday interactions. Techniques include fostering a loving vision of the self and others, as well as non-self-visualisation.

Mind Moment Analysis (MMA)

Lee (2020) discussed the objective and the distinct processes of MMA for counselling based on Buddhist teachings in his article on Mind Moment Analysis. The mind moment is an Abhidhamma (Buddhist sutras containing ancient Buddhist scriptures including extensive scholastic treatments of doctrinal topics) concept that describes how a perceptual process proceeds through a series of cognitive operations. A 'mind moment' in MMA and Note, Know, Choose is defined as a moment that provides the observers and participants the potential to observe, choose, and pause. The goal of MMA is to relieve the mind of excessive conceptual proliferation. Practicing not taking pleasure in welcoming or clinging to conceptual proliferations is one way to reduce suffering (Karunadasa, 2013). As a first step, MMA identifies an incident in which the client has been assaulted by and dominated by conceptual proliferation. The responses of the client to these instances serve as a source of data. As the client examines them, they gradually identify the body-mind components that contribute to an unwholesome (Akushal) state, identify the root causes (particularly the craving), and identify choices that will allow them to be released from a conceptually proliferated mental state. In MMA, participants learn about how mental activities cause suffering, change, and end when mental and behavioural practices are adapted. This meditative practice should be introduced by the therapist through the counselling skills like active listening, dialogue, questioning and providing insights so that the clients can cultivate the flexibility necessary to take out attention from concepts and be grounded in the current moment. The seven steps delineated in MMA are:

(a) *Mind education*: Using mind education a person can understand the nature of the mind through the standpoint of dependent arising, which allows one to create a mental space between the present moment and conceptual propagations.
(b) *Identifying a critical incident of disturbance*: It is a technique for training a client's ability to identify and observe multiple factors that contribute to suffering, including the environment, body, and mind. A recent enough incident must be identified for the clients to remember the details clearly.
(c) *Locating sensory contacts*: This is the junction of the sense object, the sense organ, and consciousness at which cognitive processes begin (Karunadasa, 2013). For example, an auditory object, the ears, and attention together provide auditory information. The six types of senses according to Buddhism are sight, hearing, smell, touch, taste, and mind. The mind is able to experience all other senses as well as create mental objects like images, inner voices, and other ideas. As a result of misinterpretations and creations of sense objects, suffering results from the mind's inordinate desire to conceptualise, which leads to distortions or rejections of the original sense representation.
(d) *Expanding awareness of bodily sensations and feeling*: 'Rūpakkhandha' or body is summative of corporeality, form, or material quality (Karunadasa, 2013). The five sense organs have their respective external objects. When sense organs, sense objects, and consciousness join, sense contact occurs, which is a prerequisite for the next aggregate, vedanā (suffering/pain). In the Satipathana Sutta, attending to bodily sensations by being attentive to the present moment is an effective way to regain the scattered attention of the mind (Anālayo, 2010). Mindfulness of one's body during an anxious state is key to understanding the conceptualised power of anxiety.
(e) *Noting cognitions*: Cognition illustrates the processes of perception, initial and sustained thoughts driven by an individual's past experiences. Individuals have unique knowledge systems, so that the same sensory input can give rise to completely different cognitions, and sometimes those cognitions are not reflective of reality. The inner voices or internal monologues that manifest in cognitions vary in their intensity and nature. These voices may be subtle, neutral, or loud, such as a pleasant voice recognising a person or an unpleasant retaliating voice disliking that person.
(f) *Knowing conceptual proliferations*: To gain knowledge of root causes and their effects, the therapist and client examine and analyse conceptual proliferations jointly. The goal is to deconstruct phenomenal, experiential, and conceptual proliferations and determine the motivations that underpin them. Clients' proliferations are usually listened to by the therapist and themes are drawn out, the expectations and needs of the client are examined, and clients are guided to recognise the craving embodied within their meanings and values. The therapist uses this reflective dialectical process to examine the creations of conceptual proliferations made by clients so they can gain an understanding of the discrepancy between their expectations and reality.
(g) *Choosing new actions*: A therapist usually helps clients see beyond their own mental proliferations, examines the network of cognitive processes to find entry points to alternative thought patterns, and assigns homework to foster mindfulness in responding to future incidents.

Mindfulness has been suggested by Buddha as a path to liberation and relief from suffering. It takes greater effort and understanding than the practice of tranquillity and insight meditation. The human mind is usually preoccupied with the thoughts of the past or the future. Mindfulness controls one's mind to the present moment. Only then can we observe the true nature of the mind. The five hindrances of life are sensual desire; antagonism and anger; sloth and torpor; doubts and restlessness; and worry. A way of security to these is through noting and observing the breath followed by moral conduct. Following the meditation, the focus is more on liberation than normal mindfulness practices applied to therapy. Precise and vigilant mindfulness practice helps in relaxing the mind and mental dispositions.

By applying the wisdom of mind and body, Kabat-Zinn (2005) developed a practical guide to meditation, mindfulness, and healing through the stress-reduction programme. Mindfulness is translated as sati in the Buddhist scriptures, written in Pali language of Buddhism. This programme focuses on developing the ability to be mindful, client, non-striving acceptance, being mindful of the current moment, and having a beginner's mind, which includes seeing each step in meditation as if it were the first time, and letting go of the past. The aim of mindfulness practice should be to restrain negative thoughts and emotions, abandon them once they arise, and develop new positive skills once they have been developed. Through regulation of breath, one can achieve solace through meditation as it helps to extend the scope of conscious control of the body. When practising formal meditation, one closes their eyes and keeps their senses quiet, allowing the breath and body sensations to become conscious. Systematically, as this practice is continued, feelings and thoughts become the focus of mindfulness. Mindfulness practices begin with the body, move to emotions, then thoughts, and then push to the nature of phenomena and the laws that govern how the body and mind work: mindfulness of the body, mindfulness of emotions, mindfulness of thoughts, and mindfulness of the nature of phenomena.

Stress in daily life has become one of the most common problems disturbing the balance of human lives. Mindfulness meditation can be helpful to gain equilibrium as it can help raise awareness about one's cognition, emotion, and behaviour and develop a sense of liveliness of the body and world around us. According to Buddhist psychology, emotional and behavioural difficulties like worry, doubt, hate, misperception, confusion, envy, agitation, and so on arise in three primary areas that are unhealthy psychological states – grasping (greed or hanging onto things), aversion (hatred or mentally pushing things that are beneficial away) and delusion (ignorance, not seeing things as they truly are especially related to oneself). Healthy psychological states which are the opposites of the unhealthy states respectively include – generosity ('Dana – giving without expectation of return), love (holiness, care, compassion, warmth, goodwill towards others), and wisdom (insight via mindfulness) that lead to mindfulness, confidence, clarity, adaptability, equanimity, flexibility, insight, joy, kindness and so on. Counsellors working from a Buddhist psychological perspective can incorporate this concept in their counselling or therapy sessions by identifying the unhealthy states in their clients and helping them to achieve mindfulness in all states. After attaining mindfulness, one can transform the negative or unhealthy states into healthy ones.

The counsellor can notice slight bits of the health states like generosity towards another by pointing it out subtly to the clients, making them aware of them, and helping them deepen that state. This helps the mind become more open, clear, and less reactive, increasing the capacity for quality decision making. It can be used to even deepen the therapeutic relationship by helping them develop warmth, openness, compassion, empathy, etc. This is done by first concentrating on a specific aspect of an experience, which can improve counsellors' attention in clinical sessions. Open monitoring can expand attention to include the full range of experiences including sensory aspects, helping to improve the ability to notice and stay open to uncertainty in clinical sessions. Finally, developing compassionate acceptance can help reduce resistance to difficult emotions like pain. It can help subside the initial symptoms of pain (emotional or physical) in the clients which can aid in bringing them to a better state – physically as well as mentally, easing the entry into the counselling process. An unintended consequence of this mindfulness is a sort of awareness that opens a new perspective to deal with various aspects of existence: dukkha according to Buddha (Batchelor, 1997). Being able to attend to one's emotions rather than being overwhelmed by them leads to the possibility of experiencing inner freedom which would lead to tasting Nirvana (Batchelor, 1997). According to Fromm, meditative techniques of psychotherapy that seek to achieve a high degree of non-attachment and serve to reach a higher level of being are associated with Buddhist mindfulness practices. Through mindfulness meditation, the client can become more aware of their thoughts, feelings, and behaviours, for example, a client with a problem of binge eating would notice that they begin eating junk food when they are anxious or bored, following which they can curb these urges.

The healing effect of meditation and mindfulness on stress and suffering has been extensively studied throughout the years. Mindfulness as a therapy became famous after the Mindfulness-Based Stress Reduction (MBSR) programme by Kabat-Zinn. Mindfulness-Based Stress Reduction (MBSR) is a concept that has its roots in Buddhist teachings (Vipasana) and was adopted by Kabat-Zinn who later developed it into an 8-week programme. This programme aims to practice moment-to-moment awareness to own every experience irrespective of whether they are good or bad. Research suggests that this technique has proven effective for people dealing with depression and anxiety disorders. (Segal et al., 2012).

Buddhist psychology has been applied to anger management problems faced by clients. One of the tools involves the visualisation process – using the practice of internalising sacred figures, embodying their spiritual essence, wisdom, and inner peace. This, in turn, can nullify and stop strong emotions like anger and hatred as the client now has internalised a calm posture via visualisation. This can be replicated by the client in anger-provoking situations, for example, they can visualise embodying a figure of great person like Sri Aurobindo in situations where they feel like getting violent, once they internalise the personality of Aurobindo, they would be less likely to then commit an act of violence.

Michelle McDonald, the Vipassana teacher developed the **RAIN method** as part of the mindfulness movement in the early 2000s which emphasises maintaining awareness of one's surroundings, thoughts, and the feelings that accompany them without judgement. This method stands for *Recognise* what is happening, *Allowing life* to be just as it is, *Investigate* inner experience, and *Non-identification* with difficult emotional states that obstructs well-being. This four-step practice can bring a sense of inner peace and calm in the times when the clients may feel stressed, agitated, frustrated, or helpless. The clients are first made to recognise and label what it is that they are feeling or experiencing (e.g., worried, anxious, angry, etc.), working with a difficult emotion is to recognise when it is present. The next step involves 'accept', 'acknowledge', and 'allow'. In this context, acceptance means acknowledging what is already present and allowing it to continue to be. Even though one acknowledges or acknowledges something is present, this does not imply that one supports or agrees with it;

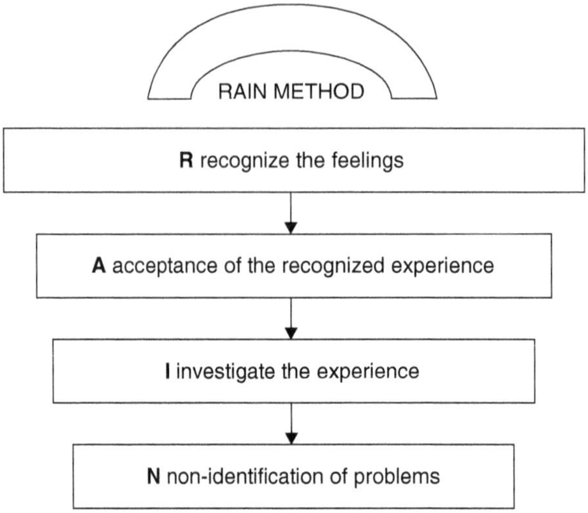

Figure 2.25 RAIN Method

rather, acknowledges what is right now. The third step investigates the experience on a deeper level, exploring without judgement, and asking oneself questions about feelings and experiences. The fourth phase of non-identification includes not taking emotions personally and realising that everyone experiences and shares emotions. This step helps clients to realise that what they are going through is not unique and there may be others who have gone through similar situations. They are also made aware that this suffering is impermanent and will not last forever; they see it as a painful but not defining experience. Once the clients reach this stage successfully, they are in a much better state of accepting their situation as it is and can understand and take in the reality. This method can help increase mindfulness in clients, help them gain new insight, and become more flexible.

Unlike psychologists, who emphasise actively confronting negative distorted thoughts and replacing them with more positive ones, Buddhist counselling emphasises separating oneself from all thoughts to achieve a condition of calm conducive to ultimate self-understanding, or enlightenment. As a result of gaining some mental control and clarity, people are guided to become more aware of the content and functioning of their minds. Clients will be able to better manage their moods and emotions and enhance their general mental health after they understand the relationship between their mind contents, action, and consciousness.

Application

Buddhist Counselling can be useful for a variety of concerns including daily hassles and stress, poor sleep, anxiety, depression, existential issues, substance abuse, and more. Therapy based on Buddhism is very effective in helping individuals to alleviate the suffering that they experience. Throughout history, Buddhism has provided a very large number of people with an extraordinary message, a set of values, and a path towards living a fulfilling life in which suffering can be dealt with, minimised, and overcome.

An Integral Approach to Counselling

Integrative therapy involves applying techniques from different therapeutic orientations according to the client's problems and adapting the methods depending on the client's preferences and needs. Psychotherapy integration is defined as an effort to look beyond the boundaries of solitary-school approaches to explore what can be added or learned from other viewpoints (Stricker, 1994). It is characterised by openness to different approaches to combining multiple theories and practices. What differentiates the integrated approach from the eclectic approach is the way it uses psychotherapy. In an eclectic approach, counsellors choose interventions because they work. Counsellors do not need a theoretical basis for using techniques other than efficacy. Integrative counsellors aim to produce the greatest benefit by customising treatment to the individuals. Integrative therapy combines elements of different schools of psychology to create a more flexible, inclusive treatment approach compared to more traditional, singular forms of psychotherapy. Integrative psychotherapy also refers to the integration of a person's emotive, cognitive, behavioural, and physiological systems, as well as the social and transpersonal components of the systems that surround them. These ideas are applied to a human development perspective in which each stage of life brings with it new developmental challenges, need sensitivities, crises, and possibilities for new learning.

The Goal of Integrative Therapy

Integrative psychotherapy aims to promote wholeness by maximising the quality of a person's being and functioning in the intrapsychic, interpersonal, and socio-political arena while considering everyone's unique limits and environmental constraints.

Modes of Psychotherapy Integration

Psychotherapy integration comes in four different forms. These are known as modes, and they describe how theory and technique have been combined in general. The four modes are *technical eclecticism, the common-factors approach, theoretical integration, and assimilative integration* (Stricker & Gold, 2019). Integration of psychotherapy is based on these modes. Each integrative approach to psychotherapy is viewed as one of these modes, although the distinctions between them may be unclear at times.

1. Technical Eclecticism

According to the APA Dictionary of Psychology, in integrative psychotherapy, techniques are used to address the complicated challenges of clients using a variety of theoretical frameworks. Technical eclecticism developed by psychologist Arnold Allan Lazarus (1932–2013) employs a methodical and well-considered strategy that strikes a balance between theoretical perspectives and therapeutic procedures. It is the most clinically and technically focused kind of psychotherapy integration, with the least amount of conceptual or theoretical integration. Following a thorough assessment of the clients, clinical methods, and procedures from two or more therapies are performed sequentially or in combination. The relationship between the issues to be addressed and the clients' psychological (cognitive, behavioural, emotional) and social (interpersonal) characteristics are investigated in this assessment. Based on clinical knowledge and research findings, techniques are chosen according to the ones that are best suited to the needs of each client, regardless of the theoretical origin. Its distinctive nature is in its focus on specific therapy procedures rather than broad treatment packages and theories, as well as in its search for specific factors rather than common contributors to efficacy. This type of integrative psychotherapy is best exemplified by the following: (1) multimodal therapy (2) transtheoretical psychotherapy, and (3) prescriptive psychotherapy and systematic treatment selection.

i. Multimodal Therapy

Lazarus (2006) developed multimodal therapy to supplement behavioural interventions with cognitive, imagery-based, and experiential techniques. According to Lazarus, clients' biopsychosocial functioning is assessed in seven areas (BASIC ID, which stands for Behaviour, Affect, Sensation, Imagery, Cognition, Interpersonal Relations, and Drugs/Biology). A treatment plan is developed based on the experimental literature, clinical guidelines, and experience. Lazarus maintained that this type of therapy provided the most accurate and focused assessment of the clients and their immediate adjustment, as well as allowed the counsellor to make customised treatment plans based on the unique excesses, deficits, and eccentricities of each client.

ii. Transtheoretical Psychotherapy

Prochaska and DiClemente (2002) defined transtheoretical psychotherapy as an applied framework for determining the optimal fit between clients' characteristics and certain therapeutic models and approaches. According to this model (known as the model of readiness for change), making changes in health-related behaviour is a complex process. People make such changes gradually and nonlinear order. Prochaska and DiClemente have identified 'ten change processes that dominate in many therapies: consciousness-raising, dramatic relief, self-re-evaluation, environmental re-evaluation, self-liberation, social liberation, counterconditioning, stimulus control, reinforcement management, and the helping relationship' (Stricker & Gold, 2019). The theory includes six stages: pre-contemplation, contemplation, preparation, action, maintenance, and termination and the client arrives in therapy at one of the stages. In the pre-contemplation stage, the clients are not ready to think about change, in the contemplation stage though they think of change but are not yet ready to take initiative. In the preparation stage, they take all steps to gather energy and resources for change; in the action stage, they make overt use of therapy. In maintenance therapy, they continue with the change, and at last in the termination phase, they close the therapy. In this approach, an assessment is made to know the levels of change that are required for each client. This concept refers to the specific kind of psychological issues that the clients are dealing with. The areas of symptoms and situational difficulties, maladaptive cognitions, interpersonal conflicts, and intrapersonal conflicts are all assessed as essential levels of change in this paradigm. Clients are assessed in these three domains- processes, stages, and degrees of change, via specially designed self-report questionnaires, and a personalised treatment plan is developed using all possible psychotherapy procedures (Prochaska & DiClemente, 2002).

iii. Prescriptive Psychotherapy

Larry Beutler, Forrester Gallagher-Thompson, Thompson and Tomlins (2012) developed a system of adapting therapy to the client's characteristics, which they call prescriptive psychotherapy. Prescriptive psychotherapy aims to the best match of therapist, strategies, and procedures for the client's problems and characteristics. Disparities in four aspects of a wide range of psychotherapies are considered while assessing each client's characteristics. These therapeutic characteristics include (1) the therapy's required intensity, (2) the therapy's focus on insight or skill and behaviour modification, (3) the therapist's directiveness and (4) changes in how clients' emotions are managed within sessions (Gold & Stricker, 2020). Prescriptive psychotherapy recommendations involve matching clients and therapy characteristics in prescribed ways. Clients' characteristics are described as resistance, coping style, distress, and problem complexity. Considering the degree of functional impairment of clients, different therapies can be recommended such as going for pharmacotherapy or psychotherapy. To help clients in distress, in the case of high levels of distress, interventions will target emotion regulation, whereas, for low levels of distress, interventions will increase awareness of emotions. In externalising clients, treatments are recommended that address external behaviours or symptoms without requiring the clients to engage in any introspection. Treatments are recommended for internalising clients that emphasise insight, awareness, self-understanding, and emotional arousal. When the clients exhibit little or no resistance, the counsellors can adopt a more directive approach, whereas when the clients exhibit more reactance, the counsellors can adopt a more nondirective approach. Furthermore, motivation to participate in therapy and to change is enhanced by using techniques that maintain clients' emotional arousal to a moderate level throughout the therapy process (Beutler et al., 2012).

2. Common-Factors Approach to Integration

This approach aims to identify the common elements among different therapies with the goal of creating more efficient and effective treatments. According to this approach, common factors are more important to explain treatment outcomes than the factors that differentiate them. In the identification of the most important common factors, the counsellor looks at a variety of interventions and psychotherapy encounters to determine those that have been demonstrated to promote and contain those ingredients. In 2015, Wampold identified several factors that have been found to have a moderate to large impact on treatment. There are several factors that facilitate change in treatment, including therapeutic cooperation; the client's exposure to prior problems followed by a new remedial emotional experience; the counsellor and the client's expectation for a positive change; favourable qualities of a counsellor (attention, empathy, and positive regard); and the facility to the client of a rationale for problems. Duncan et al. (2010) argue that the therapeutic alliance and client engagement represent the crucial change factors in all types of psychotherapies. The impact of psychotherapy depends on the counsellors' interest and ability to monitor these factors, as well as the clients' sense of engagement, by soliciting feedback from the clients regarding the state of the therapeutic relationship.

3. Theoretical Integration

Among all modes of psychotherapy integration, theoretical integration is the most challenging and sophisticated. Integrative psychotherapies synthesise aspects of different personality theories, combine psychopathological models, and combine psychological transformation techniques from two or more traditional systems. Innovative integrative theories may suggest that environmental, motivational, cognitive, and affective factors interact. Integrative psychotherapy systems employ interventions drawn from each of their components and propose original techniques that can supplement the technical selection of the traditional therapeutic schools used in this new approach.

4. Assimilative Integration

Both theoretical integration and technical eclecticism are derived from assimilative integration (Messer, 2001, 2015; Stricker & Gold, 2019). A therapeutic strategy called assimilative integration combines a strong ground in one theoretical perspective with a readiness to incorporate strategies from different therapeutic systems. Assimilative approaches combine new strategies into an existing therapeutic programme. When procedures are employed clinically in a theoretical context that differs from the setting in which they were conceived, the meaning, impact, and application of an intervention can be fundamentally altered. Motivating interviews, for example, may be assimilated into acceptance and commitment therapy in which case the meaning, impact, and purpose of the intervention may be changed by the changes in the context and the outlook of the therapist. The premise that there is no one-size-fits-all therapy is implicit in this. Assimilative integration is particularly beneficial in determining the client's needs, after which numerous different techniques can be used to create a therapy that is tailored to that understanding. It is essential to locate the clients' psychology and psychopathology within an individualised social and cultural framework to intervene successfully with any obstacles associated with issues of diversity and discrimination (Stricker & Gold, 2019). Throughout the treatment, the treatment plan must be revised as the clients' understanding grows more complete and profound.

Role of Integrative Approach Towards Psychological Health and Psychopathology

> Integrationists characterise psychological health as the ability to define one's goals; successfully jettison, modify, or retain goals depending on their (individual and social) adaptive benefit; develop plans to obtain and actively seek out these goals; learn from self-generated and other-generated feedback; and attain them without intrapersonal or interpersonal interference.
>
> (Stricker & Gold, 2019)

Psychological and environmental elements would be combined to focus on aspects that limit an individual's freedom of experience and reactivity, resulting in psychological and behavioural redundancy. According to Wachtel (2014), most integrative theorists emphasise how childhood and adolescent events set down the foundations for different cognitive abilities (perception, thinking) and motivation that lead to psychopathology. Negative, unpleasant, anxious, and defeated interpersonal experiences, according to these theorists, are internalised and become part of the client's cognitive and emotional representation systems. In many interpersonal situations, this negative representational system results in ongoing predictions of danger (shame, blame, embarrassment, rejection, etc.). The clients become avoidant, defensive, and ultimately self-defeating (Wachtel, 2014).

The focus of integrative therapy is the individual, with a sense that it is impossible to understand a person in isolation from the interpersonal context in which they exist. Regarding the nature and specifics of the goals set for each client, the various integrative therapies vary significantly. From an integrative therapy perspective, the best way to set goals is to involve the clients in a collaborative process in which the therapist takes the lead in the evaluation phase, but is open and respectful of the needs, wishes, and ideas of the clients, especially when they involve the client's efforts to modify or reject the therapist's plan. Several therapeutic goals are discussed explicitly by integrative counsellors. A therapeutic alliance is formed when trust, respect, and communication are established. Discussions tend to focus on goals that are tied to the client's overt behaviour, conscious feelings, and relationships. Discussing the clients' desire to deal with unpleasant feelings or the difficulty in relationships provide clear goals for the client and therapist. One of the major advantages of this approach is the ability to set goals at any level of experience, such as relational, behavioural, cognitive, affective, and motivational. Based on a predetermined theoretical perspective, there is no reason to eliminate, dismiss, or designate goals as superficial or insignificant.

Integrative counsellors use cognitive restructuring, skills-building interventions, and exposure methods from cognitive-behavioural approaches, as well as experiential methods such as empty chair and two-chair dialogue methods from Gestalt therapy, and client-centred therapy practices such as empathising, holding, and reflecting on feelings, to name a few of the more prominent interventions. During the session, the clients may learn techniques to cope with anxiety caused by fear of confrontation with someone in a meeting (imaginal desensitisation), develop assertiveness skills (assertiveness training), or resolve a long-standing grief reaction by talking with the deceased parent across the room. It may be more beneficial to treat a client's excessive self-criticism during a session, or in a later session, by pointing out the 'should' and 'must' that dominate their minds and teaching them to recognise these misconceptions and replace them with more soothing and realistic ideas. This selection would have been guided by each individual's central, pressing clinical need and by the identification of the technique that would best meet that need if these interventions had been performed within the framework of a technically eclectic approach or a common-factors approach. Choosing that technique in an integrated theory would be based on its effect on the identification of the problem as well as the meaning of the psychological experience.

Mindfulness meditation and Buddhist psychology, according to Germer (2005), have interesting points of convergence with a variety of psychotherapy approaches, including psychodynamic, cognitive-behavioural, humanistic, family systems, and narrative approaches. They also point out that mindfulness can be included in therapeutic practice without clients having to learn mindfulness skills. Some counsellors use meditation to help them be more attentive, receptive, and compassionate during therapy sessions, as well as to improve their own mental health and well-being in ways that benefit the therapy they deliver. Others use mindfulness or Buddhist psychology ideas in their theoretical frameworks without teaching mindfulness to their clients.

Integrated therapy is a participatory process that mainly relies on the client's input. During this type of treatment, the therapists may inquire about the client's past experiences, preferences, requirements, and other things that could impact the therapeutic tactics that are best for them. Because integrative therapy is more eclectic, the treatment may not follow a set timetable or pattern. In a single session, multiple techniques may be used, and the goals and treatment strategy may change as the therapists evaluate the progress and requirements.

The psychotherapy integration movement emphasises that psychotherapy integration is more than just combining techniques from many models and using them as needed, it also includes a focus on the relationship between theory, evidence, and technique. The aim of psychotherapy integration is the interaction between successful practice and its theoretical and empirical underpinnings (Norcross & Goldfried, 2005).

Integrative counselling often necessitates a significant time investment on the part of the client due to the in-depth analysis of issues and development of goals. As a result, it may not be appropriate for those seeking a rapid, solution-oriented approach to personal development.

Application

Integrative psychotherapy approaches can be used in practically any sort of therapy with children, adolescents, and adults, whether in an individual or group context. Such strategies have been found to be useful in the treatment of different mental problems, including depression, social anxiety, generalised anxiety, and personality disorders, according to research. This shows that integrative therapy can help with a variety of ailments.

References

Adams, M. (2014). *A concise introduction to existential counselling*. Sage.

Adler, A. (1956). *The individual psychology of alfred adler: A systematic presentation in selections from his writings*. Basic Books.

Adler, A. (1958). *What life should mean to you*. Capricorn

Albahari, M. (2006). *Analytical Buddhism: The two-tiered illusion of self*. Palgrave Macmillan.

Analayo. (2010). *Satipatthana: The direct path to realisation*. Windhorse Publications.

Anderson, H. (2005). The myth of not-knowing. *Family Process*, *44*(4), 497–504.

Anderson, H. (2006). A postmodern umbrella: Language and knowledge as relational and generative, and inherently transforming. In H. Anderson & D. Gehart (Eds.), *Collaborative therapy: Relationships and conversations that make a difference* (pp. 7–20). Routledge.

Anderson, H. (2007). The heart and spirit of collaborative therapy: The philosophical stance – 'A way of being' in relationship and conversation. In H. Anderson & D. Gehart (Eds.), *Collaborative therapy: Relationships and conversations that make a difference* (pp. 43–59). Routledge/Taylor & Francis Group.

Antony, M. M., Roemer, L., & Lenton-Brym, A. P. (2020). Behavior therapy: Traditional approaches. In S. B. Messer & N. J. Kaslow (Eds.), *Essential psychotherapies: Theory and practice* (pp. 111–141). The Guilford Press.

Antshel, K. M., & Remer, R. (2003). Social skills training in children with attention deficit hyperactivity disorder: A randomised controlled trial. *Journal of Clinical Child and Adolescent Psychology*, *32*, 153–165.

Baer, R. A., & Huss, D. B. (2008). Mindfulness- and acceptance-based therapy. In Jay L. Lebow (Ed.), *Twenty-first century psychotherapies: Contemporary approaches to theory and practice* (pp. 8–42). Wiley & Sons, Inc.

Bandura, A. (1986). *Social foundations of thought and action: A social cognitive theory*. Prentice Hall.

Bandura, A. (1997). *Self-efficacy: The exercise of control*. Freeman.

Barber, J. P., Muran, C., McCarthy, K. S., & Keefe, J. R. (2013). Research on dynamic therapies. In M. J. Lambert (Ed.). *Bergin and Garfield's handbook of psychotherapy and behaviour change* (6th ed.). Wiley.

Barlow, D. H., & Cerny, J. A. (1988). *Psychological treatment of panic.* Guilford Press.

Batchelor, S. (1997). *Buddhism without beliefs: A contemporary guide to awakening.* Riverhead Books.

Beck, A. T. (1967). *Depression: Clinical, experimental, and theoretical aspects.* Harper and Row.

Beck, A. T. (1976). *Cognitive therapy and the emotional disorders.* New American Library.

Beck, J. S. (2011). *Cognitive behaviour therapy: Basics and beyond.* Guilford Press.

Beck, A. T. & Weishaar, M. (1989). *Comprehensive handbook of cognitive therapy.* In A. Freeman et al. (Eds.), Springer Science+Business Media.

Beidel, D. C., Alfano, C. A., Kofler, M. J., & Rao, P. A. (2014). The impact of social skills training for a social anxiety disorder: A randomised controlled trial. *Journal of Anxiety Disorders, 28,* 908–918.

Berg I. K. (1994). *Family based services; A solution-focused approach.* W. W. Norton.

Beutler, L. E., Forrester, B., Gallagher-Thompson, D., Thompson, L., & Tomlins, J. (2012). Common, specific, and treatment fit variables in psychotherapy outcome. *Journal of Psychotherapy Integration, 22,* 255–281.

Billig, M. (2002). Freud and the language of humour. *The Psychologist, 15*(9), 452–455. http://www.lboro.ac.uk/departments/ss.

Binswanger, L. (1946). *The existential analysis school of thought.* Basic Books.

Binswanger, L. (1958). The existential analysis school of thought. In R. May, E. Angel, & H. F. Ellenberger (Eds.), *Existence: A new dimension in psychiatry and psychology* (pp. 191–213). Basic Books/Hachette Book Group. https://doi.org/10.1037/11321-007.

Binswanger, L. (1963) *Being-in-the-world.* Basic Books.

Bornstein, R. F., Denckla, C. A., & Chung, W.-J. (2013). Psychodynamic models of personality. In H. Tennen, J. Suls, & I. B. Weiner (Eds.), *Handbook of psychology: Personality and social psychology* (pp. 43–64). John Wiley & Sons, Inc.

Bozarth, J. D., Zimring, F. M., & Tausch, R. (2001). Client-centered therapy: The evolution of a revolution. In D. J. Cain & J. Seeman (Eds.), *Humanistic psychotherapies: Handbook of research and practice* (pp. 147–188). American Psychological Association.

Bugental, J. F.T. (1978) *Psychotherapy and process: The fundamentals of an existential–humanistic approach.* McGraw-Hill.

Capuzzi, D. & Stauffer, M. D. (2016). *Counselling and psychotherapy: Theories and interventions.* Wiley.

Carlson, J., & Englar-Carlson, M. (2017). *Adlerian psychotherapy.* American Psychological Association.

Chakkarath, P. (2014). *Buddhist psychology encyclopedia of critical psychology.* Thomas Teo (Ed). Springer.

Cole, G. (2016). Existential dissonance: A dimension of inauthenticity. *The Humanistic Psychologist, 44*(3), 296–302.

Cooper, M. (2007). Humanising psychotherapy. *Journal of Contemporary Psychotherapy, 37,* 11–16.

Corey, G. (2017). *Theory and practice of counselling and psychotherapy* (10th ed.). Cengage.

Corsini, R. J., & Wedding, D. (2000). *Current psychotherapies.* (6th ed.). Thomson Learning, Inc.

Cowperthwait, C. M., Wyatt, K. P., Fang, C. M., & Neacsiu, A. D. (2019). Skills training in DBT principles and practicalities. In Michaela A. Swales (Ed), *The Oxford handbook of dialectical behaviour therapy.* Oxford University Press.

Cramer, P. (2015). Defence mechanisms: 40 years of empirical research. *Journal of Personality Assessment, 97*(2),1–9.

Craske, M. G. (2017). *Cognitive-behavioural therapy.* American Psychological Association.

David, D., Kangas, M., Schnur, J. B., & Montgomery, G. H. (2004). *REBT depression manual: Managing depression using rational emotive behavior therapy*. Babes-Bolyai University (BBU).
De Jong, P., & Kim Berg, I. (2002). *Interviewing for solutions* (2nd ed.). Brooks Cole.
de Shazer, S., Dolan, Y., Korman, H., McCollum, E., Trepper, T., & Berg, I. K. (2007). *More than miracles: The state of the art of solution-focused brief therapy*. Haworth.
de Silva. P. (2014). *An introduction to Buddhist psychology and counselling pathways of mindfulness-based therapies*. Palgrave Macmillan.
DeAngelis, T. (2014). A blend of Buddhism and psychology. *Monitor on Psychology*, *45*(2).
Deurzen. (2002). *Existential counselling & psychotherapy in Practice*. Sage.
Deurzen, E. van. (2009). *Psychotherapy and the quest for happiness*. Sage.
Deurzen, E. van. (2010) *Everyday mysteries: Existential dimensions of psychotherapy*. Routledge.
Deurzen, E. van. (2012) *Existential counselling and psychotherapy in practice* (3rd edn.) Sage.
Deurzen, E. van. & Adams, M. (2011) *Skills in existential counselling and psychotherapy*. Sage.
Deurzen, E. V. & Adams, M. (2016). *Skills in existential counselling & psychotherapy*. Sage
Deurzen-Smith E. van. (1988). *Existential counselling in practice*. Sage Publications.
Deurzen-Smith, E. van. (1984). Existential therapy. In Dryden, W. (Ed.) *Individual therapy in Britain*. Harper and Row
Di Giuseppe, M., Perry, J. C., Conversano, C., Gelo, O. C. G., & Gennaro, A. (2020). Defence mechanisms, gender, and adaptiveness in emerging personality disorders in adolescent outpatients. *The Journal of Nervous and Mental Disease*, *208*(12), 933–941. https://doi.org/10.1097/NMD.0000000000001230.
Dreyfus, H. L. (2006). The roots of existentialism. In Dreyfus, H. L. & Wrathall, M. A. (Eds.), *A companion to phenomenology and existentialism* (pp. 135–161). Blackwell Publishing Ltd.
Duncan, B. L., Miller, S. D., Wampold, B. E., & Hubble, M. A. (2010). *The heart and soul of change* (2nd ed.). American Psychological Association.
Ellis, A. (1955). New approaches to psychotherapy techniques. *Journal of Clinical Psychology*, *11*, 207–260.
Ellis, A. (2002). The role of irrational beliefs in perfectionism. In G. L. Flett & P. L. Hewitt (Eds.), *Perfectionism: Theory, research, and treatment* (pp. 217–229). American Psychological Association. https://doi.org/10.1037/10458-009.
Ellis, A. (2003). Early theories and practices of rational emotive behavior therapy and how they have been augmented and revised during the last three decades. *Journal of Rational-Emotive & Cognitive-Behavior Therapy*, *21*(3/4), 219–243.
Ferrandiz, P. (2004). Classical conditioning. *Encyclopaedia of applied psychology*, vol. 1. Elsevier Inc.
Fiedler, F. E. (1950) A comparison of therapeutic relationships in psychoanalytic, non-directive and Adlerian therapy. *Journal of Consulting Psychology*, *14*, 436–445.
Finlay, L. (2011). *Phenomenology for counsellors: Researching the lived world*. Wiley-Blackwell.
Freire, E. S. (2007). Empathy. In M. Cooper, M. O'Hara, P. F. Schmid, & G. Wyatt (Eds.), *The handbook of person-centered psychotherapy and counselling* (pp. 194–206). Palgrave Macmillan.
Fromm, E., Suzuki, D. T. (1960). *Zen Buddhism & psychoanalysis*. Harper.
Gergen, K. (1991). *The saturated self*. Basic Books.
Germer, C. K. (2005). Mindfulness; What is it? Does it matter? In C. K. Germer, R. D. Siegel, & P. R. Fulton (Eds.), *Mindfulness and psychotherapy*. Guilford Press.
Gethin, R. (1998). *The foundations of Buddhism*. Oxford University Press.
Gethin, R. (2015). *Buddhist conceptualisations of mindfulness. Handbook of mindfulness: Theory, research, and practice* (edited by Kirk Warren Brown, J. David Creswell, & Richard M. Ryan). The Guilford Press.
Gillon, E. (2007). *Person-centered counselling psychology: An introduction*. Sage.
Glasser, W. (1965). *Reality therapy*. Harper & Row.
Glasser, W. (1972). *The identity society*. Harper & Row.

Glasser, W. (1992). Reality therapy. In J. K. Zeig (Ed.), *The evolution of psychotherapy: The second conference* (pp. 270–283). Brunner/Mazel.

Glasser, W. (1998). *Choice theory*. Harper Collins.

Glasser, W. (2000). *Reality therapy in action*. Harper Collins.

Glasser, W. (2003). *Warning: Psychiatry can be hazardous to your mental health*. HarperCollins.

Goel, A. K., and Helms, M. E. (2013). Theories, models, programs and tools of design: Views from artificial intelligence, cognitive science, and human-centered computing. In A. Chakrabarti, L. T. M. Blessing (Eds). *An anthology of theories and models of design: Philosophy, approaches, and empirical explorations* (pp 415–430). Springer.

Gold, J. & Stricker, G. (2020). Integrative approaches to psychotherapy. In S. B. Messer & N. J. Kaslow (Eds.), *Essential psychotherapies theory and practice* (pp. 443–480). The Guilford Press

Goldfried, M. R., & Davison, G. C. (1994). *Clinical behavior therapy* (revised ed.). Wiley-Interscience.

Goldschmidt G (2013) Modelling the role of sketching in design idea generation. In A. Chakrabarti & L. T. M. Blessing (Eds.), *An anthology of theories and models of design: Philosophy, approaches, and empirical explorations* (pp 431–448). Springer.

Griffith, J. & Powers, R. (2007). *The lexicon of Adlerian psychology: 106 terms associated with the individual psychology of Alfred Adler* (2nd ed.). Adlerian Psychology Associates Ltd.

Grondin, J. (1995). *Sources of hermeneutics*. State University of New York Press.

Harris, R. (2009). *ACT made simple: An easy-to-read-primer on acceptance and commitment therapy*. New Harbinger Publications, Inc.

Harvey, P. (2013). *An introduction to Buddhism: Teachings, history and practices* (2nd ed.). Cambridge University Press.

Hayes, S. C. (1987). A contextual approach to therapeutic change. In N. Jacobson (Ed.), *Psychotherapists in clinical practice: Cognitive and behavioral perspectives*. Guilford Press

Hayes, S. C. & Smith. S. (2005). *Get out of your mind & into your life the new acceptance & commitment therapy*. New Harbinger Publications, Inc.

Hayes, S.C., Barnes-Holmes, D., & Roche, B. (2001). *Relational frame theory: A post-Skinnerian account of human language and cognition*. Kluwer Academic/Plenum.

Hayes, S. C., Bissett, R. T., Korn, Z., Zettle, R. D., Rosenfarb, I. S., Cooper, L. D., & Grundt, A. M. (1999). The impact of acceptance versus control rationales on pain tolerance. *The Psychological Record*, 49(1), 33–47.

Hayes, S. C., Strosahl, K., & Wilson, K. G. (1999). *Acceptance and commitment therapy: An experiential approach to behavior change*. Guilford Press.

Heidegger, M. (1962). *Being and time* (translated by John Macquarrie & Edward Robinson). SCM Press.

Hoffman, L. (1990). Constructing realities: An art of lenses. *Family Process*, *29*, 1–12.

Josephs, L., & Weinberger, J. (2013). Psychodynamic psychotherapy. In G. Stricker & T. A. Widiger (Eds.), *Handbook of psychology*, Vol. 8: *Clinical psychology* (2nd ed.). Wiley.

Kabat-Zinn, J. (1982). An outclient program in behavioral medicine for chronic pain clients based on the practice of mindfulness meditation: Theoretical considerations and preliminary results. *General Hospital Psychiatry*, 4, 33–47.

Kabat-Zinn, J. (1994). *Wherever you go, there you are*. Piatkus.

Kabat-Zinn, J. (2005). *Coming to our senses: Healing ourselves and the world through mindfulness*. Piatkus.

Kalama Sutta: The Buddha's charter of free inquiry, translated from the Pali by Soma Thera. Access to Insight (BCBS Edition), 30 November 2013, http://www.accesstoinsight.org/lib/authors/soma/wheel008.html .

Karunadasa, Y. (2013). *Early Buddist teachings: The middle position in theory and practice*. Centre of Buddhist Studies, University of Hong Kong.

Kierkegaard, S. (1843). Journals 43 IV A 164. In *Papers and journals: A selection* (translated by A. Hannay). Penguin.

Kottman, T., & Ashby, J. (2015). Adlerian play therapy. In D. Crenshaw & A. Stewart (Eds.), *Play therapy: A comprehensive guide to theory and practice* (pp. 32–47). Guilford Press.
Lazarsfeld, S. (1966). The courage for imperfection. *American Journal of Individual Psychology*, *22*(2).
Lazarus, A. A. (1966). Behaviour rehearsal vs. Non-directive therapy vs. Advice in effecting behaviour change. *Behaviour Research and Therapy*, *4*(3), 209–212.
Lazarus, A. A. (2006). Multimodal therapy: A seven-point integration. In G. Stricker & J. Gold (Eds.), *A Casebook of Psychotherapy Integration* (pp. 17–28). American Psychological Association
Lee, K. C. (2020) Introduction to a Buddhist counselling technique based on early buddhist teachings: mind moment analysis. *Contemporary Buddhism*, *21*, 1–2, 241–262, https://doi.org/10.1080/14639947.2021.1981062.
Lee, K. C. & Ong, C. K. (2019). The Satipaṭṭhāna Sutta: An application of Buddhist mindfulness for counsellors. *Journal of Contemporary Buddhism*, *19*(2), 327–341. https://doi.org/10.1080/14639947.2018.1576292.
Lee, K. C. (G.), Oh, A., Zhao, Q., Wu, F.-Y., Chen, S., Diaz, T., & Ong, C. K. (2017). Buddhist counselling: Implications for mental health professionals. *Spirituality in Clinical Practice, 4*(2), 113–128. https://doi.org/10.1037/scp0000124.
Lee, K. C. (G.), & Tang, J. L. K. (2021). Note, know, choose: A psychospiritual treatment model based on early Buddhist teachings. *Spirituality in Clinical Practice*. https://doi.org/10.1037/scp0000220.
Linehan, M. M. (1993). *Cognitive-behavioral treatment of borderline personality disorder*. Guilford Press.
Linehan, M. M. (2015). *DBT skills training manual* (2nd ed.). Guilford Press.
Lorenzo-Luaces, L., German, R. E., & Derubeis, R. J. (2015). It's complicated: The relation between cognitive change procedures, cognitive change, and symptom change in cognitive therapy for depression. *Clinical Psychology Review*, *41*, 3–15. https://doi.org/10.1016/j.cpr.2014.12.003.
Lucas, M. (2004) *The therapeutic frame in the clinical context: Integrative perspectives*. Routledge
Lynch, T. R., Morse, J. Q., Mendelson, T., & Robins, C. J. (2003). Dialectical behavior therapy for depressed older adults. *The American Journal of Geriatric Psychiatry*, *11*, 33–45.http://dx.doi.org/10.1097/00019442-200301000-00006.
Maddi, S.R. (1980). *Personality theories: A comparative analysis* (4th ed.). Dorsey.
Maddi, S.R. (1996). *Personality theories: A comparative analysis* (6th ed.). Brooks/Cole Publishing Co.
Manaster, G. & Corsini, R. J. (1982). (Eds.). *Individual psychology: Theory and practice*. Peacock.
Maniacci, M. P., Sackett-Maniacci, L., & Mosak, H. H. (2014). Adlerian psychotherapy. In D. Wedding & R. J. Corisini (Eds.), *Current psychotherapies* (10th edn.) (pp. 55–94). Cengage Learning.
Masserman, J. H. (1943). *Behavior and neurosis: An experimental psychoanalytic approach to psychobiologic principles*. University of Chicago Press. https://doi.org/10.1037/10797-000.
Mearns, D. & M. Cooper (2005). *Working at relational depth in counselling and psychotherapy*. Sage.
Messer, S. B. (2015). How I have changed over time as a psychotherapist. *Journal of Clinical Psychology*, *71*(11), 1104–1114.
Messer, S. B. (Ed.). (2001). Assimilative integration [Special issue]. *Journal of Psychotherapy Integration*, *11*, 1–4.
Misiak, H., & Sexton, V. S. (1973). *Phenomenological, existential, and humanistic psychologies: A historical survey*. Grune & Stratton.
Morgan, A. (2000). *What is narrative therapy? An easy to-read introduction*. Dulwich Centre Publications.
Mueser, K. T., Deavers, F., Penn, D. L., & Cassisi, J. E. (2013). Psychosocial treatments for schizophrenia. *Annual Review of Clinical Psychology*, *9*, 465–497. doi:10.1146/annurev-clinpsy-050212-185620.

Murdock, N. L. (2009). *Theories of counselling and psychotherapy: A case approach* (2nd ed.) Pearson.
Murgatroyd, W. (2001). The Buddhist spiritual path: A counsellor's reflection on meditation, spirituality, and the nature of life. *Counselling and Values*, *45*(2).
Neacsiu, A. D., Bohus, M., & Linehan, M. M., (Eds.) (2013). *Dialectical behaviour therapy skills: an intervention for emotion dysregulation*, Vol. 2. Guilford Press.
Norcross J. C. & Goldfried M. R. (2005). *Handbook of psychotherapy integration* (2nd ed.). Oxford University Press.
Otero, T. L., Schatz, R. B., Merrill, A. C., & Bellini, S.(2015). Social skills training for youth with autism spectrum disorders: A follow-up. *Child and Adolescent Psychiatric Clinics of North America*, *24*(1), 99–115.
Paré, D., & Tarragona, M. (2006). Generous pedagogy: Teaching and learning postmodern therapies. *Journal of Systemic Therapies*, *25* (4), 1–7.
Pavlov, I. P. (1906). The scientific investigation of psychical faculties or processes in the higher animals. *Science*, *24*, 613–619
Payne, M. (2006). *Narrative therapy: An introduction for counsellors*. Sage.
Perls, F. (1973). *The Gestalt approach and eye witness to therapy*. Science and Behavior Books.
Perls, F. S. (1969). *Gestalt therapy verbatim*. Real People Press.
Pierce, W. D., & Cheney, C. D. (2017). *Behaviour analysis and learning: A biobehavioural approach* (6th ed, pp. 1–622). Routledge.
Popper, K. R. (1965). *Conjectures and refutations: The growth of scientific knowledge*. Harper Torchbooks.
Prochaska, J. O., & DiClemente, C. C. (2002). Transtheoretical therapy. In J. Lebow (Ed.), *Comprehensive handbook of psychotherapy*, Vol. 4. Integrative–eclectic (pp. 165–184). Wiley.
Robins, C. J. (2002). Zen principles and mindfulness practice in dialectical behavior therapy. *Cognitive and Behavioral Practice*, *9*, 50–57.
Rogers, C. R. (1942). *Counselling and psychotherapy: New concepts in practice*. Houghton Mifflin
Rogers, C. R. (1957). The necessary and sufficient conditions of therapeutic personality change. *Journal of Consulting Psychology*, *21*, 95–103.
Rogers, C. R. (1961). *On becoming a person*. Houghton Mifflin
Rogers, C. R. (1966). Client-centered therapy. In S. Arieti (Ed.), *American handbook of psychiatry* (Vol. 3, pp. 183–200). Basic Books.
Rogers, C. R. (1970). *Carl Rogers on encounter groups*. Harper & Row.
Rogers, C. R. & Jerome Freiberg, J. H. (1994). *Freedom to learn*. Maxwell Macmillan International.
Rogers, C. R. (1975). Empathic: An unappreciated way of being. *The Counselling Psychologist* https://doi.org/10.1177/001100007500500202.
Russell, S., & Carey, M. (2004). *Narrative therapy: Responding to your questions*. Dulwich Centre.
Salter, A. (1949). *Conditioned reflex therapy, the direct approach to the reconstruction of personality*. Creative Age Press.
Samberg, E., & Marcus, E. R. (2005). Process, resistance, and interpretation. In E. S. Person, A. M. Cooper, & G. O. Gabbard (Eds.), *Textbook of psychoanalysis*. American Psychiatric Publishing.
Sartre, J.-P. (1973). *Existentialism and humanism* (translated by P. Mairet). Methuen. (Originally published 1946.)
Sartre, J.-P. (2003) *Being and nothingness: An essay in phenomenological ontology* (translated by H. E. Barnes). Routledge. (Originally published 1943.)
Schneider, K. J. (2011). Existential-humanistic psychotherapies. In S. B. Messer & A. S. Gurman (Eds.), *Essential psychotherapies: Theory and practice* (pp. 1–34). Guilford Press.
Segal, Z. V., Williams, J. M. G., & Teasdale, J. D. (2012). *Mindfulness-based cognitive therapy for depression* (2nd ed.). The Guilford Press.
Seligman,L.W. & Reichenberg, L.W. (2014). *Theories of counselling and psychotherapy: Systems, strategies, and skills* (4th ed.). Pearson.
Shedler, J. (2010). The efficacy of psychodynamic psychotherapy. *American Psychologist*, *65*(2), 98–109.

Skinner, B. F. (1953). *Science and human behavior*. Macmillan.
Skinner, B. F. (1974). *About behaviorism*. Knopf.
Skinner, B. F. (1990). Can psychology be a science of mind? *American Psychologist*, *45*, 1206–1210.
Sonalkar, N., Jung, M., Mabogunje, A., & Leifer, L. (2013). A structure for design theory. In A. Chakrabarti & L. T. M. Blessing (Eds.), *An anthology of theories and models of design: Philosophy, approaches, and empirical explorations* (pp. 67–82). Springer.
Speedy, J. (2008). *Narrative inquiry & psychotherapy*. Palgrave Macmillan
Sperry, L. (2015). Diagnosis, case conceptualisation, culture, and treatment. In L. Sperry, J. Carlson, J. D. Sauerheber, & J. Sperry (Eds.). *Psychopathology and psychotherapy DSM-5 diagnosis, case conceptualisation, and treatment*. Routledge.
Spiegler, M.D. & Guevremont, D.C. (2010). *Contemporary behavior therapy* (5th ed.). Wadsworth, Cengage Learning.
Spinelli, E. (2005) *The interpreted world: An introduction to phenomenological psychology*. Sage.
Stein, M. (2017). Where East meets West: In the house of individuation. *The Journal of Analytical Psychology*, *62*(1), 67–87.
Stricker, G. (1994). Reflections on psychotherapy integration. *Clinical Psychology: Science and Practice*, *1*(1), 3–12. https://doi.org/10.1111/j.1468-2850.1994.tb00002.x.
Stricker, G., & Gold, J. (2019). Assimilative psychodynamic psychotherapy. In J. C. Norcross & M. R. Goldfried (Eds.), *Handbook of psychotherapy integration* (3rd ed., pp. 207–227). Oxford University Press
Suzuki, D. T.(1960). *Manual of Zen Buddhism*. Grove Press INC.
Swales, M. A., & Heard, H. L. (2017). *Dialectical behaviour therapy: Distinctive features* (2nd ed.). Routledge.
Tanphaichitr, K. (2005). *Essence of life: Mindfulness & self-awareness*. Horatanachai Printing,
Tarragona, M. (2008) Postmodern/poststructuralist therapies. In Jay L. Lebow (Ed.), *Twenty-first century psychotherapies: Contemporary approaches to theory and practice* (pp. 167–205). Wiley & Sons, Inc.
Thase, M. E. (2012). Social skills training for depression and comparative efficacy research: A 30-year retrospective. *Behavior Modification*, *36*, 545–557.
Volungis, A. M. (2019). *Cognitive-behavioural therapy: Theory into practice*. The Rowman & Littlefield Publishing Group, Inc.
Wachtel, P. L. (2014). *Cyclical psychodynamic and the contextual self*. Routledge.
Wampold, B. E. (2015). How important are the common factors in psychotherapy? An update. *World Psychiatry*, *14*, 270–277.
Warnock, M. (1970). *Existentialism*. Oxford University Press.
Watson, J. C. (2002). Re-visioning empathy. In D. J. Cain (Ed.), *Humanistic psychotherapies: Handbook of research and practice* (pp. 445–471). American Psychological Association. https://doi.org/10.1037/10439-014.
Weiten, W., Dunn, D. S. & Hammer, E. Y. (2018). *Psychology applied to modern life adjustment in the 21st century*. Cengage Learning
White, M. & Epston, D. (1989). *Literate means to therapeutic ends*. Dulwich Centre.
White, M. (1995). *Re-authoring lives: Interviews and essays*. Dulwich Centre.
White, M. (2000). *Reflections on narrative practice: Essays and interviews*. Dulwich Centre.
White, M. (2004). *Narrative practice and exotic lives: Resurrecting diversity in everyday life*. Dulwich Centre.
White, M., & Epston, D. (1990). *Narrative means to therapeutic ends*. Norton.
Williams, M. and Penman, D. (2010). *Mindfulness: An eight week plan for finding peace in a frantic world*. Kindle.
Wolpe, J. (1958). *Psychotherapy by reciprocal inhibition*. Stanford University Press.
Wolter, J. A., DiLollo, A. & Apel, K. (2006). A narrative therapy approach to counselling: A model for working with adolescents and adults with language-literacy deficits. *Language, Speech, and Hearing Services in Schools*, *37*, (3)168–177.

Wubbolding, R. (1991). *Understanding reality therapy*. HarperCollins.

Wubbolding, R. E. (1988). *Using reality therapy*. Harper & Row Publishers.

Wubbolding, R. (2000). Brief reality therapy. In J. Carlson & L. Sperry (Eds.), *Brief therapy with individuals and couples* (pp. 264–286). Zeig, Tucker & Theisen.

Wubbolding, R.E. (2017). *Reality therapy and self-evaluation: The key to client change*. American Counselling Association.

Wubbolding, R. E., & Brickell, J. D. (2015). *Counselling with reality therapy* (2nd ed.). Speechmark.

Yu, F. (2019). Miracle question in couple and family therapy. In J. L. Lebow, A. L. Chambers, & D. C. Breunlin (Eds.), *Encyclopedia of couple and family therapy*. Springer.

Zettle, R. D. and Hayes, S. C. (1986). Dysfunctional control by client verbal behavior: The context of reason giving. *Analysis of Verbal Behavior*, 4, 30–38. doi: 10.1007/BF03392813.

Zinbarg, R. E. & Griffith, J. W. (2008). Behaviour therapy. In J. L. Lebow (Ed.), *Twenty-first century psychotherapies: Contemporary approaches to theory and practice* (pp. 8–42). Wiley & Sons, Inc.

3 Building a Partnership

The quality of the relationship between the counsellor and the client is the basis for a good therapeutic alliance. Engaging the client in such a therapeutic alliance requires an active partnership between the counsellor and the client. The goal of such a relationship is to assist the client in working towards a better life. The entire therapeutic alliance will depend on how the counsellor provides a safe, open, and non-judgemental setting, and encourages the client to explore and share the story. This setting helps the client feel safe, important, accepted, and understood.

The concept of therapeutic alliance can be traced back to history. Freud (1912) described the therapeutic relationship as a 'friendly affectionate feeling'. Freud used the term transference in the psychoanalytic theory. Though the term transference had a negative connotation initially, at a later stage, it was regarded as a possible factor for developing a beneficial relationship between the counsellor and the client. Freud, in his letter to Carl Jung wrote that 'healing is achieved through love'. Edward (1937) was the first to popularise the term 'therapeutic alliance'. According to Jung (1933), both the counsellor and the client mutually influence, each other, their states of consciousness merge, becoming an essential component of therapy. Such an alliance is necessary for establishing trust and a mutual transformation between the counsellor and the client. Jung compared the association between a therapist and a client to a chemical reaction wherein the therapist and the client are transformed (Jung, 1938). Adler's model of counselling identified that the first step in the counselling process is the formation of a strong and collaborative relationship of which care, involvement and empathy are the foundations. During the Second World War, Zetzel (1956) used therapeutic alliance in the initial stage of psychoanalytic therapy. According to her, a therapeutic alliance was like a 'mother's instinct for her child'; she added that it was a basic condition for a therapeutic process.

Gestalt therapists view the client-counsellor relationship as a dialogic relationship and consider it the main tool in promoting growth and transformation in the client and attaining the goals. This significant positive personality change can occur only through a well-established therapeutic relationship (Rogers, 1967). The strength of a therapeutic alliance is found to be a predictor for effective therapy and client outcomes (Norcross, 2010). Horvath et al. (2011) defined therapeutic alliance as the overall bonding between the counsellor and the client. In their meta-analysis, Baier et al. (2020) suggest that a therapeutic alliance 'can be an independent driver to change the client'.

The treatment outcome is significantly related to the type of association between the client and the counsellor (Horvath & Symonds, 1991). A strong bond between the client and the counsellor is beneficial to both. To summarise, the therapist and the client can be framed as two equal and accomplished individuals to share a platform in the counselling

DOI: 10.4324/9781003459415-3

process where both have the capability to grow and be enriched by the process (Rogers, 1961). In his theory of the 'person-centered approach', Rogers (1967) described the therapeutic relationship by stating that 'at least one of the parties has the intent of promoting growth, development, maturity, improved functioning, improved coping with the life of the other'. Through his clinical and research experience, Rogers endorsed that for a constructive personality change, certain 'psychological conditions' are necessary and these conditions are provided by the counsellor. The therapeutic relationship can bring a definite change in the client when these core conditions are met.

Characteristics of an Effective Counsellor

Counsellors' characteristics play a major role in a client-counsellor relationship. To promote therapeutic change, counsellors need to own some characteristics which according to person-centred theory as the core conditions for a counselling process. Some of these characteristics are so fundamental to the counselling process that it becomes important for counsellors to imbibe these attributes and translate them into values. Values have an immense influence on how the counsellor views the client, the interaction with clients, the therapeutic process, the interventions and goals (Corey, 2001). In Chapter 1, the core values of the counsellor are described by the authors as *Saptapadis*. In this chapter the core values along with the other characteristics will be elaborated on. These characteristics go beyond the diagnosis and therapy and help the counsellor focus on the manner in which clients act in their world with others, the way they can move forward in constructive ways, and how they deal with blocks and move towards a change. We will use Rogers' (1967) six prepositions, for a 'constructive personality change', to understand the importance and need for counsellors to imbibe the attributes, integrate them and translate them into their core values. When there is greater integration and lesser internal conflict, the counsellor has more energy available to bring about a personality change in the client. Let's discuss the six conditions mentioned by Rogers.

The first condition specifies that for any therapeutic relationship, a psychological contract must exist between the counsellor and the client. This condition is the primary step towards the development of a continuing and enduring relationship. The second to sixth conditions describe the characteristics of the relationship. The six propositions are listed in Box 3.1. and are explained in the next section.

The first proposition proposes the presence of 'psychological contact' between the counsellor and the client. Rogers names it as a precondition for any therapeutic change to occur in the client. The word 'psychological contact' simply means that both the client and the counsellor have entered an intensely personal and subjective relationship. This relationship is *person-to-person*, wherein both are aware of their roles and expectations from each other, and there is a readiness for therapy. Psychological contact is a valuable factor for building trust and initiating a sense of responsibility in the counsellor and the client.

As we move on from propositions 2–6 in Box 3.1, we can observe that all these five propositions define the characteristics of the counsellor-client relationship. A successful counsellor-client relationship can be established when the three central components (Rogers, 1957), congruence or genuineness; unconditional positive regard or acceptance with respect; and empathy or a deep understanding, are integrated into the therapeutic process. The three components mentioned in propositions 2–5 in Box 3.1 are called the facilitative conditions to enhance the counselling process and are also observed as the

Box 3.1 Values Congenial for Therapeutic Relationship

S.No	*Core Values*	*Explanation*
1.	*The two persons are in psychological contact.*	The client and the counsellor are aware of each other's role and are willing to participate in the counselling process.
2.	*The first, whom we shall term the client, is in a state of incongruence, being vulnerable or anxious.*	A client is in a state of inappropriateness. In Rogers' words, the client lacks alignment between the real and ideal self.
3.	*The second person, whom we shall term the 'counsellor', is congruent or integrated into the relationship.*	The counsellor is integrated and genuine, without any façade. S/he is non-defensive and open to experience.
4.	*The counsellor experiences unconditional positive regard for the client.*	The counsellor suspends all judgements and accepts the client with respect.
5.	*The counsellor experiences an empathic understanding of the client's internal frame of reference and endeavours to communicate this experience to the client.*	The counsellor sees the world as the client does and can understand the client's perceptions, feelings, and behaviour.
6.	*The communication to the client of the counsellor's empathic understanding and unconditional positive regard is to a minimal degree achieved.*	The counsellor is in a state to communicate the understanding of the client's perceptions and feelings through his/her verbal and non-verbal behaviours.

essential qualities of an effective counsellor (Figure 3.1). All the above conditions are discussed elaborately in the following section.

Congruence

Proposition 2 describes the client's psychological state. The client approaches a counsellor in a highly fluid state. Roger calls it 'a state of incongruence'. The client is in a demoralised state and is unable to accept himself or others or the present situation. He or she is defensive, confused, frustrated, overwhelmed, fearful, judgemental, anxious, have feelings of insecurity or stigma, is unable to accept himself or herself, and may have a history of difficult therapeutic experiences. This state of mind inhibits the client from sharing information related to self. Regardless of the client's state he or she can be helped to change. A successful counselling outcome can be achieved only if the counsellor can establish an accurate therapeutic relationship, and the counsellor 'is congruent and integrated with the relationship'. When the counsellor is more integrated than the others (Rogers, 1957), he or she is

- in better control of his feelings
- is self-aware
- can accept feelings whether good or bad or right or wrong
- can communicate them to others when appropriate
- can provide a stable humanistic element to the relationship
- can help the client solve most of their dilemmas

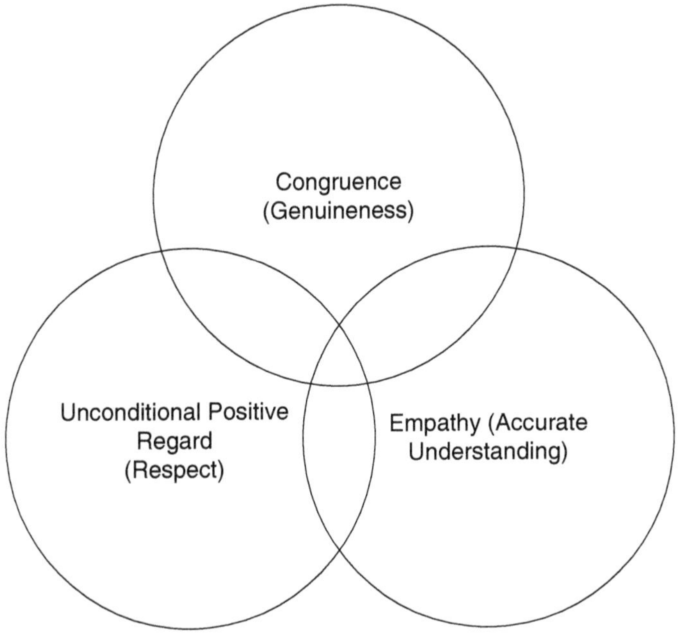

Figure 3.1 Core Conditions for Effective Counselling

Congruence is a primary quality indicating that the counsellor is integrated, is in harmony with self, and implies that the counsellor is projecting his/her real self. As Rogers says, congruence is 'avoiding the temptation to present a façade or hide behind a false mask of professionalism or an attitude of superiority'. In other words, it is the ability of the counsellor to be aware of his/her thoughts and feelings and express them without any filters. Congruence is also a state wherein there is a similarity in the inner understanding and the external manifestation. Being accepting and comfortable with oneself, the counsellor allows others to be 'at home' and unrestricted. By doing so, the counsellor models genuine behaviour giving scope for the client to be genuine, open up and share. As the process of counselling progresses, the genuineness of the counsellor helps in dismantling the client's defences and allows the client to explore the problem. Let's see the example.

Case study: Laaj is an adolescent girl from a remote tribal village in Adilabad, Telangana. She is referred to the College counsellor Mohana. The session goes as follows

Laaj: What do you know about my culture and my background? I know you will be branding me as a tribal girl who doesn't know anything about the city culture.

Mohana: I very well understand what you are saying. You are saying that we are two different people from different cultures and backgrounds. Probably I have never interacted with anyone from your village, and I have never been there. But I would like to understand your culture and know more about it from you. And as I get to learn more about your background, there is a possibility that I can help you. It will be great if you can help me understand your culture.

Mohana, as a counsellor is in harmony with her feelings. By agreeing that she and Laaj are from different cultures and by acknowledging her lack of knowledge about Laaj's cultural background, Mohana is translating her feelings in a spontaneous manner, which captures the sense of the moment and the context. Her natural way of expressing thoughts also indicates her sincere intention to help, and Laaj can now trust Mohana because she finds herself in safe hands. A congruent individual is open to experience and authentic during his/her interaction with the client, and when the client can experience the genuine expression communicated by the counsellor, he/she is encouraged to trust the counsellor and share her feelings and experiences. By doing so, the counsellor also becomes a role model for the client, who is then able to express his/her thoughts and feelings without fear of expression. Such a well-established therapeutic relationship will enhance the process and outcome of therapy. It is not possible or necessary that the therapist practices congruence in all spheres of life, but it is important that the counsellor should be congruent, within the framework of his or her relationship with the client.

Unconditional Positive Regard

Is defined as acceptance in the therapist's attitude towards the client, wherein no standards are required to be met by the client, and the counsellor lays no conditions to demonstrate this regard for the client. It is a complete non-judgemental acceptance of the client. The counsellor prizes the client as a person of self-worth, without any ifs or buts in the way.

In Rogers' words, 'A caring which is not possessive, which demands no personal gratification ... It involves an acceptance of and a caring for the client as a separate person, with permission for him to have his own feelings and experiences and to find his own meanings for them' (Rogers, 1967).

The concept of unconditional positive regard can be best explained with the example of the mother's equation with the child. The mother sees through the strengths and weaknesses of her children as they grow and develop. Though she does not approve of certain characteristics of the child, she nevertheless accepts the child wholeheartedly 'as is and how is'. Similarly, in the context of counselling, the counsellor should have an unconditional acceptance of the client with all the potential strengths and weaknesses. This gives rise to a positive attitude where the client is accepted with no judgement against any standard yardstick, with no conditions applied to express respect and accept the client. As a counsellor, one must understand that the client is going through challenging experiences, due to which he/she may have low self-esteem, low confidence, guilt or shame, irrational beliefs, and lack of trust. In such circumstances is important that the counsellor refrains from any judgement; this will allow the client to open up and express his/her thoughts and feelings without fear of being judged or criticised.

Empathy

Empathy is the ability to understand the clients from their point of view rather than the counsellor's, or in simple words, he sees the world as if he were the client. It is referred to as entering the 'phenomenological field' of the client and understanding the client's 'frame of reference' (Rogers, 1967), wherein the counsellor is not considering his/her feelings but rather tries to understand 'how the client feels'. Roger (1951) adds, 'We think we listen, but very rarely do we listen with real understanding, true empathy. Yet listening, of this very special kind, is one of the most potent forces for change that I know'.

Empathy can also be described as adopting the perspective of the client and getting associated with the role he/she is playing in life. Empathetic understanding includes getting an insight into the client's cognitions, feelings, and behaviour (Brodley, 1999). Empathy hence gives an accurate perception of the client's problem, which in turn helps to precisely understand the problem, and once there is a comprehensive understanding, the expression or communication of this understanding to the client is accurate. Empathy is a useful tool for the counsellor to create a caring environment and develop a trustful relationship and is found to have a significant client outcome (Bohart et al., 2002). Along with congruence and unconditional positive regard, empathy is identified as an important 'nonspecific factor' (Bohart et al., 2002), meaning that it has to be the most important natural ingredient in the counselling process. Empathy is expressed through the counsellor's warmth and genuineness and is the goal of any helping relationship. Empathy as a skill and its application will be discussed in the next few chapters.

Communicate the Understanding

The sixth condition describes the counsellor's ability to communicate empathetic understanding, and unconditional positive regard to the client and the client's experience of the counsellor's unconditional positive regard and accurate empathy. One of the very important aspects of a successful therapeutic relationship is the client's perception of the counsellors understanding. The empathetic circuit is said to be completed only when the counsellor is able to communicate the understanding to the client and the client is able to perceive this understanding (Figure 3.2).

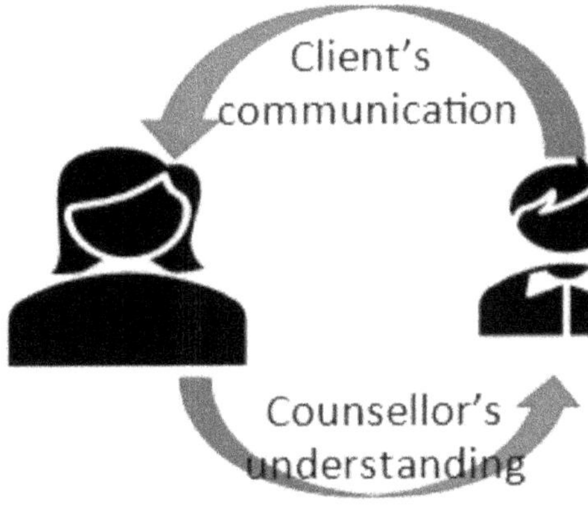

Figure 3.2 The Empathetic Circuit

Other Competencies of an Effective Counsellor

Counsellors work with diverse clients and diverse situations, and it is imperative that they possess the qualities and attributes necessary to handle the varied clientele. Effective counsellors are individuals who have not only gained the know-how of all the technical skills of counselling but also achieved intrapersonal and interpersonal skills. In this section, we will explore some of the other core characteristics of an effective counsellor.

The conditions to facilitate a therapeutic relationship in counselling are genuineness, congruence, patience, warmth, honesty, and passion for their work. The other qualities of an effective counsellor include competence, self-awareness, the ability to draw boundaries in relationships, the ability for self-disclosure, a non-judgemental attitude, and psychological flexibility. According to Corey (2012), effective counsellors are open to experience and willing to learn from their mistakes, they have a sense of humour and are sensitive to diverse cultures, races, and gender are successful. In the next section, we will discuss a few more facilitative conditions.

Counsellor's Competence

Counsellor's competence is central to the entire helping process. The skill and knowledge required to deliver help, by maintaining minimal standards and achieving the expected change in the client can be called a counsellor's competence. Counsellor's or therapist competence is 'the extent to which a therapist has the knowledge and skill required to deliver a treatment to the standard needed for it to achieve its expected effects' (Fairburn & Cooper, 2011). Counsellor's competence includes proficiency, expertise, educational qualification, and ability to demonstrate the required skills. According to Nagy (2012), competence is not static, it is dynamic and always in a state of fluidity.

The counsellor's competency in knowledge, skill, and practice can be assessed using the clinical competency model proposed by Miller (1990). The 'Pyramid Model', as it is known, explains the progress of a therapist's competence from knowledge to performance (Figure 3.3). The four-level model provides a framework for assessing clinical competence can be well applied in a counselling set up. The first level named as 'knows', is related to knowledge, i.e., acquiring knowledge to perform is the primary task of competent counselling. The second level is 'know-how', which relates to the use of knowledge to understand, diagnose and interpret the client's problems and issues. The third level 'shows how' deals with the integration of knowledge and skill into clinical practice. The last level of the model 'does' is related to the therapist's clinical performance and the application of skills in practice. This level also evaluates how the counsellor reviews the client's progress, and follow-up treatment, and provides quality care to all the clients. Although Miller's model (Figure 3.3) has been applied in medical education to assist medical professionals, the framework can be well applied in a counselling setting since when we deliberate about as counsellors' competence, also includes knowledge, skill, performance, and provision of quality support.

The competency of a counsellor also includes aspects like self-awareness and assessment of one's strengths and weaknesses which are discussed in the next section.

Self-Awareness

Self-awareness, also referred to as self-knowledge or introspection, is one of the important attributes of an effective counsellor. Self-awareness is all about understanding one's own

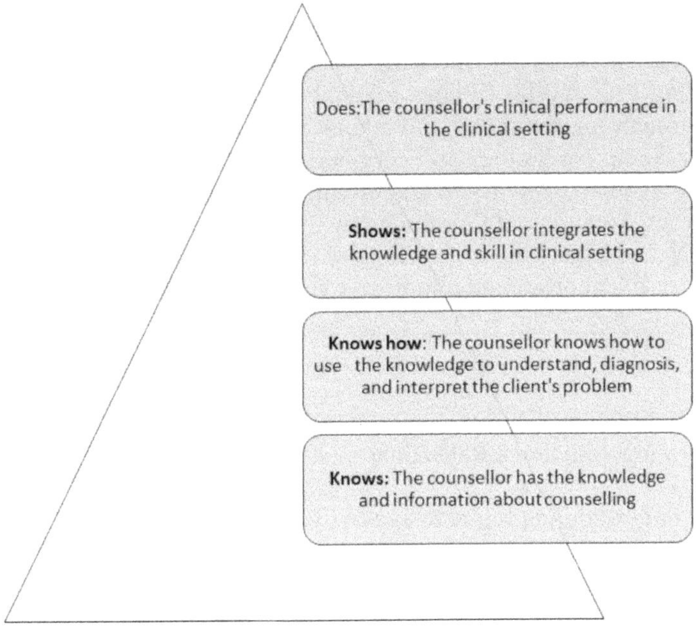

Figure 3.3 The Counsellor's Competence Pyramid

feelings, motives, needs, and desires. Such awareness helps the individual understand and adapt to life situations by bringing about positive behavioural changes. It is important to understand that any response given by the client can impact or trigger responses in the counsellor too. There may be many painful incidents in the counsellor's life, and when similar incidents are recited by the client, these may trigger responses in the counsellor. Unless the counsellor has dealt with those incidents, he or she may not be able to handle the client.

For example, Raghav comes to the counsellor and talks about how he has been physically and psychologically abused by his father for his poor performance in the exams, in such a case, if the counsellor has a life story similar to that of the client, then the counsellor will not be able to help the client in dealing with the trauma unless she herself has resolved her own traumatic feelings.

Saritha was counselling a client who was revealing her experience of sexual abuse during childhood. Saritha herself went through abuse when she was a child and when she realised that her client too, was going through similar trauma, her own unresolved experiences came in the way of her client's experiences. For Saritha being unable to help the client was quite frustrating.

Every individual is exposed to a range of experiences in their personal, educational, and professional lives, and these experiences contribute to shaping the individual. The sense these experiences make to the individual and the insights they get from these experiences influence their psychological growth and their understanding of self. These experiences also have an impact on the individual's attitudes, values, and beliefs. The case study explains how past experiences impact the counsellor's attitudes and values.

Case Study

Atul comes from an orthodox family, where there were strict rules and restrictions. All decisions regarding Atul and his siblings were taken by his father. Atul always felt suffocated all through his childhood and adolescence. After his school education, he decided to take up psychology and continued it as a career. In one of the counselling sessions, when an 18-year-old adolescent shared his conflicts and relationship with his father, Atul advised the young boy to leave home and take charge of his own life. Atul's own experience, the feelings of frustration, and not having an insight into his own problem prompted him to give such advice to his client.

Box 3.2 Life Exploration with Some Reflections

The best method of understanding self is to explore your life experiences. You can be more aware of yourself by taking up the following activities.

1. Draw a life map. A life map is a graphic organiser where you place all the significant events of your life. You start the life map from the day of your birth and place all the events till the present date. The life map helps you to understand your life experiences, the blocks in life, your choices and decisions, your values, beliefs, and significant information about your life goals. After drawing the map do a thorough introspection of how you dealt with each of these experiences, check if you are able to get an understanding of your feelings, the experience that you went through, and the action or behaviour that followed. What strategies did you use to resolve and, were these the right strategies? If not, how can you look at these with a different perspective?
2. Write an autobiography. Writing an autobiography is an exercise where you write the story of your life. Writing an autobiography is an innovative therapeutic technique and acts as a process of catharsis. It is also called expressive writing, wherein you can write down all the positive and negative experiences of life to the present day. After writing the autobiography, take time to review the experiences and unresolved conflicts. In case you observe any unresolved conflict, take immediate help. Discussing with your supervisor or a trusted friend or colleague can be helpful.

Unresolved feelings and experiences can often influence the counsellor's behaviour towards the clients. Boxes 3.4 and 3.5 present an exercise in self-exploration and reflection, which can help counsellors to enhance self-awareness. Cormier et al. (2016) explain that every individual goes through experiences in the past and has healthy or unhealthy ways of dealing with it; the most important point is that the individual is aware of his/her limitations and is able to acknowledge these limitations. The case examples cited above explain how life experiences influence attitudes and beliefs and how important it is for practicing counsellors, to resolve these painful experiences so that they do not cause any damage to their clients and their professional lives. As a professional, one should also keep in mind the motives for entering into the helping profession. According to Norcross and Farber (2005), the common motives to enter the helping profession are: self-healing, self-growth, altruism, and healing others, while Day (1995) points out the following: to do for others what someone has to me; to do for others what I wish had been done for me; to share with others certain insights I have gained. Cormier and Day (1995, 2012), also cautions professionals entering a helping profession to be aware of their intentions and motivation to take up the profession, the intention should be that of attaining some self-sufficient goals.

Helping professionals' own attitudes and behaviours will either aid or interfere with the helping process. Hence identification and awareness of one's attitudes and behaviour is the first step towards professional growth. Awareness of one's own strengths and limitations will help the counsellor to be more sensitive to the experiences of clients. Self-awareness also helps the counsellor to reflect client's experiences and provide the right interventions. Burnard (1994) points out that self-awareness helps in identifying the boundaries and discriminates against the counsellors' and clients' needs. The 'conscious use of self', as described by Heron (1994), helps the counsellor in paying attention and increases sensitivity towards the client's needs, and becomes more tactful in dealing with the clients.

Box 3.3

The question given below will help you to explore the various aspects of your life. There is no right or wrong answer to any of these questions. Answering the questions will help you to introspect and get an understanding of some of the events in the past

Question	*Response*
1. Write about an incident/experience/ event and record your response/ behaviour towards it.	
2. Were you happy with your behaviour/ were you happy with the way you handled it?	
3. If yes, mention the outcome and how the outcome was beneficial to you.	
4. If no, how could you handle it in a better way?	
5. If a similar event occurs again how well are you equipped to handle it?	
6. If a client comes to you with a similar issue, will you be ready to help?	

Drawing and Setting Boundaries

Boundaries help to define identity, bring order, and protect oneself from the control of others. Boundaries also help to maintain respect and preserve one's purpose. Effective counsellors can set boundaries for themselves and honour the boundaries of others. Setting the right kind of boundaries implies not only being entirely present with the client but also getting disengaged when required. Box 3.4 has some questions pertaining to some real-life situations; answering these questions will help counsellors think and evaluate how they handle their personal boundaries.

Box 3.4 Setting Effective Boundaries

Answer the questions below:

1. Are you excessively attached or detached in your relationships (in a group, family, or your relationships with others)?
2. Do you feel your physical or emotional space is being violated?
3. Do you identify yourself as a violated victim, and do you accept your victimisation?
4. Think of some area in your life where you can try to push or extend your boundaries.
5. Loose and open boundaries will lead to getting too involved in others' problems. Do you have difficulty saying 'no'? Are you unable to say 'no' because there is a need to please others, because you fear rejection, or there has been too much self-disclosure, which has left you vulnerable before others?
6. Check which of your boundaries (physical, relational, emotional) are permeable and which are rigid.
   Rigid boundaries will keep you at a distance from others, and you may be detached even from your close partners. Rigid boundaries lead to voiding close relations and having few close relations.
7. How healthy/unhealthy are your boundaries?
8. Discuss with your peer and explore ways to set or strengthen your boundaries.

Supportive techniques to manage boundaries:

- Reiterate your expectation from yourselves and others
- Say 'no' whenever needed
- Value yourself because there is a fine line between giving value and being taken advantage of
- Set your priorities/be clear with your priorities
- Identify your point of exhaustion and stress, stop, and take help
- Withdraw emotionally to keep your objectivity
- Speak up when there is discomfort
- Retreat and relax and start fresh whenever the situation call for it
- Suspend privileges whenever needed
- You may have some discomfort while you set your boundaries, you may even feel awkward because it is not your usual self, and people may not accept your behaviour but you need to be consistent and remind yourself about the positives of healthy boundaries.

The Personal Self as the First Impression

When a counsellor contacts the client, the first response is primarily related to the physical appearance. Personal grooming, body posture, and style of clothing speak many words and have an impact on the client (Johnson et al., 2008). Counsellors should keep in mind that personal appearance has both positive and negative impacts on the client. Hutchinson (2014) mentions that when he appeared before his client dressed in a 'tie', thinking that he would look more professional, his client reacted by saying, 'I hate ties'. On exploring, Hutchinson found that for his client the appearance was more like an authority figure trying to control and run his life. Smriti was a young counsellor and had tattoos on her arm. When Saroj, a 65-year-old woman, came to her for counselling, she felt that Smriti was too 'bold' and may not be able to understand her. Saroj felt she was 'old fashioned' and she may not be comfortable with Smriti. Tattooed and pierced professionals were perceived to be less caring, skilled, and knowledgeable (Wittman-Price et al, 2012). A recent study by Zidenberg et al., (2021) found that counsellors with tattoos were more open, confident, and likable. However cultural differences do play a major role in the acceptability or non-acceptability of the above. Yet another counsellor Lata was very thoughtful about her appearance before her clients. She took care that she dressed up appropriately for her sessions; for her client Karisma, she was a role model. Clients can develop trust, get attracted or distracted or reject the counsellor based on some social stereotypes like age, gender, caste or race, and appearance. Maintaining a neutral position and multicultural know-how is best recommended for a counsellor.

Box 3.5 Am I Comfortable with Myself?

Stand in front of a mirror and look at yourself. Observe your physical appearance. How do you see yourselves? Look at your posture, your general physical appearance, your hairstyle, your facial expression, and your sense of dress, and get a general impression about yourself. Reflect on what you like or do not like about your physical appearance. How do you think others or a client will react to your appearance? Do you think you should make some changes in your appearance, especially when you are presenting yourself before a client? Write down your reflections on a piece of paper. Discuss them with a peer and take their input. Your reflections will help you become more comfortable with your appearance and help you present yourselves before your clients in a better way.

Non-judgemental Acceptance

Counselling is a profession where the counsellor interacts with varied varieties of clients. Clients come from different cultural and geographic backgrounds, socio-economic strata, ages, gender, and sexual orientations. Clients also differ in their beliefs, attitudes, and behaviour and the counsellor's judgement in evaluating these differences in his/her client's stands is important in the course of the client-counsellor relationship. To make it simpler, a non-judgemental attitude is simply a way of accepting people without reflecting on one's own preconceptions or biases, in other words accepting 'what is said rather than who said it'. Non-judgemental attitude ensures clients are valued, respected, and accepted even if they have some shortcomings, which helps clients build up their self-confidence and self-esteem and motivates them to bring about the required changes to reach their goals. The skill of non-judgemental acceptance can be achieved when the counsellor:

- Listens to the client without being distracted by one's own thoughts and experiences
- Helps the client express his/her values and beliefs even if they contradict the counsellor's own values and beliefs
- Allows the client to speak without interruption and understand what is being said
- Enables the client to speak freely without being judged

Psychological Flexibility

A very significant attribute of a counsellor's competence is psychological flexibility and the know-how of multicultural counselling contributes to it. Psychological flexibility is the individual's ability to be in the present moment, be aware of thoughts and emotions without changing or controlling them, and at the same time deal with challenges without compromising one's values. It is the ability to be in the present moment. Psychological flexibility is thus the ability to manage distress without breaking or impacting one's behaviour. When an individual is psychologically flexible, he/she is able to accept the emotions, sensations, and thoughts even though they are distressing and work with their behaviour in accordance with their values. Hayes et al. (2006) define psychological flexibility as the capacity to behave consistently with one's preferred values, even in the presence of unwanted internal experiences.

Need for Personal Counselling for Counsellors

It is essential to embark on a journey of self-awareness to become an effective counsellor. The counsellor's own interpersonal as well as intrapersonal awareness and levels of insight, guide the process of counselling as much as, or probably more than, the formal training does. As discussed earlier, unexamined and residual feelings from any unfinished business from the past can easily slip into the client-counsellor relationship, ultimately causing a surfeit of consequences. Consequently, there is inauthenticity of the process, mistrust, second-guessing, projection, and/or countertransference, and each of them not only renders the counselling relationship ineffective but also potentially causes serious harm and damage, while simultaneously undermining the entire art and science of the therapeutic process. In this light, it becomes vital that the counsellor trainee undergoes in-depth counselling or therapy as part of his/her journey of becoming an effective and compassionate counsellor. The individual counselling or therapy sessions, help the counsellor trainee get in touch with the inner self and work on his/her own unresolved personal or professional issues that may continue to interfere in the present context of relating to people. In addition to unresolved issues, the counselling sessions also empower the therapeutic process by keeping the counsellor trainee firmly entrenched in understanding the benefits and effects of being on the receiving end of such a relationship. Too often, counsellors become jaded in their knowledge of the craft and forget what it may be like to be the person seeking help. To understand, accept, forgive, and work through one's own humanness is at the core of personal therapy sessions. In group therapy, the counsellor's own interpersonal styles are brought to the fore by being a member of a facilitated group. The universality of issues, catharsis achieved by way of working through shared experience, understanding the influence of external dynamics, and parallel processing are all a part of the healing process. To be there for the client, the counsellor needs to be sharply aware of his/ her boundaries, limitations, areas of conflict, strengths, and weaknesses so as to be able to use that very knowledge to further the process for the greater good of the client. There is no shame in knowing when to step back from the territory shaky ground for the counsellor and referring the client to another counsellor. On the other hand, once one is able to light the darkest recesses of the mind, one's strengths shine brightly, and one is able to touch stones, guide, and become an empathetic witness to another's tale.

Professionalising the Counselling Relationship: Initiating the Counselling Process

Rapport Building

The most critical part of the counselling process is to initiate a therapeutic relationship. Rapport building is an essential component of a healthy counsellor-client relationship. Rapport is the ability to build an environment of faith and mutual trust. According to Youell and Youell (2011), rapport is being on the same 'wavelength' as the individual in conversation and making him/her feel understood. While the meaning of rapport is being in harmony with one other, it does not imply that we respond to them as desired by them. Rapport includes a trusted environment, a smooth flow of conversation, and establishing a psychological connection. Rapport building is like an ice-breaking session and helps ease out the tension so as to help the client feel relaxed and open for further communication. Counsellors in their initial years of practice may be confused between rapport building and questioning, one has to understand that rapport building is not questioning and getting answers. It is a conscious process that includes establishing a connection at an emotional level and being on the same wavelength or in tune with the client. Rapport building can be understood with a simple example. Think of how you listen to music using a bluetooth. Bluetooth helps to sync one instrument to another, similarly, rapport building is like a bluetooth that connects a counsellor with a client with a complete sync. Rapport building thus is a critical component of counsellor-client relationships and it promotes open communication, a sense of trust, and a desire to work towards a positive change.

Building a rapport cannot be done rapidly. It is important that counsellors are patient and do not rush the process. The entire process is systematic wherein the counsellor uses some specified skills and facilitates a positive change. During the process, the counsellor with his/her personal attributes and professional skills minimises the client's anxiety and fear. According to Yalom (1980), the most important lesson counsellors should learn in their initial stage is 'it is the relationship that heals the client', and by communicating with a counsellor who is receptive and engaging, the client gets into the mode of healing oneself. Some of the skills required for building a rapport viz. unconditional positive regard, congruence, empathy, and non-judgemental attitude have been discussed under the characteristics of a good counsellor in the initial part of the chapter, and some of the skills will be discussed in the coming chapters. However, the skills and the benefits of these skills are summarised in Box 3.6. Attributes such as openness, respect, genuineness, and an inclination towards helping are the building blocks for a good therapeutic relationship. As emphasised by Rogers, the quality of the relationship is the key to a therapeutic alliance. Counsellors must understand that these skills are required in every session and can be enhanced with practice.

The other important feature of a therapeutic relationship is its collaborative nature. The client and the counsellor work together towards the goal. According to Egan (2014), the helpers do not 'cure' the client, rather they are facilitators in problem management. The outcome of the relationship depends upon the counsellor's competence, the

Box 3.6 Rapport Building Skills

Rapport Building Skills	*Benefits*
1. ***Initiating***: Ability to facilitate a conversation	A non-threatening talk initial talk helps clients open up and puts them at ease
2. ***Non-judgemental attitude***: The ability to accept the client in spite of the differences in values, morals, and beliefs	Builds trust and confidence in clients. The client feels cared for and respected
3. ***Self-awareness:*** The ability to introspect and understand oneself	Helps the counsellor become aware of his/her inner feelings and unresolved conflicts. Gains and ability to resolve them. This awareness helps the counsellor work with the clients' issues
4. ***Active-listening***: Listening to the client without filters and without getting distracted	Clients understand that the counsellor is focused, interested, and attending to him/her
5. ***Non-verbal skills***: Awareness about one's own body language and self-generated cues	Understanding non-verbal communication helps the counsellor in estimating the impact of issue
6. ***Responding with empathy***: Ability to understand the clients' experiences, thoughts, and feelings from his/her own perspective	Provides support and the client feels understood. It helps clients explore and encourages them to share their experiences
7. ***Self-disclosure***: Ability to share personal experiences when necessary	Builds trust and provides validation to the client that it's normal to feel the way he/she is feeling and that is not alone. Also helps reduce the power difference between the client and the counsellor

motivation of the client, and the quality of the relationship. Egan also calls the therapeutic relationship 'a forum for relearning'. The helpers are role models whose attributes and behaviour are transferred to the client through social learning and social influence. If the clients find the relationship a safe platform, they are motivated to share and experiment with their behaviour.

Clients' needs vary hence counsellors should understand these varied needs and extend help. Egan calls this *relationship flexibility*. According to Egan, some clients need plenty of warmth, while others fear intimacy. There are clients who are highly objective, while a few are dependent. Counsellors need to understand the needs of the clients and extend help. To explain further, if a client who has a fear of intimacy is provided with too much empathy, the client may feel uncomfortable. According to Norcross (1993), 'therapist integrated relationship stance and therapeutic techniques based on client's requirements, are beneficial in therapy'.

Multicultural Competencies

The American Psychological Association (APA, 2003) defines multicultural competency as the knowledge, skills, and personal attributes needed to live and work in a diverse world. Sue et al. (1982) introduced the term 'multicultural competency', which led to mandating multicultural training. Pedersen (2000) recognised multicultural competencies in counselling as a 'fourth force' after psychoanalysis, behaviourism, and humanism. Counsellors who are culturally competent must be aware of their cultural heritage and the diversity between themselves and their clients (Sue, 2001). Sue examines the importance of how counsellors should respect the religious and spiritual practices of different cultures. A competent counsellor has the capability to understand the culturally based meanings of clients.

A client is a product of his/her cultural and ethnic background, and personal experiences do affect therapeutic experiences. Geographic background, socio-economic background, gender, religion, values, and belief system of the counsellor may influence the counsellor's approach and attitude towards the client. While dealing with the client, it is important to understand that the client's cultural context and background are as important as his/her psychological or emotional encounters. Carr (1977) describes the inability of counsellors to recognise cultural differences as 'colour-blindness', and this may have a damaging effect on their counselling practice. Sue et al. (1998) developed a framework for multicultural competence (Figure 3.3). They elaborated that multicultural competence has three levels and begins with awareness of one's own culture and its relationship with others and the influence of these cultural beliefs and assumptions on one's life. The first level includes the counsellor's ability: to understand and interpret verbal and non-verbal communication; recognise cultural and linguistic differences, myths, and stereotypes, develop cultural sensitivity and appreciate multicultural education; and develop awareness about one's acceptance of other cultures.

The second level is about knowledge and information, and how one comprehends that knowledge and information. This stage assesses the counsellor's knowledge about cultural assumptions, for example, the history, values, attitudes, and behaviours; how members of other cultures interpret their own rules and customs. The third level describes the counsellor's ability to use this comprehension to develop skills and practice. Multicultural competence hence depends on the counsellor's accurate assessment of awareness of self, and others, gaining knowledge and information of facts, and using this awareness and knowledge in the day-to-day practice. The three levels of development of multicultural competencies are explained in Figure 3.4.

Pedersen (2000) adds that placing all clients on a similar 'hypothetical standard', expecting the individual to adjust to a 'fit system', lack of interdisciplinary collaboration, and disregard for the individual's cultural background and social context, are some of the reasons for a failure in maintaining multicultural standards. The assumption that an individualistic approach is more fitting in a counselling context than a collectivistic approach is extremely pertinent when dealing with clients of Indian origin (Pedersen, 2000). The approach used in an individualistic culture cannot be applied to clients who are from a collectivistic culture. The APA (2017) guidelines make it mandatory for counsellors to

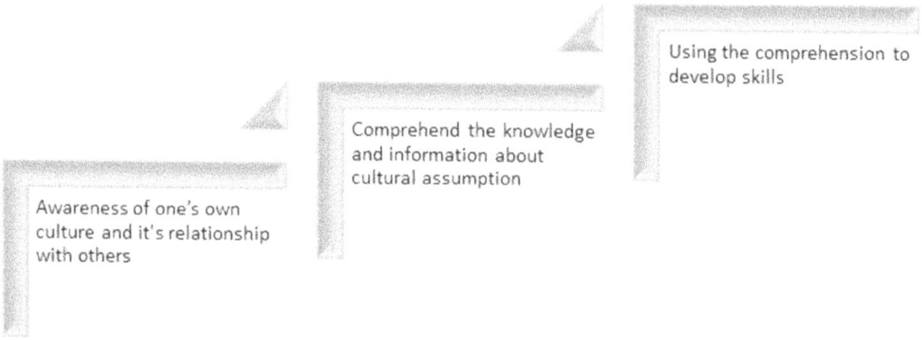

Figure 3.4 Levels Multicultural Competencies

understand the diverse nature of individuals and communities and approach them with the necessary skills.

Another integrative model developed by D'Andrea and Daniels (1997) helps recognise the multidimensional perspective of clients. The RESPECTFUL model addresses human diversity and helps counsellors develop multicultural competencies. The model has ten components and is listed as an acronym RESPECTFUL these factors are considered because they influence the psychosocial development and well-being of the client. The model, though developed about three decades ago still holds good ground in dealing with diverse clients. The ten components in the model are present in Box 3.7 and are elaborated on in the next section.

Box 3.7 The RESPECTFUL Model for Multicultural Competencies

R Religious/spiritual identity
E Economic class background
S Sexual identity
P Psychological maturity
E Ethnic/racial identity
C Chronological/developmental challenges
T Trauma and threat to well-being
F Family background and history
U Unique physical characteristics
L Location of residence and language differences

- ***Religious/spiritual identity***: Is the first component, which states that individuals identify themselves with a religious belief that transcends beyond their physical entity and gives them an existential meaning. Since religious beliefs are important factors to give life experiences a meaning, counsellors must understand how these beliefs transcend into the client's life experiences, and make a positive or negative impact on the client.
- ***Economic class background***: Research has shown that personal attributes, values, and beliefs are shaped by socio-economic status, and have a multidimensional impact on

the individual. And recognising them is important for a counsellor. It's important that counsellors recognise their own assumptions, prejudices, and views about the socio-economic class before they deal with their clients.

- *Sexual identity*: Sexual identity refers to the individual's subjective sense of gender identity, gender role, and sexual orientation (D'Andrea & Daniels, 2001). Sexual identity influences the development and is an important aspect to be paid attention to while counselling.
- *Psychological maturity*: Clients who come for counselling have different levels of psychological maturity. Counsellors need to assess the client's level of psychological maturity to develop rapport, set goals and plan interventions.
- *Ethnic/racial identity*: Individual differences exists among people coming from different ethnic backgrounds. These differences are related to physical, psychological, and social development. Counsellors should understand the clients in the context of pluralistic culture.
- *Chronological or developmental challenges*: Chronological challenges refer to age-related tasks, which impact the individual at various stages of the lifespan. These changes are related to changes in physical growth, cognitive competencies, and emotional maturation and have a tremendous influence on their self-worth. Counsellors should be aware of these chronological challenges and work with the clients accordingly.
- *Trauma and other threats*: Individuals often have traumatic experiences in their lives. These experiences leave deep scars and memories in their lives. Incidences of such a kind make the individual vulnerable. Counsellors need to work effectively with such at-risk groups and assess the various psychosocial factors that impact them and plan the right interventions.
- *Family background and history*: Families have the most important influence on the growth and development of individuals. The type of family, family relationships, and the client's interpersonal relationship with the members of the family have a major impact on individuals. Counsellors' personal experiences and biases shouldn't come in the way of his/her therapeutic relationship.
- *Unique physical characteristics*: Characteristics like obesity, severely low weight skinny appearance, differences in height, or challenges due to physical disabilities negatively affect the sense of self. Such clients can be assisted to develop their identity and build their personal strengths.
- *Location of residence and language differences*: Counsellors in India may find this as one of the common factors influencing client characteristics. As D'Andrea and Daniels identified five major geographical areas in the United States, and people belonging to these areas differ with respect to climate patterns, terrain, occupation, and industry. A similar concept can be applied to the clientele in India. India is one of the most diverse countries with varied geographical locations, languages, cultural values, and traditions. Stereotypical biases, predispositions, and myths develop due to these differences. Counsellors should develop sensitivity towards people from other cultural and geographical backgrounds while being able to articulate elements of their own culture and should be able to recognise and understand the relationship between diverse cultures.

Obstacles in Establishing a Counselling Relationship

Establishing a relationship with a client is not just about deepening the relationship but also strengthening it. Every client who comes to counselling has different stories which they are either willing or not willing to share. Clients can be categorised into a) voluntary clients: who are open to sharing their problems and motivated to resolve them. The client experiences discomfort and pain, he/she is motivated to see a counsellor and relieve himself or herself, such actions are also called self-initiated actions. These clients have a greater chance of bringing about change and resolving problems, the counsellor is a facilitator and a medium to help the client understand and resolve the problem; b) involuntary client: is the client who either actively opposes the intrusion or interference of the counsellor and resists complying; or the reluctant client who hesitates to talk, share or disclose.

When we look back on certain incidences in our life, we can recall times when someone suggested we bring about a change in our behaviour or our attire; when parents or members of our family restrained us from meeting someone or asked us to stop using a cell phone. We can recall how we reacted to their advice, we would have reacted in anger, we may have resisted their suggestions, or we may have been annoyed about their interference in our activities. A change necessitates giving up our old behaviours and adopting a new one which requires adjustment, adaptation, and modification of many of our day-to-day activities and bringing a change in our perceptions, beliefs and thoughts.

Let's take this case example, Sudeep was a 23-year-old young man very confident and sure of what he was doing. He loved driving and was a good and confident driver. He drove his car almost every day on the same route. On Sunday morning, he planned to visit his friend on his birthday, so he took the car and left home. He was driving on the same route which he used to go every day, but at one point he lost control of his car and bumped into a road divider. Thankfully he was safe but the car was very damaged. Sudeep was in shock. Though he was dismayed and troubled, he was hesitant to share his feelings with anyone. He resisted talking about the incident and told everyone that he was fine. Shame, guilt, denial, and hesitancy to speak about the incident were some reasons for not sharing his feelings. Reluctance and resistance are behaviours exhibited by clients, to block therapy. Blocks to attending counselling may also be because of a lack of understanding of the counselling process, denial or distortion of the problem, or lack of trust in the counsellor. Counsellors should be aware of the fact that there are clients who are difficult, and it is the counsellor's responsibility to deal with resistant and reluctant clients. Apart from the client's state, the counsellors may have difficulty in dealing with the client because of their own resistance and reluctance, their own emotional state, or a lack of experience in the counselling setting.

Many clients remain in a static state and get twined into their problem situation. They continue to remain in this state unless some external force acts upon them and helps them move out of this state. Egan (1990) calls it '*inertia*' or a state of rest. This is a state when the client is unwilling to act on the problem and remains in a troubled state. In the coming section, we will discuss some obstacles in counselling relationships viz. resistance and reluctance; transference and countertransference

Resistance and Reluctance

Resistance and reluctance are two sides of the same coin. Resistance and reluctance though used interchangeably, connote different meanings. While resistance is active opposition to authority or unwillingness expressed by the client towards the therapeutic process, reluctance is the hesitancy or unwillingness of the client to seek help or participate in therapy or the tasks related to the therapeutic session. Cormier et al. (2016) conceptualised that when an individual's freedom is threatened, they exhibit feelings like frustration and rage and behaviour like disobedience and opposition.

Resistance

The concept of resistance is central to the psychoanalytic theory. The psychoanalytic approach considers resistance as any feeling, behaviour or thought either conscious or unconscious, that is preventing the individual from moving towards the process of change. Resistance in a client is also viewed as a process of protecting oneself from anxiety and fear of change. Any behaviour that interferes with individual growth can be called resistance (Engle & Arkowitz, 2009). According to the cognitive behaviouristic approach, resistance is the client's attempt to safeguard his/her integrity, safety, and freedom. Resistance clients are non-compliant, refuse to participate in sessions, have a confronting attitude, and are unreasonably demanding (Newman, 2002). Egan, (2014) names it as a 'push back' from the client when he or she is pressured. Resistance can be looked at in two ways; one is the client's emotional or psychological state and the second is the characteristics of the counsellor. The first one is either a stable disposition or a temporary state (Beutler & Harwood, 2000). Resistance can be perceived as a temporary state for the reason that, when the client comes to the counsellor, he/she is not sure of the process of counselling, having trust in the counsellor and disclosing to someone whom they have met for the first time is not easy for the client (Watson, 2006). The reasons for resistance as described by Egan (1994) are:

- Dislike for the person who has referred.
- No conviction on the need to see the counsellor.
- Feels visiting a counsellor is admitting weakness or failure.
- Consider counselling as a stigma.
- Views counselling as an intrusion or imposition.
- Has no trust in the counsellor or had a negative experience in the past.
- Has a history of rebellious behaviour.
- Has a suspicious or negative attitude towards the authority.
- Conflicts in the goals of the client and the counsellor.
- Conflict of power or need for power.
- A difference in socio-cultural variables like gender, socio-economic status, religion, caste, beliefs, and values.
- Does not know the art of participating in the counselling set up.
- Refusal to move out of the comfort zone.
- Incidents in the client's social or family environment like a death, abuse, separation or a divorce.

Some examples to explain resistance are given below:

Suhas: *I don't know why the principal has asked me to see you. There's no big deal. I don't think it's a big problem, I am just wasting my time sitting here, I know I can handle this myself.*

Counsellor: *Suhas you are annoyed that the principal has asked you to see me because you think you are capable to handle it and by coming here you are wasting your time.*

Suhas: *Yes of course. Its no big deal. I am old enough to handle things, I don't think I need anyone's help.*

The client is a 12-year-old boy who has been asked to see the counsellor by an authority figure which is quite upsetting for him. The client seems quite resentful about it and is disrespecting the authority.

Client: *My wife is the reason for the problem I am facing now. I don't know what she has told you about me that I am here, sitting in front of you without any fault of mine. You are a counsellor; how can you help me? I think only the court can help us.*

Counsellor: *So you think the problem is with your wife and not you and the court is the only place where you can get help.*

The client here is blaming his wife for the current situation. He does not have any intention to cooperate to bring about a constructive change.

Client: *I've been to see counsellors, but as always, I don't think it's going to work this time either. I don't think anyone can help me out of this, and I don't even know why I am trying this out again.*

Counsellor: *Ravi, seeing a counsellor hasn't helped you earlier and you think it's going to be the same again, but you feel you have to try something.*

In the above example, the client has been seeing counsellors but there hasn't been any positive experience for him.

As explained in the example clients have many reasons to show resistance to counselling. Some indications of resistance are resentment, rebellious behaviour, stubbornness, disrespect, sabotage of the helping process by being non-cooperative setting unrealistic goals, talking carefully, or on speak only about low-priority issues. Resistant clients are more often seen in schools or colleges, where students are referred by the teachers or the school administration, or in marital counselling where clients may not be willing to share or admit reality or change from their comfort zone.

Though resistance is seen as a behaviour of the client, counsellors often fail to understand that resistance or the unwillingness to change may sometimes be triggered by the counsellor, which is the second reason for resistance and can be explained by taking the view of interaction theorists who define resistance as 'the psychological forces aroused in the client that restrain acceptance of influence (counsellor's suggestions) and are generated by the way the suggestion is stated and by the characteristics of the counsellor stating it' (Strong and Mastross, 1973). Resistance thus is viewed as the outcome of the counsellor's interaction style, which hampers the process of counselling. The counsellors should be aware and become counteractive in changing their interaction style. As theorised by Strupp and Hadley (1979), there are certain specific factors that influence the therapeutic relationship. Counsellors' personal characteristics, competence, and nature of therapeutic alliance have an influence on the outcome of therapy (Chatoor & Krupnick, 2001) Strupp (2001) also adds that positive interaction by the counsellors brings about a positive attitude in the client. Miller and Rollnick (2002) name the 'helper's style' as one of the important determinants of resistance. Counsellors' non-verbal communication, lack of empathetic understanding, and counsellor's therapeutic approach can also be reasons for resistance. For example, a student who is referred to the school counsellor by the school principal may be threatened by the power of the authority and experience a sense of insecurity leading to resistant behaviour. The interaction theorists define resistance as 'the psychological forces aroused in the client that restrain acceptance of influence (counsellor's suggestions) and are generated by the way the suggestion is stated and by the characteristics of the counsellor stating it' (Strong & Mastross, 1973). Arkowitz (2002) adds that it is important for therapists to understand and interpret resistance in the right way by picking up the right cues so that the client's concerns are resolved. Otani (1989), describes four categories of resistance: response quality resistance; response content resistance; response style resistance, and logistic management resistance.

1. *Response Quality Resistance*
   When clients do not comply with the change process it is called response quality resistance. Clients in this category use silence, talk minimally and use pauses between their descriptions. Otani (1989) adds that minimal information helps the client control the session and avoid discussion on emotionally painful topics.
2. *Response Content Resistance*
   The clients in their responses try to restrict the content of information. Talking about irrelevant issues, gossiping, discussing problems in an abstract manner, and displaying emotions like crying and anger are some methods of response content resistance. Clients with this type of resistance ramble, ask meaningless questions and also ruminate about their past. By doing so clients try to manipulate the session and give them little chance for the counsellor to take the session forward.
3. *Response Style Resistance*
   This kind of resistance is related to the manner in which the information is communicated by the client. Discounting, externalising, thought censoring, not disclosing or disclosing at the last minute, showing seductive behaviour, flattering, and making false promises are the forms of response style resistance. The use of this type of resistance helps the client in discouraging the counsellor from getting to areas that are uncomfortable for the client to speak about. The counsellors become 'soft' and do not push the client beyond a point.
4. *Logistic Management Resistance*
   Clients show their resistance by violating some of the procedures of the counselling process. Clients ask for favours and break the basic rules like delaying payment, and not keeping to the time schedule. Clients use these techniques to disobey or rebel against the counsellor.

Reluctance

Reluctance is regarded as the ambivalence or hesitancy of the client, to be a part of the counselling process. Clients who are reluctant, either avoid participation in the counselling process or are overly cooperative. They do not focus on the issue that is actually affecting them, rather they choose to deal with the lowest priority issue. According to Egan (2014), reluctant clients have no goals or may set unrealistic goals, shun responsibilities, and leave tasks unfinished. Counsellors should be observant of verbal and non-verbal behaviour to understand reluctance. Some clients show silence as behaviour towards reluctance, silence can mean anything from fear, shame, guilt, hostility or defence to disrespect and anger (Manthei & Matthews, 1982). Interpretation of the client's verbal and non-verbal behaviour will give the counsellor an understanding of discrepancies in the overt and covert behaviours of the client. Ucar (2017) adds that most reluctant clients place the blame for their shortcomings on external factors such as parents, family, friends, or school and they even complain about the existing social system for their problems. The reluctant clients are manipulative, they distort and mislead the therapist.

Reluctant behaviour often has its underpinnings in some beliefs such as being named, being in pain, and emotional strain, expected during the session, the clients then have a perception that the session will not be useful or in their favour. Signs of reluctance can be seen when clients do not come for the session at the time of the appointment. Missing sessions, talking about issues that are unimportant, doing a safety talk, and being purposefully late for the session are some important signs of reluctance (Ucar, 2017). Miron and Brehm (2006) add another component of 'reactance' a 'motivational state', where the client doesn't wish to invest energy into the therapeutic activity, and the authors call it a 'freedom restoration behaviour'. Some of the causes for reluctance are listed below:

- Referral by an authority figure viz. teacher, the parent, or school authority
- Lack of trust in the counsellor
- Guilt, shame, and or being a guard
- A fear of change
- Fear of intensity

Handling Resistance and Reluctance

Counsellors' reactions to resistance and reluctance may appear in the form of irritation, frustration, impatience, and inaction. Counsellors who are under training lose confidence and in the process tend to appease and accept the client and succumb to their manipulative behaviour, or become helpless, give up, and terminate the client by blaming the client for not collaborating. Irrational assumptions and self-defeating behaviours for example clients should trust and like the counsellor, all clients should be willing to follow the change process, and counsellors should be able to deal with all kinds of clients, are some of the negative reactions in the counsellors while dealing with resistant clients (Egan, 1994). To deal with resistant or reluctant clients, counsellors can try to get an understanding of their own resistance and reluctance. Counsellors can try by recalling their own reactions. Here are some self-questions to understand your own reluctance and resistance.

- What did you do when someone tried to force you to do something which you didn't want to do?
- How did you feel when someone tried to intrude into your personal space?
- What were the verbal or non-verbal messages you used towards the person to avoid coercion?
- Can you recall and recollect the reasons or the underlying avoidance behaviours for your resistance?

Answering the above questions will help counsellors understand that reluctant and resistant behaviour is natural. Counsellors cannot be rigid, and impose upon the client to bring a change. Being realistic and understanding their personal and professional limits, can help counsellors avoid situations when clients' behaviour starts affecting them and triggers unhelpful responses. According to Corey (2001), clients use resistance to block the threatening memories or experiences from coming to awareness. These blocks can be addressed by the counsellor to help client overcome the fears. To prevent the client from denial and help the client understand resistant behaviour, the counsellors can first deal with the most apparent and observable behaviour. Egan (1994) adds that counsellors can observe the quality of the interventions extended to the client, and check if they are committing mistakes while attending or probing. Reinforcing positive behaviour, acknowledging achievements, setting goals that have immediate pay-off, generating an alternative method if the present is not working, and redefining the problem so that the clients can see the blind spots or blocks are some methods of overcoming the challenges of dealing with resistance and reluctance.

Transference and Countertransference

Raj had been seeing his counsellor Reema for the past six months. Raj's mother died of cancer six months ago. Initially, Raj was very resistant and refused to visit the counsellor, Reema with her skills and competence could help Raj open up and deal with the loss. As the sessions progressed Raj was trying to place Reema in his mother's position. He expressed that whenever he was with Reema he never missed his mother. Here we can see Raj transferring his feelings of love and affection to the therapist.

When feelings for a specific person are redirected or projected towards the counsellor, it is referred to as transference. Transference is a phenomenon when emotions and feelings are redirected unconsciously from a significant person in the past to another and in the case of counselling, it is towards the therapist. Freud (1895) described the concept of transference as deep and intense unconscious feelings developed towards the therapist. The client develops these feelings by means that he/she may see the counsellor as one of the most prominent people in his or her life, who could be a mentor, a parent, or a lover. Transference may also be negative, wherein the client directs feelings of anger, irritation, and frustration onto the counsellor. Transference can arise out of dependence, unmet relational needs, or nurturing needs. It is important that counsellors recognise these needs in clients and help clients handle them. Maintaining boundaries, as discussed in the earlier part of this chapter is one method of dealing with transference. Gelso et al. (1999) described five important ways of dealing with transference: focusing on relationships, interpreting the right meaning, promoting insight, educating, and self-disclosure as some methods which are useful to deal with transference.

Countertransference

This is described as the therapist's feelings and reactions towards the client. Countertransference may be a realistic response to transference or the genuine feelings of the counsellor towards the client. Even though these feelings arise due to the psychological connection between the counsellor and the client they may sometimes be useful and sometimes harmful. Countertransference may lead to a situation wherein the counsellor may start inappropriate self-disclosure, start feeling responsible for the client's progress, or may not be able to set boundaries with the client. Counsellors must be aware of such situations and prevent damage to the client. Self-awareness and personal counselling are some means of dealing with countertransference. Counsellors can also take help from their supervisors to deal with feelings of countertransference.

Goals of Counselling

Clients who seek counselling come from different backgrounds with wide-ranging problems. The expectations from a counselling session are different for different individuals, e.g., if a parent comes to a counsellor with his child, the expectations of the parent are different from that of a child. According to Nelson-Jones (1979), counsellors need to understand the difference between 'responsibility to' and 'responsibility for'. The goal of counselling is not to impose ideas and judgements on the client, rather the goal is to make the client responsible for his behaviour and action. Reducing clients' anxiety, increasing self-acceptance, exploring options for problem-solving, and helping them identify their strengths and resources are some of the ways to enhance clients' self-responsibility are some of the universal goals of counselling. The goal of counselling is not to advise and interfere in what the clients do, rather the goal of counselling is to bring about desired behaviour change, and help them to make independent decisions. As discussed earlier in the chapter the above goals can only be achieved by building a trustful relationship, an empathetic response and a non-judgemental attitude. Using the core-competencies like unconditional regard, empathy and genuineness, counsellors can create a space which is emotionally safe, this will help the counsellor and client explore, understand and discover their fears and concerns. Once the major goals are defined, the specific goals can be determined and the client can initiate strategies to achieve these goals. Some of the major goals of counselling are discussed below:

- *Enhancing coping skills*: When a client comes, they are in a helpless state and charged emotionally. The clients use statements like 'I am shattered'; 'I am in a mess and no one can help me'; 'I think all good things have come to an end and I don't see any light on the other side'. Looking at these statements we can understand that they are in a state where emotions are at their peak, which lowers the capacity to think logically and reason out. The immediate goal here is to reduce the emotional state of the client and calm him/her down. Engaging the client in emotional expression and ventilation will help the client to a certain extent, but what is important here is to enhance their coping techniques. Identifying the maladaptive coping strategies, unlearning the maladaptive coping and learning the adaptive coping methods are some of the ways to enhance coping.
- *Facilitating behaviour change*: There are a wide number of factors that determine an individual's behaviour. Behaviour is a product of complex interactions between an individual's knowledge, beliefs, attitudes, social interactions, and environmental influences. Change in behaviours is required in many domains, e.g., maintaining health and well-being, maintaining interpersonal relationships, managing conflicts and modifying risk behaviours and so on. Though behaviour change is time-taking, when facilitating a change in behaviour is set as a primary goal the consequences can observe in many other aspects of life.
- *Improving relationships*: Strong interpersonal relationships bring in feelings of happiness and are a great source of social support. When the client has issues with his/her interpersonal relationships, it impacts their well-being. Poor self-esteem, inappropriate management of boundaries, and unrealistic expectations are some of the causes of interpersonal conflicts. Enhancing and improving interpersonal relationships will help clients to gain social support and enhance their self-esteem which gives them the confidence to gain solutions for further problems.
- *Promoting decision making*: Clients come with multiple issues and in most situations, they are unable to make the right decisions. The reason could be anything like- fear of the unknown, fear of change, unable to get clarity of the right and wrong choice or lack of confidence and trust. Motivating the clients, providing them with the right information, weighing the pros and cons of the options available, identifying the behaviour,

attitudes, and emotions influencing decision making and enhancing assertive skills are some methods to promote decision making.

- *Facilitating the potentialities of the client:* According to Rogers' assumptions about human nature, 'An individual is an accrue force of energy-oriented towards future goals and self-directed purposes'. Every individual has an innate potential that if allowed to unfold brings optimal development in the personality. Counsellors can tap this potential in every client and help him/her develop to the fullest potential (Ucar, 2017).

The outcome of counselling is heavily based on how the counsellor shapes the therapeutic relationship with the client. There are various ingredients like respect, empathy, genuineness, competence, and a non-judgemental attitude, which have to be dispensed in the right amount and at the right time so that the relationship is qualitative and the outcome is in favour of the client. Nevertheless, the counsellor's knowledge, attitude, skills, and training do play an important role in the sustenance of the counselling relationship. Enhancing knowledge, developing the right skills and techniques and keeping themselves updated with the theoretical developments and research that underpins the counselling process.

References

American Psychological Association. (2003). Guidelines on multicultural education, training, research, practice, and organisational change for psychologists. *The American Psychologist, 58(5)*, 377–402.

American Psychological Association (APA) (2017). https://www.apa.org/about/policy/multicultural-guidelines.

Arkowitz, H. (2002). Toward an integrative perspective on resistance to change. *Journal of Clinical Psychology, 58*(2), 219–227.

Baier, A. L., Kline, A. C., & Feeny, N. C. (2020). Therapeutic alliance as a mediator of change: A systematic review and evaluation of research. *Clinical psychology review, 82*, 101921.

Bischoff, M. M., & Tracey, T. J. (1995). Client resistance as predicted by therapist behavior: A study of sequential dependence. *Journal of Counseling Psychology, 42*(4), 487–495. https://doi.org/10.1037/0022-0167.42.4.487.

Black, J. & Enns, G. (1997) *Better boundaries: Owning and treasuring your life*. Raincoast Books.

Bodie, G. D. (2011). The Active-Empathic Listening Scale (AELS): Conceptualization and evidence of validity within the interpersonal domain. *Communication Quarterly, 59*(3), 277–295.

Bohart, A., Elliott, R., Greenberg, L.S., & Watson, J. C. (2002). Empathy. In Norcross J. C. (Ed.). *Psychotherapy relationships that work: Therapist contributions and responsiveness to patients* (pp. 89–108). Oxford University Press.

Bradshaw, K. M., Donohue, B., & Wilks, C. (2014). A review of quality assurance methods to assist professional record keeping: Implications for providers of interpersonal violence treatment. *Aggression and Violent Behavior, 19*(3), 242–250. https://doi.org/10.1016/j.avb.2014.04.010.

Brodley, B. T. (1999). Reasons for responses expressing the therapist's frame of reference in client-centered therapy. *Person-Centered Journal, 6*(1), 4–27.

Burnard P. (1994) Counselling and self-awareness. In *Counselling skills for health professionals*. Springer. https://doi.org/10.1007/978-1-4899-3334-8_4.

Carr, A. (1997). *Family Therapy and Systemic Practice: Readings of Child Protection, Clinical Techniques, and Empirical Foundations*. University Press of America.

Chatoor, I., & Krupnick, J. (2001). The role of non-specific factors in treatment outcome of psychotherapy studies. *European Child & Adolescent Psychiatry, 10*(1), I19–I25. https://doi.org/10.1007/s007870170004.

Corey, G. (2001). *Theory and practice of counseling and psychotherapy*. Brooks/Cole.

Cormier, S., Nurius, P. S., & Osborn, C. J. (2016). *Interviewing and change strategies for helpers*. Cengage Learning.

D'Andrea, M., & Daniels, J. (2001). RESPECTFUL counselling: An integrative model for counsellors. In D. Pope-Davis & H. Coleman (Eds.), *The interface of class, culture and gender in counselling* (pp. 417–466). Sage.

Day, J. M. (1994). Obligation and motivation: Obstacles and resources for counselor well-being and effectiveness. *Journal of Counseling & Development*, *73*(1), 108–111.

Edward, B. (1937). Contribution to the symposium on the theory of the therapeutic results of psycho-analysis. *International Journal of Psycho-Analysis*, *18*, 170–189.

Egan G. (2014). *The skilled helper. A client-centered approach*. Cengage Learning.

Elliott, R., Bohart, A. C., Watson, J. C., & Greenberg, L. S. (2011). Empathy. *Psychotherapy*, *48*(1), 43–49. https://doi.org/10.1037/a0022187.

Fairburn, C. G., & Cooper, Z. (2011). Therapist competence, therapy quality, and therapist training. *Behaviour research and therapy*, *49*(6–7), 373–378. https://doi.org/10.1016/j.brat.2011.03.005.

Folstein, M. F., Folstein, S. E., & McHugh, P. R. (1975). 'Mini-mental state'. A practical method for grading the cognitive state of patients for the clinician. *Journal of Psychiatric Research*, *12*(3), 189–198. https://doi.org/10.1016/0022-3956(75)90026-6.

Gehart, D. R. (2017). *Mastering competencies in family therapy: A practical approach to theory and clinical case documentation*. Cengage Learning.

Gelso, C. J., Hill, C. E., Mohr, J. J., Rochlen, A. B., & Zack, J. (1999). Describing the face of transference: Psychodynamic therapists' recollections about transference in cases of successful long-term therapy. *Journal of Counseling Psychology*, *46*(2), 257.

Heron, J. (1994). *Catharsis in human development*. Human Potential Research Project.

Horvath, A. O., Del Re, A. C., Flückiger, C., & Symonds, D. (2011). Alliance in individual psychotherapy. *Psychotherapy*, *48*(1), 9.

Hutchinson, D. (2014). *The essential counselor: Process, skills, and techniques*. Sage Publications.

Ivey, A. E., Ivey, M. B., & Zalaquett, C. P. (2013). *Intentional interviewing and counseling: Facilitating client development in a multicultural society*. Cengage Learning.

Jacobs, L. (2009). Interview with Lawrence Weed, MD – the father of the problem-oriented medical record looks ahead. *The Permanente Journal*, *13*(3), 84. https://doi.org/10.7812/TPP/09-068.

Johnson, K. K., Yoo, J. J., Kim, M., & Lennon, S. J. (2008). Dress and human behavior: A review and critique. *Clothing and Textiles Research Journal*, *26*(1), 3–22. https://doi.org/10.1177/0887302X07303626.

Manthei, R. J., & Matthews, D. A. (1982). Helping the reluctant client to engage in counselling. *British Journal of Guidance & Counselling*, *10*(1), 44–50. https://doi.org/10.1080/03069888200760051.

Miron, A. M., & Brehm, J. W. (2006). Reactance theory-40 years later. *Zeitschrift für Sozialpsychologie*, *37*(1), 9–18.

Nagy, T. F. (2005). Competence. *Journal of Aggression, Maltreatment & Trauma*, *11*(1–2), 27–49. https://doi.org/10.1300/J146v11n01_03.

Nagy, T. F. (2012). Competence. In S. J. Knapp, M. C. Gottlieb, M. M. Handelsman, & L. D. VandeCreek (Eds.), *APA handbook of ethics in psychology, Vol. 1. Moral foundations and common themes* (pp. 147–174). American Psychological Association.

Nelson-Jones, R. (1979). Goals for counselling, psychotherapy and psychological education: Responsibility as an integrating concept. *British Journal of Guidance & Counselling*, *7*(2), 153–168. https://doi.org/10.1080/03069887900760181.

Norcross, J. C. (1993). Tailoring relationship stances to client needs: An introduction [Editorial]. *Psychotherapy: Theory, Research, Practice, Training*, *30*(3), 402–403. https://doi.org/10.1037/h0092300.

Otani, A. (1989). Client resistance in counseling: Its theoretical rationale and taxonomic classification. *Journal of Counseling & Development, 67*(8), 458–461. https://doi.org/10.1002/j.1556-6676.1989.tb02117.x.
Pedersen, P. (Ed.). (2000). Review of *Multiculturalism as a fourth force* [Review of the book *Multiculturalism as a fourth force,* by P. Pedersen (Ed.)]. *Cultural Diversity and Ethnic Minority Psychology, 6*(1), 102–104. https://doi.org/10.1037/1099-9809.6.1.102.
Ritchie, M. H. (1986). Counseling the involuntary client. *Journal of Counseling & Development, 64*(8), 516–518. https://doi.org/10.1002/j.1556-6676.1986.tb01186.x.
Rogers, C. (1951). *Client centered therapy.* Houghton Mifflin.
Rogers, C. (1967). *On becoming a person: A therapist's view of psychotherapy.* Constable.
Rogers, C. (1957). The necessary and sufficient conditions of therapeutic personality change. *Journal of Consulting Psychology, 21*(2), 95–103. https://doi.org/10.1037/h0045357.
Strong, S. R., & Matross, R. P. (1973). Change processes in counseling and psychotherapy. *Journal of Counseling Psychology, 20*(1), 25–37. https://doi.org/10.1037/h0034055.
Strupp, H. H., & Hadley, S. W. (1979). Specific vs nonspecific factors in psychotherapy. A controlled study of outcome. *Archives of General Psychiatry, 36*(10), 1125–1136. https://doi.org/10.1001/archpsyc.1979.01780100095009.
Sue, D. W. (2001). Multidimensional facets of cultural competence. *The counseling psychologist, 29*(6), 790–821.
Sue, D. W., Carter, R. T., Casas, J. M., Fouad, N. A., Ivey, A. E., Jensen, M., ... & Vazquez-Nutall, E. (1998). *Multicultural counseling competencies: Individual and organizational development* (Vol. 11). Sage Publications.
Ucar, S. (2017). Reluctance and resistance: Challenges to change in psychotherapy. *Journal of Psychology and Clinical Psychiatry, 7*(6). DOI:10.15406/jpcpy.2017.07.00464.
Watson, J. C. (2006). Addressing client resistance: Recognising and processing in-session occurrences. http://www.counseling.org/knowledge-center/vistas.
Wheeler, A. M., & Bertram, B. (2019). *The counselor and the law: A guide to legal and ethical practice.* John Wiley & Sons.
Wittmann-Price, R. A., Gittings, K. K., & Collins, K. M. (2012). Nurses and body art: What's your perception?. *Nursing Management, 43*(10), 44–47.
Yalom, I. D. (2020). *Existential psychotherapy.* Hachette UK.
Youell, R., & Youell, C. (2013). *Effective NLP skills* (Vol. 141). Kogan Page Publishers.
Zetzel, E. R. (2018). Current concepts of transference. In *Influential papers from the 1950s* (pp. 109–123). Routledge.
Zidenberg, A. M., Dutrisac, S., & Olver, M. (2022). 'No regrets': Public perceptions of tattooed mental health professionals. *Professional Psychology: Research and Practice, 53*(3), 304.

4 Pre-Counselling Skills

The helping process involves appropriate communication between the counsellor and the client. According to Egan (1990), communication skills are essential tools at every stage of the counselling process and help to develop and augment the client-counselling relationship. A counsellor needs to be in '*conscious communication*' with the client. When communication is '*conscious*', the person is wholly present with the client, and this presence is '*in the moment*' (Lewis, 2009). In conscious communication, an individual is not only aware of his/her feelings and expressions but can get a complete understanding of the perspective of the person he/she is talking to. Conscious communication helps the counsellor in responding accurately and is supportive of a strong and trustful relationship. Egan (2013) stresses the importance of the counsellor's competence in interpersonal communication, a good interpersonal interaction has four important requirements. The first is *mutual interaction*, wherein both the counsellor and client equally participate. Mutual interaction or mutual conversation helps the counsellor understand the client's problem, and the client get a space to express his/her concerns. Mutual interaction not only prevents the counsellor from overpowering the client but also stops the client from rattling. The second requirement of a good interpersonal interaction is a *mutual connection*, wherein the responses of the counsellor and the client complement, and the alliance is productive. The third requirement is *mutual influence*, wherein the counsellor can bring in new learning to the client through social influence, and at the same time, both are open to new learning. The fourth requirement is *creating beneficial outcomes*. Here the counsellor's role as a facilitator helps the client to find solutions to the problem and accomplish goals, which is a beneficial outcome for the client. In a counselling context, these communication skills are called 'micro-skills' or the units of communication and are considered to be the foundations for the development of a trustful goal-oriented relationship between the counsellor and the client. Communication skills are described differently in various models of counselling. While Carkuff's model (1987) describes communication skills as pre-processing skills, Ivey and Ivey (2013) call it a micro-skill approach, the RUC model and the five stage DASIE models by Nelson & Jones (2000), are the lifeskills model of counselling, and Egan (1990), on the other hand, describes them as basic communication skills. According to Egan (1990), basic communication skills or micro-skills are tools to enhance the relationship and help clients deal with problems and achieve their goals. Carkuff, Egan's, and Ivey's models have the micro-skills entrenched into the attending skills, which are the first step in the helping model of counselling. Box 4.1 describes the basic models of counselling and how each of these models describes the skills required for the counselling process.

While the skills in the first few stages of all the three models are the basic skills, the later stages of the models are oriented towards focusing, understanding, and getting clarity

DOI: 10.4324/9781003459415-4

Box 4.1 A Comparison of the Basic Counselling Skills in Carkuff, Ivey, and Egan's Models of Counselling

Carkuff's Model	*Ivey & Ivey model*	*Egan's Model*
1. Counsellor Attending: physical attending, observing, learning client involvement 2. Counsellor responding: responding to meaning, feeling, and content Client exploring self and self-experience 3. Counsellor personalising: personalising meanings, goals. Internalising experience Client's understanding of the goals 4. Counsellor initiating: defining goals, planning, implementation, and action Client: participate in goal defining, and planning. Act to accomplish goals 5. Feedback: recycling, understanding, and action	1. Attending and empathy: these are at the base level and are beneficial to use at every stage of counselling 2. Observation skills 3. The basic listening skills comprise: questioning, observation, encouraging, paraphrasing, summarising, and reflection of feelings. 4. Focusing: contextualising the client's story, empathetic confrontation, or challenging 5. Influencing skills: a reflection of meaning, interpretation, reframing, and self-disclosure 6. Skills for integration: application of the skills in theories and interventions	1. Attending 2. Listening 3. Empathy understanding feeling, meaning, and behaviour 4. Probing and summarising: nudging, focusing, and direction 5. Challenging, accurate empathy and self-disclosure 6. Leverage or focusing 7. Goal-setting and decision making 8. Strategies for action 9. Termination

about the client's problem and influencing the client's feelings, behaviour and thoughts, and getting the clients to an *action* mode. The skills in these steps help the client understand and state the problem in meaningful terms, get a new perspective, and move towards a commitment to solving the issue. Hutchinson, (2014), on the other hand, has differentiated these skills as skills for developing relationships and skills for deepening relationships. The skills stated in all the above models are a framework to guide the counsellors for easy progression. The counsellor can integrate the therapies and interventions into all these models to help the client. Egan (2014) extends by stating that the model is an open framework wherein there is a scope for incorporating and integrating the therapies, techniques, and interventions. Counsellors under training must understand that it is important to

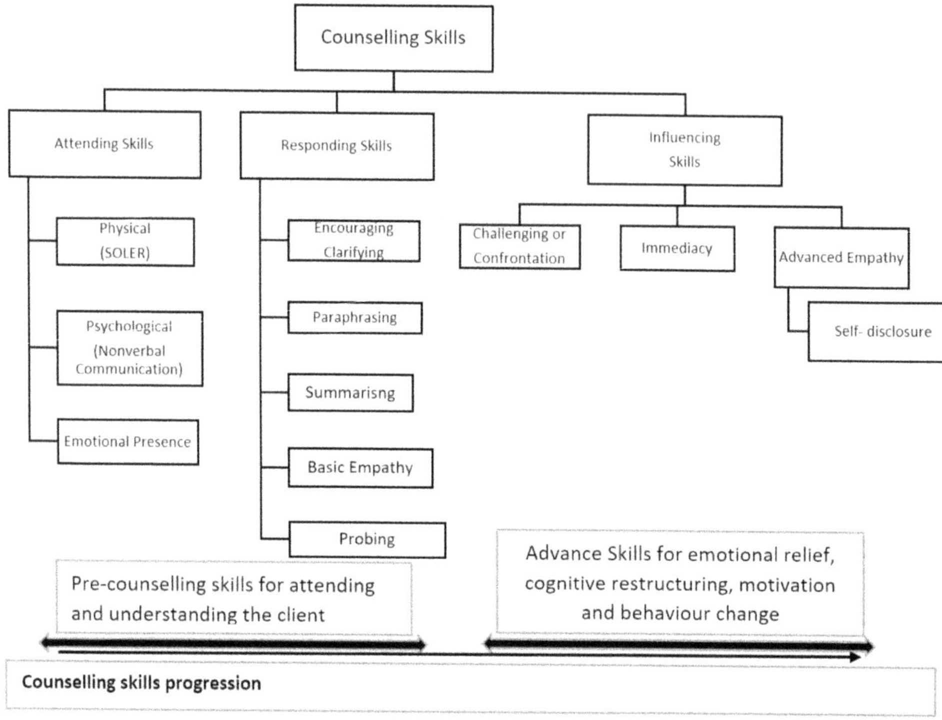

Figure 4.1 Basic Counselling Skills: Progression from Attending and Understanding

gain competency in each of the skills to effectively help the client. While the basic counselling skills, stated as the pre-counselling skills in this unit are important not only in the initial process of building a therapeutic relationship, but their use is significant at every step or stage of counselling. The influencing skills, also known as advanced skills, will be discussed in the next chapters of this book. In the next section, we will be exploring the pre-counselling skills and their usage and practice in the counselling process. Figure 4.1 gives a diagrammatic representation of the basic counselling skills.

Attending Skills

We often hear people saying – 'the doctor is attending to the patient', 'The lawyer is attending to his client before the court meeting', or 'I am attending a spiritual discourse'. Looking at these statements, we can understand how common the word attending is. While attending commonly means focusing, being present at, or taking part in, the term attending has a great significance in counselling. In simple terms, attending in counselling specifically means being with the client and giving full attention to what they are saying or doing. Egan (1991) describes attending as the 'physical and psychological presence' with the client. When the counsellor is physically available, the client can *observe the presence,* and when the counsellor is psychologically available, the client can *experience the presence.* While attending, both physical and psychological presence are equally important for the counsellor and the client.

Attending, in simple terms, means *simply being there* for someone who is in need. It can be as simple as extending a helping hand to someone who fell from a bicycle or being beside someone who is sick and is in the hospital. Let's see this example: Sasha lost her father after he was infected with the COVID virus. Her friend Nandita felt that her presence was required. She just went and stayed by Sasha's side to comfort her. Though not many words were spoken between them, the emotional and physical presence helped Sasha in her time of grief. Clients who seek help are distressed, worried, and confused. When a client is in such a state of pain and anguish, the counsellor's unconditional presence, which includes being with the client physically and psychologically (Bradford, 2007), gives the client undistracted and undivided attention. As stated by Geller and Greenberg (2012), attending is being there with the client on multiple levels or investing one's 'whole', this includes being there for the client physically, psychologically, cognitively, and spiritually. An unconditional presence which includes an open, perceptive, and receptive presence, has one of the most powerful and immeasurable effects on the therapeutic process (Nanda, 2009).

As described earlier, attending skills include the physical and psychological presence of the counsellor. These have been defined by authors in different ways. For example, Egan (1990) explains attending skills as a visible tuning to the client's needs and describes them as the micro-skills of attending. Egan uses the acronym SOLER to explain physical attending in a simple manner, where S: sitting squarely, O: open posture, L: lean forward, E: Eye contact, and R: relaxed posture. Ivey and Ivey (2013) views attending behaviour as the most critical phase of counselling. The authors explain communication of attending using an equation:

Attending = 3v's + B

The 3 Vs include:

- visual contact (facial expressions, eye contact)
- vocal quality (tone of voice, pitch, tonal quality)
- verbal tracking (the content, the words used)

and B is the body language (body posture, gestures).
Attending includes physical attending or visibly tuning, non-verbal communication, and the quality of presence.

Physical Attending

Physical attending is all about how the counsellor demonstrates physical presence through body posture or physical orientation. The counsellor's posture indicates the quality of involvement with the client. The posture includes the counsellor's sitting position, the distance between the counsellor and the client, and the quality of presence. Figure 4.2 shows the seating position in counselling.

In a counselling setting, the physical setting, the distance between the counsellor and the client, the seating arrangement and the ambience of the room are considered to be vital.

1. Physical distance and touching*:* The physical setting of the room has an impact on the client. An environment can be arousing or non-arousing for a client. According to the Mehrabian-Russell stimulus-response model, a moderately arousing environment

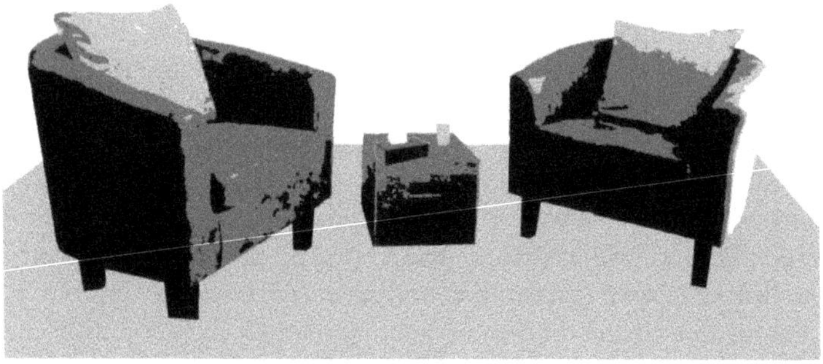

Figure 4.2 The Counselling Setting

is recommended to help the client feel relaxed and get an insight into his problem (Mehrabian, 1976). These include the design of the room, the ambiance, the lighting, the seating arrangement and the noise level. Paying attention to the multicultural perspective is an important consideration while planning the physical setting; the setting should be non-threatening and preferably devoid of objects, pictures, or items that can lead to cultural prejudices. Barriers like a table or a desk between the counsellor and the client, reduce the openness and create a block between them. Moreover, it increases formality and affects the emotional distance between the counsellor and the client. An accessible and barrier-free environment is associated with an increased perception of empathy (Pressly and Heesacker, 2001). A barrier-free setting where there are no physical barriers between the counsellor and client should be considered.

To conclude, the physical setting should be comfortable and non-threatening, where privacy and confidentiality are maintained. Regardless of the physical setting, it is a universal requirement that the sessions should be uninterrupted by phone calls or people walking in and out. For complete self-disclosure, auditory and visual privacy is mandatory (Benjamin, 1987; Shertzer & Stone, 1980).

2. Distance between the helper: An optimum distance of 4–5 feet is recommended between the counsellor and the client. Maintaining such a distance will help prevent proximity anxiety and intimidation in the client. Clients often feel edgy and pressurised when the counsellor faces them straight. To reduce this feeling of intimidation, a slightly turned or a 5 o'clock position is preferable. The position is called '*facing squarely*', and this position helps to avoid a direct stare (Figures 4.2 and 4.4). The slightly angular position helps the counsellor to look at the client directly and at the same time, not in a threatening manner, this setting also helps in reducing the dominant position of the counsellor. The counsellor must understand that angles or positions are designed for the comfort of the client; what is more important is the quality of presence and communication that says 'I am there for you'.

Psychological Attending

Psychological attending is attending to the verbal and non-verbal communication of the counsellor and the client. Psychological attending involves observation and understanding of the client's verbal and non-verbal communication and at the same time counsellor's own awareness of his/her verbal and non-verbal behaviour. Psychological attending is all about connecting to the phenomenological field of the client, which helps the client to get an understanding that the counsellor is there for him/her.

Open Posture

Imagine you are talking to a friend about a serious issue that has been bothering you. You are completely involved in your story and are sharing it with your friend, but you find her shut and slouched. She is crossed-armed, fidgeting, her head is tilted to a side, and she is clicking a pen in her hand and shaking her leg. You understand that your friend is not interested in your problem; you find her closed and uninvolved (Figure 4.3). One's body posture gives an insight into whether the individual is attentive and interested in taking the dialogue or the conversation forward. An open posture is used to communicate that one has an openness and interest in attending, and indicates a willingness to listen. An erect, open posture with an open torso indicates non-defensiveness, and signifies readiness for interaction (Figure 4.3). Keeping arms beside your body or folded on the lap communicates involvement; crossing arms indicates defensiveness or being closed off, and expanded arms may point out that the counsellor is commanding and impends the client. Grounded feet and pointing the feet towards the client are considered to be an open posture and show willingness and attention. Sitting cross-legged indicates less involvement, hence may show a lack of interest in some cultures, which may send signals of negation and repudiation, while the same posture may demonstrate confidence, dominance, and a relaxed attitude in some other cultures. It is important that the counsellor uses his/her discretion and adopts the right posture. Some authors consider posture synchrony or posture congruence as a significant body orientation (Maurer & Tindall, 1983). Posture congruence is stated as 'mirroring the client's position' or adopting the client's posture. Studies have shown that when there is greater synchrony in the counsellor's and client's posture, the rapport between them increases (Tickle-Degen & Rosenthal, 1990; Sharpley

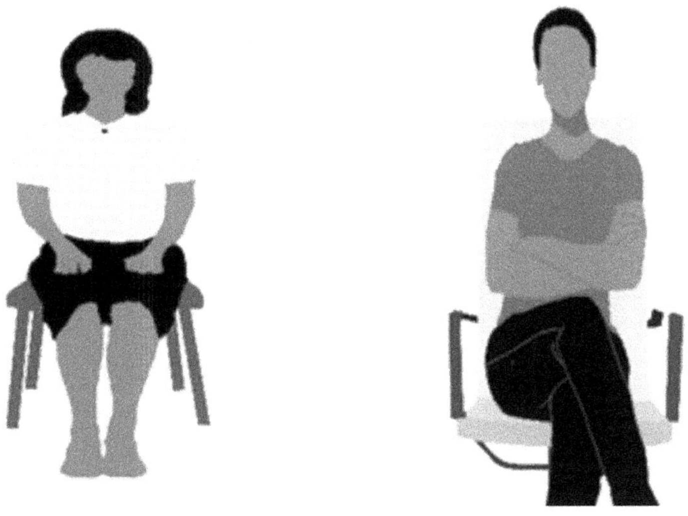

Figure 4.3 Open and Closed Body Posture

et al., 2001). Maurer and Tindall (1983) further add that posture congruence increases the perceived empathy in clients.

Lean Forward

When a group of friends have a discussion, and when the topic is of interest, unconsciously, some of them lean forward and listen. This body posture indicates an interest in the topic being discussed. Leaning forward is a sign of readiness to participation in the discussion, conveys trust and influences the client to talk. Leaning forward with a slight bend in the upper torso is a sign of involvement, Egan (1990) refers to it as bodily flexibility and adds that bodily flexibility demonstrates mental flexibility. While leaning forward gives the client a sense that the counsellor is ready to listen, leaning too forward may create a sense of anxiety or may frighten the client, and imply an entry into the personal space of the client. Hall's (1966) proxemic theory suggests that humans are culturally patterned, and cultural frameworks are used to define and outline one's space, which is internalised in people at an unconscious level. Violation or crossing of this space may create a barrier or failure in communication.

Relaxed and Natural Behaviour

Counsellors should be sensitive to the client's needs, but at the same time, they should feel relaxed and comfortable in understanding these needs by displaying a natural style. The counsellor's body itself is a vehicle of expression (Egan, 1990), by exhibiting a relaxed posture, the counsellor not only conveys that he/she is at ease but also sends a message of willingness to listen. A relaxed posture is one where the counsellor is not fidgeting or edgy, or anxious. A relaxed posture conveys to the client that 'Sitting before you is a person who will take all the emotional outbursts'. Figure 4.4 depicts a typical counselling

Figure 4.4 SOLER

setting where the counsellor is in an open posture, slightly leaning forward. There is eye contact between the client and the counsellor is in a relaxed state.

Eye Contact

The eyes are often called '*the windows to the soul*' and reveal plenty of information about an individual's feelings and thinking. In any conversation, healthy and direct eye contact is an indication of readiness to listen and engage in a conversation. Let's take this example: Pranay, an 11-year-old boy, comes running to his mother who is working in the kitchen, to share how he presented his project in his school and how he was appreciated by his principal, teachers, and friends. While sharing his joy, he finds his mother completely involved in her work and not looking at him. He holds his mother's face, turns her head towards him, looks into her eyes, and asks, 'Are you listening?' His mother says, 'Yes' She looks at Pranay for a few seconds and turns back to her work. Pranay continued to talk, but after some time, he paused and kept silent. His mother again looked at him and said, 'I am listening', and returned to her work. Pranay is angry and upset. He had come to his mother to share his achievements, but his mother was not giving him the attention he wanted. He left the kitchen disappointed, and all the excitement with which he had when he came to share his joy with his mother died down. The above example shows how eye contact is vital in communication. Had Pranay's mother stopped her work, made eye contact, and listened to what her son had to say, she would have made her presence felt for her son and conveyed her interest and attention; as a result, Pranay would have shared all his feelings and experiences. Eye contact is a simple way of saying, 'I am with you'; or 'I am listening to you'. Looking away from the person and not maintaining eye contact indicates a lack of interest, lack of confidence, or feeling uncomfortable about a topic. Though eye contact is considered an important micro skill to build a rapport between the counsellor and the client, one must be cautious about the intensity of eye contact. In a situation where the client is disclosing some part of their life story that they feel will be judged by the counsellor or sharing a story will lead to a negative outcome, an intense eye contact may leave the client anxious or apprehended, as clients may think that they are being stared or gazed. It is essential that counsellors take the necessary precautions about the frequency, length, and intensity of eye contact. The cultural connotation of eye contact has been a point of discussion. Studies show that in Western culture, eye contact is considered to be a sign of confidence and interest and is an important component of social interaction (Argyle et al., 1986), while in some Asian/ Eastern cultures looking into the eyes of elders and speaking, is a sign of disrespect or disobedience towards elders or an authority figure (Sue & Sue, 1990; Watson, 1970). Eye contact can vary based on the context. It was found that eye contact was better during listening than speaking (Hessels et al., 2019), suggesting that speech affects eye contact. Yet in another study, when cognitively challenging questions were asked, mutual gaze was found to be less in Eastern participants than in Western (McCarthy et al., 2008). Current studies, however have also looked into the cultural differences in mutual eye contact among Eastern Asians and Western Caucasians, showing that Eastern Asians engaged in eye contact for a longer period of time than Western Caucasians while telling a story, and both cultures had a mutual eye gaze while speaking and listening (Haensel et al., 2022). The study suggests that contextual factors should be considered to understand eye contact. Differences in cultural variables may manifest the eye contact patterns, and counsellors need to consider these influences. However, Wainwright (2010) has put forward some universal rules of eye contact (Box 4.2), and these principles can be applied in any context.

Box 4.2 Universal Principles of Eye Contact

1. Eye contact
   - too much indicates: disobedience, superiority feelings, and threat
   - too little indicates: inattentiveness, dishonesty, nervousness, or anxiety
2. People have steady eye contact when
   - there is mutual interest in the conversations
   - comfortable with the topic of discussion
   - one is trying to influence the other
   - interest in the other person
3. People have less eye contact when
   - the topic of discussion is uneasy
   - they do not like the person
   - they are not interested in the person
   - they feel overpowered by the other person
   - they want to avoid communication

Tone and Pitch

Apart from the spoken words, the delivery of the words or sentences is an important aspect of any communication. The way the counsellor uses his/her voice impacts the clients. The right intensity of speaking or voice conveys warmth, clarity, respect, and genuineness. The tone, pitch, inflexion, speed of speaking, pause, silence, and fluency communicate the emotional state of the counsellor.

For example, let us see the instructions given by Sudhir (the Director) to Madhu (his assistant)

Sudhir: (puts the file on the table) 'I want you to complete this work before you leave'.

The meaning of the sentence can change based on the tone and pitch, and inflection. If Sudhir pitches the words '*I want you to complete*' and '*before you leave*', the message conveyed will be harsher. The research adds that counsellor should be able to convey empathy through a calm, relaxed, and clear voice.

Touch

This has not been discussed in many of the models as it is open to interpretation. Though touch has a sensitive angle about its use, it does communicate concern and care in situations of grief or crisis. If used precisely, it can have a positive influence on the client and enhance the bonding between the counsellor and the client (Driscoll, Newman, & Seals, 1988). Stickley (2011) introduced a model on the basis of the SOLER framework and proposed the acronym 'SURETY', where S stands for 'sitting at an angle'; U stands for 'uncrossed legs and arms'; R stands for 'relax'; E stands for 'eye contact'; T stands for 'touch', and Y stands for 'your intuition'. He proposed the model for the nursing population, which includes the appropriate use of touch and also emphasises on the individual's intuition. Though there are no ethical guidelines for the use of touch in therapy, it is important to understand that touch should be appropriate to the situation. For example, touch can be used for grounding the client or to bring him/her back from an overwhelming state to the present moment. For a client who has been crying for a long time and is in an uncontrollably overwhelming state, a slight touch on the knee or shoulder can comfort the client (Zur & Nordmarken, 2011). However, counsellors must be aware that touch may also lead to expression of greater intimacy and sometimes convey a negative message to the client. Appropriate use of touch has an impact on the client however the counsellors can use their discretion in the use of touch in a counselling session.

Silence

Silence often makes communication uncomfortable. Counsellors who are new to the field often try to rush up to fill up the discomfort of silence. Counsellors feel they need to support or make the client speak and end up either in an inappropriate response or they do not give the client time to respond at his or her pace. The client may sometimes value silence and not want to rush. They may want to think about what they want to say or how they want to say it. Interrupting silence tends to reduce the disclosure of personal feelings that clients may want to share. Crowding the client with an immediate response during silence may interrupt the client from processing their thoughts. Cormier (2016) categorised silence as 'helper induced silence' and 'client induced silence'. The former is seen when the counsellor intentionally remains silent either to get some time to process and comprehend the information received from the client or because the counsellor does not get the right words to respond, it can also be because the counsellor has decided to deliberately remain silent in order to be less active and give the client time to reveal and get an insight. The reasons for client-induced silence can be intentional when the client tries to avoid speaking about issues because of discomfort or deflect attention, or it is a result of the client getting a new insight into his problem and taking time to process the understanding.

Silence should be taken as a tool to help the client focus rather than using it to direct a session and if used judiciously, has the same effect as an encourager. Silence, when used in the right way, has the following advantages:

- It demonstrates the capacity of the counsellor to attend and to listen to the client. Silence plays a receptive role and provides the client an opportunity to gear up and speak about the problem or focus on the area that is troubling him/her.
- Silence is useful in dealing with clients who are reluctant, by remaining silent the counsellor gives time and space for the client to open up and speak.
- Silence sometimes motivates the client to speak. Silence conveys a message that the client is significant and worthy, and he or she will be heard. For a client who cannot articulate well, silence also gives a space to speak.
- Silence has a reflective use; by using silence, the counsellor provides an opportunity for the client to clarify or sort out his/her thoughts and feelings.

- Silence can be used for inquiring or probing. When the client speaks about his story, silence from the counsellor helps the client to get deeper into his thoughts, process them and give the appropriate information and become more focused.
- Silence is very helpful when both the client and counsellor are cognitively and emotionally fatigued. It gives a breather to both to get on to the next phase.

Listening and Responding Skills

> *So when you are listening to somebody, completely, attentively, then you are listening not only to the words but also to the feeling of what is being conveyed, to the whole of it, not part of it.*
>
> Jiddu Krishnamurti

Before we understand the importance of listening in counselling, let us differentiate between hearing and listening. Hearing is an autonomic brain response and requires no effort. We keep hearing many sounds, but we ignore them unless we really have a need to hear those sounds. Listening, on the other hand, is more active, focused, voluntary, and intentional. The listener not only pays attention to the story narrated by the speaker but also pays attention to the use of words, language, voice modulations, and context to which is related. Rogers (1980) named listening as one of the most potent forces for change. When someone actually listens to us, we feel comforted and reassured. Think of a situation when someone told you, 'You're not listening to me'. Go back in the timeline and think about why you were accused of not listening or what state were you in that you were not able to completely listen to what the person was telling you. There could be many reasons for not listening to the person: you didn't pay attention, hence you didn't receive and process the information; you were not interested in the conversation; you were preoccupied with something more important; or you felt that whatever the person was telling you was not worth listening. Whatever may be the cause, you didn't listen to the person. Now you can also recall times when you felt wonderful simply because someone who means something to you stood or sat with you and really listened. Conversely, you also can remember instances in which you felt frustrated because someone close to you was inattentive and distracted when you wanted to share an important incident. Listening is a basic skill that commences at the time the client comes to the counselling session. It involves attending, hearing, and understanding the verbal and non-verbal messages sent by the client. The client pours out a volume of messages, out of which some may be highly relevant to the context, some may be cues for future understanding, and some may also be irrelevant. Counsellors need to listen to every cue and clue presented by the client, sort out the information, and decide what will add to build the hypothesis for the case and what has to be omitted.

The skills of listening and responding are

- Active listening
- Encouragers
- Paraphrasing
- Summarising
- Basic empathy or reflection of feeling

Active Listening

Listening is considered to be a prerequisite to a helping relationship. Neukrug and Schwitzer, (2006) call it the best method to collect information without the need for questioning. Listening in a counselling scenario is called active listening, which has a price; it heals, it helps clients ventilate, and helps the client feels understood and valued. In active listening, the counsellor is actively involved in the communication process, which helps the counsellor get an understanding of what is being said, and what is not being said. Active listening is one of the most important facilitative conditions. It comprises suspending one's thoughts, desires, and judgement and existing for the other person. Active listening helps establish trust and encourages the client to open up and talk without any fears and filters. This, in turn, helps gather valuable information and aids the counselling process. Active listening aids in understanding the client's story, connecting the bits and pieces of information given by the client, and understanding the client's strengths and weaknesses. Egan (1990) advocates that counsellors often fail in their listening skills. The reasons for this failure are that counsellors only hear and don't listen, they interrupt the clients, speak more than required, or do not accurately listen to the content and feelings of the client.

In any interaction, the listener needs to be consciously and emotionally involved, and this involvement should be perceived by the client (Bodie, 2011). Bodie defined the above as Active-Empathetic Listening, which includes three aspects: *sensing, processing*, and *responding*. In *sensing,* the counsellor attends to the verbal and non-verbal cues presented by the client; *processing* involves remembering, integrating, and understanding the meaning and emotions of the words spoken by the client; and *responding* involves communicating that the client is understood the client's perspective.

Active listening comprises listening and understanding the client's messages. These messages could be verbal, as told by the client, non-verbal, as expressed by the client or hidden, as untold by the client. The components of active listening are presented in Box 4.3 and the following text gives an explanation.

Box 4.3 Components of Active Listening

a. Listening and understanding the client's verbal messages
b. Observing and interpreting the client's non-verbal behaviour
c. Listening to clients' strengths, opportunities, and resources
d. The context or the milieu
e. Listening to breaches and gaps
f. Reflective Listening

a. *Listening and understanding the client's verbal messages*: Clients come to counsellors with their issues, often called a story in a counselling situation. Listening helps in bringing out this story (Ivey et al.,1993). The stories are descriptions of their experience, feelings, and behaviour. Let us take this example:

Client: *I failed to clear the civil service examination. This is the third time I failed. I have been preparing for almost three years. I am avoiding going home because I can't face my parents. I haven't lived up to their expectations, and I feel ashamed and frustrated.*

The client's narration talks about how he failed to clear his civil services examination for the third time (*experience*), how he is avoiding meeting his parents (*behaviour*), and how he feels ashamed and frustrated (*feelings*). The content of the client's story includes the client's experience, behaviour and feelings.

Experiences: Experiences of the clients tell us about what the clients are doing or have done in the past; experiences talk about the situations, which may or may not be in the client's control; experiences also talk about the people involved in the client's story and how the clients focus on whether they or the people around them are responsible for the problem. When clients relate their experiences, they may focus on their achievements, problems, failures, or sometimes even see themselves as victims. It is important that counsellors listen to the narration and understand the experiences of the clients because when these experiences are rightly identified, the counsellors can address the genuine concerns of the client. The following statements are examples of experiences

Client: *I was unable to sleep last night as I and my husband, had an argument regarding my work timings.*

Client: *My daughter is all by herself now. She doesn't talk to the family members and doesn't participate in family get-togethers. She just stays in her room all the time. I am upset with her behaviour and I am wondering if there is something seriously wrong.*

Client: *There are too many people visiting our house every other day, and I am unable to concentrate on my office work.*

Client: *I injured my back, and the treatment is quite expensive; I don't think I have the finances to go for the treatment.*

Client: *The cynical comments by my boss keep bothering me. I am unable to keep them off from my mind.*

Behaviour: Behaviour is a response, reaction, or action taken by the individual towards a person, a particular situation, or a stimulus. Most of these responses or reactions help the individual to resolve or get out of the problem or the disturbing situation. Behaviours can be categorised into three types: the action approaches, such as taking medication for an illness, preparing for an examination, or going to see a therapist; the emotional approaches, like for example crying, throwing objects when angry, hostility, arguing, aggression or impulsivity; and the avoidance strategies like withdrawal, emotional restraint, procrastination, escaping situations, social isolation, use of alcohol or drugs, daydreaming. The behaviour responses are explained with some examples:

Client: *I'd rather stay back at my office and go home late; at least I don't have to hear all the bickering from my wife.*

Client: *My daughter came home very late last night; when her father questioned her, she started arguing with him, she was very aggressive and spoke rudely, and when he followed her to her room, she banged the door on him.*

Client: *I lost Saha last year; she was everything to me. We had such a good time in the short period of our marriage. The day passes off with all the work at the office, but the evenings and nights are haunting, so I started drinking.*

Feelings: Feelings are conscious, intense, and enduring reactions to the emotional state. They are the subjective responses to a situation and vary from person to person, and the subjective responses can be based on how the individual interprets the event or the situation. According to Egan (2013), feelings give a colour to the client's emotional and behavioural state. Given below are some examples of feeling responses:

Client: *My entire day goes in either doing the day-to-day chores at home or the work in my office, but at the end of the day, no one appreciates me; it's so disgusting.*
Client: *My daughter has been coming home late these days; when I ask her, she says she is in the library studying, I know she is lying, and I am worried about her.*

Clients' stories are a combination of their experiences, behaviour, and feelings, they present their problems in unique ways and the expression of their experience, behaviour and feelings are not always clear. They may narrate the story in bits and pieces, without order or structure, with an emotional outburst, with blurred emotions or feelings, hidden messages, and vague statements, or they may be totally numbed. Clients may not be able to talk about their feelings or emotions, but it may be observed in their non-verbal behaviour or in the way they present the story. Whatsoever the state of the client, it is the responsibility of the counsellor to listen to and understand the client. Counsellors understanding of the core messages and themes, identifying the feelings and emotions, and conveying this understanding to the client will help the client describe their missing experiences and identify their feelings and emotions. The latter part of this chapter and the following chapters will explain the above in detail.

b. Listening to, observing, and interpreting the client's non-verbal behaviour:

> *Fie, fie upon her!There's language in her eye, her cheek, her lip, Nay, her foot speaks; her wanton spirits look out At every joint and motive of her body.*
>
> William Shakespeare (Troilus and Cressida)

The above lines from William Shakespeare describe how an individual's face and body are powerful communicative tools. Albert Mehrabian's 7-38-55 Communication Model (1971) describes how the non-verbal component of communication has a more powerful impact compared to the accompanying verbal behaviour. According to the model, only 7% of the expression of feelings and attitudes takes place through words, 38% takes place through the tone and voice, and the remaining 55% is through facial expressions, body, and gestures (see Figure 4.5).

When non-verbal behaviours are such important components of communication, it is imperative that counsellors develop a capacity to distinguish various non-verbal behaviours of the clients and their probable connotations. The need to recognise these behaviours is explained in Box 4.4.

The importance or power of non-verbal messages has been explained in Box 4.4, nonetheless, these messages can also be combined with verbal messages to get a better understanding of the client's issue. Non-verbal messages are interrelated and can complement or support each other (Knapp & Hall, 1992).

Non-Verbal Messages as Modifiers of Verbal Messages

1. Repetition: Non-verbal behaviour is said to reinforce verbal behaviour. For example, when the counsellor asks, 'Did your friend greet you when you met him last time?' The client may say *'yes'* and at the same time nods his head, or for example, the counsellor may ask the student, 'Did you argue with your teacher in the class yesterday?' The student may say 'no' and *nod* his head.

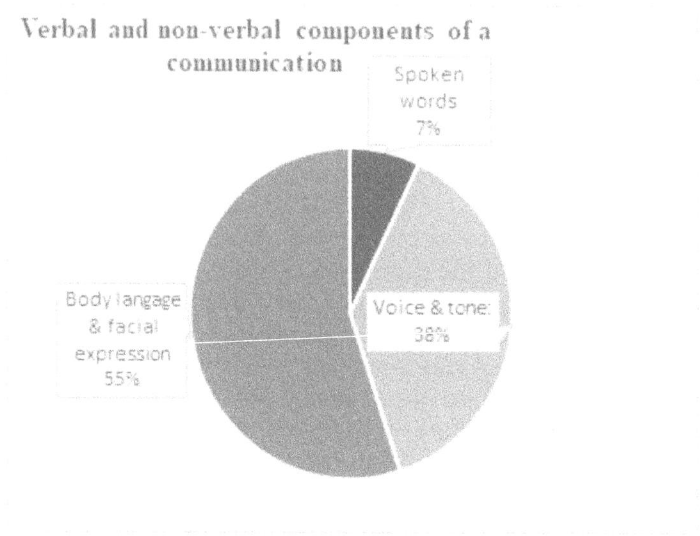

Figure 4.5 Verbal and Non-Verbal Components of Communication

> **Box 4.4 Power of Non-Verbal Behaviour**
>
> Non-verbal behaviours are:
>
> 1. Expression of oneself
> 2. More spontaneous than verbal behaviour
> 3. Clues to emotions and feelings
> 4. Concealed or hidden to the client but obvious to the counsellor
> 5. Leakages to verbal behaviour, hence can give a complete understanding of the clients' behaviour
> 6. Not sent intentionally so the right meaning can be elicited by the counsellor

2. Contradiction: In many instances, the non-verbal and verbal messages contradict each other. Awareness about this aspect will help the counsellor become cognisant of the relation between what the client has said verbally and the unintentional non-verbal message of the client. For example:

   Client: *My father really cares for me.*

   But while saying this, if the client frowns, grinds her teeth, or clenches her fists, the client is sending a different meaning.
3. Substitution: Non-verbal expressions become a substitution for verbal communication. For example:

Counsellor:	*You must have had a good time with your husband; you both got some time to spend together after a long gap.*
Client:	Smiles and has a gleam in her eyes. Both these non-verbal expressions are a substitute for verbal communication *Yes, I did, and I cherish those moments.*

Accents: Non-verbal messages can be used to convey the intensity of emotion that is expressed in verbal communication. The verbal message can get stronger, along with the non-verbal message. For example Payal, who is not allowed to go to a late-night party with her friends, may shout back at her parents and, at the same time, clench her fist and start hitting the wall:

Counsellor to the student:	*Did you argue with your teacher in the class yesterday?*
Student:	*No*. The student may raise his head, and frown

Such non-verbal messages make the verbal message stronger and have a higher impact.

4. Complementation: Non-verbal messages also help clients to convey uncomfortable verbal messages or messages they want to avoid talking about, and sometimes non-verbal messages are used to emphasise the meaning of the verbal message. For example, if a client is uncomfortable sharing an incident that may be traumatic, he/she may fumble and then remain silent, avoid eye contact, or bend his/her head and remain calm. In another case, a student who has got the news that she is being awarded a gold medal may say, 'I am so happy and excited', and immediately jump with joy and hug her mother.
5. Regulation: Some of the non-verbal messages help to regulate verbal messages or regulate the flow of the conversation. For example, when the client is speaking to the counsellor, and the counsellor nods her head as an affirmation that she is listening, the client will continue to talk; on the other hand, if the counsellor turns away her head or starts looking at her watch, it would indicate that the counsellor wants to end the conversation.
6. Deceiving: Some non-verbal cues purposefully disguise or mislead the counsellor. A client may be talking about his breached relationship with his wife with a smile on his face. Or the client may say that he is not upset about what is happening between him and his wife but his tone may be low.

c. *Listening to clients' strengths, opportunities, and resources*: Rogers, in his client-centred theory, pronounces that every individual is purposive, forward-looking, progressive, has an innate potential, and when this potential is allowed to unfold, there can be a change in the personality. Captivating this aspect of Rogers' theory, one can say that the client who comes for counselling with unresolved issues has the potential strength and capability to resolve the issue. The counsellor is only a medium to help clients identify these strengths and potentials. When encountering problems, clients are in an emotional or traumatic state, and their thoughts are so focused on the problem that they degrade their potential and feel totally exhausted and emotionally drained. It is for the counsellor to listen to the client's story and identify the strengths and resources, which can be tapped at a later stage of counselling to achieve the goals. Optimism, high self-esteem, humour, gratitude, high intellectual capabilities, creativity, self-control, a good friendship network, support from family, and a secure job or finances can be identified as some of the strengths and resources. The following example explains:

Suja: *I have not been able to complete any work on time. I feel I have become very clumsy and disorganised and keep slogging with my work till late in the night. There were days when I had time to relax and read my favourite book before I sleep, but now, by the time I get to bed, I feel half dead. I was very particular about my fitness, diet, and overall personality, but now I lost interest in everything. Neither I am taking care of my health, nor my work or my home. I feel so disgusted with myself.*

The client's statements talk about her organisation skills, her ability to meet deadlines by completing her work on time, and her interest in reading and fitness. The client may have given up on these for some time, but these resources can be tapped if needed during the course of the counselling sessions.

d. *The context or the milieu*: The client gives a fragmented piece of information in the form of verbal and non-verbal messages. But it is important for the counsellor to get a holistic understanding of the client's experiences, behaviour, and feelings in the context of his/her social setting. Context is the background or the situations of the client's life. The social context and the cultural framework have a huge impact on the client's perception of the problem, and the counsellor needs to take the social and cultural context and regional variations into perspective while dealing with the client.

Pratima: *My daughter is not listening to me. My in-laws and husband are very particular about my daughter coming home on time. They don't like her coming home late. I understand that youngsters like to hang around with friends, but my in-laws and husband are from the old school of thought. I am unable to make my daughter understand. I am torn apart between my daughter and my family.*

The client is talking about certain cultural and social aspects which are important to the family. Family values and beliefs need to be taken into consideration while dealing with the client's problem. Getting a holistic understanding of the client's feelings, experiences, and behaviour in the context of his/her social setting gives a larger picture of the client's issues.

Client: *I come from a close-knit family. I am the only daughter of my parents. My parents imbibed a number of values in me. I was taught about the equality of men and women. Two years back, I was married into a rich family. My husband and my in-laws believe that as a daughter-in-law I have to just follow their commands, I have no role in any of the decisions made in the family. I have no identity of my own and I feel suffocated.*

- Observe what the client is talking about the social context.
- Look at the background of the client.
- Also, look at the emotional context.

e. *Reflective Listening*: Reflective listening emphasises understanding the accurate message from the client's story. The counsellor here pays attention to the content and the feeling expressed by the client and communicates this understanding to the client. This communication is done by responding and by reflecting on the thoughts, feelings, and non-verbal behaviour. Reflective listening cannot be accomplished unless the counsellor can sense, process, and understand the client's statements. The uses of reflective listening are presented in Box 4.5.

Box 4.5 Reflective Listening

Helps the counsellor *check out* and verify if he/she has accurately understood the client's communication.
Helps the client feel understood.
Gives the client an opportunity to identify emotions and thoughts effectively.
Helps the counsellor and the client to be at the same pace.
Helps the counsellor achieve the outcomes.

f. Listening to breaches and gaps: When a client narrates a story, some of the content may be true and close to reality, and some may be unrealistic assumptions. There may be distortions and contradictions in some of the content of the client's narration.

Client: *I have always been a topper and scored well in my papers. Now I am in this job, but my boss doesn't trust me. He thinks I am not capable of presenting the project in the coming meeting.*

In the above example, there are some gaps in the client's narration; for example, in reality, is the client competent enough to make the presentation? If so, is the client aware of his abilities?

Counsellors must be able to listen to these gaps and breaches, which are a part of clients' experiences. Even though the counsellor identifies these gaps and is cognisant of the fact that the clients understanding or perceptions are not accurate, challenging or confronting the client is done at a later stage. The use of challenging is explained in Chapter 6. Listening to the gaps in the stories helps the client and the counsellor to be grounded and stay close to reality.

Blocks to Listening

Active listening is a skill that can be acquired with practice. Counsellors are bound to get distracted or not pay attention to what the client is saying. There could be many explanations for a counsellor to get unfocused or side-tracked while listening to the clients. The text below explains the reasons for ineffective listening.

Insufficient Listening

Many times, when we listen, we get distracted or get preoccupied with our thoughts. Yet sometimes, when someone is speaking to us, we contemplate some other work that is on our priority list. Whatever the case, we do not pay attention to what the other person is speaking. We may get remarks such as 'Why aren't you listening to me?' Or 'Are you listening to what I am saying?' Lack of interest, fatigue, being distracted or attracted by the client, are some reasons for insufficient listening. Some counsellors may be preoccupied with their own issues, which leaves them emotionally unavailable to the client. Inadequate listening can also be observed in counsellors who are in a hurry to respond to the client and end up either interrupting the client or not listening entirely to the client's issue. The other reason for inadequate listening is the cultural differences between the client and the counsellor. Culturally skilled counsellors or counsellors with multicultural awareness have the knowledge of how one's own cultural background and experiences influence attitudes, values, and biases about psychological processes. They can recognise their sources of discomfort due to the differences that exist between themselves and their clients in terms of race, ethnicity, and culture and work towards resolving these discomforts.

Judgemental Listening

When a person narrates or talks, we often critic as to whether the person is correct or incorrect, whether his/her acts are moral or immoral, or whether his/her behaviour is appropriate or inappropriate. Counsellors, like any other human beings, have a tendency to become judgemental at times. They may find it tough to view an opinion that is unacceptable or against their own morals and values. In such a situation, counsellors get into the mode of advising or moralising the client. According to Egan (2007), it may not always be possible for the counsellor to be non-judgemental, but what can be done is to suspend the judgement for some time and understand the client from his/her perspective.

Amateur Listening

Counsellors in their initial training stage often end up rehearsing or preparing themselves to respond to the client. Egan (2007) adds that some counsellors while thinking about the 'perfect response' end up not listening to the client. Counsellors may have some self-questions, for example, 'The client is so overwhelmed. What kind of response should I give?' or 'What can be my next question?' Cormier (2016) adds that helpers who are frenetic or restless end up in amateur listening because they are either too distracted or too reactive in their approach. Cormier also adds that helpers who are self-centered or self-absorbed are also inattentive and amateur in their listening. They either put across their own ideals and principles to the clients, or they experience too much 'internal noise' that they are emotionally unavailable to the clients.

Responding Skills

Clients come with their stories, and the counsellor attends and listens to the narrations. We have seen how listening helps the counsellor get an understanding of the client's problem; however, it's not just listening; the counsellor's response to what they listened to is also important. Counsellors respond to the clients in different ways: sharing their understanding, checking to make sure that they've got things right, and summarising the issues that were discussed. Responding skills are not only useful in telling the client that he/she has been listened to accurately but also pave the way for making decisions and setting goals. The text below will discuss some of the responding skills listed below:

1. Encouraging
2. Clarification

3. Paraphrasing
4. Summarisation
5. Empathy
6. Probing

Encouraging

Encouragers are verbal and non-verbal prompts by which the client is helped to continue to talk about his thoughts, feelings, and behaviour, with minimum interruption or influence from the counsellor's end. Encouragers have minimal word responses along with non-verbal responses, that help to keep the focus on the client and help the client elaborate on the topic of discussion. Some examples of encouragers are given below.

'Tell me more'; 'Go on' (use hand gestures)
'Um-hum'; 'Uh-huh' (accompanied by a nod of the head)
'OK.......'. 'And......'; 'Then......?'; 'Oh......?'

Repetition of the last few words or two keywords:

Client: *I was trying to be very patient with my daughter, even though she is headstrong and always does what she wants to. Yesterday she came home very late from college. I tried to talk to her and find out if everything was fine but just look at her, she just shouts back and asks me not to interfere. What do I do?*

Counsellor: She shouted back and it upsets you.
Restatements of the exact words used by the client.... *You want to go and talk to her again?*
You are upset about what she said.
Give me an example;
for instance....
And to you, that means......?

Apart from the above facial expression, vocal tone, a smile, and the counsellor's demonstration of care and warmth are effective encouragers. Encouragers, if given on time, help in communicating to the client that he is being listened to and help maintain the flow of the conversation between the client and the counsellor.

Clarification

Clients speak from their internal frame of reference, i.e., they try to see the problem or the issue from their perceptual world, and as a result, the messages are mixed, confusing, and ambiguous. A clarification response from the counsellor will help to make the message explicit. Clarification is the understanding of the content of the message that is conveyed by the client (Dickinson, 2007). It is a basic skill that can be used, especially in the first session, and when the counsellor knows very little about the client. It allows the counsellor to illicit detailed and accurate information from the client. Clarification is used to check the accuracy of the counsellor's perception when the counsellor is not sure of the client's response or wants to verify the response, interpret a statement, or ask the client to elaborate on what he/she has said. A clarification can begin with a phrase, or it can be a question, for example the counsellor can use phrases such as:

> *Tell me if I understand it right..........*
> *Could you explain what you mean by giving up on your son?*
> *You said your relationship with your son is strained. Can you elaborate on that?*
> *Correct me if I am wrong, but you said that your husband doesn't trust you, and yet you believe that he is the best person in your life.*

Clarification responses help the counsellor and the client to precisely understand the message being communicated, help eliminate assumptions and, at the same time, check if any information has not been explored (Cormier, 2016). Clarification has four steps:

1. Identifying the content of the verbal and non-verbal message. Here the counsellor can ask himself/herself, *'What is the client saying?'*
2. Once the counsellor identifies the content, he/she has to check if there are any missing links or vague statements.
3. Choose the required response.
4. Check if the response is accurate or useful.

Hrithik: *My parents still think that I am a kid. They don't trust me and never give me any responsibility, and are always checking on me.*
Counsellor: *You said that your parents always check on you. Could you elaborate on what you mean by 'checking on you'?*

In this example the counsellor is trying to seek more information and elaboration on the vague response *'checking on you'*

Shruti: *I am totally disorganised nowadays; I haven't had a proper routine for the past six months. It is as though I have no control over my life.*
Counsellor: *Your life seems to be quite a mess these days. Am I right?*

In the above example the counsellor is trying to get a clarity if her response was accurate.

Paraphrase

Paraphrasing is rephrasing the client's key words, content, and thoughts. The counsellor responds by choosing the most important details of what the client has just said and reproduces them back to the client, but at the same time, stays focused on the essence of what is being said. When the counsellor responds to the client as a paraphrase, the client often says, *'That's right'*, or validates the response by stating it to be correct or wrong. Ivey et al. (1997) call it the cognitive part of the message, which helps to get the cognitive essence of what the client has said which can include, the description of the situation, the people involved, the events that took place, and so on. The message may also have the affective component or the feeling towards an incident or the person and is known as a reflection of feelings which will be discussed later in the chapter.

1. ***Client:*** *I had enough of this relationship, and I have decided to put an end to it. But I don't understand how I should tell him about it. I don't know what he would do.*

   Counsellor Paraphrase: *It sounds like you haven't found a way to tell your husband that you want to end the relationship because of his possible reaction. Is that right?*

2. ***Client:*** *I ended my relationship with Abhishek last month. There was no dignity in the relationship. I lost my identity altogether. I feel so much better now.*

   Counsellor's Paraphrase: *You feel much better after your break up with Abhishek; it must have been difficult to stay with a person who didn't value you.*

An accurate paraphrase thus has a sentence stem that introduces the paraphrase, for example: *'It seems like....'*, *'From what I see......'*, *'Tell me if I am right.......'*. Some of the sentences are presented in Box 4.6.

The sentence stem is followed by the restatement of the keywords used by the client to describe the situation; the counsellor then presents the essence of what the client said in his/her own words and then checks out for accuracy. Paraphrasing thus helps the counsellor communicate that he/she has understood of the client's story; once there is a communication of the understanding, the client can simplify, focus and crystalise what they wish to say. The client can then further elaborate and discuss the key ideas, events, or behaviours. Paraphrasing not only enhances the focus but also helps to keep the client on track (Cormier, 2016). By getting the essence of the problem through paraphrasing, the counsellor and the client can make decisions regarding the counselling goals.

Box 4.6 Phrases and Sentence Stems for Paraphrasing

- *It seems like*
- *It appears as though*
- *From what I see*
- *Sounds like*
- *From what I hear*
- *Looks like*
- *Tell me if I am right*
- *I sense that*
- *So, you are thinking that*
- *In other words, what you are saying is*
- *So, it's as though*
- *In other words, can I say that*
- *What appears to be coming across*
- *Would it be right if I said?*
- *I have a feeling that*
- *What I seem to be hearing*
- *So, in effect, what you are saying is*

Summarising

While narrating the story, the client comes up with strings of messages, the messages may be vague and ambiguous, or they may be in certain patterns or themes. Summarising involves taking what the client has said over a prolonged period which may be in the form of themes or vague messages, then condensing these key messages and restating them to the client as accurately as possible. The main purpose of summarisation is to check the accuracy of the content, feeling, behaviour, and experience of the client. The following example shows how the counsellor summarises the story narrated by the client in a session.

The client is a young girl who is upset about her parents, who are planning to part ways. Observe her statements during her sessions and note the steps in summarisation

Client at the beginning of the session:

Supriya: *My parents have constant fights, and now they have decided to part ways. I don't understand why they have made this decision.*

Client during the session:

Supriya: *Most of the time, I am the cause of their fights. Maybe I'm the reason they don't want to live together anymore. I wish I could do something to bring them together.*

Note:

a) *the key content*: Wants parents to stay together and key affect: feels sad, upset, responsible
b) *the patterns or themes*: She thinks she is responsible for her parents' separation
c) *use an appropriate sentence stem and verbalise the summarisation response*: Example: 'I sense' or 'You feel'

> *Counsellor's Summarisation: If we can recall, earlier today, you said you didn't know why your parents didn't want to live together. But now I sense that you are holding yourself responsible for their break-up, and this thought is upsetting you.*

d) Assess the effectiveness of the summarisation.

Summarisation can be used to *begin a session*. For example

Counsellor: *Anita, in our last session you spoke about how you felt when your daughter never cared for your words, and you also spoke about how your husband and in-laws support your daughter, and you feel unhappy and upset about it. We decided on some homework too. So how have things been in the past few days.*

Summarisation can be used in the *middle of a session*; for example

Counsellor: *From what we discussed, Anita, I can understand that more than the way your daughter responds to you, your main concern is about your*

husband and in-laws' behaviour. You are also annoyed that they discuss you right in front of your daughter. You think that your daughter can be handled better if they support you.

Summarisation can be used at the *end of a session,* for example

Counsellor: *Anita, from what we talked about today, it seems like your entire efforts to bring about a change in your daughter's behaviour are futile. You are frustrated that you don't have any support from your family, and your daughter is taking advantage of that. In spite of all this, you want to continue your efforts because you are concerned about your daughter's future.*

Summarisation thus helps in letting the client know they've been heard and understood. It not only helps the clients to clarify without the counsellor directing them but also helps them get clarity about what's going on. Some of the uses of summarisation are presented in Box 4.7.

Box 4.7 Uses of Summarisation

- To tie together multiple elements of client messages
- To identify a common theme or pattern
- To interrupt excessive rambling
- To start a session
- To end a session
- To pace a session
- To review progress
- To serve as a transition when changing topics

Basic Empathy

In the earlier sections, we have seen how attending and listening responses are strong supporting skills for the counsellor and how these skills enable the counsellor to build trust and get in touch with the client's world. While these skills help the counsellor to attend to, listen, and understand the client's problem, what becomes important is to communicate this understanding to the client. According to Rogers, the most important part of counselling is sensing the acute feeling and meaning experienced by the client and communicating the accurate understanding to the client. The important skill used to communicate this understanding is called empathy. The definition and significance of empathy have been discussed in Chapter 3, but in this section, the importance of empathy as a skill will be discussed in detail.

Empathy comes from the German word '*einfuhlung*' which means 'inner feeling'. In simple terms, to empathise is to recognise or understand another person's emotions, 'put oneself in another's shoes' or 'the ability to see the world through someone else's eyes'. But the expression of empathy is not easy. 'Empathy is the capacity to think and feel oneself into the inner life of another person' Kohut (2009). Kohut adds that understanding a person's inner world is more than what our sensory organs do by seeing, hearing, or touching. A person's inner world can be understood by himself/herself through introspection and can be understood by others through empathy. According to Rogers, when any person is hurt, disturbed, anxious, feels isolated, or has a doubt about his identity or self-worth, then it is important to understand and address the person. Such an understanding is called empathy, and it helps heal and empower the clients and places them in a position to understand their own emotions and the meaning of their experiences. Empathy thus is 'a special way of coming to know another and ourselves, a kind of attuning and understanding'. Rogers (1957) describes empathy as an ability 'to sense the client's "private world" as if it were your own but without ever losing the "as if" quality'. Two important phrases used in the above definition turn out to be the most important facts of empathy. The first phrase, 'private world', includes the individual's deep feelings, thoughts, beliefs, perceptions, and experiences. This inner realm is also called the 'inscape'. Empathy is entering this inscape. By extending empathy, the counsellor makes a metaphysical entry into the client's private perceptual world, a world that is unique and personal to the client, and understands the feelings, perceptions, and experiences in totality. The second phrase, 'without ever losing the "as if" quality', talks about how the counsellor, even while experiencing the client's personal world, maintains the balance by remaining congruent and integrated. In doing so, the counsellor is doing two important things: 1. being sensitive and temporarily connected, experiencing the other person's feelings, and 2. not getting influenced by the emotions of the client by maintaining an external perspective. Box 4.8 gives a simple exercise for counsellors to check their empathy.

According to Rogers (1957), constructive change is more likely to occur when therapists can get to the client's private world, a world that the client feels and experiences. An empathetic presence sends a message that the counsellor is a confident companion to the client and is accompanying the client in his/her search and exploration (Rogers, 1980). To sum up, empathy is entering into the 'other person's world', experiencing the world bit by bit, and moving in the world non-judgementally to understand the experience effectively.

Empathy = attention + listening + communicating your understanding (response)

Empathetic Response

The essential component of empathetic understanding is to imbibe the feelings of the client, which itself becomes a cue for participation. Responding with empathy does not mean seeking information to know the story or to prolong the conversation. It requires accuracy. Missing out on the right feeling, behaviour, or experience and not communicating the understanding will leave the client in discomfort. Below are outlined some prerequisites to responding with empathy.

Prerequisites for Empathetical Responses

Accuracy of perception of the client's feeling and emotions

Case Study 1

Client: *Yesterday, I went to the bank to close one of my accounts, but the concerned person was not in their seat. Once the person came, he said that the server was down and the systems were not working. I waited for almost three hours, but my work wasn't done. It was just a waste of time.*

Counsellor 1:	*You were angry with the way things were going on.*
Client:	*No, I am not angry but see how I wasted the entire morning, and yet the work wasn't done.*
Counsellor 2:	*You were frustrated that your valuable time went in vain, and you couldn't complete the bank work.*
Client:	*Yeah, it's so frustrating when you plan so much for the day, and your entire time is spent unproductively.*

Case Study 2

Client:	*I haven't been well for the past few days. But nobody really cares about me. I have severe pain in my joints, and I am suffering a lot. When I tell this to my son, he thinks I am bluffing.*
Counsellor 1:	*Did you try to talk to your son and explain your condition?*
Client:	*What is the point in talking to him?*
Counsellor 2:	*You feel miserable; on one side, you are suffering with pain, and on the other hand, your son thinks you are making it all up.*
Client:	*Yeah, it's a miserable feeling. I am in so much pain, and how can he think I am bluffing?*

In both the above examples, Counsellor 2 could accurately perceive the client's feelings and experiences.

Counsellors' accurate perception ensures the client that he/she is listened to and understood. This feeling of being understood creates a platform for the client to open up and share. Counsellors basic intelligence, social intelligence, emotional maturity, individual experience, objectivity, listening, being in harmony with the client's emotional experience, being attuned to the client's needs and objectivity help enhance perceptiveness.

Box 4.8 Check your Empathy

Counsellors can use these simple self-assessment questions to check their levels of empathy

- Am I sensitive to other people's issues?
- Before I condemn others, do I try to imagine how I would feel if someone condemned me?
- Are people ready to come and share their problems with me?
- Do I have a concern about what others are going through?
- When someone is in difficulty, am I able to see things from their perspective?
- When I see someone in crisis or difficulty, do I have a strong urge to help them?

Accurate Skill to Communicate Understanding

The second requisite of empathy is the skill of communication. Accurate perception helps the counsellor to be aware of the client's feelings and experiences; once the counsellor has the knowledge of the kind of response called for, he/she will be able to deliver it.

Egan calls it a translation of understanding into words. In the above example, when Counsellor 1 said, 'You are angry,' the client immediately negated it and said, 'No, I am not angry.' Here the counsellor could not interpret the feeling. Precise interpretation of the feeling is an important skill and a vital skill for communicating empathy.

Accurate Assertion

The third requisite is assertiveness. Counsellors' perceptions and knowledge or skill aren't of any use if they are not used rightly. When a counsellor is able to perceive the right feeling and emotions and has the knowledge to translate them into words, he or she should also be able to translate them into a response. Assertiveness is about sharing one's intuitions and hunches with the client without any hesitation. Assertiveness is applicable when there is a need to challenge the client (explained in Chapter 6). If the counsellor is not assertive, he or she hesitates to challenge.

Given the three prerequisites, which are the essential conditions for responding with empathy, Barnett-Lennard (1993) delineated three phases for responding with empathy. A complete empathetic process between a client and a counsellor requires three important phases: *empathetic resonance, empathy received,* and *empathy expressed.* In empathetic resonance, the counsellor actively listens to the client's expression of feelings and experiences. It is an inner process of empathetic listening wherein the counsellor is listening to the clients who are expressing their feelings and experience in their own way. Barnett-Lennard calls it 'active openness in knowing a particular other in their own inside' this phase is followed by 'empathy received' where the counsellor receives and recognises the client's felt experience and meaning, almost similar to the perceptiveness as explained by Egan. The final phase is empathy expressed, which is the counsellor's expression of the empathetic response, where the client is communicated about the counsellor reception of the feelings and experience. This concludes the cycle of responding with empathy. The prerequisites of empathy help in creating a connection between the client and the counsellor and help the client understand that he/she is not alone.

The Formula for Empathetic Response

Responding with empathy is a challenge for counsellors. The challenges are poor attending and listening skills, poor understanding skills, and poor choice of words for communicating empathy. Counsellors demonstrate incorrect empathy responses in their settings. As we have seen that perception of feelings and experience is one of the prerequisites of empathy, Egan (1990) included some elements of empathy to help counsellors respond with empathy. Once the counsellor listens to the core message, the accuracy can be checked using a standard statement or formula which has two parts; the first part labels the feelings the counsellor senses the client is dealing with: excited, overwhelmed, upset, annoyed, confused, and so on (the feelings are variations of the four basic emotions: anger, fear, sorrow, and joy explained in Chapter 5, Box 5.1) and the second part has the key experience, behaviour, and thought of the client which leads to the feeling.

The formula to express empathy comprises:

The feelings: Identify the right feeling from the category of feelings (Chapter 5, Box 5.1) and recognise the intensity of the feeling.

The experience: Note down the experience of the client in the situation that he or she is.
The behaviour: Perceive the behaviour of the client; the behaviour might have further aggravated the problem situation or helped to resolve the problem.
The thought: Perceive the thoughts; the client's thoughts/cognition may have either aroused an emotion or may have evoked a behaviour.

Let's look at the statements for responding with empathy:

You feel......(insert the correct feeling expressed by the client with the right intensity) because............(insert the key experience, behaviour, and thought of the client which leads to the feeling).

You *feel hurt* because *your opinion is not taken in any of the decisions made in the family.*

You feel *dejected* because *you have no support either from your family or from your friends.*

You are *confused* because *both the courses are of your interest and you are unable to decide which one to choose.*

You are *proud* that *you could achieve your goals even though you had no support from your family and you had to manage your work and home all by yourself.*

You are *angry with yourselves* because *you are unable to tell your family that their behaviour hurts you.*

You are *concerned* about *how your daughter is going to manage her new family.*

Examples of empathy:

Example 1

Client: *I have been running pillar to post to complete the formalities for the past two days, and yet I was unable to put up the papers on time. I am sick of this entire system.*

Counsellor: *You feel frustrated because all your efforts of running from one office to the other to complete formalities went in vain, and you couldn't put the papers on time.*

Example 2

Client: *I still remember the day after the divorce. Life seemed so empty and dark. Maybe I wasn't having any feelings. At one moment, I even decided to leave my child in my parent's home and just disappear.*

Counsellor: *Your world seemed to be completely desolated, and you felt totally helpless that you wanted to send your child away and get away from all this.*

Example 3

Client: *For writing an important email or a letter, I always ask my brother to do it for me. I know he gets irritated, but I am afraid I will goof up everything if I do it myself.*

Counsellor: *You've always doubted yourself and been afraid of messing things up, so you thought it is better to play safe by depending on your brother.*

Some authors mention empathy as a reflection of feelings, which is defined as understanding the client's emotions, experiencing them, and communicating this understanding back to the client. The counsellor's reflection includes the *receiver's skills* and the *sender's skills.* The receiver's skills involve the counsellor's understanding of the face, body, verbal and vocal messages. Understand the emotional reactions, context, and underlying meaning of the client's message. The sender's skills involve conveying the message back to the client by picking up the client's feeling words or phrases, using the right feeling word or expression of emotion, using appropriate non-verbal behaviour and finally checking for the accuracy of the understanding. While using the feeling word, it is important to check for the intensity of the client's feeling for example, the word distraught is of a higher intensity emotion than the word upset, which is of moderate intensity. Sometimes clients come up with phrases which need to be labelled as an emotion or come up with mixed feelings two examples are given below

Client: *Finally, it's done. I got all my medical tests done and yesterday I got my reports. All my reports are clear. I feel like a huge weight has come down my head.*

Counsellor: *For the past few days I could sense the anxiety in you. You seemed to so relieved now.*

The counsellor's use of the word relieve is the right expression of the client's phrase '*a huge weight coming down*'.

Client: *I am so happy I got admission to the best university in the US; I don't know how I will stay away from my family.*

Counsellor: *You seemed to have some mixed feelings; on the one hand you are glad that you have got admission to the best university but on the other you are worried about leaving your family.*

In many instances, clients talk at length. They have a number of messages in the one they are stating. Counsellors should pick up the core message and respond. For example:

Client: *Yesterday my boss called me. He never seems to be happy with what I do. He had a list of things to tell me and it was never-ending. I don't know what the real meaning of the meeting. I felt he called me only to point out the mistakes that he thinks I have made, and tells me about how organised he is. I am really fed up with all this. I better resign from the job. I think that's the best solution to my problem.*

Counsellor: *You seem to be frustrated with your boss' behaviour and you think resigning from the job is the only solution to come out of it.*

Responding with empathy includes reflections of accurate feeling and accurate meaning, which not only helps to increase the client's responses but also deepens the relationship. The client unfolds the story, giving the counsellor a chance to explore and understand and take the client closer to the process of change. Effective empathy is nothing but accurate, reliable care which results in an outcome that is favourable to the client.

Probing

Probes are verbal and non-verbal techniques used to assist clients to talk more freely and concretely about an issue and help the clients express their concerns in concrete terms. Probing is a skill that can be used in every stage of counselling and helps the counsellor to begin a session, clarify a statement, get the accuracy of perception, get a leverage, enhance the quality of the information given by the clients. It is a strategy used to bring additional or specific information to the client's story, address an issue that is of utmost importance, encounter blocks, explore goals, and challenge the client to reflect. Probing is also used in the intake and the assessment process. Though probing is an essential skill, it needs to be used judiciously and with caution. Probing need not always be in the form of a question. For example, probes can be in the form of:

- A statement to seek clarification: 'I am not sure I understand what you are saying…'.
- A statement of request: 'Please help me understand what you mean by being confused'.
- Non-verbal: The raising of an eyebrow, leaning forward, or a frown.
- Verbal interjections*:*

Client: *Since yesterday, I have been sensing that everything is 'not as good' as it should be.*
Counsellor: *Not as good?*

- As a question: Questions can be open-ended or closed-ended

Open-ended questions are those which cannot be answered in one or two words. These questions encourage clients to elaborate and provide the maximum information.

1. **Counsellor:** *Could you tell me more about how you felt when your boss insulted you in front of your colleague?*
   Client: *I was dismayed by the way she was supporting my colleague. How can she insult and blame me for messing up things when she very well knows that the one who goofed up everything was my colleague, and not me?*
2. **Client:** *I think I am done. I have tried everything to change his behaviour but nothing worked.*
   Counsellor: *You have decided not to put up with your husband, who comes home drunk every night. What makes you think you can do it this time?*

Probes are helpful tools in counselling, but they should be used as minimum intervention and not as a question-and-answer session. Probes, in combination with empathy, can help the counsellor structure the sessions in a meaningful and focused direction.

Context for Probing

When the context suggests that there is a lack of clarity, concreteness, and quality in the narration of the client, the counsellor uses probing. Figure 4.6 gives a comprehensive idea of the contexts in which probing is used.

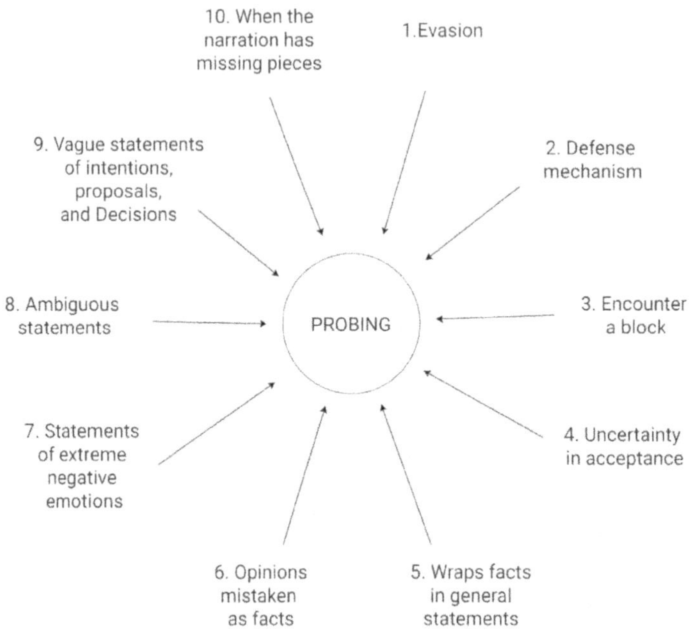

Figure 4.6 Contexts for Probing

As seen in Figure 4.6, probing is used in different contexts. It is important to mention that the skill is used in many other contexts, and what is shown in the figure and discussed here is only suggestive but not exhaustive.

Evasion to Talk

One of the contexts to use probing is when the client shows signs of evading while presenting the facts. The evasion may happen due to the embarrassment the content causes or due to apprehension of non-acceptance by the counsellor.

(The client came to the counsellor unable to manage her emotions after a breakup with her boyfriend)

Client: *Perhaps I was the reason for the breakup. We were going steady. We loved each other so much that very soon, we planned to inform our families and plan to get married.*
Counsellor: *That sounds like things were good between you.*
Client: *Yes. Everything was perfect. I thought we understood each other well; our interests and tastes matched. He was so loving and caring. But......... everything collapsed suddenly.*
Counsellor: *Umhumm.*
Client: *I felt he mistook me for a different type.*
Counsellor: *Different type?*
Client: *Yes. He thought I was like one of those girls who are ok with things.......*

Counsellor: *Suja, you are talking about 'different type', 'ok with things', etc. Can you tell what exactly is 'different type' or 'ok with things', please?*
Client: *........... How can I say? Well...... it is a part of love.....*
Counsellor: *Part of love?*
Client: *You see, it is about the physical relationship....... He has been insisting on it. I felt very hurt and offended. I am not a person to compromise on my values... He failed to understand that...*
Counsellor: *So, you were in a situation where the personal values of both were different, and neither of you was ready to compromise on it.*

In the above example, the client, coming from an orthodox middle-class family, had inhibitions in discussing the intricate aspects of the breakup, which was the crux of the problem. Unless these aspects of the problem in the relationship are discussed, the session cannot progress. The client was talking in generic terms, and counsellor had to use the right probes to elicit the facts and move forward in the session. It may be relevant to mention here that the client who tried to evade discussing the physical relationship could, in fact, talk about it in response to the counsellor's probing. Having done that and also having seen that there was no reaction of shock or embarrassment in the counsellor may also have contributed to a new insight about the way sexual relationships are perceived by people other than her boyfriend. While holding on to her value system, she may gain an understanding that people do not react sharply to the topic on this aspect. This insight may be inadvertent in the process of counselling. This is to reiterate that the counsellor's behaviour can be a great source of social influence on the client.

Use of a Defense Mechanism

There are occasions when the client has misperceptions and misrepresentations of the stressful situation because he/she has been blinded by the use of defense mechanisms. When the counsellor spots this, the best way to unblind the client is to use probing. The following example will throw light on the situations

(The husband has been diagnosed with the initial stage of Alzheimer's disease)

Counsellor: *Your wife's worry is that you insist on taking your medicines by yourself but skipping the doses often.*
Husband: *Look, I wish to put myself on alert. Don't want to be dependent.*
Counsellor: *That is perfectly fine, as long as you are able to follow the prescription meticulously.*
Husband: *Most of the time, I do comply with the prescription. Anyhow, this is a progressive disease. It does not cause any damage if the doses are skipped once in a way.... (Smiles)*
Counsellor: *Is that why you are skipping doses deliberately?*
Husband: *(Worried)* No. *In fact, I want to be regular with my medication. But there are times, I feel confused when I try to remember if I had taken the dose. I try my best to remember....... but....... I think the disease is progressing. I feel ...angry. I cannot lose grip on my memory...... wish to be sure about it and....and I get rigid about not being helped by my wife.... lose my temper... (Breaks into sobs)*

In the above example, the patient is found to be using rationalisation by stating that the disease is anyway progressive and hence low compliance actually does not matter. There seems to be also an element of repression. Only when the counsellor probed if the skipping of doses was deliberate did the husband get the clarity that he had been missing medicines because of his progressive forgetfulness. That probing from the counsellor helped in giving vent to the emotions that could have been under the carpet due to repression.

Encountered a Block

Sometimes, the client may be stuck with an idea and unable to move forward with a decision because of an emotional block that stops further thinking. In such cases, the decision-making process can be initiated only by helping the client to remove the block. Once the flow of thinking is obstacle free, the emotion is handled, and the decision is made. The following example helps in bringing clarity to this aspect.

(The client is a faculty in a university)

Counsellor: *You feel that the university has been very unfair in blocking your well-deserved promotion.*
Client: *Yes. Not once, but twice. I have appealed to the administration and the executive council, but to no consequence. The only option is to approach the court of law.*
Counsellor: *So, are you going to file a case?*
Client: *Well, that is what I think.....but*
Counsellor: *But?*
Client: *....I am a bit scared..... Firstly, I have never been to court. Don't know how it will be. But... the main thing is, our Vice-Chancellor is a dangerous person. He will not take it kindly. He.... may do anything...*
Counsellor: *He may do anything? What do you think he would do if you approach the court?*
Client: *ummm...... I don't know, really.*
Counsellor: *Can you think of the possible reactions from him?*
Client: *Well, perhaps he would call me and question...... But there is also a possibility that he would stop causing any harm because the court may view it differently.*

In the above example it is very evident that the client, burdened by his emotions, was stuck at the idea of taking the help of the judiciary because he was burdened with the emotion of fear. The counsellor, with the probing, pushed him towards thinking of the possible reactions from the Vice-Chancellor in case he approached the court. Removal of the emotional block of fear helped him in thinking realistically. This would help him forward in initiating action or deciding against it by carefully weighing the pros and cons. This will be worked out with the help of the counsellor.

Uncertainty in Acceptance

There are chances that the client puts off certain actions because the outcome of the action is uncertain. The client may have high stakes in it, so he/she is unable to accept one of the possible outcomes. In such cases, the counsellor's probing helps the client to visualise the consequences of the worst possible outcome in a supportive and empathetic condition. An onset of thinking is likely to aid in logically assessing the probability of consequences as well as preparing one to cope with the worst consequences. The example below explains the situation with clarity.

(The client is a 42-year-old woman)

Counsellor:	*So, you have the problem of sleepless nights, lack of appetite, and feeling anxious. Any specific stress?*
Client:	*Yes. ...something that I always was apprehensive about.*
Counsellor:	*Ummhmm?*
Client:	*I....I...have discovered a lump in my right breast.... (Breathes heavily)*
Counsellor:	*Ok. You feel it could be a matter of concern?*
Client:	*I am very scared.*
Counsellor:	*You are scared about...?*
Client:	*.... I...I am scared that it could be cancer.*
Counsellor:	*Have you gone through the tests?*
Client:	*......No. That's what I am scared of.*
Counsellor:	*The diagnosis is what would tell you if it is malignant or benign. There is a chance that it is found to be benign and an equal chance that it is malignant. What is the worst that could happen with the diagnosis?*
Client:	*(In tears) It may turn out to be malignant.*
Counsellor:	*In case, ... In case it is diagnosed as malignant, what do you think the doctor would advise?*
Client:	*.........(Silent)*
Counsellor:	*There are many aspects related to the diagnosis of malignancy. Stages, types, treatment options..., etc. So, what do you think could be the worst?*
Client:	*It could be the last stage...... (sobs). May require chemotherapy...... painful...... (Sobs)......... But....but there are also other possibilities, no? Could be benign..... even if malignant, may be in initial stage......*
Counsellor:	*But how would you come to know the facts?*
Client:	*...Perhaps I should face the diagnosis......*

In this example, one sees that the counsellor's probing (what is the worst that could happen with the diagnosis?) worked as a propeller to stimulate thinking and acceptance of action orientation in the client. The non-acceptance of the possible diagnosis of malignancy pushed the client to inaction and anxiety. With the thinking prompted by the counsellor, the client gets to logically think in terms of probabilities, raising some hope against the worst consequence, which leads to the essential action initiation.

Wrapping the Facts in General Statements

The client may sometimes present the situation in a way where the statements are very general, which does not make much sense to the counsellor. In such instances, a probe from the counsellor will accelerate the session and direct it in a meaningful way.

(The client is the daughter-in-law of a middle-class family)

Client:	*She (referring to the mother-in-law) treats me very badly, and my husband is fully aware of it. Yet, he remains silent. That is something not acceptable to me.*

Counsellor: *You are saying she treats you badly. Can you elaborate on what does she actually does to you?*
Client: *She speaks ill of me behind my back. She projects me in bad light among relatives and friends, while she is very sweet to me in her behaviour.*

The client here would not have come up with the facts without the probe. 'Treating badly' is a statement that leaves a lot to one's imagination. Without the right probing, the counsellor would not have known the facts based on the initial presentation by the client. When facts are wrapped in general terms such as 'bad treatment', 'inconsiderate behaviour', and 'suffered a lot of pain', they are not the specific facts but are the perceptions and interpretations of the clients. Though they are significant in understanding the feelings of the client, it is important to know the experiences and behaviour in the context. Therefore, it is important to use probes in such contexts.

Opinions Presented as Facts

It is very common for the clients to narrate their plight in terms of their opinions rather than presenting the facts. Expressions such as 'she is very stubborn', 'he is very lazy', and 'he is not sensitive to others' needs' put forth one's opinions than the facts as they occur. Many times, when references for counselling come to us, there are statements such as 'she does weird things; she is quarrelsome, not adjusting……has no concern for others….'. Normally the counsellors ask them to describe what they mean by it and request them to describe it in behavioural terms. Unless this is done, it is not easy to have an idea about the nature of the problem. Similar things happen in counselling sessions when the client explains the problem. In such cases, the counsellor's probing would bring the client to explain things in behavioural terms, which sometimes may not match the initial description.

(The client is the father of an adolescent son)

Counsellor: *You said your son is the source of your stress. Please carry on…*
Client: *He is not focused in his studies. He has distractions.*
Counsellor: *What makes you think so?*
Client: *He can hardly study for three hours at a stretch. He says he cannot concentrate beyond one hour. Needs a break for at least ten minutes after an hour or so, but he can watch a movie continuously for two hours without blinking. I think he needs the breaks to speak to his friends every hour. Perhaps, has a girlfriend. That is his major distraction from academics.*
Counsellor: *So, you are not sure about it. You guess that he has a girlfriend who is distracting him after a full hour of studying.*

Based on his observations, the father has formed some opinion that not being able to focus beyond one hour on studies is a loss of focus. The fact that the son uses his phone during every break suggests that he talks to his girlfriend. The counsellor's probe helps the father to explain further. The opinion of the father is that the length of time spent on the phone and taking breaks to speak to his girlfriend is the reason for his son's distraction. This opinion, which is not based on any facts, is causing stress to him. The probe here further helps the counsellor help the client with cognitive reorientation.

Statements of Extreme Negative Emotions

Clients with irrational beliefs, may culminate in repetitive thoughts. These repetitive thoughts invoke negative emotions. Carried away by the negative emotions, the client may sometimes make statements that are emotionally charged. Such statements are devoid of rationality. To bring the client back to rational and logical thinking, the counsellor uses probes.

(The client is a middle-aged homemaker of an alcoholic husband)

Client: *The story repeats every night. He is drunk, and he is violent. I and my children have suffered enough. During the day time when he is sober, he promises to go for a deaddiction, he promises to take care of the family, but evenings, he is a different person. My children are put to so much suffering. I have no peace and no interest in life. He has made everyone's life miserable. There is no way to reform him. There is no way to restore peace in the family. I am fed up.....fed up for life. Enough is enough.... Next time,.... Before he gets violent,...I think I will stab him with the knife and stab myself too. Let the children go to the orphanage...*

Counsellor: *You seemed to be totally vexed with the situation at home, but is that what you have come here for?*

Client: *(Calms down). Sorry.... I think I lost control over my emotions. I need a respite from this problem. I am here to seek a solution.*

In this context, the timely probing question by the counsellor, puts the client back in stable thinking. Without this intervention from the counsellor, the client is likely to continue the emotionally guided thoughts, which may further enhance the anxiety than bring clarity in purpose and action.

Ambiguous Statements

When in a state of emotional turmoil, cognition gets blurred. The individual cannot have a clear perspective on events and incidents. As a result, the statements are likely to be ambiguous. Probing helps in bringing clarity. Asking the correct question turns the client to view the specific aspects of the event and organise the field more systematically. This more or less resembles general statements. But ambiguous statements also have an element of uncertainty.

(The client is the husband of an IT executive)

Client: *We married two years ago, going against our parents. We certainly love and care for each other. She is good to me normally. But, in the presence of her colleagues, she behaves with me differently. It hurts.*

Counsellor: *Could you elaborate on what you mean when you say she behaves differently?*

Client: *Ok,......she belittles me. Sort of ridicules.... Maybe makes fun of me.... Well, I don't know...*

Counsellor: *You say you don't know, can you elaborate?*

Client: *Ummm... I don't know if .... If it is behaviour that is different, or I feel that way...*

The client, who has been nurturing the hurt feelings related to his wife's way of interacting in the presence of her colleagues, got stimulated by the probing by the counsellor. This may take him to examine if the reality lies in the wife's behaviour or his own feelings. This is a step towards bringing clarity to cognition.

Vague Statements of Intentions, Proposals, and Decisions

The client may sometimes appear very serious in the statement of a new decision, proposal, or intention made, but the statement itself may lack concreteness. The progression of the session in terms of action orientation would be difficult unless the counsellor takes definite initiative in bringing specific meaning to the client's statement.

(The client is a young obese patient)

Counsellor: *You are upset because you had a breakup in your relationship for the second time and you feel it is because you are overweight.*
Client: *I cannot take it any further. I will not continue to carry this weight of mine anymore.*
Counsellor: *If you think your being overweight is causing the problem, how do you plan to stop being obese?*
Client: *I need to think of some drastic action.*
Counsellor: *Can you explain what you mean by drastic action?*
Client: *Yes. It may cost me substantial expenditure and inconvenience, but I need to join some good weight reduction programme.*
Counsellor: *Have you decided the sort of programme you want to join?*
Client: *I don't know.... I really don't know.*
Counsellor: *So what do you think, how will you decide?*
Client: *Perhaps I need to find out.....with all seriousness. I will give myself just a week to identify the suitable one for me.*

In the example, we see the counsellor using probing at several points to make the client think concretely in terms of action. With the use of probing, the counsellor could bring the client from the stage of being as ambiguous as the 'I don't want to be obese' stage to 'I will fix a suitable weight reduction programme for myself in a week's time'.

Missing Pieces in the Narration

While narrating the story, the client normally elaborates on the aspects he/she has been focusing on, and misses out on other aspects which, according to him/her, may not be significant but actually constitutes a very relevant part of a complete understanding of the situation. The counsellor sometimes finds the absence of crucial information without which the logical sequence does not fall in place. If the client is allowed to carry on in his/her direction, the missing part may get lost, making it difficult to have a comprehension of the situation being described. Probing by the counsellor helps the client speak about the missing link in the story, which brings a new meaning to the entire narration.

(The client is a young mother)

Client: *I have tried every method to put a stop to his throwing tantrums. But nothing seems to be working with this boy. He is just three years old, and he manages to have his way. Be it the mall, be it a party, or be it an*

	occasion when the relatives are at home, if he wants to have something, he just throws himself on the floor and creates a ruckus.
Counsellor:	*You said you tried every method; can you explain the methods you used?*
Client:	*As we decided last time, every time he shows such behaviour, I just go out of that place so that he does not get that attention. It is not working. I am really losing my patience. He is thoroughly spoiled by the pampering by my in-laws. He seems to be out of my control.*
Counsellor:	*Can you explain what your in-laws do to make him behave that way?*
Client:	*Nothing specific. But they generally pamper him a lot.*
Counsellor:	*Ok, tell me what happened after you left the place when he threw himself on the floor and cried?*
Client:	*He continues to cry. I ask my husband to be around and keep a watch. You see, my husband is a busy person. There are times when he gets a call during these episodes. He has to attend official calls. Cannot have the wailing child in the background. So, he carries him and pacifies him before answering the call.*

Without the appropriate probe, the counsellor would not have known the reason behind the failure of the well-tested technique in weakening the child's tantrum behaviour. The husband's official phone call may be so significant for the mother that his violation of the rule was not taken significantly by her until asked by the counsellor through probing. Now with the complete information about the scenario, it would be easy for the counsellor to explain to the client the cause of the strategy failure, which in turn would make her realise the logic behind the method and the cause for its failure. This is nothing but cognitive restructuring with regard to the technique advised to be applied to weaken the child's undesirable behaviour.

The Art of Probing

The English meaning of probing is to 'examine, inquire or explore'. In the context of counselling, in view of the goals of probing, the meaning of 'to explore' is more appropriate for the word. The counsellor uses probing so that the client explores oneself more to reveal more information that adds to the content and quality of the narration. The general idea of probing is to use an explicit question. While that certainly is one of the obvious methods, probing is used by adopting various means. There are various techniques of probing, as depicted in Box 4.9.

Box 4.9 Probing Techniques

NON-VERBAL	VERBAL
A forward-leaning of the body	An open-ended question
A nod	A request
Raise of the eye-brow	A statement
Gesture with hand to carry on	Single worded prompts
A pause with good eye contact	Certain sounds suggesting to carry on

Probing: The Non-Verbal Techniques

A skilled counsellor spontaneously applies probe. Many a time, it need not be a spoken sentence or a word. An appropriate expression sometimes carries more power than a spoken word. An appropriate gesture, expression, or movement will function as probing. Following are a few examples.

Example 1:

Client: *It is not the lack of trust, nor it is the absence of love for my husband, but...... something in me, some part of me is no more alive.... I don't know how to explain it... (Looks at the counsellor).*
Counsellor: *(Makes a small forward movement of the upper part of her body)*
Client: *There is a general lowering of my libido. Perhaps a menopausal symptom. But he feels that I am no more the loving wife I have been. He gets very irritable. Passes sarcastic remarks in front of my growing children. They are no more kids. What if they understand what is going on between their parents?*

In this example, the non-verbal probe from the counsellor gave a clue to the client that she is being listened to and there is unconditional acceptance giving confidence to the client to share delicate details about the ongoing relationship between her and her husband.

Example 2:

Client: *Before my retirement, we used to have household help, cook, and gardener. That was a luxury the family enjoyed, and it was my position that gave them all the luxury (chokes and there is a shiver in the voice indicating hurt, pauses)*
Counsellor: *(Gives a nod with a long blink)*
Client: *Now,... I am retired and am of no consequence because I don't give them the same life.*

The nod with a long blink is a signal of acceptance and approval to go ahead. The elderly client was hesitant to make the statement, perhaps because the counsellor was approximately the age of his son and hence may not like such statements. But the non-verbal probe indicated that he is understood and accepted. This may even be construed as a gesture of empathy and acceptance. Communication, whether verbal or non-verbal, cannot be exclusively categorised into one or the other as it sometimes carries a package of a cluster of messages.

Probing: Verbal Techniques

Asking a question is not a great deal. But what makes it professional in the context of counselling is asking the right question in the right time in the right way so that the response adds to the quality and quantity of content presented by the client. A question of probe need not necessarily be a complete grammatically correct interrogative statement. What is important in the context is that it should serve the purpose of dissipating the inhibition, explore into the preserved information, encouraging the client to volunteer information, unravel the untold story in more detail to enrich the quality. To achieve this, the counsellor needs to judiciously apply the skills of probing verbally. A few examples and explanations will help in comprehending the skill appropriately.

Example 1:

Client: *I don't deny that I have got a seat in the best university in the country. I know that the department there enjoys an international reputation and that the faculty are world-class quality. All that is true, but I am not happy. I don't know why, but I don't want to be away from my parents.*

Counsellor: *Is there something bothering you about your parents?*

Client: *Well, ... Not really. But, ...my mother may miss me very badly and become lonely. My father hardly cares for her. Always busy with his work and social engagements. She is recently diagnosed with blocks in her arteries....*

A straight question from the counsellor is what warrants the situation to bring the hidden fears of the young boy out.

Example 2:

Client: *I was not looking for a movie-type of romantic relationship in the marriage. I am a typical homemaker. I am all right with the joint family arrangement. I am fine with looking after the parents-in-law. I am also ready for anything they expect from me. But...... I am not able to adjust to the suffocation of my marriage becoming a bit too crowded...*

Counsellor: *Could you please explain what you mean by marriage becoming too crowded?*

Client: *...What to say? I realised that my husband was not permitted to marry the woman he was in love with. They forced him to marry me......... Now, having married me, he is unable to reconcile.... He continues his relationship with his lady love.... something, something, very difficult for me to accept.*

It is difficult to interpret statements like 'marriage getting crowded'. Apparently, the client used that expression to soften the impact on herself. It is essential to get clarity on this central theme of the client's communication. Probing in the form of a direct request is very appropriately used by the counsellor, who not only conveys to the client the seriousness with which the counsellor was listening but also that it is important for the counsellor that the client speaks in specific terms.

Example 3:

Client: *He (the son) moved to a rented flat along with his wife four months ago. But most of the time, both of them stay here with us. Earlier, they used to stay as family members, and now as guests. The burden is so much on me now to prepare meals for all. Moreover, their coming and going are unannounced. They should understand.*

Counsellor: *Well, it is not clear to me whether you intend is to let them know it is causing you problems or leave it to their realisation.*

Client: *I want to tell them. But they should not feel hurt or unwanted. Not that I want to keep them out. I just don't know how to tell them.*

Box 4.10 Practice Exercises

1. Divide yourself into triads, conduct a role play where each one of you will be a counsellor, client and an observer. Note the skills of each one of you while play the role of the counsellor and the client. Discuss the key skills demonstrated by the counsellor and the responses of the client, discuss the discrepancies.
2. Look at the responses of the three counsellors and tick the correct response. Explain your understanding.

Client:	I am really discouraged. I can't find a good decent place to live. I've looked at so many apartments, but they are all so expensive. I'm tired and I don't know where to turn.
Counsellor 1:	You feel tired and discouraged.
Counsellor 2:	Searching for an apartment simply hasn't been successful, they are all so expensive.
Counsellor 3:	You look tired and discouraged, you've looked hard but haven't been able to find an apartment you can afford.

When the client's statements are not clear in their intention, and when the client expresses some clear feelings with a tentative action, the counsellor has to probe further so that clarity emerges in probable action points. In this case, the counsellor uses probing by making a statement that clearly points out the point of ambiguity in the client's statement. Such straight statements are sure to elicit specific responses from the client that brings clarity to both and take the session forward.

The discussion till now is related to the use of the skill of probing. The use of this skill requires a good amount of training through exposure to simulated situations, followed by application under expert supervision, before one can apply it independently.

Pre-counselling skills, viz. attending and responding skills, help the counsellor to understand the client story by getting an insight into the client's situation. The pre-counselling skills are a set of skills that the counsellor can use at any stage of counselling. If used judiciously these skills equip the counsellor to take the sessions forward smoothly. The influencing skills, which are also a part of counselling skills which include challenging, accurate empathy, self-disclosure, and immediacy, will be discussed in the coming chapters.

References

Argyle, M., Henderson, M., Bond, M., Iisuka, Y., & Contarello, A. (1986). Cross-cultural variations in relationship rules. *International Journal of Psychology*, *21*(1–4), 287–315.

Barrett-Lennard, G. T. (1993). The phases and focus of empathy. *British Journal of Medical Psychology*, *66*(1), 3–14.

Cormier, L. S. (2016). *Counseling strategies and interventions for professional helpers*. Pearson.

Cormier, S., Nurius, P. S., & Osborn, C. J. (2016). *Interviewing and change strategies for helpers*, Cengage Learning.

Driscoll, M. S., Newman, D. L., & Seals, J. M. (1988). The effect of touch on perception of counsellors. *Counsellor Education and Supervision*, *27*(4), 344–354.

Egan, G. (1990). *The skilled helper: A systematic approach to effective helping.* Thomson Brooks/Cole Publishing Co.

Egan, G. (2013). *The skilled helper: A problem-management and opportunity-development approach to helping.* Cengage Learning.

Evans, D. R., Hearn, M. T., Uhlemann, M. R., & Ivey, A. E. (2016). *Essential interviewing: A programmed approach to effective communication.* Cengage Learning.

Geller, Shari M., and Leslie S. Greenberg (2002) Therapeutic presence: Therapists' experience of presence in the psychotherapy encounter. *Person-Centred and Experiential Therapies, 1*(1–2), 71–86. https://doi.org/10.1080/14779757.2002. 9688279.

Haensel, J. X., Smith, T. J., & Senju, A. (2022) Cultural differences in mutual gaze during face-to-face interactions: A dual head-mounted eye-tracking study. *Visual Cognition, 30*(1–2), 100–115, https://doi.org/10.1080/13506285.2021.1928354.

Hall, E. T. (1966). *The hidden dimension* (Vol. 609). Anchor.

Hutchinson, D. (2014). *The essential counsellor: Process, skills, and techniques.* Sage Publications.

Ivey, A. E., Ivey, M. B., & Zalaquett, C. P. (2013). *Intentional interviewing and counseling: Facilitating client development in a multicultural society.* Cengage Learning.

Knapp, M. L., & Hall, J. A. (1992). *Nonverbal communication in human interaction.* Holt, Rinehard and Winston.

Kohut, H. (2009). *The restoration of the self.* University of Chicago Press.

Lewis, L. T. (2009). *Living life consciously.* Author House.

Maurer, R. E., & Tindall, J. H. (1983). Effect of postural congruence on client's perception of counsellor empathy. *Journal of Counseling Psychology, 30*(2), 158.

Mehrabian, A. (1971). *Silent messages.* Wadsworth.

Neukrug, E. S., & Schwitzer, A. M. (2006). *Skills and tools for today's counselors and psychotherapists: From natural helping to professional counseling.* Thomson Brooks/Cole.

Pressly, P. K., & Heesacker, M. (2001). The physical environment and counseling: A review of theory and research. *Journal of Counseling and Development, 79*(2), 148–160. https://doi.org/10.1002/j.1556-6676.2001.tb01954.x.

Rogers, C. R. (1957). The necessary and sufficient conditions of therapeutic personality change. *Journal of Consulting Psychology, 21*(2), 95.

Stickley, T. (2011). From soler to surety for effective non-verbal communication. *Nurse Education in Practice, 11*(6), 395–398.

Tickle-Degnen, L., & Rosenthal, R. (1990). The nature of rapport and its nonverbal correlates. *Psychological Inquiry, 1*(4), 285–293.

Wainwright, G. (2010). *Understand body language: Teach yourself.* Hachette.

Zur, O. & Nordmarken, N. (2011, February). To touch or not to touch: Exploring the myth of prohibition on touch in psychotherapy and counseling. http://www.zurinstitute.com/touchintherapy.html.

5 Skills for Emotional Relief

There has been so much emphasis on cognition that emotion, which pervades almost every change in our lives, is still awaiting its importance. The emotionality associated with thoughts and actions need to be handled with care because, to a large extent, it contributes to an individual's quality of life. Very often, the client approaches the counsellor because of the persistent negative emotions that interfere with the effectiveness and productivity of life. Emotions can be compared with smoke that blurs the vision. The more it is accumulated with no outlet, the more it blocks the perception, thereby causing a negative impact on cognition. It is easier for the client to work on restructuring cognition with the emotions released. Emotions are complex phenomena. As long as they are unexpressed, they remain as feelings influencing thoughts. Only when the complexity of these closely held feelings starts unfolding and manifesting in various emotions does the client gain new insight about the impact of the experience that invoked a host of emotions. There are occasions when the client starts with one identified emotion but gradually, as the session progresses, starts endorsing the coexistence of other emotions as they unfold themselves. It is common for the client to start with one emotion and then realise and support emotions contrary to the one endorsed in the beginning. Many factors, such as self-esteem, and ego defense mechanism, may camouflage the real emotions which are bottled up.

Let us explain with a description of a case of a young medical doctor. The doctor, a young neurosurgeon, was caught and booked by the security guards of a women's hostel on the complaint of the woman for being physically abused by him in front of many other inmates. Based on the complaint, he was detained at the police station for a few hours. He was referred by the Registrar of the University to the counsellor. The doctor walked into the counsellor's office in crumpled clothes; his hair appeared to have been ungroomed for days, his face indicated that he had not shaved for days. He walked in with the shoulders dropped, eyes sunk and red. He sat down with his eyes fixed on the floor. He was accompanied by his brother. The gist of the story, as narrated by the brother, was that the doctor had been in a relationship with a girl for two years. He was deeply in love and had proposed to her. They were to get married the following year. In the meantime, the girl moved to another state to pursue her post-graduation at a university. They continued their contact on a daily basis over the phone. However, a few months later, the calls and responses from the girl started getting cold. At one point, she told him she was no longer interested in continuing the relationship. The doctor could not take it and insisted on meeting her once. In this context, he travelled from his state to meet his girlfriend.

The doctor describing the incidence of 'abuse' said that on seeing him as the 'visitor', his girlfriend was first shocked. Later she welcomed him and spent the whole day with him 'as if the relationship continued'. The following day he went to the hostel to meet her

DOI: 10.4324/9781003459415-5

again. Then, she asked him to get out of her life and turned around to return to her room. The doctor wanted to stop her physically and tried to hold her from behind, but he could hold only her hair and pulled her towards him. According to the doctor, all this happened at such a speed that before he realised the girl started screaming, the security staff rushed to the spot. The following is the interaction between the counsellor and the client:

Counsellor: *The report from the Registrar's office says that you hurt her physically. Were you angry with her?*

Client: *No, never. She is my love; how can I ever be angry with her? I just wanted to stop her because I did not want her to disappear like that.....*

Counsellor: *Okay. Is it that you did not expect her to leave that way?*

Client: *True. She was so loving towards me even the previous day..... I thought we would have one more day together..... and...... she behaved so differently....... (tears flow down his eyes). Someone.....someone is perhaps influencing her.......she is good.....she loves me.....(stops talking and sobs with his face covered with both hands)*

Counsellor: *(After giving a good pause)..... It's alright, doctor. It's okay.....(hands him the tissue paper. Waits for the client to calm down, and then offers him a glass of water).*

After a few more exchanges between them in the next half-an-hour to 40 minutes, the following is the extract from further conversation:

Client: *She..... she used me....exploited me for two years....... she just used me. And I was a fool......*

Counsellor: *You feel that she was not really in love with you?*

Client: *It was I who always longed for her company. I was deeply in love with her, madam. Never did I suspect that she would find someone else and dump me this way...*

Counsellor: *You seem to be thinking that her severing relationship with you is because she has developed another relationship. Did I get you right?*

Client: *Yes, yes, yes. Definitely. She is a b.......(impolite word). She has no business playing with my life. (His face turns red with anger). True that I did not intend to hurt her physically...but now I feel...I should have slapped her in the face. I should have... for the insult she caused me...for the hurt she gave me and for all the days she used me....(stamps his foot)*

Counsellor: *You feel furious that you allowed her to exploit you in many ways and feel no regret for causing the physical hurt...*

Client: *I never intended to harm her. It just happened. But, what about the hurt that I am carrying, madam? They put me in police custody. What about my reputation? What about my self-esteem? She just does not care? I never listened to my sister who warned me about this woman's character.....so much so that I started avoiding my sister! Cha! What a person I was to distance myself from my sister, whom I love so much?................*

The above excerpts from the case show that the doctor carried a host of emotions, such as love, sorrow, anger, frustration and guilt, each tumbling out as he started talking. It may be noted that he only acknowledged his love for the girlfriend when he began. As the session progressed, his other emotions started unfolding, such as anger, hurt and sorrow, shame, and guilt. This is a case where the emotions started manifesting with relative ease. This may not happen in every case. Some clients need the little trigger to express their emotions while some may be guided by their inhibitions due to cultural expectations, protection of family honour, and sense of shame preventing the expression of real emotions while yet others may be so overwhelmed that they experience what can be called 'emotional numbness' caused by the situation.

Emotions are significant factors contributing to life. They are closely associated with perceptions of situations, experiences and events tagged to needs, expectations, achievements, affiliations and the outcome of such experiences. Emotions have an overreaching influence on thoughts, motivation and behaviour. Bottling up emotions is considered undesirable in view of the individual's health and well-being. Figure 5.1 explains the changes in various systems in the body associated with emotions.

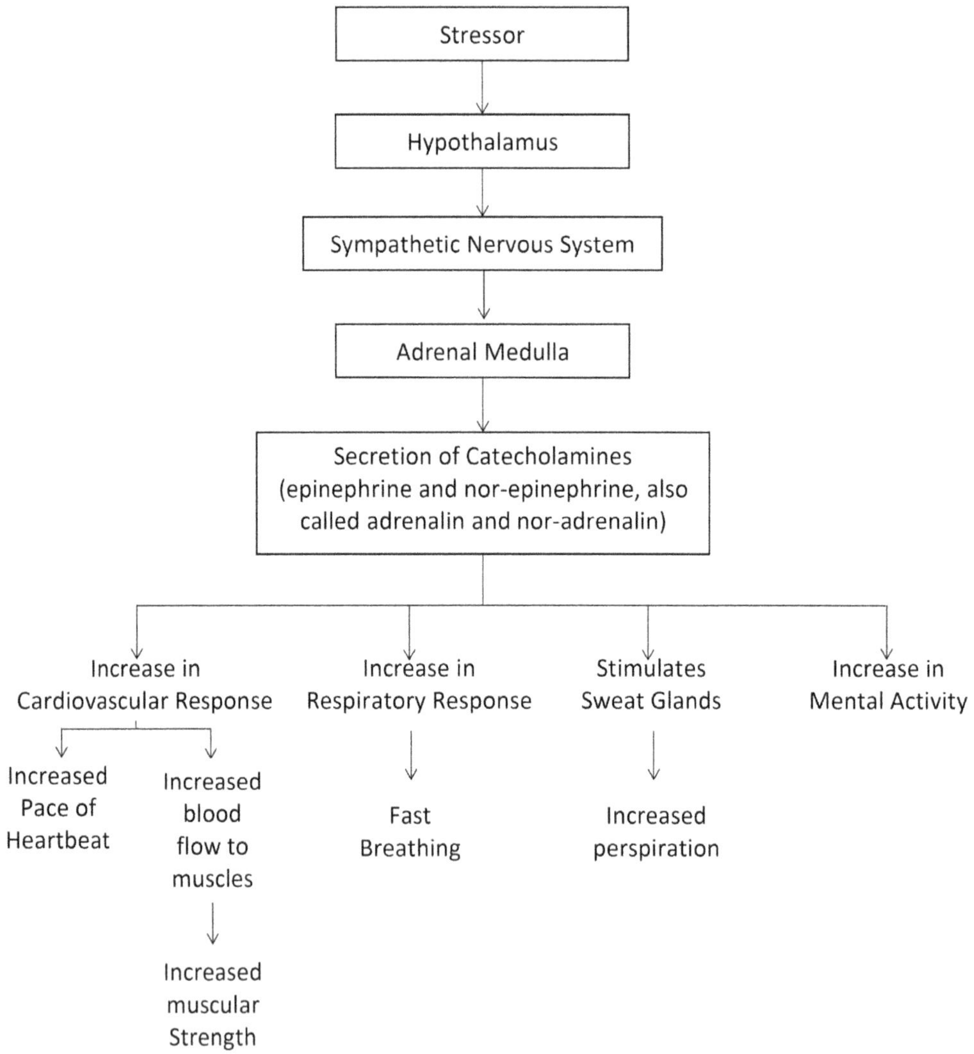

Figure 5.1 Physiological Response to Emotions

As explained in Figure 5.1, when an individual is emotionally disturbed, the message of emotion reaches the hypothalamus, then the sympathetic nervous system, which stimulates adrenal glands situated at the top of the kidneys. Adrenal glands secrete adrenaline and noradrenaline. These secretions get into the bloodstream and travel all over the body and impact a number of systems in the body. The impact on the cardiovascular system results in an increased pace of heartbeat and increased flow of blood into the muscles. The impact on the respiratory system is seen in hyperventilation (fast breathing). The influence on sweat glands results in increased sweating while the brain experiences increased mental activity.

If an individual is in a state of emotional disturbance for a longer duration, it is likely to have an adverse effect on health, causing various problems. This is depicted in Figure 5.2. The details in the figure clearly imply that the client who approaches the counsellor after experiencing prolonged stress may have suffered an impact on the physical health, alongside the psychological state.

The client's disposition may be described with one or a combination of a few states such as exhausted, low in energy level, low in immunity level, frustrated, dejected, angry, sad, feeling helpless/hopeless, apprehensive, anxious, depressed and low in self-efficacy. It is not an exhaustive list but is a common experience which may be present either in isolation or in combinations. If there is any unanimity about counselling among various theorists, it is about one aspect that the counsellor should facilitate the client to release emotions. Helping the client release the emotions thus assumes the priority in the counselling process. In the traditional psychoanalytic approach by Freud, emotional release is given prime importance. The concept of catharsis gained popularity, and several therapies were designed to facilitate emotional catharsis in the client to restore well-being.

On the other hand, there are therapies that believe that negative emotions can be handled by working on the thoughts which are said to be the source of emotions. Cognitive Behaviour Therapy (CBT) and Rational Emotive Therapy (RET) are based on the premise that repetitive thoughts have a close association with negative emotions. In view of the physiological and biochemical response and the associated anxiety and depressive consequences, it may not be an exaggeration to term intense and prolonged emotional upheavals as toxic states. In the interest of restoration of equilibrium in the individual, such toxicity should be released from time to time. Counselling setup should provide the right platform for this. Kottler and Shepard stated, 'The one place in the world where people feel safe to cry and honestly express their pain is in the counsellor's office' (Kottler & Shepard, 2008, p. 15). This is very true because any other place has the potential for reactions from others. At the same time, the supportive environment in the counselling session expects and encourages the client to shun all inhibitions and emote freely. If the counsellor applies the right skills, the clients break all inhibitions. They are seen crying, screaming, thumping the table, stamping their feet, expressing remorse, showing their hurt and exposing their shame and guilt, giving complete vent to their emotional energy. The competent counsellor normally absorbs this with ease and comfort until the client experiences a sense of relief. Counselling is one context where such emotional expressions are indications of the process going in the right direction. Counsellor's clinic is where the ventilation of all emotions (particularly negative) is considered normal, and the absence is viewed as the client experiencing some discomfort.

The client, while approaching the counsellor, has a complex affect state. For example, the doctor in the case cited at the beginning of the chapter initially thought all he had for his estranged girlfriend was only love. As the session progressed, he started to express his hurt, anger, shame and guilt as part of the entire episode, from courtship to estrangement.

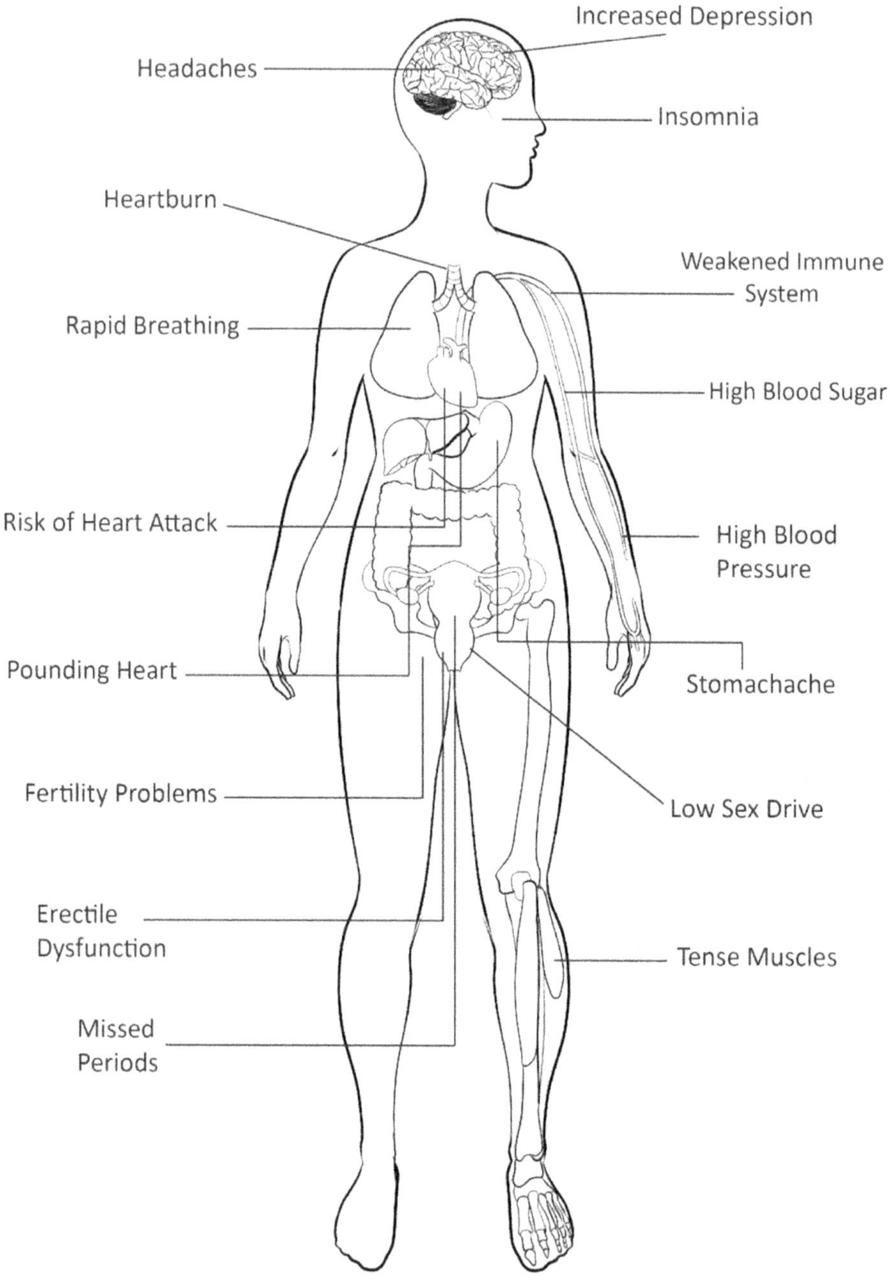

Figure 5.2 Impact of Emotional Experience on Various Organs

In many cases, the client may not even know about the range of emotions harboured by them until they start ventilating in the counsellor's clinic. It is not rare when a client is surprised to discover the hitherto unacknowledged emotion surfacing in a counselling session. In majority of cases, the client experiences a new insight about one's emotions associated with an issue and also feels a sense of relief as well as 'an emotional drain out' after intense emotional ventilation.

The counsellor's skills play a crucial role in touching the right chord of the client to trigger emotional expressions. These skills can be classified into verbal and non-verbal. Though many of these skills are natural characteristics of a counsellor, one can be trained in acquiring these skills.

Non-Verbal Skills

Non-verbal skills for the emotional release can be defined as those expressions, gestures, postures and movements of the counsellor that gives a cue of acceptance and encouragement for the spontaneous expressions of the client.

Being There

Some skills originate from the natural gestures of friends and relatives in affiliation-oriented societies when someone is in crisis. For example, just 'being there' physically with the family that lost a member is considered to be very comforting. Often, a family member in shock at the sudden death of the father/mother/spouse will have all the emotions coming out in a gush on seeing a close friend who visits their home. The counsellor's psychological presence encourages free expression. Egan (2010) refers to the robustness and intensity of the presence of the counsellor, which communicates to the client that the counsellor is 'tuned in' to him/her or that the counsellor is 'with him/her'. This is communicated clearly with the non-verbal factors of attention that include positioning face-to-face with the client, maintaining a physically open posture, leaning forward, making eye contact and manifesting the commitment to receive the communication from the client. This projects to the client the importance he/she receives from the counsellor. Gaining importance in the eyes of the other individual helps the client break the barriers of being guarded.

The counsellor will have to start the assessment of the client's emotional state from the time he/she walks into the clinic. The physical appearance gives a clue to self-grooming; the gait throws light on the mental status (whether the client is depressed, anxious, hopeless, panicking, etc.); the eye contact suggests confidence level; sitting posture, voice quality gives an insight on the mental state, inhibitions or emotional state. The counsellor's first goal is to instil trust and confidentiality in a client who manifests a high emotional state. Here is where the counsellor can have a great social influence on the client by maintaining a relaxed disposition combined with complete attention. The composure of the counsellor influences the client by relaxing him/her a bit. If the client still manifests tension, the counsellor's offering a glass of water will comfort the client significantly. If the initial observation suggests an intense emotional state in the client, rather than starting the verbal interaction immediately, a pause of a few seconds interspersed with a nod of acceptance or smile from the counsellor is a good foundation for building a relationship to allow the client to manage the complex emotional state. It communicates to the client the counsellor's acceptance of the emotional condition, thus easing the situation. Further, it communicates to the client that the counsellor is in no hurry to 'finish

Box 5.1 Non-Verbal Emotional Expressions of the Client

- General grooming and hygiene of self
- Gait
- Eye contact, sustenance of eye contact, restless eye movements
- Fixing of gaze (on the floor or into a distance)
- Frown
- Voice culture, tone, pitch, frequency, fluency, pauses, silence, intensity
- Muscular flexibility/rigidity
- Shoulder position (dropping, slagging, rigid)
- Sitting posture (relaxed/tense)
- Facial expressions (relaxed/nervous/depressed)
- Facial changes (redness/paleness – indicating anger/fear)
- Fast/heavy breathing
- Restless and fidgeting
- Mannerisms (shaking the legs/biting nails/clutching the arms)

the job' and move on to the next client. Such feelings strengthen the perception that 'the counsellor is there to listen to me'.

It is not uncommon for the client to express emotions non-verbally. A number of factors in the client reflect their emotional expressions. A range of cues starting from the general appearance to observable reactions to internal physiological responses constitute the client's emotional expressions non-verbally. Box 5.1 summarises the non-verbal cues of the client indicating the emotional state.

All the non-verbal behaviour listed in Box 5.1 are expressions of specific emotions like sorrow, anger, nervousness, hopelessness, fear, frustration, shame, guilt, remorse, etc. However, non-verbal expressions may be common for a few emotions. Hence it isn't easy to understand the underlying emotions based only on non-verbal cues. The non-verbal cues from the client should be considered as indications of significant emotions, which should be encouraged to be ventilated explicitly for a better understanding of the client. The feelings can be explicit when the client starts speaking about the problem. The client's narration of the story presents the content of the events/incidents and situations, while the form in which the client presents the story contains sufficient components to infer the feelings, emotions and experiences of the client.

Listening to the Emotions

The phrase 'listening to emotions' may sound poetic, but it has a definite meaning in the context of counselling. The emotional expressions are usually written loud and clear in the non-verbal expressions of the client. However, as already discussed, non-verbal cues are only indicators. Only when combined with the verbal expressions of the client will they give a definitive interpretation of the correct emotions. Listening to verbal expressions contributes to the 'accurate perception' of the counsellor. Thus, listening to emotions refers to listening to the contents of the client's narration in combination with the non-verbal expressions that constitute the 'form' of the client's expression. The counsellor's focus is not limited to what the client narrates in terms of content, but also the listening should extend to the type of emotions, the intensity of it and their impact on the client. 'Listening to the emotions' requires the counsellor to tune in to the various aspects, such as the client's voice, facial expressions, gestures and movements. For example, when a client speaks about the estranged relationship, his statement (content), 'I don't care .....or long to continue my relationship with her', when accompanied by a high-pitched voice, throwing the hands out and the face going red communicates one emotion which is certainly different when it is accompanied by a low pitch voice, eyes fixed to the floor and hands clutching to the arms of the chair. In the first case, it indicates anger and rage, while in the second case, it suggests sorrow, uncertainty, and lack of confidence in self.

Listening to emotions by studying non-verbal communication assumes significance because often, particularly in the initial sessions, the clients tend not to express their emotions openly. One may be harbouring a range of emotions such as fear, anger, guilt, shame, jealousy and hurt but have reservations speaking about them either because they have not yet started feeling secure in the environment or because the self-esteem blocks the explicit expression of the same or even because of issues related to social desirability. The absence of expression can also be because of the client's frozen state or lack of communication skills in translating emotions into speech. In spite of this, the emotional experience tends to show up through non-verbal communication. This is the advantage of the counsellor, who should use the cues to help the client verbalise the emotions.

Verbal Skills

Verbal skills refer to the counsellor's verbal expressions to the client in terms of initiating communication and responding to the client's non-verbal and verbal cues. For example, when the counsellor finds the client showing signs of anxiety through body language, he/she may initiate verbal communication with statements like: *(every statement can be an add-on to the previous statement depending on the need)*

1. You seem to be very tense.......
2. You seem to be tense...... please take your time to relax
3. Can I offer you a glass of water?
4. I wish to reiterate that the confidentiality of the client constitutes an essential value of counselling.
5. (In case the non-verbal communication of emotionality is seen to be prolonged) Is something in the surroundings bothering you? Or
6. You seem to be very restless for some reason, and I am here to help you.

The initiative can be any of the above statements or something similar to it. There is no formula or standard for initiating communication with a client who appears to be emotional. However, the principles that apply are to be sensitive, accurate, and empathetic to the client while initiating verbal communication.

The client who is overwhelmed with problems may not understand where to start the story. The following example gives an insight.

> Example: The client is a young woman who feels surrounded by problems. She has been diagnosed recently with a rare disease called 'Retinitis Pigmentosa' where the retina develops pigmentation causing problems in vision. The disease that is progressive in nature has no known cure. It may lead to total loss of vision sooner or later.

She was newly married. It was just by chance that her disease was diagnosed when she, along with her newly wedded husband, went for a normal vision test requiring a change of specs. When her husband heard about this diagnosis, he was shocked. He informed his parents. His parents started suspecting that she and her parents were, in fact, aware of the problem and concealed it from them. They started blaming the girl's parents for this. Unable to handle the stress of the diagnosis and the in-laws blaming her and her parents for cheating, she picked up a fight with them. One fine morning after a fight, she walked out of the house in a fit of anger and reached her parents' place. Her father, who was in his fifties, was unable to take the bleak future of his daughter, who may lose vision and also staked her marriage. He died after a massive heart attack. The stress mounted up with the death of the father. After a few weeks, the mother of the girl started to express her unhappiness with the daughter, and things gradually reached a stage when the mother started to openly blame the daughter for the father's death. It is at this point that the young girl in her mid-twenties sought an appointment with the counsellor. She pleaded with the counsellor to advance her appointment because she wanted to meet the counsellor immediately since she was unable to take the stress any more. We will call the client by the pseudo name Saroja.

Saroja:	*(Gives an awkward smile and clutches her handbag)*
Counsellor:	*(Smiles back) Well, on your request, we advanced your visit. Looks like you found it difficult to wait for two more days (Smiles)*
Saroja:	*Yes (Eyes downcast)*
Counsellor:	*Well, I am here to listen*
Saroja:	*(Silently moves her toe on the floor in a semi-circular way)*
Counsellor:	*You seem to be hesitating. Any reason?*
Saroja:	*(Looks up with tearful eyes and trying to control)*
Counsellor:	*(Offers her a glass of water) It is okay.... Take your time. There's no hurry*
Saroja:	*(Takes a sip of water) I... I want to talk....*
Counsellor:	*Please....*
Saroja:	*I.... I don't know where to begin and where to end....... There is so much....to tell*
Counsellor:	*You can begin anywhere. Whatever comes to your mind naturally.... Whatever you feel comfortable with*
Saroja:	*I have not slept well for weeks.....I....think life is unfair to me.......*

Now we see that the client, after the right responses from the counsellor, could make the opening remark. The story came out gradually. The client was slow and calm initially, loud and shrill in the middle, had spells of crying in between, and was relatively composed towards the end. What is important at this point is to take into cognisance the way the counsellor broke the silence to bring her to make the beginning of her narrating the emotion-filled story. What are the essential verbal skills to be used in helping the client vent their emotions?

Empathy

Though we have already discussed the skill of empathy, it is important to know how to apply empathy in helping the client shun all inhibitions and ventilate his/her emotions. When the client starts to tell the story, the contents consist of the client's perceptions, interpretations, thoughts, imaginations, feelings, experiences, and actions. They may not name the feelings or emotions associated with a certain experience or the mood that persisted in the aftermath, but an empathetic counsellor should be able to perceive them. Accuracy in empathy is of great importance. Let us understand this concept.

Accurate Empathy

Accurate empathy requires accuracy in perception and expression (communicating it back to the client). The counsellor should perceive the client's emotions accurately. This will happen if the counsellor identifies the correct family of emotion in the client and perceives it to the right degree. Family of emotions refer to the types of emotions, such as happiness, sorrow, anger, fear, love, and so on, which are mutually exclusive. Each of these emotions varies in its degree. For example, happiness can be experienced in different degrees, happiness, pleasure, joy, enjoyment, thrill, excitement, and ecstasy. When the counsellor perceives happiness in the client, he/she should assess the degree to which the client is happy. Once the assessment is done, they should use the most appropriate word to express the perception of this emotion to the right degree. Table 5.1 presents six families of emotions and the words to describe various degrees of emotions within these families.

The counsellor's expression of empathy should correctly capture the right word. Let us explain with a hypothetical example of a client saying the following in a high pitch:

Client: *I know very well that the management is bent on proving me wrong. They all have ganged up against me because I exposed their corruption. As the vigilance officer of the organisation, it is my duty to catch them. I have done the right thing. But I never knew that the management at the top level is hand in glove with this group. Do they want to trouble me?*

Table 5.1 Words that Express the Degrees of Emotions in Various Families

Happiness	*Sadness*	*Fear*	*Disgust*	*Anger*	*Surprise*
Bliss	Sad	Afraid	Aversion	Annoyance	Dismayed
Joy	Disappointed	Alarmed	Abhorrence	Agitated	Appalled
Pleasure	Lonely	Scared	Distaste	Irritated	Astonished
Satisfaction	Upset	Dreaded	Dislike	Fury	Amazed
Glad	Hurt	Anxious	Displeasure	Wrath	Stunned
Rejoice	Gloomy	Apprehensive	Loathing	Infuriated	Flabbergasted
Cheerful	Discouraged	Panic	Sickening	Outraged	Nonplussed
Peace	Miserable	Petrified	Nauseating	Exasperated	Astounded
Delight	Despairing	Horrified	Repulsive	Raged	Shocked
Elation	Heartbroken	Terrified	Repelling	Maddened	Startled
Optimism	Dejected	Wary	Resentful	Enraged	Dazed
Glee	Woeful	Jittery	Hatred	Irked	Stupefied
Enjoyment	Disheartened	Unnerved	Repugnance	Piqued	Wondered
Contentment	Crushed	Nervous	Fed up	Provoked	Bewildered
Exhilaration	Crestfallen	Peevish	Weary	Hostile	Awestruck
Euphoria	Worried	Ferocious	Tired of	Cheesed off	Dumbfounded
Enchantment	Stressed		Vexed	Bitter	Marvelled
Tranquillity	Distressed		Animosity	Vengeful	
	Shattered			Spiteful	

Let them. These corrupt people in the organisation should not be spared, come what may. I may lose my job and become a pauper, but I will go to any level to teach a lesson to these people. Let them take me out of my job if they can, but I will not spare them.

Counsellor 1: *You are angry with them for their corrupt practices and afraid you may lose your job.*

Counsellor 2: *You feel annoyed with the management for the way they are getting away with the corrupt practices.*

Counsellor 3: *You seem to be irritated with the management along the hierarchy for their dishonesty and vindictiveness.*

Counsellor 4: *You are mad at the people along the management hierarchy for their corruption and mutual support, so much so that you are even ready to stake your job to take on them but not spare anyone!*

Counsellor 1, while identifying one emotion (angry) correctly, has erred by stating '....also afraid that you may lose your job' (fear). Counsellor 2, though identifying the right family of emotion (angry), committed a mistake in assessing the degree of anger by labelling it as an annoyance, which is far milder in its form than the client's expression. Thus, the intensity of the emotion is under-assessed. While Counsellor 3's statement is comprehensive by including 'vindictiveness', the degree of anger as perceived and expressed (irritated) is much lower than what the client experienced (as evidenced in the high pitch of voice and the choice of words). The absence of accuracy in the perception of the client's emotion and expression of empathy compromises the effect empathy has in triggering the pent-up emotion and encouraging its expression. The client is likely to feel 'not adequately understood' by the counsellor, and hence the spontaneity of expression may be interrupted. On the other hand, Counsellor 4 used the expression 'you seem to be mad at the people.....'. This reflects accurate perception and expression. Further, her choice of language in saying '.....so much so that you are even ready to stake your job to take on them but not spare anyone' also communicates the perception of the intensity of the anger that is even ready to stake the security of job should there be any vindictive action. Such accurate empathy, when communicated, helps the client release emotions with ease.

Explicating the Emotions

The counsellor sometimes has to name the specific emotion to the client whose verbal and non-verbal communications only suggest the emotion without obviously stating it. The skill of doing it is closely related to perceptual accuracy.

Very often, when the clients describe their stories, they do it in terms of their experiences. They express in statements like:

- My children really don't care for me
- My wife fails to understand me
- My boss does not see merit in me
- My parents feel I am a dud

These expressions involve others, mostly responsible for these experiences. It is difficult to infer the associated emotions, and by assuming them, objectivity and accuracy are lost. For example, the client whose children do not care for her may feel angry, hurt, apprehensive or a combination. Unless the counsellor stimulates the client appropriately, the emotions associated with it may not surface in the client's description. In other words, the counsellor should bring the implicit emotion to the surface and make it explicit. A somewhat neutral interception from the counsellor, such as 'I can see that you don't like it' helps the client to focus on the emotion that he/she goes through with the experience.

Sometimes, the client may describe the story in terms of experiences and behaviour without referencing the associated feelings and emotions. Following are some examples:

Client: *When my wife gets to nag me too much, I dash towards the bar, get drunk and return late at night only to head straight to sleep.*

Counsellor: *I fail to see any direct relationship.*

Client: *Maybe. But it gets on my nerves. When I get really angry, I tend to react very aggressively. When I see my anger rising, I get out of home lest I may react very badly. Having gone out of home, I still have the anger. Perhaps I feel humiliated too because I have to take her criticisms every time without any retort. It triggers the thoughts about my marriage with her..... and all the flashback.....which I don't want. I feel like putting everything behind.....The best way is to have a few drinks......*

Counsellor: *What about the flashback about your marriage?*

Client: *I was forced into this marriage. She is related to me. I was almost forced to marry her because their family was in trouble after losing her father suddenly. I was ....in fact in love with another girl.... I feel very guilty that I... cheated on her. She committed suicide. I feel guilty and sad...*

Counsellor: *Oh! That must be hurting. So, you wish to get away from those memories and guilt?*

The client here described the story in terms of his behaviour of getting drunk. A counsellor who lacks competence is likely to assume the emotion of anger at the nagging of the wife. But a competent counsellor uses the skill of empathy to elicit the right feelings and information. In this case, it happened to be a host of emotions, such as anger, guilt, and sorrow, which the client cannot handle in situations of this kind. Unless the client was encouraged to express more, he would not have spoken about his past and the associated emotions.

It is implausible for the client to explicitly state that he/she is angry/sad or scared. The counsellor has to perceive it based on non-verbal cues and the choice of language.

Following is an excerpt from the case of Saroja discussed in the preceding pages:

Saroja: *I first could not comprehend the diagnosis of the doctor. Once he said I might gradually lose my vision, I thought he was wrong.....how could I become blind when I am able to see perfectly with my glasses? As he started explaining, the fact sunk in. I felt like the ground under my feet was caving in, and I was falling. I did not ask anything, even when the doctor offered to answer questions. Perhaps, I was in shock. I could barely walk. But ...... you know what? My husband did not say a word, leave alone any attempts of comforting me ....After reaching home, I had no energy left. I shut myself in the room. But he? ....He sat down with his parents and discussed the issue...... That's it.....*

Here though Saroja never stated her emotional state, it is evident that she was distressed at the diagnosis. It is apparent that she was disappointed with the absolute insensitivity and lack of emotional support from her husband. Her anger with him for choosing to share the matter with his parents without being a support to her during such a crisis is also visible. What should be the empathetic expression of the counsellor to help her out with more emotional expression? Let us examine the hypothetical responses of a few counsellors.

Counsellor 1: *You were in shock and hence could not discuss anything with your husband while he discussed it with his parents.*

This response of the counsellor is content focused. It missed out on the perception of the emotions that were expressed implicitly. Such responses may not encourage the client to express emotions.

Counsellor 2: *You went into a shock and could not act, while your husband acted, which made you angry.*

In this case, the counsellor perceived and communicated only a part of the emotional reaction of Saroja. This probably would help Saroja in expressing more of that emotion which was endorsed.

Counsellor 3: *While the diagnosis about you shattered you, you expected the much-needed support from your husband, the absence of which added to your distress. Perhaps you were hurt? And seeing him talking about it to his parents seems to have angered you a lot.*

In this case, the counsellor communicated accurate empathy by capturing the right families of emotions in their correct degrees. This is evident in the choice of her words, such as 'shattered', 'distressed', 'hurt', 'angered'. Such a response encourages the client to explain the experience in detail, express the emotions in their intensity and shun inhibition in revealing their behaviour in response to the situation. The accurate perception of the emotions is likely to make the client 'feel accepted'. This feeling of acceptance comes from the realisation that if the other person could feel the exact pulse of the moment, it should be something which is not out of place. Thus, the first principle of empathy is the perception of the accurate emotion and communication, leaving scope for correction by the client. Here we can observe the tentative tone of the counsellor with the use of words like 'perhaps' and a question seeking clarification. Such responses are preceded by total attention to the client.

Selective Response to Core Emotions

This is a skill of identifying the prominent emotions from a long-winding expression of the client's story and responding in a way that stimulates further expression. It is said that though we mention it in singular, the term 'problem' in real life is always plural. The client who approaches the counsellor typically does so with multiple problems. Some present the problems in sequence, while others present them as a mixed bundle. Since the client describes the problem from his/her perspective, it comes out as an overwhelming personal experience of the client. There are times when the client's presentation of problems (in a long winding way or when it tumbles out as a gush) leaves no scope for the counsellor to intervene and paraphrase. In such instances, the counsellor has to apply the skills of listening with all its characteristics and give a response at the end which is both crisp and comprehensive, so that the client feels that he/she was listened to correctly. The response should communicate empathy and encouragement to speak further to release more emotions. The following example may drive the point better:

Example 1:

Client: *I was going through a very bad phase in my career. It appeared like an ever-lasting conflict with my boss. That was the time my father suffered a massive heart attack, and I had to travel to his place and be with my parents for about three weeks. I was getting tense about the impact it would have on my office work. By the second week, my wife started to complain that she was finding it difficult to manage things alone. Before I planned my return, my son had a fall in the school and had multiple fractures in the left leg, which had to be operated upon. My boss threw a fit when I sought an extension of leave. Had a huge showdown with him. That was exactly the time when my neighbour chose to file a case against me for the dispute over the boundary wall. I.... I felt as if I was being torn into pieces. There was nothing positive in life. There were days when I wished I never woke up in the morning to face a fresh day to attend to problems. (Sighs and pauses)*

Counsellor: *That.... is a bit too much! It must have been overwhelming.*

Client: *Overwhelming! I spent nights without a wink of sleep; I spent hours walking on the streets aimlessly; there were occasions when I sat alone in the park and allowed my tears to flow generously; there were days when in my fantasy, I showered blows on my boss....... I was all alone in this fight. My wife is from a small town and not well educated. Her idea of being a wife is to take care of household needs and look after children. She cannot go beyond this. I...I still feel lonely... orphaned... when handling my stress.*

One statement from the counsellor here could summarise the trauma the client experienced within a period. This is called selective response to emotions. The counsellor cannot identify, name, and endorse every emotion associated with various experiences. If he/she does so, it would appear unnatural and defeat the purpose of encouraging the client to continue the expression of emotions. The short and crisp statement of the counsellor, on the other hand, was comprehensive, natural and spontaneous. Selective response to emotions calls for intent listening, spontaneity, and genuineness besides the expression of accurate empathy.

Probing

Probing is a skill that is used in many contexts. It can be used to trigger the expression of emotions too. Sometimes the clients are found to speak in terms of their experiences, observations and inferences. It is important to understand the emotions and feelings associated with the experiences. The counsellor can use probing to get the client to focus on the emotional experiences. Let us explain with the example of Saroja.

Saroja:	*My husband has never tried to understand me. For him, I don't matter. This I have been observing since the day of my marriage.*
Counsellor 1:	*You think that your husband makes no attempt to understand you.*
Counsellor 2:	*You feel your husband has no concern for you, and that disappoints you.*
Counsellor 3:	*Oh! Can you explain that, please?*

The response of the first counsellor has no reference to the feelings, while the second counsellor though, refers to the feelings, lacks perception and expression of accurate empathy. The third focused on the general statement that her husband has no concern for her, which she has been experiencing ever since marriage. This statement seems like an inference drawn on the basis of some experiences. Each experience must be associated with certain emotions, which probably had no opportunity for expression and have been weighing heavy on the client. The response of the third counsellor has combined empathy with probing. The statement communicates the counsellor's accurate perception and communication of the client's experience of repeated disappointments with her husband, which has no details. The probing in the form of a request to explain more on that aspect encourages the client to elaborate on the experience and recount and relive the emotions associated. Thus, the third counsellor is in the right direction of helping the client release the bottled-up emotions.

There are times when the client fails to understand what is going on in his/her emotional front beyond the experience of discomfort. With the right probing, the counsellor can make the client speak about the experiences in such a way that the associated emotions emerge with good clarity. Let us examine it in the case of an elderly woman who lost her husband during the second wave of COVID-19. As per her description of the story, her husband had quit his job very long ago, when he was young, after a few years of their marriage. She was employed and supported a family of four that included the couple and two children. According to her, he 'had some psychological problem and was under treatment'. He was highly dominating and never allowed her any personal space. As a result, she had to confine herself to her job and family. She almost killed her desire to be associated with her maternal family, leave alone socialise with relatives and friends. She said she had no complaints because she almost got used to this life and joined a spiritual Guru, who helped her progress. The husband developed cardiac problems and was under medication. He developed co-morbidities. They continued the marriage this way for about four decades. Just before the first wave of COVID, he had a fall and fractured his hip bone which had to be operated upon. Subsequently, he developed post-surgical complications. The children were located in another city. Hence, she was the sole caregiver of her husband. His death happened a few minutes after she had her second session of tele counselling. She had her third session four days after his death. Following is a part of tele counselling (Jayanti is a pseudonym).

Jayanti:	*You would have heard him calling out for me when I was in a session with you last week. I had to request you close the session.*
Counsellor:	*Yes, I remember.*
Jayanti:	*He developed breathlessness, and I tried to connect the oxygen. But it did not help, and he passed away. (She paused briefly)*
Counsellor:	*I am so sorry. You were alone with him. Right?*
Jayanti:	*Yes. He never allowed even any helper. Though it is not COVID-related death, no one would visit for condolence because of COVID condition in*

the city and the lockdown. So, I called the driver. We both helped the body into the car. The driver was the one who did the cremation. I did not even try to accompany him.

Counsellor: *Was that very tough on you? Normally one needs a lot of support from people during such time.*

Jayanti: *I don't know. Perhaps not. I even asked my children not to come because it requires permission from authorities, RTPCR test, etc., to travel to another state. I was only thinking of the next course of action. Did not even cry. The neighbours sent me food after the driver took the body for cremation. They continued for the second day too. But I asked them to stop because I thought I was normal enough to cook for myself. Strangely, I slept the whole night and the whole day. I woke up, had my bath and went to have a good walk on the terrace. I picked up a book and started reading. Yes, I do miss him; I am sad that I lost him. After all we were married for forty long years! But why is it that I am not crying? Why is it that I am eating and sleeping so well? Why am I engaging myself in rearranging the house? I am sure I am not happy. I am also able to feel that sense of loss, but......... sometimes I feel that I may be abnormal in the way I am behaving in such a situation.... Madam, am I normal?*

Counsellor: *Ms. Jayanti, can you recall when is it that you cried last?*

Jayanti: *(After a long pause) I am unable to recollect.*

Counsellor: *When is the last time that you were sad?*

Jayanti: *Many occasions. I was sad when my son fought with his father and left home, when my husband did not let me go and see my ailing brother, ... when he had the fracture and the surgery......many occasions.*

Counsellor: *How did you express your sorrow on these occasions?*

Jayanti: *(Short pause) Did nothing.... Just moved on....... (Voice slightly raised) Do you mean to say I have stopped expressing my feelings for a long?........ Yes, perhaps....... Yes, yes, you are right. I don't remember crying ....getting angry..... oh...no.....yes....I have stopped expressing my feelings! Is that so?*

Counsellor: *Is that what you think?*

Jayanti: *Yes. I realise now..... In a way.... Perhaps I practised that to.... have peace at home and accommodated myself to my husband's needs.*

Counsellor: *Is that something you have realised now?*

Jayanti: *Yes... (voice choked) but why? I.....I seem to have submerged myself in his mental illness........ lost a precious part of my life to his illness......*

Counsellor: *Ms. Jayanti, are you feeling bad about it? Regretting the fact of being what you have been?*

Jayanti: *No, no. No regrets. But now, ...at least now, I should allow my emotions .... without any fear...Don't you think so?*

Counsellor: *What do YOU think?*

Jayanti: *Madam...... I.....I think, while.....I am sad for his death.......somewhere ....somewhere deep down.... I (lowered the voice) am also feeling a sense of relief...... To be honest, I feel I am liberated........ perhaps a newfound freedom......some lightness...you know......I feel scared ....of such a reaction. Yes, I am scared of myself.....apprehensive that...I may be ....not normal... perhaps like my husband?*

The counsellor diligently used the skills of probing to help the client identify and endorse a kind of emotional vacuum in her, which she started imbibing through practice because that was the need of the time to maintain peace at home. The client's experience of lack of emotion followed by the doubt if she was normal in fact concluded with the finding that it was an issue of fear and apprehension if her experience of a sense of relief with the death of her husband was normal and acceptable. The emotion of fear like the other emotions, seems to have got camouflaged with her non-emotional disposition. The sense of relief was something strange to her. This strange feeling combined with her association and experience with her husband who was under treatment for mental illness, created fear in her driving her to contact the counsellor. She could not identify this ambiguous feeling as the emotion of fear until she named it while interacting with the counsellor. The probing from the counsellor that asked her to check when did she cry last or felt sad last triggered the insight about her consciously practising blocking of emotional expressions. The subsequent questions by the counsellor helped in contrasting the feelings of subjugation in her husband's presence and the absence of it now, leading to identification and endorsement of enjoying the newfound freedom, which was strange and scary for her. It may be noted that nowhere in the interaction the counsellor imposed her opinion or thinking on the client. The probing skills of the counsellor here facilitated the client to explore her emotional life and endorse the changes in two important stages of her life.

Invoking Positive Emotion

While it is the responsibility of the counsellor to help elicit the right emotions from the client, the counsellor also invokes positive emotions in the client. This can be done by responding to the client's strengths, opportunities and resources. Very often, when the client narrates the story, he/she highlights the woes in terms of failures, exploitations, restrictions, limitations, helplessness and weaknesses. Hidden in those stories are the unidentified strengths, unused resources, and unseen opportunities. A competent counsellor identifies them and projects them back to the client to contemplate upon.

> Example: The client is a busy hardware consultant. He had to undergo major surgery, after which he was advised to rest for eight weeks. He could spend two weeks binding himself to home. But once he was comfortable with his mobility and had no pain, he started feeling restless. Though he continued his meetings online, he missed his driving, his outstation travel, meeting new clients and socialising. By the beginning of the fourth week, he got irritable, had sleep problems, and lost his appetite. His urge to go out was starting to get the better of him. He had arguments with his wife on his attempt to go out. His expression to the counsellor was ' I feel caged'. Following is a part of the exchanges between him and the counsellor.

Client: *I feel caged.*
Counsellor: *You don't seem to like the medical advice of complete rest.*
Client: *I have never been confined to home this way at any time in my life.*
Counsellor: *This sort of rest is out of sync with your lifestyle?*
Client: *Yes. I get mad at everyone around me. I feel like taking my car out and reaching the place of the meetings. What is there to occupy my attention after completing the few virtual meetings during the day? There is emptiness and emptiness all around...... I feel lost. This helplessness is something*

that is very new to me. I am a person who is always in control of things in my life..... But now, see I am bound by the medical advice........ I feel I am just wasting my productive time.....

Counsellor: *You said you have never been confined to home this way ever in your life.*

Client: *Yes. That is the problem.*

Counsellor: *You are not likely to face such a situation in future, right?*

Client: *Hopefully.*

Counsellor: *Then, could it be a one-time opportunity in life?*

Client: *What?*

Counsellor: *I was looking at your profile. I understand that besides being an engineer, you are also a good artist.*

Client: *That was long ago. I have not touched the colours for quite some time.*

Counsellor: *A singer, and you seem good at photography and mimicry ...That is a lot of things....*

Client: *(Long pause) oh yes...... I understand what you are hinting at. I can utilise the time to catch up with these things (with a glow in his eyes). Why did I not think of it? Some hesitation... maybe I should ..... the very thought is so exciting....*

Counsellor: *You know that during the freedom movement, the best of the writings from the leaders came when they were in prison?*

Client: *Turn the prison into a prism and pass light through it to emanate colours of versatility....*

Counsellor: *You seem to be already in the mood to write a poem.*

In this case, had the counsellor not seen the profile of the client he could have started with a probe like 'in earlier days when you had plenty of time in hand what were you doing' or a straight question like 'what are your hobbies?' In case the client does not mention any hobby, the probe could be about the friend circle, socialising, the best time in his life and writing about it. There cannot be any definite formula, but the counsellor can certainly identify the strengths and opportunities.

In another case, the client, a patient who suffered a paralytic attack and recovering from it, was narrating about his struggle in life.

Client: *I have gone through many struggles in my life... Now that I am comfortable and enjoy life, should I face this challenge? (Voice choked. Tries to control his emotion by pausing). As a young boy from a small town, I took the challenge of doing the engineering course and earned to pay my fees by working during the weekends and spare time. Never did I become a burden on my father. Getting a job was easy, but I did not see any future in that job. I decided to complete my post-graduation and then Ph.D. from USA.*

Counsellor: *That sounds great.*

Client: *Not really. People assume great things there in America. But living there and pursuing studies has its own challenges. There were times when I wanted to quit. It was just my tolerance that saw me through. Then, my qualification itself became a disadvantage to find a suitable placement in India..... At last, I crossed that hurdle too. And now.... This?*

Counsellor: *You have every reason to feel distressed with your present situation. But, tell me one thing, the struggle you went through in the past may not have* *been a physical illness, but that was no less a challenge. You seem to be having the grit to face challenges and come out successfully.*

Client: *(Suddenly looks straight into the counsellor's eyes)... Did you say grit? Yes. You are right. That will see me through this problem too. Why not?*

Such a dramatic response may not come from every client, though some clients can surprise the counsellor with such sudden insights. All that the counsellor did here was to emphasise the strength of the client, who perhaps was blinded because of his physical condition and pain. Unblinding this strength brought a new sense of confidence in the client, who was already on the path to recovery. The physical condition and lack of active engagement perhaps were responsible for the client's getting into a trap of self-pity. The counsellor's skill of emphasising the positive strength in the client could help him rediscover the internal resource that was unused in this situation. This helps in replacing helplessness with determination and reinstates hope in the client.

Therapeutic Interventions for Emotional Release

The importance of emotional release was long identified. For instance, Freud introduced the theory of catharsis. The phrase 'Emotional catharsis' as a treatment for many mental and physical illnesses was suggested based on the positive impact of the emotional release of patients during hypnosis. Taking a clue from here, a number of psychologists have come up with therapeutic approaches to help the client have the much-needed emotional release. However, the debate on the impact of the cathartic release of emotions such as aggression continues and has inconclusive evidence. Some found the emotional release providing relief, while others found that the relief is temporary and the sense of relief functions as reinforcement to see aggression recurring.

Many experiences trigger emotions. Immediate release of negative emotion in its raw form does not have social approval. In a civilised society, the individual experiencing the emotions processes, regulates, and expresses only if it suits the context. Thus, the need for emotional regulation often ends up in the individual suppressing a lot of emotions. This suppression builds pressure or tension in the individual, causing substantial stress that impacts a number of physiological changes. The tension continues to build up in the person until emotions are released in an unthreatening environment. The counsellor can provide a therapeutic set-up that triggers a safe release of emotions in the client. This can be done in many ways by adopting what is called 'Expressive Therapy' (Kottler & Shepard, 2008). It includes the following:

- Art therapy
- Play therapy
- Physical exercise
- Bibliotherapy

Expressive Art Therapy

While language is normally perceived as a facilitator for expression, it may also be the greatest barrier to expression. There are occasions when the experienced emotions are so intense and intertwined with many other emotions that it gets suppressed for want of adequate expression in language. Following is a situation when actions speak louder than words.

> Dheeraj was a middle-aged bank employee. He had only one son who was in his mid-twenties and was pursuing a professional course. That is the time when Dheeraj's alcoholic brother died after a brief illness. After losing the elder son, Dheeraj's parents started placing high demands of financial support on Dheeraj. There was a bad altercation after which Dheeraj's parents disowned him. Around the same time the college where his son studied called the parents to report some behavioural deviations of their son, who was subsequently placed under psychiatric treatment. Owing to the son's treatment, Dheeraj had to take leave from his office and move to a city where his son was undergoing treatment. It was Dheeraj's wife who was taking care of their son totally. She had no other support since the relationship with her in-laws was severed. About one year passed, and the treatment was showing results. This is the time Dheeraj's health started showing some symptoms, which was diagnosed as cancer in the advanced stage. His wife took this stoically. He had to undergo surgery which led to surgical complications. He was put through radiation and chemotherapy. All the savings were almost spent. In the meanwhile, Dheeraj exhausted all his leave and had to go on a loss of pay, which they could not afford at this stage. Since the cancer site was oral, Dheeraj lost his clarity of speech following the surgery. It was his wife who contacted the bank, spoke to the officials and requested a transfer to the place where they were taking treatment for their son and father for two different problems. The bank did not believe the reasons until substantiated with medical records. It was nearly a wait of four to five months. Dheeraj's wife had to take care of her husband's physical pain on one hand and insulate him from the stress by giving him hope that the transfer would materialise while protecting her son from any impact of stress. She would keep a brave front to her husband while venting out her sorrow to her siblings in private. After a wait of four to five months, when she received a call from her husband's bank communicating that the transfer order was ready, she screamed and cried after hanging up the phone. She started shouting 'It is done...it is done.....' and started hitting her sister who was present there. Everyone around found her reaction strange, and they had to physically control her. They started asking why she was crying and hitting people in anger when she was expected to be happy. She only said, 'I don't know'.

The distress of several months, the anger towards the suspicious employers of her husband, and the feelings of helplessness and hopelessness suppressed over months found a release in her actions. Her feelings and emotions at that point are certainly difficult to express in words. Her emotional reaction might not have logically fitted the context, but the release was spontaneous and came out like an explosion at the least expected time and in a least expected form. It was a combination of sorrow, fear, anger and happiness.

In another case, a young boy from a highly religious family background, after completing the course in a reputed IIT was showing the symptoms of depression. Even otherwise he was not good with his communication skills. It was a drawing that gave a clue to the counsellor that he was experiencing a conflict deep down. Figure 5.3 is the reconstruction of the picture drawn by this student.

Based on this drawing, the counsellor could progress in the sessions. It was found that this young boy got initiated into visiting sex workers and was unable to get his libido under control. This was clearly against the values of his highly religious family. This put him through severe conflict. Besides his problems with communication, the emotions of shame and guilt prevented him from expressing the experience verbally. Thus, Art

Figure 5.3 Client's Depiction of Conflict between Id, Ego, and Superego

therapy comes in handy to facilitate express the complex emotions. The picture he drew depicted the constant conflict between his libidinal energy and family values.

Art includes several forms, such as (drawing/painting), dance, drama, music, and writing.

Art Therapy

Art therapy relates to drawings and paintings and as a part of expressive art therapy, which includes various forms of art as described above. Feelings and emotions are found to reflect in the drawings and paintings where the individual speaks through the images (Case & Dalley, 2006; Waller, 2006) and colours. The use of art therapy has been found helpful in emotionally healing injuries (Camic, 2008) and restoring emotional balance (Gross & Swartz, 1982). The therapy has been found successful with children. Research in the field revealed that art therapists, through art, could elicit positive and negative emotional expressions of varying intensities reflected in the product. Some drawings indicated impulsivity in dynamic terms (Pénzes et al., 2018). The therapists interpret the emotions by analysing several details such as the placement of the picture on the paper, the pressure used in drawing the lines, the type and the size of the pictures, the slanting of the pictures, details illustrated in the pictures, colour scheming, etc. Art therapy is used on children and adults. The client need not be an artist to express himself in drawings. The counsellor resorts to art therapy when verbal expressions are inadequate and ineffective.

Art therapy is effective on anyone with built-up emotions of any intensity ranging from grief after losing a loved one or exhaustion with the disproportional demands of daily life. Apart from helping the client express emotions, it also seems to involve a healing process. The total attention and concentration on the strokes of the pencil or the paintbrush are said to be similar to the mindfulness experience, which has a calming impact on the person. Thus, the effect of art therapy satisfies the expression of conflicts involving complex emotions, as in the case of the IIT student discussed above and also provided the opportunity for a meditative experience and distraction from intense negative thoughts.

Dance and Music Therapy

The two most popular and most common recreations across the globe are music and dance. Music and dance are potentially therapeutic. The cultural integration of music and dance in moments of happiness and sorrow is a testimony to their therapeutic characteristics. Functions such as marriages, engagements, and birthdays in any Indian culture, by default, integrated music and dance in the form of *Shahnai and baraath dance* (in Northern India) and *Nadaswaram* (in South India) and *Band baja and bara jaathri dance* (in Eastern India). Similarly, in many regions in India, drums and dance lead the funeral processions. Needless to say, the moods of the music and dance are different in these two contexts. Thus, music and dance are the accepted forms of expression both on happy and sad occasions.

There may be instances when one feels overwhelmed with emotions, and music comes as a natural expression. For some, a brisk walk or workout in a gym provides the much-needed emotional relief. Following is a typical case where the expression through dancing brings great emotional relief to the person.

> Pratyusha was a psychologist and also a dancer. She was working in a research organisation. As a well-known dancer, she used to give public performances too. When she was 55 years old, she consulted the doctor for the weakness of her limbs and two mild epileptic attacks.
>
> She was diagnosed with a malignant tumour in her brain. When the news of the diagnosis was broken, she was in shock. The doctor asked them to decide on the surgery while also disclosing the fact about not-so-encouraging prognosis of the type of cancer she had. She shut herself in a room. She went into a shell for a couple of days. Her son and husband tried talking to her positively with statements like 'Things would be alright' 'let us do our best', 'we are with you', etc. While she knew that they, too, were going through the trauma, she said she was too preoccupied with her psychological state. According to her, she found that her head was crowded with thoughts. She asked her husband and son to give her time to organise her thoughts. One day when they both were away, she closed herself in her room, fixed her 'ghunguroo' (metallic bells strung together on the anklets worn by classical Indian dancers) to her ankles, played her favourite music and started dancing. She continued until she felt exhausted and satisfied. In the end, she was sweating profusely and found tears flowing down her eyes continuously. It was only after this episode that she could sit with her family and discuss further course of action.

When the emotion is at the peak, the cognition gets blurred, making decisions difficult. Pratyusha could not express her emotions in any other way. Even her weak limbs could not prevent her from expressing herself through aggressive dance that helped her ventilate her emotions adequately. She found expression through dance and music more suitable than verbal expressions to her loved ones to get solace and support. What she needed much was self-expression. Besides expression, dance also functions as a therapy for the highly stressed. Indian classical dances give significance to the expression of emotions through typical themes. *Navarasas* (the nine emotions) are typically designed to express various emotions in many Indian dance forms. For example, '*Rudra Thandava*' is a typical dance for the expression of anger. Dance helps release endorphin and oxytocin, which enhances the positive affect state. However, the neurochemical impact of dance and music is yet to be confirmed with more Randomised Control Trials (RCTs).

Music is yet another art to be used for therapeutic purposes. Music impacts multisensory processes and influences emotional processing in the brain (Koelsch, 2009). Research investigating the relationship between neuro activity and music is still in its nascent stage. Yet, the positive connection between music and emotion is suggested. Music can modulate the limbic and paralimbic system, which is the control centre of emotions (Sammler et al., 2007; Ball et al., 2007; Koelsch et al., 2007; Eldar et al., 2007). The emotions are triggered, maintained, modulated and terminated in the limbic system. This input is encouraging for initiatives in music therapy. Listening to music was found to influence limbic and paralimbic activities both in musicians and laypersons. Different parts of the limbic system get stimulated depending on the pitch, beat and tune of the music. Indian classical music identifies specific *ragas* (a combination of tonic intervals) associated with different emotions.

Music helps the client in emotional regulation. It has the potential to energise, calm down, and relax to induce sleep by stimulating the brain to produce alpha or beta waves to excite or relax a person. It was observed that an individual who experiences the emotion of sorrow without being able to express the same when exposed to a piece of sad music could reach catharsis. Heshmath (2019) found that a sad individual listening to music that has lyrics to resonate with one's sad experience finds the right expressions for his/her experience, which otherwise would not have been possible. Mathur et al. (2015) found that the *ragas* have the potential to elicit specific emotions while the tempo and rhythmic regularity contribute to the level of arousal. The client can be an active or passive participant in music therapy (Shankar, 2010). She identified certain specific *ragas* for certain typical problems as listed in Box 5.2.

The *ragas* mentioned for the problems are suggestive. They are yet to be validated through randomised controlled studies.

Box 5.2 Some *Carnatic Ragas* as Interventions

Name of the Raga	**Type of Problem**
Karaharapriya	Worry and distress
Desh	Provides Positive Energy, Peace & Calmness
Saveri	Anxiety
Kalyani	Fear/Frustration
Neelambari	Sleep problems
Charukesi, Arabhi	Anger
Amrutavarshini	Emotional suppression

Source: Shankar (2010)

For a counsellor to apply music therapy effectively, special training in the field is essential. In case the counsellor feels that verbal expressions are not effective in emotional release in a client, he/she can be referred to an expert in music therapy.

Play Therapy

Play is a natural and spontaneous expression in children. Virginia Axline pioneered play therapy. Her book *Dibs; in search of self* is a biography of a young boy whose emotional suppression and non-communicative state resulted in branding him as unfit to study in a normal school. The therapist's application of play therapy helped him release his pent-up emotions in a therapeutic set-up, after which he was in fact found to be a gifted child.

Play therapy has no limitation on the age of the client; it is normally used on children under 12 years of age. Young children between 2 and 12 are not well equipped with language competence to express their experiences, feelings, and emotions. When they face challenges, they tend to behave weirdly and yet find it difficult to express their feelings verbally. In such cases, play therapy is found to be appropriate. In play therapy, the therapist creates a situation where the child is encouraged to explore events in his/her life which might have caused an impact on the child's behaviour in the present situation. The pace of this exploration is left to the child. In the secure presence of the therapist (who invests substantial time in establishing rapport with the child), the child explores his/her traumatic experiences, pent-up emotions, and troubling thoughts, giving them a non-verbal release and verbal expressions. The child is left in the specially created playroom with selected toys and materials. The child's interactions with the various toys are observed by the therapist. Very often the child acts out the traumatic experiences in the interaction with the toys. These interactions with the toys are considered 'symbolic words'. In non-directive therapy, the child is allowed to play as per his/her own wish. In directive therapy, in which the initial part is left to the child's choice of play, the therapist gradually introduces the play material to suit the problems encountered by the child. In directive therapy, the progress of the sessions is faster. Play therapy is likely to be effective in cases where the child has possibly gone through a trauma (victim of kidnap, sexual abuse, violence, ill-treatment, bullying, grief, or separation from loved ones, having to connect to a new person, etc.) where the child is unaware of the actual emotions or feels inhibited due to a feeling of shame, guilt or fear.

Like adults, children, too, feel the emotion of anger. However, they cannot express it as adults do in a safe environment. Aggressive play therapy helps them to vent their anger in a secure environment. Aggressive play therapy situations have certain aggressive toys like dinosaurs, tigers, lions, etc. Placed in such a situation, the child can freely express anger and feel relief while learning the boundaries and the way to regulate emotions such as anger. A child who is exposed to frequent fights between parents may choose to act out the conflicts between two aggressive animals, reliving the situation. The child will have the scope to use aggressive gadgets like rubber knives, swords, etc., to express aggression through action. The children are also found to move and sway their bodies in different ways that help them release the aggression building up in their bodies. The therapist will have to facilitate the release of emotions through appropriate prompts and guidance.

The counsellor using play therapy has to be trained in observation, probing and interpretation to be effective. For example, a six-year-old boy who developed a fear of going to school held back some experiences which he did not know how to express. While playing with the dolls, he picked up a male doll, took out all its clothes, and placed it in a corner of the room. The therapist, during the conversation, very gently broached the subject of the doll whose clothes were off. The boy responded by revealing that his neighbour whom he addressed as 'uncle' did it to him. And he added 'I don't like Kamalesh uncle' and started pouring sand from the sand pit over another male doll with adult features.

In another case, a seven-year-old girl in her play session was clinging to a female adult doll all the time. In the interaction that followed the play session, she told the therapist that it was her grandmother. 'I don't want her to die', she said. She was nurturing an apprehension that she would lose her grandmother soon because recently her grandfather had died suddenly, after which the grandmother was often found crying. The child seemed to have heard her grandmother telling someone she could not live without her husband.

Play therapy has been successful in bringing emotional release, particularly in children who are otherwise not verbally expressive, for various reasons, including a lack of language skills.

Physical Exercise

Any physical exercise, such as walking, jogging, aerobics, mass drill, swimming, and outdoor games such as badminton, football, tennis, etc., have therapeutic potential (Anshel, 1995). Physical exercise is a good proactive coping that prevents and minimises the impulsive reaction to stress manifested in irritability, anger and depression (Hariharan & Rath, 2008). Physical exercise has been identified as a good intervention to enhance creativity, confidence and well-being and minimise negative affect states such as anxiety, depression and addictions (Annesi, 2005; Sachs & Buflone, 1984; Stathopoulou et al., 2006). Accordingly, the physical exercises occupied an integral part of therapeutic intervention either during or in between counselling sessions or after the termination of counselling as an attempt to rejuvenate the client.

Clients with significant pent-up emotions can be prescribed suitable physical exercise as homework between the counselling sessions. Physical exercise in group sessions is also significant in handling non-clinical depression and anxiety.

Hariharan and Rath (2008) have suggested variants of physical exercise for handling stress in individuals. Simple breathing exercises such as deep breathing and exhalation breathing are prescribed to calm down and relax the individual. Suppose the client is found to be in a state of nervous agitation and unable to express themself adequately, in that case, the counsellor can introduce simple breathing exercises as a crisis intervention measure to first bring down the anxiety in the client. Stretching exercises relieve the client of muscular tension that piles up due to overwork or stress. It can be prescribed for clients who show symptoms of rigidity in muscles or those who show signs of high inertia. Walking was identified as the best medicine for humanity by Hippocrates two thousand years ago. Walking tones up all the skeletal and muscular areas of the body and is identified as a good contributor to almost all physiological systems in the body. The therapeutic ingredient of walking is not only to the physiological system but also to the psychological health of the client. Walking constitutes a type of mindfulness meditation if carried out in a proper way. Concentration on the rhythm of the steps, opening the sense organs to the physical environment to experience nature around in the form of flora and fauna, listening to the sounds of nature, feeling the temperature and the wind brushing against the body, inhaling the mild natural smell of the mud, flowers, water, etc. brings in some relaxation in the client. Clients who are depressed, anxious or overwhelmed may be prescribed solitary walks at least once a day during the morning or evening. While prescribing walking, the counsellor should train the client to experience the sensory inputs during the walks to optimise the impact.

Bibliotherapy

Bibliotherapy refers to the suggestion of selected reading material to the client that is considered to be helpful in dealing with their present state of stress.

In this era of 'education by search engines', bibliotherapy is the most relevant prescription for the client. It is very common for patients diagnosed with a chronic or even a terminal illness or a client undergoing counselling sessions who wish to know the technical aspects of the treatment and the prognosis but cannot discuss the same with the doctor or counsellor to take recourse to the popular 'Google search'. More often than not, they encounter information flooding. Unable to screen the relevant from the unwanted, they end up feeling the 'burden of the information' that leaves them more confused than before. Bibliotherapy, in a way, can be called an effective step to screening the relevant contents and preventing burdening the client with information overload.

The counsellor can suggest some self-help books. The suggested books are listed depending on the unique need of the client. For example, for a client who is going through severe stress after the diagnosis of cancer, which is in stage 2 and a milder form, the counsellor can suggest *Quantum Healing* by Deepak Chopra which inspires the patient to fight the disease. Children who lack social competence may be suggested to read *Panchatantra stories* where social skills are imparted through animal characters. When the client is a woman feeling deprived and helpless, the biography of Sindhu Tai may be suggested to understand the development of resilience in self. An elderly client suffering 'empty nest syndrome' after her grown-up children left home in pursuit of their careers may feel encouraged to tap her unused resources by reading the biography of another client who started publishing her story books at the age of 80 after her children settled down in their lives. The counsellors can prepare biographies of their clients and use them as reading material for other clients if found useful. In such cases, the only care the counsellor has to take is to mask the identity of the client whose biography is prepared and obtain written permission from the client to have the whole story documented and shared with others as reading material.

Bibliotherapy works well in helping the client release emotions when the client identifies with the main character in the reading material. The client who otherwise could not express the emotions may feel the vicarious effect and emote well while reading the story.

These are some therapies to be applied when the client is not verbally expressive; hence the emotional release is either unlikely or marginal through conventional counselling sessions. These therapies can also be used in combination with counselling. The counselling sessions can be interspersed with therapeutic interventions, or the therapies can be suggested as homework for the client in between the sessions. The only caution to be taken by the counsellor is that the client needs to be properly apprised of how to practice the therapy. Further, unless the counsellor is trained and competent in a particular therapy, one should avoid trying it out on the client. In such cases, the counsellor can always refer the client to a competent therapist who is trained in the method and take inputs about the outcome from the therapist to supplement the counselling.

Exercises

Following are some excerpts from counselling sessions. The dialogue between the client and the counsellor is presented, and the context is explained. The responses of more than one counsellor are presented. Read them carefully and identify which of the counsellors has responded correctly and what skill(s)is/are applied in the context. Also, discuss why the other counsellor is wrong.

Exercise 1

Client (a 45-year University teacher who is physically challenged). I am so fed up that I sometimes feel this life is not worth living. This world has no place for honesty and forthrightness. I am a serious researcher and have a good reputation as a teacher. But that has absolutely no value in the University system. This system is so rotten with caste and regional feelings that you tend to get your rightful place only on those criteria. Since I do not join any such group, I am treated as an outcast. They denied me my promotion, and they disallowed my bills, they instigated students against me, they harassed me for every small thing.....so much so that I experienced hell in the department day after day... (Pauses and then resumes in a reflective tone). I know how much I had to struggle to reach this stage. I put my foot down and convinced my parents to pursue higher education in that remote village. I made it a point to clear national-level entrance examinations to get a seat in Ph.D. It was a different ball game to go on a Commonwealth fellowship for my postdoctoral research. Then, I got this job purely on my merit........not under the reservation for the physically challenged...... I am in no way inferior to these people..... But they make me feel so ...everyday (Chokes)...stops

Counsellor 1: You know how to fight and overcome adverse situations. You have been doing it all the way. Then, how come you suddenly feel that this life is not worth living?

Counsellor 2: Why do you think those people are troubling you?

Exercise 2

Client: (a University student) I ......I feel baffled....What is happening in my life? I came to this university with great hopes of excelling academically, as I have always stood first in class. But, ever since I joined, ...I am put through different experiences. Before I realised I found myself entering into a relationship. I spent long hours in the company of my boyfriend. I....... I don't know, but I did things I would never have imagined........ The other day, I joined the students protesting against the management....only because my boyfriend was taking the lead. The police were called, and I was booked along with the others. My teacher called me the other day and said that my performance in the examination was very poor. I.......don't know how to tell this to my father... My father has sent me here with so much hope that I will excel. How would he feel? I have lost a lot of time in all these things. I think I am entangled now......Cannot get out of this rut. I cannot dissatisfy my friend, and I cannot dissatisfy my father or sacrifice my dreams...... I am doomed...... (Sobs)

Counsellor 1: (after giving a decent pause) Oh! It's all very upsetting, right?

Counsellor 2: The only wrong step taken by you is entering into a relationship rather than concentrating on your studies.

References

Annesi, J. J. (2005). Changes in depressed mood associated with ten weeks of moderate cardiovascular exercise in formerly sedentary adults. *Psychological Reports, 96*, 855–862.

Anshel, M. H. (1995). Effect of regular aerobic exercise and progressive relaxation on motor performance and affect following acute stress. *Behavioural Medicine, 21*(4), 186–196.

Ball, T., Rahm, B., Eickhoff, S. B., Schulze-Bonhage, A., Speck, O., & Mutschler, I. (2007). Response properties of human amygdala subregions: Evidence based on functional MRI combined with probabilistic anatomical maps. *PLoS ONE, 2*(3), e307.

Camic, P. M. (2008). Playing in the mud: Health psychology, the arts and creative approaches to health care. *Journal of Health Psychology, 13*(2), 287–298.

Eldar, E., Ganor, O., Admon, R., Bleich, A., & Hendler, T. (2007). Feeling the real world: Limbic response to music depends on related content. *Cerebral Cortex, 17*(12), 2828–2840. https://doi.org/10.1093/cercor/bhm011.

Gross, J., & Swartz, R. (1982). The effects of music therapy on anxiety in chronically ill patients. *Music Therapy, 2*, 43–52.

Hariharan, M., & Rath, R. (2008). *Coping with life stress: An Indian experience*. Sage.

Hariharan, M., Padmaja, G., & Padhy, M. (Eds.). (2011). *Trauma and pain: Biopsychosocial perspectives*. Global Vision.

Heshmat, S. (2019). Music, emotion, and well-being: How does music affect the way we think, feel, and behave?, *Psychology Today*. https://www.psychologytoday.com/us/blog/science-choice/201908/music-emotion-and-well-being.

Koelsch, S., Remppis, A., Sammler, D., Jentschke, S., Mietchen, D., Fritz, T., Bonnemeier, H., & Siebel, W. A. (2007). A cardiac signature of emotionality. *The European Journal of Neuroscience, 26*(11), 3328–3338. https://doi.org/10.1111/j.1460-9568.2007.05889.x.

Koelsch, S. (2009). A neuroscientific perspective on music therapy. *Annals of the New York Academy of Sciences, 1169*, 374–384. https://doi.org/10.1111/j.1749-6632.2009.04592.x.

Kottler, J. A., & Shepard, D. S. (2008). *Introduction to counselling: Voices from the field*. Thomson Corporation.

Mathur, A., Vijayakumar, S. H., Chakrabarti, B., & Singh, N. C. (2015). Emotional responses to Hindustani raga music: The role of musical structure. *Frontiers in Psychology, 6*. https://doi.org/10.3389/fpsyg.2015.00513.

Pénzes, I., Hooren, S. V., Dokter, D., & Hutschemaekers, G. (2018). How art therapists observe mental health using formal elements in art products: Structure and variation as indicators for balance and adaptability. *Frontiers in Psychology, 9*. https://doi.org/10.3389/fpsyg.2018.01611.

Sachs, M. L. & Buffone, C. W. (Eds.) (1984). *Running as therapy*. The University of Nebraska Press.

Sammler, D., Grigutsch, M., Fritz, T., & Koelsch, S. (2007). Music and emotion: Electrophysiological correlates of the processing of pleasant and unpleasant music. *Psychophysiology, 44*(2), 293–304. https://doi.org/10.1111/j.1469-8986.2007.00497.x.

Stathopoulou, G., Powers, M. B., Berry, A. C., Smits, J. A. J., & Otto, M. W. (2006). Exercise interventions for mental health: A quantitative and qualitative review. *Clinical Psychology, 13*, 179–193.

6 Cognitive Restructuring

Rashmi is an 18-year-old student and the elder daughter of the two children of Sanjeev and Sravanthy. At the age of 18, her father, Sanjeev died in an accident. Rashmi has been unable to reconcile to the fact of losing him for ever. While she was grieving his death, she also started being rude to her uncles, aunts, and cousins. At the same time, she complained that her mother, sister and she were left alone, and no one in the family actually cared for them. She went into depression and consulted the counsellor. The counsellor encouraged her to describe incidents that subscribed to her conclusion that she and her family is deserted by all. While she described the incidents, she would tone down the initiatives from her relatives in offering help. She would also justify her reactions of stonewalling every gesture of support and kindness from her relatives. The counsellor highlighted to her the facts of the positive gestures from the relatives. She asked Rashmi to check if her negative reactions could be a manifestation of her grief, helplessness of not having her father around. During the course of the session the counsellor even asked Rashmi if she was looking for a substitute for her father in everyone who tried to support and offer help. After two to three sessions, Rashmi, started to introspect and found that she assessed every offer for help as trivial compared to saving her father's life which was not possible. Gradually she started to realise that given the situation, she needs to create a lot of goodwill and support from family by being positively responsive to them rather than being rude which resulted in distancing from all.

This change in Rashmi's thinking did not come in a day. It was a process through several sessions. This change happened because of change in the perception, objective analysis of facts and application of logic. This is cognitive restructuring. This happened through the process of counselling where the counsellor was a catalyst through use of the appropriate skills.

Cognitive Restructuring is a process of identification and disputation of irrational and negative thoughts that are responsible for triggering negative emotions in the individual. This process is used in Cognitive Behaviour Therapy, Rational Emotive Therapy, etc. The process applies a number of strategies and techniques. The rationale behind this is that certain (repetitive) thoughts are responsible for negative affect leading to inducing stress, sometimes posing a challenge to the individual's mental health. Hence, one way to break this vicious circle between cognition and emotion is to change the cognition. When irrational and negative thoughts are challenged, alternative thoughts develop and replace them. These alternative thoughts are either positive or neutral, with no power to invoke negative emotions. Thus, the process involves demolishing the faulty cognitive structure and rebuilding the cognition with substitute thoughts that have no inherent

DOI: 10.4324/9781003459415-6

negative emotions. Since it involves replacing a set of thoughts with the other, the term 'Restructuring' is appropriate.

Are there inputs from theories of counselling that suggest cognitive restructuring? To answer this question, it may be ideal to examine the commonality among some of the very popular theories of counselling.

Why Cognitive Restructuring? Suggestions from Theories

The Gestalt Approach

Gestalt therapy is not identical to Gestalt psychology, though one has to agree that Gestalt psychology has certainly contributed to the development of Gestalt therapy. Gestalt psychology is built on the premise that the whole is greater than the sum of its parts. According to Gestalt principle, human perceptions are guided by certain principles such as proximity, similarity, closure, etc. despite the fact that the stimuli are not organised that way. The human mind has the capacity to perceive even the not-so organised stimuli in an organised way. This is done automatically to provide and sustain the psychological equilibrium at the cost of distorting the real arrangement of the stimuli. The principle goes beyond visual field, about which the students are familiar. Example of the application of this principle to the auditory field is the game that many of you might have played in school. Children sit in circle. One child chooses to whisper something (a word or a short sentence) into the ear of the one sitting next, who is supposed to transmit the same to the next. The process continues until the whispering completes the circle. The last person announces what is whispered into his/her ear. Seldom it matches the content at the origin. The content must have gone through transformations at various points. Yet, the transmission continues with multi-level distortions at various degrees lest the child experiences psychological disequilibrium. Whatever is not clear gets substituted/filled by the listener before the next level of transmission, thus causing a distortion in the end product. The same principle applies at the thought level too. The gaps in perceptions automatically get filled with content which may not match the reality, thus resulting in irrational thoughts. These irrational thoughts when negative, stimulate the associated negative emotions. These negative thoughts have the potential to block the self-awareness of the individual which constitutes the central theme of Gestalt therapy.

Gestalt approach functions on the assumption of unification of mind body and soul, thinking, feeling and action. Awareness of the self lies in integration and understanding of these three components as a unit. Self-awareness constitutes the corner stone of Gestalt approach. The awareness refers to individual's understanding of his/her thoughts, feelings and actions at present. Very often, the individual cannot be perceived in isolation. The individual's present experience has a connectivity with the past. Two factors that block self-awareness in the individual are preoccupation with the past and low self-esteem. The individual's present is perceived against the background of a context, which is the past experience. Many a time the individual gets stuck with the unfinished tasks of the past which interferes with his/her present. In such instances, the thoughts about the past invoke negative emotions which are disruptive for personal growth. According to Gestalt approach the individual has a personal responsibility in developing an awareness about one's thoughts feelings and actions in the present 'as they are and how they are' rather than indulging in the past. To explain in very simple terms, the individual cannot proceed further if he/she believes 'My past has been problematic; I cannot change the past; therefore, I cannot grow and develop'. Instead, one should be ready to develop awareness about 'here and now' of thoughts, feelings and actions. This helps in instilling the ownership of one's own thoughts feelings and actions. Once this is done, the individual is likely to accept responsibility for what he/she is at present. This in turn invokes the motivation to change which subsequently results in changing the thought process. It is through self-awareness and acceptance that one gets motivated to change the existing perspective than when a change is forced upon the person (resulting in resistance than motivation). The process involves the old meanings being replaced with new and development initiated through new insights. Thus, the Gestalt approach advocates cognitive restructuring through self-awareness and offers a number of techniques. The techniques emphasise on helping the client talk about the thoughts, feelings and actions of the present than digging into the past. This is a striking deviation from psychoanalysis.

Existential Approach

Existential approach is an intersection of philosophical and psychological approach to life. The fundamental assumption on which the whole approach stands is that we are the architects of our lives. This basic postulate is extremely important in this context because, being the builders of our own lives there is a need to understand, assess and exercise choice in structuring our lives at various points.

Existential approach premises that every individual has a self-awareness in terms of one's own potentials that are unique and the actions to realise these potentials that rests on one's choice. The individual is bestowed with the freedom of choice and hence is fixed with the responsibility to choose from the environment as it presents to the person. The master motive is to exercise the choice and preserve one's existence and develop by realising the potential. In the process of preserving the existence, the individual encounters the paradoxes of life. They are – while there is complete freedom, that is also bound by the responsibility; alongside the need for preservation, there is the reality of death; simultaneous with the reality of being alone in the world, there is a need to be connected; and while life is meaningless in the face of certainty of death, there is a quest of meaning through actions. Caught in these paradoxes, the individual experiences 'existential crisis', feeling trapped in the prisons of lives. The existential philosophy argues that these 'prisons' are the individual's own creation either by their incapability or by refusal in assuming responsibilities or by surrendering their choices in life. Thus, they are found to depart from what is called 'the authentic existence'. The outcome of this is experience of anxiety, depression or deviation from the state of well-being. Helping the person out of this state of anxiety involves development of new insights into life forces to understand the inauthenticity with their antecedents, accepting the same, developing a new self-awareness or rediscovering one's own potentials, making meaning of actions to organise life more systematically. This process is followed with a clear understanding that every individual is unique and needs to be understood and handled in a unique way. The common factor of this approach with the Cognitive and Gestalt approach is its advocacy for cognitive restructuring.

Box 6.1 Cognitive Distortions

Cognitive Distortions	Examples
1. All or none thinking	*Either I get a promotion or I am useless*
2. Emotional Reasoning	*I feel apprehensive about marriage. My marriage is not going to work*
3. Mind reading	*I am sure my wife is thinking that I am incompetent to get a better job*
4. 'Should and must' statements	*I should be successful in all my attempts*
5. Catastrophising	*The doctor said it looks a benign tumour, but the biopsy report will prove it malignant*
6. Labelling	*I am just a good-for-nothing person*
7. Personalisation	*I saw mom in tears to day. Must be because of my poor performance in exams*
8. Disqualifying the positives	*I am unhappy with my project report. I missed one unique point, though rest was ok*
9. Magnification	*I failed to convince the consumer. I am a horrible sales person*
10. Fortune telling	*I will not be able to complete all answers in exams, the bell will ring when I start my last answer*

Cognitive Behavioural Approach

The basic premise on which the cognitive-behavioural approach stands is that there is a close connection between cognition, emotion, and behaviour. The individual experiences negative emotions due to automatic thoughts which are negative and irrational. Hence it is important to capture and work on these thoughts of the clients. Automatic thoughts are assumed to have their origin in childhood beliefs constituting schemas. The daily life events are interpreted and understood against the background of these schemas and surface as thoughts following the events. Sometimes, some self-critical beliefs of childhood get triggered by certain events and situations, culminating in automatic thoughts. These negative thoughts generate negative affect states such as anxiety, fear, anger, frustration and so on. The best way to handle such situations is to dispute these irrational beliefs at the core in a systematic and logical way so that the equilibrium is restored through emotional relief. This is popularly known as the A, B, C, D, E model, where A stands for the activating event (Antecedent), B for Belief, C for Consequence of the belief (anxiety, fear, etc.), D for Disputation of the belief (by using appropriate counselling skills) and E for Emotional effect.

Blumenthal et al. (1999) described ten broad cognitive distortions that one might engage in. Box 6.1 lists them with examples.

Left unattended, these cognitive distortions invoke negative affect, disturbing the emotional equilibrium. As a result, the client may engage in self-denigration or demeaning others, indulge in expectations of perfection from self and others, and undermine the potential in self or the intentions of others. This creates an unreal world for oneself that lowers one's own well-being.

Given such circumstances, the counsellor needs to address and question the client's irrational way of thinking, challenging the logical fallacy therein until the client comes to a stage to appreciate and endorse the absence of logic and distorted perspective and is willing to take an alternative perspective. While applying the skills in this process, the counsellor is careful in limiting his/her role to that of a facilitator in driving the clients to discover their faulty thought process. This is what Beck and Weishaar (2005) called 'Collaborative empiricism', connoting a collaborative relationship between the counsellor and the client. The goal of the counsellor is to provide the client with a cognitive reorientation. This is done by questioning the automatic thoughts and also the schemas that constitute the base for them. The cognitive restructuring may take place in any one of these following ways:

1. Reinterpretation of schemas (application of schemas to a suitable context)

   Example: *While a stranger approaches for help, one need not trust completely*

2. Modification of schema (parts of the schema changes)

   Example: *Not all strangers seeking help are bad; some are genuine and can be trusted*

3. Restructuring of the schema (total replacement of schema)

   Example: *People, in general, are good and can be trusted*

Thus, the major approaches to counselling justify the need for cognitive restructuring as an essential component of counselling. There are various methods and skills to be applied to attain this goal. The counsellor needs to exercise professionalism in the process of choosing the right skills for cognitive restructuring. Many factors, such as the personality of the client, the emotional state they are in, the level of motivation, resistance manifested, will have to be taken into consideration. The skills advocated by various approaches are consolidated and discussed in this chapter.

Concreteness: The Corner Stone in Cognitive Restructuring

When do clients approach the counsellor? This happens only after he/she tried out all methods to handle the problem. The client approaches the counsellor when the distress caused by the situation is found to interfere with the day-to-day functioning. The counsellor is approached when either the clients or their well-wishers realise that the well-being of the person is at stake. Consultation with a counsellor precedes many unsuccessful attempts to resolve the problem by using the available resources or when the problem is left unattended until it becomes unmanageable. Now, it is not difficult to visualise the cognitive and emotional state of the client at the point of the first consultation. The client, in extreme cases, is likely to experience one or more of the following: confused about the dynamics of the problem, clueless about the reasons for unsuccessful attempts in resolving it, not having a total understanding of the stressful situation, and yet assuming to have a good comprehension because some gaps are filled with beliefs, opinions, and feelings, erratically guided by thoughts leading to inferences, the presumption of having tried all the resources under control, feelings of hopelessness, helplessness, distress, dejection, fatigue, disinterest due to depression or inattentiveness due to anxiety. Just visualise a situation where the client in such a cognitive and emotional state meets the counsellor, who expects him/her first to apprise the problem.

The client presents the problem in a way that is in synchrony with his/her psychological state. Every client is found to be unique in the way they present the problem. There may be some who would go chronologically and present the facts as they unfolded; there may be others who narrate the current situation and go into a flashback. In case of these two categories, the narration may or may not be interspersed by emotional outbursts. Either way, these two categories of clients can be labeled with some degree of cognitive structure. But there may be some who do not know where to start and may not have an idea on what is relevant to narrate. There may be others who start at a point and then add bits and pieces as and when they remember, with no order or structure. Yet others may be so distraught and overwhelmed that they can hardly speak and burst into sobs. For a few others, the overburdening stress finds an outlet like a gush of a volcano. Whatever may be the characteristics of the client, one likely common feature is some element of subjectivity in the narration of the problem. The subjectivity will include irrational beliefs, assumptions, inferences, closures, opinions, projections, generalisations, concealed messages, ambiguous contents, conscious evasions, safe statements, and contradictory statements, to mention a few.

In this context, the counsellor is responsible for systematically guiding the client to clarity from ambiguity, reality from distortions, and acceptance from evasion; in summary, concreteness from confusion, abstraction, and generalisation. There are two aspects in the client's narration that demand the attention of the counsellor: Content and form. The form of the presentation reveals the emotional state of the client, while the content of it is in a way the manifestation of the cognitive clarity. Concreteness is judged by the content of the presentation. The counsellor, while taking note of the form of narration, also looks for the core messages in the client's narration. However, very often, the presentation of the client is so highly emotionally overpowered that the content in it is insignificant. The counsellor has to ensure the presence of content in the narration. This can be elicited if the counsellor helps translate the narration in terms of feelings, experiences, and behaviour (FEB). The following examples may be of help in understanding the way concreteness is achieved.

Example 1:

Client: *It is not once; it is not twice... but it is the third time that the management has denied me the promotion. They have the power, and they can use or misuse it. They have a coterie, and I am not a part of it. They are powerful men, and they can deny the women their rightful growth. Everyone endorses to me that it is injustice, but only in whispers. Nobody has the courage to come together as a team and fight the injustice- not even all the women employees.*

Counsellor: *You feel mad at the management and yet helpless and silent because you are unable to get support from colleagues who are playing it safe.*

Example 2:

Client: *I know that I am good at my subject, but I am not very confident about teaching in the corporate school. They teach in English.*

Counsellor: *You hesitate to accept the job in the school because you feel inadequate in communicating in English as you did not study in English medium.*

Example 3:

Client: *I have been following a disciplined lifestyle. I never ever had even a head ache in my forty years of life. I have never smoked, never do I drink, very keen on nutritious food and exercise......then, how? How can a person like me get cancer? I have friends who smoke, drink, have junk food, and have all sorts of bad habits. They are all fine..... Why? Why?*

Counsellor: *You are shocked with the diagnosis because you thought a health-abiding person like you would not get diseases like cancer.*

In all three examples above, the counsellor extracted the core message and gave concreteness to the expressions of the client by applying a simple formula 'You feel...... because......'. By transforming the client's statements into this templete, the counsellor could bring concreteness in terms of how the client felt, the experience that the client was put through, and the consequent behaviour. In the first example, the paraphrasing of the counsellor includes the emotion of the client(Feeling mad at and yet helpless), the experience (indifferent colleagues), and the inaction on the part of the client (silent). In the second example, the cousellor brings to the surface the feelings (feeling inadequate), the background experience (not studied in English medium), and behaviour (hesitation in accepting the job). Similarly, in the third example, the counsellor points to the feelings of shock, past experience of healthy habits, and behaviour of non-acceptance of the diagnosis of cancer in the client. This way of concretising the narration helps the client speak further and understand the problem in a perspective that constitutes facts about the whole situation.

Concreteness is also likely to evolve in the client as he/she gives an expression of language to the thoughts and feelings. It is important to encourage the client to narrate the story. Very often, while translating the thoughts, feelings, situations, and experiences into speech, the entire episode takes shape, which can throw a new insight into the whole problem leading the client to take a different perspective about the whole problem. Besides this, the counsellor intervenes at various points so as to unravel the facts camouflaged by assumptions, affect, and beliefs. This is done in the most professional manner by applying various skills suitable to the context. The role of the counsellor is one of the facilitators who, through the skills, helps the client unblind the blind spots and gain new insights that help him/her to revise the earlier perspective about one's stressful situation and take a different stand in understanding the problem through the gained insight. To be successful in the progression of the session, the counsellor has to attain two major goals- 1. Cognitive restructuring, and 2. Changing the attitude of the client towards the stressful situation. Let us now elaborate on the skills the counsellor applies to attain these two goals.

Box 6.2 Case Study 1

Malini is a 17-year-old girl from an underprivileged background. She is a second-generation learner. She is the youngest of four children in the family. Father was an employee with the state Government but died when Malini was in school. Mother is a homemaker. All the older siblings of Malini are educated. Mother is highly encouraging about children's education, though she had no schooling. Malini is highly social and developed a good social network. She actively participated in sports and cultural activities in school and college. However, academically, she was considered only an average performer. Malini did not perform well in her Intermediate examinations. What followed the announcement of the results was her suicide attempt. She had sent her mother out on some pretext and tried to hang herself behind the locked door. Fortunately, her mother, smelling something fishy about her behaviour, returned home without finishing the task for which Malini had sent her. Not getting a response to the door bell, she sensed that something was amiss and alerted the neighbours, who broke open the door and saved Malini at the nick of the moment. Following is a part of the interaction between Malini and the counsellor:

Malini: *(Her looks fixed on the floor) I feel embarrassed to stir out of the house. The entire colony knows about it now........ My mother created a big scene.....*
Counsellor: *What do you think will happen if you go out of the house?*
Malini: *Everyone may get curious......(does not complete the sentence)*
Counsellor: *Curious about what?*
Malini: *........ My action.*
Counsellor: *What will they be curious about? The cause of your attempt?*
Malini: *Well, not that. My mother seems to have told them the reason for it on the very day when everyone assembled to break the door......*
Counsellor: *Then? What will they be curious about?*
Malini: *They may talk about it on seeing me.....*
Counsellor: *Talk to whom? You?*
Malini: *They may not talk to me....will be talking to each other.......*
Counsellor: *Ok. Did you hear them talking to each other about it on seeing you?*
Malini: *Not really. .... but, I saw them talking to each other.....*
Counsellor: *Do you think they would not interact with each other when you are not seen outside?*
Malini: *Why not? They do talk. May be on many issues.*
Counsellor: *Now, please tell me how true it is that people in the colony talk to each other about you when you get out of the house.*
Malini: *Well, I think it is my feeling.....I guess.*
Counsellor: *Does this guess or feeling help you in getting back to your normal activities?*
Malini: *No. In fact, it stops.*
Counsellor: *What is it that is stopping you from resuming normal activities?*
Malini: *Welll...... I suppose... it is my imagination and ...... perhaps my own feelings...*

Counsellor: *Now that you acknowledge that it is not the people outside, but it is your own feelings and imagination that are preventing you from returning to your normal life, we need to talk about handling these feelings and imagination in you.*

After further interaction, Malini and the counsellor decided that Malini would take a walk in the colony along with her friend in the evening, counting the steps manually from the time of leaving the house until they finished counting 3,000 steps. On the return, they did not have to count the steps. This was given as homework to Malini.

The following is a part of the interaction between Malini and the counsellor.

Counsellor: *Well, as we decided today, we will try to understand the cause of your attempt to take your life. What made you take the extreme step?*
Malini: *I think I felt ashamed. All my friends could pass, and I was the only one who failed.*
Counsellor: *Well, the sense of shame? Can you tell me more about feeling ashamed?*
Malini: *I thought...... I am dumb compared to my friends. I am good-for-nothing. They would take admission to the graduation course right away. I will have to appear in the supplementary exams. That spoils my career. The label of 'supplementary candidate' ...... is unbearable. Once supplementary, always so. None of my friends would ..... like me anymore. I felt I have let down my mother, sisters, and brother. They have to answer all fiends and relatives. And........ more than anything, my cousin, who is a bright student, may just dump me......*
Counsellor: *Ok. There are a few statements you have made. Like- that you are good-for-nothing, that once supplementary, always supplementary; that your career is spoiled; that you have let down your siblings; and that you will be dropped by your cousin and not liked by your friends anymore. Shall we examine each of them?*

In the case study mentioned in Box 6.2, the counsellor's responses are in the direction of cognitive restructuring. In this case, the client is found to be guided by a number of irrational thoughts, and assumptions, which are considered to be real. The counsellor took the client in the direction of realism. We shall subsequently discuss the skills applied by the counsellor.

We will discuss two major skills under separate heads and combine the other skills under one head used to attain the counsellor's goals:

- Probing
- Challenging
- Other skills

Probing

Probing is a cue used by the counsellor with the purpose of stimulating the client to elicit expression that provides both quantity and quality of communication from the client. It is a skill that helps the client express and communicate the relevant aspects of the problem. It is essential to mention here that the skill of probing in counselling differs from the one in police or judicial investigation, where it is done to get the truth out of the person trying to conceal it consciously. In a counselling setting, probing is done to help the person refine or supplement the narrations to enrich the conceptualised, perceived, and presented facts causing distress to the client. In case of an inquiry or investigation, probing helps the investigator, while in a counselling set up, the probing helps the client being probed by creating opportunities for new insights. As stated by Egan (2010), probes are tactics that help clients express themselves freely and concretely.

The goals of using the probe are:

- To help the client think
- To help the client distinguish facts from others
- To help the session progress

The client assumes a perspective about the situation. It may have partial facts, whole bits and pieces of the event may lack inputs. These gaps are filled by the client with aspects not contributing to facts. In such situations, when the counsellor uses probes, it makes the client think, realise, discard, and substitute the 'non-fact' parts in the narration. The following example which is the extension of Case Study 1 presented in Box 6.2 explains it further.

Example:

Malini: *Once supplementary, always so.*
Counsellor: *Can you please explain to me what is meant by 'once supplementary, always so'?*
Malini: *If I take supplementary exams to pass my intermediate, I will be doing the same even in graduation and thereafter.*
Counsellor: *May I know why is it so?*
Malini: *Well, that's how it will go........ perhaps one gets into the 'failure mode'.*
Counsellor: *Shall we talk about what determines the outcome in an examination?*
Malini: *It is the hard work and effort put in terms of preparation for the exams. One needs to be regular in classes, prompt in studying and good in preparing for exams, and of course, a little luck....*
Counsellor: *Tell me now, which of the ones you mentioned contributes to your statement 'once supplementary, always so'?*
Malini: *.......I think .... I dont know.......may be.......my apprehension.*

In the above example, Malini assumed her apprehension to be a fact and believed it. This gave rise to many other negative thoughts subscribing to automatic thinking, perpetuating negative affect. The counsellor used the skills of probing to make her think in a realistic way. This thinking helped her to the realisation that she believed a self-inflicted apprehension to be a fact. The counsellor, through probe, first elicited the factors contributing to the success of the examination. Then, the next probe made the client think about the logical relationship between the ingredients for success and her generalised statement indicating that failure breeds failure. This triggered thinking in Malini, and she identified and accepted the fallacy in the logic and made a statement distinguishing between fact and apprehension.

There are instances when the session does not move forward. One of the reasons for this is the client presents the problem in long winding statements, without having the focus on the crux of the problem. This may happen either because the client is not good in communication skills or because there is ambiguity in the thoughts itself. In such contexts, it is the counsellor's responsibility to ensure progress in the session. Towards this goal, the counsellor uses a probe. The following example will help bring clarity to this point.

Example: (The client is a working woman who is the sole earner in the family. The husband is unemployed)

Counsellor: *You said that the home environment is the cause of all your stress and frequent migraine. Shall we discuss that?*

Client: *I complete all the household chores in the morning, pack my lunch, and rush to the office by 8.30 in the morning. The minute I reach the office, there is work waiting for me. I get involved, and there is no time to think about the home front. In fact, I enjoy my work and the reputation in the office. I hardly have any time for myself except the half-an-hour during the lunch break. I have no problem with it, either. On my return from the office, I stop by to buy vegetables and other things for home. By the time I return, it is already seven in the evening. I have no energy left. The whole atmosphere turns negative. I find it difficult. Why should things be like that?*

Counsellor: *Can you be clearer on the atmosphere being negative? What is negative?*

Client: *Well, how do I explain?...........*

Counsellor: *Tell me what makes it negative.*

Client: *I see my husband sitting and watching the TV. The volume is loud.*

Counsellor: *What is it that you perceive as negative?*

Client: *My husband's attitude. He stays home the whole day. Does not go to work. Yet, contributes nothing, even to household chores. At least he could make a cup of tea for me. Rather he expects me to give his evening tea on my return. I am tired....... I feel unloved..... I feel exploited.....*

In the above example, the client went on narrating the problem in a long winding description without the mention of the crucial aspect related to her husband's unemployment and attitude until the counsellor probed with a question, 'What is negative in the atmosphere?' With this question, the client had to be specific, and that brought the focus to the session. In such cases, had the counsellor limited the interventions to that of expression of empathy by paraphrasing the client, it would fail to take the session forward. It is the intervention with probing from the counsellor that helps the session move forward, with the client mentioning the cause of the negative atmosphere.

The counsellor's intervention through probing at the appropriate time when the session seems to miss the spotlight helped bring the focus back. Regaining the focus in a way leaves no option to the client but to pay attention to the facts of the problem. This smoothly turns the perceptions and thoughts into an objective and logical path, where the client starts identifying and endorsing some details that were missed in initial perception and rethinking the attributions, generalisations, apprehensions, and opinions that were earlier misinterpreted as facts. Such cognitive restructuring takes place very gradually and is triggered by probing. Probing as a technique can be integrated into challenging.

Challenging

Challenging is a concept with a positive connotation. It is different from confrontation which has an element of intimidation. Egan (2010) in his explanation about challenging feels that it is a positive intervention to prevent gross mistakes from being committed. There is a saying that a real friend is compared to a shadow and a mirror. While the shadow refers to the constant companion and support, the mirror refers to the function of reflecting reality. This can be applied to the role of a counsellor. A counsellor, through unconditional acceptance and empathy, manifests strong support to the client. Empathy and support, while considered essential, are not sufficient by themselves. The softness of empathy, combined with the context-appropriate skill, helps the client to be unblinded, see the reality, look within, introspect, and identify the major and minor flaws. This lays the foundation for him/her to change the perspective on the problem, reassess the situation, and contemplate a change in the approach to it.

Challenging as a counselling skill can be defined as an invitation to the client to endorse the self-defeating attitudes, ideas, feelings, and behaviour in oneself so as to view the problem from a different perspective. It is an important skill to be applied to bring cognitive restructuring. While explaining the skill, it is very important to reiterate the absence of the characteristics of confrontation, intimidation, and putting down the client. It is the skill of the counsellor to combine firmness and compassion to say difficult things to the client in a non-judgemental way (Finn, 2005). Applied this way, challenging brings the best results in cognitive restructuring.

The rationale behind challenging are:

- There is a tendency to have an exaggerated perception of the emotional turmoil, vulnerability, and helplessness of the client
- The resources of the client are often underused
- Change is possible, and one can move towards the change only when one identifies and acknowledges the lacunae and feels the need to overcome the same through initiating change

The rationale can be explained with an example. A client who lost his job feels depressed that all his attempts to find a new job failed. Further details on the efforts put in by him reveal that he has been responding to newspaper advertisements without even receiving a call for an interview. Unless the client is made to assess the efforts and accept that the attempts are not adequate and pragmatic, he may not even realise so as to make amends. He may have more achievements than reflected in his resume. He may have the potential to revise his resume to make it more attractive to the employer. All these are possible only when he is challenged to assess the adequacy and impact of his past attempts. Figure 6.1 explains the functioning of challenging.

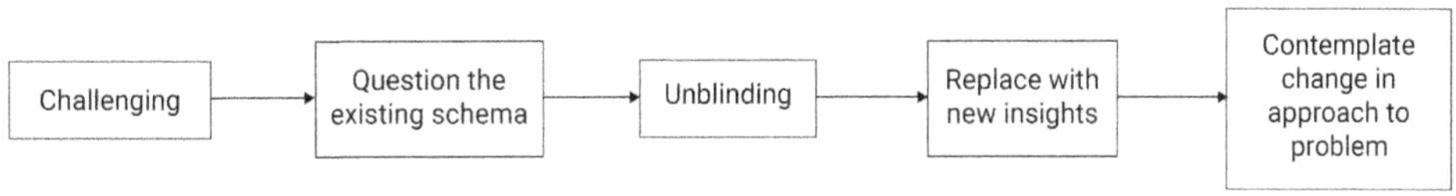

Figure 6.1 Functions of Challenging

Goals of Challenging

The goals of challenging can be broadly divided into two: goals for achieving covert change and goals for achieving overt change. Covert change refers to internal changes, while overt changes refer to observable change. The internal changes translate to observable changes. Figure 6.2 explains it further.

As depicted in the figure, challenging has two major goals, which are interconnected. Challenging brings the client to take a relook at one's ways of thinking, feeling, and the attitudes about self and the world. This is likely to direct one to a more objective assessment followed by the realisation about the self-defeating pattern, irrationality or negativity in thinking and the subsequent emotion or the hitherto held attitudes that are devoid of logic and rationality. There is a quest to replace such covert functioning. Neutral or constructive thinking with concomitant emotions and attitudes is likely to substitute them, resulting in a cognitive reorientation and a changed perspective on the problem. Challenging also brings in a change in the expression of thoughts, emotions, and attitudes in the client, leading to a behavioural change in the approach to the problem. Questioning the existing pattern of thinking, feeling, and attitudes also drives the need to change the expression and manifestation of these covert activities. The change may either start at the covert level or overt expression of the same. Either way, the outcome is positive and desirable.

Similarly, the restructuring at the cognitive level reflects in the changed approach to the problem. The double-edged goal is to bring changes at a covert and overt level. As long as the intervention of challenging attains the goal, it is immaterial where the change originated. In a nutshell, the goal of challenging is to bring in a change in the internal

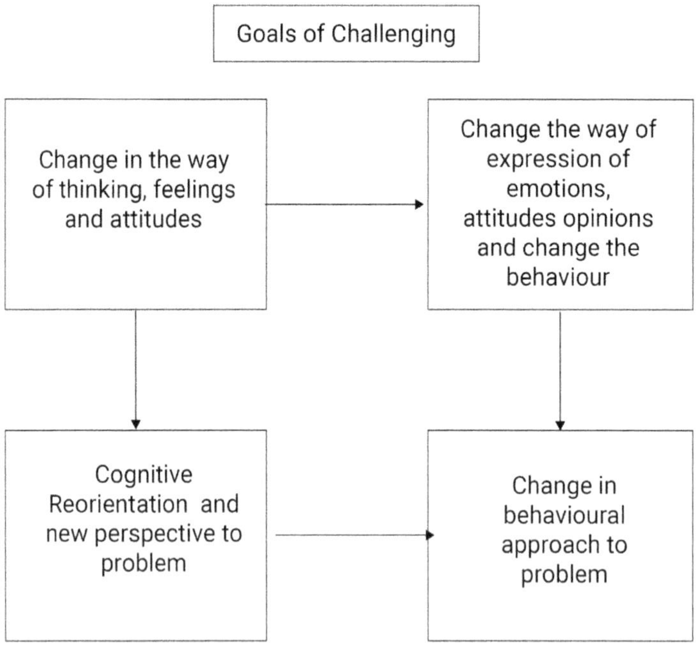

Figure 6.2 Goals of Challenging

and external behaviour of the client. The challenging skills applied by him/her impact in a way that makes the client challenge himself/herself. This self-challenging is what brings cognitive reorientation in the client. Since it is self-initiated, it is likely to be sustainable. Anything forced on the client by the counsellor is likely to be countered with resistance. To attain this sustainable outcome, the role of the counsellor has to be one of a catalyst.

What is to be Challenged?

A question of practical importance is what should be challenged. How does the counsellor know that the skill of challenging has to be applied? What are the indications for the counsellor to use the skills? The guiding principle here is that the challenging should not target the client but the covert and overt behaviour of the client. When this constitutes the thumb rule, the question of intimidation and chances of offending the client are ruled out. Following are the contexts for using the skill of challenging:

- Not ready to own the problem
- Presenting the problem as insolvable
- Misinterpretation of feelings, experiences, and behaviour
- Distorted perception of the external world
- Discrepancies in thoughts, feelings, and behaviour
- Unused resources
- Not acknowledging the consequences of behaviour
- Self-defeating expression of feelings and emotions
- Irrational Beliefs
- Resistance and Reluctance

NOT READY TO OWN THE PROBLEM

It is very common to see the clients presenting the problem as somebody's creation. The stress one experiences are often depicted as infliction by someone else. Such descriptions of stories are not likely to go beyond the purpose of serving emotional release because as long as the problem is perceived as originating from others, the locus of control is never internal. Hence, either no move can be contemplated in changing the other's behaviour, or any such initiative may not meet with any success. The only way to consider reducing stress is to examine the extent of the contribution of self to the problem, either in creating or in precipitating it. When the client is made to successfully identify one's own role in the existing stress, he/she is ready to own the problem. The counsellor's use of challenging is likely to unblind the client to change the position from not owning the problem to owning the problem. This is a major cognitive restructuring that enables the client to view the problem as within the purview of internal control, calling for a definite goal followed by a strategy and action plan to mitigate the situation. The counsellor's identification of the context of 'not ready to own the problem' and the challenging skill is depicted in the following example.

Example 1 (The client is an alcoholic addict)

Client: *I have no intention of getting violent. I have told my wife several times not to provoke me when I am a little 'high'. But she never heeds. She loses her*

	temper when I ask her for something. If only she was a bit tactful, why would I be violent?
Counsellor:	*What I understand from your statement is that YOU go home in a drunken state, YOU ask her for something to which she gets provoked and responds with irritation, and when you see her irritable, YOU don't like it, and YOU take to violence.*
Client:	*Do you mean to say that I provoked her and then beat her up too?*

The counsellor's emphasis on the word 'YOU' is to drive home the fact of the part played by the client in the whole episode of domestic violence in contrast to the role of his wife on whom he was blaming the provocative role.

Example 2 (The client is a fresher in the university sharing her room with a senior)

Client:	*I think the covered way in which the ragging continues has crossed all thresholds. I have been patient all these days.*
Counsellor:	*You said the ragging goes on under some cover. Can you explain, please?*
Client:	*Yes. They do not do it in groups. They do it to the freshers in the respective hostel rooms. My senior roommate makes me copy her notes, wash her clothes, bring her food from the mess, and wash her plate. Why should I do all this? It is so demeaning.*
Counsellor:	*Oh, correct me if I am wrong. You felt helpless in this exploitation, and you are angry with yourself for allowing your senior roommate to dictate things to you.*
Client:	*...Perhaps yes. I am aware of the anti-ragging campaign. Could have silently complained....*

In this example, the counsellor has mildly challenged the client by changing the statement to a passive voice to highlight the role of the client in the existing situation. While the client described the situation as a demand from the senior, the counsellor projected it as compliance from the client. By doing so, the counsellor emphasised the partnership role portrayed by the client in creating the stressful situation. In both examples, the skill of challenging is used without intimidating the client. The goal of the challenging here was to project to the clients the flaw in believing that the other person is responsible for one's behaviour/stress. With this challenging, the clients in both cases seem to have taken the suggestion about their role.

PRESENTING THE PROBLEM AS INSOLVABLE

The client, when approaching the counsellor, is in a state of helplessness, anxiety, or distress. It is natural that a person in such a state presents the problem with heavy subjectivity where they projects themselves as victims of circumstances and others as perpetrators. The fact that the client approached the counsellor is an admission for the client that the problem is grave. Hence, inadvertently, there will be a tendency in many clients to present the problem as difficult, complex, and not easy to solve. The presentation of the problem takes shape where the present is the product of the past, or what faces the client is a dead-end or a situation that has frozen the client totally. Responding only with pure empathy in such situations is likely to reinforce self-pity leading to sympathy-seeking behaviour, which may not bring any productive outcome. So, the counsellor's challenging should prompt the client to shift the attention from the past to the present, translate the presentation to one of specific feelings, experiences, and behaviour which are all dynamic, or redefine the problem in a way that identifies the components that have the flexibility of change.

Example 1:

Client: *I have been through a tough childhood. My mother is schizophrenic. My father left her and married another woman. I grew up in an atmosphere where there was no warmth or love, guidance, or discipline. Thanks to my teacher, who provided support for my education because I was doing well in class. One thing that I was taught thoroughly by my father was that somehow, I should give the medicines to my mother and take her to the doctor at regular intervals so that peace is preserved at home. How do you expect a person grown in such a challenging environment to have a great bonding with her husband's family?*

Counsellor: *Family bonding is something you have missed in your childhood. Should that decide that you miss it when there is an opportunity?*

Client: *No..... perhaps I do not want to miss it........ perhaps I do not know how to initiate, how to respond....how to sustain... Could it be so?*

In this example, the client's initial presentation, by and large, communicated that 'I am what I am because of my past, which cannot be edited now. So, how can I be different?'. This stand was challenged by the counsellor by pointing at the opportunity. Once the opportunity missed earlier is highlighted, the client starts to look within and identify the actual source of the problem, which is related to the approach to participate in the process of family bonding, which is genuine and yet can be helped. Thus the problem was changed from the state of insolvability to that of solvable.

Example 2 (The client had a break up of a relationship)

Client: *She promised never to part. We had dreams of marrying, having a family, and pursuing careers for ourselves....... We had a great time in the past one year.... Now how can she just call it 'quits'? I cannot believe this. I cannot live without her. I cannot forget her. I am unable to eat, sleep, read, work, ...go out...I cannot do anything......*

Counsellor: *You said that you could not forget her and are unable to eat, sleep and do anything. Why do you say so? What happens when you try to sleep, for example?*

Client: *When I close my eyes, I see the flashback of our time together...... it runs as a movie reel. I keep tossing in bed. See the clock ticking till wee hours.... (Has tears in eyes)*

Counsellor: *This break up was totally unexpected, and you are very upset about it. Shall we talk about the specific problems you are having with your basic routine related to health...for example, sleep, eating, etc?*

In this case, the counsellor used the skill of challenging to shift the thinking of the client in terms of the complexity of the problem (expressed in terms of the absolute impossibility of 'cannot') to specific real problems being experienced at present that are interfering with the essential day to day activities for which there are techniques to overcome. Not having an appetite, not being able to concentrate, or being unable to fall asleep are the problems that can be worked out, but 'cannot forget, cannot live without.....' are the problems that cannot be talked about in concrete terms. Challenging the client has shifted his thought pattern from the impossibility of accepting the inevitable reality to focusing on the specific current manifestations that actually constitute the present problem for the client.

Example 3 (The client is the only daughter married to a US-based professional)

Client: *I imagined a different life in the US. But there is no one to help with the daily chores. I have to wash vessels, clean the house and bathrooms, empty the garbage...... My God! I have never done these things at my parent's place. I cannot cope with this life.*
Counsellor: *Well, I do understand that you have no experience doing household chores. Are you mistaking the lack of experience for a lack of ability?*
Client: *...Ummmmmm? (Looks at the counsellor silently)*

The counsellor chose to challenge the cognition of the client directly. The client in this example presents the case as if she has reached the dead-end of the marriage as she is unable to cope with the new demands because the reality is contrary to her expectations. She really feels that the real situation in life warrants avoidance behaviour of withdrawing from the scene at whatever cost. Such self-defeating thoughts need to be challenged by pointing out the major fallacy in it. The response of the client is a hint that the challenging by the counsellor struck the right chord.

MISINTERPRETATION OF FEELINGS, EXPERIENCES, AND BEHAVIOUR

Clients often misread their own feelings, experiences, and behaviour. That may sometimes mean an opportunity missed. The client may be blind to that. Unless that is challenged and brought to the forefront, the client may continue to cling to the concept of 'the poor me', which is a non-initiator of action. Misinterpretations happen not only about one's own feelings, experiences, and behaviour but also with regard to others' feelings, experiences, and behaviour.

Example 1 (The client is a woman reporting her husband's extra-marital affair)

Client: *This relationship with his business partner has been there for the past few years. I was naïve and a fool not to have realised it. Since she is our neighbour and also a widow, my husband would always suggest including her in our family outings. Many times, during the outings, I used to find to my discomfort, that while I was busy helping the children with their dinner or dessert, these two would freak out to the dancing floor or buffet table, ignoring my presence totally. They shared the food and dessert while I was asked to share with the children.*
Counsellor: *You never had an idea? But wait a minute; you said their behaviour during your family outings was 'to your discomfort'. That suggests that you perhaps had an inkling, and yet you chose not to entertain that idea for some specific reason...Could it be so?*
Client: *......Hummmm. May be. Some neighbours also hinted at their affair to me. But... the children were young. The business was taking off. My husband*

had a minor cardiac issue. I did not want to bring this conflict and chose to protect my apple cart.

The counsellor here, while challenging directly, also chose to be tentative to soften the impact of the directness. Without adding the tentativeness, the counsellor would have opened the scope for the client to take a defensive stand which would have defeated the purpose of challenging.

DISTORTED PERCEPTION OF THE EXTERNAL WORLD

One of the driving forces behind any human action is the protection of one's self-esteem. In this process, there may be occasions when the individual has to take a stand of 'I am ok; You are not ok', where 'you' represents the world outside. This perception of 'you are not ok' is often distorted and yet necessary to preserve the positivity about self. Such distortions, though may serve an immediate purpose for the client are harmful in resolving the problem or crisis in the long run. Hence the counsellor chooses to challenge them.

Example (The client is a schoolgirl with a kleptomaniac tendency)

Client: *This school is highly discriminatory. They don't like children coming from backward communities. They try to blame them for everything. I just hate this school.*
Counsellor: *Last year you were in a different school. You did not like that school either.*
Client: *Yes, that was a bad school, too, though not as bad as this school.*
Counsellor: *We are actually talking about the recent incident of your taking away the marker pens and pen-drives from the classrooms. Every time we talk about it, you seem to be talking about the school being bad.*
Client: *Yes. .... What else do you want me to say? The school leaves everything out in the open and puts the blame on a few children. Why should they do that?*
Counsellor: *What happens when they leave things openly?*
Client: *That IS the problem. I...I cannot control myself........ I....I don't want to be bad.... But....*

The counsellor used challenging skills thrice in this context. The first time she challenged her by pointing out her inappropriate response of talking ill of the school whenever the topic of stealing things came up. The second time the counsellor challenged the client by pointing out the fact that she disliked even the previous school. Third time by questioning what happens when the things in the classroom are left accessible. This made the child reveal about the anxiety she experienced until stealing the thing. The young child first showed her distorted view of the schools by pointing out their casteist characteristic. When challenged, she came down to specifics of the schools leaving things open to the children, while the actual problem was her own urge to act in a particular way that violates the social norm.

DISCREPANCIES IN THOUGHTS, FEELINGS, AND BEHAVIOUR

The client in an emotionally charged state may not be in a position to detect certain discrepancies between what one believes and what exactly one feels and whether the behaviour concurs with the thoughts and feelings. A competent counsellor will be able to identify the discrepancies between the thoughts, feelings, and actions of the client. It is pertinent to challenge these discrepancies so as to help the client bring some clarity and convergence between these three disintegrated psychological processes so as to understand his/her own stand on the issue. Sometimes the discord between the three processes may be the result of the use of a defense mechanism by the client, while some other times it could result from a conscious effort on the part of the client to conceal or mis represent the thought, feelings, or behaviour in a stressful situation. This is often seen in clients manifesting reluctance or resistance.

Example (The clients are a couple in marital counselling)

Husband: *I always treated her with respect. But it is always her inferiority complex that makes her feel that I don't respect or care for her feelings. It is...*

Wife: *What I feel is....*

Husband: *Wait. Can't you? Do not interrupt when I am putting forth my points. This is disgusting.*

Counsellor: *Is it that you always WANT to treat her with respect, but when it comes to practice, your irritation gets the better of you?*

In this example, the counsellor could perceive the discrepancy between what the husband believed (treating his wife with respect) and how he behaved (disrespectfully) in a counselling situation. However, the gentle method of challenging that the counsellor chose is something to be noted. An incompetent counsellor could have pointed out the behaviour in the situation and challenged by questioning the client's 'then and there behaviour' with a statement, 'Is this the way to respect the wife?'. This would only push the husband to a defensive position where he may start justifying his irritability or would shame him, where he may freeze and become resistant or reluctant. The discrepancy between cognition and feeling can be observed when the client while describing the problem, may say, 'I am not bothered about the relationship. I can live alone and give a penny to my marriage......' but while making these statements may have a choked voice, and tearful eyes, indicating hurt and feelings of loss. The counsellor can use challenging by pointing out the same with a statement such as 'The possible break up seems to have deeply hurt you somewhere, which you wish was not the case.' The choice of words of the counsellor, while challenging, is very crucial for the right impact of the skill.

UNUSED RESOURCES

It is not unusual for the client to assume that he/she has exhausted all the available methods in coping with the stress, while there may actually be some effective methods yet untried because some very effective resources remain unendorsed. These resources may be internal or external. Unless identified and suggested by the counsellor, the client may not even realise the presence of such a resource. Even if the client knew about the presence of the internal resources (for example, good communication skills) they may not realise that it can be used as a 'resource' in handling the situation.

Example (Client is a middle-aged single woman who lost her husband, the only-earning member, and had only a graduation degree through distance education)

Counsellor: *You stated a while ago that you had done your diploma course in music. Then how can you say that you do not have the qualifications to start a career?*
Client: *You mean to say my diploma in music is a qualification?*

In this example, the client presented a helpless state after the demise of her husband since she would not have actually given any importance to her interest in music and the diploma that she procured since that was never put to use in the past. Thinking along those lines can be initiated with the challenge posed by the counsellor. Thus, the challenging by the counsellor helps in bringing an alternative perspective to the client which is an indication of cognitive restructuring. The counsellor has to be alert to identify the unused resources in the client. A competent counsellor always chooses to challenge the strengths of the clients, which aids in finally empowering the client.

NOT ACKNOWLEDGING CONSEQUENCES OF BEHAVIOUR

The counsellor has to challenge the client when he/she is not ready to see through the outcome of the behaviour chosen to handle the stress. Many times, a faulty coping strategy proves counterproductive. While under stress, the probability of reacting rather than responding to the crisis situation is very common. Such reactions normally are not the outcome of any proper assessment of the conditions or consequences. Hence the chances of precipitating the stressful situation or adding new stress to the situation are high. In his/her anxiety to act, the client may not give much consideration to the consequences of an action. Challenging the client to associate the action with the consequences is a skill that may draw the attention of the client to the right aspect. The client may or may not revise the action, yet, the action then would be an informed decision than a knee-jerk reaction so that there is some degree of readiness on the part of the client to absorb or respond to the consequences.

Example:

Client: *My boss has given feedback to the management that I have a quick temper and cannot get along with people in the team and that I need some intervention in interpersonal relations.*
Counsellor: *Ummhmm.*
Client: *Damn it! How biased! I want to confront him. I wish to go into record that it is he who has gender bias and hence has such views about me.*
Counsellor: *Well, do you want to prove to him right that you do not have good interpersonal skills?*
Client: *(Pauses) No. That would give him a chance...right?*

The counsellor challenged the client here by directly pointing out the consequences of her confrontational action. When highly stressed out, the client may not be able to estimate the result of one's chosen action until pointed out.

SELF-DEFEATING EXPRESSION OF FEELINGS AND EMOTIONS

Emotional regulation constitutes an important ingredient in building one's social network. Lack of these skills may end up in the absence of social support or even negative support. Expression of the right emotion in the right proportion in the right context is not a skill everyone possesses. The absence of emotional regulation is indicated by the suppression of feelings or inappropriate expression of feelings and emotions. While bottling up is directly harmful to the self in terms of manifesting in psychophysiological symptoms, inappropriate expressions lead to distancing of the potential support groups. Both are negative contributors to the state of well-being. The counsellor, when finds them harmful should challenge.

Example (A 13-year-old boy with a rare disease where his GI system cannot digest any adult food except milk)

Client:	*Ever since I changed my school, I face this problem of being bullied by the class mates for carrying a bottle of milk as my lunch. I feel miserable.*
Counsellor:	*Miserable means?*
Client:	*humiliated, angry, helpless.....*
Counsellor:	*So, what do you do?*
Client:	*Nothing. Try to walk away silently. Pretend not to hear them....*
Counsellor:	*Does it help you in any way?*
Client:	*Not at all. I cry alone at night. Sometimes I just cannot sleep at night and feel like screaming at all my friends and telling them why I have to rely on just milk for the next two years....that I am under treatment......*
Counsellor:	*What will happen if you do so?*
Client:	*Ummm? ....Don't know.......may be.......well, I really don't know.*

The counsellor may take the discussion forward until the client realises that his reaction and feelings are, in fact, self-defeating.

IRRATIONAL BELIEFS

There are cases where the client is guided by one or a set of irrational beliefs and thoughts. The feelings and actions originate from these irrational beliefs. They need to be necessarily challenged so as to prevent the client from indulging in such affect state and behaviour. Ellis (2004a, 2004b), who developed Rational-Emotional-Behaviour Therapy (REBT), identified a set of such irrational beliefs which are self-defeating and dysfunctional in their characteristics. Box 6.4 presents the list of irrational beliefs based on Ellis' model.

The counsellor can challenge any of the irrational beliefs listed above. It must be remembered that there may be other irrational beliefs not listed here, which also need to be challenged.

MANIFESTATION OF RESISTANCE/RELUCTANCE

Resistance and reluctance are identified as major hiccups in developing rapport between the client and the counsellor. There are many reasons for the client to take shelter under resistance and reluctance. This becomes a major obstacle in creating a cognitive reorientation for the client. The counsellor has to identify the manifestation of this behaviour and challenge them in combination with empathy and support.

Example (The client is a college student caught with marijuana in his hostel room)

Counsellor:	*You are asked by your Warden to meet me. Right? Do you want to tell me something?*
Client:	*Yes, it is the Warden who sent me to you. Perhaps he would tell you what his problem is.*

Counsellor: *Well, the Warden already spoke to me. I wish to hear from you.*
Client: *From me? Why? It is the Warden who had a problem with me. I don't have a problem with anyone. What will I have to say?*
Counsellor: *You seem to be very angry with your Warden for some reason. You are showing that anger here. Shall we talk about why you are angry with the Warden?*
Client: *Angry? I am, in fact, very angry with him. He is highly biased. He listens to the tales of his favorite students.*

In this case, the client is resistant because he is angry with the person who referred him to the counsellor. That constitutes the first point of his cognitive distortion. Unless the client's resistance is challenged, proceeding further with the session will be totally blocked. Hence, the counsellor tactfully challenged the client's resistance and brought him to discuss the anger with the Warden first. It will be easier to carry forward the discussion on the central theme thereafter.

Box 6.4 Irrational Beliefs to be Challenged

Irrational Belief	*Example*
Being loved	I must be loved by all
Being competent	I must be an achiever, or else it is worthless
Bad persons	People committing wrong are evil and should be punished
Having one's own way	When things don't go the way I desire, it is awful
Being trouble-free	I should face no problems. If so, should have quick solutions
Avoidance	Better to avoid a situation than to take responsibility
Being a victim	Others are the cause of my misery. No one can take advantage of me
Impact of the past	I am shaped by my past. Because of it, I feel & behave the way I do
Perfection	There is only one right solution to problems. It will be disastrous not to have it
Fair & just world	The world has to be fair & just. Cannot tolerate otherwise
Hurt-free & pain-free	I should never have pain or face hurt. Cannot take it
Being passive	I should be passive and have no commitment to be happy

Example 2 (The client has a sensitive issue of sexuality)

Counsellor: *In our last session, we were discussing the problem between you and your close friend and the issue that you have with your wife, who has left home upset with you. Shall we take these issues forward by discussing the specifics?*

Client: *(With a smile). These are, in fact, very common things in relationships, right? Love and hate are part of life. Everything will be ok soon. It is just a question of time. (Tries to make light of the issue)*

Counsellor: *When we were discussing this in our last session, you said at the end that these are sensitive issues and you would be ready to talk about the details in the next session. You are trying to put it off again today because they cause some discomfort to you. Am I right? I am listening. Please go ahead without any inhibition. (Leans forward)*

The client's reluctance is seen in his self-contradictory statements. The counsellor's challenge with support communicates his acceptance. The non-verbal communication of the client is a good complement to his verbal support and challenge that would stimulate the client to open up with some degree of confidence.

We discussed the above ten different contexts where the counsellor applied challenging. It is important to mention here that the skill of challenging can be used in helping cognitive restructuring whenever there is an indication of causing a hurdle to it. The ten situations mentioned above are only suggestive but not exhaustive. A competent counsellor may identify an obstacle to cognitive restructuring in many other contexts and may decide to use the skill of challenging.

How to Challenge: Specific Skills

In this section, we will discuss the methods of challenging. This refers to the 'How?' of challenging. The first and foremost aspect is to remember the goals of challenging, which is to stimulate the client that results in thinking, taking a relook, contemplating, revising, identifying, or endorsing, all helping in cognitive restructuring. With this in the background, one would be cautious not to create any aberration to the very purpose of challenging. Hence, challenging should be done with a good blend of empathy and support. The constructive use of challenging inciting new insights helps the client transform the blind spots into revised perspectives. The signs of this may be seen in internal functions such as changed attitudes or external actions such as regulated emotional expressions or modified overt behaviour. This is also known as 'second-level learning' (Argyris, 1999). The process is called 'Frame breaking' (Egan, 2005). Though there are many other nomenclatures, these two are worth a special mention because of their aptness. The appropriateness of the term second learning is because the client relearns the problem leading to a totally different perspective. Frame breaking gains its importance because the counsellor, through challenging, breaks the erstwhile frame of reference to the problem.

The counsellor uses various techniques to challenge the client. Egan (1990, 2010) has brought the skills under a few broad heads. We will explain the most significant ones here. Figure 6.3 gives a comprehensive picture of these methods.

As shown in the figure, Egan (1990) discussed five methods of challenging: Sharing Information, Self-disclosure, Advanced empathy, Immediacy, and Asocial Response. Out of this, Advanced Empathy, Immediacy, and Asocial Response adopt three major techniques each. Let us discuss each of them in detail.

SHARING INFORMATION

One way of empowering oneself is to have the right information. Information brings clarity to an ambiguous situation. Most of the client's confusion and indecisiveness crop

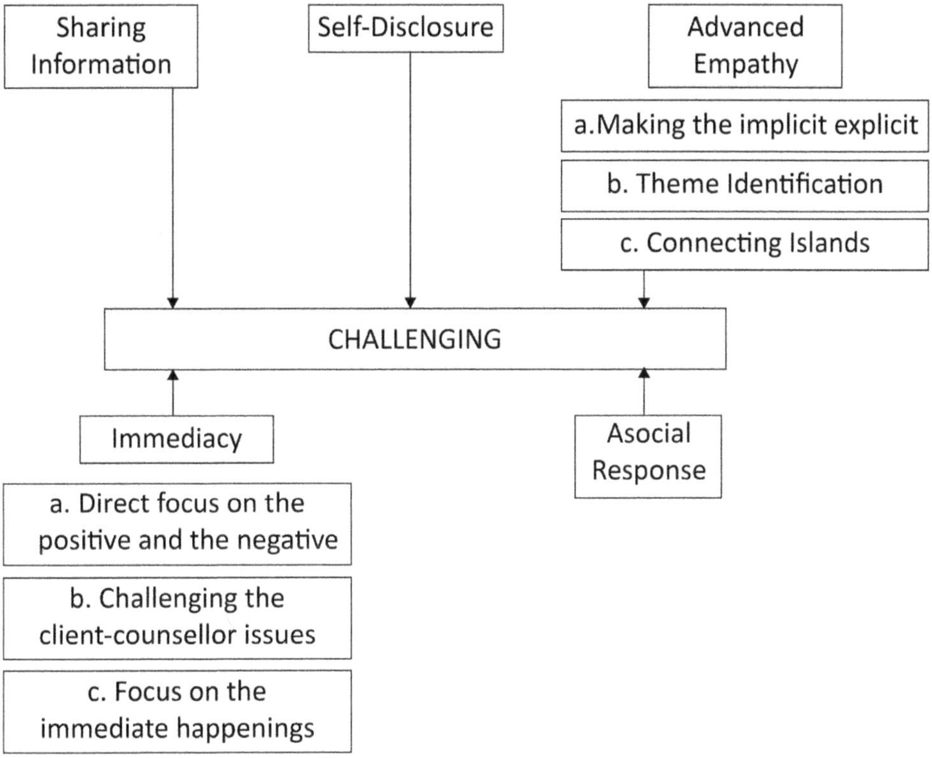

Figure 6.3 Methods of Challenging

from the absence of information, and inadequate or wrong information, which creates hurdles in exploring the problem and working on a solution. The counsellor's challenging by sharing information either fills the total gap of the information vacuum, enriches the existing information inadequacy or replaces the wrong one through information correction. In all three cases, the challenging by information sharing empowers the client. Incomplete information generates stress, while wrong information misleads the client. In either case, the client's actions are blocked, while the action is the much-needed outcome of the counselling process. For example, when a patient for the first time hears that he/she has cancer, the existing information on cancer that had been inadvertently gathered during the course of the time is inadequate. The type of information needed when one is diagnosed with the disease differs significantly from what is gathered out of curiosity or academic interest. One needs to know information on the grade, stage, implications, treatment options, funds required, prognosis, treatment time, and many more in connection with the specific diagnosis related to self. Many hospitals have the provision of information sharing with the cancer patient with the participation of the doctor and a counsellor. The following points are very crucial in information sharing:

1. The shared information should be relevant
2. Presentation of information should be organised
3. Quantity of information should not be too much

4. The client should be given adequate time to process the information
5. Ascertain that the client does not leave with any wrong information
6. Information sharing should be distinguished from advice

The counsellor should use discretion in deciding the contents so that the clause of relevance is adhered to. The spacing of the content presentation should match the information processing ability of the client so that it does not take the shape of information flooding. While the information is shared, the counsellor needs to be dispassionate so that there is no scope for influencing the client with the personal choice of the counsellor.

Sharing new information with the client creates a psychological disequilibrium in the client, which may be temporary. It is this consequence of the skill that adds to the challenge of the counsellor. The counsellor should be adequately skilled to handle the cognitive, emotional, and behavioural outcomes of such disequilibrium. For example, when the client is given the information of the diagnosis of cancer, the reaction may vary from emotional freezing to emotional explosion. The counsellor should be ready to respond to reactions of any degree. Further, during the discussion of treatment options and prognosis, the counsellor needs to use discretion on the content and form of presentation, taking care of the facts and objectivity without causing undue emotional trauma to the client. It is relevant to mention here that the responsibility of the counsellor does not end with providing the information. It extends to assessment and assistance in processing and assimilating the information. Some examples related to challenging with sharing information are discussed below.

Example:

Client:	*The fact that I failed to crack the medical entrance examination is difficult to absorb.*
Counsellor:	*Why do you think so?*
Client:	*Look, my entire community had so much hope on me. I was considered a brilliant student in the town for the last ten years. Now....see....*
Counsellor:	*Does your failure to crack through medical entrance exams wipe out your brilliance?*
Client:	*If I were really brilliant, I would have made it.*
Counsellor:	*Well, do you have any idea of the number of candidates who apply and the number of seats available in the country. Let us have a look at this data and the rank you got in this exam. Perhaps you will be able to assess yourself correctly. (Shows the data). Just check this sheet having the numbers of applications against the seats this year.*
Client:	*Oh God! More than sixteen lakh applications for less than fifty thousand seats in Govt. colleges!*
Counsellor:	*And... what was your rank in the list?*
Client:	*Two lakh seventeen.*
Counsellor:	*So?*
Client:	*(Smiles) Thank you. I understand.*

In this example, it is very natural for a student from a small town to feel that failure to get a seat is a failure in itself. However, the counsellor's challenge, wrapped with good support, enlightened the student on his relative position in a situation of tough competition, where there are lakhs of candidates screened out against few thousands who were selected. The challenging brought to light for the boy that though he could not obtain a seat, he should still be considered brilliant as he procured a rank that was ahead of more than ten lakh applicants from the entire country. This is cognitive reorientation that resulted from replacing a wrong schema due to inadequate information combined with irrational belief (I cannot fail in anything). It is the information sharing by the counsellor that could have the right impact. Any amount of empathy and listening or emotional ventilation would not have brought this change in the client.

SELF-DISCLOSURE

The counsellor invariably has a social influence on the client. Though not intended, the personality disposition of the counsellor, the behaviour, responses and reactions of him/her can be called inadvertent self-disclosure of the counsellor. Through his/her continuous interaction with the client, the counsellor reveals certain dimensions of his/her characteristics. This is indirect disclosure. This will influence the client in many way not only in his/her relationship with the counsellor but also in the way one approaches life. In addition to this, the counsellor can choose to challenge the client through self-disclosure. Counsellor self-disclosure refers to sharing some of the counsellor's thoughts, experiences, and behaviours with the client with a goal to change the direction of the client's thinking, feeling, and behaviour (Farber, 2006; Kelly & Rodriguez, 2007). This skill has been adopted by many counsellors in the past few decades. The counsellor more or less serves as a role model to the client. This skill of challenging has to be applied following certain guidelines:

1. Use self-disclosure judiciously: The counsellor should apply this only if the context warrants. It should happen very spontaneously, naturally, and effortlessly than contemplated. Further, the counsellor has to be cautious about the quantity and quality of disclosure. It is desirable to be crisp. Though it amounts to disclosing something personal, the counsellor should retain the professionalism. Violation of this principle may place the client in discomfort. There are instances where elaborate disclosures by the counsellor resulted in the client decision to discontinue the sessions.

   Example:

   Client: *The very thought of going for cardiac intervention is giving me jitters. I am unable to sleep.*

   Counsellor A: *You said you are advised to get an angiogram done, Right? I have been through it six months back. Actually, it is a diagnostic procedure. Not a treatment but a diagnosis with accuracy.*

   Counsellor B: *Angiogram is a simple procedure. I was asked to have it. What they do is send a dye through your arteries. They poke somewhere in your leg through which they inject the dye, which travels to the heart. If there are any blocks, the dye shows it to them on the screen. If they find the blocks very significant, they seek your informed consent to do the angioplasty procedure right away. Your family members have to sign an informed consent form. There is some amount of*

> *risk, of course. But every procedure has its risk. Those allergic to dye will have some problems.*

In the above case, both counsellor A and B have put forth the facts. But while counsellor A's intervention helps the client reframe the concept of the procedure to put him to ease, counsellor B's intervention changes the frame of thinking to create more anxiety and panic. This is because the quantity and quality of information from counsellor B are overwhelming.

2. Verify the cultural appropriateness of the disclosure: The purpose of self-disclosure is to equip the client with glaring positive evidence related to an issue that has been a source of stress. The client's cognitive activity is likely to take stock of the similarities and differences between the experience of the counsellor and the present situation that he/she confronts. The natural human resistance may catch up on the differences, if any, resulting in resistance to change the perspective. For this reason, the counsellor has to be sensitive to the cultural differences between the client and himself/herself so that self-disclosure does not prove futile. For example, when the counsellor is a male and the client a transgender and is reporting a situation of lack of social support during a health crisis, and the counsellor applies self-disclosure, it may just boomerang because social support is determined by several factors related to societal sensitivities and acceptance.
3. Choose the appropriate time: Counsellor self-disclosure too early in the counselling process is not likely to be successful. There should be sufficient rapport built between the counsellor and the client so that the counsellor's social influence on the client is already on. In such cases, self-disclosure is more likely to have the desired effect.
4. Meet counselling goals rather than counsellor's goals: The content and form of self-disclosure should be crisp and relevant. The objective is to instill confidence in the client about alternative thoughts, experiences, and behaviour. Since the challenge is supposed to be spontaneous, and the skill involves the disclosure of personal experience, there is a likelihood of taking an unprofessional path and going tangent about one's experience and reliving the same. Such reminiscence may be of help to the counsellor but not the client, who may either withdraw attention or find it amusing in a professional setup.
5. Use the skill sparingly: Self-disclosure is not recommended to be applied frequently. Frequent use of this skill may defeat professionalism and end up in the client becoming informal with the counsellor, which is not desirable in a counselling context. Frequent application of the skill may prompt the client to perceive the counsellor as self-centred, immature (Egan, 2010), or no different from many self-styled counsellors like teachers, superiors in the office, elders in the family, who often relate the problems of others to their own experience and indulge in advising the person encountering the problem.
6. Use discretion on whom to use the skill: Not every client will be able to accept and process self-disclosure. Some may get overwhelmed by being subjected to listen the experience of the other person. Some may tend to get too curious and seek unwarranted details, while others may take it in the right spirit. The counsellor should apply the skill only to the third category of clients. There is a possibility of the clients perceiving it as the counsellor unloading his/her burden while the client is dealing with his/her own.

ADVANCED EMPATHY

Advanced empathy is different from primary empathy in its form and purpose. Primary empathy is used to communicate to the client that the counsellor understands, feels, and experiences the situation that the client encounters. This helps the client develop trust in the counsellor, and encourages the client to express more and progress in the session. Advanced empathy is used to take the client beyond the concrete expressions and explore what is not stated, identification of a common theme, and thread together the isolated events/experiences with a common factor responsible. The purpose of the advanced empathy can be compared to the excavation of the thoughts, feelings, experiences, and behaviour concealed and camouflaged by other factors. Advanced Empathy is a method used for challenging the client to understand the message concealed behind the one expressed.

The blind spots of the client include both positive and negative factors. The client may be blind to his short-temperedness on the one hand and his great potential for managerial skills on the other. He may, while stating his feelings for his mother, express his appreciation and love for her selfless disposition while trying to conceal his irritation for her over-indulgence in caring for him.

The alert counsellor, while the client is narrating the story, should make a note of the many aspects that the client is either blind to or is not presenting clearly. Box 6.5 presents the identifiable blind spots of the client. They can be detected in the client's description of the problem. Box 6.5 presents them in two categories – first, messages in incomplete disclosures, and second, messages concealed in expressed statements.

The counsellor, after identifying the hints, hesitations, and confusion in the descriptions of the client, challenges them on these aspects. It is very important to reiterate here that identifying the gaps mentioned above is not equivalent to an interpretation of the same. A competent counsellor would be able to spot not only feelings, experiences, and behaviours expressed but also those hidden behind the expressions. For example, a student who is upset about the broken relationship and expressing her longing for a revival may make a statement like 'I spend a lot of time in the library and that I have been missing in the last one year. But.....It is difficult not to have him beside me while going for a long walk. I think I should call him and give a trial' (the last part of the statement is faint and unsure). The tone and tenor of expression are indicative of the ambivalence in the student. The counsellor may challenge this by saying, 'Well, you sounded quite happy about the gained time for the library, but you seem to be a bit unsure of attempts of reviving the relationship.' Here the counsellor did not interpret anything but caught the communication expressed through the form of communication.

Box 6.5 Client's Blind Spots Fit for Advanced Empathy

Messages in incomplete statements	*Resources untapped*
Statements in the form of hints	Dreams unrealised
Confused statements	Wishes unfulfilled
Statements with a tinge of hesitation	Potentials unrealised
Incomplete or half statements	Support unused
Statements calling for reading between the lines	Competence ignored
	Opportunities not availed

Challenging through advanced empathy can be through different techniques.

From Implicit to Explicit: The counsellor captures from the client what is being implied in the communication rather than expressed concretely. The same is put back to the client with a question directed, seeking an answer to what was unstated. This can be explained with the following example, where the couple was to be present for marital counselling. The husband turns up, but the wife does not.

Example:

Husband: *I have asked her to be here by 11 am sharp....... She agreed. Perhaps she is stuck in some traffic..... (uncertainly) She will come.*

Counsellor: *Well, you do not sound very confident about her turning up. Anything you wish to say?*

Husband: *Yeah....... Last two occasions, the same thing happened. She promised to come but just gave it a miss....Of course, she gave some excuses.....I was in two minds about whether to go and pick her up myself to ensure her presence, but somehow believed her when she said anyway she had to come to this side to meet someone... I am sorry, even this time, it looks like an appointment was not honoured by us.*

In this example, the counsellor, by capturing the tentativeness in the tone of the husband, challenged him to speak out about what he was hesitating to. Without this, the husband could have extended the time of waiting than accepting that this is yet another time his wife avoided meeting the counsellor.

Theme Identification: Advanced empathy works when clients endorse what the counsellor identifies and challenges. Hence, counsellors have to be careful in their accuracy of perceptions. Very often, the client's description of problems has multiple experiences and behaviours. If the counsellor listens intently, he/she may identify a common theme that may constitute the centrality. Once identified, the counsellor may challenge the client by projecting the central theme. This is likely to set the client to take a revised look at the whole problem.

Example:

Client: *I feel very lonely sometimes. I have no one to turn to or relax with, you know?*

Counsellor: *Let us talk about it.*

Client: *My wife is hardly an intellectual companion to me. The topics my colleagues discuss ...like movies, malls, or tourist spots, are so boring for me. My college friends are long lost... and my neighbours? It is always children's education, competition, and cultural events..... I feel so sad that there is no one who matches my mindset.*

Counsellor: *What is your mindset?*

Client: *It is so different. ....I like to think, contemplate......*

Counsellor: *Are you sure you are not really indicating your lack of social skill that fails to relate well to others?*

Client: *I.....I find it difficult. I get upset when people do not agree with me......*

In the example above, the counsellor intently listened to the client's absence of good social contact, starting from home, neighbours to colleagues, where the others are blamed for inadequacies. Yet, the client was unable to explain 'the different mindset' that he attributed to himself. The client cited various causes for not relating to others. The varied contexts and the varied reasons for his lack of making friends, supplemented by his statement that his mindset is to engage in thinking and contemplating rather than interacting, spoke about his lack of social skills. This was put back to the client straight. The response of the client to this started to bring out the exact problem. More is likely to come too. Only when the client is challenged did the client start directing the thoughts to the facts experienced. It is important to place these facts before the client so that the problem can be helped. Egan (1990) states that the themes can relate to affect states such as anxiety, depression or hurt, experiences such as being a victim, subject to seduction, failure, behaviour indicating domination, control, and avoidance. The counsellor should be alert. On identifying any self-defeating patterns in thoughts, feelings, or actions, they can be ascertained through challenging. This requires alertness, empathy, assertiveness, and above all, the tact for the right communication.

Connecting the Thread: While presenting the situation, the client may present a few experiences that are independent and isolated. None of them may be responsible for certain outcomes in the form of hurt, anxiety, exhaustion, or indulgent behaviour, while the combination of them might culminate in such outcome. When such indications are perceived, the counsellor can challenge them by questioning or suggesting such possible connectivity. This helps the client fill in the missing link and review and revise their perspective about the problem.

Example (The client has a husband diagnosed with bipolar and a daughter with a personality disorder)

Client: *My daughter has been extremely demanding of late. She just does not care for my feelings. My husband, who is a bipolar patient, pampers her despite my repeated warnings. He is so vulnerable to her manipulative behaviour. But neither of them respects my words. As a result, there is some crisis or the other that they create on almost a daily basis. This is a very trying period for me. I am tired. But now is the time for my son, who joined his new job and is seeking my support to be with him in Bangalore until he settles down and gets used to managing his office and home. I want to go. But I feel that I am being irresponsible, leaving my husband and daughter to themselves to create havoc here. I don't know why, but I want to go to my son....Am I a good mother? Good wife?..... Don't know....*

Counsellor: *You have had your platter filled by your daughter and husband. You are unable to help the situation here. Now, your son's call appears to be a welcome break from this situation. Is that right?*

Client: *I am fed up with both of them. She aids him in skipping medications, knowing fully well the implications. He returns the favour by giving her money, knowing fully well that she spends lavishly on drinks. All these are happening right under my nose! I feel absolutely redundant. Sometimes I feel that they would learn only when their mutually aiding behaviour leads to some crisis. Why do I not protect my sanity when there is an opportunity?*

The client here presented two unconnected situations-one at home and one with her son, both demanding her attention and time, though in different ways. The counsellor tried to connect the two with a common thread of her unpleasant experience and helplessness and feelings of being inconsequential and identification of a temporary relief route. When she describes her dilemma of where to be present, the counsellor, by connecting the two separate needs with her thoughts of need for respite, brings clarity to the cognition.

IMMEDIACY

Immediacy refers to a package of skills used by the counsellor to explore what is happening to the relationship between him/her and the client in the immediate situation of counselling (Egan, 1990). Human relationships and interactions are the screens where the individual's personality and behaviour patterns get projected. The way the client relates and interacts with the counsellor is likely to provide a sample of the client's interaction in the outside world. Hence it is pertinent to explore deeply into the identified discords and unexpected feelings and behaviour shown by the client towards the counsellor. Challenging the client on this is termed as Immediacy, which was advocated by Carkhuff (1969), Anthony et al. (1979), while Higgins, Ivey and Uhlemann (1970) called it 'direct mutual communication'. Called by any name, immediacy is used to put back to the client the unexpected way he/she relates to or behaves with the counsellor in the counselling setup. The response of the client may sometimes extend to the experience, feelings, and behaviour with the world outside.

A few methods of challenging through immediacy are discussed below.

Focused Challenge on Positives and Negatives: The positive aspects of behaviour during the counselling process are clues to the client's motivation and efforts. They need to be sustained by appropriate reinforcement. The counsellor's focus on this is considered as a challenge to the client because the communication that is passed through this is the expectation of the counsellor to maintain the same. Thus, it becomes challenge to the client. Further, it triggers the thoughts to identify and confirm the positive feelings and behaviour pointed out by the counsellor.

Example 1 (The client is an adolescent student who is struggling with himself in communicating to his father that he wishes to quit his Engineering course because he wants to pursue Fine Arts where his heart is)

Client: *I could not sleep the whole night because, in the last session, we decided that I should tell my father about my passion and my dislike for engineering. I was trying to figure out how to initiate the conversation. Finally, I thought that it was impossible not to disappoint him in whatever way I revealed my mind, so it is important that I speak my mind spontaneously rather than preparing and rehearsing. Having made that final decision, I could fall asleep, ...perhaps in the wee hours. But, by the time I woke up, my father had already left for work. Thus, I failed to keep up with the earlier milestone of communicating to him before coming for this session. I think I have disappointed you. Sorry for that.*

Counsellor: *That is fine. But I really like the clarity that you arrived at after a long night's thinking. The way you communicate with me now is something* *that is good. This spontaneity perhaps will help you with clarity even when you interact with your father.*

In this example, the client's reporting majorly highlighted the failure or missing the opportunity to communicate with the father, ending with an apologetic note for not being able to stick to the decided action. However, the counsellor, highlighted the positive behaviour in the client and communicated his expectation of retaining it when he has to face his father. Here what the counsellor has done is to focus on the positive behaviour of the client in the immediate context in relating to the counsellor. This assumes importance because the same positivity needs to be extended in a situation of interaction with the father, which constitutes the major issue at this point in time. The counsellor could have emphasised the negative part of the failure to initiate communication with the father. That would contribute to the already existing thought pattern in negative lines. But applying immediacy by focusing on what is already achieved in terms of coming out of a confused state contributes to the cognition in changing the perspective from 'Can I?' to 'I can'.

Example 2:

Counsellor: *One thing I wish to share with you today is my own reactions when you describe your problem to me. I don't know why, but there are times I feel intimidated. Can you see any reason for it?*

Client: *This is something I am familiar with, you see. Even my friends say that I annoy them when I narrate something. ....Perhaps it is true... that it is my style of communication. Should we try to see what it is?*

The counsellor can apply immediacy not only from the point of the way the client relates him/her but also can mention the reaction it is producing in the counsellor. In this case, the counsellor focused on the negative reaction that the client was invoking in him through his narration. This enabled the client to relate similar reactions to his friends. This indicates a new insight. Further, the client's initiative that this aspect be explored, in fact, lays the path forward in the progression of the session.

The counsellor sharing the inexplicable reactions to the client was even used by Carl Rogers. Once, he seems to have expressed to his client the boredom that he experienced while listening to the story's narration by the client. To this, the client responded that his narration is bland, flat, and uninteresting because he did not think that the listener was ever interested to know what he spoke. Such revelations bring to the forefront a new schema of the client related to interpersonal relationships. Both the client and the counsellor get a new perspective on the problem in question.

Relationship Immediacy: This refers to the counsellor challenging the client based on the relationship that developed between him/her and the client over the sessions. This sometimes can be extended to a relationship in real life situation. Challenging this aspect helps the client to review through comparison and thereby explain, attempt, and modify the behaviour in the outside world.

Example:

Counsellor: *Tell me something; you say that you never get along with your father, and you feel that it is because of the huge age gap between the two of you. But,*

	for the past two sessions, we have been interacting. In the process, I might have asked you uncomfortable questions, and you have openly disagreed with me, yet we are going on with our interaction without major problems. Then why is it that you are unable to sit and talk with your dad?
Client:	*.....That is because ......may be...I don't like him. You are treating me with respect. How can I have a problem with you? Perhaps I....hate him. ...... hate him because of the way he treats my mom.....*

The new perspective the client got is that the strain in the relationship between him and his dad is not so much due to the age difference but due to his disrespectful way of treating his mother and him. This could be brought when the counsellor directly challenges by comparing the relationship shared with him under similar conditions of age differences.

Focus on Immediate Happenings: This is also known as 'here and now immediacy' (Egan, 1990). This technique of immediacy involves the counsellor's challenge to the client on what is presently going on between the client and him/her. Thus, the focus of challenge is the immediate happening during the session, aptly phrased as 'here and now' rather than the relationship itself. It is important to challenge the immediate happening at certain points when the happening itself is perceived as an impediment to the progress of the session. The specific 'happening' can be a behaviour, a feeling, an experience, or a combination of them in the client perceived by the counsellor or the the behavioiur, experience or feeling of the counsellor. Such experiences, feelings, and behaviour are more likely to be a reaction to the client's open or camouflaged expressions. Challenging the client by bringing this to the forefront helps in drawing the attention of the client to the factor for immediate corrections in the covert or overt behaviour, which is very important in the overall relationship between the client and the counsellor.

Example 1:

Counsellor:	*(Interrupting the client in the middle) I am sorry to interrupt you, but I thought it was important to bring this up. I see that you are speaking very guardedly today. This is very unlike you. What is the matter?*
Client:	*You are right. I can hear someone moving on the other side of the partition of the room. I feel that privacy is intruded.*
Counsellor:	*Well, that is my secretary. She is typing some report from the Dictaphone with her earphone on. I can ask her to stop that and wait in the office until we are through with the session so that you feel comfortable. Will that help?*

In this example, it was very appropriate for the counsellor to have noticed the change in the normal pattern of speaking in the client and challenge the same and subsequently remove the hurdle. If the session continued in the same way, the client's narration would have suffered spontaneity and transparency, making the whole interaction suboptimal.

Example 2:

Counsellor:	*I think I would just side-track a bit to make the session a bit smooth.*
Client:	*What is it?*
Counsellor:	*For the past ten minutes or so, I have been feeling a little inhibited in responding to you. I feel a bit intimidated by your stern stare at me when*

I say something with the intention of understanding you better. Is there something you are communicating through the stern looks thrown at me?

Client: *Umm....! Did I do that? I normally do that to stop my wife when she is in a mode of communication leading to severe nagging. That helps in controlling the situation. Actually, I have no such intention to do that to you. Now that you have pointed it out I will be conscious and try not to resist inconvenient questions.*

The client sometimes inadvertently uses some of the behaviour that works in normal life situations, which is not appropriate in a formal context of counselling. When the counsellor finds himself responding/reacting to it adversely impacting professionalism, he/she uses immediacy in challenging so that the issue is resolved from both sides. In this case, the male client was unintentionally applying the behaviour to control the nagging of his wife when the lady counsellor was applying probing/challenging, which might have put him in some degree of discomfort. The similarity of age, gender of the counsellor, and the experience of being probed/challenged must have spontaneously made the client apply the same reactions in the context of the wife's nagging. Until challenged, the client was not even aware of what he was doing. Timely challenging by the counsellor helped in the client's realisation of his behaviour and its impact on the counsellor, and also helped him in consciously avoiding it in the interest of the smooth progress of the session.

Immediacy is one of the essential challenging skills that can be compared with 'action research' that provides scope for midterm corrections so as to sustain the scientific approach in counselling.

ASOCIAL RESPONSE

The name itself suggests the type of challenging. This is an unconventional approach to challenging and is normally used very sparingly by expert counsellors. However, even beginners can benefit from it when used judiciously. When used, the intended communication is actually contradictory. The use of asocial response is to make the client take a counter view and to get an outcome that is not in line with the actual challenge. We will discuss three types of challenging under this head.

Contradictory Response: When the client goes into a long-winding description of a complaint about the other person, the counsellor sometimes sees a need to cut down on the indulgence. In a way, this is done after understanding the standing of the client, who seems to be taking a position of single-track thoughts.

Example:

Client: *I am now elevated to a high position. Need to host VIPs off and on. But she (the wife) is just a high school passed. She is so unsophisticated. Sometimes it is so embarrassing for me to see her naivety in her interactions. True that we have been married for 15 years. But, I wish.......Hmmm.....what is the point.......*

Counsellor: *You are right. You can do away with her. Yes.*

Client: *What? What are you saying? How can I do it? What will happen to the children? .....I...I must admit that though she is not educated, she is one of* *the best mothers. She is a good homemaker. Takes care of all of us with so much affection.....*

The counsellor's challenging with explicitly saying what the client has been trying to say, not so much to mean it but out of frustration, touched the right chord of the client, who instantly took a U-turn and started spelling out the positives in his wife. The purpose of challenging is thus served by making the client reorganise the thought process by highlighting the positives in his wife. This helps the client handle the repetitive negative thoughts about his wife's unsophisticated behaviour in social groups or thinking in the lines of training her in essential social skills. The challenge of the counsellor was through an asocial response.

Box 6.6 presents a case where one of the authors successfully used a Contradictory Response.

Box 6.6 Contradictory Response Case

Janani (pseudonym for the purpose of confidentiality) is a young woman in her early thirties from a middle-class family. She was married by her parents when she had not even graduated. Soon after she had a girl child. But she found her marriage in trouble because of the cultural differences with her in-law's family. She decided to walk out of the marriage and pursue her studies. With the support of her parents, she completed her graduation and joined a course in journalism. While in her journalism course she met her classmate who got close to her. They decided to get married after two years of courtship. Her husband was very understanding and caring. According to her own description he was a 'gentle man to the core'. He legally adopted her daughter through her first marriage and was very affectionate towards the child.

Janani had a great passion for journalism and wanted to pursue her post graduation and doctorate in the subject. Endorsing her potential for the discipline, her husband encouraged her to apply for further studies in one of the American Universities, while he joined as a journalist in a national newspaper. She got a seat. The understanding was that her husband would take care of the six year old daughter in India while Janani pursued her higher studies in America.

The arrangement seemed to work well with Janani's parents extending support once in a while in taking care of the child. Janani used to visit India every six months to spend time with her family. However, once she completed her post graduation and joined the doctoral programme, she was increasingly getting hard pressed for time and her visits to India was getting more and more spaced. In one such visits to India she made an appointment with the counselor just two days before her scheduled return journey.

The summary of the story she narrated was that she was friendly with an Indian man in US. The friendship grew intense and turned into a relationship. The following is the excerpt of the relevant parts of the counseling session between Janani and the counselor.

Janani:	*Nitin is so caring and intellectually so superior. He has the perfect chivalry that fits a civilised man.*
Counselor:	*Ummhmmm.*
Janani:	*His love for me is something that won me totally. He knows what exactly I want. He perfectly understands my taste. He is such a great companion and talks so well. More than anything, he is so romantic. You see...... the sexual relation should not be confined to the bedroom.... It should start in drawing room, kitchen......and end up in bedroom. Otherwise it is so unromantic and monotonous. My husband just has no idea about it. My husband is a good person, but is so quiet and reserved. We hardly have much conversation.... See, ...I....I would say, it is something like a 'mute marriage' between us. Nitin is not married. He has proposed to me. Now, I....I don't know..... what to do.... (Cries)*
Counselor:	*So?*
Client:	*I....I don't want to lose Nitin. I cannot part with him....... He is my great support in a land of no friends. He got me so many friends there. He is a superb person. (Cries)*
Counselor:	*(After a considerable pause for her to stop crying and continue speaking. When it did not happen, the counsellor spoke) Then, what are you waiting for? Why don't you go ahead and marry him?*
Client:	*(Looking straight into the face of the counselor) How can you say this? My husband has so much trust in me and sent me to US. He is looking after my daughter in my absence.....A perfect family man. A good father. A loving husband in the real sense. What if he is not romantic? Is that everything in life?.......*

In the case study described, the counsellor could stimulate the client sufficiently to bring the other side of the argument to the surface. The crying spells of the client and some of the statements made by her were indicative of her attachment and respect for her husband and her rationalising about the developed intimacy with Nitin. This conflict has been going on in her. However, what surfaced in her description is a sort of justification for the newly developed relationship. This certainly is useful in protecting her self-esteem.

From the counsellor's point of view, this is the only session she would have with Janani as she would be leaving the next day or so. There is not much time that the counsellor will have to help the client resolve her conflicts with cognitive restructuring in a systematic long-drawn process. Under such circumstances, the counsellor in fact, took a calculated risk in challenging the client with a contradictory response which normally is not used in the first session. The timing of challenging seems to be right to give the desirable outcome. A word of caution in using a contradictory statement is that it has to be timed and aimed well for the best outcome. Failing that, it may boomerang.

Paradoxical Interventions: A paradox is a situation containing two opposite facts or two opposite characteristics, making it difficult to understand. The interventions are introduced with the expectation that the client would comply with the suggestions and directions of the counsellor for an outcome contrary to what seems obvious. We will discuss three different techniques under this. They aim for cognitive reorientation as well as behavioural change.

Reframing: This is a skill applied in some typical contexts where the counsellor helps the client to reinterpret some of the negative factors by attributing positive connotations. For example, anxiety may be interpreted as someone's keenness to have a desirable outcome. Depression may be given a connotation of somebody's extreme sensitivity to internal feelings. Such reinterpretations break the thread of the thoughts triggering negative emotions and perpetuating the same. The skill seems to be effective for clients who manifest resistance to interpersonal influence.

Symptom Prescription: In this, the counsellor prescribes the problematic symptoms to be experienced/enacted by the client(s). Paradoxical intervention in counselling setup refers to the intervention of the counsellor advocating the continuation or worsening of the problem situation rather than mitigating it. The idea of the intervention is to decontextualise the problem by changing the context and the environment so that the problem loses its negative value. It should be noted here that the intention of the counsellor is opposite to what is advocated. Hence it is called paradoxical intentions. For example, when a couple comes for marital counselling and their problem is getting on to each other's nerves, the counsellor suggests that they both keep a record of all irritants of the spouse and set a specified time in a day during which they can engage in fighting. Now, with this arrangement, though the counsellor is advocating to continue fighting, the time set aside for fighting and the place identified for it would weaken the very behaviour of fighting, which normally gains strength in their natural settings and spontaneity or impulsivity in expression. This is called symptom scheduling.

Symptom Reframing: The other variant of symptom prescription is Symptom Reframing. In this, the client is asked to express the problem behaviour in an exaggerated way. The intention here is to facilitate the client to gain control over the behaviour/situation. The two together is called Symptom prescription.

These skills help in cognitive restructuring. In all these contexts, the chain between cognition, affect, and behaviour is broken through a change in the context of the behaviour. Having lost the power of the original context of the problematic behaviour, the meaning of the behaviour is likely to change, thus resulting in cognitive restructuring.

Possible Client Reactions to Challenging

Challenging, though packed with empathy and support, has its consequences of placing the client in an uncomfortable position. The expected human reaction to any discomfort is resistance, counterattack, or finding escape routes. When the skill of challenging misses the bull's eye, there is a possibility of such basic reactions from the client. Being aware of these possible unexpected outcomes of challenging is like equipping oneself with the techniques for handling them. Following are some of the possibilities:

Discredit the Challenger with a Counterattack

A client who is challenged with advanced empathy that her descriptions suggest that there is more domination than concern in the way she relates to her husband may retort. She may respond by saying that the counsellor being a man, would not be able to understand a woman's plight with a simpleton as a husband, who, by default, commits mistakes in almost every action.

Attempts to Change the Challenger's Views

The client who is challenged by the identification of a theme that it is the complaisance in him that is resulting in underachievement may try to reason with the counsellor. He may say that it is not right for him to run after achievement, which may further damage his hypertension. Adverse effects of hypertension may end up making him a liability for the family, while underachievement is at least not doing it.

Devalue the Very Issue

The client who is advised to totally abstain from smoking after having an angioplasty, when challenged on his 'freaking out', may totally devalue the impact of occasional smoking.

Take Shelter under Others' Support

The clients who are challenged by the counsellor may come back to the next session with some defensive stand. A client who is challenged for being assertive to the point of being rigid may come back for the next session and say, 'I discussed with my mother about being over-assertive. She said it is perfectly ok to be so in order to live in this tough world.'

Agree with the Challenger without Acting

It is not uncommon to find clients who endorse the reason for the challenge and yet indicate their intention not to change. A client who is challenged to link the problem to his past may say, 'You may be right in saying that the past cannot be changed; hence I should focus on the present, but I am unable to get over my past. That's it!'

The counsellor should expect many such reactions from the client and be ready to handle them. This is possible when the counsellor goes with the assumption that defence and resistance are the natural arms of human beings. In instances of such reactions, the counsellor needs to go into some self-evaluation about where he/she has gone wrong in challenging so as to elicit these reactions in the client.

Principles of Challenging

Challenging is one of the major skills used by professional counsellors, which distinguishes the professional from a self-styled counsellor. Hence it needs to be used in combination with empathy and support, which are the essential ingredients to mellow down the tone of it. The counsellor should always leave scope for the client to correct the statement, clarify, or add information when the counsellor goes wrong in perception. The tone and tenor should not be devoid of respect and concern. The skills of challenging are used not only in the context of cognitive restructuring but in many other contexts. Counsellor's

Box 6.7 Principles of Challenging

1. Always comply with the goals of challenging
2. Use the skill after establishing a good rapport with the client
3. Make the statements of challenge in such a way as to encourage the client to challenge self
4. Choose to use tentative statements so that there is scope for the client to correct
5. Be specific while challenging
6. Emphasise strengths than the weaknesses
7. Respect the client's values
8. Expect and deal with the client's defensiveness
9. Use support and empathy as combinations
10. Evaluate the outcome of challenging

challenging should follow certain basic principles so that the chances of defensive reactions or resistance are minimised. Box 6.7 presents the principles of challenging.

A beginner should be very conscious of the principles of counselling to ensure the appropriate use of the skills. As one moves forward in practice, the principles are likely to get automatically integrated as they get assimilated into the cognition of the counsellor with the efforts and alertness put into the initial stages. The skill of challenging being one of the frequently applied skills, one needs to be thoroughly trained under expert guidance in the use of the skill. Application of the skill under simulation and using the skill on the clients as an intern under an expert are some possibilities to gain competence in the skill.

Other Skills

Techniques other than the ones discussed so far, by and large, aim at cognitive restructuring. Some of them are suitable to be applied by the counsellor in the counselling context, while some others can be given as homework to the client. Almost all skills in this miscellaneous category are advocated by the Cognitive Behaviour Approach to counselling. Some of them are also integrated into the skills already discussed under probing and challenging. We will briefly explain the remaining few skills.

Maintaining a Cognitive Diary

The counsellor can orient the client to various types of cognitive distortions. Then guide the client to maintain a cognitive diary that keeps a record of the initial distorted thoughts and the substituted rational thought with the ratings of both on the level of distress. The idea is to bring the clients to experience and make the relief one feels evident by restructuring one's cognition with healthy thoughts. Box 6.8 provides a template of one such proforma to be filled by the client. The box also has the columns filled for a day by a client to show how the diary might look. The columns are filled for one event just to demonstrate how it looks.

Box 6.8 Cognitive Diary

Instructions: This diary is for you to record your disturbing thoughts. Write these thoughts in column 1 whenever you get it. These thoughts are associated with some negative feelings. These thoughts belong to one of the categories of irrational thoughts which I discussed with you. (Readers may refer to Box 6.1 that lists ten types of cognitive distortions.) Identify the category to which this thought of yours belongs. Mention that in column 2. Identify the feelings and write it in column 3 and rate it on a ten-point scale of distress (where 1 is least distressing and 10 is most distressing). Having identified the thought as irrational and distorted, you have to substitute it with a more rational thought with your reinterpretation. Mention that substituted thought in column 4. Fill column 5 with the ratings of distress associated with the substituted thought on the same 10-point rating scale. Maintain this diary regularly. Bring this along when you come for your next counselling session.

Initial Irrational Thought	Category of Thought	Associated Feeling and Distress Rating	Rational Thought Substitution	Distress Rating
I will not be able to crack this exam	Fortune-telling	Nervousness rating: 8	The chances of my performing well are high since I have prepared well	Nervousness rating: 4

A client who fills this diary on a daily basis will have evidence of the reduced distress levels associated with the reinterpretation of the events triggering the distorted thoughts. That would be a good motivation to practice identifying and changing cognitive distortions. This homework will be useful for clients who are found to indulge in irrational thoughts.

Engage in Socratic Dialogue

The counsellor continuously challenges the client on thoughts that do not merit logic and reasoning. The counsellor engages with the client in a dialogue until the client realises the flaw in his/her argument and replaces the same with one that conforms to logic and rationality. A number of examples related to this were given in earlier paragraphs while explaining the skills of challenging.

Evidence Testing

When the client makes sweeping statements that are imaginary and far from facts, the counsellor may involve the client in an action of evidence testing so that the unrealistic thoughts are challenged not by the counsellor directly, but the evidence gathered by the client itself would pose a challenge. For example, when a client makes a sweeping statement that ALL her attempts for SUCCESS IN LIFE have always been a failure, the counsellor asks the client to make a list of milestones in her life and write next to it if it fetched positive or negative results. It is very likely that the list would have a combination of both, though they may vary in frequency. Yet, the challenge of the 'All' or 'Always' statement may still stand. This skill is used in many such contexts where the client is found to indulge in over generalisations.

Statement Reorganisation

The client's sweeping statements can also be questioned by the counsellor in a different way by modifying the language. This minor revision can sometimes reorient the client and help him/her understand the flaw in one's own stand and make changes. For example, when the client makes a statement such as 'I long to have peace. But my son makes me angry all the time', has a technical flaw in the language. An expression such as 'someone making you angry' has a fallacy if one analyses the same. Anger is an emotion. It is expressed by the person experiencing certain physiological changes after perceiving something amiss. The perceiver, experiences, and the expresser are the self. Then, how correct is one in saying that someone else 'makes' one angry. Questioning the minute aspects may help the client realise the fact that the emotion originates with perception, moves to interpretation, goes through experience, and manifests in expression, with the involvement of the self at every step. In such a case, a change at any level of the process has the potential to stop the experience and expression of anger. This change in thought amounts to cognitive restructuring. However, the use of this skill should be applied with care so that it is not viewed as a playful comment.

More research in the field is called for to standardise more techniques for cognitive restructuring. However, the number of skills and their variants already in use are good contributions to the field of counselling.

Exercises

Following are the excerpts from the dialogue between the client and counsellor. For each client, there are two counsellor responses. Read them carefully. Try to identify which of the two counsellors is correct and why. What is the exact skill used? Identify the specific skill. Discuss why the other counsellor is wrong.

Exercise 1

Client: *(A newly married bride) I find things very bizarre in my in-law's family. It may not appear as a major problem to many when the*

	family sits together in the evening having drinks.... Sharing all sorts of jokes. Sometimes I ....find the behaviour of the men folk .....sort of.......different. .... They behave.........uninhibitedly... I am unable to take it. I don't belong to that category of family, you see..
Counsellor 1:	*What category of family?*
Counsellor 2:	*You feel awkward being part of the drinking sessions of the family because you do not belong to that category of family*

Exercise 2

Client:	*(A middle-aged woman who recently lost her husband and none of her children want to take her to stay with their family) Well, as a mother, it was not just my duty but my pleasure to bring them up and see them grow in their lives. There must be some flaw in my bringing it up. Otherwise, why will they all desert me this way? I am not hurt or angry with them. I am angry with myself. I don't think I deserve this sort of treatment from my own flesh and blood... (Breaks into sobs)*
Counsellor 1:	*While you say that you are not hurt, you seem to be deeply hurt. Am I right?*
Counsellor 2:	*You feel angry with yourself but not with your children because you feel you must have committed some mistake in the way you brought them up.*

References

Anthony, W. A., Pierce, R. M., & Cohen, M. R. (1979). *The skills of rehabilitation programming.* Carkhuff Institute of Human Technology.

Argyris, C. (1999). *On organisational learning*, Blackwell Publishing.

Blumenthal, S., Gudjonsson, G., & Burns, J. (1999). Cognitive distortions and blame attribution in sex offenders against adults and children. *Child Abuse & Neglect, 23*(2), 129–143.

Carkhuff, R. R. (1969). Helper communication as a function of helper affect and content. *Journal of Counselling Psychology, 16*(2, Pt.1), 126–131. https://doi.org/10.1037/h0027200.

Corsini, R. J., & Wedding, D. (Eds.) (2005). *Current psychotherapies*, Thomson Brooks/Cole Publishing Co.

Egan, G. (1990). *The skilled helper: A systematic approach to effective helping,* Brooks/Cole Publishing Company, A Division of Wadsworth, Inc.

Egan (2010). *The skilled helper: The problem management and opportunity development approach to helping.* Brooks/Cole Cengage Learning.

Ellis, A. (2004a). *Rational emotive behaviour therapy: It works for me, it can work for you,* Prometheus Books.

Ellis, A. (2004b). *The road to tolerance,* Prometheus Books.

Farber, B. A. (2006). *Self-disclosure in psychotherapy.* The Guilford Press.

Finn, S. E. (2005). How psychological assessment taught me compassion and firmness. *Journal of Personality Assessment, 84*(1) 29–32, 33–36. https://doi.org/10.1207/s15327752jpa8401_07.

Higgins, W. H., Ivey, A. E., & Uhlemann, M. R. (1970). Media therapy: A programmed approach to teaching behavioural skills. *Journal of Counselling Psychology, 17*(1), 20–26. https://doi.org/10.1037/h0028632.

Kelly, A. E., & Rodriguez, R. R. (2007). Do therapists self-disclose more to clients with greater symptomatology? *Psychotherapy: Theory, Research, Practice, Training, 44*(4), 470–475. https://doi.org/10.1037/0033-3204.44.4.470.

7 Skills for Motivating the Client

'If motivation is taken care of, I can handle humans in any situation'. This is a statement from an academician and psychologist. Motivation occupies the nucleus of human behaviour. It may be relevant to spend some time recapitulating and understanding the phenomenon of motivation before we discuss the skills used to motivate the client in a counselling setting.

Initiation of a new behaviour, ceasing an old behaviour, modification of existing behaviour, learning a new behaviour/skill, and avoidance of learning a new behaviour – are all guided by the individual's level of motivation. It is the driving force behind every action. It consists of biological, emotional, cognitive, and social forces that drive an individual to behave in a chosen way. To elaborate, various disequilibrium created in the body, manifested as hunger, thirst, and sexual urge, drive the individual to restore homeostasis by seeking food, water, or a sexual partner and the actions of eating, drinking, or participating in sexual activity. Similarly, emotions such as fear lead to avoidance of exposure to fear-inducing stimuli, while the feeling of anger leads the person to target the perpetrator through action. The significant factor associated with movement is the belief or cognition on the part of the individual (Miller, 2008). Thus, motivation is a complex phenomenon influenced by biopsychosocial forces.

Motivation theorists have explained the force behind the individual's action differently. Maslow's theory organised human needs in a hierarchy where the satisfaction of basic needs is fundamental for moving up the pyramid to attend to higher-order needs. Safety needs relate to protection, and affiliation needs call for mutuality in love and attachment. Control and competence in life are required to satisfy self-esteem needs. For the sustenance of well-being and emotional health, it is essential to meet these needs (Crandall et al., 2020). Alderfer reorganised Maslow's theory and presented the requirements into three categories in ERG (Existence, Relatedness, and Growth) theory. Self-Determination Theory is highly relevant in the context of counselling (Deci & Ryan, 1985). This theory advocates that for the individual's well-being, the satisfaction of three psychological needs motivates the person to action. They are autonomy, competence, and relatedness. Fulfilment of these psychological needs is determined by the social climate, which either supports the need for autonomy, control and relatedness or is controlling in nature. In a supportive climate, the individual is guided by autonomous motivation, where the actions are taken for their intrinsic satisfaction. In a controlling climate, one gets guided by a motivation where actions are contingent upon external rewards and avoidance of punishments. Actions triggered by intrinsic factors are sustainable because the individual reaps pleasure in the action itself, which is missing in the

DOI: 10.4324/9781003459415-7

actions driven by extrinsic factors. This takes us to explain motivation in the context of counselling.

In the counselling set-up, clients are burdened with a problem when they approach the counsellor. Having encountered either failure or suboptimal outcomes from the various methods adopted in resolving the issue, it is very likely that the client's levels of hope are low. Having encountered the problem and meeting with one or repeated failures is likely to place the client emotionally charged. Being under severe stress and hopelessness is not a congenial condition for a high level of motivation. Hence the counsellor's responsibility is to awaken the inspiration in the client and rekindle the hope that is faded due to failed attempts. The assumption under which the counsellor should work on it is that motivation in an individual is never zero. Life experiences cause the incentive to shift positions between low and high on a continuum. Taylor (2019) states that the client approaches the counsellor either because they have a problem and have to find a way out, because others have a problem, and a way should be found to change others, or because they are referred to counselling. In either of the three cases, the very fact that the client has come to the counsellor is evidence of some degree of motivation. The counsellor has to start from this positive assumption of the essential motivation in the client.

The client approaching the counsellor in a state of stress spends the initial time in the counselling session narrating the situation with the feelings associated with it, experiences the situation put one through and the behavioural response to the problem. Very often, the encountered problem and the crisis are so painful and anxiety provoking that the client goes through the residual pain while narrating it or, when the stress experienced is continuing, the situation is projected as an ongoing painful process. The client's consulting the counsellor is to minimise the stress and relieve the negative emotions triggered by the stress. The client's experience of the past is unchangeable, and the present is painful or problematic. Hence the way forward is to shape the future. Building the future has to be designed by the client. However, often, the client, in a state of stress, is not able to envisage a future free from the present problem. Professional skills will have to be used to help the client work out for a future free from the present stress. This process of motivating the client has to be a systematic gradual move that ferries the client smoothly from the unchangeable past and problematic present in which he/she is stuck. This is what distinguishes a professional counsellor from amateur or self-styled non-professional counsellors who show the tendency to take a direct leap from the problem to reaching the solution. The layperson's approach from the problem to a solution normally meets with an unsuccessful or transient positive outcome. This happens for many reasons, such as:

- Inadequate effort is invested in creating hope in the client
- A strong need is not yet created in the client to drive towards action
- Sufficient time has not been spent in helping the client formulate a goal
- Absence of conviction that things can be better, and the client not owning up to the goal

Steps to motivate the client to initiate action to minimise the stress involve the following:

1. Help the client visualise a situation where the present stress is handled
2. Help the client set definite goals with regard to easing the current stressful situation
3. Help the client evaluate the set goals in terms of probable outcomes

Skills for Motivating the Client

Motivating the client is a challenging task for the counsellor because very often when approaching the counsellor, the client is in a state of anxiety, depression, sadness, helplessness, or hopelessness which are all antithetical to a motivated state. The counsellor has to gently guide the client from such a state to a state of conviction that things can be worked out for the better. This conviction is essential to drive the client to a state of 'wanting to work for a better future'. The experience of this 'need' holds a promise for contemplating, generating and considering concrete goals and tagging them to action points to be implemented to attain the goals. Towards this, the counsellor has to use three broad skills: viz. nudging, probing, and challenging. Nudging refers to encouraging the client to do something that enhances the motivation in oneself. The counsellor gently elicits a response from the client which functions as a stimulus for the client to trigger a new hope and pushes the client to set a new goal or revive an old one. Probing in this context refers to a cue used by the counsellor to stimulate the client's thinking that surfaces the need to do something about the problem situation. Challenging in the context of motivating the client is an invitation to the client to think, imagine and set a goal to achieve a state where the problem is resolved and the stress minimised. The argument of Benson-Stott and Stott (2007) supports the need for invoking the motivation in the client to get out of the present troubled life to a more desirable future. They indicated that the therapy should aim at breaking the strongholds of traumatic experiences of life to facilitate the beginning of a reconnecting that restores more freedom and wellness. For easier understanding, the skills have to be discussed contextually. Egan (1990, 2010, 2018) discussed the skills of motivation in his Developmental Model in Stage 2 under three steps: Possibilities, Agenda, and Commitment. This discussion revolved around how to help the client move from a description of the problematic stressful situation to where one wishes to be, i.e., a 'problem-free' future. The discussion majorly revolved around what the counsellor has to do to help the client envisage a positive future, how to reach there and commit oneself to reaching there. This is the gist of invoking the motivation in the client. We will discuss the three identified skills under four headings: motivating through visualising a positive future, formulating goals to enhance motivation, enhancing client compliance to the set goals, and motivational interviewing.

Motivating through Visualising a Positive Future

This refers to experiencing a visual transition from the problematic past to a positive future.

Before we plunge into the core discussion on visualising the positive possibilities, a preamble on why people normally lack the motivation to act will be helpful. People, in general, avoid, postpone or resist action and instead continue with the inconvenience caused by a problem because of one or a combination of the following reasons:

- General inertia
- No conviction about an attractive future
- Getting used to the inconvenience caused by the problem
- Hesitant to invest effort and time that the new action demands
- Unsure of the outcome
- Inhibited by the possible obstacles
- Lack of faith in personal abilities

The individual often does not think much about the action because of natural inertia. Further, the outcome of the action in terms of a changed scenario remains an unknown factor. As long as the person does not make a conscious effort to visualise the likely outcome of the steps to resolve the problem situation, it tends to remain neutral. A person who has made a few unsuccessful attempts views the outcome as negative or suboptimal. Neither of these has the potential to motivate the person to act.

In the initial phase of counselling, the client elaborates on the problematic situation. It could be an interpersonal conflict, financial problem, addiction in a family member, chronic health problem, inability to come to terms with the loss of a loved one, etc. The presence of the problem and its adverse impact on life cannot be denied. The problematic situation has already occurred. Its impact is being suffered now. The event that caused emotional upheaval and disturbed cognitive functioning cannot be undone. The impact of it on cognition, affect state, and behaviour is something that the client wants to handle and minimise. This is possible only when the present situation is handled deftly. Cognitive restructuring and emotional release (discussed in earlier chapters) certainly contribute to helping the client with perceptual clarity. However, the client, while feeling better after emotional release and gaining new insight that enables them to reassess the problem, is still not sure about the new approach to the problem situation, which is different from the methods already applied without a satisfactory outcome. The massive question before the client continues to be, 'is there a way out?' 'Is it possible?'. This is a state where the client viewing the problem from a different perspective and understanding the opportunities missed, is yet to figure out the route map of a probable solution because there is not yet a belief in the existence of a way out. The first thing to be initiated in such a situation is to build a conviction. Here is where the 'Art of counselling' can take the front seat. One method that would relocate the client from indulging in the problem is the imagination of a situation where there is no problem. The greatest blessing unique to humans is fantasising. The capacity to derive pleasure from something in the absence of it is unique to human beings. For example, while in the thick of the problems, one can imagine overcoming the problem. During the process of this fantasy, one experiences relief from the stress. Fantasising is an art that paves the path for scientific innovations. The imagination and fantasy of the scientist precede every new scientific invention. From this imagination evolves pragmatism and feasibility. Applying the same principle, helping the client to imagine a situation where the present situation is already handled is assumed to lay the foundation for evolving a sketch for future action. Triggering the positive images in the client is done by using the skills of nudging and probing in isolation and in combination. These two skills are explained in the context of motivating the client in the following paragraphs.

Nudging

The counsellor uses the skills of nudging to trigger imagination in the client to envisage a situation when the problem does not exist. The following case is a good example of the use of nudging to trigger motivation in the client.

Box 7.1 Client Motivated for Cardiac Surgery

Sumitra Devi is a 70-year-old woman from an upper-middle-class family. Her husband was a doctor and died when she was in her mid-fifties. Though she had just completed primary school, she was a highly capable woman who effectively raised her four children and also helped many of her relatives from her village by facilitating their stay in her residence in the city until they completed their education. She is known among her relatives as a cheerful, happy and energetic person who is always ready to help. She is highly orthodox. When she was 72, she had a severe cardiac attack. After going through all the diagnostic tests, the cardiologist concluded that she had severe blocks in the arteries, which warranted a bypass surgery. The doctors explained the need for one-week hospitalisation, follow-up review meetings and the other post-operation precautions and also the expenditure involved. Sumitra Devi, who is otherwise a very confident woman, was quite upset after the visit to the doctor. What upset her the most was the hospital rules during the one-week hospitalisation. They strictly prohibit outside food for the patient. The patients have to eat the food provided by the hospital. Sumitra Devi being very orthodox, had objections to this restriction. She said, 'In my 72 years, I have never eaten anything from outside the home. I am not ready to violate this family tradition in this last leap of life. If the hospital is so rigid about the food, I would rather not have the surgery'. Every attempt by her children to reason out with her met with failure. Sumitra Devi continued her life without surgery. Her condition deteriorated slowly. Her activities in daily life started progressively declining. She found it difficult even to walk to their gate, which is a few yards from the main door. She found life very difficult. Started feeling depressed. Hated being dependent. They were worried about she being bedridden. Following is the excerpt of a conversation with the counsellor:

Sumitra Devi: *I hate to be sick. I don't deserve this.*
Counsellor: *Can you explain your illness, please?*
Sumitra Devi: *Cardiac problem. I am taking medicines. But no use.*
Counsellor: *Oh! Heart ailment. Do you mean to say the medicines are not giving any relief?*
Sumitra Devi: *Well, the doctor said that the medicines wouldn't work. They need to do heart surgery.*
Counsellor: *Then?*
Sumitra Devi: *Well, I did not agree to the surgery. Not that I am scared of the surgery, but I refused to go for it.*
Counsellor: *Umhummm?*
Sumitra Devi: *I come from a very traditional family and married into a traditional family too. In our family, the women never eat food from outside. At least till my generation, no one has done it. The hospitalisation would force me to eat the food provided in the hospital. How can I? So, I refused to get operated on.*
Counsellor: *How do you feel about your present condition?*
Sumitra Devi: *I feel miserable. I have never been so dependent. I can barely carry out the essential activities for myself...like bathing, combing, etc. Even a slight exertion like cooking leaves me exhausted......*

Counsellor:	*Just assume that the blockage of arteries is not there...... or removed..... how would your life be on a typical day?*
Sumitra Devi:	*..... Normal. I would wake up at 4 am as I used to. Have my bath. Spend the next hour doing my daily pooja. Prepare breakfast and lunch.....Go to the temple in the evening, teach music to my grandson in the afternoon..... Full of activities. There is never any time to sit and brood about anything. Life will be so easy. (With a bright smile)*
Counsellor:	*The thought itself is so pleasant, right?*
Sumitra Devi:	*Absolutely! I almost went back to those times. (Enthusiastically)*

Let us briefly analyse the interaction between the counsellor and the client presented in Box 7.1. The interaction shows that the counsellor used a combination of probing and nudging skills. All the interactions except the last two from the counsellor made effective use of probing in order to elicit more expression and communication from the client. The purpose of this is to add quality and quantity to the communication so that the essential feelings, experiences and behaviour of the client going through the crisis of ill health come to the surface. Once that is attained, the counsellor nudged the client to imagine a situation free from the present state of illness-causing exhaustion, dependence and restriction of active life. Such imagination, as stated by the client, took her back to those busy days. Now, the counsellor skillfully and gradually brought the conversation to a stage where he could take her to visualise an illness-free situation. This experience of fantasy apparently invoked a pleasant experience in the client. This positive experience functions as a reward and helps in creating motivation in the client to think of a positive move (either by altering one's stand on compromising with eating hospital food or by exploring alternatives to get the same surgeon to conduct the surgery in a different hospital or considering a change of cardiologist located in a relatively liberal hospital). Thus, probing and nudging helped the client to move from a state of acceptance of 'an inevitable doomed situation' to 'a possible positive situation'. Such thinking can be termed as 'hope'. Hope refers to the belief that things will improve. It is not a wish that things should improve. It has the elements of knowledge and feeling gradually leading the person towards working for things to change to positive. Confronted with problems, hope goes into a dormant state. Its fantastic strength needs to be beckoned to instill the faith that one can circumvent and persevere through the obstacles encountered. Hope helps the thoughts to gravitate to optimism. This is the exact effect of nudging the client to visualise a positive situation free of the problem. The impact of visualising a positive future is made through nudging and probing skills. The strategy brings better results when the probing lays down the present painful situation followed by a contrasting problem-free situation of the future visualised. This is made possible when probing and nudging are used in combination in this context.

Probing and Challenging

Nudging the client to envision a positive future can be done by posing relevant questions that lead to thinking in terms of 'what is to be done/changed'. The counsellor should contextually guide the client to tune the thoughts/imagination to explore and identify the new actions/behaviour to be initiated, the new decisions to be taken, the new opportunities to be created, new resources to be put to use, new places to be explored and new abilities to be developed or the existing abilities to be refined and improved. Nudging is done very gently by using appropriate probes. When the client is either hesitant to fantasise or imagine, the counsellor can challenge the client on his/her ability to do so. In the context of the case presented in Box 7.1, the counsellor continued the session in the following way:

Counsellor: *Well, what, according to you, should change so that once again you will be able to enjoy an illness-free normal life?*

Sumitra Devi: *Certainly not compromising on the hospital diet. My conscience does not permit me to do so.*

Counsellor: *Well, leaving that aside, is there any other way?*

Sumitra Devi: *Any other thing? Perhaps we should think of other hospitals where we can consult. We are keen on this doctor who is good. Perhaps we can find out if he is a consultant in any other hospital.*

The counsellor did not make any attempts to talk the client out of her decision to reject the surgery in the hospital that would not allow outside food because the decision was linked to her family values. The counsellor followed the ethics by accepting her values though it sounded unscientific and unconvincing to him. Now, the client's thoughts are triggered to alternatives and consider the best alternative. This could be done without much difficulty because the initial visualisation triggered hope in the client. Through this line of future-oriented thinking, hope gains strength, and motivation gets a boost. Nudging and probing can be used in stimulating imagination related to the behavioural change in self, resources to be mobilised, attitudes to be changed, skills to be developed, habits to be dropped, etc., depending upon the client's needs.

The client can be encouraged by the counsellor to visualise a positive future by adopting many methods. Some of them are discussed below.

Identify Successful Models

Sometimes when the future looks bleak, a flash that someone else in similar situation has successfully dealt with it brings a ray of hope for the future. There are many instances where things that work wonderfully well for others do not work for us. We then tend to think of why does it works successfully with others? Only then do we identify the difference between the approach, methods and handling between us and the others. For example, we see that a plant we bought from the nursery and placed on our balcony is growing long in a single string. We have tried different ways but failed. We were about to give up on it and discard the plant when we visited a friend in the neighbourhood, where we found a similar plant that was green, bushy and healthy. Only when we enquired that we realise that the neighbours are regularly trimming the plant so that the branches are developing. We also found that they nurture the soil with kitchen waste while we have been using chemicals. With this additional knowledge, we gained hope of changing the fate of our plant by adopting a new approach to plant care similar to that of the neighbours. The same principle applies in case of troubled situations in life where we emulate a successful model. However, very often, this does not strike our minds. Just like the way we were about to give up on the unhealthy plant, we also tend to give up on the problem and assume a 'doomed' position. The counsellor's nudging can help us to look around and identify a successful model to be emulated. The following example helps in understanding how the counsellor helped the client identify successful models.

Client: *(A young mother of a mentally challenged child) I could successfully manage her for 11 years. But now, she is showing spurts of aggression. Sometimes her physical strength scares me. The other day, for some reason, she got angry with her grandfather and pinned him down to the floor and held his neck. He was terrified, and I could not control her physically.*

Counsellor: *Oh! That must have been a very difficult situation for you. Naturally, you are bothered.*

Client: *I am now worried that in case such a situation repeats in my absence, what would happen to my old and fragile father? My daughter's hyperactivity is now increased.*

Counsellor: *You are a member of the support group of parents, if I remember correctly. Have you come across any similar cases? How are the parents managing such children?*

Client: *I know of one such family with a 16-year-old boy. The doctor they consulted put him on medication to keep the hyperactivity under control. They are using some homoeopathy medicine.*

Counsellor: *Umhmm.*

Client: *Should I go for it?*

Counsellor: *What do you think?*

Client: *....Perhaps we should consult the same homoeopathy doctor.*

The successful models can be found among friends, relatives, neighbours, colleagues, and acquaintances. Sometimes it may not naturally strike the clients to emulate known others or borrow knowledge from others. The reasons for this could be anything ranging from the idea not striking to the fact that the two situations, though similar, are not identical, like in the case cited above, where the two children differ in age and gender. In such cases, the counsellor's nudging helps.

Following is another example where the mother and her adolescent daughter have the problem of continuous arguments.

Client: *I am worried about her impulsive behaviour. I try my best to reason with her. But she feels she knows everything. She takes decisions without considering the repercussions. When I caution her, she feels I treat her like a child. Not a single day passes without fights and arguments between us. I was also a teenager. I never behaved this way. I was so obedient to my mother.*

Counsellor: *Do you know other families with adolescent girls going through the same phase but with better relationships?*

Client: *Yes, of course. My own brother's family.*

Counsellor: *How are they managing?*

Client: *My sister-in-law is a homemaker. She has all the time at her disposal. Spends a lot of time with her daughter. She says she does not immediately respond when her daughter does or plans to do something that is not acceptable. She talks about it after a while and explains the pros and cons, leaving the final call to her. She says the teens should be given time to sink the facts. But this calls for a change in approach at my end. Right?*

Counsellor: *If so, would it be possible?*

Client: *Not easy, yet possible. (Smiles)*

In this example, the situations are almost identical. The client is nudged to identify a model as close as her brother's family. The difference in mothers' responses is correctly pointed out by the client. Emulating a model, though it sounds simple, is not really easy to practice because the dynamics of the personalities do not work in the same way. Here the client correctly assessed the feasibility of emulating the model, which is termed by her as 'not easy, yet possible'. This is a realistic assessment. The client, in this case, seems to have broadly assessed the possible hurdles in emulating the model. This needs to be viewed positively because when the possible hurdles are endorsed, the client is likely to develop a sense of readiness to encounter the hurdles. The motivation, in this case, will be stronger, resulting in better perseverance and effective outcome.

Reviewing the Positive Past

Very often, when one faces a difficult situation, one tends to compare the present hardship with the past trouble-free time. Such colourful past sometimes can be used to the advantage in dreaming of a positive future. Helping the client review the positive past can motivate him/her to work for a similar future.

Life poses dynamic situations and relationships. Interpersonal relationships have peculiar dynamics. With more and more interactions, it gains strength in the initial phase up to a certain point. The care, concern and adjustments one adopts to make the other person happy makes the recipient happy, which in turn results in drawing the two closer emotionally. However, after a stage, things done by one to make the other happy start to become basic, and more is expected from each other. This leads to frustrations and disappointments, culminating in conflicts.

For example, in a marital relationship, if the wife, wanting to make her husband happy, irons his clothes and keeps them ready before he goes to the office, on the first day, the husband is pleasantly surprised, expresses his happiness and thanks his wife and also perhaps praises her for her presence of mind in front of their familiar friends. This reinforcement makes the wife repeat this help day after day. Gradually, the husband stops the reinforcement and starts expecting the ironed clothes by the time he gets ready for the office. He would however express his happiness when the wife begins to ensure that he carries his valet and cautions him about the fuel in the car. After a few weeks, this is added to the husband's expectations from his wife. Over a period of time, they start taking each other's help for granted in every aspect. The relationship gradually gets stale. Monotony and frustration take the place of surprises and happiness. The pleasant past gets buried while the present unpleasantness of monotony and dissatisfaction glare at the couple. Given such circumstances, if only the troubled couple takes time to peep into their positive past, will they see the absence of actions that made them happy in the past. It is very unlikely for the couple to remember the past while indulgence in the problematic present occupies all the attention. It is the responsibility of the counsellor to help them review their history and identify the antecedent actions and efforts that made the past a pleasant time – having done that, and the counsellor should help them borrow the pages from the past to write a pleasant experience in the present. The following example will be relevant.

The unhappy wife comes to the counsellor who feels vexed with her husband after seven years of marriage.

Client: *I feel absolutely lonely in this marriage. So much change in him. He used to be so caring and loving, full of fun. Now, his full attention is on his* *work. When he has leisure time, he prefers to be with his friends. I also have a job. But I give my time to my kids. Take care of their studies. Should he not do it too? He seems just not interested... either in the kids or me! I am unable to take the burden any more. I need some emotional support from him.*

Counsellor: *Well, you said that he used to be caring and full of fun ..... perhaps you referred to some earlier part of your life together. What are the things that you used to do to have fun in life and how were you caring for each other?*

Client: *(Trying to recollect) Ummm...... We used to plan weekend outings... like ... long drives..... badminton with friends, and poolside party.... Oh, a variety of things. I used to make it a point to spring a pleasant surprise on him once in a way ....and that used to excite him so much that he would come up with a weekend plan..... Well, those days were different.....*

Counsellor: *Is it possible to bring back those experiences?*

Client: *Do you think it would work? .....*

The counsellor took the clue from the client, who made a passing remark on better times in the past and gently pushed the client to recall the pleasant times of the past. This enabled the client to compare the initiatives that she took those days, which are, in fact missing in the present time. Once the motivators are identified, it calls for the person to invest some effort in a primary initiative to revive the action and reinvent the positive past in contemporary times.

Things may not work out as easily as they did in this particular case. But, reviewing better past times certainly kindles the hope because when a positive experience was possible once, it should be possible to repeat. There may be several changes in the situation, such as added responsibilities, financial status, health condition and so on. These changes may not allow the clients to bring back the replica of past activities. Yet, the counsellor may challenge the client to think divergently to come up with suitable variations in the actions. The use of challenging skills in this context can be understood better by citing the extended conversation with the client in the same example.

Client: *Maybe, I should give it a try? But the problem now is that my husband now tends to oppose anything that I propose. He would immediately negate anything that I asked him to do. How can I convince him to revive the old practices of planning the weekends?*

Counsellor: *Are you sure he enjoyed those trips as much as you did?*

Client: *Of course, yes. He was the one who wanted them the most.*

Counsellor: *In that case, he, too, must be nurturing the pleasant memories of that phase in your married life. Can you think of any other methods than suggesting to him directly?*

Client: *What could it be....? Really cannot think of anything that makes him realise the pleasure of doing things together.*

Counsellor: *What is it that you would respond positively in such a situation? Keep thinking, and you may come out with some innovative idea.*

(Later, the client informed the counsellor that she picked up some of the photographs of their great weekends and put them on the collage. They discussed the pictures along with the children. The children were excited to hear the stories of their fishing expedition, bird watching and a game

of football with village children. They proposed that they all could do it together once again. That initiated the first-weekend plan after so many years. The whole family enjoyed the trip.)

In this case, the counsellor challenged the client to think innovatively. The counsellor challenged her to place herself in her husband's shoes. In a way, the challenge to the client is to own up to the problem and take the first initiative to bring about a change in the situation. Though it did not seem to bring an immediate trigger to an innovative idea, it did work in the mind of the client, who came up with a productive concrete idea in the end. Motivation need not always spark up during the counselling session. The stimulus may continue to work and drive the client towards an action bringing a positive outcome.

Using nudging, probing, and challenging to review the pleasant past can be adopted by the counsellor easily when the client makes a passing remark about better times in earlier days. Even when the client does not give such cues, the counsellor can use probing skills to ask if there were any better times that one remembers. Probes such as 'Were the things so bad right from the beginning, or have there been any time that you recall with pleasure?' Reviewing the positive past is adopted by the counsellor when the issue relates to interpersonal problems in a marriage set-up, between the parents and children, siblings, friends, colleagues, etc.

Futuristic Writing

Fantasy and imagination used for motivating the client can be extended to fantasising about advancing in time zone and taking writing approaches by 'living in the future'. Nudging to futuristic writing will be effective on clients who manifest inertia and are deficient in foresight on life in the future. It is effective in the case of those where the gap between the ego ideal and reality is high, those who lack a road map for growth and achievement. It can also be applied successfully in those cases where the client is unable to estimate the long-term consequences of the present inaction or wrong actions.

Futuristic writing includes writing about one's own self in a future time zone that may span anything between the following month to several years from the present time, depending upon the context. For example, if the client is a patient who is undergoing treatment for the preliminary stages of cancer and is depressed because of the various side effects of the treatment that would last for three months, a writing approach spanning three to six months from the present period may create an opportunity for the client to imagine the time that is free from the treatment and the temporary side effects. This helps in enhancing the motivation of the client to inculcate patience and endurance of the painful treatment in view of the desirable life after a few months of treatment. In case a client is a person who just entered the post-retirement and is unable to cope with it, a time zone of five to ten years from the present may be taken, and the client may be asked to write about his post-retirement life's achievements visualising five years from now. Such exercise tunes and motivates the client to plan the time and have a road map for future life.

The counsellor may nudge the client to imagine and write anything from a daily journal between now and two months later to an autobiography written a decade later to the way one wishes one's obituary to be. The following examples help in bringing clarity to the skills applied.

Example 1: The client is a newly married woman who relocated herself to the place of her husband. She resigned from her job to join her husband after marriage with the hope of finding a suitable placement in the city where her husband is located. She was experiencing a vacuum in her life as she had to spend the whole day alone after he left for work in the morning.

Client: *I never imagined my married life so boring. I am just reduced to a nobody in my new role. My sudden transition from a busy life to such a leisurely phase is something I am not able to cope with. Very unusually, I have become very irritable and am showing my unhappiness to him.*

Counsellor: *Supposing you start writing about the major activities of life and maintain a journal, what do you think your journal will prominently have a month from now?*

Client: *Well, I think it will fill with details on the dishes I make and the frustration shown on my husband.*

Counsellor: *As a contrast, what do you wish to be prominent in your journal in the next month?*

Client: *Oh! I suddenly feel lost........ wait ....wait a minute.... I think I would like it to be filled with my various attempts to get a job. Preparing and sending in my resume, having interviews with some organisations, negotiating the pay packages, choosing from various offers, discussing these offers with my husband....... Well, well.... I think I know now what to do to get out of this situation...*

Example 2: The other day, I asked my class of postgraduate students in their final year about their plans for the future. When I asked the class how many wished to pursue the line of research, out of 24 in the class, about six to seven hands went up. I asked the rest what they wanted to do after they completed their Master's in Health Psychology. There was a stoic silence, and I observed that most students avoided eye contact with me.

I told them, 'Let us have some fun now. Imagine that this is a different time zone, and we are meeting in this classroom when you all came for an alumnus meeting ten years from now. Now, I wanted you all to submit your biodata for the record of the University. Please prepare your biodata imagining that you are ten years ahead of the present time'. Initially, there was some awkward silence in the class. Some wry smiles, looking at each other amusedly, etc., took a couple of minutes. But I persisted by waiting in silence, communicating in a way that I was serious about the task. Gradually everyone turned to their notebooks and got busy writing. After about 15 minutes, when everyone appeared to have completed their report, I posed the same question – what they wished to be after completing their Master's in Health Psychology. Almost everyone had an answer, whether tentative or definite. This time none tried to avoid eye contact with me. Later we discussed career planning. Some of them confessed that until they were asked to write their resume with a future date, they did not take up the matter seriously. Some said that they realised that they had a plan at a subliminal level which manifested while writing the resume. One of them said that she felt pretty excited writing the resume with a future dateline, so much so that she now understands the efforts that need to be invested right from now on to be able to have a resume envisioned. Though the fact remains that all of them may or may not attain the position to have a resume they wrote for them today, certainly, the task of writing a futuristic resume churned their imagination and woke them up to the reality of the need for a road map. Here the teacher's nudging worked to trigger the motivation of the students to draw a road map for their careers.

Example 3: A client is an older adult in his mid-sixties. He retired as Chief Engineer from the public sector. Throughout his active working life, he never spent time with family owing to work on his job front. He enjoyed the power and benefited from the position. Post-retirement, when all the perks were removed, he felt deprived. Not having established a bonding with his children and grandchildren, there was little communication with family members. He felt lonely and longed for the attention and care of others. He could get their attention whenever he fell sick. Within a year, he became a hypochondriac. He felt that he had vertigo. He believed that he would fall if he went for a walk alone. He started demanding the services of his family members and complained that he was being neglected by them. The family started seeing him as a constant pain. He came to see the counsellor. Following is a small excerpt from a counselling session.

Client: *No one at home really cares for me. They know that I am a sick person. Still, they never help me. On the contrary, they expect me to lend a helping hand in household chores.*

Counsellor: *You seem to be very bitter about how people relate to you.*

Client: Yes. *People who used to hover around me in the office have not bothered even to make a single phone call after I retired. Does it not matter for these people even if I die?*

Counsellor: *Since you are talking about death, I wish to ask you something related to it. How do you want people to remember you after you are gone?*

Client: *..........(Long silence) An intelligent person, Efficient officer......... Friendly...... Helpful........Pleasant... Sociable...*

Counsellor: *What do you think you need to do to be remembered the way you wish to be remembered?*

Client: *(Murmured) Nothing that I am doing now would help me .....*

In this example, the nudging and probing by the counsellor helped the client to realise the huge gap between his wish and his methods of relating to people in realising the wish. This will likely generate a disequilibrium driving him to contemplate a behaviour change. However, there is a possibility that the client may just identify the gaps or needs and yet not initiate action. In this case, though the client endorsed the need for change in his attitude and behaviour towards people so that people may remember him the way he wished, he refused to take any initiative to change his equation with others.

Visualising the Future Through Guided Imagery

Guided imagery is a therapeutic technique that helps the client visualise things by inducing all sensory experiences. In this context, the imaginary sensory expertise is replaced with the imaginary general experience. This technique can be used to enhance the motivation of clients who can mention their goal but are unable to fantasise and visualise the future after attaining the goal. In such cases, the counsellor can ask the client to go through the experience in their imagination, following the guided instructions of the counsellor. Here the counsellor narrates each detail of the situation that leads to a pleasant experience. For example, a student who wishes to top the examinations but is not investing the required efforts and needs a boost to do so may be given the guided imagery in the following way:

> *Close your eyes and imagine the situation as I narrate. You are waiting for the day for the results to be out. A day before the results, you are feeling very anxious. You have done very well in the exams, yet you are not sure because the other student who stood first in the last examination also has a chance of topping the list. Now, you have woken up in the morning. Tension is building up in you. You are waiting for the clock to strike ten so that the results are declared........... The list is put on the website. You have opened the website with all anxiety. Your heart beats fast. You are feeling weak in your limbs. 'What if I don't get it...' is the question that comes to mind repeatedly. Now, the list is on the screen. You are reading the name in the serial order......... Yes, it is your name............You jump in excitement. Your friends are cheering you up. Your phone is ringing.....and it is a call from your father... 'Daddy......' you said in an emotional voice, and rest is spoken by your father, who is overwhelmed........*

When the counsellor gives such descriptions to the client who has to experience it in imagination, the excitement and pleasure invoked function as a motivator to work for such experience in reality. The counsellor has to ensure that the narration is close to the real life of the client so that it has an effect.

Experience through Experiments

It is not uncommon for people to postpone a decision related to a major change in life due to apprehensions about the change itself. For example, a pregnant woman contemplating joining *yoga* classes that promise the ease of natural delivery, an Engineering graduate postponing the decision to join the executive MBA classes in the evening, and a homemaker wanting to join a spoken English course to improve her language skills are found to postpone the final decision as they are unsure of its impact. The pregnant mother may be worried about the safety of the foetus, and the engineering graduate may be unsure of adjusting the time between his job and classes, the homemaker may be apprehensive that she would be the only one in the age group of forty years and find it embarrassing to sit with the other youngsters in the class. There may be many such reasons preventing people from moving forward. These are all motivation blockers. They need to be handled carefully. Any attempts to coerce may meet with stiff resistance. Further, the coercive approach is not ethical in counselling. Hence the counsellor can gently nudge the client towards choosing to experience a sample of the situation about which there is apprehension and hesitation. Such sample experience may be taken up without any commitment on the part of the client. Having gone through a sample experience, the client would be able to assess if the apprehensions are actual or imaginary. In case the apprehensions are true, the decision may be taken against the action so that alternatives can be identified. In case the apprehensions are found to have no ground, the client's motivation may drive him/her to action. The following example discusses the issue of a student in 10th class whose parents had to move to a village set up in the middle of the academic session. To avoid disruption to his studies in the crucial 10th standard, they decided to change his school and put him in a residential school of high reputation in the city. Ever since this decision was taken, the boy started worrying about being ragged and bullied by the other students in the hostel and being subjected to a regimented life by the Wardens in the hostel, etc. His anxiety impacted his sleep, and he was getting very irritable with his younger sister, who would be moving along with her parents to the rural set-up. Following is the excerpt from a session:

Counsellor: *So, this sudden development of your parents having to move to the village to set up their work is something that was unexpected?*
Client: *(Nods)*
Counsellor: *How do you feel about the arrangement to move to the boarding school?*
Client: *I don't like it. I want to continue in my school.*
Counsellor: *But your school has no residential facility.*
Client: *(Silent and looks down)*
Counsellor: *Now, let us talk something about the future. How do you think things would be if you moved to the boarding school?*
Client: *I will be new there. All others have their friends, and I will be alone.*
Counsellor: *So?*
Client: *They may all gang up and rag me. You know... how ragging is in boarding schools...*
Counsellor: *Ok. What else?*
Client: *I may not be able to play in the evenings. Perhaps the Warden keeps a watch and always pushes me to study....tenth class...no? I will be all alone.... Will miss my parents and friends. I may not be allowed to meet my friends from my present school... (Silence) My friend who was shifted to boarding school in eighth class told me how strict things are in residential school. He could not continue there and came back to our school. But...for me, there is no choice. Dad says that it is a matter of just one year.*
Counsellor: *Well, was your friend who experienced the boarding school go to the same one that your parents are going to put you in?*
Client: *No, no. It is a different school. Not here in the city.*
Counsellor: *Have you been to this boarding school? Have you seen the hostel or met the other students, teachers or the Warden?*
Client: *No, no. I have not yet joined. I will meet after joining.*
Counsellor: *Would it be a good idea to make a visit and meet them all once? Perhaps your dad can even take special permission for you to spend a weekend in the hostel sometime next week or so when your parents are still around? Would that help give you an idea about life in the hostel?*
Client: *With my parents in the hostel?*
Counsellor: *No, no. Your parents will be at home. You may spend a couple of days in the hostel before your parents shift from the city and put you in the hostel. That may give some scope to discuss the experience with your parents.*
Client: *Maybe. That will give me an idea. If it is very bad there, I can tell my parents.*
Counsellor: *Yes. Who knows, you may even find things to your liking...*
Client: *I think it is a good idea.*

Experimenting with experience involves minimum stakes. Hence the clients are mostly willing to take this up. There is a chance that the experience happens to be negative. In such a case, the outcome of dropping the option also is good because the client gets relief from the uncertainty and would contemplate creating other new opportunities. This also is counted as a motivation to act.

Thus, nudging the client to conceptualise a positive future functions as a propeller to create a need to live in a positive future. As per the theories of motivation (Hull, 1952), the need, once created, would generate unrest and push the individual to action to satisfy it. Thus, the counsellor's use of nudging, probing and challenging the client to imagine a positive future helps in creating this need and drives the client to 'want to experience' the positive future. From here onwards, the counsellor should take the responsibility of helping the client to formulate a concrete goal. Seligman and Reichenberg make a strong argument in favour of invoking the client's conceptualisation of a positive future. In their words: 'As they become cognisant of the possibilities for positive change, their empowerment and motivation increase correspondingly, creating a beneficial circle; positive change fuels people's belief that change can happen, which enhances their motivation and efforts to change, which in turn leads to more positive changes' (Seligman & Reichenberg, 2013, p. 242).

Formulating Goals to Enhance Motivation

Once the counsellor successfully creates the need for creating a positive future, the client is likely to experience a psychological disequilibrium due to the striking contrast between the painful present and the pleasant future envisaged. This is the right time for the counsellor to stimulate the client to evolve concrete goals related to satisfying the needs created within through visualisation. Whatever the approach is, the counsellor recognises, endorses and optimises the client's efforts and involvement in the process of counselling. Goal setting is also considered an important step in behaviour therapy. Solution-focused behaviour therapy (SFBT) lays due emphasis on client involvement for sustaining motivation. Such involvement ensures the ownership of the decision by the client, which has a close association with motivation.

Adequate care needs to be taken while helping the client to give shape to the goals. The counsellor should use all pre-helping skills, probing, and challenging, in order to drive the client to formulate goals that are pragmatic and concrete. Rief (2021) recommended that the training of professional psychotherapists should now shift the focus from theoretical inputs to the practical training of competencies such as client's motivation and goals. Goal setting is identified as one of the priority steps in therapeutic interventions (Cooper & Law, 2018; Grey et al., 2018). Renger and Macaskill (2021) found the effectiveness of guided goal setting. Counsellor-guided goal setting is effective because through nudging, probing and challenging, the counsellor helps the client to form goals that are pragmatic in every respect. It should be remembered that the goals are formulated and owned by the client. The counsellor assumes the role of a facilitator.

Why should the client formulate a goal? Once the client has an emotional release and is subjected to a cognitive reorientation in the counselling, is he/she not ready to identify the solution to the problem rather than spending time in goal setting? What else can be the goal of any client except reaching the solution to the problem? These are some of the questions that may come to the mind of any novice.

Though goals are future-oriented, the articulation of the goals helps in changing the present condition of the person (Presbury et al., 2002). Bachel (2001) enumerates the significance of goal setting by stating that the goal stretches the person out of one's comfort zone, changes the outlook of life, gives a purpose for life, boosts self-confidence, instils trust in the decision, strengthens self-reliance, and increases the sense of satisfaction.

Investing time and energy in setting goals has certain definite advantages for the client. This intermediary step functions as a conservation ground for physical and psychic energy that would later go into real action towards problem resolution and stress reduction. The advantages are summarised into the following points:

- ***Provides a direction for the actions in the next step***: Only when the goals are set would one understand the way to direct one's thinking and action for a solution. For example, for a client facing a financial crunch to meet the monthly expenditure, the final aim is to have adequate money. But only when the client identifies the various methods of improving the financial status, such as taking up a weekend job, taking a bank loan, starting a small side business, offering online tuition to school children, giving a musical performance in star hotels after the office hours, etc..... will he/she have a specific direction to channel the thinking and efforts. Until the formulation of specific goals, the client, though would know what he/she wants, may not know how to get it. Goal setting helps the client with an idea of what to do, where to go, and how to reach it. This enables to strengthen the dream to be realised.
- ***Creates a readiness to initiate action***: When the goals are set, the client tends to visualise the road to attain the goal. In that process, he/she is likely to identify the possible obstacles and the way to overcome the same. By chalking out the goal, the client would have a mental assessment of the required resources and the feasibility of mobilising the same. Resources can refer to external resources such as material, money, and social support or internal resources such as abilities, skills, stamina, energy, etc. A realistic assessment of the same helps in enhancing the motivation of the client, particularly when the resources are available. In case there is uncertainty about resource availability, it sets the client to think of alternative goal setting. In either case, the exercise of goal setting contributes to motivating the client.
- ***Mobilises energy***: This can be explained with a simple experiment to be tried by you individually. Imagine that you are taken to a room where three suitcases are placed on the floor. You are told that the suitcases are quite heavy. You are asked to lift the first one. When you lift it with your hand, you find that it is empty and is not heavy. But when you lift it, you find that your hand goes up with the suitcase to a height not intended. This happens because, since you were told that the suitcase is very heavy, inadvertently, you invested more energy in your attempt to lift the suitcase. Thus, the expectation of doing a task has a tendency to mobilise the estimated energy for the task. When the client builds the goals, inadvertently, he/she also conserves the physical and psychic energy for executing the task. This minimises the probability of failure in reaching the goal and resolving the problem. This would not happen in a situation where the client gropes for a solution as soon as one encounters the problem.
- ***Functions as a motivator and enhances perseverance***: Once the client sets the goals in concrete terms, the need to attain the goal starts unrest and drives him/her to action. Thus, goal setting functions as an action initiator and a perseverance enhancer. Having identified the probable obstacles, they fail to have the surprise element for the client. That also enables one to plan a contingency or the methods of handling the hurdles, managing the restraining forces more effectively than when one is caught unawares by the stumbling blocks.
- ***Creates a sense of autonomy***: When the client approaches the counsellor, he/she is almost in a state of diffidence because of failures in resolving the problem. There is research evidence suggesting that goal setting helps in the enhancement of well-being in clients and satisfies the need for autonomy (Sheldon & Elliot, 1999). The counsellor's intervention in goal setting helps the client to face one's anxieties in a supportive environment. The process of goal setting helps the client gain new insights, enhance the sense of mastery and self-efficacy, and minimise demoralisation (Kleinke, 1994).

- ***Objectivity enhancer*:** Formulating the goals and learning to evaluate them develops a sense of objectivity towards the problem assessment in the client. This enables the client to function from a changed perspective which is a positive change. A relatively dispassionate view of the problem brings in more ideas to handle them, and the probability of resolving would thus get a boost.

Principles of Goal-Setting

All the advantages of goal setting can be reaped when it is professionally guided by a competent counsellor. The counsellor must ascertain that the client is guided to formulate goals that have the best characteristics of pragmatism and effectiveness. Goal-setting theory postulates the characteristics of effective goals. They include specificity, measurability, attainability, result-orientation and time-boundness (Locke & Lathan, 2002). They can be summarised into the acronym – SMART. We add to this the characteristics of being substantial and realistic too. We will discuss in detail the skills used by the counsellor to help the client formulate 'smart' goals.

Goals to be Specified

An attempt at helping the clients set goals is likely to elicit a first reaction from the client, who would state the goal as 'I want to get out of the situation'. This, at best, can qualify the general 'intent' of the client. An intent suggests the general inclination of the client, indicating the presence of motivation to work for the solution of the problem. The counsellor can take that as a positive indication to guide the client to move further in crystalising the goal. Some other clients may give a slightly better expression indicating their role in coming out of the problem. For example, statements such as 'I need to do something to change the situation' is a better pointer to the client's motivation. Statements of this type can be classified as the aim of the client. While this certainly is a positive indication, it is not sufficient to drive the client to action. These statements, in a way, refer to 'where' the client wants to be. While that is the valid first step, in order to link to the associated action, the client should be guided to spell out 'what' one wants, 'how and when' one wishes to reach the goal using 'what' resources. This would make the goal specific. Following is an example of guiding the client on this path.

Client: *I have troubled my family enough! Now, I want to have some peace and respite from my alcohol addiction.*
Counsellor: *That is really nice. What do you want to do about it?*
Client: *I think I should go for some deaddiction programme.*
Counsellor: *Good idea. Any specific plan for the place?*
Client: *I must make enquiries and identify the best place.*
Counsellor: *How do you plan to carry out this enquiry?*
Client: *I think I should look up the internet source.*
Counsellor: *Any other way?*
Client: *I will speak to a friend who underwent the same two years ago. Perhaps I must also ask my wife's friend, who is a psychologist.*
Counsellor: *Ok, that looks good. But how would you choose 'the best' from the list you would prepare from the enquiries?*
Client: *Ummmm.... Perhaps ... would look at the location, the reviews, affordability... and the most important thing is I should like the place.*

Counsellor: *To check if the place is to your liking, you may have to plan a visit.*
Client: *Yes. Only after that can I take the call.*
Counsellor: *Do you have any time target for all these jobs?*
Client: *I should have. Maybe. I should make the decision in the next week.*
Counsellor: *If I may sum up, you wish and you want to join a deaddiction centre to get rid of your drinking habit and wish to identify the best-suited institution in the next week.*

In the above counselling session, the client started an intent with an expression that he would like to give his family some relief from his drinking habit, shaped as his setting a specific goal of joining the best deaddiction centre, the identification of which will complete in a week. The trajectory from the intent to the specific goal is like a funnel with a broad opening and then narrowing down at the other end. The counsellor here used the skills of probing to stimulate the client to think more intensely about the intent expressed and give it a concrete shape. The intent expressed by the client in the first instance, 'to give the family respite from his habit of drinking', is idealistic. Though sounds good, it has nothing to pursue yet. Hence it is likely to be evaporated in procrastination. The intent and aim can be compared with a porridge state, while the goal in specific terms leads the client to freeze and pursue it.

Goals to be Substantial

Motivation to act is likely to reinforce itself if the outcome of an action is visible. The outcome should be such that it impacts life adequately in a positive direction. However, sometimes the goal set by the client is such that the impact is marginal. The marginal impact of the first goal has the potential to weaken the next goal or sustenance of action for the first goal itself. Goals set too high or too low fail to motivate the client. Too high goals are difficult to attain, and too low goals fail to make any impact on life. The characteristic of being 'Substantial' is not limited to just the quantity. It connotes the quality of the goal too. For example, an intelligent student whose grades fell down to 'C' from 'A+' wishes to set a goal to improve the grades to 'B' from 'C' is considered marginal from a quantitative perspective. A working mother who has a complaint from the children that she is not home most of the time decides to stay home for the whole week and work from home. Working from home is not setting a substantial goal because the goal is not satisfying the need for quality time with the children. The counsellor must be competent enough to help the client balance the quantity and quality aspects while satisfying the characteristic of setting a substantial goal. When the client is choosing a goal that does not satisfy the criteria, the counsellor can apply the skill of challenging to make the client realise the lack of strength in the goal. The following example relates to a situation where the counsellor challenges the client on this ground.

Client: *I understand that my daughter feels I am not spending time at home as her friends' mothers do. But she does not understand that her mother is a CEO of a big organisation.*
Counsellor: *You mean to say that your daughter's demand is from her mother, and she does not see the other role that the mother plays? How do you plan to make her accept it?*

Client: *Difficult to make a ten-year-old understand. I think I need to somehow satisfy her.*
Counsellor: *Oh! Good. What do you plan to do?*
Client: *Well, I plan to stay home for a week.*
Counsellor: *That sounds really good. What do you plan to do with your daughter for the whole week?*
Client: *(Surprised) Well, staying home means.... Working from home. I have several meetings scheduled for the next two months...*
Counsellor: *Is that what your daughter meant when she referred to you not spending time with her?*
Client: *.....I know.....but ....then...*
Counsellor: *Is there any way that you spend time WITH her than spending time AT HOME?*
Client: *Perhaps I should take one day off and club it with the weekend and plan a trip. But that cannot be done in the next two weeks.*
Counsellor: *Well, that plan sounds substantial. When will it be possible?*
Client: *First week of next month.*
Counsellor: *How do you think your daughter would react when you announce it to her?*
Client: *She would start talking about the trip from today itself and continue till the day we go. (Laughs)*

Very often, clients tend to stick to their comfort zone and not set a substantial goal that demands moving out of their comfort zone. The counsellor's challenge helps jolt them out of their comfort zone. Here the two interjections by the counsellor ('Is that what your daughter meant....?' And 'Is there any way you spend time WITH her than spending time AT HOME?') brought the client to identify the blind spot and reset her goal. Though the goal does not promise immediate satiation, it is substantial to make a difference in the life of the client in fulfilling the role of a single parent. Sometimes a delayed satisfaction of a substantial goal has the potential to enhance motivation more than the immediate satisfaction of a marginal goal.

Goal to be Measurable

A measurable goal has the advantage of monitoring the progress of both the client and the counsellor. Monitoring the change brings the advantage of strengthening motivation because the positive outcome reinforces the behavioural change. Once the client witnesses the impact in terms of change that is measured, confidence and self-efficacy are reinforced. In such cases, though the client finds the action needing effort that is slightly beyond one's capacity, the outcome measured infuses more energy into the client to sustain the action. Hence the counsellor should nudge the client to spell the goal in terms of measurable outcomes. Let us understand the phenomenon with the following example:

Counsellor: *You feel that your grades will have to improve, and you need to work for it. How do you plan to go about it?*
Client: *I should increase my study hours.*
Counsellor: *That's right. Can you be more specific?*
Client: *I should add four hours more to my studies.*
Counsellor: *Well, how many hours are you spending studying at present?*

Client: *Two hours.*
Counsellor: *Oh! Do you wish to increase it to six hours now?*
Client: *Yes.*

The counsellor used the skills of nudging and probing in combination with support to compare the newly set goal with the baseline, which is two hours. Having decided on the time to be spent in studies, the client will now be driven to schedule the stipulated six hours so as to attain the goal. The goal in this form is more attainable than when it was in its initial form of 'I have to increase my study hours'. The goal in the present form is more motivating and action-oriented than in its raw form of intent.

Not all goals can be mentioned in measurable terms. For example, if the issue in question is time to be spent, money to be earned, grades to be achieved, or weight to be lost, it is possible to quantify the variable. Very often, the issue in question relates to anxiety being reduced, interpersonal relations to be improved, depression to be lowered, satisfaction to be enhanced, and pain to be managed. In such instances, it is difficult to quantify the goal. Here is where the counsellor can train the client in measuring the experience using a subjective rating scale. For example, if the counsellor is helping the client to set a goal to reduce the distress level in the primary caregiver while attending to a terminally ill patient, a rating scale is constructed with the help of the client. The left part of the continuum refers to the presently existing state, while the right part refers to the desired state to be attained. The counsellor can prepare a ten-point scale or a visual analogue and ask the client to indicate where he/she is at the point in time and where one desires to reach in a matter of one week, a fortnight, a month and so on.

The following example may help you understand the process clearly:

Counsellor: *You feel that your distress over the state of your husband is now perceivable by him, and you want to manage your distress effectively so that you present it to him in a pleasant form.*
Client: *(Nods)*
Counsellor: *Well, I am showing you a series of facial expressions that range from a highly distressed state to a pleasant state. Can you assess your distress level at present, selecting one expression among the ones on the left side of the strip? (presents the visual analogue to her)*
Client: *(Points to the second from the left with a rating of 8)*
Counsellor: *Ok. That is quite high in distress. You already started on the relaxation therapy last week. Besides that, we shall have our sessions. Both interventions would help you. Now, from this state of high distress, how much progress do you want to make to improve the distress level in the next week? While you identify this, I would request you to be reasonable by taking into account your efforts, the time, and the impact the relaxation is having on you.*
Client: *I find the relaxation therapy sessions very useful. And I am also very keen to manage my distress effectively. So,......by next week, I wish to be..... here. (Points to the rating of 4)*

With such goal setting, it would be easy for both the client and the counsellor to cross-check the goal attainment compared to the goal set. Thus, the counsellor creates a scope for subjective measurement of goals set for the management of feelings and experiences.

Goals to be Attainable

Attainability connotes the feasibility of reaching the goal in terms of internal and external resources and the individual's enterprise in availing these resources. Sometimes in the pursuit of shaping the goal as substantial, the client's resource availability may escape attention. In such a case, the goal remains unattainable. Unattainable goals may add to frustration in the client. For example, if a student whose grades have been consistently 'D' sets a goal to top the class in the forthcoming semester, the probability of attaining the goal remains low. But, if the students set the goal to get a grade of 'B+', then, the probability of attaining it is higher. When the client tries to set the goal too high, the counsellor should use the skills of probing and challenging to draw the attention of the client to resource mobilisation. Following is an excerpt where the client is challenged and probed about the resources, after which she resets the goal as attainable. A client is an obese person. She has joined a weight reduction programme.

Counsellor: *It is a good initiative from your side to have joined the weight reduction programme.*

Client: *I had to do it because I need to reduce my weight and look trim for my brother's marriage which will be on July 7th.*

Counsellor: *Oh! That is just two months away. How much weight do you expect to lose within two months?*

Client: *My instructor said that I should lose 15 kgs to have the right weight.*

Counsellor: *Did your instructor give two monthly timelines for that?*

Client: *No. She did not give a time frame. But I thought I must attain it in two months so that I look trim in the marriage.*

Counsellor: *Ok. That means, on average, you should be losing more than 7 kgs per month. When did you join the programme?*

Client: *Ten days ago.*

Counsellor: *How many kgs have you lost in the last ten days?*

Client: *The weighing machine does not show any weight loss yet. I checked just yesterday.*

Counsellor: *So?*

Client: *Is the programme ineffective?*

Counsellor: *How is your experience? Are you feeling the impact in any way?*

Client: *I do feel the impact... like, I feel more active now. I don't feel the heaviness in my stomach after I have adopted the diet schedule.... But it is not showing in the weight....*

Counsellor: *Could it be that your expectation of impact in terms of weight loss is a bit high since it is linked to 'looking trim in the marriage'?*

Client: *....I think so. Perhaps I should just expect to be able to participate in the events of the marriage and lose only around three to four kgs of weight?*

Counsellor: *So, you want to revise your goal?*

Client: *Yes. Feeling agile is more important in participating and enjoying the marriage. Even three to four kgs would be visible.*

Counsellor: *Visible for who? Others or your own experience?*

Client: *Well, I understand....my own experience and feelings are more important than whether others perceive the change in my looks or not. (Smiles)*

In the case cited above, the counsellor not only challenged the client to reset the goal in terms of feasibility but also challenged her to change her orientation from extrinsic to intrinsic motivation. This helps in attainable target and also assess goal attainment more in terms of personal satisfaction based on the experience with oneself than the observations of others where the locus of control is external.

Guiding the clients to set attainable goals is important for all clients. It assumes an added significance in the context of Sports Psychology, where athletes will have to be helped in moving their goals to higher levels, each time checking on the attainability.

Goals to be Result-Oriented

This is closely related to the clause of 'substantial goal'. The goals set by the client should be based on the impact it brings in his/her life as well as that of the significant others in his/her life. To trigger the motivation of the client further, the counsellor can use the skills of probing to identify the positive impact the set goal would have in his/her life and the lives of significant others. Following is a case of an alcoholic who desires to get rid of his addiction.

Counsellor: *What turn do you think your life would take after you are de-addicted?*

Client: *I would be sober. Behave gently with others. My relationship with my wife and kids would be far better. In my job, my efficiency would go up, and I would be respected.*

Counsellor: *That sounds very encouraging. Now, can you describe the way it impacts your family?*

Client: *Family?..... Of course, they would be happy. It would leave a lot of time to be together. We can plan the evenings in a better way. The kids can get my help in their academics. .....Then...then, the family will have more money... because I will be saving all that I used to spend on my drinks. We can plan holidays.....dining out....Oh! Life would really be so good.*

This description and imagination of the client would strengthen his motivation sufficiently to push him to action to realise the results.

Goals to be Realistic

Realistic goals are those which are in tune with the resource availability and Locus of Control of the client. Cooper (2019) advocates that the client's set goals should conform to the internal Locus of control. For example, if the client sets a goal such as 'My children should show respect for me' or something like 'My organisation should give me a pay hike' the goal is anchored on the actions of others, which is not under the control of the client. So, these goals do not stand the test of being realistic. In such cases, the counsellor should challenge the client to own the problem so that the goal setting would have his/her involvement as the nucleus of action to give it a realistic flavour. Further, the counsellor should assess the number of goals set by the client. The number and the level should conform to the resources and the time frame. Too many goals, even though minor, may be difficult to sustain. In case the client's ambition goes beyond realistic limits, the counsellor can challenge by nudging the client to structure a time frame for the same and by envisaging the consequences of so many changes in behaviour/life events.

Goals to have a Time Frame

A good way of goal setting is to make it time-bound. A goal gains in its meaningfulness when it is tagged to a clearly specified date and time of achievement (Fried & Slowik, 2004). Without the timeline, the goals may get lost in time. Attaining a goal at an appropriate time retains its value. Attaining it after a considerable lapse of time may render the achievement redundant. For example, an employee aiming for a salary hike along with his counterparts in the office gets it two years after his colleagues receive the hike will not feel happy because he would not be on par with the colleagues with whom he joined the organisation. In order to retain the value of the goal and sustain the motivation, it may be a good idea for the counsellor to help the client identify a long-term goal with a distant timeline and break and link it into short-term and immediate goals, each with a timeline. This way, the client need not wait for a prolonged time for goal satisfaction and also derive satiation intermittently while attaining the immediate and short-term goals logically leading to long-term goals. For example, the client who wants to lose 15 kg of weight to look trim for her brother's wedding around the corner can be helped to derive short-term and immediate goals of losing 15 kg that have a long-term time frame of six months. The immediate goal for the next month can be feeling energetic and light and being active with good participation in preparation for marriage. A short-term goal can be losing four kgs of weight in three months under the guidance of a weight reduction programme coach. Having to work on a longer timeline requires a long wait for goal attainment, making it difficult to sustain motivation. Introducing short and immediate goals thus fills the gap of prolonged waiting and function as a reinforcer to strengthen motivation.

Enhancing Client Compliance with the Set Goals

Goals are like assignments. They need to be pursued with an action plan. Goals formulated without many considerations remain either as non-starters or dropped mid-way. The best examples that testify to this are New Year or birthday resolutions which are made without much consideration of resource availability, feasibility, possible obstacles, etc. hence abiding by them becomes difficult. A competent counsellor should understand the factors that contribute to strengthening the client's commitment to the goals and apply appropriate skills in shaping the client's goals in a way that enhances client compliance with them.

Client-owned Goals have Better Compliance

The underlying principle is the natural human tendency to preserve and protect that which is owned by us. The goals owned by the client are more likely to be pursued and attained. Many counsellors observed that when the client is in the stage of goal setting, he/she has a tendency to seek endorsement from the counsellor on the chosen goal. The counsellor has to respond very carefully in such a situation so that in the process of encouraging the client to set the goal, the counsellor does not own the goal. If that happens, the client will be likely not to own the responsibility of reaching the goal successfully. There are occasions when the client while setting the goal, would explicitly state that the goal is set to satisfy someone in his/her life (father/spouse/boss). Such goals do not take the client forward towards successfully mitigating the problem. The following examples give insight about the way it happens in real practice.

Client: *So, it is my poor communication skills that make me unfit for job interviews. I need to improve.*
Counsellor: *What do you want to do to improve your communication skills?*
Client: *Go for English language classes. Personal effectiveness classes.*
Counsellor: *So, you want to join English language classes to improve your language and personal effectiveness classes to overcome your shyness.*
Client: *Yes.*
Counsellor: *Do you have any specific place in mind?*
Client: *I have enquired. Classes at EL university are good for English. I will join that. Of my shyness, ...want to join the Life Skill course...online. It is free. What do you think?*
Counsellor: *What I THINK is not important here. WHAT DO YOU THINK IS. Have you made proper enquiries about the online classes and their suitability of it for your purpose?*
Client: *Actually, no. I only thought of taking it because it is free anyway. But will enquire. But I don't know, when online, how will it help shyness? Maybe, I should see for something else.... Direct classes.*

In this example, we see that the client setting the goal of joining a course for overcoming his shyness was driven not by the main objective of whether the course helps one in overcoming shyness but by the fact that it was offered free. Somewhere he was aware that the choice was not correct. Hence, he tried to seek the approval of the counsellor. Had the counsellor given her nod, he would have joined the course only to get back with an observation that it did not help him. However, the counsellor was alert and made it clear that the set goal should be owned by the client and not by the counsellor. This helped the client to become cautious and revise the goal set in haste. Since the client made an informed choice of joining a particular English language course, he is likely to pursue it religiously. Similarly, only when he chooses the personal effectiveness course gathering all information and the review by those who took the course, would he own up to that goal. The counsellor will have to use listening skills well and respond with assertions on recommending, suggesting or pushing a goal.

In the following example, the client is challenged by the counsellor for making it very obvious that he is setting a goal owned by his father.

Client: *Finally, I think I will reconcile to become an engineer.*
Counsellor: *Reconcile?*
Client: *Yes. What else? There is so much pressure from my father. He wants to see me as an engineer.*
Counsellor: *But what do YOU want to become?*
Client: *Well......... How does it matter anyway? I want to become an artist...a cartoonist.*
Counsellor: *Then?*
Client: *Then? My father throws a fit at the mention of it. He says I will be ruining my life. He is talking about spending so much on me to get coaching for the*

	engineering entrance test where I could get a decent rank. He feels I have the aptitude for engineering.
Counsellor:	*But what do YOU think about your career?*
Client:	*Fine arts is my passion. I have wanted to go in that line..... but....*
Counsellor:	*Do you think you can give your best in case you go into the line chosen by your father?*
Client:	*No.*
Counsellor:	*Then?*
Client:	*Difficult to convince him. I feel doomed.*
Counsellor:	*Are you equating 'difficult with impossible'?*
Client:	*(Silent spell) Do you think I should try various other methods?*
Counsellor:	*What do YOU think?*
Client:	*Perhaps I should.*

In this case, the client was ready to pursue the goals his father set for him. The counsellor challenged it. Later, the client also tried to seek the counsellor's approval for his immediate goal of persuading his father. The counsellor asserted and made him own up to the immediate goal too.

Appealing Goals have Better Compliance

New goals set by the client demand resources. Resources (be it material resources, time, or skills) are limited in supply. Thus, the new goals will have to compete with the existing ones in attracting investment of resources. The client would have a tendency to favour the new goal only if it is relatively more attractive than the existing one when he/she has to divert the resources from the old to the new. There is a subjectivity involved in perceiving the attractiveness of the goals. The responsibility of the counsellor lies in helping the client compare the existing status with the outcome of the new goal in order to highlight the advantageous outcome of the new goal. In that process, sometimes the counsellor may have to help the client endorse the negatives in the present status and the positive outcome of the newly set goal. Here is an example of a patient who has been postponing her knee replacement because of her fear of surgery.

Client:	*I am almost immovable now. Severe pain. This sort of dependence is something that I am unable to accept. I have never depended on anyone in my whole life. And ....now...... even to go to the washroom... I need help. (Her voice chokes)*
Counsellor:	*You are unable to accept the loss of your autonomy. This is something you are unable to come to terms with.*
Client:	*Sometimes I feel that I should rather die... than be so dependent. No medicine is there. The doctor says only surgery is the answer.*
Counsellor:	*Oh! You have the option of surgery as the treatment.*
Client:	*Yes. The only option. But I am so scared. Scared of the general anaesthesia. One of my uncles died due to that.*
Counsellor:	*Well, when the doctor has given you the option of surgery, you have hesitation. You opt for the dependent life due to the fear of a few hours of surgery under general anaesthesia.*

Client: *I know.... But....*

Counsellor: *Well, let us, for a minute, assume that you have successfully undergone surgery. How would your life be thereafter?*

Client: *I will be mobile. I will be on my own. Move around in the house....Go out shopping... Play with my grandchildren.... Make dishes in the kitchen..... (Breaks down into sobs)*

Counsellor: *(After waiting for a while till she stopped sobbing) Does that make you feel sad?*

Client: *No, no. I broke down because I am still suffering and not able to opt for surgery.*

Counsellor: *Do you think it is a good idea for us to first address your fear if there is no other reason for your not opting for surgery?*

Client: *I think I will first say 'yes' to the surgery, and we will work on my fear between now and the date of the surgery. It is easier to handle my fear than the continuous pain and distress of immobility.*

The counsellor's challenge to the client by contrasting the persistent pain with irrational fear leaned the client towards opting for surgery as the visualisation of the post-surgical life appeared attractive compared to the painful present. Thus, when the client is hesitant to set a proper goal, the counsellor should challenge and help the client compare the appealing future with the painful present.

Goals with Pain Reduction Potential Have Better Compliance

Pain can be physical or psychological. When the individual suffers from prolonged pain, anything that has a promise of giving respite from the pain would motivate the person. In many cases, people narrate stories of their initial stages of addiction to alcohol or drugs, citing the reason that they provide temporary relief from the pain/distress they experience. Pain reduction thus becomes a significant motivation. In the example of knee replacement cited above, it is the hope of pain reduction that made the client come around to fight her fear of surgery. The counsellor has to place before the client the repulsive pain that one experiences at present and contrast with the promise the goal holds in reducing the pain and making that big change in life.

Better Compliance with Goals where Disincentives are Managed

Clients hesitate to set the goals because they foresee some obstacles and some adverse effects of the newly set goals. The client is not motivated enough to set the goal because it has some inherent disincentives. For example, a young woman is not inclined to set the goal of having a baby after marriage because she sees it coming with certain responsibilities as having to forgo sleep for several nights, losing body shape, going through labour, etc. Similarly, a person at the peak of his career is hesitant to set the goal of changing his job because that would demand relocation to another place where his old parents will not accompany him. Once the client is helped to express these perceived disincentives, the counsellor can use empathy, support, probes and challenges to bring a cognitive restructuring so that the client changes the perspective and gets motivated towards pursuing the goal.

Motivational Interviewing

Motivational Interviewing (MI) is a therapeutical approach to counselling with the objective of enhancing the client's motivation to change behaviour. The client, after being helped to have a cognitive reorientation, views the problem from a different perspective and develops a desire to approach the situation differently. Yet, the uncertainty of the outcome, the need for investing efforts and the natural resistance to change pull the clients back from moving forward towards the behaviour change. Thus, the client gets stuck with ambivalence. Ambivalence refers to a state of opposing feelings and attitudes that coexist in the person who wants to change but at the same time does not want to change. This state is particularly pronounced in situations where an immediate reward for behaviour is in conflict with the adverse consequences in the long run. It is a state where the individual experiences uncertainty because of indecisiveness. Any attempt to convince or coerce the person has more chances of being counterproductive because the more the person is pressurised to change, the more defensive one would become because the ambivalent state has a stock of arguments for not changing, which would actively surface and strengthen playing a defensive role. Motivational interviewing helps the client come out of this ambivalence and insecurity associated with the change in behaviour and strengthens the drive for change in behaviour. Motivational interviewing is a technique that flows with the person-centred approach of Carl Rogers, where the control over the agenda rests with the client, with the counsellor playing the role of a facilitator. Miller and Rollnick (1991) originally came up with MI as an intervention for addictive behaviour and later (Miller & Rollnick, 2002) extended its scope of it to a variety of behaviour changes.

Theoretical Basis

Motivational interviewing is based on the assumption that change in behaviour is not an easy process and does not occur as an 'all-or-none' phenomenon. Change is an incremental process that is determined by the decision of the person concerned. This syncs well with the trans-theoretical model or stages of change model of behaviour change advocated by Prochaska and DiClemente (1982, 1983). According to this theory, the individual's change in behaviour is dynamic as the person's cognition/thinking moves in its direction. The theory postulates five stages as pre-contemplation (a person not thinking in terms of change), contemplation (a person considering the change in behaviour), preparation (a person inclined towards change and is ready to change), action (a change in behaviour is initiated), and maintenance (the behaviour change is sustained). The progression need not follow the hierarchical order because, at any point, the person may relapse into one earlier stage and change the decision. It may happen between the stages of pre-contemplation and contemplation; contemplation and preparation; preparation and action, action and maintenance, or even at the stage of maintenance. For example, a client who is a heavy smoker is medically advised to stop smoking in view of his deteriorating cardiac health. The individual who has adequate health information on the harm smoking causes is in the stage of contemplation but is not very sure if he could give up smoking at this point where he needs to smoke while in his peak of creative work as he is conditioned that way. He has to complete a creative deadline task in the next six months and is not sure if he could risk his work by trying to quit smoking at this time. Now, in this situation, if his wife tries to put pressure on him to quit smoking as she is concerned about his health or if the counsellor tries to 'educate' him about the urgency of quitting smoking as the cardiac attack he suffered recently was quite bad, the person may get more defensive on the significance of completing his work on time and may tend to move back to the pre-contemplation stage from the contemplation stage. Similarly, a person who quit smoking on medical advice (Action) may slide into the habit of smoking when he has to cope with severe work pressure. Thus, the behaviour change according to the transtheoretical model totally rests on the decision of the individual. Motivational Interviewing is completely in sync with this and advocates that the technique of motivational Interviewing should respect the autonomy of the client at all costs.

Assumptions and the Spirit of Motivational Interviewing

Motivational interviewing is based on the following assumptions:

- Behaviour can be changed/modified
- Clients desire to be healthy and wish to change
- The key to behaviour change is the motivation
- Motivation is dynamic
- Motivation can be influenced by social interaction
- The client's motivation is influenced by the counsellor's style

The above assumptions help in evolving the spirit of MI. The counsellor applies the technique guided by the spirit of MI. The underpinning principle guiding it is respect for the client and his/her autonomy. The counsellor banks on the intrinsic motivation of the client. The counsellor respects the client's non-inclination to change as much as his intent to change. Yet, the counsellor works on eliciting the intrinsic resources of the client. The counsellor functions on the understanding that if the client is not inclined to adopt any change at a point, he/she must have some reasons for it, which is not known to the counsellor. Hence the counsellor shall not take a patriarchal view on the issue. The approach adopted by the counsellor is non-confrontational, non-coercive and non-challenging. The spirit of MI is collaborative, evocative and respectful of patient autonomy. Table 7.1 draws a contrast between the style adopted in MI and other styles.

An example in the form of a case study may provide a deeper insight into the spirit of MI. A 41-year-old IT employee who had a cardiac episode was advised to quit smoking. He expressed his desire to do so, yet continued to smoke with the well-known procrastinating statement of 'I shall quit soon'. It is very natural and also easy to conclude that the person lacks the motivation, does not understand the seriousness of the consequences, or really does not care. A counsellor who starts with such assumptions is likely to warn the client about the consequences and the need for a change in behaviour. When that does not bring the desired results, it is quite natural to brand the client as unmotivated and give up on him. In contrast, in MI, the client's behaviour of expressing the desire to quit smoking and action contrary to it is viewed as 'unresolved ambivalence' rather than 'lack of motivation'. The very fact that he expressed the desire to quit is an indication of motivation. The counsellor works on this unresolved ambivalence in the client. As a first step, the counsellor respects the autonomy of the client and accepts the fact that the decision to quit or continue to smoke is the responsibility of the client. Hence, the counsellor avoids the authoritarian approach. The counsellor, using MI, tries to elicit reasons for his expression of a desire to quit. Once the client

Table 7.1 Motivational Interviewing and Other Styles

MI Style	*Other Style*
Client Autonomy: The counsellor may provide information but finally leaves the decision to the client with a clear communication that says 'It is up to you to change or not to', clearly indicating the freedom and right bestowed on him/her.	**Counsellor Authority:** The counsellor feels empowered and instructs the client to initiate the change for the benefit of themself and others. Expects the client to comply with the suggestions/advice/instructions.
Collaborative: The counsellor assumes the role of a collaborative partner. Decisions are taken jointly between the client and counsellor. The counsellor respects the client's expertise on matters related to self. The counsellor assumes the facilitating role and lets the client take the lead role in final decision making.	**Confrontative:** The counsellor assumes that the client's perspective has shortcomings and lacks insight. Tries to impose on the client 'what is best'. Tries to impose the counsellor's perspective through persuasion and coercion. Challenges the client for resistance to change.
Evocative: The counsellor's attempt is to evoke the client's own motivation to change. In this process, the counsellor tries to project to the client the contrast between his/her values and wants and the status quo, which defeats compliance with what he/she really cares.	**Educative:** The counsellor assumes ignorance on the part of the client. Thinks that the client lacks the much-needed insight as well as the knowledge and skill required. Hence the counsellor imparts the knowledge and educates the client on the need for change and how to go about it.

enumerates the reasons for his desire to quit, the counsellor identifies the values and needs embedded in the expression of desire. The client is also stimulated to think and enumerate the reasons for not quitting smoking. This turns into a collaborative effort between the client and the counsellor to identify and weigh the pros and cons of continuing to smoke, by which the unresolved ambivalence is worked. For example, if the client stated that his expression of the desire to quit smoking had in mind to contribute to coaching his 13-year-old daughter as a badminton player or achieving a new goal in his trekking expedition, the counsellor focuses the discussion on how his continuing to smoke may come as an obstacle to theses values and goals set by him in life. The job of the counsellor stops here. Rather than pushing his arguments to elicit a resolve to stop smoking, the counsellor here totally leaves it to the client with the message 'it is up to you'. This helps the client to contemplate, if not immediately, at a later time. MI adopts an invitational style of working with clients. It has the scope for addressing the impasses of the clients with alternative problem-solving approaches. The congenial approach towards this is a collaborative functioning between the client and the counsellor where the client takes the major role, while the counsellor plays the role of a propeller who triggers the thinking and talking in the client. Miller and Rollnick believe that 'MI is about arranging conversations so that people talk themselves into change, based on their own values and interests' (Miller & Rollnick, 2013, p. 4). The unique feature of MI is that the counsellors here assist the clients in becoming their own advocates of change. The counsellor functions on the premise that every individual has the capacity to change by invoking intrinsic motivation within oneself. The process of MI is permeated with the sense of shared hope and optimism between the client and the counsellor that change is possible. Once the client starts to believe that a change is what is desired and one has the ability to change, he/she will initiate the action. The counsellor helps in tuning the client to such thinking and initiating the change.

The spirit of MI can be summarised in an acronym-PACE, which stands for Partnership, Acceptance, Compassion, and Evocation. The counsellor should assume an equal partnership with the client and make the process collaborative. Second, there should be unconditional acceptance of the client irrespective of his/her choice to change or not to change. The counsellor must have compassion for the client for all the struggles one has undergone in life and also the present struggle one faces in adopting the change decision. The counsellor should be guided by the principle of helping to evoke the client's values, desires, obstacles and resources, which gradually dissipates his/her state of ambivalence.

Application of Motivational Interviewing (MI)

The application of MI rests on the pillars of the basic assumptions, the spirit, principles and skills of MI. The assumptions and the spirit are discussed in the preceding paragraphs. We will discuss here the principles and skills of MI here.

Principles of Motivational interviewing (MI)

Rollnick, Miller and Butler (2008) developed four basic guiding principles for the practitioners of MI. It is easily remembered as an acronym: RULE representing **Resisting** the righting reflex, **Understanding** the client's motivation, **Listening** with empathy, and **Empowering** the patient.

i. Resisting the righting reflex: When an individual presents the desire to change the behaviour and yet is showing some resistance to commit to the change, the very normal tendency on the part of the listener is to 'fix the person' by correcting the fallacy in the issue. However, in MI, the counsellor should resist this tendency to persuade or argue with the client because this would only reinforce the resistance in the client by emphasising the reasons for maintaining the status quo. It should be remembered that it is very natural for any individual to put up a defence against any attempts of persuasion. The counsellor operating the MI should consciously suppress such righting reflex so that it is possible to move to explore the client's motivation to change which takes the session in a positive direction of emphasising the change.
ii. Understanding the client's motivation: The counsellor's focus should be on understanding the client's motivation. There is a need to explore the client's concerns, values and interests, which prompted one to express the desire to change. Identification of these aspects would provide the counsellor with an insight into the client's motivation.
iii. Listening with empathy: The general thumb rule in MI is that the counsellor should equally balance the consultation time between listening and talking. Listening intently to the client would help the counsellor understand and appreciate the client's ambivalent situation better. Empathetic listening helps the counsellor to place himself/herself in the position of the client and appreciate the ambivalence in him/her. This prevents the counsellor from the righting reflex too. Empathy should not be mistaken for endorsing the client's resistance to change. Understanding the reasons for resistance is different from subscribing to or supporting it.
iv. Empowering the client: The counsellor's way of empowering the client is by following a collaborative approach where the client plays the role of a collaborator than

a compiler. This calls for the counsellor to explore the ideas of the client on the approach to the intended change, the past experience of the client in bringing any change in the behaviour or the obstacles that one faced when an attempt was made the previous time. Communication in this direction invokes in the client a sense of personal responsibility in initiating the change, which has the power to motivate the client better.

Skills of Motivational Interviewing (MI): General

The skills of MI are not drastically different from the general skills of counselling. However, as in the case of counselling in general, contextualising the skills is very important. They can be discussed under eight subheads. The first four skills are the general ones that need to be applied in the context.

1. *Develop discrepancies:* The counsellor should 'tip the balance towards change' by clearly bringing to the notice of the client the discrepancies between his/her interests, values and goals as a person playing various roles (parent, spouse, employee) and the present behaviour (Hall, Gibbie & Lubman, 2012). They are effectively used as teasers to their existing ambivalence to move them towards expressing their concerns about the present behaviour. Thus, the counsellor's objective is to make the client realise and 'create the want to change' from within. The following example may help in bringing clarity to its application:

Client: *The doctor has cautioned me that my liver will not be able to tolerate alcohol any more. That is a strong warning. I know I need to abstain.*
Counsellor: *So, how are you going to do it? And when?*
Client: *I will do it. Gradually... sooner or later..... It is not that easy....a habit of 20 years.*
Counsellor: *Yes, I understand. But can you tell me what made you say that you need to abstain?*
Client: *My failing health, as per the medical report.*
Counsellor: *What else?*
Client: *My family. My children are in their crucial stage of education. They need my support.*
Counsellor: *That is right. Any other reason?*
Client: *My son is now 16 years old. I sometimes worry that he may get tempted and follow me in this habit.*
Counsellor: *Correct me if I am wrong, but the reason for your desire to quit is your failing health which needs immediate attention; you feel you cannot afford to risk your health and life because you have a responsibility towards your children, who are at a stage where they need your support; and you are concerned about your son who you think may role model you. All of them are quite genuine and call for immediate attention.*
Client: *I understand. But I am really scared of the withdrawal symptoms. And.... I may also lose out on some of my important friends.....*
Counsellor: *While you desire to give up drinking to save your liver and strengthen your children's career, the withdrawal symptoms that you may have*

during the process of cessation and the possibility of losing some friends are stopping you from going ahead.

Client: *I am not sure if I can tolerate the withdrawal syndrome.... I believe it is very painful....*

Counsellor: *Maybe. Have there been any occasions when you tolerated the pain to achieve something?*

Client: *Yes. I used to be a heavy smoker. I had a block in my blood vessels in the ankle and had severe pain in my lower back and legs. Could not walk due to pain. Had to undergo stenting near the ankle. The doctor said he would perform the procedure only if I was very sure of giving up smoking totally and would not smoke even a single cigarette because it could be fatal. He asked me to return for the procedure only if I was very sure of abstaining from smoking. I took one week to think. Then, I was determined to give up smoking because I did not want to become immobile. I did it. It was no doubt very difficult. But, my wife and siblings stood as strong support. Underwent withdrawal syndrome for almost a couple of months. I should say that my family really tolerated all my irritable behaviour and tantrums.*

Counsellor: *Oh! You have the precedence where your willpower triumphed. And you have the strong support of your family too.*

Client: *Yes, that is my real advantage. If I really decide, I can and shall do it, and my family will stand with me.*

Counsellor: *What if you take – say few more months to decide on getting out of your habit of drinking?*

Client: *(A quick look at the counsellor)....... I may lose out .....my liver condition worsens and ....I may not have a chance.... An option to mend things...*

In the above example, the counsellor, with his one question, evoked from the client the strengths that he is bestowed with for initiating the change and the main obstacles that he foresees. The counsellor once again contrasts with the client by questioning him on the consequences of delaying the change in behaviour, eliciting from the client a response of how his interest and values may have to be sacrificed by choosing not to change. At this point, the client's motivation is sufficiently invoked.

2. *Roll with the resistance:* In practice, sometimes it may so happen that the counsellor may perceive the urgency for the client to change either because of time pressure or the risk of continuing the behaviour is perceived to be very high (for example, involvement in criminal activity such as transporting drugs). In such cases, the counsellor is likely to have a tendency to inadvertently pressurise the client or apply coercive methods. When the counsellor brings in the skills of showing the discrepancy or assumes a proactive role by describing the ill effects of the behaviour, the reaction of the client is likely to be that of resistance. Resistance is manifested in many ways. The client may mobilise all the arguments as to why the status quo should be maintained; may interrupt the counsellor; discount the expertise of the counsellor; trivialise the consequences of their behaviour; blame others for their behaviour; express lack of confidence in one's ability to change or even express unwillingness to change.

   Resistance is not something that is static in the client. It emerges during the process of communication. It is possible that neither the client nor the counsellor would know the reason for resistance. One thing the counsellor can do is to identify it when it manifests in the client. The manner in which the counsellor responds to it initially has a great impact on the further progress of the session. Hence the counsellor should respond professionally to it rather than reacting to it, which is very unprofessional. When faced with such resistance, the counsellor in MI rolls with the resistance. This means the counsellor resists any attempt to win over the client with counter-arguments or abandon the client based on any judgement. Instead, the counsellor goes with the flow by reflecting and putting back to the client the expressed resistance. There are many ways of applying it.

- Simple rephrasing (reflecting back) of the client's statement (example 1: This idea is not to your liking; example 2: You do not agree with this method)
- Project the tone of the client in the reflection (example: You are very unhappy about being in this situation)
- Project the client's ambivalence in the reflection (example: On the one hand, you want to quit smoking while on the other, you are scared of the possible irritable behaviour during the abstinence)
- Acknowledge the resistance in the reflection (example: Looks like we are entering into an argument. That is not what I intend to do)
- Reflect and support the client's choice (example: Finally, it is your choice. You are the one who should decide whether to change or not. It is up to you)

Thus, shifting the focus of the discussion or reframing what is expressed by the client may help sustain the focus of the discussion without it getting drifted into arguments based on resistance. The principle to keep in mind is that the focus of the counsellor is the behaviour/problem/issue but not the client. Hence moving with the client's resistance helps in bringing back the attention to change from indulgence to 'not change'. If the counsellor observes that the resistance is stiff or the client is upset or getting agitated, it is always wise not to stretch it any further and leave the client that way for the next two or three days. The client is likely to calm down, ruminate and start seeing the merits of changing the behaviour during this incubation time. Rolling with resistance is a very effective skill for handling resistance as it is likely to reduce the client's defensiveness (Corbett, 2016).

3. *Express empathy:* It is not enough if the counsellor listens with empathy. The empathetic understanding should be communicated to the client through appropriate paraphrasing. The counsellor, while listening to the client, expresses his/her understanding through non-verbal communication, asking questions that project the counsellor's interest to know and understand the counsellor's emotions, experiences and feelings in more detail. Such expression creates an environment of security where the client feels comfortable being open and expressing better
4. *Support client self-efficacy:* Self-efficacy refers to the individual's belief in one's own ability to do and achieve something. MI emphasises enhancing the client's agency for change. The counsellor strives to draw the attention of the client to one's own resources and put them to full use in executing the change. The counsellor using appropriate probes, helps the client formulate their own goals, identify the resources to attain the goals, and also invoke confidence and faith in oneself in attaining the goal. The counsellor focuses on the strength of the client and highlights the ability present in him/her. This boosts the morale of the client and reinforces self-efficacy. The process of doing it is evident in the example cited under 'Developing Discrepancies' where the

counsellor probed the client with a question if there had been any occasion when the client tolerated pain to achieve something. The client then gave a long description of his experience with smoking cessation. Invoking this experience fresh in the memory helped the client to revive the confidence in his ability to successfully meet the withdrawal syndrome of quitting drinks. The counsellor's endorsement of the ability of the client is a powerful promoter of self-efficacy in the client.

5. *Open-ended questions to be asked:* The counsellor should pose open-ended questions that elicit descriptive responses from the client. This would create a situation where the client does most of the speaking. The process of answering open-ended questions stimulates thinking in the client. Sometimes the client may express the fears and apprehensions that have been dormant and never had a chance to surface, which helps in gaining new insight into self. The following contrast between the two counsellors may help in appreciating the power of open-ended questions:

Counsellor 1:	*You are here to explore the possibilities of controlling your habit of drinking. Does your habit worry you?*
Client:	*Yes.*
Counsellor 2:	*You are here in the context of handling your habit of drinking. What are your worries and concerns about it?*
Client:	*It worries me on many counts. Of late, I tend to get violent after drinking. There were two occasions when I was physical with others. I am losing control.....it is evident. But I don't see it easy to stop drinking now. ....I.....I have become sort of dependent on it. I....I feel trapped.*

The closed question from the first counsellor elicited only a monosyllable response from the client, while the open-ended question from the second counsellor could bring out the behaviour, experience and feelings, want and hopelessness of the client related to the present condition and the future. It is easier for the counsellor to continue the engagement with the client in this case.

6. *Affirmations to be used*: Affirmations from the counsellor are encouraging for the client, particularly when they reiterate the client's strengths, efforts, intentions, and goals. The counsellor's affirmations function as reinforcements for the client to move towards change. They also strengthen the self-efficacy of the client. Used in appropriate contexts and in adequate measures, they consolidate the client's resolve to change. The following example will be of relevance.

Client:	*Don't you think I am the one who is actually put to difficulty because of my obesity? I certainly want to reduce my weight. I tried last year. Went on a drastic diet and exercise regime. I continued for about one month. But then, that was the time when my brother's wedding was fixed. I gave up....gave up because it was impossible to stick to a regimented lifestyle when the atmosphere was one of joy and merriment. And now, my mother is so cut up with me because she sees my body shape as a major issue to my marriage prospects.*
Counsellor 1:	*The very fact that you feel the strong need to reduce your weight is a real positive point. Also, your one-month trial just before your brother's wedding is proof that you can do it.*

Counsellor 2: *But why did you not resume your programme after your brother's wedding? You tried for one month, but then, you did not do anything for one full year!*

Counsellor 1, by affirming the strong desire in the client to reduce the weight and the effort made in the past (though unsuccessful), helped in rekindling the desire to reset the goal in the client. On the contrary, the second counsellor, by emphasising the negative dampened the motivation of the client. The first counsellor is a competent motivational interviewer.

7. *Use of Reflections:* Reflections are mirroring to the client their statements, feelings, intentions, desires and apprehensions as expressed by them. Many a time, when we are caught unawares by a mirror, we tend to respond with a startle. This startling response is elicited as a reaction to catching the stranger in ourselves. When we consciously stand before the mirror, we do tend to adjust our posture and expressions to our liking. That is the reason we are startled when the mirror catches us suddenly, giving us no time to 'pose'. Something similar happens to the client when the counsellor uses reflections in the form of reframing, rephrasing and restating the expressions of the client in the process of 'change talk'. The client may identify the hidden desire to change, the dormant fear preventing him/her from taking the initiative, the timidity in him/her unknown before and the struggle between the 'want' and the 'apprehensions' associated with the behaviour change. The advantages of the counsellor's reflections can be summarised into the following points:

   - Reflections make the implicit meanings of the client's statements explicit. Thus, it gives scope for understanding self better
   - Reflections encourage further exploration into the unknown areas of motivation
   - Reflections reinforce the motivation to change in the client
   - Reflections are testimony of the counsellor's involvement in the process of counselling and help in strengthening the rapport between the client and the counsellor.

   As explained under the head of 'rolling with resistance', reflections can capture not only the content of the client's expression but also the feelings, resistance, ambivalence, desires, apprehensions and so on. Thus, the counsellor's use of reflections mirrors to the client one's position with regard to change in totality. Hence it is insightful.
8. *Use of summarising:* The technique of summarising is used by the counsellor to keep the flow of the counselling process intact. Summarising as a technique helps in linking the two sessions held on different days. It provides feedback to the client about the counsellor's active involvement in the process. It brings the client the discrepancies between the present status of himself/herself in contrast to the goals set by one. Thus, the perception of a gap between the goal and the status helps in creating a disequilibrium and drive towards the goal.

The last four skills mentioned above are termed 'change talk' between the client and the counsellor (Dean, 2015). They can be remembered with the acronym OARS referring to use of Open-ended questions, Affirmations, Reflections, and Summarising. The first four can be remembered with the acronym DRES referring to Developing Discrepancies, Roll with Resistance, Empathy all along and Supporting Self-Efficacy in the client.

The principles, skills, and techniques are applied to enhance the client's motivation to change. Making the client realise the need for the new goal is one milestone reached, but thereafter, the client's motivation to change needs to translate to commitment to change. In order to attain this goal, the counsellor in a MI uses several probes to elicit responses from the client that concentrates on the change. The questions relate to the following areas:

- Disadvantages of continuing the existing harmful/unproductive/ineffective behaviour (*example: What worries you about the way things are right now?*)
- Areas of change being contemplated (*example: What specific change are you thinking of bringing in first?*)
- Immediate goal (*example: What do you wish to do as the next point of action?*)
- Short/long term goal (*example: Where do you want to go from here?*)
- Advantages of changing the behaviour (*example: How do you think things would turn after you make the change?*)
- Optimism (*example: When was the last time that you could bring in a significant positive change in your life? How did you bring that?*)
- Intentions to change (*example: How should your life shape up, say.. about five years from now?*)
- Obstacles: (*example: What are the things that you can foresee as obstacles in changing your life?*)
- Strengths (*example: How do you think those obstacles can be managed by you?/How do you think you would handle the roadblocks in reaching your goals?/What are the major strengths in you to overcome any obstacle to reach your goal?*)

The change talk can also be sharpened a little by introducing quantitative methods. Using the quantitative scales helps the counsellor in assessing the client's present position, desire to change, intention to change and self-efficacy with better accuracy. The counsellor here uses a scale of ten points on different parameters. The examples explain the method clearly.

Present Status

Counsellor: *On a scale of one to ten, where a score of one indicates 'Very bad' and ten indicates 'Very good', where do you place yourself with regard to your present problem of compliance with medical advice for your diabetes?*
Client: *Ummm....I think I will put myself on seven.*
Counsellor: *Why do you think you are on seven and not on ten?*
Client: *Because I am not totally non-adherent. I do take insulin regularly though I am careless about my diet and exercise.*

Need for change:

Counsellor: *On a scale of ten, where a score of one represents 'Not at all important' and ten signifies 'Very important', what would be your rating on the importance of adhering to a diet and following the prescribed physical exercise?*
Client: *Well, I know it is ten.*

Desire to change:

Counsellor: *on a scale of ten, where One stands for 'Do not want' and ten stands for 'Very much desire', where do you place yourself in wanting to change your habits of diet and exercise that suits a diabetic?*
Client: *Perhaps eight.*
Counsellor: *Why is it that you do not place yourself on ten?*
Client: *Honestly speaking, I have a severe weakness for sweets. I cannot deprive myself.*

Ability:

Counsellor: *On a scale of ten, where a score of one stands for 'Not at all possible' and ten stands for 'Very much possible', how do you rate yourself in your ability to totally comply with the medical advice related to diabetes?*
Client: *I will put myself on ten.*
Counsellor: *So, you can control your weakness for sweets?*
Client: *Once I am determined, I know I can. I should only take that resolve.*

The counsellor may ask questions to understand the incentives and the disincentives associated with change and the status quo, the steps one is ready to take as the initiative for change, and the steps already taken to promote the change. Questions associated with change move the client towards commitment to change. However, the counsellor should time these questions appropriately. If these questions come too early in the process, there is a likelihood of the client assuming a resistant mode.

MI is a method that is found to have brought encouraging results in terms of economy of time, positive outcome, and client-friendly; it calls for the counsellor to go with the spirit of it and desist from challenging the client with resistance. What helps the counsellor to accept the method of MI is to understand that there is innate resistance to change in everyone, including the counsellor, and this consolidates itself when someone applies pressure. Second, every human being encounters ambivalence in many situations of decision making. A strong knowledge base and the creation of cognitive dissonance in the person helps one to move towards change. Choosing change is not a sudden occurrence. It goes through a process. The counsellor in MI sails the client through the process systematically and progressively. Finally, there is a presence of motivation in every individual. However, it is not always clearly visible. When it is in a dormant state, it is possible to awaken, arise and make it functional to set a healthy goal for oneself to change from a bad state to a better one.

Exercises

Following are the exercises. You can take the cue and do a role-play which requires two people. One will play the role of the counsellor, and one will be the client. The initial conversation is given in the exercise. You should prolong the session to a level where the client's motivation shows an enhancement.

Exercise 1: Use Motivational Interviewing

Client: *I know pretty well that my present job does not promise a good future. If I have to grow in my career, I must quit and choose a better future. But, you see..... this is a government job.*

Counsellor: *Though you don't see many prospects in the present job, you are inclined to stick to it because it brings you the security of being a government job. Can you describe the security part of it?*

(You must continue from here. The person playing the counsellor should try to use the skills of MI to handle the ambivalence in the client. It is important that both the players live their roles genuinely so that the simulation would be effective)

Exercise 2: Help the Client Formulate Goals

The client is a young student from a university who got addicted to spending the whole night watching porno sites on the Internet.

Counsellor: *You feel that since you are awake and active the whole night, you are unable to attend classes in the daytime. Now, tell me, if this problem was not there, how would your day be?*

Client: *I wake up very early, around 5.30 every morning. I enjoy my morning game of badminton. On the way back we, the four of us...me and three friends, have breakfast in the canteen. Then, by 8.30, I am ready for my class. Spend the evening in the library. I would again be my studious self. My teachers appreciate my participation in the classroom. I will be in the company of the Ph.D students in the lab...*

Counsellor: *Tell me, how do you feel about getting back to that state? What does it take to get back that life?*

(Continue from here. Remember that the counsellor's objective is to guide the client through formulating a goal with all its necessary characteristics)

References

Bachel, B. K. (2001). *What do you really want? How do you set a goal and go for it! A guide for the teens.* Free Spirit Publishing.

Benson-Stott, E., & Stott, J. (2020). *Engaging the client through connecting spirited practices,* Routledge.

Cooper, M. (2019). *Integrating counselling & psychotherapy: Directionality, synergy and social change,* Sage.

Cooper, M., & Law, D. (Eds.) (2018). *Working with goals in psychotherapy and counselling.* Oxford University Press.

Crandall, A., Powell, E. A., Bradford, G. C., Magnusson, B. M., Hanson, C. L., Barnes, M. D., Novilla, M. L., & Bean, R. A. (2020). Maslow's hierarchy of needs as a framework for understanding adolescent depressive symptoms over time. *Journal of Child and Family Studies*, *29*(2) 273–281. https://doi.org/10.1007/s10826-019-01577-4.

Deci, E. L., & Ryan, R. M. (1985). *Intrinsic motivation and self-determination in human behavior*, Plenum.

Fried, Y. & Slowik, L. H. (2004). Enriching goal setting theory with time: An integrated approach. *Academy of Management Review*, *29*(3), 404–422.

Hall, K., Gibbie, T., & Lubman, D. I. (2012). Motivational interviewing techniques facilitating behaviour change in the general practice setting. *Australian Family Physician*, *41*(9), 660–667.

Hull, C. L. (1952). *A behavior system: An introduction to behavior theory*. Yale University Press.

Kleinke, C. L. (1994). *Common principles of psychotherapy*. Brooks/Co.

Marini. I. & M. A. Stebnicki. M. A. (2016). (Eds.), *The professional counselor's desk references*, Springer.

Miller, C. (2008). Motivation in agents. *Noûs*, *42*(2), 222–266. https://doi.org/10.1111/j.1468-0068.2008.00679.x.

Miller, W. R., & Rollnick, S. (1991). *Motivational interviewing: Preparing people to change addictive behaviour*. Guilford Press.

Miller, W. R., & Rollnick, S. (2002). *Motivational interviewing: Preparing people for change* (2nd ed.). Guilford Press.

Miller, W. R., & Rollnick, S. (2013). *Motivational interviewing: Preparing people for change* (3rd ed.). Guilford Press.

Neukrug, E. (Ed.) (2015). *The Sage encyclopedia of theory in counseling and psychotherapy*. Sage.

Presbury, J. H., Echterling, L. G., & Mc Kee, J. E. (2002). *Ideas and tools for brief counselling*, Merrill Prentice Hall.

Prochaska, J. O., & DiClemente, C. C. (1982). Transtheoretical therapy: Toward a more integrative model of change. *Psychotherapy: Theory, Research and Practice*, *19*(3), 276.

Prochaska, J. O., & DiClemente, C. C. (1983). Stages and process of self-change of smoking: Toward an integrative model of change. *Journal of Consulting and Clinical Psychology*, *51*(3), 390.

Renger, S., & Macaskill, A. (2021). Guided goal setting in therapy towards being fully functioning. *Journal of Contemporary Psychotherapy*, *51*, 357–364. https://doi.org/10.1007/s10879-021-09505-8.

Rief, W. (2021). Moving from tradition-based to competence-based psychotherapy. *Evidence-Based Mental Health*. https://doi.org/10. 1136/ebmental-2020-300219.

Rollnick, S., Miller, W. R., & Butler, C. C. (2008). *Motivational interviewing in health care: Helping patients change behavior*. The Guilford Press.

Seligman, L., & Reichenberg, L. (2013). *Theories of counseling and psychotherapy: Systems, strategies, and skill.*, Pearson.

Sheldon, K. M., & Elliot, A. J. (1999). Goal striving, need satisfaction and longitudinal well-being: The self-concordance model. *Journal of Personality and Social Psychology*, 47, 227–239.

Taylor, E. (2019) Motivating the client. *Solution-focused therapy with children and adolescents* (pp.59–65), Routledge. DOI:10.4324/9781315166674-6.

8 Skills for Behaviour Change

'My daughter is all the time glued to her mobile phone engaged in playing games or chatting with friends. That is the major source of my irritation and a constant source of conflict between us'. This was the complaint of the mother of an adolescent daughter. The daughter, in her interaction, told me, 'I feel happy interacting with my friends. There is so much in common between us to exchange. And playing games on my mobile? Well, it is so much fun. I enjoy. Every time I win, I get a kick out of it'. One can infer from it that the *behaviour that results in giving pleasure is something that one likes to continue.* Behaviourists believe that we respond in a particular way and strengthen such responses because of the gains we experience in the form of pleasure, material gain or rewarding feedback, or successful results.

An alcoholic was describing the process that got him into addiction. He said, 'I am mediocre while my wife is considered to be very intelligent. Thus, I never met her expectations in any field. She became a constant critique of me. While at home, she never missed an opportunity to nag me with something or the other. Very humiliating for me in the presence of children. That is the time I developed a friendship with a colleague of mine who stayed in the neighbourhood. He was not a great company either. But he used to come home every weekend during the afternoon and call me to go out with him. I used to jump at the invitation because that helped me escape from my wife. Initially, I used to go and sit with him in the club while he had drinks. Slowly I was inducted into the habit which rescued me from my wife for long hours…'.

This narration leads one to assume that *behaviour that gives relief from pain is something one is ready to embrace.* Behaviourists explained that certain behaviour is triggered and sustained because it helps one to escape or avoid unpleasant consequences. This is called negative reinforcement.

Once in my conversation with a religious leader his response to me to a query was 'when you have your fistful of valuables, and someone offers you to grab another variety of valuables from a platter, you will be willing to empty your already filled fist only if you judge what is in the platter more valuable than what you have in your hand. If not, you would be happy to hold on to what you already have in your hands and let go of the offer'. This example is very relevant to behavioural change. The individual weighs the relative benefit (investment in terms of time and effort) of the existing behaviour and the proposed change before initiating the new behaviour. We may term it as 'behavioural economics'.

Resistance to change is a natural reaction in a human being. It applies to the call for change in behaviour. Discarding the comfort zone of a behaviour, habit, or pattern of response to entering into a new or unknown zone of behaviour or response involves effort

DOI: 10.4324/9781003459415-8

and initiative. Certain amount of risk is perceived in it, particularly when the new behaviour is in an unknown zone where the predictability factor is low. In such circumstances of competition between the old and new behaviour, the old behaviour is likely to gain power due to its familiarity while the new stands fragile on that ground. This can be termed as 'politics of behaviour'.

Behaviour change, or initiation and sustenance of new behaviour thus, is a complex process where a number of factors operate in the decision making of the client in choosing and committing to the new behaviour. Hence, the counsellor has to be judicious and pragmatic in using the skills to help the client initiate and sustain action. The client's want for a change in the situation is not as much a problem as the client's willingness to take the initiative to bring about that much-needed change. Counselling is considered successful only when the verbalisation of the client's commitment to action during the session is transferred to application in their day-to-day life (Kottler & Shepard, 2008). Once the counsellor is successful in helping the client ventilate emotions, gain new insights and have the motivation to act in a desirable manner, the counsellor has to apply skills to help them initiate the much-awaited action. In the process the counsellor needs to assess the strength of the undesirable behaviour, identify the reinforcers that help in sustaining them, locate the possible reinforcers for the proposed desirable behaviour, involve the client in exploring the various possible actions to act upon the stressful situation, help the client in identifying the likely obstacles in initiating and sustaining the desirable behaviour in the real life environment, plan a strategy to circumvent them so that the action is initiated. Once initiated, the counsellor also needs to help the client in planning preventing measures from relapsing to the old behaviour. In the process of successfully carrying out this responsibility, the counsellor uses several skills and relies on the application of behavioural principles such as reinforcement, conditioning, deconditioning, extinction, etc.

Skills for Initiating Action in the Client

A change in the client's behaviour is needed for one of the following reasons:

- The existing behaviour is inefficient
- The existing behaviour is deficient
- The existing behaviour is pathological.

The approach of the counsellor is different for the three contexts. The difference in the contexts is summarised in Table 8.1. The deficient and inefficient behaviour can be combined into non-pathological behaviour, and various related aspects can be compared with the behavioural change where pathology is present.

Intervention for Behaviour Inefficiency

Very often the problem with the client is not so much about not wanting to act to a situation but acting to the situation without much thought and proper direction. This either fails to bring a desirable outcome or boomerangs. Clients tend to approach the counsellor after repeated failures from such experiences of knee-jerk responses. They are vexed, feel hopeless, distressed, and are exhausted from the unsuccessful trials. It may

Table 8.1 Contrast Between Pathological and Non-Pathological Behaviour Change

Change in Non-pathological Behaviour	*Change in Pathological Behaviour*
Replace the old behaviour with the new	Replace the old behaviour with the new
Collaboration between the counsellor and the client	Collaboration between the counsellor and the client
The intervention goal is correction in behaviour that is unproductive or filling in the skills the client is deficient in	The intervention goal is to replace the pathological behaviour
The counsellor helps the client choose alternative action from a wide range of options identified by the client	The counsellor helps in weakening the pathological behaviour and strengthening the normal behaviour
Behaviour change is approached through cognitive and motivational intervention	In majority of cases behaviour change is approached through direct intervention
Behaviour change is applied in day-to-day life	Behaviour change is applied in day-to-day life

be reiterated here that the client in such instance is a normal person with the emotional equilibrium disturbed temporarily owing to the stressful situation. The counsellor's use of specific skills in helping the client ventilate emotions, provide cognitive reorientation, and motivate the client to see the possibilities of handling the stressful condition effectively readies him/her to envisage an action that approaches the problem from a new-found perspective. Now, the role of the counsellor is to trigger action in the client. The counsellor follows the following steps in triggering action.

Change in Covert Behaviour

In the context of counselling where the client functions as an active partner in a decision on the choice of the changed behaviour in approaching the problem, the change in behaviour in the real environment should precede a change in covert behaviour. It is important here to distinguish between covert behaviour and a restructured cognition, which the counsellor is assumed to have succeeded. A restructured cognition (as explained in Chapter 6, titled Cognitive Restructuring) refers to the client's ability to view the entire problem from a perspective different from how it has been perceived till now. It refers to the client's understanding of the situation from a different viewpoint. It is all about conceptualising the problem in a different way. Covert behaviour, on the other hand refers to the client's mental planning of the action or behavioural response to the problem. It is the thought process of the client with regard to the possible action related to the problem. In the background of the restructured cognition, the client is encouraged to take an expedition of various possible actions at a covert level before initiating the real behaviour in the live situation. This calls for a certain ability to be imaginative, creative, and think divergently. Divergent thinking is paradoxically opposite to convergent thinking. While convergent thinking looks for one single correct answer for a problem, divergent thinking explores to identification of multiple approaches that may suggest solutions for the problem. Divergent thinking is based on the premise that a problem can be approached in multiple ways. Every approach is important in the sense that each one has some valid suggestion for the solution to the problem. Convergent thinking, on the other hand, is based on the premise that there is only one correct solution for

Table 8.2 Contrast Between Characteristics of the Client and the Creative Person

Characteristics of Creative Person	*Characteristics of the Client in Counselling*
Optimism	Pessimism
Energetic	Exhausted
Enthusiastic	Anxious
Flexible	Rigid
Drive for Persistence	Ready to give up
Explorative	Confined
Ready to take challenges and risks	Apprehensive of challenges and risks
High self-confidence	Low self-confidence
Positive emotions dominant	Negative emotions dominant
Ready for action	Hesitant to act

every problem, and competence lies in spotting and applying 'that one correct solution'. Real-life problems are too complex to have a fixed formula of one correct solution. What works successfully in one case need not do so in another identical case because of the individual differences in their perception, emotion, and behavioural response and reactions. Hence, divergent thinking is highly appropriate while exploring a solution to a problem. In fact, the absence of application of divergent thinking contributes to many failures in the client's initial response to complex problems.

While divergent thinking is essential in a changed behavioural approach to the real-life situation, it is not as easy as said in facilitating the client think divergently. Table 8.2 depicts the contrast between the characteristics of divergent thinking, an ingredient in creativity, and the client's mental state.

The very first obligation of the counsellor is to acknowledge this psychological state of the client and assume the challenge of triggering divergent thinking and covert action in the client with all his characteristics contrasting the pre-requisite for divergent thinking. Following are some techniques used by the counsellor.

Brainstorming

Brainstorming is a technique by which the individual is stimulated to generate many ideas within a short time. The ideas in this context relate to possible alternate actions that can address the problem in hand. The counsellor can apply the probing and challenging skills in triggering and sustaining brainstorming activity in the client. The following example will bring clarity to the process involved in brainstorming.

Counsellor: *Your goal is to stop subjecting yourself to the violent acts of your husband. Shall we try to think of various possibilities for it?*
Client: *Perhaps I should go to my parents' place.*
Counsellor: *Well, that is one way. What other possibilities?*
Client: *Hit him back or start screaming to attract the neighbour's attention which would shock and embarrass him.*
Counsellor: *Sounds good. What other ways?*
Client: *Disappear from home in the evenings...*

Counsellor: *Well, what does it exactly mean?*
Client: *Don't return home from the workplace for a few evenings... (Laughs)*
Counsellor: *Well, that is also fine. Carry on; you are doing well. Think, think... What other ways?*
Client: *Call the police? ...yes, call the police. That may be an extreme step, but yes... calling the police is yet another possibility.*
Counsellor: *Of course, yes. We are only trying to explore the various possibilities. You can come up with many such ideas. Come on, more ideas...*
Client: *Have some friends at home every evening so that he cannot indulge in violence in the presence of others. And... yes, why not request his sister to come and stay with us for a month? That would ensure the presence of someone all the time...*

As seen in the example, with encouragement from the counsellor, the client who started slowly is able to use one idea to generate the next. While applying the skill of brainstorming the counsellor should follow certain guidelines so that the process is smooth and free-flowing.

- The client may not be fluent or spontaneous and may even be hesitant to express ideas. This may be because he/she is unable to think. Here is where the encouragement from the counsellor functions as a good reinforcer. The counsellor should gently challenge the potential of the client and express trust in the client's ability
- The important principle in brainstorming is a non-judgemental disposition. The counsellor and the client should converge on taking cognisance of every idea without any critical assessment. This helps in preventing inhibitions for fear of criticism
- While the suspension of judgement is the thumb rule, it should not prevent the counsellor from seeking clarification
- The client should be appraised that the ideas triggered by brainstorming must be realistic. The client, at the outset, should be oriented to the distinction between ideas and wishes. Wishes can be unrealistic, while ideas are rooted in reality though they may vary in the difficulty of attainability
- It is very likely for the client to reach saturation very quickly. This is the time the counsellor should challenge the creative potential of the client. In such situation, the counsellor should change the direction of the challenge. Rather than continuing to place the demand for new ideas, the counsellor should change the approach by asking the client to close the natural and spontaneous flow of ideas. However, the counsellor should ask the client to come up with what Egan (1990) called 'wild ideas'. Wild ideas can be explained to the client as out-of-the-box thinking. The client is asked to come out of the beaten track and think of some unconventional ideas which are not usually tried in such situations. Many a time, unconventional ideas prove effective in real-life situations.

Turning Ideas into Feasible Actions

Brainstorming will result in a variety of ideas on possible action. The feasibility of these ideas needs to be examined. In many instances, the exhausted client may show little persistence in following up on the generated ideas and be ready to dump them as non-implementable either due to lack of confidence or due to lack of information. The counsellor's role assumes significance in the client's sustaining enthusiasm after the brainstorming. The counsellor should help the client translate the ideas into the feasibility of the actions. This is possible through the application of the following skills.

Use of Probes and Prompts

Probes and prompts stimulate the client to think deeper into the nitty gritty of an issue at hand. Probes can target specific issues related to the idea forcing the client to think in a particular direction and identify a variety of possible sources. These probes can ask leading questions with 'what, who, where, when'. The following example will throw more light on the skill.

Client: *I feel so overwhelmed with the pressure of work, demands of family members, and the lousy climate in the place to top it all that I wish I had wings to fly away from here to a distant place of fairies who would take care of me!*
Counsellor: *I guess you are hinting at having a holiday all by yourself.*
Client: *That is a far-fetched goal anyway!*

The counsellor at this point encouraged the client to think of some possibilities for making it happen and used brainstorming. After the client came up with some broad and vague ideas, she got stuck and said 'Leave it. It is not going to happen anyway'. Here is where the counsellor applied the skills of probes and prompts. Following is the conversation between them.

Client: *Leave it. It is not going to happen anyway.*
Counsellor: *Why do you think so?*
Client: *First is financial problem. The hotels are costly. Moreover, I cannot stay alone in a hotel. My husband won't like it.*
Counsellor: *Is there a place where you can go on a holiday and yet need not stay in a hotel?*
Client: *Ummm... Wait! Maybe. Can think of guest houses or hostels in the university campus!*
Counsellor: *Where can you possibly get such a campus?*
Client: *Uttarakhand! Nice place. Nice guesthouse.*
Counsellor: *Is there someone who would be willing to host you there?*
Client: *Yes. I know someone there who had invited me to visit the campus.*
Counsellor: *What places you plan to visit there?*
Client: *There are many places close to nature. That is exactly how I wish to spend a few days... all alone with the nature...*

There are instances where the client needs to be stimulated to identify external resources and use internal resources such as abilities, skills, and talents. Probes and prompts function as good propellers in this context. The details of a case reported in box 8.1 enable one to understand and apply the skill appropriately.

Box 8.1 Elderly Couple and Terminal Illness

Many elderly people in Indian metropolitan cities are living alone with their children working in other countries. Raghuveer and Romila are one such couple. Raghuveer is 80 years old and Romila is 72. Romila enjoys good health, while Raghuveer has a history of cardiovascular disease with two cardiac surgeries, two episodes of cardiac attacks, and one episode of stroke. They were managing their life quite well though their children were settled abroad. They were in for a severe shock when Raghuveer was diagnosed with cancer in its fourth stage. He was advised chemotherapy and radiation. Romila was at her wits end thinking about the need for managing hospital visits, patient care, attending to possible emergencies, and financial burden. She considered the option of moving to a place where everything can be taken care of.

The counsellor then asked her questions on who are the people who would be willing to support her if they moved to a place of her choice. The counsellor further asked what would be the financial requirement and how she plans to mobilise finances. Which are the hospitals she was considering. Following is the excerpt from further conversation between her and the counsellor

Counsellor: *Well, some elderly couples in such situations opt for retirement homes. How about that?*

Romila: *I don't know. Perhaps we can consider it seriously.*

Counsellor: *Are you aware or familiar with organisations in the city that involves in care giving for the elderly and the sick?*

Romila: *Ummm... yes, yes... The other day my neighbour was mentioning about a few of them her sister-in-law was considering. I did not give much attention then. Perhaps I should talk to her.*

Romila: *Hospital and medical treatment is one aspect while my confidence level in managing the patient well is another factor that weighs heavy on me.*

Counsellor: *What exactly you mean by this?*

Romila: *I am ....sort of blank! I only know that something needs to be done because I am not confident of managing the situation efficiently.*

In the case mentioned in Box 8.1, the counsellor is found to use the skill of prompt and fade (*Well, some elderly couples in such situations opt for retirement homes. How about that?*). Using prompts and fade is different from giving suggestions. Here the counsellor while informing about the choice of a few elderly, fades out by asking the client 'How about that?'. The second noticeable skill of the counsellor here is the use of a probe. The counsellor asked the client to think if she knows of any organisation in the city that cares for the elderly and the sick. This is like stirring the steam so that it surfaces. That is exactly what seems to have happened when the client suddenly recalled a vague conversation with her neighbour which was not of interest to her then. This recall helps in initiating action in the client who planned to revoke the same conversation with her neighbour. The counsellor can include probes and prompts that stimulate the client to explore and identify a variety of resources relevant to the context. For example, the client can be probed to explore the social network and identify people who would help in a situation, contemplate on places, organisations, institutes that offer what is being searched for. For example, this is a case of a woman who has to accompany her husband to a deaddiction centre for an in-house treatment, but unable to implement it because she has school-going children to be taken care of. In such instance, a query like 'who do you think will be willingly taking care of your children for a month when you have to accompany your husband admitted into a deaddiction centre?' is a probe that stimulates the client to go through a mental scan of the social contacts.

Assessment of Action Options

As mentioned, the client is very unlikely to seek counselling soon after encountering a complex problem. It is very natural for any human being to first give one's own trials before realising that these attempts are futile and the situation in the meantime is turning more complex and the emotions are turning more intense. It is at such a juncture that one is likely to seek professional help. The difference between the layperson's response to the problem and the professional approach lies in restraining the pattern of stimulus-response and activating the appraisal that mediates between the stimulus and the response. The common pattern of responding or reacting immediately to the stimulus may miss out on assessing a number of factors that may have the potential for neutralising the expected positive outcome of the behavioural response. Repeated occurrence of this results in feelings of hopelessness, dejection, anxiety, and depression in the client. Hence, in a professional set up the counsellor scrupulously avoids repetition of such experience for the client. Assessment of the opted action is what makes the professional approach distinct from the commonplace approach.

Once the client helped by brainstorming has identified a wide range of actions, the logical step is to run them through the scanner of feasibility of the action and willingness on the client's part. Every new behavioural option is likely to face certain inherent obstacles in the form of weak reinforcement or punishment, getting defeated in the politics of behaviour, judged less attractive in the assessment of behavioural economics or lose its priority in the competition of alternatives as discussed in the examples delineated at the beginning of this chapter. The client should be encouraged by the counsellor to have a first level of broad assessment and screen out those actions that are judged as having very low feasibility. Scanning the remaining options in terms of various factors named above constitutes a sound assessment. This helps the client in making an informed decision on the final choice of behaviour to be tried in the real-life situation. This calls for the preparation of a nominal balance sheet. The counsellor must help the client in developing such behavioural balance sheet. Probing, challenging, support and brainstorming skills can be used to elicit responses from the client to develop the balance sheet. The behavioural balance sheet may look something like what is depicted in table 8.3. This table is developed for an alcoholic male who wished to give up drinking behaviour.

The behavioural balance sheet mentioned above can be developed by the counsellor by using the skill of probing and eliciting answers intermittently in the course of counselling once the client completes the first level of screening of the possible actions elicited through brainstorming. The following example helps in understanding the skill clearly.

The client is a young mother subjected to humiliation and disrespect by her underqualified and unemployed husband. This resulted in the client progressively losing her self- esteem, indulging in self-doubt about her credibility and efficiency as a good wife and mother, culminating in panic attacks and suicidal ideation. During the counselling

Table 8.3 Behavioural Balance Sheet for Deaddiction from Alcoholism

Factors Associated with Behaviour	*Self*	*Family*	*Society*
Stakes with the present behaviour (Alcoholism)	1. Failing health 2. Disrespect from children 3. Societal scorn 4. Job insecurity	1. Persistent conflict 2. Poverty 3. Unhealthy environment 4. Impact on children's academics	1. Neglect of work in office 2. Nuisance in the neighbourhood
Efforts for behavioural change	1. Convincing the boss for leave 2. Stay in the de-addiction centre 3. Following a routine in the centre	1. Wife to accompany the patient 2. Leave from job for wife 3. Care-taker to be arranged for children	1. Finding a substitute for the work
Cost involved	1. Rs 50,000/- for the treatment	1. Rs 50,000/- to be arranged	Nil
Obstacles	1. Fear of possible withdrawal syndrome 2. Facing social stigma 3. Oscillation of trust in the outcome	1. Difficulties in leave sanction 2. Convincing a relative to take care of children during treatment period	1. Lack of sufficient staff 2. Procedural hurdles in hiring on ad hoc basis
Resources	1. Will Power 2. Self-confidence 3. Perseverance	1. Strong family bonding 2. Supportive friends 3. Understanding extended family	1. Accommodating boss
Gains with behaviour change	1. Restoration of physical and mental well-being 2. Regain respect from society 3. Resume participation in social events 4. Re-establish healthy relationship with family 5. Enhance self-esteem 6. Enjoy job security	1. Restore healthy family environment 2. Save money that drained out in alcohol and recover from poverty	1. Enhanced efficiency and output of the rehabilitated employee
Concerns following the behavioural change	1. Managing withdrawal syndrome 2. Possibility of relapse 3. Planning alternative activities to fill the time spent in drinking	1. Changing the attitude towards the rehabilitated head of the family 2. Renewing the relationship 3. Extending the support to prevent a relapse	1. Changing the attitude towards the rehabilitated employee/colleague 2. Extending the support to prevent a relapse

session it was decided that she has to attend to her painful panic attacks on priority. Brainstorming came up with certain broad possible actions such as taking leave and going to her parents where she would seek professional intervention; continuing to stay at her place where she would seek professional intervention; Going to her friend's place and seek professional intervention in that city. Following is the extract of a relevant portion of the interaction between the counsellor and the client.

Counsellor: *What do you think would be the advantages to you if you decide to go to your parents' place on leave?*
Client: *I feel reassured.*
Counsellor: *Ok. What else? You can list them all.*
Client: *I have my parents to take care of my two-year-old child. I can rest any time I want without any hesitation. But... But I have these spells of crying... That may disturb my parents. Would that be fair to cause them distress?*
Counsellor: *Well, we will classify that as a negative point for your parents. But now, let us identify the personal benefits to you.*
Client: *Ok.... One of the benefits would be that it is a metropolitan city where I can get professional help easily. But then, my parents would come to know about my psychological state... which I wish to avoid.*
Counsellor: *I get your point. That also we shall classify under the negative impact on your parents.*
Client: *One thing that bothers me is ... if I take such long leave and go to stay at my parents' place I will not be available at my office in case of any emergency for my team.*
Counsellor: *We will take that too into account. But it is not a personal problem to you, but the problem your office would face. We shall consider it under that. But apart from personal benefit, will your going to the parents' place do any good for them and to your office?*
Client: *Good to the office? (Laughs) Perhaps my team members will learn to be more independent.*
Counsellor: *Yes. I noted the point.*
Client: *My parents will be very happy to have their grandchild with them and enjoy playing with him.*

As the counsellor probes and elicits the responses from the client he/she makes note of them and after the session, the responses can be given a shape of the behavioural balance sheet. Alternatively, with clients who are found to be more cognitively focused, the counsellor may hand over the format of the balance sheet at the end of the session and give homework to the client to come with the details filled. The balance sheet can be discussed with the client to help in selecting the behaviour from the list of possibilities drawn from brainstorming. Working on the balance sheet enables the client to have an objective assessment of the options and make an informed choice of behaviour with which the situation should be responded to minimise stress. In case lack of clarity still prevails, the client can be encouraged to adopt what can be termed as trying 'behavioural sampling'. Behavioural sampling refers to trying out a few options to get a hang of it. Egan (1990), who calls it strategy sampling mentions an alcoholic who wishes to quit drinking trying out various options such as attending the meetings of Alcoholics Anonymous, visiting the hospital that provided treatment, attending a fitness programme before deciding on a particular approach to the problem. This method is used particularly when the client is unable to spell out the merits, obstacles, efforts, etc.

Sampling helps in getting a broad idea about the demands that the new behaviour places on the client and the family contributing to a realistic assessment.

Strategising the Behaviour

The concept of strategy is closely associated with war situations. It refers to the detailed and pragmatic action plan in an adverse condition of war. In a war situation, the planning of action has to be very meticulous, detailing every move while considering the unknown adverse situation arising due to many factors, including the action from the enemy. It is justified to have a strategic plan for the behaviour change in the client because the client has to execute the action in adverse conditions with some ambiguity regarding its impact on the others involved or the stress-inducing situation involving a host of factors. It may not be an exaggeration to describe that the client is at war with the world out there or, in some cases, with themselves.

Developing action strategies involves micro level planning. The counsellor may adopt the following steps in strategising the behaviour change.

Goal Recapitulation and Action Matching

Recapitulation of the major goal and the sub-goals already specified by the client in an attempt of the counsellor to invoke and sustain the client motivation is an essential first step in planning the strategy. This is because the action plan should corroborate with the set goal to successfully bring the desired outcome. Once the client exercises his option for a particular action plan, the counsellor should help him/her match the action plan with the already set goal. In the example cited above related to the panic attacks of the young mother, the following part refers to the counsellor's use of challenging skills in helping the client match the chosen action with the set goal.

Client: *I think, instead of my going to my parent's place, I can leave my child under their care for some time and take on my husband for the mental torture he is causing me.*
Counsellor: *That is one option you have if you feel that it meets your major goal.*
Client: *Oh! (Looking perplexed) But my main aim is to get rid of my panic attacks.*
Counsellor: *Yes.*
Client: *By leaving my child with my parents and confronting him for his unacceptable behaviour might increase my anxiety.*
Counsellor: *It might.*
Client: *So that cannot be the course of immediate action. I should go away with my child to a place where I get professional help.*
Counsellor: *Well, that brings us to an action point where you have to think of choosing a place where you have good access to professional help.*
Client: *My parents' place seems quite suitable.*
Counsellor: *Ok. If it is Hyderabad where your parents live, the next thing is for you to think of identifying the available professional help and choosing from the list.*

In this interaction, it is observed how the first choice of the client loses its context when matched with the major objective once the counsellor challenges the client gently. It is very pertinent that the client's choice of the action plan is unambiguous and specific.

For example, an action statement that matches the goal of weight reduction as 'I must start some physical exercise by making some time during the day' is a vague action. The specific alternative to that is 'I must join the Zumba dance classes run in the clubhouse during the mornings and evenings'.

Example:

Client: *I should allocate some time during the day for physical exercise.*

Counsellor: *'Some time' and 'some physical exercise' sounds a bit vague. Can you focus more and come up with something more specific?*

Client: *(Laughs) There are options like a one-hour morning walk daily, joining the Zumba class during the early morning slot, or doing skipping jumps in the garden in the evenings...*

The counsellor smoothly brought the client from an ambiguous to specific action statement, which can be matched with the major goal.

Strategising is possible by adopting any or a combination of the following steps.

Action Fractioning

A statement of a specific major action is certainly a good development in bringing a behavioural change. But strategising involves breaking the major action into small fragments. By doing so, the focus is taken to the details, which is a significant ingredient in developing strategy.

In the example of physical exercise, the counsellor may ferry the client through a behavioural balance sheet to have a relative assessment of the three options. When the client, after an assessment, chooses to join the early morning Zumba session, the counsellor should help strategise the action taking into consideration the obstacles identified in the balance sheet against the early morning Zumba dance option. For example, in case one of the inherent obstacles is waking up in the mornings, the actions should be fractioned into small strategies such as setting a loud alarm that goes off every morning, drinking a lot of water at night that fills the bladder, compelling one to get up, arranging someone close to make a phone call every day at an early hour, going to bed early so that the required sleep is completed, buying an expensive outfit for the Zumba session so that one feels guilty if it is not used. The list of action fractions is only suggestive. Each client can be innovative in one's own way. Action fractions can be discussed from another perspective. For example, joining early morning Zumba sessions in the clubhouse has several steps, such as Enquiring the clubhouse about the availability of slots during the early morning class, meeting the Zumba trainer and assessing the competence, finding out about the fee structure and the duration of the course, meeting those already enrolled in the class to assess the effectiveness of it in weight loss. Once the major action is fragmented in this manner, the client may be encouraged by the counsellor to tag a timeline for each fraction of action.

Example:

Client: *Joining the Zumba dance classes in the clubhouse looks like the best option in terms of its timings.*

Counsellor: *Are there any other considerations apart from the timings?*

Client: *Yes. I must like the instructor.*

Counsellor: *Well, sounds important. Any other?*

Client:	*Many. I should be able to afford it. I must like the company of those in the session. I should find it good for weight reduction. I am not going to join for fun and entertainment.*
Counsellor:	*Absolutely. Carry on. Is there anything more?*
Client:	*(Laughs) First of all, the early morning sessions should have a vacant seat for me.*
Counsellor:	*So, what should be done to get clarity on these aspects?*
Client:	*I should plan a visit to the clubhouse to enquire.*
Counsellor:	*When do you plan to do it?*
Client:	*Why not? This evening.*
Counsellor?	*What else do you need to do?*
Client:	*Meet the trainer and the participants. So, I must go during the session. Perhaps this weekend.*
Counsellor:	*Is there any other step?*
Client:	*I prefer to meet some participants privately outside the class. I can plan it after I come to know who are all there on my visit.*

In this example, the action plan of taking up some physical exercise for weight reduction first takes the shape of a specific action of joining the Zumba class in the clubhouse in the early morning slot, then divided into certain strategic steps such as preliminary inquiry in the clubhouse in the same evening, visiting the class while on a session during the weekend, and meeting the participants privately after looking for familiar faces there. Once the action fractioning is done, automatically it gets arranged in a hierarchical order, as seen in the example. Hierarchy follows either the order of priority or the essential chronology as per the demand of the case.

Fractioning the action is a good strategising measure for many reasons. Primarily, it is relatively easy to analyse and estimate the feasibility, obstacles, investment of effort, and time involved in minor actions. The demand for time and effort looks smaller in fractions of action than in the major action. This helps in sustaining the motivation of the client. Tagging each fraction of action to a timeline places some pressure for action on the part of the client leading to the conservation of energy at every step. More important than any, every fraction of accomplished action functions as a reinforcement for encouraging the next step of action. This enhances the self-efficacy of the client now on the path of action or behavioural change.

Planning Contingencies

Drawing a contingency plan is an integral part of strategising. Every war strategy will have an alternative plan to be operated just in case the original plan fails or has to be changed in the last-minute owing to some unforeseen circumstances. In order to minimise any possible failure related depression or demotivation, it is desirable to equip the client with contingency plan. Just as the major action, the contingency plan is also chosen by the client from among the brainstormed action plans. The client's owning up the chosen action plan is important, be it the first option or the contingency, because self-owned actions have self-accountability. Actions chosen by the clients have higher probability of execution with commitment resulting in successful outcomes. Contingency plans constituting back-up are to ensure the execution of action in the field by the client. It is a precaution against the possible withdrawal of the client from action should the original plan fails to take off or has to be suspended mid-way. Egan (1990) emphasises a contingency plan, particularly in a situation where the client pursues a high-risk action chasing a critical goal. The case study is described in Box 8.2.

Having a contingency plan is like having some savings in the bank account, which will come in handy in case of exigency. The following interaction between the counsellor and the client at the crossroad of choosing a career helps appreciate the need for a contingency plan and also understand the skills used by the counsellor in enabling the client to develop a contingency plan. The following excerpt gives an insight into the significance of contingency plan.

Counsellor:	*Well, your resolve to become a doctor is strong. You said you could not crack the entrance test in the past two years. You are now gearing yourself for the third attempt, right?*
Client:	*Yes. That is what is making me nervous. While I feel strongly that I should get it this time, sometimes, I feel very uncertain about my chances. I cannot take a failure yet again.*
Counsellor:	*The probability of failure to get through seems to be bothering you.*
Client:	*Yes. The very thought of not clearing the entrance this year is so scary that it disturbs my focus on my studies. A lot of time gets wasted because of such disturbing thoughts.*
Counsellor:	*While you put in all your best efforts and hope that you would get a seat in a medical college this year, let us, for a minute, think that it does not happen that way this time too, then what do you think you would do?*
Client:	*My only dream is to go in the medical field. I have no other choice... I... I... cannot take it...*
Counsellor:	*You said 'Medical field', right?*
Client:	*Yes.*
Counsellor:	*Medical field is very vast. The profession of a doctor is one of them. Can you name some roles in the medical profession other than the doctor?*
Client:	*Nurse?*
Counsellor:	*That's right. Any other?*
Client:	*Physiotherapist?*
Counsellor:	*That's fine. Go on; there are many others. Name them.*
Client:	*Nutritionist, Dentist, Dietician, Psychologist, Lab technician, Pharmacist, Biochemist, hospital manager....administrator.... I don't know what they are called.*
Counsellor:	*Carry on; you can go beyond the walls of the hospital.*
Client:	*Community health workers, ... Can I name those who do research in the field of health?*
Counsellor:	*Sure, carry on.*
Client:	*Health Psychologists, public health researchers, ... therapists... speech therapists. (Takes a big sigh)*
Counsellor:	*Now, do you think your opportunities are closed just in case you cannot clear the examination to join MBBS course?*
Client:	*I... I understand. But then I must think in parallel lines.*
Counsellor:	*Can you please elaborate?*
Client:	*I must apply also for a seat in an undergraduate college or other colleges like the college of pharmacy.*

Counsellor: *How does that feel?*
Client: *Not as good as a medical college, but not bad either.*
Counsellor: *Out of so many other health-related professions, you should first screen and scan to select the most appropriate ones. Shall we take off from there?*

Box 8.2 Terminally Ill Patient Needs Continuous Vigil: Contingency Plan

The doctors have done their best for Rajeev, who successfully fought cancer for nearly seven years. He enjoyed a good quality of life and was labelled as a 'cancer survivor'. He suddenly developed secondaries during the COVID pandemic when it missed timely detection due to difficulty in accessing routine medical care. He underwent chemotherapy, radiation, minor surgery, and immune therapy. The progression was controlled with the treatment. However, after the oncology department of the hospital exhausted all available treatment, the disease started spreading fast, and Rajeev was put into palliative care. It was a blow to the family even to think of the inevitable. Rajeev, discharged from the hospital, was put under home care by his family with the assistance of a full-time caregiver. At one point, the doctors pronounced that nothing could be predicted about his life anymore. The family decided on one goal that Rajeev should not go without any family members by his side. They decided on a day and night vigil and ensured that at least one family member was by the bedside at any moment. The night shifts were planned. The son and the wife took turns to keep awake, sitting by his side. Weeks passed by with Rajeev intermittently getting better and slipping back to a worse condition. The two members of the family were getting exhausted with the night shifts, emotional draining, and the other household chores. It was realised that their energy levels were thinning down when they found themselves engaging in arguments with each other, having spells of breakdown, and the quality of caregiving coming down. In discussion with the psychologist, they were helped to identify sources for a backup in caregiving as intermittent relief to them. They identified two sets of contingent support from extended family. The first set was the relatives who were local residents. They decided on requesting local relatives to support them in the shifts while alerting the close relatives in a close-by city to stand by in case of any need. This ensured their goal that Rajeev would not go unattended because it was a strong value that there should be prayers from the family members when one takes the ultimate journey, which was followed in the case of others in the family.

With the help of the counsellor the client chose the alternative of applying for a seat in BSc course with Psychology and Biology as essential subjects, which will open many opportunities at the postgraduate level and for Ph.D. The contingency plan, in fact, helped the client handle his anxiety attacks during the preparation for the medical entrance examinations and could finally obtain a seat in a medical college. Thus, a contingency plan is not only a good strategy to ensure action but the backup itself is an intervention to dissipate the anxiety arising out of failure apprehension. Further, the contingency plan helps to create a readiness in the client to face failure, which will otherwise induce disappointment and frustration leading to inaction. A contingency plan keeps the action alive in the client, insulating one from the adverse consequences of failure of plan A. The counsellor can apply brainstorming and challenging skills to elicit possible alternative plans from the client. The client may not be ready with the alternatives in mind. It calls for some priming, prompting, and probing from the counsellor.

Change in Overt Behaviour

Change in overt behaviour that leads to effective coping and minimising the stress is the final goal of the counselling. The counsellor adopts one or the combination of some skills discussed below.

Force Field Analysis

Strategising an action is one thing, and initiating the action is yet another thing. Initiating a new behaviour is an essential change. However, resistance to change is inherent in every individual despite concurring with the essentiality of the new behaviour. The politics of behaviour has the potential to defer, stall or suspend the chosen behaviour midway. It is desirable that the counsellor foresees it and takes preventive steps. One approach is stimulating the cognition of the client and helping him/her in check-mating such a scenario where the action has to wade through a tough set of obstacles. This is done by applying what is known as force field analysis. The premise on which this technique is applied is that action initiation is not an isolated decision and function of the individual in question. The physical, social and psychological factors have an influence on the successful execution or otherwise of the action. These physical and psychosocial forces may operate independently as well as in combination. There may be a number of factors that contribute towards the successful execution of action. Many of these forces may also interfere with the execution of the action by throwing a spanner into the wheel of action, which either causes temporary interruption or total stalling of the action. These forces include external elements such as the physical environment, social norms, significant others objecting to it or ridiculing the action thus demotivating the client. It could also be the individual's tendency of procrastination, losing motivation in between the action, lack of energy and so on. Force field analysis is a technique introduced by Lewin (1951) to manage change. It involves identifying all the forces that contribute positively as well as negatively to the change, and analysing their relative strength, and thereafter applying strategies to add to the strength of supporting factors and weaken the factors opposing the change. The counsellor should operate the force field analysis using the following guiding steps:

- Help the client identify and define the new behaviour to be adopted
- Strategise the actions and contingencies
- Brainstorm with the client to identify and list all the driving forces that would support the change in behaviour
- Brainstorm with the client to identify and list all forces that are likely to restrain him/her from initiating/sustaining the decided action
- Encourage the client to quantify the strength of each driving force as well as a restraining force by giving a rating ranging from 1 to 5. At the end, add up the ratings of the driving and restraining forces separately to know their relative total strength
- Encourage the client to estimate his/her power of influence on each of the identified force in terms of enhancing its strength (for driving forces) and weakening its influence (Restraining Forces) on the action chosen as new behaviour

- Encourage the client to come up with strategies for weakening the restraining forces and adding strength to the driving forces

The counsellor can help the client prepare a visual chart of the force field analysis for enhancing the motivation level to initiate action. Figure 8.1 portrays the visual illustration of the force field analysis.

Figure 8.1 portrays the force field analysis for a young boy who felt that his girlfriend has been using money from his account liberally that left him in a financial crunch and accountable to his parents. He chose the strategy of taking back his debit card from her. This action, while guaranteed to prevent her from operating his account, comes with a number of factors that may force him either to retrieve his card or to return it after a short while. The counsellor brainstormed with him to identify his driving forces. She also helped him assess the strength of each of the forces. She then went ahead brainstorming with him to identify the restraining forces and rate their power in preventing his action and estimate his power or influence in countering the restraining forces. Following is the last part of the interaction between the counsellor and the client. This is an example of the counsellor boosting the self-efficacy of the client by using the skill of challenging with support.

Counsellor: *You plan to take back your debit card from your friend. What are the possible factors that may stand in the way?*
Client: *My soft corner for her. I cannot be harsh on her. Taking it back would be harsh.*
Counsellor: *Ok. What else?*
Client: *I … I don't want to lose my friendship with her.*
Counsellor: *You feel that this step from you has the threat of losing her forever?*
Client: *Maybe. What if she bad-mouths me? My friends will dissuade me from doing it… and what if she approaches me for money for some emergency expenses?*
Counsellor: *Like?*
Client: *Like… Some health problem…*

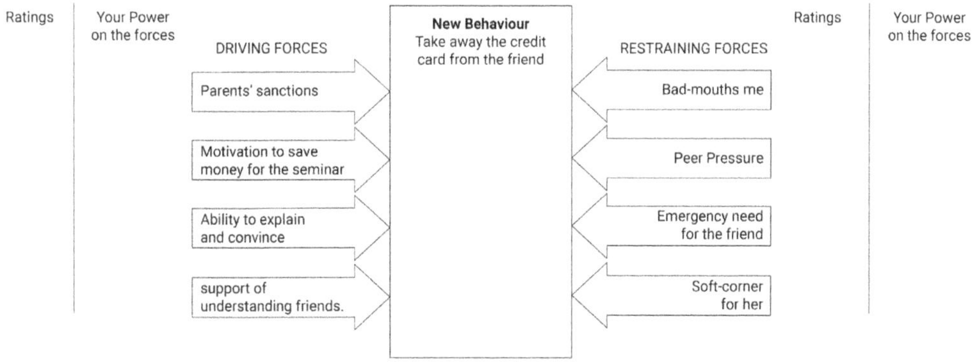

Figure 8.1 Force Field Analysis

Counsellor: *Well, all these are possibilities. Each one has a strength of its influence on your action of not allowing her to operate your account.*

Counsellor: *Let us imagine that they do happen, then would you be just seeing them happen or would you try to stop, or control it by minimising the damage. Now, I have made a list of all the possible negative forces you named. We assume that you have some influence in preventing it. If not, at least minimising the impact of such forces in stopping you from action. Can you assess your power in countering the debilitating effect by giving a rating for each of it on a 5-point scale where 5 is the highest influence and 1 is the least influence? (Hands him over the list of restraining forces summarised from the client's responses)*

Client: *(After spending time on working on it returns the paper to the counsellor)*

Counsellor: *(After scrutinising the ratings) Well, I find that you have given a rating of 5 to your fear of losing her while your influence on the fear is rated as 2 on a 5-point scale. Can you explain this, please?*

Client: *That fear is very intense in me. I don't want to lose her.*

Counsellor: *But that is YOUR fear, right? By giving it a rating of 2 you are saying that YOU have very little influence on YOUR fear.*

Client: *That fear is continuously increasing. That's why.....*

Counsellor: *What can you do to prevent that fear intensifying?*

Client: *What can I do?... Don't know...*

Counsellor: *Ok, let us understand first why do you have that fear.*

Client: *She will feel offended if I ask her to return my debit card. She may even suspect that I do it to help my other friend who is also a girl....*

Counsellor: *What do you think you need to do to prevent such misunderstanding in her?*

Client: *First talk to her about my need for saving for the trip.*

Counsellor: *Ok. What do you think will happen then?*

Client: *She may understand and cooperate for the time being. But that would only be for some time. I have six months to go before taking the trip. She may borrow money from others and ask me to repay later. I will have pressure from peer group who are actually not very happy that my paper is accepted while theirs got rejected.*

Counsellor: *Are they your close friends?*

Client: *No. Close friends do not feel jealous.*

Counsellor: *So?*

Client: *I need not bother. Can just ignore them.*

Counsellor: *Let us now get back to your fear of losing her over which you felt you have very little influence. Do you think her emotional attachment to you is not as strong as yours for her?*

Client: *No no no. She is as much attached to me.*

Counsellor: *Do you think she would break with you for your act of taking back the debit card for your need?*

Client: *May not... break ... she needs me not just for money but... I give her good support otherwise, too.*

Counsellor: *How much do you think your 'support otherwise' is valued by her?*

Client: *Very much. We have been bonding for nearly eight years. It is not easy to break...*

Counsellor: *Think of it rationally. After which, you can tell me if you wish to revise your rating of 2 for your influence on the fear of losing her.*
Client: *I wish to change it. I have all the influence to handle my fear. It is 5.*

The counsellor here used the skills of probing and challenging in getting the client to revisit his ratings. This is the way in which the counsellor helps the client to weaken the restraining forces that pose a threat to implementing action in the field. Weakening the restraining forces call for certain action points which the client would plan and execute before initiating action or while initiating action as the situation demands. The same method is followed in enhancing the facilitating forces. The counsellor should brainstorm with the client to identify all possible forces that have the potential to drive the client to the behaviour change. For example, a school student who has set a goal to improve the grades should be asked to explore all possibilities that contribute to a focus in preparing for the examinations. The counsellor may help him to identify behaviours that contribute to sustaining the focus ranging from drawing a definite timetable to follow study hours to keeping association with studious classmates, arranging with the older sibling to follow up on the daily progress, and planning minor and major incentives proportionate to the goal achievements on a daily or weekly basis. Force field analysis thus equips the client by enhancing the strength of the proposed changed behaviour by carefully protecting it from debilitating influence.

Behavioural correction is what is intended in the interventions for behaviour that lacks in efficiency. The interventions suggested above are when the client is found to respond with an incorrect behaviour either in one's haste to respond to the situation or because of a lack of understanding of the situation. Hence the interventions are aimed at identifying and substituting the old behaviour with the new with due precautions of understanding the potentials of the proposed new behaviour in an attempt to optimise the outcome of the behaviour. Now, let us try to know the approaches and skills used by the counsellor when the client's behaviour manifests deficiency.

Interventions for Deficiencies in Behaviour

Deficiency in behaviour connotes inappropriate responses or behaviour due to a lack of skills. There is no pathology involved in such cases. This is different from 'behavioural deficit' that indicates the absence of age-specific behaviour due to physical and mental impairment.

Very often, what is labelled as the client's 'faulty behaviour' are the consequences of a lack of knowledge and skill about the correct behaviour. The inappropriate action by the client in handling a stressful situation fails to bring the desirable outcome pushing the client to experience anxiety, depression, and adverse effects on health and well-being. The consequent anxiety and depression in such cases cannot be labelled as pathological. They are rather the repercussions of the deficiency in their behaviour. These behaviours can be modified, improved, or changed with behavioural intervention. Assertiveness is a behaviour in which many people may be deficient. Not being able to be assertive has the risk of being caught in a number of situations that one may not desire. This induces a lot of stress. For example, being unassertive with a sexual partner may force the person to have unsafe sex and contract HIV/AIDS. Mohapi and Pitsoane (2017), in their study on university students, found that training in assertiveness helps in practicing the behaviour that has the potential to prevent them from being vulnerable to HIV/AIDS. Many people end up doing a sloppy job not because they want to be that way but because they fail to manage their time judiciously. Training in time management skills will equip them to execute the job more carefully. It is very common to see people getting nervous, anxious, and slipping into depression because of their inappropriate behaviour or apprehension of it. When such clients approach the counsellor, the primary responsibility of the counsellor is to assess the situation and identify and ascertain the deficiency in the behaviour. The best way to intervene in such cases is to provide them an opportunity to get trained in the behaviour where they are found deficient.

The examples of behavioural training for the client are plenty. An obese client needing disciplined physical exercise and diet control can be referred to a professional slimming centre. A subdued and inhibited employee in a corporate sector depressed for not getting the due promotions can be referred to a communication skill training that includes self-enhancement. The couple seeking marital counselling found to be harbouring dissatisfaction against each other can be suggested interpersonal communication training for the married couple. The couple getting into frequent financial mess can be oriented to financial management. Parents being abusive to their children can be trained in anger management. Family members unable to manage the critically ill patient can be trained in basic care giving skills. There are plenty of opportunities for skill training in a variety of fields. The counsellor should keep himself/herself abreast of the availability of such facilities so that the clients can have a ready referral. The counsellor has to decide on training for deficiency in behaviour based on the following guidelines.

- Explore the strength of the existing undesirable behaviour
- Assess the client's feelings associated with the existing behaviour
- Assess the client's internal resources to change the behaviour
- In case the assessment outcome indicates negative feelings, weak internal resources, and low strength of the existing behaviour, the counsellor should contemplate behavioural change through training
- Where necessary, put the client through short orientation as part of counselling session
- Refer the client to appropriate professional or organisations with established professional competence
- While referring the client, provide options from which he/she should choose
- Team up with the skill trainers to exchange feedback on the client to make the intervention comprehensive
- Link the behavioural training to SMART goals for an objective outcome assessment
- Take feedback from the client on the skill training
- Compare the pre and post training assessment to evaluate the impact of training and share with the client

Training in skills should be applied only in cases where the deficiency is ascertained after due assessment of the client. The counsellor should exercise due caution in preventing any labelling of the client by anyone. The following example gives further insight into the process followed by the counsellor in suggesting skill training to the client.

Counsellor: *You said you are unable to restrain yourself when your son back answers you, and you end up being physical with him.*

Client: *It is not that I want to hit him. I know that he is in his adolescence, and beating him at this age will have a bad impact. Every time I do it, I end* *up haunted by guilt until I make it up to him, sometimes even apologise to him. Now he knows that I would say sorry later, and he thinks his behaviour is correct and I am wrong.*

Counsellor: *Oh! You mean to say that your apology is in fact rewarding his wrong behaviour?*

Client: *Yes. Now I see that he provokes me to get hit by me and then demands whatever he wants. I know it is all going in the wrong way. I try my best not to react with anger... but each time, the situation is so bad that I am unable to help...*

Counsellor: *You said you are unable to stop getting angry. Can you explain?*

Client: *Explain? How? After every episode, I make a promise to myself that next time I should not react with anger... but while facing reality, I do get angry....Perhaps my nature?*

Counsellor: *Do you do anything during the episode to stop getting angry?*

Client: *During the episodes? Things happen so fast that there is no time to do anything except get angry. Actually, I am not getting your question.*

Counsellor: *Well, there are some techniques people use to prevent an angry reaction in themselves. Are you aware of or do you use any such?*

Client: *I warn him not to back the answer. Repeat my warning, and when he persists, I burst out in anger. Is that what you mean by 'technique'?*

Counsellor: *Not really. Would you like to learn those techniques? It is called anger management. One can be trained in it.*

In the above example, we see the broad assessment of the client's knowledge of the skill of anger management by the counsellor. Only after ascertaining that the client has no clue that there can be techniques to manage anger did the counsellor put forward her suggestion for anger management training.

The counsellor talks about the study skills to a student in the following example.

Counsellor: *You are frustrated because however much you study you cannot get good marks. Could this be because your hard work is not showing in your performance in the examinations?*

Client: *I am unable to move up from a B grade. I try to recollect everything I read and write in the exam. I keep leaving gaps in every answer and fill it up as and when I remember that point while attempting the other questions. In this process of shifting from one question to the other I get confused.*

Counsellor: *How do you plan your study time?*

Client: *(Smiles) Planning... no. I go to my study table and pick up the subject that comes to my mind. Read for an hour or so then pick up another book and read that for an hour... like that...*

Counsellor: *Study time can be planned systematically. There are some tips, if followed, one would remember better whatever is studied.*

Client: *Can you give me those tips?*

Counsellor: *Sure.*

In the above example, the client is already sufficiently motivated to initiate action that takes him to his goal. He knew that there is some deficiency in the action that he has adopted. Hence, he showed an interest to adopt the new techniques if the counsellor is ready to share. Thus, the counsellor by assessing the motivation level of the client can either take advantage of it or build motivation in the client.

There is a possibility of misinterpreting the deficiency in behaviour as pathology. Sometimes the deficiency is perceived as a disability or a trait that cannot be filled. Here is where the counsellor needs to exercise caution in assessing if the deficiency has its base in ignorance about the skill or inability to use the skill. Further plan for training or orientation should follow this preliminary assessment by the counsellor.

Interventions for Pathological Behaviour

When pathological behaviours get strengthened and establish as patterns it may go beyond the individual's ability to replace them. They turn for professional intervention. The counselling approach in bringing a change in the behaviour in such cases are different from the cases where an inefficiency or deficiency in the behaviour is noticed.

Pathological behaviours may strengthen in the individual not so much due to genetic predisposition but majorly due to faulty associations or reinforcement of a wrong behaviour. For example, an individual manifesting panic behaviour every time on board a plane may have the antecedence of watching a ghastly plane crash on the television news. In this case, the individual might not have experienced a plane crash but still responds with anxiety during the plane journey because of the classical conditioning and association of the shock and anxiety one experienced while watching the visuals of a plane crash. A middle-aged daily wage labourer involved in violence against his wife every evening after having drinks when constantly protected by his mother saying that it is male-appropriate behaviour will indulge in the pathological behaviour of alcoholism and domestic violence. This behaviour in him is strengthened to set into a pattern because of the positive reinforcement that followed the behaviour. However, the same behaviour can be adopted by his son who has been watching the father's behaviour and grandmother's protection every day. This happens because the child goes through a social learning of the pathological behaviour as per Bandura's social cognitive theory (Bandura, 1977, 1982).

Some clients may manifest behaviour that cannot be classified as normal. For example, symptoms of obsession, phobia, borderline personality disorder, alcoholism, drug addiction, sexual perversions, depression, anxiety, or compulsive lying and so on. In such cases the counsellor has to go beyond counselling. The first step on the part of the counsellor is to assess the severity of the problem. In cases where the cognitive functioning of the client is found to have been blurred or impacted otherwise because of the intense emotional turmoil, the immediate step should preferably be an assessment by the psychiatrist who would decide if the condition warrants medication. In such conditions, psychotherapy and counselling can either follow psychiatric intervention or be administered simultaneously as decided jointly by the psychiatrist and the counsellor.

When the client presents a problem suggesting a certain degree of pathology in the behaviour, the counsellor has a choice to take behavioural counselling. Behavioural counselling was introduced by Krumboltz (1965). According to him, all counselling is ultimately behavioural because the goal of counselling is to bring a change in the behaviour of the client in real life context. Thus, the behavioural perspective is to view counselling not as a philosophy of life but as a set of principles that the counsellor applies to suit the specific situational demands. Following are the basic principles of this approach:

- Emphasise the importance of the individual
- Recognise the role of the environment

- Identify the significance of the interaction between the individual and the environment
- Focus on the present problem rather than getting into the cause of the problem rooted in the past
- Identify the factors in the environment that are contributing to the present behaviour
- Identify the factors in the environment that can be used as a reward for the changed behaviour
- The goal is to target the specific dysfunctional behaviour
- Provision has to be made to document the changes in the behaviour in a systematic way

The major premise on which the behavioural counselling is based is that the problem behaviour of the client is a maladaptive learning pattern. Hence, the intervention can be planned in two parts: unlearning the dysfunctional behaviour and learning new skills. This is possible by adopting the following steps:

- Weakening the reinforcement of the existing dysfunctional behaviour
- Introducing or enhancing the reinforcement for the target behaviour
- Suggesting/executing the environmental changes that would weaken the dysfunctional behaviour and optimise the target behaviour
- Exposing the client to models with the target behaviour
- Training in skills required for target behaviour

Though the approach of behavioural counselling is described in simple terms, it may not be as simple and smooth in its application. Client's resistance to change remains the common factor, whether it is behavioural pathology or deficiency. Hence the counsellor should make adequate provisions to isolate and minimise client resistance. The approach lays significance on the environment and its interaction with the individual. It should be expected that the client's environment is not systematically organised so that the reinforcers of the dysfunctional and the targeted behaviour are clearly visible. There may be a number of distracting variables among the reinforcements and the target behaviour. So, the counsellor should make an effort to modify the distracting variables. In case of any need, the counsellor should also have a contingency plan to make changes in the intervention plan (Gottman & Leiblum, 1974; Spiegler & Guevremont, 2003).

Behavioural counselling is a specialised approach. Here the interventions are individually tailored to suit a specific problem of a specific person taking into consideration the unique characteristics of the individual and his/her environment. The points to be considered in the context are very well described by Paul (1967, p. 111). He stated it in simple terms: 'What treatment, by whom, is the most effective for this individual with that specific problem and under which set of circumstances?'. The roles of the counsellor and the client are well defined. The counsellor plays a major role in identifying the intervention for the client. The client's participation in the process is of great significance. The client unlearns the old behaviour/learns the new behaviour, practices the new behaviour out of the counselling sessions until the new skill is learnt thoroughly. The counsellor makes continuous assessments to document the progress of the client and shares it with the client to sustain the motivation. The counsellor encourages the client to apply the newly learned behaviour in real-life situations. This is an index of final goal achievement of the behavioural interventions. The counsellor may even help in applying the behavioural change directly in a real-life situation by reorganising the reinforcement in the environment in such a way that the undesirable behaviour is weakened or the desirable behaviour gains strength.

What the counsellor applies is largely the principles of learning based on classical conditioning, operant conditioning and social cognitive approach. We will examine some of the following principles used by the counsellor in bringing behavioural change in the client.

- Reinforcing the positive behaviour
- Removing the reinforcer for the existing behaviour
- Punishing undesirable behaviour
- Using social modelling
- Use of desensitisation

Reinforcing Positive Behaviour

The objective of the intervention is to help the client acquire the behaviour which he/she is unable to respond with for some reason. The steps to follow broadly are:

1. Clearly define the target behaviour that needs to be learned by the client
2. Identify through the client or his/her close aids the rewards that function as an incentive
3. Arrange the environment in a way that the reinforcement is presented to the client soon after the right behaviour is manifested every time
4. Gradually wean the client from the reward so as to ensure making the behaviour natural independent of the reward

The case presented in Box 8.3 helps in familiarising one with this technique.

This process of reinforcing the positive behaviour is called Shaping. Not every positive reinforcement follows the method of shaping. The reinforcement can also be placed contingent to the new behaviour. For example, a child with juvenile diabetes who fusses a lot for taking the insulin can be rewarded with a permission to play a video game every time he takes the shot voluntarily. The contingent reward of the video games can be gradually reduced and withdrawn at a point.

Removing the Reinforcer of the Existing Behaviour

When the client's existing behaviour is problematic which he/she is unable to cease, it is certain that this problematic behaviour is receiving some positive reinforcement from the existing environmental setup. The main responsibility of counsellor in such cases is to scan the current environmental events and identify the factors that are contributing to maintaining the faulty behaviour of the client. Once this is done, the second step for the counsellor is to introduce changes in the environment by removing the events from the environment which have been rewarding the existing behaviour. This is called functional assessment or behavioural analysis (Wolpe, 1990). The case described in Box 8.4 explains the principle well.

It should be observed that the boy's undesirable behaviour was sustained because of the reinforcement of the parent's attention and giving in to his tantrums. Once that is removed, the behaviour is expected to weaken. But this did not happen. The parents' report indicated an increase in the undesirable behaviour soon after the removal of the

Box 8.3 Shaping Maternal Behaviour

This is the case of a woman who lost her two children within few months of their birth. A few of her relatives commented in her earshot that the children did not survive because the mother's contact is a bad omen for them. However, her immediate family was very supportive of her. She conceived for the third time and gave birth to a healthy female child. However, she was not ready to hold the baby or feed her. She was overpowered by some fear and would start shivering if the baby was brought near her and ended up crying a lot. The baby was unable to get nutrition because the formula milk did not suit the baby. There was a risk of the baby being deprived of nutrition. The counsellor in the first two sessions helped her ventilate her emotions, addressed her irrational fears, and helped cognitive restructuring. Yet, the mother found it difficult to come in physical proximity with the child. The counsellor and the mother agreed that she would take a progressive approach in acquiring the behaviour of nurturing the child. She would first see the baby to her satisfaction sitting in her bed. In the second step, she would take a few steps to the cradle and see the baby from a close distance. In the third step, she would go near the baby and touch her. In the fourth phase, she would hold her in her hands lifting her slightly from the base of the cradle. In the next step, the nurse would place the baby in her lap. In the final step, she would feed the baby. Every time she achieved the small part of the target behaviour, the family members have a small celebration by distributing sweets, playing music and congratulating her for her motherhood. The mother could very soon start feeding her baby which is a natural maternal behaviour.

Box 8.4 Stopping Tantrums

The parents of a child with Attention Deficit Hyperactivity Disorder (ADHD) from a rural area approached the counsellor with the problem of the child's throwing severe tantrums every time the local ice cream vendor comes to the colony with a loud bell indicating his entry. The child is advised against ice cream because of his weak respiratory condition. The parents complained that the child threw himself down on the floor outside the gate and cried until he was allowed to have the ice cream by the parents who feel embarrassed with the comments of the neighbours and commuters on the street. The counsellor explained to the parents that their giving in to his tantrums is the main cause of his persisting tantrums. They argued how difficult it is to manage the situation. The counsellor and the parents agreed that in the next seven days, the parents would stay strong and determined not to give in and stick to their position whatever be the behaviour of the child and report back after seven days. The parents reported back saying that it was a very difficult situation for the first three days when the child would never stop crying, hit the parents, pushed them out, spat all around and banged the doors and rolled on the floor until he got tired and slipped into sleep, crying. The fourth day he did cry but did not show so much aggression. The tantrums reduced in intensity and on the sixth day he did not cry, though he was looking at the parents with hope that they would be 'kind'. The parents were asked to continue their stand for the next one week too. By the end of the second week, the boy stopped his tantrums.

reinforcement. This is expected because the child intensified the behaviour with a hope that it would help him get the reward. Only when he found the reinforcement missing consistently, the undesirable behaviour started weakening.

Punishing Undesirable Behaviour

Punishment strategies are expected to reduce the frequency of the undesirable behaviour. However, counsellors use this method very judiciously and rarely because research findings have proved that though punishment reduces the behaviour immediately, it may reappear more vigorously at a later point. Gershoff (2002), in his review of studies related to corporal punishment, discovered that though it was successful in bringing compliance in children, it had a long-term impact when they grew into adults. It was found that these children indulged in physical assault on their children and spouse. The method adopted should very carefully isolate the behaviour for punishment without involving the self-esteem of the person. Corporal punishment causes a dent to the self-esteem of the child. The long-term impact could be because of the scars it creates. A competent counsellor can successfully isolate the behaviour to receive the punishment. The example of a doctor couple introducing punishment to their daughter's truant behaviour throws light on the skill of isolating the behaviour. This girl in her sixth standard was found to bunk school very often on the pretext of stomach ache. The parents got her tested medically and found no reason for her complaint. Her appetite and digestion were good. All the medical investigations gave normal results. But no amount of persuasion from parents resulted in the girl's confiding that she was faking. The parents finally adopted a method for the next two occasions when she refused to go to school due to 'stomach ache'. They gave her a 'medicine' for her problem, which was actually a purgative. She started having loose motions. She was not allowed to have her regular lunch where the parents made sure that the choicest of her favourite dishes were made. She could not go for playing with friends. Two such repeated events stopped her from faking stomach ache.

Though the parents were successful in this case it is not advisable to use this technique without the involvement of a competent counsellor due to its potential long term implications.

Using Social Modelling

We have understood the use of modelling in the context of motivating the client. Use of modelling in this context is to help the client learn the behavioural skills from the successful models who fit the context. Very often a faulty behaviour is adopted by the client which does not fetch the desired results. But the client who adopts a dysfunctional behaviour tends to maintain the status quo because of unawareness of an acceptable and productive alternative behaviour. In such instances, exposing the client to a successful model undergoing a similar experience helps in emulating the behaviour. The following example explains the context and the approach.

Muscular dystrophy is a progressive disease of weakening of muscles in the body leading to physical disability in male children. The progressive disease impacts all the muscles including the muscles of the vital organs at some point causing death in the person. It is a genetic disorder where women are the carriers of the genes. A mother of a child with muscular dystrophy was devastated by the diagnosis of her son. In earlier stages when the disability was manageable, she was able to manage the situation. But as the boy started to grow into his adolescence, and the disease progressed fast incapacitating the patient to make any movements, he was totally dependent on the parents for every locomotion. Due to lack of exercise, the boy put on a lot of weight. The father of the boy had a touring job because of which the mother had to be constantly engaged with the boy. The woman had to drop all her career ambitions, hobbies, socialisation, and even leisure activities. She went into severe depression. She thought she was doomed. She felt suffocated. There were instances when she would just disappear from home for about a week without informing anyone. This was repeating. The family, and particularly the boy with muscular dystrophy was feeling increasingly apprehensive and insecure about this behaviour of the mother. But the mother said that she does it when things are too overwhelming. She said she felt a sense of aggression and a need to 'punish' everyone for the distressing condition she was trapped in. This mother was introduced to a woman senior to her in age and managing her twin sons, both affected by the disorder. The senior woman requested her to spend a weekend with her in her house. This was an opportunity for the woman to observe the way the senior woman behaved with her sons and the way she managed her time, resources, and social contacts. She found that the senior woman equipped her house with certain mechanical and technical support such as a remote bed elevator, a motorised wheelchair, and a pulley fixed to the ceiling to pick up the grown-up sons and place them wherever they want, the way she engaged her neighbours who visited their place in turns to support her in her hobbies like music and painting, her online classes of mathematics where she taught children from other countries, etc. This helped her gain insight as well as contribute to the self-efficacy that she could manage her own son much more effectively when the senior woman was doing it with her two sons.

The outcome of behavioural change will be more rewarding if the conditions of the model are closer to that of the client.

Use of Desensitisation

Systematic desensitisation is a technique that is built on the principles of classical conditioning. Wolpe popularised this technique which though time-consuming has been found to be very effective. In this technique, the anxiety-provoking behaviour is linked to another behaviour which is either neutral or positive. The anxiety-provoking condition is exposed alongside the positive behaviour. The neutral/positive behaviour competes with the anxiety. Repeated exposure to the simultaneous presentation of anxiety-provoking condition and the neutral/positive behaviour gradually makes the anxiety lose its relevance. This is the process of desensitisation. The clients are desensitised in a systematic way where the anxiety-inducing situation is ordered from the least to the highest anxiety-provoking condition. For example, for a client with having phobia for the ocean, who has to travel on sea accompanying her husband, the systematic exposure to the ocean will be the picture of the ocean, the video clipping of it, then a visit to the seashore, followed by wetting the feet, having a bath in the sea, taking a short trip on the boat, each of this accompanied by her requirement to trim the fur of the toys that she makes as a hobby.

In the above example, her anxiety of getting exposed to the ocean competes with her pleasant feelings of giving the finishing touch to the toys she loves to make. Continuous presentation of the two together weakens the power of the anxiety-provoking characteristic of the ocean. This technique is mostly used in the context of dissipating phobias (Cormier et al., 2013; Spiegler, 2016).

The counsellor follows a process involving a few steps before administering it to the client. The counsellor spends more than one session interviewing the client to understand him/her and have detailed information about the phobia. Then, information is collected about various conditions that produce anxiety related to the particular stimulus. The counsellor then assesses the relative power each of the situations has in revoking anxiety in the client. These events are then hierarchically arranged in ascending manner (low to high). The counsellor trains the client in relaxation procedures. Presentation of the anxiety-provoking stimuli is done in a systematic way after the client is totally relaxed (Head & Gross, 2008).

There are many other processes in desensitising the client such as in vivo exposure, flooding, etc. A word of caution to be placed here is that only a trained counsellor should administer these behaviour techniques to the client. If the counsellor is not trained, one should refer the client to a trained counsellor.

The skills the counsellor uses to trigger a change in the behaviour range from basic skills like skill training to therapeutic behavioural techniques. Whatever be the approach, the path followed is a collaboration between the client and the counsellor. The outcome of the intervention rests on how well each of them understands, accepts, and plays their roles.

Exercises

Following are two cases presented to the counsellor. Place yourself as the counsellor. Describe your approach.

Exercise 1

The problem is about a 13-year-old boy. He has been doing well in his studies. Suddenly his performance dropped drastically. The parents discovered that after school this boy was in the company of a group of university students much older than him. They were taking him out of the colony on their bike to the park where he said they all played cricket. They dropped him back home after it is dark. The parents tried their best to convince him that he should be playing with the boys of his age and stop being in the company of the older boys. On inquiry, he said that those older boys never forced him to join them but he liked to go with them to 'play cricket'. His parents tried to convince him to play the same game of cricket with his age group and even offered to buy him the cricket set from a sports shop. He agreed. Got the cricket set and played with his colony friends. But it lasted only for two days. He was seen again going out with the older boys. Parents approached the counsellor to help him resume his association with his age-group friends and his good performance in academics.

Exercise 2

The client is a young IT employee who started his career two years ago. After two years he is now a victim of attrition. His company has given him the notice to quit. He feels so depressed that he has no energy left after returning from the office to sit and look out for opportunities elsewhere. He says that there is always insecurity in the IT sector. One day he wants to join some other industry, another day he dreams about starting his own business and yet another day he says he would go into farming. One month passed and he lost his job. After losing his job, he stayed home and gradually got used to it. Slowly inertia set in and he needed effort to do even small errands for the family. He was aware of his condition and wanted to get over it and start looking for a job. But he did not know where to begin and how to begin. He has come to the counsellor.

Two members can volunteer to have a role play, one as the client and the other as the counsellor. The objective of the counsellor is to bring about a change in the behaviour of the client.

References

Bandura, A. (1977). Self-efficacy: Toward a unifying theory of behavioral change. *Psychological Review*, *84*(2), 191–215. https://doi.org/10.1037//0033-295X.84.2.191.

Bandura, A. (1982). Self-efficacy mechanism in human agency. *American Psychologist*, *37*(2), 122–147.

Cormier, S., Nurius, P. S., & Osborn, C. (2013). *Interviewing and change strategies for helpers*, Cengage Learning.

Egan, G. (1990). *The skilled helper: A systematic approach to effective helping*, Thomson Brooks/Cole Publishing Co.

Gershoff, E. T. (2002). Corporal punishment by parents and associated child behaviors and experiences: A theoretical review. *Psychological Bulletin*, *128*, 539–579.

Gottman, J. M., & Leiblum, S. R. (1974). *How to do psychotherapy and how to evaluate it.* Rinehart & Winston.

Kottler, J. A. & Shepard, D. S. (2008). *Introduction to counselling: Voices from the field.* Thomson Brooks/Cole.

Krumboltz, J. D. (1965). Behavioral counseling: Rationale and research. *Personnel and Guidance Journal*, *44*, 373–387.

Mohapi, B. J. & Pitsoane, E. M. (2017). Life skills as a behaviour change strategy in the prevention of HIV and AIDS: Perceptions of students in an open and distance learning institution. *SAHARA-J: Journal of Social Aspects of HIV/AIDS*, *14*(1), 77–84. https://doi.org/10.1080/17290376.2017.1374878.

O'Donohue, W. & Fisher, J. E. (Eds.) (2008). *Cognitive behavior therapy: Applying empirically supported techniques in your practice.* Wiley.

Paul, G. L. (1967). Insight versus desensitization in psychotherapy two years after termination. Journal of Consulting Psychology, 31(4), 333–348. https://doi.org/10.1037/h0024855

Spiegler, M. D., & Guevremont, D. C. (2003). *Contemporary behavior therapy.* Brooks/Cole.

Spiegler, M. D. (2016). *Contemporary behavior therapy.* Cengage Learning.

Wolpe, J. (1990). *The practice of behavior therapy.* Pergamon Press.

9 Winding up and Termination

It may be observed from the case studies and examples cited throughout the book that counselling services are sought when the individual faces an aberration in the process of development, an interruption in the effective functioning of life, or a disruption in well-being, placing an individual in a conflict, dilemma, or crisis. Hence, counselling services can best be called an intervention that facilitates an individual to resume life, equipped with new coping skills to handle life's challenges or adapt to life changes more productively and effectively. The emphasis is on 'resuming life'. The competence of the counsellor lies in equipping the client to apply the skills in real-life situations, not only in the problem area for which intervention was provided but also in other similar situations as and when they arise. This demands the application of the learned skills and the transfer of the skills in real-life situations. A counsellor to whom the client keeps repeatedly returning with one problem or the other cannot be acclaimed as a competent professional for the simple reason that he/she could not facilitate the client with skills appropriately applied and transferred to suit life's challenges. To fulfil this professional obligation, the counsellor must organise a professionally sound process into the system of winding up the counselling sessions to give it a healthy and meaningful conclusion so that the client is appropriately armed with the knowledge and skills to encounter life's challenges and avail of life's opportunities. Assigning an entire chapter for winding up and termination may, at the outset, appear very trivial. Still, the following example will help us appreciate the thought that should go into the process so that the aftermath of termination attains the goal of any intervention.

The example is about learning the skill of driving a car. A young friend of mine who wanted to escape the problems of the public transport system wanted to buy a car. She had no experience even riding a bicycle, let alone driving a car. She had to undergo driving training classes on the road. She found the experience quite exciting. The trainer who sat beside her had the second set of accelerator, brake and clutch under his feet and used them as and when required. As the classes progressed, my friend could manage driving the car very well. According to the trainer there was no need for him to use the brake, clutch or accelerator since she was doing it all 'perfectly'. She could finally be trained to the satisfaction of the trainer, who also helped her get a driving licence which was part of the training package. Within a week of the training, my friend got the delivery of her new car, which was driven to her garage by the showroom's driver. The actual problem started from the time the car was parked in her garage. She was supposed to use the car as she had the training and the licence to drive. The following day there was a slight rain, and therefore she decided not to take the 'new car' out. The next day she had to go to a different office for a meeting, so she 'could not' take her car. Following that was

DOI: 10.4324/9781003459415-9

the weekend when she stayed home. The whole of the following week, there was some reason or the other for her not to take the car. After a week, she had to be pointed out by her friend that she was avoiding driving for some reason best known to her. Thinking about it, she realised that though she had acquired the skill of driving, she got so used to the presence of the trainer, and the reassurance of the presence of the second set of the control system with the trainer that would rescue her should there be any error, that she was unable to go it all alone on the road. To overcome that fear, she had to call back her trainer and make him sit next to her while she drove her car (which did not have the second set of control systems) for the first few days. After that, the trainer helped her by gradually weaning her out of his presence. He appraised her of the potential problems of driving at night, operating in the rain, managing traffic jams, parking in narrow spaces, etc. and gave proper instructions on overcoming these normal setbacks. My friend could gradually get onto the wheels and is now a good driver.

The above example reveals that it is just not the training in driving that would really 'make one drive in the traffic', but there are several hidden factors that need to be addressed to bring the readiness for driving in an individual. The same situation can be extrapolated to the condition of counselling, where the client undergoes emotional release, cognitive restructuring, goal setting, and action plan and is found ready for action with all the strategies drawn well on the paper. Satisfied with the progress, the counsellor terminates the sessions with the hope that the client, now equipped with the action plan, must just implement it in life. The client, armed with new cognition, rekindled motivation and a carefully chalked-out action plan, may either fail to initiate action or drop out mid-way. This may not happen with all clients (just as the way all those trained in driving may not avoid going alone into the traffic), but this is very likely to occur with many of the clients if they are not prepared well to act in real life situations that may pose unforeseen challenges. Hence, the counsellor should pay particular focus on the process of winding up and termination of counselling in a systematic and scientific way by applying the skills appropriately. What should go into the package of the counsellor is foresight, identification of the probable action-blockers and preparing and skilling the client to encounter them successfully.

Post-Counselling Probabilities

Post-counselling probabilities refer to the factors that challenge the client in initiating or sustaining action for which the strategies are drawn, facilitating and restraining forces are identified, and contingency plans are worked out. While the client may feel that they are all ready to initiate action on termination of counselling, implementing the action in the absence of counsellor support may place the client in a totally different disposition. The client experiences a new-found freedom from being accountable to the counsellor combined with self-doubts about one's ability to execute the action and its possible outcome. This may be supplemented with the unimagined and unforeseen situations standing between the client's goal and action. This has the potential to dampen the motivation, find excuses for postponing the action, or suspend an already initiated behaviour. If these factors confluence with the client's efforts to protect one's self-esteem, it may lead to the process of rationalisation, where the very goal of the action may be discounted.

Following are some of the possibilities that inhibit action from the client in the aftermath of counselling. The list is suggestive but not exhaustive.

- Learned helplessness and client dependence on counsellor
- Inability to transfer skills learned in the counselling
- Non-initiation and procrastination
- Natural decay curve
- Entropy
- Relapse and rationalisation

Counsellor Dependency and Learned Helplessness

Counsellor support throughout the counselling process works as an excellent strength for the client. The social influence of the counsellor, the empathy, unconditional acceptance, respect, and understanding of the counsellor, while functions as a great source of confidence and booster of self-efficacy, also inculcate in the clients the habit of looking for the unspoken acceptance of the counsellor to boost their morale. Since the counsellor's support during the counselling process is continuous, the client is likely to get conditioned to this cue from the counsellor for any action or initiative. Now, on termination of counselling, suddenly caught alone in a real situation, the client may find action initiative difficult without the cue from the counsellor. Logically, it is not the counsellor who in any way is concretely contributing to the new behaviour. Yet, the physical presence starts to matter because of the client's dependency on the counsellor. This can be compared with the school children unable to do the homework if the mother is not sitting next to them because they get conditioned to a situation where the homework is done in the physical presence of the mother. This is a learned helplessness syndrome. This has the characteristic of preventing any initiative. The following case illustrates the way it operates in a live situation

Box 9.1 Client's Dependency on the Counsellor

A young aspirant to build a career in academics approached the counsellor with problems of self-efficacy, symptoms of anxiety and depression forming into a vicious circle. He has been consistently a good student. After completing his doctorate, he has been trying for a faculty position in various colleges and universities. However, he was not effective in his interview performance. During the counselling sessions, the counsellor helped him to chalk out a plan of action that had meticulous planning of preparation for the interview, trained him in stress inoculation technique, and boosted his self-esteem. He was now ready to face any interview. About a week after the counselling session was terminated, the counsellor received a call from him. He sounded anxious and disappointed. He narrated to the counsellor that he went to attend an interview in the northern part of the country. He was full of confidence and was almost sure that he would perform well until he saw the experts entering the interview hall. One of them was his teacher at the university. He said, 'I felt very awkward. I was prepared to face the strangers in the interview board. But when I saw my teacher, I was not sure...... I wanted to talk to you badly. I tried to call you, but there was no network. I wanted to ask if the same techniques would work with a familiar person. I was not sure....... I thought it would put me down to face yet another failure........ So, I returned without appearing in the interview'.

This is a typical example of counsellor dependency. The training of simple transfer of skills either was not provided or failed to work. Such instances are not definite evidence of the client's inadequacy, but they may also indicate an inadequate emphasis on the winding-up process. Egan (1990) aptly termed it as 'trapeze feeling', similar to that of a trapeze player in transition between leaving one trapeze bar and catching the other. The experience of being in the air without any support is something that impacts the player. If the player is caught with the fear of hanging in the air, he/she would never be willing to let go of the bar from which one hangs. Leaving the secure approval of the counsellor and transiting to the new behaviour sends the seminal feeling of insecurity and dependency.

Transfer of Skills Problem

The above example also applies to the lack of ability to transfer skills. Many a time, a learned skill is trans situationally applicable. One should have the presence of mind to utilise the skill across situations. The clients often get so deeply glued to their existing problem that they associate the learned skill only with that one problem discussed in the counselling session. Training in assertiveness, anger management, relaxation, mindfulness etc., can be applied across situations, the message of which needs to be ingrained in the movement itself. A manager in an IT firm trained in anger management should be able to practice it not only in the workplace but also in a family situation. A person who applies it in his office environment but gives full vent to his anger with his wife and children is displacing his anger than managing it. One may rationalise that he chooses not to apply the skill in a non-threatening condition like a family setup. But anger management is a skill when trained, can be used in every anger-provoking situation to improve one's emotional quotient.

The Problem of Non-Initiation and Procrastination

There may be innumerable excuses for not accomplishing something, but only one strong reason for doing something. The competitive strength of the two decides which side of the balance is heavier. Some clients initiate the behaviour with high enthusiasm but drop it as quickly in the face of a single adversity. Some clients build up the spirit up to the planning stage but experience a total lack of energy regarding execution. Yet others have the confidence and the other resources, but mere resistance to change builds sufficient inertia to put off the work perpetually. The causes for this may be any or many, such as weak self-efficacy, lack of strength in commitment, experience, fear of failure, fear of success, non-assertiveness, giving in to pressure, lack of social support, lack of will, few coping techniques in one's repertoire, emphasis on the wrong factors, failure to contingent the rewards and punishments, lack of discipline, poor time management technique, counsellor dependency or Inability to reorganise the environment. There may be many other reasons too.

Self-control is one of the significant factors that prevents or drives the individual to decisive action. What precedes the action initiation is the decision to act. At a psychological level, conscious non-habitual decision making calls for self-control, self-regulation, and emotional regulation. In initiating action as per the action plan, one can discuss two types of self-control. The first is redressive self-control. In this, the individual exercises self-control, self-regulation and emotional regulation to resume the standard functions that have been disrupted due to stress or crisis. The second is reformative self-control.

As the name suggests, this refers to breaking old habits and replacing them with more effective new behaviours. Executing the planned behaviour, be it the resumption of old productive behaviour or replacement of the old behaviour with the new behaviour, calls for the use of resources in the form of self-regulation of one's cognitive and emotional responses in the face of stress, application of problem-solving skills, and choice of more meaningful delayed gratification in place of immediate satiation (Rosenbaum, 1989). Clients who are low on these resources may fail to take off in executing the action after the termination of counselling.

Studies have shown that once a conscious decision is made, it results in the depletion of self-control, self-regulation and emotional regulation, physical stamina, persistence and increased level of procrastination (Vohs et al., 2014). The adverse impact on self-control, though is seen during the thinking and deliberation about the decision, and the depletion is found to be significantly associated with the act of decision making. Thus, the slowing down or non-action following the action plan should be considered a natural human response rather than a sign of retraction of the client because he/she does not want to implement the action plan.

Decay Curve

The decay curve is the greatest reality of life. It is very natural and universal. Any programme or action that starts at a high enthusiasm level has certain limit in sustaining the same level for long. This is because, at the initial stages, the behavioural response to the new stimulus generates interest because of the value of the novelty of the object. The response persists as long as the stimulus sustains its novelty. After a while, the stimulus gradually tends to lose its value of novelty, bringing along with it a gradual decline in the intensity, frequency and rigour of the behavioural response. This can be explained with the example of a young student's enthusiasm for maintaining a bike recently gifted by the parent. The overwhelmed student spends time in dusting, washing and keeping the bike clean in the first week and takes pride in displaying the shining bike to friends. But gradually, after the initial excitement passes, the bike is not given so much attention by the same student. The cleaning behaviour weans out from twice daily to once, alternate days, weekly and then occasionally. This is an expected natural behaviour. But one need not be surprised if the same pattern is seen when the same student is gifted a car on the next birthday. The pattern is associated with the factor of novelty. A similar pattern can be observed in birthday or New Year's resolutions that many of us make.

Chalking out the strategies and action plans are visualisations. With the support and encouragement of the counsellor, things may appear simple and easy for the client. Identification of possible obstacles and keeping a contingency plan ready enhances the pragmatism of the plan drafted. However, once the client is out of the counselling support, and faces the real situation, what appeared so easy and simple may start to look very complex and insurmountable. Every attempt may demand efforts manifold than bargained for. When the outcome of each effort is only a promise of gratification in future, the motivation to sustain the behaviour that fails to show any immediate result gradually withers out. This impacts the conduct's frequency and intensity, leading to a decay curve that slopes down across time. For example, an obese person with an action plan of following the diet chart meticulously worked on and an exercise regimen drawn with all the possible obstacles in mind tends to adhere to it strictly for the first two to three weeks. But, with the impact of it not being seen in the weighing balance for the next month dampens the client's motivation. Further, inadvertent comments from others about the futility of the weight reduction mission function as an added demotivation. As a result, the client may revert to his/her binge eating and sedentary life.

A competent counsellor can apprehend the decay curve and plan a prophylactic in the winding-up process to prevent it from optimising the counselling outcome.

Entropy

The concept of entropy can be traced to thermodynamics. It describes the extent of uncertainty and disorder in a system. The idea can be adapted to the discipline of Psychology, where the 'system' refers to the organism's response to the environment. The uncertainty in this system is entropy. There is a constant interplay between the individual and the environment. Uncertainty emerges when the individual's perception enters a conflict with his/her probable action on the object in the environment. For example, a client who has given up smoking meets a group of his old friends who are discussing the past days while many among them are smoking. The client's perception of this situation comes in conflict with his resolve to abstain from smoking. This uncertainty is inversely proportional to the clarity of the goal of abstinence. If the goal of quitting smoking is very clear with a strong commitment, the entropy is low.

On the other hand, if the goal and resolve lack strength, then there is every likelihood of uncertainty translating into the subjective experience of anxiety (Hirsh et al., 2012), leading to behaviour accordance. Unlike the decay curve which shows a progressive decline, the entropy is a sudden downward drop. The client may have maintained the new behaviour successfully for a good length of time, after which there is a sudden slope. The risk with entropy is the sudden slope not picking up to the maintenance level but continuing the downward trend. This is what is termed a transition from lapse to relapse. The client falling back to the old behaviour may not stop with that one stray occasion but has the risk of pushing him/her to the original dysfunctional state. Figure 9.1 shows the difference between the decay curve and the entropy giving rise to the decay curve.

Entropy turns out to be the major challenge in sustaining the new behaviour in the client post-termination of counselling sessions. In many cases, a single violation of discipline in the client is seen to result in relapse. This is true in cases where the client relapses to dysfunctional behaviour after successfully breaking a habit such as smoking, drugs, etc. It is as much seen in issues where the clients who successfully learnt a new behaviour relapses to the old inaction as in the cases of cultivating the habit of regular physical exercise after a cardiac episode and stopping it totally after a break of two days when one must engage some unexpected guests.

The client should have multiple orientations to handle entropy situations to sustain the new behaviour.

Relapse to Rationalisation

The client who relapses into the old behaviour owing to the decay curve or entropy may experience a dent in self-esteem due to guilt feelings, lowering of self-efficacy, and poor willpower. If entertained and sustained, this is anxiety-inducing and disruptive to maintaining equilibrium. So, in many instances, the client who relapses into the old behaviour following the termination of counselling takes recourse to rationalisation.

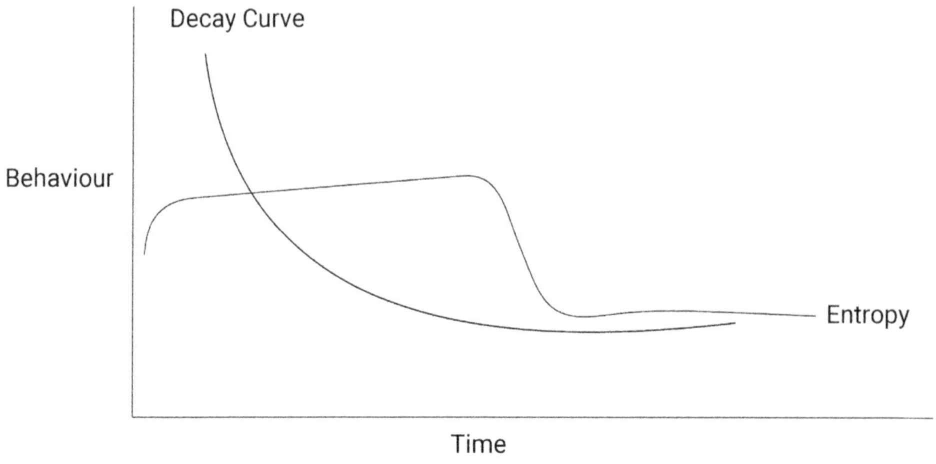

Figure 9.1 Decay Curve and Entropy

Box 9.2 Smoker's Rationalisation

A middle-aged IT employee who has been a smoker set a goal of quitting smoking in his counselling session. After he quit smoking, he suffered and withstood the withdrawal symptoms very well. It was about six months since he quit smoking. He reported regaining a good appetite, sound sleep and, more importantly, no 'urge' to smoke. He was happy about lowering the risk of cardiac health problems. A few months later, he was found resuming his smoking after attending an alumni meet at his college. His logic was that smoking has the most negligible contribution to the cardiac problem because two of his classmates who followed a healthy lifestyle died of cardiac arrest. Many of his acquaintances have been heavy smokers for decades but had no cardiac issues. He argued that since he was not obese and had no family history of cardiac problems, just a condition of an arterial block does not warrant cessation of smoking. It was found that during the alumni meeting, when he was amidst his peer group who smoked, he experienced entropy and gave in to his temptation.

They may tend to discount or denounce the very goal of the new behaviour and justify the old deficient, inefficient, or dysfunctional behaviour. The case presented in Box 9.2 is an example of this.

Entropy is a natural phenomenon. One should be sensitised about its probability and trained to deal with it effectively. If one does not know how to demolish entropy, it will demolish one.

Arming the Client to Handle Post-Counselling Adversities

A competent counsellor takes good cognisance of the post-termination possibilities of the client losing behavioural strength. This knowledge helps the counsellor arm the client with appropriate skills to cope with the adversities successfully. We have deliberately used the term 'cope' here to indicate clearly that the actions of the client should aim at changing the adverse environment than changing oneself or the set goal (Hariharan & Rath, 2008). These can be divided into the skills to be used before, during and after the execution of action in a real-life environment. For clarity, we call them protective armours, promotive armours and preventive armours. Protective armours are the adversities the counsellor helps the client foresee and develop some preparatory steps. For example, a client who shows high anxiety after being selected for a reality show on television may be helped in finding various ways of acquainting oneself with the facts about the show. For this, the client may choose one or more options like meeting a person who has gone through it, visiting the studio a week prior to participation, identifying others who are co-participants in the show and contacting and getting to know them, etc. These preparatory steps protect the client from the anxiety of sudden exposure to the strange physical and social environment in which he/she should perform. This can also be achieved through stress inoculation techniques that involve the steps of education, rehearsal and implementation (Hariharan & Rath, 2008). Promotive armours are the planned behavioural strategy for overcoming anxiety during the actual action. The counsellor prepares the client to expect some unforeseen adversities in the environment where one has to operate with a behavioural change and be prepared with some definite strategies to shift the action plan to suit the demand. For example, the anxious client called for an interview for a faculty position in a university goes prepared with a PowerPoint presentation of their achievements as mentioned in the discussions. The counsellor also mentally prepares him/her so that in case of any difficulties, the Board may ask him/her to demonstrate a concept to the class in a simulated environment. This preparedness promotes the client's performance despite the sudden shift in the focus of the Board. Hence such training or strategies can be termed as promotive armour. The last type is preventive armour. This is useful in the phase following the action/behaviour. There are occasions when the client, after making a decision and taking the first decisive step, starts negatively evaluating the decision and gets into regret and depression. This is called post-decisional depression. For example, in a strained marriage, ending up in a divorce, one spouse may regret not giving it one more try after signing the divorce papers. A young woman may feel high anxiety about repaying after taking a heavy bank loan to purchase a house. A person starting a career may feel that he/she made a wrong choice after joining the office. All these may lead to high anxiety and depression. The counsellor should foresee this and equip the client with the skills to prevent such adverse reactions following a well-contemplated behaviour.

A competent counsellor takes care of these possibilities culminating in client inaction and sensitises, orients, trains and prepares him/her to cope with such necessities. Some ways of preparing the client for the possibilities are discussed below.

Flexibility to Encounter Changed Scenario

Life situations are dynamic. They keep changing contingent on several factors such as time, persons involved, policies, organisational structure or management, health, or well-being status of the other person in an interpersonal situation, etc., to mention a few. The strategy and action plan chalked out by the client with the support of the counsellor is based on the circumstances described by the client's experience at a point in time. There may be instances where these situations undergo minor or major changes at the time the client returns to act upon the environment. The counsellor should equip the client with what Egan (1990, 2010) calls 'tactics'. He defines tactics as 'the art of adapting a plan to the immediate situation' (Egan, 1990, p. 377). It calls for a flexible disposition, quick thinking and the presence of mind to rework the strategy, develop an alternative, evaluate its efficacy and execute the same. One needs to have not only a predisposition to be flexible but also build the necessary strength and preparedness for risk-taking behaviour. The rule of thumb here is to prepare the client to remain steadfast in pursuing the goals set while changing the action when the environment turns either irrelevant to the original strategy. The counsellor, before terminating the counselling, should take necessary steps to boost the self-efficacy of the client by engaging him/her in some tasks where one has to necessarily modify the original strategy and achieve the original goal. The tactics of the client in such situations rewarded by the counsellor boosts one's self-efficacy.

> Example: A student showing examination anxiety is given the task of coming prepared for an hour-long examination. When he comes all prepared for a written examination, he is asked to face an oral examination where the examiner in the simulated situation asks him questions. Though the student at the beginning finds himself lost with the change in the mode of examination, he settles down and gradually starts answering the questions comfortably without giving vent to anxiety.

The counsellor analyses the situation for the student and gives feedback on how quickly he could adapt to the changed situation without being impacted by the initial stress. This is only one example of helping the client to use the potential tactics. The counsellor can plan to discuss such possible changed scenarios about the health status of a loved one to a client who is the primary caregiver, policy changes in the organisations when the client is an employee facing problems of assertion in getting the promotion, change in the mood of the other person when the client is planning the strategy of improving the relationship.

Along with the tactics, the client should be apprised of using the logistics. Egan (1990, 2010) defines logistics as 'the art of being able to provide the resources needed for the implementation of the plan in a timely way' (Egan, 1990, p. 377). It may be appropriate to state that while tactics are gathering one's internal resources such as flexibility, presence of mind and ability to think fast, logistics is gathering external resources such as finances, time, social support, etc. The alternative strategy may require resources different from what the original plan gathered. Without these resources, the alternative action remains unimplemented. The client's cognition should be so trained that he/she will be able to quickly assess the availability of alternative resources and applies the same in executing the new strategy. In one of the episodes of the reality show for the chefs, the participants are asked to choose their ingredients from the store and plan the preparation of their choice of dish. Halfway through they are instructed to interchange the cooking platforms among them and they are asked to continue the dish half prepared by their co-participant without knowing what their co-participant planned for. Many a time in real life, one is placed in such situations while in the process of coping with a stressful condition. The situation keeps unfolding itself as the individual works on it, sometimes springing a total surprise. The readiness and willingness to encounter such changed scenarios help in sustaining the motivation rather than freezing or quitting. The counsellor's force-field analysis with the client in a way helps the client identify all the available resources. All that the client has to do is to identify and reorganise the choice of resources in the worst scenario of challenges of a changed environment at the time of action implementation.

Tips to Fight Procrastination

Procrastination is one of the worst enemies of the new behavioural initiatives. In the politics of old and new behaviour, the old behaviour tends to win because of its advantage of providing a comfort zone to the client. One of the methods found effective in fighting it is to apply what may be termed as 'exposure triggered motivation'. This is a process of invoking self-motivation by the client. While dealing with the students encountering ambivalence in initiating concerted preparation for the final examination that is crucial in their career this technique was applied by one of the authors and found to be effective. This works particularly with those who have the aspiration to perform well but are unable to overcome the tendency to put off the initiative to follow a schedule and start their serious preparations. The counsellor can enter into a contract with them where they need not start to plan a timetable or start their study hours with a bang. All that they need to do is to commit themselves to 'just spend a couple of hours with their books the following day', during which one thing they need to commit is that they should not physically move out of that place. Spending time with the books involves certain steps such as taking out all the text books and notebooks from their usual place like the shelf/cupboard or study table, dusting them, arranging them following any order such as subject wise, size wise, as per one's rated liking for the subject or even as per the alphabetical order. Then they should 'take care' of the books by changing the cover where they are torn, setting right the folded corners, etc. which would result in giving a better look to the book. The last step is to just flip through the pages of every book, with a promise not to read them. They have a look at the figures, illustrations, tables, and notes made in the margins, if any, but reading the book is prohibited. After the two hours, they can place the books in some organised way following any criteria. It was invariably found that this exercise of spending time with books conquers procrastination and the student begins the serious preparation. This happens because by spending time with the books, the student is physically drawn to the books. Second, by flipping through the pages, one makes an informal audited estimation of the task ahead. The contract of not reading anything on day one combined with the cognition of the volume of reading one must do, creates an unrest in mind similar to the Zeigarnik effect. In addition, changing the covers of the book introduces the novelty factor. This motivates them to make the beginning. The counsellor may apply similar techniques to the clients. Similar measures, such as helping the client to break the whole task into small implementable fragments and starting with what is assessed as the relatively easy step, can be planned as the first step. For example, an unemployed client who is not able to initiate the action of trying for jobs by sending a resume can be asked to spend a day enlisting friends and acquaintances who could give a reference, make courtesy calls to them and speak without mentioning anything about the help to fetch a job. This exercise helps the client to assess the strength of the support network and identify the likely people who would benefit.

The counsellor should foresee the possibility of procrastination and not only forewarn but also equip the client with skills and techniques to fight the same. Just forewarning and not helping the client with appropriate skills has the potential of the client mistaking the caution as an allowance to procrastinate.

Organising Rewards and Punishments in the Natural Setting

Why clients fail to initiate and sustain action after planning the strategy has already been discussed. It has been identified that when the incentives for not initiating or continuing action are stronger than the incentives to initiate or continue an action, the client tends to choose inaction. To break this circle, the counsellor helps the client to identify the powerful and feasible incentives in one's life setting. For example, one may locate tangible incentives such as having an ice cream, social incentives such as attending a party with friends, emotional incentives such as meeting one's parents, religious motivations such as visiting a long-pending place of worship, spiritual stimulus such as joining the classes of meditation. The preferences and the incentive values differ from person to person. Similarly, the accessibility and feasibility of availing the incentive and the frequency with which it can be availed, the duration of its impact etc, are highly subjective. That is one reason why the counsellor should help the client identify the incentives depending upon the type of behaviour for which the motivation has to be associated. The one strong consideration in determining the incentives is its valence in strengthening the new behaviour. The counsellor trains the client to link minor and major rewards to every step of the action in attaining the goal. The incentive attached to action should be proportionate to the efforts needed to execute and sustain the activity. For example, a husband who has chalked out the strategy to express the positives in his wife may arrange to go for half-an-hour swimming in the evening each day he does it successfully. When he is sustaining the behaviour for an entire week, he may treat himself to a game of golf in the weekend. In case it is successfully sustained for a month, he may treat himself by joining his friends on a trekking expedition during the last week. Thus, the incentives may continue until the behaviour turns into a habit and an attitude.

While rewards are found to work well in strengthening the behaviour, the role of setting punishment was not found to be very effective in strengthening the behaviour, which in fact, concurs with the principles of learning. Punishments are found to be used for weakening undesirable behaviour. However, while setting the incentives, the individual's deprival of the incentives contingent to non-adherence to the new behaviour is sufficient to strengthen the new behaviour.

Multiple Level Commitment

The individual being a social entity, change in behaviour has multilayer influences. Reinforcements for behaviour are found to be hidden in the social responses. It may be necessary at times to fine-tune the social agents in the immediate environment of the client so that the new behaviour is initiated and sustained. In such cases, the counsellor, in the process of winding up the sessions, may plan a family counselling or a group counselling involving family and school in case of children, or caregivers and professional care providers in case of a patient, family and peers, colleagues along the hierarchy in case the client is an employee. In such sessions, the counsellor discusses the strategy in the group and assigns each member a responsibility to commit himself/herself to supporting the behaviour change in the client. The case described in Box 9.3 is a good example of a client who is discharged after going through deaddiction.

Box 9.3 Multi-Level Involvement to Sustain Deaddiction Treatment

The client has been into the addiction to alcohol for about two decades. He was diagnosed with a medical condition when the doctor told him that unless he stopped his alcohol intake immediately, a good prognosis to treatment could not be expected. The client was advised to go for deaddiction. After returning from deaddiction, to prevent a relapse, the family members, and one of his close friends who lives the next door were called for group counselling. In this session, the counsellor explained to the group the probability of entropy and the role each one needs to play in order to prevent entropy and relapse. At the end of the session with the counsellor, the family agreed to plan a weekly schedule along with a contingency plan for every evening. Their plan includes outings, aggressive outdoor games, indoor fun games, visits by friends and quiet personal activities. They may bring in any innovation to the plan. The group was appraised about the possible outbursts of irritation by the client. In such instances, it was agreed that only his wife would respond and others would not interfere. The client had the practice of confiding in his friend, who was also his neighbour. The group was warned that there might be instances when he would talk to him about his increasing urge for a drink. It was agreed that the only way the friend would respond was to talk about his present liver condition, its improved state and the tremendous willpower he had shown till now in sustaining his abstinence. Every family member committed that they would restrain from being critical about his earlier addiction, and in case the topic surfaced, everyone would talk about it as a dark past and highlight the pleasant present. A commitment was also made by everyone that none would appease him or show any overprotective behaviour and be as normal as possible in all other matters.

This commitment by people within the family and the close friend created a readiness in the social environment to handle the possibility of a relapse successfully.

Identifying Social Support Agents

Support of the counsellor during the process of counselling is a source of positive reinforcement for the client's action. However, the presence of the counsellor is not possible during the time of action execution in real life. In order to make the client feel the presence of support, the counsellor helps the client to identify the sources in his/her environment. The client identifies the people in his/her life who can be relied upon for encouragement in initiating and sustaining the new behaviour. The client can confide and share the experiences with this support source which is expected to respond spontaneously and genuinely. In case of any need, the counsellor can orient the support agent in responding appropriately to the client for a productive outcome of behavioural sustenance. This is a precaution against the support agent responding in a way that would be counterproductive. The support from real-life environment can also be formal in the form of the support group for patients with chronic kidney diseases, a support group for caregivers of the terminally ill, parents' groups for autistic children, Alcoholics Anonymous, etc. The counsellor can help by informing the client about the support groups they might join.

Having a support agent or joining a support group is not an indication of the dependence of the client. In fact, the client is helped to be self-sufficient in structuring the support within one's environment rather than depending on the counsellor. This, in a way, is a step towards strengthening the natural social support structure for the client so that the dependence on the counsellor is gradually withdrawn. Further, the skill of building a support network in one's life achieves two goals, viz. maintains general well-being in life and functions as a good shock absorber for the client should there be any significant stress in their lives. It is a definite step in restoring the interpersonal bonding that has its cultural roots but is getting weakened because of the cultural, economic, and political changes brought in over a period in the past two to three decades.

Feedback on the Behaviour

Feedback from a significant person sometimes becomes the nucleus of the behaviour. Not receiving feedback has the potential to create self-doubt in any person. On one occasion, one of the authors was invited to address a group of participants from the National Industrial Security Force. After fulfilling the basic protocols like the formal introduction of the speaker, the author started her talk. In the first ten minutes, as a usual practice, she used humour to get connected with the audience. No one reacted. She tried using more humour then a heart-wrenching case study. Every participant was sitting straight with rapt attention. Except for that, there was no expected spontaneous reaction of laughter, or comment or observation. The speaker started introspecting if she was going in the right direction. Some common sense prevailed, and she decided to announce an unscheduled break in the session and requested tea for all. During this time she started interacting with the participants informally. This worked, and then they were at ease for the rest of the session and were spontaneous. She realised that had she not announced that unplanned break, the lack of reaction and absence of feedback would have dampened her spirits and because of that the session would have failed to have any impact on the participants. The same possibility operates with a client who implements the new behaviour in the field of life. If the client initiated the new behaviour in a bland indifferent environment, it would be difficult to gauge whether the behavioural change is impacting the target or the environment in general. There are two ways of keeping motivation alive in the field. First, the clients should be taught to give feedback to themself. For example, the client who initiates the new behaviour without giving way to procrastination deserves positive feedback from self. Similarly, when one continues the behaviour despite the absence of feedback from the target, one needs feedback from oneself. For example, while working on the marital conflict, if the husband is exercising restraint in being critical about the wife, but this goes unacknowledged by the wife, the husband has every reason to feel confused about the correctness of the new behaviour. Repetition of such experiences may lead to the extinction of the new behaviour. If the client is equipped with a checklist which helps him/her to objectively assess the new behaviour in terms of timing, intent, spontaneity, and some other such parameters, it works as a self-assessment and generates a sense of satisfaction derived from executing the action. Alternatively, the client may be encouraged to identify a person from the social network appropriate to evaluate the new behaviour in question which would provide the correct feedback from time to time. Whether it is self or external feedback, it should be objective. This is possible if the feedback is arranged as one of the two categories, viz. Confirmatory or Corrective.

Confirmatory Feedback

Confirmatory feedback is given when the client's behaviour is on the right track. It can be a bit elaborate to encourage the client to continue it. For example, a student of 9th standard trying to cultivate the habit of maintaining study hours can be given feedback from the mother as 'You were very punctual in maintaining your morning one-hour schedule today. It was a good strategy to keep your mobile phone switched off during the period. Then the decision to have a target for the one hour is also something that you implemented successfully'. This works better than generic feedback, such as 'I am delighted that you are following your study hour schedule and the details'. Though in both cases, the feedback confirms the new positive behaviour of the student, the inclusion of details communicates the genuineness which may be lost in the general expression. However, not every behaviour calls for detailed confirmatory feedback. For example, a depressed woman trying to fight her self-denial and social isolation makes an effort to get dressed for a social gathering. She needs confirmative feedback. In this case, a smile of appreciation from her husband with a non-verbal gesture of putting the thumb and index

Figure 9.2 Effective Non-Verbal Feedback

finger together will be sufficient. In this context, the subtlety of the feedback will be more potent than the detailed confirmatory feedback.

Corrective Feedback

Corrective feedback is given with the intention to correct/refine or finetune the behaviour of the client in the field. Corrective feedback should strictly confine to the behaviour in question and never extend to the personality, attitude or intentions inferred on the basis of the behaviour. It should be crisp and specific. Including the logical reason for the suggested correction may add value to the feedback. This can be explained with a case reported in Box 9.4.

In the case cited in Box 9.4, the feedback was just limited to the behaviour. Had the grandfather elaborated by explaining that the confidence was missing because the mother was apprehensive about the reaction of her daughter or a bit of advice that she should be firmer with her daughter like with the others could have turned her defensive or made her weaker. The crisp feedback on the behaviour is more likely to make the mother ponder about the ways of being more effective the next time.

Box 9.4 Corrective Feedback

The parents of an adolescent daughter who neglected her academics because of her addiction to mobile phone and social media approached the counsellor. They complained that their attempts to discipline her failed miserably because she would create a big scene shouting at them, sulking and starving herself, and finally threatening them that she would leave the house. With that threat, parents have always given in, and she got back to her mobile that kept her awake the whole night. The counsellor and the mother entered into a contract. The mother would insist on the mobile phone of all family members be kept away under her disposal for a few hours during the evening until dinner time. The new family rule was supposed to be implemented the following week after a discussion among the members. On the first day, the mother had to ask all the family members to switch off their mobiles and put them all in the designated place. Everyone did it willingly while the daughter started to grumble. Finally, she complied after a showdown she had with the mother. The grandfather, who was supposed to provide the feedback, later told the mother, 'You were asking each one to put away their phones. But, when you addressed her, the confidence was missing in your voice which was there when you addressed the others'.

Progressive Weaning Process

While many clients have the ability to use the techniques and implement the new behaviour in the field, some may need continuation of counsellor support until they feel comfortable in implementing the new behaviour in the field. Termination of counselling in such cases should be preceded by process of gradual weaning. Following are some tips for the counsellor.

Continuation of Sessions

The counsellor allows the clients to continue the sessions, but the sessions get progressively spaced. This process helps the client to continue drawing support from the counsellor who goes through gradual fading. This process is helpful for those clients who measure low on social skills and have a weaker support networks in their social environment.

Joining Support Group

Some clients with specific needs can be helped by the counsellor to join some self-help group or support group. This helps them continue specific behaviour change programmes such as adherence to a diabetic diet and exercise for a chronic diabetic by joining the self-help group of diabetics in the city. This may even be topped with a need-based supportive counselling session with the counsellor.

Occasional Sessions with the Counsellor

The counsellor may agree to have occasional sessions with some clients when they absolutely feel the need for it. This can be a personal session, a video session or even a tele counselling, depending on the need. However, the counsellor needs to use the utmost discretion in using this because this allowance should work to instil confidence in the client rather than making one dependent.

A counsellor who applies the techniques with discretion appropriate to the individual cases will be able to wind up the counselling in a manner that leaves satisfaction both for the counsellor and the client. It enables the client to gain the required strength to cope effectively with the real-life situation and overcome dysfunctional behaviour.

Termination

The two most important questions about terminating counselling sessions are: 'when?' and 'how?'. The timing of termination and the process are issues to be handled with care. Let us address the first question first. How many sessions are required on average to make counselling effective? Our search for such statistics on Indian clients drew a blank. About American population Phillips (1988), in the context of psychotherapy, mentioned that the average number of sessions per client varies between four and six. We have come across reports where the clients required only a single session, after which they could comfortably go ahead with the new behaviour without any hiccup. There are also instances where the counselling sessions go beyond 20. A young woman battling marital conflicts who consulted a clinical psychologist was assessed and diagnosed with severe anxiety and depression. She was informed that she had to go through 20 sessions with the psychologist. The client had two sessions with the psychologist, and 'felt nice' after the sessions but slid back to the panic attacks the following mornings. She felt that the sessions were not going to help her and consulted another psychologist, who, after reading her scores on depression and anxiety, thought that she needed medication for her condition and referred her to the psychiatrist and promised to see her after the symptoms reduced. Thus, a decision on the number of sessions and the time to terminate is something that has no definite standard and hence can be debated.

One may talk in terms of short-term and long-term counselling. Yet, these terms are not linked to any specific numbers. Hence, the use of these terminologies will not be of much help either. But one can go by the contemporary need of the clients seeking professional help. With a drastic change in the pace of life, clients facing new challenges in every dimension of life and unable to handle life stress are increasingly seeking professional help. They have time constraints and wish to match their pace of life in managing their stress-related issues too. The counsellor should plan the number of sessions with these client requirements in mind. Unlike some of the earlier approaches, counselling in contemporary times is not aimed at resolving the conflicts fixated at an early stage of life. They are more concerned with changing the behaviour and helping the client cope effectively with life situations. Thus, the counsellor, after the first one or two sessions, should be able to have a rough plan of the significant goals. Once this is done, the approach is decided. The counsellor, going by the primary counselling goal and the assessment of the client, will be able to estimate a time plan. This time plan, in terms of the approximate number of sessions, should be discussed with the client. The counsellor can tell the client that it may require about three to four sessions, after which there will be a review. The client should also be informed if the sessions are planned weekly/bi-weekly, or daily. This provides the client with a broad idea about what to expect. Further, by discussing the number of sessions, the counsellor, in a way, is building into the contract the time for termination too. When this is done, the termination does not come as a surprise to the client.

It is good practice to inform the client about termination in advance so that the counsellor does not have to make it look like an abrupt closure by declaring that this is the last session for the client. Some counsellors integrate an exclusive closure session with the client where the counsellor summarises the action plans for the client and reiterates the techniques of overcoming the obstacles in implementing them, and the client is given an opportunity to seek any clarification. Further, the closure session is also used as a 'booster dose' by the counsellor. This is done to enhance the client's self-efficacy by emphasising the strengths in the form of abilities and resources. This is done by the counsellor as part of the process of summarising. At the point of termination, while the counsellor discourages the client from falling back on the counsellor for life's minor problems, the door is also not shut permanently on the client. Leaving scope for the client to approach the counsellor differs from leaving an open invitation to the client. Here are a few examples of parting statements by the counsellor.

> You have come a long way from where we started the counselling. You now have a definite goal and the chosen strategy to attain the goal. All that you need to do is to go and get started.

> You now have the know-how of starting the action. You also know how to meet challenges should there be any.

> You have worked pretty well on resolving your emotional upheaval. Now you are ready to take that initiative to bring the much-needed change in your environment. It is time for action. You have the new skills to aid you in this.

> You worked on your emotions much better than expected. Your learning skills are found to be quite good. The goals you have set for yourself are very sound, and the action strategies are quite pragmatic. You should now get started.

The examples are just indications. There is no standard set of statements to conclude the session. The counsellor can be spontaneous and genuine while making the parting statements.

It is good practice to use a checklist before termination of the session. The counsellor may evolve their own checklist. We have constructed a checklist in Box 9.5 that can help to assess if the client is ready for termination of the sessions.

Certain items in the checklist need to be filled by the counsellor through observation. Some items will have to be checked by verifying the pre and post counselling assessment scores. Some other items related to the feelings of the client may have to be responded to after cross-checking with the client.

The counsellors in pursuit of constant improvement may desire feedback on the counselling sessions from the client. Box 9.6 provides a client feedback form. Counsellors can evolve their feedback forms. While doing so, they need to remember that the information sought should be specific, objective, measurable and useful for the counsellor for further refinement of skills.

The counselling session ends with feedback from the client. The counsellor can identify the areas where the ratings are high and where the counsellor needs to strengthen their skills. The counsellor should see oneself as a constant learner so that there is a scope for continuous progress and professional growth.

Box 9.5 Pre-Termination Checklist

1. Have the symptoms in the client reduced?
2. Has the client managed/been confident to handle the problems?
3. Has the stress level come down?
4. Are the emotions managed?
5. Is there a better understanding of self?
6. Is there a better cognition of internal and external resources?
7. Does the client have a clear goal?
8. Is the client confident about the action plan?
9. Does the client have an orientation about the possible obstacles?
10. Does the client have the ability to transfer the learnt skills in real life?
11. Does the client have a positive outlook on life in general?
12. Is the client maintaining better relationships with others than before?
13. Has the self-esteem of the client improved?
14. Has the self-efficacy of the client improved?
15. Is the client more effective with the tasks in life than before?
16. Is the client showing more interest in life than before?
17. Have the scores on the parameters that he/she was assessed earlier improved?
18. Is there a positive change in the grooming of the client?
19. Is there a positive change in the affect state of the client?
20. Is there an improvement in the energy levels felt by the client?

Box 9.6 Client Feedback Form

Here are some statements related to your feelings, experiences and outcomes related to the counselling sessions. Read them all carefully. Rate them on a five-point scale ranging from 'Very True = 5' to 'Not at all True = 1'. Your responses are purely your subjective experiences. So please be honest and spontaneous in responding. Please note your rating points in the brackets against the statements.

1. I felt comfortable with the counsellor ( )
2. I felt emotionally relieved ( )
3. The counsellor gave me good attention ( )
4. I felt that my feelings and experiences were understood by the counsellor ( )
5. I was given adequate opportunity to express myself ( )
6. The counsellor was never in a hurry ( )
7. The counsellor sometimes surprised me with questions that made me introspect ( )
8. The interventions by the counsellor helped me bring clarity to my expressions ( )
9. Some of my efforts to be evasive were handled well ( )
10. The counsellor had good communication skills ( )
11. The sessions helped me rethink about the problem ( )
12. The sessions gave me hope that things can be better ( )
13. The sessions made me think about different ways of approaching the problem ( )
14. The sessions helped me identify the problem correctly ( )
15. I was obliged to set a definite goal ( )
16. I was obliged to work out various possible action plans ( )
17. I am happy about the correctness of the dream I have set ( )
18. The action plan that I have set appears very feasible ( )
19. I feel I can work on my problem confidently ( )
20. Overall I am happy that I sought counselling here ( )

References

Hirsh, J. B., Mar, R. A., & Peterson, J. B. (2012). Psychological entropy: A framework for understanding uncertainty-related anxiety. *Psychological Review*, *119*(2), 304–320. https://doi.org/10.1037/a0026767.

Phillips, E. L. (1988). Length of psychotherapy and outcome: Observations stimulated by Howard, Kopta, Krause and Orlinsky. *American Psychologist, 43,* 669–670.

Rosenbaum, M. (1989). Self-control under stress: The role of learned resourcefulness. *Advances in Behaviour Research and Therapy*, *11*(4), 249–258.

Vohs, K. D., Baumeister, R. F., Schmeichel, B. J., Twenge, J. M., Nelson, N. M., & Tice, D. M. (2014). Making choices impairs subsequent self-control: A limited-resource account of decision making, self-regulation, and active initiative. *Motivation Science, 1*(S), 19–42. https://doi.org/10.1037/2333-8113.1.S.19.

10 Counselling in Different Settings

The examples presented in Box 10.1 help us to understand the diversity in the need for counselling and help us to understand the scope of counselling. Case 1 is in a school setting, wherein the issue is about the child's behaviour in the classroom, Cases 2 and 3 are about decisions about one's choice of career and Case 4 is about interpersonal issues in an organisation, Case 5 is about a couple who are facing issues about the family and family dynamics, wherein a family counselling is required, and Case 6 is in a hospital setting where there is a need for an intervention of a health psychologist. Though all the cases are primarily concerned with an individual, the issues are related to a particular situation and context, and the counsellor has to have the expertise to deal with the context. Counselling is a broad category that encompasses many specialised subfields, for example, community counselling, group counselling, grief counselling, premarital counselling, counselling in a health setting, and counselling for special needs to name a few. Each of these special settings has its own work-related tasks and expertise. Counsellors can choose to specialise in any of the settings based on their competence, interest, and proficiency. This chapter will delineate the specialised areas of counselling and discuss how each of these areas requires special know-how and proficiency.

School Counselling

School counselling is a discipline that branched out from vocational guidance, the area developed by Frank Parsons (1909), the details are presented in Chapter 1. During the 1960s and 1970s, there was a paradigm shift from vocational guidance to psychological support. The United States of America established the American School Counsellor's Association (ASCA) in 1952. The ASCA released a national school counselling programme model in 2003, which provided standards for school counselling across the country. The ASCA model, which was revised in 2005, 2013, and 2019 placed some important roles for the school counsellors in the areas of personal and social development, academic achievement, and career planning of students. ASCA delineated that school counselling is systematic, clearly defined, sequential, and accountable. The programme is proactive and preventive in nature and involves individual and group counselling, and consultation, and includes coordination between the student, teachers, parents, and the school. The concept of school counselling as a profession is still in its initial stages in India, but the informal practices of school counselling can be dated back to the Vedic period when the *Gurukula* or the *Guru-Shishya* system was prevalent. The *Guru* (teacher) at the *Gurukula* guided and mentored the *Shishya* (students) through close and continuous interaction. Such interactions helped the student's personal, intellectual,

DOI: 10.4324/9781003459415-10

Box 10.1 Case Studies in Varied Settings

Case 1: Anjali is a 10-year-old girl studying at a reputed school. She was a brilliant student, active in her class. She was very friendly, and all her classmates loved to interact with her. Over the past few days, the teacher observed a change in her behaviour. She found Anjali not her usual self. She kept herself isolated and aloof, did not concentrate in class, showed disinterest in school activities, and always seemed muddled. Anjali was referred to the school counsellor, who found that she had lost her aunt, with whom she was very close. Anjali had spent all her childhood with her aunt; her aunt took care of her day-to-day needs and also was a great support to her. The school counsellor helped Anjali come out of her grief.

Case 2: Sameer, a 19-year-old student in his fourth semester of engineering, met the counsellor and said, 'I don't think I want to continue this course. I have no aptitude for any of these subjects, nor a passion for becoming an engineer, I feel I am wasting my time here. I think I have messed up my life'. Sameer's understanding that he did not have an aptitude for engineering left him in a state of confusion. He was upset about his decision to take up the course. He was unable to decide what he should be doing next. The college counsellor helped him in come out of the confusion and reset his goals.

Case 3: Urmilla was a 40-year-old homemaker with two children and a loving husband. She spent all her married life taking care of her husband and children. Now her children were going to school, and she had a lot of time for herself. She was a qualified interior designer. She met the counsellor and said, 'All these days, I thought I should give my time to my children because they were growing and needed my support. Now that they have grown up, I feel I should use my time doing what I like and enjoy. My husband also feels the same and is very supportive. I want to start my career as an interior designer, but I am confused and unsure if I really can. I need someone to help me get some clarity about what I should do to attain my goal'. Urmilla took the help of the career counsellor to plan and start her new career.

Case 4: Satish to the counsellor 'I am very upset about how things are going in my organisation. There was a time when I used to proudly tell that I am working here, but now I feel the entire place has fallen apart. You know we spend most of the day at work, and if the relationships at the workplace are strained, how do we go about it? Every day I carry the stress home. My family is not happy, and it is impacting my health. I feel like quitting my job, but I am unable to decide'. Satish approached the counsellor in his organisation to deal with the stress at his workplace.

Case 5: Ramesh to the counsellor 'Last night my wife said she wants a divorce. I was shocked. She says she is tired of managing the office, household work, children, and my parents. She doesn't want my parents to be with us. She says she has done enough for them. How can I leave my parents all alone, they are very old. I think all these days, when we needed them and when our children needed their care, my wife was quite fine, and now that the children no longer need their care and they are on their own, my wife thinks they are a burden. How can parents be a burden to us? We have been having arguments about this for almost two years. Now she is giving me an ultimatum either you leave your parents, or I will file a divorce. I really don't know what to do'. Ramesh sought the help of the family counsellor to see if there was any way he could reconcile his relationship with his wife and save his marriage.

Case 6: Rupa to the counsellor 'My husband had a kidney transplant two days back. We suddenly found a donor, and he got the surgery. But the prognosis is not good. The doctors are not telling me what the issue is. They say he is stable, but he is kept on the ventilator. My children are not in India, my daughter is a doctor, and she is coming tomorrow. She is in touch with the doctors here, but no one is telling me anything. I am really worried about my husband. Hope this decision of going for the transplant was correct'. Rupa's apprehension of her husband's health and her uncertainty regarding the outcome of the transplant were handled by the health psychologist of the hospital.

social, and spiritual growth. The guidance and mentoring helped the student not only in the learning process but also helped them gain skills like communication, discipline, values, planning, and decision-making. The introduction of the English education system in 1835, brought in huge transformations in the entire education system, which not only changed the teacher-student ratio but also reduced the quality of teacher-student interaction. Apart from the school the traditional family system in India, was strong and grounded and gave a great source of support to the overall growth and development of children. Children had their parents, grandparents, aunts, or siblings to share their concerns, and most of the issues were handled with strong support from the family. Globalisation and urbanisation brought rapid social, cultural, and economic changes. Families no longer sit together at the dinner table and share how their day has been, as the dinner is usually in the living room while the family watches the TV shows; siblings no longer share their emotions and feelings along with sharing their rooms, as every child has his/her own room and private space; grandmothers or aunts no longer sit with the children and tell or read out stories, share or pass on values. The consequences of globalisation brought changes in almost all areas of the life of an individual. It led to a shift in the family system from a collectivistic organisation to a nuclear family system, an increase in the number of divorce rates, single-parent families, immense pressure due to competition in every field, increased pressure from peers, parents, and schools, and increased interference from social media. The above has left huge imprints on mental health of children and adolescents. A study on child and adolescent mental health reported that nearly 50 million children in India suffer from some type of mental health issue (Hossain & Purohit, 2008). A 2016 National Health Survey reported a prevalence of 7.3% of mental health disorders among children between the ages of 13 and 17 (Gururaj et al., 2016). The necessity of a counsellor in school is quite evident from the above studies. The school counsellor with his/her expertise plays a fundamental role in promoting the psychological, social, and emotional development of students from pre-primary to secondary school students. They provide individual and group counselling and work in collaboration with the parents, teachers, and the school administration.

Types of School Counselling

School counselling can be directive or non-directive. Directive counselling usually comprises meeting students individually. Individual problems are addressed on a confidential basis.

Non-directive counselling services include group counselling, wherein a small group is addressed based on the needs and requirements of the group. Group counselling is effective in addressing issues related to academics, career, and social issues; multiple students of similar age, who are dealing with similar issues are grouped. Non-directive counselling also comprises meeting parents and teachers to resolve academic, behavioural, and social issues. School counselling stems from the specific needs of children and adolescents. To cater to these needs of students, school counselling outlines the following goals:

- promote a safe environment
- help children in school adjustment
- provide assistance for the academic, social, and emotional concerns
- promote academic, career, and personal development
- assist the school administration in creating a safe and responsive school environment
- provide support in remediation

The role of school counsellors varies depending on the educational setting in which they work. The next section of the chapter discusses the responsibilities of school counsellors at various levels of education viz. primary school, middle school, and high school.

Counselling in Primary School

Primary school is a crucial period in the child's intellectual, mental, and emotional development. Children learn socialising skills which include communication and interaction with others, developing relationships with friends and teachers, and group behaviour. The major developmental tasks of a primary school child are to attain the necessary physical skills, develop the skills of reading, writing, and mathematics, get along with their classmates, and develop age-appropriate morals and values. While these are the expected tasks for a child to achieve in primary school, many children have the disadvantage of not being able to achieve one or more of the above tasks, resulting in adjustment issues, behaviour problems, low self-esteem, anxiety, fear, failure to perform in the classroom activities, inability to confront, and bullying to name a few. The other psychological, social and developmental issues children and adolescents go through is abuse in school or at home, family issues, social skills challenges and learning disabilities to name a few. The primary school counsellor can assist students with these difficulties by providing support through counselling and necessary interventions. The three different cases given in Box 10.2 will help the readers understand the need for a school counsellor in primary schools.

The above cases explicate some of the diverse issues faced by children in primary school. The stressors faced by children include the loss of a loved one, stressors induced due to interpersonal conflicts, injury, insecurity, fear of punishment, imposition, and performance-based stress. Furthermore, divorce or separation of parents, illness of a family member, inability to make friends, and bullying are some of the stressors to be dealt with. Children often need help to overcome these stressors. Children respond to stress in different ways. Stress brings in physiological, behavioural, and cognitive manifestations along. Box 10.3 presents some of the common reactions to stress in children. Behavioural responses include anger, crying, irritability, difficulty in communication, excess of humour, restlessness, changes in sleep patterns, or eating behaviours. Cognitive indicators include worry, racing thoughts, poor attention and concentration, reduction in cognitive flexibility, and lack of organisation.

Box 10.2 Case Studies in School Counselling

Case 1: Rishi was a second-grade student. The teacher referred him to the primary school counsellor stating that Rishi had problems with attention. She also complained that Rishi didn't pay attention to the teacher, didn't listen to what is taught in the class, and disturbed other students. The primary school counsellor in her interaction with Rishi did not find any major behavioural issues. The counsellor then decided to observe Rishi in the classroom. After a few sessions, the counsellor observed that Rishi was the first child to complete any assignment or task given in the class and was very prompt in submitting his work. The counsellor also observed that after completing his work within a span of time, Rishi was bored and went around the class talking and disturbing other students. The counsellor had an interaction with Rishi and his parents and found that he read books that children of his age were unable to comprehend. The counsellor after her initial assessment referred Rishi to a psychologist for an assessment of his IQ; the results of the assessment showed that Rishi was a gifted child. After confirming the results of the assessments, the counsellor recommended that Rishi should be given assignments that are of a higher level of difficulty than what his classmates do and recommended that if he completes his work, he should be allowed to engage himself with some interesting readings so that his interest and attention are sustained.

Case 2: Abhigna was a student in grade three. She was a very bright, cheerful, and diligent student. She came from a highly supportive family and had a good group of friends. Everything was going well till the day when Abhigna suddenly refused to go to school. Her parents made attempts to talk and find out the reason, but she wouldn't speak out. Her mother tried to come along and drop her to school, but Abhigna would start to panic and have crying spells till her mother took her back home. Abhigna's parents spoke to the school counsellor. After a lot of resistance, Abhigna agreed to speak to the counsellor. After several sessions and after gaining the trust, the girl revealed her story. The girl was in a highly traumatic state because the helper of the school bus was molesting her. The girl was then counselled. She required continuing therapy to regain her self-esteem and deal with the trauma. Apart from handling the distress of the student, the counsellor also planned collaborative interventions to train the parents, administration of the school, teachers, and non-teaching staff of the school to create awareness among students and prevent such incidents.

Case 3: Rakshit was a child from grade two. His teachers and parents were often upset with his performance in school. Rakshit scored low grades and his teachers complained that his skills were significantly below his grade level. His mother was upset about his grades, so she engaged a tutor for him. Rakshit had no time for play or co-curricular activities because of his school and tuition. He did not have good friends, and his classmates bullied him. Rakshit was referred to the school counsellor. After further counselling and assessment, Rakshit was diagnosed of specific learning disabilities. He was recommended academic support in reading and writing and curriculum-based remediation. Rakshit's parents had difficulty accepting his condition; consequently, the counsellor took special sessions for the parents. With the help of the school counsellor and the school administration the counsellor organised a workshop for the teachers to create awareness and identify children with specific learning disabilities so that early interventions could be provided.

Box 10.3 Physiological, Cognitive, and Behavioural Responses to Stress in Children

Lack of sleep
Physical complaints like headaches, stomach aches, palpitations, nausea
Bed-wetting
Loss or increase in appetite
Nail-biting or thumb sucking
Nightmares
Loss of interest, poor attention, and concentration
Irritability, anger
Fear (of being left alone, darkness, strangers, animals)
Withdrawal, clinging behaviour or attention-seeking behaviour
Regressive behaviour
Anxiety or panic

Counselling in Middle and Secondary School

School counsellors who work with middle school children face unique challenges. Students in this age group struggle with issues related to physical changes during adolescence, low self-esteem, problems with their families or peers, mood swings, bullying, peer pressure, and conflicts with peer groups. Concerns of students in secondary school include drug and alcohol use or abuse, sexual concerns, adjustment issues and issues regarding interpersonal relationship. Students also have concerns about career choices, career decision-making, decisions regarding educational pursuits, decisions about intimate relationships, and decisions about developing personal value systems. Behavioural and emotional issues including anger outbursts, violence and aggressive behaviour, motivational difficulties, anxiety, avoidance behaviour, sleep disturbances, eating disorders, sense of hopelessness, loss of confidence, negative self-talk, thrill/risk-taking behaviours, absence from school, abuse, neglect, inappropriate social skills, low motivation, and achievement indicate the need for support.

Counselling and early intervention can help children and adolescents cope with and manage stressors, behavioural and psychological issues. Counsellors can help children and adolescents in schools by providing individual or group counselling.

Individual counselling can include students who directly approach the counsellor or are referred by teachers, school authorities, or parents. The stages of individual counselling have already been mentioned in the initial chapters of the book, however, for the convenience of the reader, the steps are listed below:

1. Initial contact and rapport building
2. In-depth exploration and assessment of the problem or problem situation
3. Setting counselling and intervention goals
4. Planning intervention and action
5. Evaluation, termination, and follow up

The pre-help skills elaborated in Chapter 4 help the counsellor in exploring the nature of the problem. From the story or the narrative of the student, the counsellor can understand the strengths, resources, support system, the chain of events that resulted in the problem, how long has the problem persisted, and does it interfere with the daily life of the student. The counsellor can assess the emotional or behavioural issues or even refer the student to a psychologist (the intake form and methods of assessment are presented in Chapter 11). In-depth assessment helps the counsellor set goals and plan interventions. The earlier chapters presented detail the interventions for emotional relief, cognitive restructuring, and skills for motivating the clients. Interventions may be applied according to the need and requirements of the client. For example, in the case of Abhigna, who faced severe trauma and was totally withdrawn, she can be helped with play therapy and expressive art therapy (Chapter 5); this form of treatment is well suited for clients who are inept with words and have difficulty in communicating their feelings and emotions. Nonetheless, it is important that before any formal therapy, the counsellor gets a comprehensive understanding of the child's emotional state by 'listening to the emotions', communicating and responding to the non-verbal and verbal cues, helping the child ventilate the emotion by providing a safe and trustful platform is important. The alternative expressive technique that works immensely with children and adolescents is the scribble technique (Cane, 1983) which is an effective tool to tap the client's imagination and unconscious. In the scribble technique, the client is asked to draw a continuous fluid line without removing the pencil or crayon from the paper. When the client thinks the scribble is complete, he or she is asked to stop. The client can be asked to use colours to give some shapes and meaning to the scribble. The technique is non-threatening, wherein manifest content from shapes identified by the clients and the lines and structures of the scribbles are analysed to understand the client's issues. Working with clay, sand, and mural making are some other forms of art therapy. The technique of art therapy has already been described in Chapter 5.

Problems faced by children, and adolescents could be a product of their perceptions and thoughts. Students may have problems with their interpersonal interactions. For example, Rafik was a 9th-grade student interested in joining the basketball team to play for his school. He was a good player and had been a part of the basketball team in his previous school. When he was not selected for the team, he thought that his math teacher, who was a part of the selection panel, was responsible because he was not one of '*his favourites*' even in the math class. Ira, a 12-year-old, told the counsellor 'I have no friends. I think no one likes me because I am short and dark. All my classmates are very smart, and don't think I can match them'. Irrational thoughts and self-defeating behaviour exhibited by Rafik and Ira may lead to feelings of failure and dissatisfaction with life. REBT and CBT are effective approaches to dealing with such behaviour. One of the advantages of using REBT in a school counselling setup is that it is focused and can be carried out in a short period.

Reality therapy which is based on the concept of the choice theory developed by Glasser (1962), has been a well-used therapy for students and adolescents to improve relationships, which is one of the major issues during the adolescent period. The therapy is explained in detail in Chapter 2.

The aim of reality therapy is to assist the student to improve their choices and relationships. The association between choices and relationships is presented in Box 10.4. The choices of relationships in adolescents are based on individual needs. Counsellors can help adolescents understand their choices and behaviour and accept responsibility. Glasser's theory suggests that relationships can be improved when the 'seven unhealthy

Box 10.4 Association between Needs, Choices, and Relationships

- Choices are made consciously or unconsciously
- The basic needs of any individual are survival, belongingness, love, power, freedom, and fun
- Choices are made to fulfil the basic needs
- All behaviours are internally motivated and aim at satisfying the basic needs
- Individuals have the ability to accept responsibility for their actions and motivate others to do the same
- Individuals have the power to regulate their behaviour or choices but cannot have control over the behaviour of others
- Relationships get stronger when unpleasant behaviours become less prevalent

Box 10.5 Strengthening the Relationships by Replacing Unhealthy Habits with Caring Habits

Unhealthy Habits	*Caring Habits*
Criticising	Supporting
Blaming	Encouraging
Complaining	Listening
Nagging	Accepting
Threatening	Trusting
Punishing	Respecting
Bribing or rewarding to control	Negotiating differences

habits of external control' are substituted with 'seven caring habits of internal control' (Box 10.5).

By using internal control, individuals can stop attributing that others are the cause of their problems. By doing so, one can understand the consequence of their behaviour, and also develop accountability for their behaviour. Reality theory helps individuals to reflect on their relationships with others and, by doing so, helps them to make the right preferences.

Group counselling in schools

Schools are often burdened with issues that impact a large number of students. Group counselling makes it possible for the counsellor to address and assist a large group of children at one given point in time. While group counselling aims to address multiple students of similar age, similar issues, and similar goals, the developmental needs of the group should be taken into consideration. While group counselling has its underpinnings in Adlerian, Client Centred, Reality, Behaviour, and Cognitive theories, Pérusse et al. (2009) emanate that there are three major psychoeducational groups in schools:

1. Groups to encourage growth: Help students deal with the concerns related to physical growth and personal development, which include their day-to-day class activities, time management, learning styles, organising, prioritising, and setting goals.
2. Groups to improve the school environment: The goal of these groups is to improve the school climate. The main intention is to prevent undesirable activities such as bullying, intolerance, and immoral behaviours. Such groups also help students identify the risk behaviours and help them to deal with it. These groups can also support the school by conducting awareness programs for students.
3. Reformative groups: These groups assist students who have problems in their personal lives, which include abuse, grief, family problems which include conflict with parents and siblings, divorce, and separation.

School counsellors can effectively train, educate or develop the skills of students. Social skills, assertiveness, communication skills, peer and family relationships, problem-solving skills, setting boundaries, and teamwork are some of the topics that can be addressed in groups. Issues related to abuse, alcohol, drugs, suicide, sexual risk behaviours, and dating violence are sensitive and challenging topics and may need to be addressed in specific target groups.

Career Counselling

Madhav: *I really don't know if I have made the right decision. Everything seems to be out of my hands. I am not sure where I am heading to.*

Counsellor: *You think everything is out of your control, and you really seem to be upset.*

Madhav: *Yeah, I am in the second year of engineering, I joined engineering because my parents said this was more fetching, we can get a job immediately and also all my friends were here in this college. But now, nothing here interests me. I think I am not in the right place, and an engineer is not what I really want to be.*

Counsellor: *Madhav, you joined the engineering course because your father said it would get you to a good career, and your friends too were here, but you seem to be confused with your choice now.*

Madhav: *Yeah exactly, I really want to know if this is the career path I want to take or if I still have a chance to take up something that I am passionate about.*

A newspaper article in *Times of India* (2019) reports that India has more than 250 career options, and 93% of Indian students aged between 14 and 21 are aware of only seven options. A news article in *The Economic Times*, India (2022) reports that 71% of employees felt that they should rethink if they should remain in their career or choose a different one. 51% were wondering if their current job helps accomplish their goals, 67% questioned whether they are in the right job, and 61% even felt that there was a need to reprioritise the job so that life priorities can be achieved.

The above example and studies explicate the importance of career choices and the need for the right support and guidance. Academic and career decisions play a substantial role in a person's life. While the phase starts in childhood, as many children grow up idealising the professions of their parents or people whom they consider their role models, the real preparation for a career starts in early adolescence when academic decisions and goals are designed to accomplish career ambitions. Career decisions are largely influenced by family traditions, particularly in families where children are expected to follow the family career path or take over the family business. The other reasons for not exploring career choices are external influences, lack of planning and insight (Carpenter & Foster, 1977), or a compromise when no alternatives exist. Gati and Saka (2001) formulate that problems in career decision making arise due to three factors:

1. *Lack of readiness* which may be due to indecisiveness, lack of motivation, or dysfunctional beliefs.
2. *Lack of information* about self, the available career options and alternatives, or the process of decision making.
3. *Having inconsistent information* owing to internal and external conflicts and unreliable sources of information.

Career development is an ongoing process and needs constant evaluation at every stage of the lifespan. Choosing the right career that aligns with the aptitude, values, and interests of the individual has an immense influence on life satisfaction and overall well-being. A career counsellor helps clients explore, navigate, and strategise career goals and decisions. A career counsellor is trained to evaluate the client's personality, interests, abilities, values, and skills; assist the client in exploring career possibilities and alternatives; and help the clients choose a job where they can maximise the use of their abilities and competence.

The field is broad and encompasses student development, career placement, learning strategies, and career planning. The major perspectives of career counselling are:

- Help individuals gain awareness about their interests, aptitude, and values.
- Help individuals (students in schools) explore and gain knowledge about occupational opportunities.
- Help the individual plan their career and make the right decisions about the career which suits their interests, aptitude, and values.
- Help individuals manage their career paths and achieve positive professional growth at every stage of life.

Theories of Career Development

The theories of career development elucidate the relationship between the individual's personality, developmental factors, social and environmental factors, and the choice of career. Erik Erikson's (1980) theory of psychosocial development has made some significant contributions to the developmental perspective of career choice and vocational behaviour. In a longitudinal study, Valliant and Valliant (1981) found that successful resolution of 'industry vs. inferiority' was correlated with career adjustment, career satisfaction and positive psychological health and well-being. James Marcia's theory of identity development (Marcia et al., 1993) can be well used to explain the career decision-making process. Exploration and commitment lead to identity achievement and are the prerequisites of career decision making, but the inability of the adolescent to explore the various career options and make the right commitment leaves them in a state of confusion. Exploration is a process of a thorough examination of one's values, interests, abilities, and commitment is a way of making the right choices of behaviours that are supportive in achieving career goals. The accurate use of exploration and commitment helps the individual to achieve the right career path. Career counsellors can understand the identity status of the clients and help them explore their career choices.

Trait-and-Factor Theory

Frank Parsons (1909) assumed that client characteristics should be analysed first and then methodically matched with features inherent in various occupations. The three main factors that influence career decisions (Parsons, 1909), are an in-depth understanding of:

- Self which includes one's skills, interests, resources, and weaknesses.
- The needs, conditions for success, benefits and drawbacks, pay, opportunities, and prospects in various professions.
- A precise reasoning about the relationships between the two groups.

This theory emphasises the interpersonal nature of occupations, associated lifestyles, as well as job requirements. Whilst the theory was initially strongly supported, the decade of the 1950s saw the development of other modern theories in career counselling.

John Holland's Theory of Vocational Personalities and Work Environment

A hexagonal model developed by Holland (1997) illustrates the relationship between personality types and workplace settings. The theories comprise six personality types and relate them to the various occupations (Figure 10.1). Higher the congruence between the personality type and the work environment higher the work satisfaction.

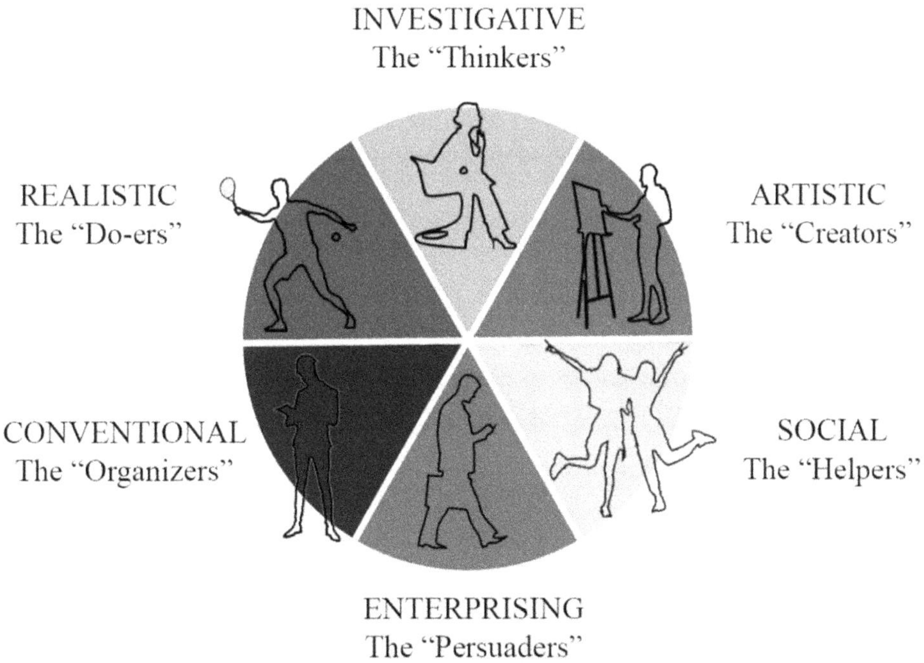

Figure 10.1 John Holland's Hexagonal Model of Career Development

According to Holland's typology, most people come under one of the six modal personality types: 1. The investigative type are the individuals who have intellectual, scientific, and analytical skills; 2. The artistic type, are individuals who possess creatine, aesthetic and imaginative skills; 3. The social type are individuals who are service oriented, social worker, counsellors, police; 4. The enterprising individuals who have skills of persuasion, are outgoing, and have good verbal skills, business executives, lawyer; 5. Conventional individuals are practical and organised, they conform to the job given to them, bank officers, data entry; 6. Realistic individuals are skilled in working with machines, tools, plants, and animals and are practical. Congruence between the personality type and the work environment enhances career satisfaction and success. John Holland's model has been used in individual and group career counselling in different cultural contexts. The theory not only helps people to make career decisions but also predict the manner in which individuals would cope with job change and adjustment.

Anne Roe's Psychodynamic Theory

The psychodynamic theory of career development (Roe, 1966) states that a child's occupational choice will depend on early childhood experiences. Vocational interest develops as a result of the interaction between parents and their children and an individual makes a career choice to satisfy the needs not met by the parents in his/her childhood. Unconscious motivation from childhood experiences influences the choice of careers where these needs can be expressed or gratified. There are three different types of parent-child relationship climates, and each of these leads to individuals getting oriented towards self, others, or towards self and others.

- Emotional concentration on the child leads to parental behaviour as: a) overprotection which increases dependency; b) over demanding, which stresses on achievement. Children who are subjected to emotional concentration choose careers that provide recognition from others, such as performing arts.
- Avoidance of the child leads to parental behaviour as: a) neglectful parents who make little effort to satisfy needs and b) rejecting parents who make no effort to satisfy needs. Children subjected to avoidance concentrate on careers that involve scientific and mechanical interests.
- Parents who accept their child are loving and encourage independence, individuals choose careers where they can balance their personal and professional life, they choose careers such as teaching or counselling.

Though the theory emphasises that the satisfaction of needs determines the degree of motivation, it does not include the socio-economic factors and the individual aptitude, interest, and values which are strong determinants of career decisions.

Ginzberg's Theory of Career Development

Ginzberg et al. (1966) regarded professional development as a lifelong process. The theory was constructed on the premise that career decisions and career development are an ongoing process and involve numerous factors. Figure 10.2 gives a description of Ginzberg's theory.

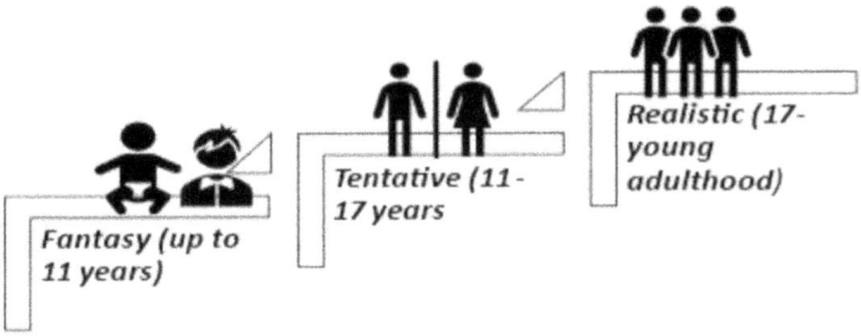

Figure 10.2 Ginzberg's Theory of Career Development

The theory postulates that there are three stages or phases involved in making a career decision:

Fantasy (up to 11 years): This is a stage of pretend or imaginative play. Children during this stage imitate the roles in various occupations, and later they try to perform the act, which the authors call a transition from playful imitation to work imitation.

Tentative (11–17 years): The adolescent is now aware of the career requirements and, at the same time, understands his own abilities, interests, and values. Early and middle adolescents understand that skills are essential to make a career choice and hence start identifying his/her abilities to relate them to the career, and values to prioritise the career choices. The process occurs by late adolescence, which is the transition period and the adolescent is ready to shoulder responsibilities and exercise choices.

Realistic (17–young adulthood): This stage can be called the integration period. Young adults narrow down their career options according to their interests. The sub-phases of this stage are exploration, crystallisation, and specification. By the end of these phases the individual makes a commitment to their career choice.

Donald Super's Theory of Career Development

Super (1990) recognised this theory as a 'lifespan view of career development'. The career phases of an individual include a job, position, activities, and occupations in the entire lifetime. The theory explains the progress of one's self-concept, which occurs as a result of an interaction between personal experiences and career choices. The stages are represented as 'the life career rainbow' (Figure 10.3) which included the five major stages of lifespan as described below:

- Stage 1 Growth (up to 15 years): The period of growth includes the individual's understanding of his/her abilities, attitudes, needs, and values. The development of the self-concept occurs during this stage, increased personal control and competency play a major role in the development of self-concept.
- Stage 2 Exploration (15–24 years): The important task of this period is to 'try out' the work interests through hobbies. The three important phases of this stage are *crystallisation* or developing and planning goals, a *specification* that includes converting general preferences to specific choices, and *implementation* of preferences through appropriate training and getting to the job position.

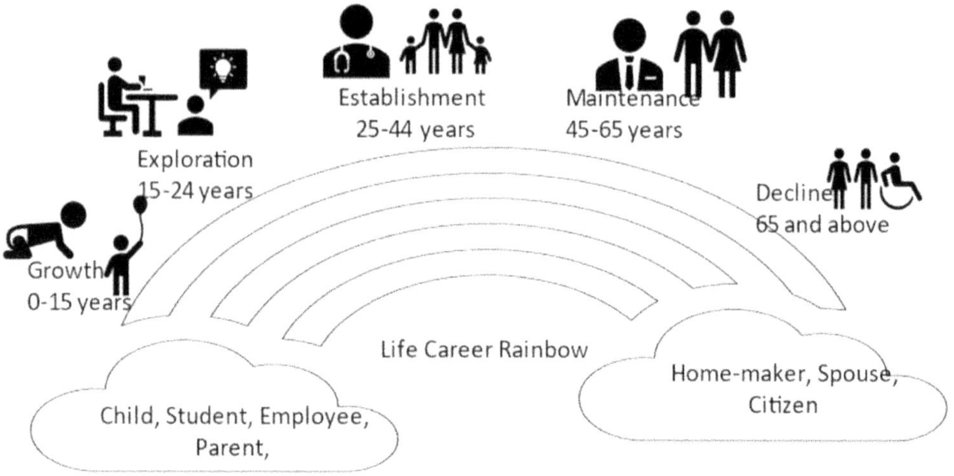

Figure 10.3 Donald Super's Life Career Rainbow

- Stage 3 Establishment (25–44 years): Having gained the job, the task now is to secure and stabilise the position, adjust to the work environment and culture, perform the duties, consolidate one's position, develop positive relationships with colleagues and prepare oneself for new responsibilities.
- Stage 4 Maintenance (45–65 years): The individual tasks are to adjust, hold the position and keep innovating at work. Since it's a stage of striving, maintaining, and facing new challenges, the individual is required to keep appraising themselves.
- Stage 5 Decline (65 and above): A period of transition when the individual is moving out to retire from responsibilities. The important tasks are to disengage and plan for retirement and face the new challenges of retired life.

The theory emphasises the tasks of the individual at various stages of the lifespan, which gives career counsellors the advantage of working with children and adults.

Socio-Cognitive Career Theory

The theory was developed on the basis of social-cognitive theory of Bandura (1989), which integrates cognitive, self-regulation, and motivational processes. The theory aims to identify the actual mediators which play a role in altering the learning experiences and impacting career behaviour. The theory is based on the causality model and, explains how variables like personal and physical attributes, environmental factors, and overt behaviour, interact with one another and influence individual growth. In addition to the genetic determinants, the course of career development is based on three important personal factors, viz. self-efficacy, outcome expectancy, and personal goals which are considered the building blocks. When all other aspects are constant, individuals with high self-efficacy and high ability perform to the highest level. The theory is significant in career counselling as it postulates a strong relationship between self-efficacy and interests. Interests can be developed either through motivation, or by performing activities that the individual considers himself/herself to be competent, or by a simpler method like modelling.

Marriage and Family Counselling

Rajshri: *I and Ravi got engaged last week. It's an arranged marriage and the wedding is going to be after two months. I am happy that I am getting married into a good family, and Ravi is a nice guy and well-settled. But I am very anxious. I know him just for two weeks, and I am apprehensive about my decision. I hope everything will be fine.*

Karisma and Adil had been married for the past four years. Both had good jobs in multinational companies and were doing very well. Just about two months ago, they decided to part ways. They had a difference of opinion on having a child. Karisma felt that if she had a child now she will have to dump her career and Adil was insisting that they have a child before they cross the age of 35 years.

Madhavi: *My husband and I are very upset with our daughter. Every time she comes home, it ends up in some sort of conflict. She comes home late almost every day, if we question her, she says she has been doing group study. I don't believe what she says. We are really worried.*

In the examples presented above we can understand how a change in the marriage system, changes in family roles, and changes in values have led to stress and conflicts in families. The cases illustrate that every stage of the family cycle comes with its own external and internal demands. Marriage, the birth of a child, children growing up and leaving home, retirement, ageing, death of a spouse or a family member, and divorce are some of the transitions in an individual's life span. Each of these changes comes up either with some virtues or crisis. The manner in which families handle the crisis or appreciate the virtues depends on how each member of the family has evolved through lifespan in the various interconnected areas such as the sociocultural and spiritual factors, the familial factors which include the beliefs shared by the family, and the decision-making process and finally the personal factors which include the personal beliefs accumulated from the childhood, in case of the parents (Dallos & Draper, 2015). The other factors which contribute to the management of problems in a family are power play and power distribution, which comprises the decision making, and performance of various duties and responsibilities; the emotional aspects including affection and intimacy and the beliefs about privacy and personal space. Over the centuries the family system has gone through several changes and these changes have impacted families and family members on various fronts. Changes in the family system in the 20th Century can be accounted to urbanisation, globalisation, and the mobility of people across continents. The traditional Indian family system which was considered to have a potential therapeutic power (Sethi, 1989), has now been replaced with nuclear families, as a result of which families have lost all the major paybacks of this system. Traditional Indian families had the unique potential of having a therapeutic milieu. The family provided social support, emotional interdependence, trust in one another, division of work, and values. Sethi (1989) adds that along with the strong emotional bond that families had, the role of the elders in disseminating religious and social values is no more available to the newer generations, and hence the deep sense of collectiveness no longer exists. The disintegration of the family, the lack of social support and the absence of someone to provide the emotional balm could be some of the reasons for the need for marriage, couple, and family counselling. The origin of marriage, couple, and family counselling can be traced to the early 20th Century. Changes in the traditional expectations in a family, changes in family roles, dual career couples, and changes in values and goals have resulted in conflicts, stress, and friction between family members. Lack of trust and the non-availability of a family member to share and emotionally ventilate have augmented the need for seeking help outside the family.

When an individual comes for therapy or counselling, the therapist takes into perspective not just the individual who comes with a problem but also tries to get to the origin of the problem, the pattern of relationships he/she has with the members of the family, the satisfaction of emotional needs, the communication patterns, the availability of support and the role of each member of the family. Understanding family dynamics gives a holistic approach to counselling and planning interventions. This takes us to the definition of marriage counselling and family therapy. Marriage and family counselling overlap each other and hence will be discussed parallelly.

Family therapy, also known as a couple and family therapy or family systems therapy, works with families and couples who have a discord and work in close relationships with them to promote growth and transformation. It tends to see change through the lens of family interaction systems and highlights the importance of family bonding in psychological well-being. Family therapy seeks to change the interaction between family members while also improving an individual's functioning that entails one to working as a group with the family. The goal of family counselling is to help the individual gain insight into the problems, facilitate a positive change; improve communication; improve the expression of thoughts and feelings; promote optimal functioning of the individual as well as the family as a whole. The major difference between family therapy and individual therapy can be explained as follows. According to family therapy external influences have a significant effect on personality development and the lives of family members, while individual therapy assumes that internal or intrapsychic thoughts, feelings, and conflicts are the key components of personality development.

Approaches to Family Therapy

Broadly, family therapies can be divided into three categories: theories that focus on behaviour patterns: The Mental research Institute's (MRI) brief therapy, strategic family therapy, structural family therapy, cognitive behavioural marital therapy, and functional family therapy; theories that focus on belief systems: epistemology, constructivism, postmodernism, Milan systemic therapy, solution-focused therapy, narrative therapy; and theories that focus on contexts: psychoanalytic family therapy, attachment-based family therapies, experiential family therapies.

Some of the above-mentioned family therapies are discussed in the following section.

Theories that Focus on Behaviour Patterns

MRI BRIEF THERAPY

The MRI brief therapy was developed at the Mental Research Institute, and the contributors are Jackson et al. (1952). It is a short-term therapy with the central idea is that unsuccessful attempts to solve problems ultimately lead to the continuation of the problems. Hence the assessment is focused on tracking both the repetitive behaviour patterns and the unproductive attempts to solve them and provide interventions to disrupt the problem behaviour patterns. For example, while a mother who is continuously worried about her adolescent son and is suspicious that he is into the wrong friendship, starts trailing him, however the child becomes more and more secretive and stops sharing any of his whereabouts which makes the mother more intrusive. Here the mother's trailing the child is an ineffective solution to her worry.

Assessment in MRI brief therapy: MRI therapy distinguishes clients as: 'customers' who have a commitment towards resolving the problem. For example, a wife who wants to sort out the issues between her and her husband and refine their relationship; and 'window-shopper' a person who attends therapy to satisfy someone (for example, an alcoholic husband who comes for therapy to satisfy his wife and has no intention to resolve the problem). The interview which is a part of the assessment is essentially conducted for the customer and not the entire family. Assessment is majorly related to identifying the repetitive problem that is responsible for maintaining behaviour patterns and also the ineffective solutions which are being used. The therapist also takes the help of the client to identify others who are trapped in this repetitive cycle of interaction. According to this theory, ineffective solutions fall into four major categories:

1. *Force oneself or others to deliberately be spontaneous*, e.g., force another family member to spontaneously feel love or respect for another.
2. *Employ risk-free solutions*, e.g., trying to cope with the anxiety of writing an exam by avoiding writing it.
3. *Using argument to resolve conflict.*
4. *Confirming an accuser's suspicions by defending oneself.* When a husband is accused of being aloof, he retorts defensively, confirming his wife's suspicions.

The goal of the therapy is to set minimalist goals and acknowledge the smallest noticeable changes. Acknowledging small achievements sends positive feedback to the client, and helps them maintain the behaviour. Interventions are more towards restraining the use of ineffective solutions and reframing the problem behaviour patterns. The MRI brief therapy is useful in dealing with behavioural and relationship problems.

STRATEGIC FAMILY THERAPY

Strategic family therapy developed by Haley (1963) assumes that families are hesitant to change because the problems serve some significant interpersonal functions for some members of the family. The therapist looks at the strengths of the family and those aspects which are healthy. For example the therapist focuses on love, symmetrical and complementary transactions, flexible management of transitions, and takes note of unhealthy functioning leading to pathological triangles. The goal of therapy is to address the problem, use family's strengths and bring about a change in the dysfunctional or problematic behaviour. Assessment involves identifying the specific problem for which the family seeks assistance, clarifying the interaction pattern surrounding the problem, clarifying the role of hierarchical incongruities, checking for lifecycle 'stuckness', and exclusive reliance on symmetrical or complementary transactions in this cycle. The therapist also assesses how the family handles power issues, the need to be loved and protected, and to repent and forgive for mistakes or shortcomings is also discussed. The treatment or intervention of strategic family therapy is oriented towards reframing problems so that there is an interruption in the interaction pattern which is responsible for the current problem. The majority of therapy sessions revolve around reframing the problem, changing the roles in pathological triangles, empowering the family, and reviewing progress. Strategic family therapy works well with children with behaviour problems, adolescents, sexual abuse, and marital problems.

STRUCTURAL FAMILY THERAPY

Structural family therapy was developed by Minuchin in 1974. Structural family therapy is used in delinquency, eating disorders, and alcoholics. Minuchin postulates that there are two types of families: enmeshed families who are emotionally connected and disengaged families that are not at all close. The primary principle of structural family therapy is that poor family organisational structures may jeopardise a family's ability to handle the problems that come with life transitions or the 'intrafamilial' or 'extrafamilial' stresses. Structural family therapists usually become a part of the family and work with families to understand their structure and the difficulties that the family has in resolving the problems. Assessment includes mapping the family structure and taking note of the rigid or diffused boundaries of parents and children, the role flexibility, and how the family members engage with each other. The preferred transaction patterns of family members, their sensitivity to the needs of others, behaviours, and attitudes of family members are also assessed. In the first session, the therapist invites those members of the family who may be most pertinent to resolve the problem. The mutual goal is to eliminate the problem. Interventions include restructuring family relations using role plays and helping the family members to use their own resources to reframe the problem. The techniques include working on boundaries which could be either too flexible or too rigid, establishing new boundaries, modifying the routines to improve the family functioning and working on the power dynamics.

Theories that Focus on Belief Systems

SOLUTION-FOCUSED BRIEF THERAPY

Solution-Focused Brief Therapy (SFBT) developed by de Shazer et al. (1985) is explained in detail in Chapter 2. The therapy concentrates on clients' strengths and earlier successes, problem-solving rather than solution-building, and a positive mindset. Clients are viewed as competent, healthy, and resourceful, with an ability to find solutions to their problems; creating solutions is more important than talking about the problem. The basic premise of the therapy is the client's desired future, not past issues or current problems. The therapist believes that no problem occurs on a consistent basis, and there are exceptions or situations in which the problem could have occurred but did not. Both the client and the therapist use this principle to generate solutions. The therapist operates from a 'not knowing position' and creates a climate of mutual respect. The relationship between the client and the therapist can be of three different kinds: a *customer type* – where the client is willing to work with the therapist to identify a problem and look for a solution; *complainant type* – a client who talks about the problem but is unable or unwilling to participate in developing a solution, he/she expects the other person to evolve a solution; *the visitor* – clients who seek treatment because someone else believes they have a problem, while they disagree about the fact that they have an issue. These positions are not fixed and keep changing. A customer may change into a complainant or a visitor and vice-versa. The therapist uses future-oriented questions to understand the problem and create the goals. Examples of future-oriented questions are given below:

- *'What will you notice when the problem is better?'*
- *'How will things be different when the problem no longer exists?'*
- *'What will you be doing differently when things are better?'*
- *'What will you be doing instead?'*
- *'How will your parents/friends tell you that things are going better?'*
- *'How will others tell when the problem is better? Tell me more about that'.*

The major interventions of solution-focused brief therapy are:

- A positive solution-focused stance: The session starts on a positive note, with a belief that individuals are resilient and they use this resilience to make changes. Resistance in clients is viewed as a way of natural protection, or the clients need to be cautious before revealing his/her problem.
- Looking for previous solutions: Every individual has resolved problems at any given point in his/her life. This may have happened at a different time, in a different place, or in a different situation. Resolving a difficulty, even if only temporarily is seen as a strength, and the therapist uses this strength to deal with the present problem.
- Looking for exceptions: An exception is something that occurs instead of the problem. It could be an event or experience where a problem should or would have occurred but has not occurred. Instead of the problem, an exception would have occurred with or without the client's knowledge or consent. An exception can also be a solution or strategy which the family has tried in the past and has worked for the family. Either the family would not have used this strategy again or they would have forgotten it. The therapist looks into these situations and strategies and tries to use them for the current problem. Since the strategies have worked earlier the client is familiar with them and also feels motivated because they have shown positive results earlier. Exception questions help the client to identify situations when things have be different for them. Here are some questions used to check for exceptions, the client is the husband who is planning for divorce but wants to see the counsellor before making a decision.

    Tell me about times when the issues between you and your wife were less troubling or when there were no issues between you both.

    Tell me about the times when you were able to handle things better even when there were arguments between you.

    Tell me what has worked between you and your wife in the past even if only for a short time.

    Tell me about a time when you felt very happy in your relationship.

    Tell me about a time when something you never expected worked for you, though you were quite surprised about it.

    Tell me about a time when you were not angry with your wife.

- Questioning is present- and future-focused: SFBT therapists pay attention to the present or the future. The emphasis is entirely on what is happening in the client's life now and what he wants for his future. The basic premise is that problems can be managed by focusing on looking at solutions that are working in the present rather than the difficulties of the past. The questions are also related to how clients want their future lives to be.

- Gentle nudging to motivate clients to look at what is working: Once SFBT therapists have established a positive frame through compliments or previous solutions and exceptions to the problem, they gently nudge the client to do more of what has previously worked, or to try changes, referred to as 'an experiment'. Therapists do not recommend or assign tasks that are not based on the client's past solutions or exceptions. Alternate ideas and assignments that come from the client, indirectly during the talk, are taken into account because these behaviours are recognised and presented by the client and not by the therapist.
- Miracle questions: Clients struggle to set clear goals. A miracle question is a method of asking the client to set goals in such a way that the client's fear about the intensity of the problem is taken into prevue, and at the same time the therapist uses prompts to help the client come up with smaller, more doable goals. The client also gets a chance to visualise the desired future. Examples of miracle questions to a woman who has conflicts with her mother and the mother doesn't interact with her.

  'Imagine you woke up tomorrow morning and you found that your mother come to greet you with a smile and a hot cup of coffee. She sits beside you and initiates a conversation'.

  This is followed by questions like:

  'What difference would you (and others) notice?'
  'What would you need to make this happen?'

- Scaling questions: Scaling questions help the client to perceive their problem and place it on a continuum and tell its intensity. They are easy and quick to ask and help in finding out the magnitude of the issue, check the levels of motivation, and defuse intense emotions or an emotionally charged atmosphere. Examples of scaling questions:

  On a scale of zero to 10, where zero is the worst you have been and 10 represents the problem being solved, how do you rate your anxiety right now?

Example: The conversation is about a couple who have difficulty in communicating, they end up in an argument.

Therapist:	*I want you to scale your problem as it stands today, on a scale of 1–10, where 1 is you never talk, argue or end up fighting, and 10 is the perfect communication, where you are able to convey what you want and don't end up in a fight.*
Husband:	*I would put my situation on 1. I don't think we ever have communicated properly with each other.*
Wife:	*I would rate my problem at 2.*
Therapist:	*Ok that seems a reasonable answer. Now I want to ask, tell me where you want to place yourself in terms of your communication, by the end of the therapy.*
Husband:	*I will be happy if I am at 7.*
Wife:	*8 will be good for me.*

Scaling questions can also be asked when a client is struggling to identify goals or exceptions to their problem.

What number were you at when the problem was at its worst?
What will you notice if you moved up one or two numbers towards your goal?

Coping questions: therapist asks clients about how they are coping with their current problems; these questions are called the 'coping questions'. The same case of the couple who decided to take a divorce is taken as an example:

In spite of the conflicts between you and your wife, there must be something that keeps you going. Can you tell me what is it?
How do you manage a day when there are many issues going on?
Who is the one person who is of great support? What is it from them which is helpful?
You said last year you both decided to live separately because things were not going well, but you still managed to stay together. What made you stay together?
Sometimes problems tend to get worse, what do you do that stops it from getting worse?

SFBT and its practice in family therapy are well-researched. Various techniques like compliments, which are empathetic statements reflecting the client's positive qualities help clients in mutual collaboration, between the therapist and client. The important intervention used is the observational task, where clients are asked to observe the occurrence of successful coping, any exception that has occurred or any factors that prevent the situation from deterioration of the problem; A positive perspective of the problem resolution, respect for the client's resources, continued encouragement by looking for exceptions and miracle situations are the strengths of solution focus brief therapy.

NARRATIVE THERAPY

Narrative therapy, developed by Harper (2009), was derived from the post-modern theory, explained in detail in Chapter 2. Individuals are viewed as having the capacity to recognise their potential, find solutions to their problems and create alternate stories to change their lives. Narrative therapy is based on the assumption that an individual's life is a story, and his or her identity is generated through the story. Problems have to be deconstructed or externalised as the problem is a problem and people are not problems. The therapist and the client work collaboratively, and the client takes responsibility for the therapeutic process. The therapy is based on the premise that healthy families have narratives about the empowerment of their families. While in unhealthy families the dominant narratives are about entrapment and there is no possibility of a narrative of empowerment.

During the assessment, the therapist helps the family member to identify the problem and look at a unique situation where the problem has not occurred in the family. The goal of the therapy is to prompt the family member to restate the narratives or stories in a positive way where the client's strengths are highlighted. He/she is helped to remodel the perceptions of himself/herself and their family member/members and to rework or change their life narratives. Therapists encourage the family member to recreate new narratives with new experiences and new possibilities that are unique to them.

Interventions: the client comes with problem-saturated stories, and the therapist uses the helping skills to listen to the narratives and help him/her to externalise the problem and view themselves as competent individuals. Roth and Epston (1996) state that 'externalising helps people experience themselves as separate from the problem'. When the client identifies that the problem is external to his self-identity and separate from the core self, he/she is able to change the perspective of the problem and this helps to counteract the effects of labelling. In narrative therapy, the past is looked at only to examine the unique outcomes or use of strengths. These unique outcomes or strengths are used to remind clients that there were times when despite the problem, they had the resource to overcome it and create new personal stories. Once the client has rewritten the stories, he/she is helped to express the new personal narrative to other people. This method of 'spreading the news' reaffirms the new view of him/herself and recognises the new change. Narrative therapy is useful in addressing trauma, as in the case of child sexual abuse or when clients blame themselves and their addictions. Narrative therapy is also used in addressing depression and anxiety in adults and improving social skills in children and adolescents. Narrative therapy is found to improve communication patterns among married women thus enhancing marital satisfaction (Ghavibazou et al., 2020)

The other therapies used in family and marital counselling are Milan's structural therapy, attachment-based family therapy, psychodynamic marital therapy, and experiential marital therapy, some of which have been explained in Chapter 2. The major goal of marital and family therapy is to increase the reciprocity between the couple or between the members of the family. Major areas which the therapist focuses on are communication between the members of the family which is the key concept. It has its influence on the other aspects of the family socialisation, relationships with children, relationships among siblings, money and finance, household chores, sexual life, and conflict resolution. The common steps of marital counselling are:

- Joining and accommodation: In the first stage is also called attending and setting the agenda wherein the therapist explores the problem, understands the family life cycle and dynamics, (a genogram is very helpful here) notes the narratives of each family member, and looks into the legal aspects of the problem in case of divorce or child custody. The therapist uses circular questions to elicit responses. Circular questions are questions to check the validity of a hypothesis about the family dynamics or the family system. Example:

    What happened next? – a question to check the sequence of interactions.
    Who was the most concerned out of all? – to check about the comparison.
    Who would agree and who would disagree with this point? – to check the agreement.
    What explanation will your family member (mother/father/wife/daughter/son) give for this?
    While using circular questions the therapist will observe who is interacting, interrupting, blaming, listening, and who does most of the talking.

- Assessment: Includes the interactions and behaviours of the family members, emotional expression and its effect on other members, family organisation, rules, expectations, roles, and boundaries are taken into account, the resources and strengths available,

along with the risks or weakness in the family. The therapist may use self-reports, observation methods, or visual devices like a genogram or an ecomap.
- Planning the interventions based on the assessment. Interventions are planned based on the approach adopted by the therapist. Interventions can include, the demonstration of appropriate or inappropriate feelings through role plays, helping the couple or family engage in recreation or a desired engagement with the family members, and a contingency contract which is a regular review.
- Termination and follow up.

Counselling in the Healthcare Setting

Physical illness can intensify psychological symptoms like stress, anxiety, trauma or depression, necessitating immediate intervention. Any disease or physical ailment can have its impression on the psychological and social spheres of the individual thus causing impairment in the individual's day-to-day functioning. The biopsychosocial model of health states that an illness or disease should be addressed beyond the biomedical perspective, and the psychosocial aspects of health need to be taken into perspective while treating a patient.

In the case of Harish, recognising the complex interaction between the physical, psychological, behavioural, and social needs is important while treating a patient. While his medical and physiological health is taken care of by the medical care professional, an intervention of a health psychologist or a counsellor will effectively resolve his psychosocial issues.

Counselling in healthcare settings is gaining prominence in recent times. The advances in behavioural medicine are paving the way towards holistic health care, and emphasising the role of a psychologist in the healthcare setting. The COVID-19 pandemic is one of the greatest examples to demonstrate the need for an intervention from a health psychologist when physical health escalates the psychological symptoms. Health Psychologists and counsellors in healthcare settings have a diverse role to play which extends from assessment and diagnosis of psychological and behavioural problems to providing interventions. The role of a Health Psychologist or a counsellor in a healthcare setting

Box 10.6 Case Study

Harish is a 60-year-old patient who had a stroke, which caused paralysis affecting the entire left side of his body. Harish was treated by the best doctors in a renowned hospital. Before his discharge doctors informed him about his medication and also recommended physiotherapy for enhancing functionality. The entire stay in the hospital was highly traumatic for Harish. It was an emergency admission into the hospital post the stroke, and he gained consciousness in the ICU. As he realised that he was unable to move one side of his body he was highly distressed, he was in a vulnerable state when he found himself at the mercy of the medical care professional for his functional needs. Even after he was back home, he re-experienced all the events of the hospital stay. At home, he found that his facial deformity and the limitations in his movements were impacting not just his functionality but also his interpersonal communication and his self-image.

is diverse. They provide individual counselling, group counselling, assessment, intervention, consultation, grief counselling and crisis intervention. In the next section, we will be discussing the diverse role of a Health Psychologist and a counsellor in a healthcare setting.

Professional Competencies for Counselling in Health Settings

Before discussing the nature of counselling in a healthcare setting it is important to understand the professional competencies required for counselling in a healthcare sector. The Arden House Conference (1983) and the Tempe Summit on Education and Training in Clinical Health Psychology (2007) delineated the distinctive competencies of health psychologists. Health Psychologists should have the knowledge and skills in the following core areas: (a) physiology of health and disease; (b) psychosocial factors of health and diseases; (c) health assessment, consultation, intervention, and evaluation; (d) health policy and the healthcare societies; the interdisciplinary nature of health and the need for multidisciplinary approach; (f) ethical, legal, and professional issues; and (g) healthcare research. Health Psychologists should obtain supervised training in providing interventions to patients and also have training in professional counselling to embrace all the characteristics of a professional counsellor. In addition, there are other specific qualities that are important for a professional health psychologist (Belar & Deardorff, 1995) some of the qualities are tolerance towards frustration; a conviction to work with physically ill patients; avoidance of fervent beliefs; tolerance to work for a demanding schedule; capacity do deal with reluctant and unreceptive patients; ability to integrate diverse conceptual models; and accepting interdependency of work.

Individuals visit a hospital to get treated when they are diagnosed with a disease. While the disease is 'an identifiable condition affecting an organ', an illness is the *patient's experience* of this physical or psychological disturbance or the disease. An illness gives rise to subjective feelings which may be physical such as pain or discomfort or psychological for example anxiety, fear, depression, etc. The symptoms of the illness may be differently perceived, evaluated, and acted upon by different kinds of people. While acute illnesses begin rapidly, have a short duration (<3 months) and are diagnosed accurately, the onset of chronic illness is gradual, the course is long, indefinite and uncertain which calls for long-term care and management. The next section of this chapter will be dealing with the factors associated with chronic illness and the need for counselling and intervention.

PSYCHOSOCIAL ISSUES IN A HEALTHCARE SETTING

Patients get admitted to a hospital with a chronic illness such as cardiac disease, cancer, or severe acute illness e.g., bronchitis, a case of dengue, surgery, or a terminal illness. Any of these illnesses have their associated psychosocial factors. For a counsellor, it is important to understand the psychosocial correlates of the illness and provide the necessary counselling and intervention. In a healthcare setting, patients with chronic illnesses have the most complicated issues which require day-to-day management, and a collaborative approach from different healthcare professionals, doctors, physiotherapists, nutritionists, psychologists, social workers, and so on. Chronic illnesses have a long-term progressive course, they are intrusive into the lives of the patient and family, and there is a chance of relapse and remission, as in the case of cancer or heart disease. Chronic illnesses are also accompanied by many other psychosocial and behavioural outcomes like anxiety, depression, dependency, uncertainty, loss of control, stigma, and isolation. These outcomes can be divided into three categories (Hariharan, 2020):

- Cognitive: Patient's knowledge, illness cognition, and perception of symptoms.
- Affective: The affective state can be explained by the direct and indirect association between chronic illness and negative emotions (Hariharan,2020), the direct association is the emotional state produced by the disease itself, for example, hormonal change, as in the case of diseases like polycystic ovarian disease, and the indirect association is the emotional state owing to one, the physical constraints which are the result of the illness. For example, restriction of movement due to paralysis, as stated in case of Harish, or the emotional state which is the result of some continuous permanent changes, as in case of patients with cardiovascular diseases or diabetes, where the patient has to make changes in his/her lifestyle, like the restriction of salt, sugar, or restriction in the quantity of food, or even giving up smoking or alcohol. The uncertainty about the disease condition or prognosis also creates negative emotions like worry, anxiety, and apprehension.
- Behavioural: Low work efficiency, and withdrawal from professional or recreational activities are the result of loss of control of self and environment, helplessness powerlessness, and vulnerability. Some of the after-effects of treatment like loss of hair or mastectomy in cancer patients has an impact on the self-image leading to isolation of self.

ASSESSMENT OF THE PSYCHOSOCIAL FACTORS

Assessment can also include understanding the functional and psychosocial state of the patient. An initial assessment is made by looking into the modifiable and non-modifiable factors that are impacting the illness. These factors may slightly vary from disease to disease but in general, there are several factors that may be common to many diseases. Some of the factors are highlighted in Box 10.7.

Clinical interviews, case reports, checklists, psychological tests to measure, personality, anxiety, depression, trauma, pain, locus of control, self-efficacy, social support, optimism, adjustment to illness, and coping are useful to understand the psychological or emotional state of the patient, behavioural aspects such as adherence to diet, medication, exercise, and sleep status. There are specific scales available for a specific disease.

Box 10.7 Modifiable and Non-Modifiable Factors of Illness

Non-Modifiable Factors	*Modifiable Factors*
Age	Overweight and obesity
Gender	Smoking
Heredity or genetic composition	Alcohol
Race or ethnicity	Sedentary lifestyle
	Diet
	Blood pressure

For example cancer-specific, diabetic-specific, and scales for arthritis are in vogue. Assessment helps the health psychologist to understand the nature of the disease and its trajectory, the effect of the healthcare setting on the patient, the presence of any psychological symptoms, the availability of resources like social support, and coping skills. Integrating all the information that is received from the initial assessment, the health psychologist should be able to get answers to the following questions.

1. How does the patient deal with pain, immobility, and other physical functions?
2. How is the patient coping with the hospital environment, the treatment procedures, and the medical professionals?
3. What is the psychological state of the patient?
4. What are the coping strategies of the patient?
5. Is the patient keeping in touch with family and friends?
6. How is the patient reacting to discharge or recovery?

Based on the clinical interview and the psychological test reports interventions can be planned. As mentioned in the previous sections, interventions are planned according to the needs of the patient. The therapeutic approach used will also depend on the category in which the disease outcome falls. All in all, the interventions planned should address the psychosocial and behavioural aspects of the illness, optimise functionality, and enhance the quality of life of the patient. Some of the interventions are underlined below.

PSYCHOEDUCATION

The right knowledge and information help patients cope with stressful medical procedures. There are two kinds of information that can be given to the patient: procedural information and sensory information. Procedural information refers to the medical diagnosis, procedures, or medication, whereas sensory information refers to the feelings or experiences the patient may undergo during or after the procedure. Sensory information is a crucial element to prepare the patient, especially in case of surgery or a procedure.

INDIVIDUAL COUNSELLING

Individual counselling works well with patients. However, counsellors should understand the physical state of the patient before starting a session. Developing rapport, and empathy will help in building trust on the basis of which the sessions can be taken forward. The set of skills and the approaches mentioned in the earlier chapters can be used by counsellors to provide individual counselling. Individual counselling can include behavioural and cognitive interventions. Cognitive restructuring, removing negative schemas, using shaping for behaviour change, and systematic desensitisation are some of the interventions. Relaxation trading, guided imagery, progressive muscular relaxation, and *yoganidra* help patients who are anxious and stressed. Relaxation training procedures are useful for patients with hypertension, migraine, irritable bowel syndrome, and insomnia. Though these procedures are well tested the health psychologist or the counsellor should have the knowledge and training to use the procedure. Behaviour techniques like contingency management help to increase adaptive behaviours. These techniques are helpful in paediatric and adolescent health care and also in modifying behaviours like diet, exercise, and smoking. Counsellors can make good use of play therapy, expressive art therapy and bibliotherapy to treat children in paediatric intensive care units, paediatric cancer units and paediatric medical care units.

SUPPORT GROUPS

Support groups work well in a hospital setting. Group discussions allow patients with similar illnesses to meet one another and share their concerns, experiences, anxieties, and coping mechanisms, as well as gather knowledge about the illness from those who have experienced it.

Counselling for Caregivers and Care Providers

Caregiving is a service provided to a patient with a chronic illness or disability. In most cases, the caregiver is a close family member who provides a voluntary service to the patient. In the entire process of caregiving, the contributions and needs of the caregiver are often overlooked and leave them in a state of physical and mental distress. Caregiving includes assistance given to the chronic or acutely ill patient who is not in a state of managing self-care needs which includes bathing and dressing and feeding needs, and medication. Along with the self-care needs caregivers also manage the financial matters, coordinate with the medical professional and family and take care of the emotional distress of the patient, which is overwhelming for the caregiver.

Caregivers can be categorised into primary caregivers – in most cases, they are the immediate family members who take care of the day-to-day needs of the patients and accompany them on a day-to-day basis; secondary care givers are the ones who assist the primary caregivers and substitute the primary caregivers when there is a need or requirement. The third category is the crisis caregivers, who assist the primary caregivers in case of a medical crisis (Hariharan, 2020). The responsibility of a caregiver may be short in case of acute illness or prolonged as in chronic illnesses like a mental health issue, physical disability, or a chronic condition such as in the case of patients of stroke, paralysis, and muscular dystrophy to name a few. Owing to the adverse physical and psychological implications caregivers themselves are hidden patients (Reinhard et al., 2008). Caregiving causes an immense strain and almost dislocates the life of the caregiver (Hariharan, 2020). Other factors that contribute to the burden of caregiving are the individual's personality. In a study by Soltys et al. (2021), it was found that individuals with high self-efficacy experienced reduced stress and depression and also had a greater commitment to caregiving. A higher level of neuroticism was related to higher stress and depression. The study also found that a sense of coherence reduced caregiver burden and prevented the development of depressive symptoms. Other factors that impact burden are the presence of social support reduced subjective burden and lowered depressive symptoms (del-Pino-Casado et al., 2018; Zhong et al., 2020). Age, financial condition, caregivers' health status, knowledge about the disease and related medical care, relationship of family members, the duration and type of disease, disease progression, prognosis and the degree of dependency of the patient were some other factors that impact caregiver burden. Caregiving invokes a series of negative emotions which include anxiety, distress, helplessness, uncertainty, anger, guilt and fear. Moreover, the caregiver affect state has an influence on the patient who internalises the emotional state of the caregivers. Caregivers generally multitask. The role they play has its influence on their work life, social life and their relationship with their children and other family members. The caregiving process can also have a positive impact on the caregiver. (Hariharan, 2020). Caregiving leaves the person with a sense of satisfaction and fulfilment and enhances the meaning and purpose of life. Disruptions in the physical, psychological, social and spiritual health of caregivers need to be attended to through assessment, counselling and psychosocial interventions. Providing optimal interventions requires a thorough assessment procedure. Assessment for caregivers includes the following-

- Assessment of the socio-economic status, age and physical health of the caregiver.
- Measurement of caregiver's knowledge regarding the disease, treatment procedures, diagnostic and other disease-related procedures, financial requirements and availability of support services.
- Assessment of personality, coping, positive and negative affect states, stress, anxiety, depression, social support. The assessment can be done using the standardised tests available to measure all the above constructs.

Assessment helps in a thorough diagnosis of the caregiver's physical and psychological health status. The diagnosis can help the health psychologists or counsellors to provide precise intervention. Prior to providing the interventions, it is important to evaluate if the interventions match the psychosocial needs of the caregivers. Caregiving is an ongoing process and caregivers may be at different stages of caregiving. Hariharan (2020) outlined five phases of caregiving which include:

- The diagnosis phase: Wherein the psychological state of the caregiver is highly fragile, because of the diagnosis of the disease. The caregiver is highly anxious or in a state of shock and will need emotional first aid.
- Treatment phase: His stage is when the treatment for the disease is initiated. The caregiver worries about the patient's response to the treatment and also about the financial implications. This phase requires a round-the-clock presence of the caregiver leading to disruption of roles and responsibilities.
- Survivorship phase: Though this phase is about the recovery of the patient, caregivers may have apprehensions about the prognosis and relapse. They may be in a state of continuous vigilance.
- Recurrent phase: Relapse or recurrence of the disease leaves the caregiver in a state of anger, hopelessness and distress. The caregiver may have feelings of guilt and doubt about his or her caregiving procedures.
- End-of-life phase: The caregiver in this phase gets an understanding that any amount of effort from his or her side or the doctors is not going to help revive the patient. The caregiver here tries to come to terms with the disease and works towards helping the patient feel comfortable. The caregiver may be in a state of increased distress and may feel hopeless and helpless. The psychological state of the caregiver will also depend on his or her relationship with the patient.

Interventions

The above categorisation helps the health psychologists or counsellors to understand the psychological state of the patient according to the phase he or she is in. This will enable them to plan a suitable intervention. The interventions should be need-based and designed according to the issues that are prevalent. Caregivers may be facing multiple concerns. In such a situation asking the client to prioritise their needs and resolve the issues may be appropriate. Psychoeducation is highly effective in a medical setting. Caregivers may have a number of informational needs which include information related to diagnosis, treatment process and cost, information related to insurance and finance, prognosis and follow-up. Providing the right information not only enhances the cognitive needs (Hariharan, 2020) of the caregivers but also gives them the confidence to get into a problem-solving mode and make the right decisions. Psychoeducation also helps caregivers in enhancing their self-efficacy in turn which helps in increasing their self-management strategies (Treanor et al., 2019).

In most cases individual counselling is advantageous. Caregivers can be provided one-on-one counselling, using the skills and approaches mentioned in chapters two to nine. Apart from psychoeducation, cognitive behaviour therapy, family therapy, relaxation techniques, and emotional and social support help in dealing with the caregiver's distress. Wiegelmann et al. (2021) in their systematic review found that interventions including psychoeducation, counselling, cognitive behaviour therapy, leisure and physical activity, befriending and peer support help in reducing caregivers' distress in dementia patients. Caregivers in Intensive Care Units are found to be benefitted from cognitive-based therapies and mindfulness training (Cox et al., 2014).

Counsellors in a hospital setting should also be equipped with techniques of pain management, dealing with issues like insomnia, coping with post-surgery and post-medication issues, adherence to diet, medication and exercise. Stress management, motivational interviews, guided imagery, behaviour analysis and modification, cognitive restructuring, crisis intervention, and grief and bereavement counselling are some of the interventions used in a hospital setting. Most of these techniques have been explained in the previous chapters, a few will be discussed in the following section.

Crisis Intervention

The perception or experience of an incident or circumstance as a hardship that transcends the person's present resources and coping skills is referred to as a crisis (James, 2008). A crisis occurs when there is a severe personal or professional loss either due to illness or the death of a family member. The term can also be applied in diverse situations. For example a disaster or adversity, sexual assault, or a medical or surgical patient who is in trauma. According to Caplan (1961), a crisis occurs when an individual faces major transitory difficulty, it is self-limiting and lasts for a minimum of four to six weeks. The crisis is seen as a major turning point or a moment when the individual has to make a crucial decision that involves the effective use of resources. Individuals use coping behaviours to respond to a threatening situation, which may be problem-focused or emotion-focused. Coping may fail when the problem situation is too demanding, too unfamiliar or profuse. In such a situation, the person may have used maladaptive coping which may have had some impact on physical or psychological health. Caplan (1961) describes four phases of crisis: the trigger or the event causes an initial increase in stress leading to an arousal phase when coping behaviours increase. If coping fails there is increased arousal or tension interfering with daily life which in turn hinders coping. There is an immediate mobilisation of internal and external resources. If unresolved, a psychological collapse may occur leading to exhaustion, and deterioration. Hobbs (1984) states that situations which precipitate a crisis can be of three types – first is the developmental which refers to transitional changes in the psychosocial stages. For example adolescent maturational crisis, childbirth, marriage, or retirement. The second type is the accidental crisis which involve unexpected life events. For example, a death, illness, accident, or a divorce. The third type of crisis is situational. For example unexpected events or disasters like floods, disasters. When there is a combination of situations like the death of the spouse when a child is born in the family the person faces severe vulnerability. The primary goal of crisis intervention is to relieve the client from distress, restore the level of function and activity that the client had prior to the crisis, and help the client cope, by helping him become aware of the internal and external resources available to him to deal with the crisis (Korchin, 1976). A crisis brings about some common problems. Understanding these problems will help counsellors provide the optimal interventions. These include:

- Loss: Loss occurs when there is a death, separation, or loss of an organ or a body part due to illness or accident. For example, amputation of a leg, accident or mastectomy, financial loss, loss of trust or sense of identity after sexual abuse. The loss sets in a pattern of responses. Lindemann (1944) describes them as shock, followed by denial and grief. If grief is worked through by providing the interventions, the individual can reorganise his or her life.
- Change: A crisis usually brings in a new situation. For example, retirement brings in a complete change in the day-to-day routine of a person or the illness of a family member may bring in a change in the roles of the other family members, death of a spouse may bring a change in the family relationships or family dynamics. The change may be threatening for the individual since it may require an adjustment to a new and unfamiliar situation. The change may also lead to shedding their own role or identity and accepting a new role or identity. The individual can work with change if he or she can see this change with a positive outlook and the expectation of a rewarding life experience.
- Interpersonal: A crisis can lead to a change in relationships. Conflicts and troubled interpersonal relations are some of the consequences of a crisis. Dealing with emotional outbursts, facilitating communication and resolving conflicts are part of an intervention.
- Conflict: Loss, change and interpersonal issues can take the individual to a situation wherein he or she has conflict in choosing alternatives, or in making decisions.

Crisis Counselling

The basic principles of crisis intervention are:

- Facilitate expression of emotions: A crisis generates an array of emotions. These emotions become problems in their own ways. An emotional upheaval has a direct impact on cognition. Individuals stop adapting coping strategies, unexpressed anger can lead to withdrawal and negative or destructive behaviour. Emotional first aid, which includes understanding the client's non-verbal cues and facilitating the expression of emotions helps the client in catharsis. Some clients do not express any emotions after a crisis, which is called emotional numbing. For example, a wife who does not cry or does not express any emotions after the death of her husband, in such a case the expression of the emotion is very important.
- Helping the client understand the problem and their responses to the problem: A crisis brings in a series of questions. For example a wife who goes through survivor's guilt

after her husband died of COVID-19, may have many questions, about the behaviour and the actions she had taken.

> *Why didn't I take him to another hospital?*
> *If I had contacted my family doctor immediately maybe he would have got better treatment.*

Guilt and self-blame are observed in survivors or family members. Helping the clients come out of their irrational beliefs using cognitive restructuring and helping them identify the problem and possible solution is important.

- Restore self-esteem and self-worth through empathetic understanding: Individuals in crisis need a thorough strengthening of their self-esteem. Identifying the strengths and assets and using them to augment self-esteem helps the client. Clients generally use unhealthy defences, which can be replaced with healthy and adaptive defences.
- Enhancing problem-solving behaviour: Emotional distress leads to inefficient cognitive responses. Anger, aggression and hostility are some of the reactions when the client is emotionally distressed. Helping the client deal with emotions and adopt the right problem-solving strategy is important. Counsellors can assist clients to comprehend the situation by disseminating knowledge and helping them to get an alternative perspective of the problem. Haaga and Davison (1986), listed a step-by-step approach to problem-solving, which include: problem orientation, problem definition and formulation, looking out for alternative solutions, decision making and implementation of the solution.

When a client is in crisis, a counsellor must assess the intensity of the cl'ent's stress symptoms and be more directive than usual. According to MacCluskie and Ingersoll (2001), people in crisis have the following characteristics:

- Introversion: The person turns inward and becomes less aware of others in her environment.
- Emotional reaching out: The person may come across as significantly more emotionally 'needy' than he normally is.
- Impulsive and unproductive behaviours: The person may be attempting to engage in problem-solving behaviours but doing so in a disorganised and unproductive manner.
- Subjective perception of excessive vulnerability: The individual may experience a profound sense of helplessness and worry in the face of a life event over which she has no control.

Different models and approaches are available for crisis intervention. But to conclude, crisis intervention includes the affective and cognitive approaches, while it is also necessary to check or resolve the social and environmental factors that contribute to the crisis so that the pre-crisis level of functioning of the client can be restored.

Grief and Bereavement Counselling

Grief is an emotional, social, and physical reaction to loss, a universal human experience which interferes with day-to-day life and causes severe physical and psychological distress. Grieving is a natural, normal, and unavoidable process that individuals go through when they lose someone close to them. The process of grief and bereavement goes through the following stages:

- Avoidance: The survivor is in an initial phase of shock and disbelief. By means of avoidance behaviour and numbing the feelings, the individual is able to provide himself with emotional anaesthesia.
- Confrontation: The survivor comes to terms with reality and tries to confront the situation. The bereaved experiences the pain that comes with grief and expresses his anxiety, anger, helplessness and yearning for the loved one. In spite of understanding that there is loss, the bereaved are unable to concentrate and are still preoccupied with the thoughts of the loved one. This phase is the most difficult phase because the loss is a reality and facing it is a tough process.
- Accommodation: The bereaved is now in a phase of accepting that the loss is real and tries to divert the emotional energies into other activities such as participating in day-to-day chores, and investing their time in new roles and responsibilities. However, grief reactions continue to surface at times and interfere in the individual's life.

Parkes-Bowlby model of bereavement (Murray, 1998), outlines five predominant reactions to grief:

- Numbness: A sense of disbelief and emptiness of feelings.
- Yearning: In this stage the bereaved may express extreme emotions like inconsolable crying, and panic.
- Agony: Accompanied by some physical reactions like pain and aches.
- Disorganisation and despair: Despair and depression are predominant in this stage, which results in difficulty in managing day-to-day activities.
- Reorganisation: In this stage the bereaved invests less emotional energy in the attachment of the loved one who is no more and instead invests one's energies into the other facets of his life.

The individual now is ready to take up new activities and new attachments or relationships.

The person who is grieving may be at different stages of life. A bereaved parent faces intense grief for their children. They may face a sense of guilt that they have outlived their children. Bereaved children and adolescents have a sense of insecurity as they have lost an attachment figure which leaves them vulnerable. People in old age may experience multiple losses. For example death of a spouse, or the death of siblings or friends leading to bereavement overload. Bereavement takes a toll on the individual. The following are the symptoms of grief and bereavement:

- Physical symptoms: Fatigue, loss of appetite and sleep, severe aches and pain in the body, restlessness, weight loss or gain, shortness of breath, nausea.
- Psychological: Anger, denial, confusion, trauma, irritability, hopelessness, fear, and resentment.
- Social: Withdrawal from social activities, isolation.
- Spiritual: Anger at God or institutions, loss of faith, spiritual confusion and search for purpose of life.

Internal factors such as gender, age, personality, coping styles, relationship with the deceased, survivor understanding of the reason for the death; and external factors such as, level of support premature, sudden or prolonged death and anticipatory grieving, place of death are some of the factors which may influence the bereavement process. Assessment of symptoms and factors helps counsellors to plan interventions. The goal of counselling is to increase the reality of loss, help the bereaved with the overt and covert experiences of loss, help the bereaved to overcome the blocks, reorganise life and make a healthy emotional withdrawal from the loved one and reinvest the physical, and emotional energy into new activities and relationships. Cognitive Behaviour Therapy, acceptance and commitment therapy, enhancing self-awareness and self-care, expressive art therapy and play therapy for children are some of the interventions for grief counselling.

In a healthcare setting, health psychologists and counsellors may also play a role in rehabilitation counselling, follow-up visits and home visits. The other important responsibilities include counselling for the healthcare professional who equally goes through distress and burnout, counselling in palliative care and hospice, and organ donation counselling. Health Psychologists have an accountable job of dealing with patients with physical illnesses. Their role is not restricted to assessment, counselling and intervention but they have a major role to play in disease prevention and health promotion. However, they need to follow ethical principles and the code of conduct.

References

71% of employees rethinking their career. (2023, March). *The Economic Times*. https://economictimes.indiatimes.com/jobs/71-of-employees-rethinking-their-careers-report/articleshow/88976325.cms?from=mdr.

Bandura, A. (1989). Human agency in social cognitive theory. *American Psychologist, 44*(9), 1175.

Belar, C. D., & Deardorff, W. W. (1995). *Clinical health psychology in medical settings: A practitioner's guidebook, Rev*. American Psychological Association.

Cane, F. (1983). *The artist in each of us* (revised ed.). Art Therapy Publications.

Caplan, G. (1961). *An approach to community mental health*. Grunne & Stratton.

Carpenter, P. & Foster, B. (1977). The career decisions of student teachers. *Educational Research and Perspectives University of Western Australia*, *4*(1), 23–33.

Cox, C. E., Porter, L. S., Buck, P. J., Hoffa, M., Jones, D., Walton, B., ... & Greeson, J. M. (2014). Development and preliminary evaluation of a telephone-based mindfulness training intervention for survivors of critical illness. *Annals of the American Thoracic Society*, *11*(2), 173–181.

Dallos, R., & Draper, R. (2015). *Ebook: An introduction to family therapy: Systemic theory and practice*. McGraw-Hill Education.

de Shazer, S. (1985). *Keys to solution in brief therapy*. Norton.

del-Pino-Casado, R., Frías-Osuna, A., Palomino-Moral, P. A., Ruzafa-Martínez, M., & Ramos-Morcillo, A. J. (2018). Social support and subjective burden in caregivers of adults and older adults: A meta-analysis. *PloS ONE*, *13*(1), e0189874.

Erikson, E. (1980). *Identity and the life cycle,* W. W. Norton & Company.

Friery, K. (2006). Workplace counselling: Who is the consumer?. *Counselling at Work*, *54*, 121–129.

Gati, I., & Saka, N. (2001). High school students' career-related decision-making difficulties. *Journal of Counseling & Development*, *79*(3), 331–340.

Ghavibazou, E., Hosseinian, S., & Abdollahi, A. (2020). Effectiveness of narrative therapy on communication patterns for women experiencing low marital satisfaction. *Australian and New Zealand Journal of Family Therapy*, *41*(2), 195–207.

Ghosh, R. (2019, May 6). India needs 15 lakh counsellors for 315 million students. *The Times of India*. https://timesofindia.indiatimes.com/education/news/india-needs-15-lakh-counsellors-for-315-million-students/articleshow/69201566.cms.
Ginsberg, E. (1966). *Toward a theory of occupational choice*, Macmillan.
Ginzberg, E., Ginsburg, S. W., Axelrad, S., & Herma, J. L. (1951). Occupational choice. In *Occupational choice*. Columbia University Press.
Gururaj, G., Varghese, M., Benegal, V., Rao, G. N., Pathak, K., Singh, L. K., Mehta, R. Y., Ram, D., Shibukumar, T. M., Kokane, A., Lenin Singh, R. K., Chavan, B. S., Sharma, P., Ramasubramanian, C., Dalal, P. K., Saha, P. K., Deuri, S. P., Giri, A. K., Kavishvar, A. B., … NMHS Collaborators Group. (2016). *National health survey of India 2015–16: Prevalence, patterns and outcomes*, NIMHANS Publication.
Haaga, D. A., & Davison, G. C. (1986). Cognitive change methods. In F. H. Kanfer & A. P. Goldstein (Eds.), *Helping people change: A textbook of methods* (3rd ed., pp. 236–282). Pergamon Press.
Haley, J. (1963). *Strategies of psychotherapy*. Grune & Stratton.
Hariharan, M. (2020). *Health psychology: Theory, practice and research*. Sage Publications.
Harper, D. (2009). Narrative therapy, family therapy and history. *Context: A Magazine for Family Therapy and Systemic Practice*, *102*(April), 17–18.
Hobbs, M. (1984). Crisis intervention in theory and practice: A selective review. *British Journal of Medical Psychology*, *57*(1), 23–34.
Holland, J. L. (1997). *Making vocational choices: A theory of vocational personalities and work environments*. (3rd ed.). Psychological Assessment Resources.
Hossain, M. M., & Purohit, N. (2019). Improving child and adolescent mental health in India: Status, services, policies, and way forward. *Indian Journal of Psychiatry*, *61*(4), 415.
Jackson, D. (1952). The relationship of the referring physician to the psychiatrist. *California Medicine*, *76*(6), 391.
Kent-Hughes, M. O. (1970). The Australian National Health Act June, 1970. *The Lancet*, *296*(7681), 1033–1034.
Korchin, S. J. (1976). *Modern clinical psychology*. Basic Books.
Lindemann, E. (1944). Symptomatology and management of acute grief. *American Journal of Psychiatry*, *101*(2), 141–148.
MacCluskie, K. C., & Ingersoll, R. E. (2001). *Becoming a 21st-century agency counselor: Personal and professional explorations*. Brooks/Cole Publishing Company.
Marcia, J. E., Waterman, A. S., Matteson, D. R., Archer, S. L., Orlofsky, J. L., & Waterman, A. S. (1993). Developmental perspectives on identity formation: From adolescence to adulthood. In *Ego identity: A handbook for psychosocial research* (pp. 42–68). Springer Science and Business Media.
Ministry of Health and Family Welfare, Government of India. *National Mental Health Survey of India; 2016*. http://www.indianmhs.nimhans.ac.in/Docs/Summary.pdf.
Minuchin, S. (1974). *Families and family therapy*. Harvard University.
Minuchin, S. (2018). *Families and family therapy*. Routledge.
Murray Parkes, C. (1998). Bereavement in adult life. *British Medical Journal*, *316*(7134), 856–859.
Parsons, F. (1909). *Choosing a vocation*. Brousson Press.
Pérusse, R., Goodnough, G. E., & Lee, V. V. (2009). Group counseling in the schools. *Psychology in the Schools*, *46*(3), 225–231.
Pew Research Center. (2023, March). The state of American jobs, how Americans view their jobs. https://www.pewresearch.org/social-trends/2016/10/06/3-how-americans-view-their-jobs/.
Reinhard, S. C., Given, B., Petlick, N. H., & Bemis, A. (2008). Supporting family caregivers in providing care. In *Patient safety and quality: An evidence-based handbook for nurses*. Agency for Healthcare Research and Quality.
Roe, A. (1966). *Early Determinants of Vocational Choice*. Macmillan Publishing Co.

Roth, S., & Epston, D. (1996). Developing externalizing conversations: An exercise. *Journal of Systemic Therapies*, *15*(1), 5–12.
Sethi, B. B. (1989). Family as a potent therapeutic force. *Indian Journal of Psychiatry*, *31*(1), 22.
Sołtys, A., Bidzan, M., & Tyburski, E. (2021). The moderating effects of personal resources on caregiver burden in carers of alzheimer's patients. *Frontiers in Psychiatry*, *12*, 772050.
Super, D. E. (1953). A theory of vocational development. *American Psychologist*, *8*(5), 185.
Super, D. E. (1990). A life-span, life-space approach to career development. In D. Brown, L. Brooks, & others (Eds.), *Career choice and development: Applying contemporary theories to practice* (2nd ed., pp. 197–261). Jossey-Bass.
Treanor, C. J., Santin, O., Prue, G., Coleman, H., Cardwell, C. R., O'Halloran, P., & Donnelly, M. (2019). Psychosocial interventions for informal caregivers of people living with cancer. *Cochrane Database of Systematic Reviews*, 6.
Valliant, G. E., & Valliant, C. O. (1981). Natural history of male psychological health, X: Work as a predictor of positive mental health. *The American Journal of Psychiatry*, *138*(11), 1433–1440.
Wiegelmann, H., Speller, S., Verhaert, L. M., Schirra-Weirich, L., & Wolf-Ostermann, K. (2021). Psychosocial interventions to support the mental health of informal caregivers of persons living with dementia – a systematic literature review. *BMC geriatrics*, *21*(1), 94. https://doi.org/10.1186/s12877-021-02020-4
Zhong, Y., Wang, J., & Nicholas, S. (2020). Social support and depressive symptoms among family caregivers of older people with disabilities in four provinces of urban China: The mediating role of caregiver burden. *BMC Geriatrics*, *20*(1), 1–10.

11 Assessment and Documentation

Assessment is the evaluation process. It is an umbrella term that includes the methods, techniques, and measurements used to collect information relating to the client. Assessment forms a basis for the entire helping process. The information collected addresses the client's issues and plans therapeutic interventions. Though most part of the assessment is done in the initial stage of counselling, collecting information is an ongoing process and may continue for the entire course of the counselling process. The assessment method includes the intake interview to assess the client's problem; conceptualising and defining the client's problem; identifying, selecting, and implementing the therapeutic interventions; and evaluation. This chapter delineates the assessment procedure, including the importance and needs of an intake interview, documentation of the information gathered from the client, and models of conceptualising and planning therapeutic interventions. Counselling is a formal process and needs an ambience and a setting which is supportive. Understanding the counselling setting or the workspace for counselling is also important before recognising the assessment procedure.

The Counselling Setting

The workspace or counselling setting can be a private space, a school setting, a community setting, a hospital or hospice, or any other public space. The counsellor has to make sure that the workspace is comfortable, is noise-proof and ensures privacy for the client. The space should be pleasing, wherein the client and the counsellor can comfortably sit and continue the sessions. The space should be free from distractions like people intruding or phone calls. Counselling is sometimes done in a home setting; under such conditions, the counsellor should ensure that the client gets a private space to continue the session so that confidentiality is not compromised. The seating arrangement can include two comfortable chairs arranged squarely at a 90^0 angle, so the client and the counsellor sit face to face. It is preferable that there is no table between the two as it may become a symbolic barrier. The counsellor and client can sit at an optimal distance (discussed in Chapter 1) uninterrupted by any auditory and visual distractions. In recent times when the world was facing the pandemic, tele-counselling and online counselling became popular because of the constraints laid by the prevailing situation. Though such modes of counselling can be handled from the counsellor's office or home, utmost care should be taken regarding privacy and confidentiality.

DOI: 10.4324/9781003459415-11

Documentation and Maintaining Records

Documentation is any material that serves as proof or a record. Documentation with reference to counselling is evidence that gives valuable information about the client. Intake forms, informed consent, case records, termination letters, and legal and ethical codes are some of the documentation in a counselling setting. Documentation in a counselling setting is necessary for conducting the counselling session aptly and helps the counsellor in maintaining evident data on the information collected from the client. It helps in keeping a record of the client's progress and serves as a protection and maintains the rights and responsibilities of the counsellor and the client. Documentation helps in the smooth transfer of information and thus is an important part of counselling practice and has a major role to play in consultation, assessment, therapy, and client's progress. Psychologists should be trained to learn the skill of documentation and record keeping. Maintaining records helps healthcare professionals abide by ethical and legal guidelines and progress. While it is proof of the accountability of the therapist, it is important to note that the documentation related to the client is kept confidential. The list of documentation is presented in Box 11.1.

Informed Consent

Informed consent is a legal and ethical document that is proof of the client's consent to participate in the therapeutic procedure. Informed consent provides the necessary information to the client or the prospective client who has the capacity to make an informed decision about his/her need to participate in the counselling process. The informed consent has a detailed description of the counselling process and the risks and benefits of counselling. It provides the client with all the required information about the roles and expectations of the counselling session and therapy. When the information is clear there is a chance of an increased collaboration between the counsellor and the client which in turn enhances the therapeutic alliance. Since it briefs the client about the counselling process, it helps in reducing the apprehensions regarding counselling. Informed consent protects the dignity and rights of the client and the counsellor and minimises ethical violations, thus protecting both parties. While preparing the consent form, care should be taken that it is clear, logical, and comprehensible; at the same time the client should give a voluntary consent. In case the client is legally, cognitively, and emotionally not competent, the parent, caregiver, attender, or legal guardian should sign the informed consent.

Box 11.1 Documentation in Counselling

1. Informed consent
2. Demographic information of the client
3. The intake interview: presenting problem; family, developmental and medical history; psychological health
4. Case notes and progress notes
5. Clinical assessment or tests
6. Diagnosis and case reports
7. Therapy or intervention planned

The information contained within the consent form:

1. Information regarding the nature of counselling, risks, benefits, and limitations.
2. The credentials of the counsellor.
3. Information regarding the outcomes of counselling.
4. Information regarding therapeutic options.
5. Information regarding fee and finance-related issues.
6. Information regarding confidentiality includes sharing information, note-taking, and audio/video recording.
7. Information about the appointments, timing, and length of sessions.
8. Information related to the decision regarding withdrawal from counselling and therapy.
9. Role and goals of the counsellor and the client.

Any other information may be updated from time to time based on the stage or phase of counselling.

Intake Interview

Interviewing the client and having the client engage in the assessment procedures are only part of the overall assessment process in counselling and therapy. The intake interview is the first step of the assessment process. It is more about seeking information than therapeutic. The intake form helps in conducting the initial assessment of the physical and psychological status of the client. It also helps in getting information related to interpersonal relationships, educational background, and details about the previous therapeutic sessions. An intake form is a useful tool wherein the counsellor can acquire information regarding past referrals and the reason for seeking counselling. The intake form is one of the simplest tools used to obtain the required information from clients. (Box 11.2), and has the following details:

- *Demographic information*: This information pertains to the identifying information about the client, including name, age, gender, nationality, religion, marital status, educational details, occupation, socio-economic status, and contact information. Details regarding the client's contact, such as phone numbers and email addresses and contact numbers of the client's family members or support, are important information and need to be recorded for any emergency or legal proceedings (Donohue et al., 2014).
- *Presenting problem*: This section includes information about the problem which is currently faced by the client. Details on the onset, precedents of the problem, the time and frequency, precipitating conditions, interference with the day-to-day functioning, therapy or counselling services have taken earlier, treatment outcomes, and reason for seeking help now.
- *Details of family and developmental history*: Includes family, family relationships and dynamics; developmental includes the details of significant events from birth the o present day; relationships between parents, siblings, children, marital relationships or discords; divorce or separation, and so on.
- *Medical and health-related history*: Includes details of health-related issues in the past and present; prescribed medication; diet, exercise, and sleep patterns.

Box 11.2 Sample of an Intake Form

Client Information Sheet

Date:

Client ID: ____
Age: _____
Gender: M ☐ F ☐
Current Address: ____
City: _______________ Pin: ___________
Mobile Phone: __________________
Email Address: ____
Permanent Address: __________________
Occupation: ________________________
Religion: _______________
Marital Status: ☐ Unmarried ☐ Married ☐ Divorced ☐ Widowed
Number of children: _________
Ages of the children:
Have you received counselling in the past? Yes ☐ No ☐
Where/When? _____
Duration: _____________________________________
Please list current medications (if any):

Presenting problem: _______________________

Developmental and family history:

- Age of parents: Mother ☐ Father ☐
- If any of your parent(s) are deceased__________
- Primary person(s) to raise you: Mother ☐ Father ☐ Brother(s) ☐ Sister(s) ☐
- Parents' relationship status:
  Married ☐ Divorced ☐ Other ☐
- No. of siblings:
- No of siblings and their age: Brother(s) __________ Sister(s) ____________
- Has anyone in your immediate family seen a psychologist or a psychiatrist?
  Yes ☐ No ☐
- If yes, please explain:
- Has anyone in your immediate family been treated for alcohol or substance abuse?
  Yes ☐ No ☐
- Have you ever been physically, emotionally, or sexually abused?
  Yes ☐ No ☐ Unsure ☐
- If yes, please explain:
- Do you use any of the following (in any amount)?
  Alcohol ☐ Other Drugs ☐ Tobacco ☐ Caffeine ☐ None ☐

Medical and health history

a. Mention any past or current medical problems if any and for how long?_____
b. Are you on any medication currently, if so specify? _____________
c. Diet, exercise and sleep patterns

Psychological health

a. Mention the current and past psychological issues if any and the length of problem: ___________
b. Details of past visits to a counsellor or psychologists: ___________________
c. Medication taken for the problem if any: _________________

YOUR REASON FOR SEEKING COUNSELLING/ REASON FOR REFERRAL:

- *Psychological Health*: Behavioural observations; past psychiatric or psychological issues; counselling or psychiatric treatment. The behavioural observations can be made using a Mental Status Examination in case of requirement. The Mental Status Examination is used to examine a client's mental status and behaviour. The mental status examination helps to identify, diagnose, and classify the signs and symptoms of any mental illness. The data is collected during the initial interview and is based on the therapist's observation of the client's behaviour. The major categories under which information is collected are the general appearance of the client, motor activity, speech, mood, thought process, affect, insight, cognition, level of consciousness, and orientation to time, place, and people. Understanding the content and functions of the mental status examination is very important for counsellors as it benefits the assessment procedure (Cormier, 2016).

Asking the client to complete the intake form prior to the initial session will help the counsellor get a briefing about the client before he/she comes for the initial session. It also helps the counsellor gather information about the client's past history, experiences, behaviour, and actions taken. The intake form also helps the counsellor understand the reason for referral, helps initiate the first interaction, and gives direction to the counselling process. Filling in the intake form is time-consuming and requires attention and effort from the client; hence appropriate time and inputs should be given accordingly. The counsellors should also be cautious about the confidentiality involved in giving and receiving the intake form.

The intake interview gives an opportunity for the counsellor to explore and understand the client and the client's problem in detail. According to Cormier (2016), there are 11 pointers on the basis of which counsellors or therapists can assess clients. The details are discussed below:

1. Explaining to the client the purpose of the interview
2. Identify the client's concerns
3. Select the issues that are of major concern
4. Identify the current problem
5. Identify the context of the problem
6. Identify the consequences of the problem

7. Incidental, secondary gains as payoffs to maintain the problem
8. Identifying previous solutions
9. Identifying the client's strengths and coping strategies
10. Identify the client's perception of the problem
11. Identify the impact of the problem in terms of its severity, frequency, and duration.

The above pointers can be used as a checklist or as a guideline. Though an interview does not impose a structure, pointers are stated in a natural so that the counsellor is focused and can elicit an accurate response.

Case Notes and Progress Notes

Note-taking is an essential component of the professional code of ethics for counsellors and helping professionals in maintaining clients' records. Client's records include case notes, case records, and case reports. The American Psychological Association (ACA) Code of Ethics (2002) states that record keeping is an integral part of therapy. American Psychological Association (APA, 2010) has designed certain guidelines which provide a framework for record keeping. Counsellors and therapists are accountable for maintaining these records. Records are essential documents; they protect and benefit both the counsellor and the client. Records help in planning, monitoring, and implementation of services provided to the clients and protect the counsellors and the clients from any legal or ethical issues (APA, 2002).

Case notes and progress notes are primary documents that help the counsellor in a stepwise maintenance of a record of assessment, diagnosis, and therapeutic interventions and can also help clients make informed decisions about their progress and treatment. While both case notes and progress notes are important documents, both differ from each other.

The progress notes are the working document which helps the counsellor conceptualise the case and evaluate the progress (Gehart, 2017). Progress notes help in maintaining continuity in case progress and are also useful in referral. Progress notes are a part of the file maintained for the client by the counsellor or the therapist. These documents can be shared among the professional helping the client as they provide information regarding the timing of starting the sessions; the client's presentation of the problem; records of the assessments performed; diagnosis and records of prescriptions, interventions, and the client's response to the interventions. In case of termination of counselling or therapy progress notes may also contain the termination summary that outlines the progress made and the goals achieved during the counselling process. This summary should be documented in the client's record. The progress notes are concise and highly structural documents accessible to the counsellor, client, the referral authority, e.g., the school principal in case of a referred student, other professionals like a doctor, nutritionist, physiotherapist, insurance companies, etc., involved in the treatment and intervention plan, legal is as in case of a divorce or custodial issues and so on. Though progress notes are accessible to health professionals or administrative or legal authorities, it is important that care is taken to protect and preserve the information in these records and use it for therapeutic interventions. An example of progress notes is presented in Box 11.3.

Box 11.3 Progress Notes

Counsellor's name
Client's first name
Session no
Presenting issue: The client had issues with two of his classmates, who called him names and bullied him. He is unable to concentrate on his academics and activities as well. His parents are upset with his performance in school.
The client looked nervous and anxious about going to school.
Assessment
Diagnosis
Treatment Plan
Interventions planned
Outcome and Responses to Interventions
Homework/Follow up
Total Sessions Taken

The case notes or therapy notes are private records of the counsellor or a therapist. These notes are prepared to keep track of each session and record information with regard to the counsellor's observation about the client's feelings, thoughts, behaviour, and the important conversations between the counsellor and the client. The case notes also include sensitive information, which include the impressions and interpretations made by the therapists/counsellors, which are not practicable to share with the client. For example, in the case of a woman coming for couple therapy, the counsellor can take a note of the sensitive aspects of the relationship or some behavioural or emotional issues between the couple that may not be required to be shared with the client. The case notes can also include the hypotheses of the counsellor based on his/her observation; his/her own thoughts about the session; queries regarding the interventions; notes on information to be furnished from other resources; and further reading about the case. Since the case notes have sensitive information, they are maintained under strict privacy protection. Information from the therapy notes is disclosed after authorisation from the client. However, in case of special circumstances, such as a threat to personal or public safety or legal issues, the disclosure of case notes does not need any authorisation. There are different methods of documentation in therapy and counselling. Some of the methods are discussed below.

SOAP notes: SOAP is an acronym for note taking in four steps – Subjective, Objective, Assessment, and Plan. The SOAP notes, which are used widely by healthcare practitioners, have originated from the POMR: Problem Originated Medical Record, which was developed by Lawrence Weed, a medical doctor who developed the tool to help medical professionals organise their diagnosis of patients with complicated medical issues (Jacob, 2009). The SOAP notes are an easy, structured, and comprehensive method of documenting the client's records as this format allows the counsellor to record the client's subjective experience, objective observations, assessments of the client's progress, and plans for future sessions. Since SOAP notes are highly structured, they provide a good framework for diagnosis and assessment. SOAP notes work well in a hospital setting; for example, the section related to objective data includes the results of tests, procedures, and diagnosis; the subjective data includes the patient's personal experience towards

Box 11.4 SOAP Notes

Name:
Age:
Setting:
Date of visit:
Presenting problem:

S: Subjective	Client's information about his present problem, and subjective experience of the problem
O: Objective	Records of past medical and psychological history, present observations
A: Assessment	Assessment and summary of the assessment
P: Plan	Setting and implementing goals and interventions

the illness, illness behaviour, adherence to medication, diet, and exercise. The next two sections are the assessment of psychological and emotional state and planning, which, as the name suggests, includes setting goals, planning interventions, and action. A sample of SOAP notes is presented in Box 11.4.

DAP notes (Data, Assessment, and Plan) are another format for documenting client progress in counselling and therapy. The first section is data. This section has information related to the client's reason for seeking counselling or therapy and observations made by the counsellor, for example, physical appearance, mental status examination, and screening. The next section is about assessment and includes diagnosis, reports of tests, and interpretation of the diagnosis. The last section is planning which includes these notes focusing on the data gathered during the session, the counsellor's assessment of the client's progress, and the plan for future sessions. DAP notes are simple and comprehensive; moreover, content can be shared, and hence they can be used as progress notes also. DAP notes can be in a counselling setup and also in a medical setting.

Documentation can be done in different ways. Counsellors can develop their own format for documentation. Some counsellors use *Narrative Notes*, a more detailed and descriptive form of documentation that provides a narrative account of the client's progress over time. These notes often include direct quotes from the client and provide a more in-depth understanding of the client's experience. Other methods of documentation are *flow charts and diagrams*, which are useful for visualising the client's progress and tracking changes over time. These simple tools can help to identify patterns and trends in the client's behaviour and provide a more comprehensive understanding of their progress. *Audio or video recordings* can be used to document counselling sessions and provide a complete record of the client's progress. However, it is important to obtain the client's informed consent and ensure that the recordings are kept confidential and secure.

Case Formulation

The information collected through the interview and other methods of documentation has no value or significance unless it is integrated with therapy. The entire period of assessment is not only about obtaining information but also using this information and generating clinical hypotheses, which leads to some tentative ideas for treatment. This entire process is called conceptualisation or formulation of the case. The process of making sense of a client's presenting problems within the context of a theoretical framework is referred to as case conceptualisation. It relates to how the client's symptoms, personality traits, cognitions, feelings, and actions are integrated with a theory to get a better understanding leading to the development of counselling objectives and intervention tactics.

The case formulation approach (like the counselling process) begins with a comprehension of the client's presenting concerns from the client's point of view. The steps in case formulation are Step 1, presenting concerns; Step 2, exploring the problem; and Step 3, identifying goals and specific interventions. The client's case is formulated from one theoretical direction at a time.

Theoretical Approaches to Case Formulation

Cognitive behaviour approach: Cognitive behaviour theory and its application in counselling has been extensively discussed in the previous chapters. From a cognitive behavioural perspective, the problems of the client are understood as the product of faulty learning that results in irrational thoughts or faulty cognitions while also taking into account environmental contingencies in the behaviour change process. The primary goal is to uncover the antecedent behaviours and cognitions that cause the maladaptive thoughts and behaviours. After establishing the theoretical framework and generating the hypotheses, interventions are designed. Unlearning the negative behaviour, replacing maladaptive cognitive schemas, cognitive restructuring, stimulus control, and self-control are some of the interventions.

Lazarus model of case formulation: The BASIC ID; Lazarus and Lazarus – (2019) developed multimodal therapy. The acronym BASIC ID has modalities such as B – behaviour; A – affect (anxiety, depression, anger, etc.); S – sensation (pleasant and unpleasant sensations like palpitations, headaches, etc.); Imagery – mental pictures, images of failure, or self-image; C – cognition (negative thoughts, attitudes and, beliefs); I – interpersonal (relationships and support); D – diet, drugs (physical health, diet, exercise, sleep, and use of alcohol or drugs). The problems of clients can fall under any one or more of these modalities, and counsellors should assess, address, and treat these modalities. The assumption of the multimodal approach is that the interventions should address these modalities.

Configurational Analysis (CA): CA is a method used in therapy that focuses on the interrelationships among the different aspects of a person's life, including their thoughts, feelings, behaviours, and interpersonal relationships. CA assumes that people's psychological difficulties arise from a configuration of factors that are interconnected and that must be understood in their unique context.

The Core Conflictual Relationship Theme (CCRT): CCRT is a concept and tool used in therapy that was developed by Luborsky and Crits-Christoph in 1998. It is based on the idea that the way a person experiences relationships with others reflects their core conflicts and patterns of behaviour. The CCRT is derived from the analysis of a patient's verbalisations during psychotherapy sessions, where the patient's perception of a significant relationship is explored. It identifies three components of the patient's interpersonal relationships: the wishes and needs they have in the relationship, the responses they expect from the other person, and the responses they receive from the other person.

The Plan Formulation Method (PFM): PFM is a collaborative process that involves the therapist and client working together to identify the client's goals, problems, and strengths. This is done through a series of assessments, including interviews, questionnaires, and psychological testing. The therapist and client work together to develop a formulation that includes the following components:

- Central conflict: It refers to the core psychological conflict underlying the client's presenting problems.
- Maladaptive coping strategies: These are the ways in which the client is currently attempting to manage their central conflict, which may be ineffective or harmful.
- Historical factors: These are past experiences or events that may have contributed to the development of the client's central conflict and maladaptive coping strategies.
- Interpersonal factors: These are current or past relationships that may be contributing to the client's problems, including family, friends, and romantic partners.
- Strengths and resources: These are the client's personal strengths, abilities, and resources that can be used to help them overcome their problems.

Overall, the choice of documentation strategy will depend on the counsellor's personal preferences, the requirements of their practice or organisation, and the specific needs of the client. Regardless of the strategy used, it is important to ensure that all documentation is accurate, objective, and respectful of the client's privacy and confidentiality.

Assessment Using Psychological Tests

The assessment also includes the use of psychological tests. Counsellors will find it necessary to conduct assessments using psychological tests. Standardised psychological tests can be classified into tests of personality, aptitude, intelligence, academic achievement, family and interpersonal relations, stress, anxiety, and depression are some of the tests which are used during the assessment. Apart from the regular assessment using standardised tests, this chapter includes some new tests developed by the authors, which include tests for children, adolescents, and the general population. The counsellors may use these tests according to the need and context. Some of the scales are attached in the next section.

Assessment Tool 1: The Self-Reliance Scale

Developed by Meera Padhy, Meena Harihara, Suma Lavanya Mutnury, Oindrila Mukherjee, Riswana NT.

Purpose:
As the title suggests, this scale measures the level of self-reliance in adults, which indicates the extent to which one can rely upon oneself and has the capability to take control of life's challenges.

Psychometric Properties:
Construct Validity – Significant positive correlations were found between self-reliance and self-regulation (.21) and resilience (.19). In both cases $p < .01$.
Reliability – Chronbach alpha of the scale is .95

Scoring:
To obtain the *total score*, sum the total scores of all the dimensions. The total score may range from 0 to 90.

To obtain the *total score of each dimension*, add the scores of all the items under that dimension.
Reverse scoring is required for items 3, 8, 9, 15, 19 and 30.

Interpretation:
Higher scores indicate higher levels of self-reliance and vice-versa.

Context:
This scale can be administered to a wide range of populations, to individuals as well as groups in counselling settings, organisations as well as educational institutes.

Self-reliance Scale:
NAME: ________________________________ AGE: ______ GENDER: ____
School/College/Organisation________________ Government/Private________
Class__________ Years of Experience______ CGPA/Percentage: ________

Instructions: Listed below are a few statements. Kindly read them carefully and respond appropriately by giving information regarding the support. You need to read each statement and select by putting a tick (✓) on a response from the four options mentioned in the columns. For example, for each of the following statements, please tick (✓) in only one box that describes you the best. Please read each sentence carefully and answer honestly.
1 = Disagree 2 = Somewhat disagree 3 = Somewhat agree 4 = Agree

	Items	Agree	Somewhat agree	Somewhat disagree	Disagree
1.	I am able to solve my problems				
2.	I trust my competence				
3.	I need someone's help when I am asked to do a work (R)				
4.	I take decisions independently				
5.	I do not rely on others				
6.	I alone can handle a situation				
7.	I never face problems if no one is there to help me				
8.	I consult my elders before taking a decision (R)				
9.	I share my problems with others so that I will not make a mistake (R)				
10.	I am ready to take challenges				
11.	I am able to control difficult issues				
12.	I finish my commitments on time				
13.	I feel to grow, one should rely on one's strengths				
14.	I am not a dependent person				
15.	I like to get as much of support as possible from others (R)				

	Items	Agree	Somewhat agree	Somewhat disagree	Disagree
16.	I try different plans to get new ideas				
17.	I learn new things to work independently				
18.	I organise my activities to finish them on time				
19.	I feel nervous to start any new activity (R)				
20.	I have strong will power to initiate new activities				
21.	I dislike to consult people for petty things				
22.	I believe independence makes one bold				
23.	I always try to achieve my goals				
24.	I feel happy when I finish my work all alone				
25.	I never give up easily				
26.	I manage my emotions				
27.	I believe that I can accomplish my work				
28.	I am able to foresee problems				
29.	I am unable to tackle problems spontaneously as they arise (R)				
30.	I am unable to convince people (R)				

R= Reverse scoring

Dimension 1. Self-efficacy (1, 2, 4, 6, 10, 11, 12, 13, 14, 16, 17, 18, 20, 21, 22, 23, 24, 25, 26, 27, 28)
Dimension 2. External dependence (3, 8, 9, 15)
Dimension 3. Self-dependence (5, 7)
Dimension 4. Self-confidence deficit (19, 29, 30)
Self-reliance (All 30 items)

Assessment Tool 2: Children's Understanding of Parents

Developed by Meena Hariharan, Suma Lavanya Mutnury, Meera Padhy, Sandra Roshni Monteiro (2022).

Purpose:
As the title suggests, this scale assesses the children's understanding of their parents within the age group of 2 to 21 years. This questionnaire is a combination of open-ended questions and close-ended questions. In order to confirm the child's responses to each of the questions, a parallel questionnaire is given to the parents to fill in their responses.

Scoring:

The scale has a total of 37 items seeking inputs on a child's understanding of his/her parents. These items are further grouped under six different sections having questions pertaining to various aspects of an individual's life that are known to people who share a close interpersonal relationship with them. Section 1 has 11 factual questions; Section 2 has seven questions related to likes and dislikes; Section 3 has nine questions related to emotions; Section 4 has five questions related to health; Section 5 has two questions related to leisure, and Section 6 has three questions related to achievement-aspiration.

Each perfectly matching response of the child with either parent's response is given a score of 1. Incompatible responses are given a zero. A partial score is given if there is an overlap in the response of the child and mother (e.g., if the mother mentioned five talents and the child's responses match with three out of those five talents, then a partial score should be allotted by computing a fraction 3/5 and a score of 0.6 will be given). The scores on this questionnaire range between zero and one.

To derive the dimension wise percentage of understanding of parents by the children, the scores of understandings (ranging from zero to one) are to be summed up for the items under that dimension.

Formula for computing the dimension wise understanding:

(Total score of the dimension/Number of items in the dimension)
Divided by the total number of pairs Multiplied by 100

Where,

The total score of the dimension = summed score of each independent item under the dimension.

Number of items in the dimension = number of items in a particular dimension

Total number of pairs = the number of parent-child pairs considered in a study.

Interpretation:

Higher scores on each dimension indicate a higher understanding of parents by the children and vice-versa.

Context:

This scale can be used to initiate a scientific exploration into the intensity to which the children understand their parents from a multidimensional perspective, which plays a crucial role in the sustenance of the relationship and acceptance of playing a reciprocal role to the parents in later life.

Children's Understanding of Parents
(To be filled by the child)

Personal Information:

1. Name of the child: ______________________________
2. Gender: ______________________________
3. Age: ______________________________
4. School: ______________________________

5. Class: ______________________________

6. Number of siblings: ______________________________

Please provide the following information about YOUR FATHER. In case you do not know the information about your father, please tick (√) in the column on the left against that sentence.

SECTION 1

Don't Know		
	1	Date of birth
	2	Educational qualifications
	3	Name of the school he passed his 10th class
	4	Name of the school he passed his 12th class
	5	Name of the college he attended
	6	His percentage of marks in 10th exam
	7	His percentage of marks in 12th exam
	8	His occupation
	9	Name of his office
	10	His designation
	11	His annual income

SECTION 2

Don't Know		
	12	His favourite subject
	13	Subject most disliked by him
	14	His favourite colour
	15	His favourite dish
	16	A dish he hates the most
	17	His favourite singer
	18	The movie he liked the best

SECTION 3

Don't Know		
	19	His happiest moment as a student
	20	His happiest moment in the past one year
	21	One thing he is very scared of
	22	One definite way you can make him happy
	23	One definite way you can make him unhappy
	24	What does he usually do when he is angry?
	25	What does he usually do when he is sad?
	26	What does he usually do when he is very happy?
	27	His greatest frustration

SECTION 4

Don't Know		
	28	Does your father have any health problem(s)? **Yes / No**
	29	If yes, what is it?

30 Does your father have any food allergies? **Yes / No**
31 If yes, what is the food he is allergic to?
32 Does your father do any of the following regularly? (Tick those that he does)
a. Yoga
b. Walking
c. Aerobics
d. Any other (specify)

SECTION 5

Don't Know

33 His hobby
34 His favourite way to relax

SECTION 6

Don't Know

35 His main aim in life
36 What does your father want you to become?
37 His most desired achievement

Please provide the following information about YOUR MOTHER. In case you do not know the information about your mother on any, please tick (√) in the column on the left against that item.

SECTION 1

Don't Know

1 Date of birth
2 Educational qualifications
3 Name of the school she passed her 10th class
4 Name of the school she passed her 12th class
5 Name of the college she attended
6 Her percentage of marks in 10th exam
7 Her percentage of marks in 12th exam
8 Her occupation
9 Name of her office
10 Her designation
11 Her annual income

SECTION 2

Don't Know

12 Her favourite subject
13 Subject most disliked by her
14 Her favourite colour
15 Her favourite dish
16 A dish she hates the most
17 Her favourite singer
18 The movie she liked the best

SECTION 3

Don't Know		
	19	Her happiest moment as a student
	20	Her happiest moment in the past one year
	21	One thing she is very scared of
	22	One definite way you can make her happy
	23	One definite way you can make her unhappy
	24	What does she usually do when she is angry?
	25	What does she usually do when she is sad?
	26	What does she usually do when she is very happy?
	27	Her greatest frustration

SECTION 4

Don't Know		
	28	Does your mother have any health problem(s)? **Yes / No**
	29	If yes, what is it?
	30	Does your mother have any food allergies? **Yes / No**
	31	If yes, what is the food she is allergic to?
	32	Does your mother do any of the following regularly? (Tick those that she does) a. Yoga b. Walking c. Aerobics d. Any other (specify)

SECTION 5

Don't Know		
	33	Her hobby
	34	Her favourite way to relax

SECTION 6

Don't Know		
	35	Her main aim in life
	36	What does your mother want you to become?
	37	Her most desired achievement

Children's Understanding Parents
(To be filled by each parent, separately)

RELATIONSHIP

Personal Information:

1. Name of the Respondent Mr / Ms: ______________________________
2. Name of the Child: ______________________________
3. Relationship with the Child: (Mother / Father)
4. Age: ______________________________
5. Occupation: ______________________________

Please provide the following information about yourself.

SECTION 1		
Don't Know		
	1	Date of birth
	2	Educational qualifications
	3	Name of the school you passed his 10th class
	4	Name of the school you passed his 12th class
	5	Name of the college you attended
	6	Percentage of marks in 10th exam
	7	Percentage of marks in 12th exam
	8	Occupation
	9	Name of the office
	10	Designation
	11	Annual income

SECTION 2		
Don't Know		
	12	Favourite subject
	13	Subject most disliked by you
	14	Favourite colour
	15	Favourite dish
	16	A dish you hate the most
	17	Talent(s) (For example, music, art, sports)
	18	Favourite singer
	19	The movie you liked the best
	20	Extracurricular activities

SECTION 3		
Don't Know		
	21	Happiest moment as a student
	22	Happiest moment in the past one year
	23	The person who inspires you
	24	One thing you are very scared of

SECTION 4		
Don't Know		
	25	One definite way your child can make you happy
	26	One definite way your child can make you unhappy
	27	What do you usually do when angry?
	28	What do you usually do when sad?
	29	What do you usually do when happy?

SECTION 5		
Don't Know		
	30	The time you wake up every morning
	31	The time you go to sleep every night

	32	One good habit of you are proud of
	33	One bad habit you have
	34	One strong superstition
	35	Most favourite possession of yours

SECTION 6

Don't Know		
	36	Do you have any health problem(s)? **Yes / No** If yes, what is it?
	37	Do you have any food allergies? **Yes / No** If yes, what is the food you are allergic to?
	38	Did you ever meet with an accident? **Yes / No** If yes, what was the injury?
	39	Were you hospitalised any time? **Yes / No** If yes, when?
	40	Do you engage in any of the following regularly? (Tick those you do) a. Yoga b. Walking c. Aerobics d. Any other (specify)

SECTION 7

Don't Know		
	41	Name of your best friend

SECTION 8

Don't Know		
	42	Your hobby
	43	Your favourite kind of music (for example, Hindustani, Carnatic, New songs)
	44	Your favourite TV show
	45	Your favourite place for a holiday
	46	Your favourite way to relax

SECTION 9

Don't Know		
	47	Your biggest regret in life
	48	Your greatest frustration

SECTION 10

Don't Know		
	49	Your main aim in life
	50	What do you want your child to become?
	51	Your most desired achievement

Assessment Tool 3: Childhood Stress Scale

Developed by Meena Hariharan, Meera Padhy, Sandra Roshni Monteiro, Laxmi Priyanka Nakka, Usha Chivukula (2018).

Purpose:
As the title suggests, the scale is developed to assess the stress levels of adolescents within the age group of 11 to 18 years of age in terms of occurrence and intensity of the stress.

Psychometric Properties:
The test-retest reliability was calculated using the Pearson correlation coefficient. The three-week test-retest reliability was .57 with correlation significant at the 0.01 level. To establish the concurrent validity of the scale Children's happiness scale (Morgan, 2014) and General health questionnaire-12 (GHQ-12) (Goldberg & Williams, 1988) were used. The childhood stress scale was negatively correlated with the Happiness scale with an r-value of –.20 and positively correlated with r-value of .29 with GHQ-12. Both correlations were found to be significant at 0.01 level. The internal consistency of the entire set of 31 items (α = .92) *was* higher than that of the individual subscales (α = .87 for Major loss induced Stress; α = .65 for Enforcement or Conflict induced Stress; α = .73 for Phobia induced stress; α = .79 for Interpersonal conflict-induced Stress; α = .51 for Punishment induced stress; α = .69 for Illness and Injury induced stress; α = .73 for Performance stress; α = .61 for Imposition induced stress, and α = .79 for Insecurity induced Stress). The reliability coefficients for each subscale were found to be within acceptable norms for individual diagnosis (Nunnally, 1994).

The ten-factor mean scores were also found to have a significant difference, $F(9,5778) = 68.48, p < .001, \eta^2 = .096$.

Scoring:
The subscale scores were cumulatively calculated by summing up the item scores of each of the factors. Overall stress level could be found out by summing the subscale scores.

Interpretation:
Higher the score in the identified stressor, the higher the stress perceived.

Context:
This scale is a holistic measure to identify the domains of stressors faced by children. Moreover, it also helps to identify the intensity perceived in the experience of stress by the child.

Childhood Stress Scale
Instructions
We have prepared a list of situations that are identified as stressful by students from 5 to 18 years of age. We are in the process of developing a measurement for the stressful situations described in the list. We request your responses to help us develop the measurement of stress.

All that you have to do is read each situation, understand it, assess the intensity of stress it causes, and give it a rating based on your judgement of the intensity of the stress. You need to assess each stressful situation on a five-point scale. Supposing the death of a parent is the most stressful situation, getting a rating of 5; what will be the rating for each of the items listed below? After you finish giving your rating, go to the second column, and tick those ratings which you have experienced in your life.

<u>Participant's details</u>
Name:
Age:
Gender: **Class:**
School/College/University:

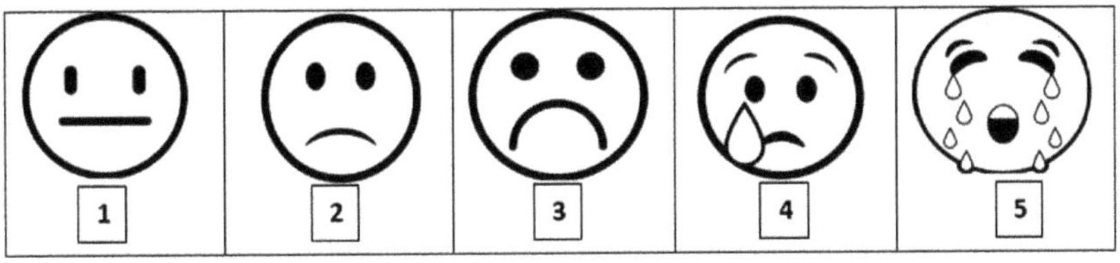

	Stressors	Your Rating	Have you experienced it in your life? Yes or No
1	Alcoholic parent(drinking problem)		
2	Beating by teacher		
3	Quarrel between parents		
4	Quarrel with friends		
5	Quarrel with parents		
6	Quarrel with brother or sister		
7	Quarrels in family		
8	Death of a family member		
9	Death of friend		
10	Death of grandparent		
11	Death of parent		
12	Failure in exams		
13	Fear of animals		
14	Fear of dark places		
15	Fear of hospitals		
16	Forced to do disliked task		
17	Forced to participate in an activity		
18	Being punished		
19	High academic pressure		
20	Ill health of self		
21	Injury to self		
22	Lack of sleep		
23	Meeting with an accident		
24	Not meeting academic expectations (self or others)		
25	Not meeting expectations in other activities (self or others)		
26	Problems with girlfriend or boyfriend		
27	Separation from loved ones (grandparents/cousins/friends)		
28	Separation from parent		
29	Someone touching me wrongly		

	Stressors	Your Rating	Have you experienced it in your life? Yes or No
30	Fear of ghosts, etc.		
31	Not getting what you had asked for		

Factor 1: Major loss Induced Stress (items 8, 9, 10, 11, 12, and 23)
Factor 2: Enforcement or conflict induced stress (items 19, 22, 26, and 31)
Factor 3: Phobic stress (items 13, 14, 15, and 30)
Factor 4: Interpersonal conflict induced stress (items 3, 4, 5, 6, and 7)
Factor 5: Punishment induced stress (items 2 and 18)
Factor 6: Illness and injury induced stress (items 20 and 21)
Factor 7: Performance stress (items 24 and 25)
Factor 8: Imposition induced stress (items 16 and 17)
Factor 9: Insecurity induced stress (items 27, 28, and 29)
Factor 10: Unhealthy environment induced stress (item 1)

Assessment Tool 4: Adolescent Stress Scale

Developed by Meena Hariharan, Meera Padhy, Sandra Roshni Monteiro, Laxmi Priyanka Nakka, Usha Chivukula (2023).

Purpose:
As the title suggests, the scale is developed to assess the stress levels of adolescents within the age group of 11 years to 18 years. The scale has 31 items in total with ten dimensions.

Psychometric Properties:
The Cronbach's α for the whole scale is 0.90, and for dimensions, it ranged from .50 to .80. The test-retest reliability for the whole scale was calculated using the Pearson correlation coefficient. The three-week test-retest reliability was .57, with correlation significant at the 0.01 level. To establish the construct validity, convergent, and discriminant validity were carried out, resulting in the r-value of .29 and –.20, respectively, with $p < 0.01$.

Scoring:
The number of items under each dimension ranges from 1 to 6. Major loss-induced stress (items 8, 9, 10, 11, 12, 23), Enforcement or Conflict induced stress(items 19, 22, 26, 31), phobic stress (items 13, 14, 15, 30), Interpersonal conflict-induced stress(items 3, 4, 5, 6, 7), Punishment induced stress (items 2 and 18), Illness and injury-induced stress (items 20 and 21), Performance stress (items 24 and 25), Imposition induced stress(items 16 and 17), Insecurity induced stress(items 27, 28, 29) and lastly, Unhealthy environment (item 1). Total scores are calculated through the sum of all items for the whole scale ranging from 31 to 155, and for the dimensions, it ranges from 1 to 30 depending on the number of items. The scale also indicates the stressors experienced by the participants.

Interpretation:
Total scores above the mean of 2.5 indicate high-stress levels, and the mean below 2.5 indicates low-stress levels.

Context:

Stress scales can be a useful tool in a counselling setting for adolescents as they offer a standard way to gauge and quantify the client's level of stress. A stress scale can help the counsellor assess the level and type of the adolescent's stress, which can then help guide treatment choices and interventions.

Instructions

This scale consists of a list of situations identified as stressful by adolescents from 11 to 18 years of age (ranging from Class 6 to University level). Please read each situation, understand it, assess the intensity of stress it causes, and give it a rating based on your judgement of the intensity of the stress. You need to assess each stressful situation on a 5-point scale. Supposing death of a parent is the most stressful situation, getting a rate of 5, what will be the rating for each of the items listed below? After you finish giving your rating, go to the second column, and tick those ratings which you have experienced in your life. Please use the visual analog scale provided below for reference while rating the intensity of the stress.

Participant's details

Name: **Age:**

Gender: **Class:**

School/College/University:

	Stressors	Your Rating	Have you experienced it in your life? Yes or No
1	Alcoholic parent (drinking problem)		
2	Beating by teacher		
3	Quarrel between parents		
4	Quarrel with friends		
5	Quarrel with parents		
6	Quarrel with brother or sister		
7	Quarrels in family		
8	Death of a family member		
9	Death of friend		
10	Death of grandparent		
11	Death of parent		
12	Failure in exams		
13	Fear of animals		
14	Fear of dark places		
15	Fear of hospitals		
16	Forced to do disliked task		

	Stressors	Your Rating	Have you experienced it in your life? Yes or No
17	Forced to participate in an activity		
18	Being punished		
19	High academic pressure		
20	Ill health of self		
21	Injury to self		
22	Lack of sleep		
23	Meeting with an accident		
24	Not meeting academic expectations (self or others)		
25	Not meeting expectations in other activities (self or others)		
26	Problems with girlfriend or boyfriend		
27	Separation from loved ones(grandparents/ cousins/friends)		
28	Separation from parent		
29	Someone touching me wrongly		
30	Fear of ghosts, etc.		
31	Not getting what you had asked for		

Assessment Tool 5: Physical Health Scale for Adolescents
Developed by Meena Hariharan and Laxmi Priyanka Nakka (2021).

Purpose:
This scale is constructed to assess the physical health status of the participants within the age group of 11 to 18 years. The scale comprises three different sections to assess the health history, health risk habits, and ill health experiences of the individuals with ten, 15, and 21 items, respectively.

Psychometric Properties:
Test-retest was carried out, which resulted in r-values of .57 ($p < 0.01$) for Part I, .63 ($p < 0.01$) for Part II, and .29 ($p < 0.05$) for Part III. The internal consistency (Cronbach's alpha) for Part I, Part II, and Part III are .68, .70, and .83, respectively.

Scoring:
Part I of the scale is a dichotomous scale with Yes or No responses where Yes = 1 and, No = 0 which indicates the health history of the participants. Part II and Part III are a four-point scale where 1 is given for 'Never', 2 for 'Rarely', 3 for 'Sometimes', and 4 for 'Almost Always'. The total scores are obtained with the sum of all the items for each part of the scale.. For Part II scores range from 15 to 70. In Part III of the scale, items 1 and 2 are reverse-scored. The scores range from 21 to 84.

Interpretation:
Higher scores in Part II and Part III of the scale imply high health risk behaviours and high ill health experiences in individuals.

Context:
In a counselling environment for adolescents, the use of this physical health scale can be a useful tool for identifying their health risk behaviours and ill health experiences. Through which, counsellors can assist them in improving their overall well-being and further improve mental and emotional health outcomes. Knowing their health history will direct counsellors in facilitating adolescents to cope with their illness and the challenges it poses.

Physical Health Scale for Adolescents
Instructions: Normally, the physical health of an individual is found to influence and be influenced by a number of factors that are psychological and social in nature. Hence, the assessment of physical health is highly significant. This particular questionnaire has three parts: Part I talks about your health history, Part II talks about your health habits, and Part III talks about your health experiences.

We wish to state very clearly that there are no standard right or wrong answers for these items. What we need is an honest response depending upon whatever is true in your case. Please remember that the outcome of our research largely depends upon your honest responses. We assure that your responses will be confidential and will be used only for research purposes.

PART I
Instructions: Please read the following items carefully and put a tick mark (✓) in the column 'Yes' if you are diagnosed with that particular health condition and put a tick mark (✓) in the column 'No' if you do not have the health condition.

	Health Conditions	Yes	No
1	High blood pressure		
2	Type 2 diabetes		
3	Arthritis		
4	Respiratory diseases (example; asthma, chronic obstructive pulmonary disease, etc.)		
5	Any chronic problem related to digestive system (example: hyper acidity, irritable bowel syndrome, etc.)		
6	Any cardiac related diseases		
7	Any problem related to reproductive system (example: polycystic ovarian syndrome/disease, etc.)		
8	Any skin disease (example: psoriasis, eczema, etc.)		
9	Migraine headache		
10	Any tumours		

PART II
Instructions: Below are some common habits adolescents are found to adapt. On the right side of the statements, you have four columns, each indicating a frequency (almost always, sometimes, rarely, and never). After reading an item, take a few moments to think and assess how frequently you go through the experience described in the statement. In case you experience it quite frequently, put a tick (✓) mark in column one (Almost always) against that item. In case you experience it only sometimes, you will have to tick (✓) in column two (Sometimes). If you experience what is described in the statement only once in a while, you have to tick (✓) in column three (Rarely). Finally, if

you have not gone through that experience ever, you will have to tick (✓) in column four against that item (Never). There are no right or wrong answers. Please respond honestly.

	Statement	Almost always	Sometimes	Rarely	Never
1	Sleeping for more than nine hours in a day				
2	Skipping meals in a day				
3	Skipping brushing in a day				
4	Skipping sleep at night				
5	Skipping bath in day				
6	Use of social media for more than 2 hours				
7	Consumption of fast food				
8	Consumption of aerated drinks (example: Coca cola, Pepsi, Sprite, etc.)				
9	Sniffing snuff				
10	Sniffing stimulants such as iodex, fevicol, nail polish, petrol, etc.				
11	Consumption of khaini				
12	Smoking cigarette, beedi or tobacco related stuff				
13	Chewing paan				
14	Consumption of gutka				
15	Consumption of alcohol				

PART III

We have mentioned below some experiences related to one's physical health. Please read them carefully and assess how frequently you experience what is described in each statement. On the right side of the statements, you have 4 columns, each indicating a frequency (almost always, sometimes, rarely, and never). After reading an item, tale a few moments to think and assess how frequently you go through the experience described in the statement. In case you experience it quite frequently, put a tick (✓) mark in column one (Almost always) against that item. In case you experience it only sometimes, you will have to tick (✓) in column two (Sometimes). If you experience what is described in the statement only once in a while, you have to tick (✓) in column three (Rarely). Finally, if you have not gone through that experience ever, you will have to tick (✓) in column four against that item (Never).

	Statement	Almost always	Sometimes	Rarely	Never
1	I feel energetic				
2	When I wake up in the morning, I look forward to the things I need to do				

	Statement	Almost always	Sometimes	Rarely	Never
3	I wake up with a headache				
4	I do not wake up feeling fresh				
5	I feel lack of appetite				
6	I experience uneasiness in stomach				
7	I suffer from abdominal pain				
8	I have body aches				
9	I feel weak				
10	I feel drowsy				
11	I have back ache				
12	I suffer from eye infection				
13	I feel emptiness in my stomach				
14	I feel heaviness in my head				
15	I have cold/cough				
16	I experience nausea				
17	I suffer from dental problems				
18	I get ulcers in the mouth				
19	I get pain in ear/throat				
20	I suffer from ear infection				
21	I suffer from skin infection				

Assessment Tool 6: Perceived Physical Environment Scale for Adolescents
Developed by Meena Hariharan, Laxmi Priyanka Nakka, Meera Padhy, Usha Chivukula (2021).

Purpose:
This scale is constructed to assess the participant's perception of their surrounding physical environment with 32 items in total in adolescents with an age range of 11 to 18 years.

Psychometric Properties:
To establish the reliability of the scale test-retest reliability was carried out, and the r-value was .44 ($p < 0.01$). The internal consistency of the scale (Cronbach's alpha) is .79.

Scoring:
This is a four-point Likert scale where 1 is 'Totally disagree' and 4 is 'Totally agree'. Items 1, 2, 3, 4, 12–21, and 31 are reverse scored. The total score of the scale is obtained by the sum of all item scores. The scores range from 32 to 128.

Interpretation:
Higher scores indicate an adverse perceived physical environment.

Context:
This scale can be used to identify specific aspects of the physical environment that may be contributing to stress, anxiety or other negative emotions of adolescents, which can be

handy to counsellors in helping their clients develop effective coping strategies to manage their environment and promote well-being.

Instructions: The scale described below has certain factors related to the physical environment. We are making an attempt to study the physical environment of adolescents. This scale described below has certain items related to your physical environment. Please read each item carefully and indicate how much you are in agreement about that description of the physical environment in your case. In case you feel that a statement described in the scale totally matches your environment, you have to tick (✓) in column one labelled as 'Totally agree'. In case the described item is more like your environment, then you will have to tick (✓) in column two labelled as 'Agree'. If you find that described item is more unlike your environment, you need to tick (✓) in column 3 labelled as 'Disagree'. On the other hand, if a given statement is not at all matching your environment, you will have to tick (✓) in column 4 'Totally disagree'.

We wish to mention clearly that there are no right or wrong answers. Whatever is true in your case is the right answer for you. Therefore we request you respond to this with utmost honesty. We assure you that your responses will be confidential and will be used only for research purposes.

	Statement	**Totally agree**	**Agree**	**Disagree**	**Totally disagree**
1	My residence is spacious				
2	I enjoy a private space in my residence				
3	My home has good ventilation				
4	We have adequate water supply in the residence				
5	There is lack of air flow inside my residence				
6	My residence is dark				
7	The bad smell in and around my residence causes discomfort				
8	The noise from the neighbourhood is disturbing				
9	I feel that my home/residence is crowded with many people living under the same roof				
10	The locality in which I live is congested				
11	The approach road to our locality is not good				
12	The locality of my residence has good street-lights				
13	There is a community park for children to play				
14	Our locality has adequate greenery				
15	Our locality is well connected with good transport facility				

	Statement	Totally agree	Agree	Disagree	Totally disagree
16	There is a good recreation club for the people of the locality				
17	The residents of the community have good relations with each other				
18	The locality of my residence caters to the daily requirements of the household				
19	There is a good medical facility nearby				
20	We live in a secure locality				
21	My residential area has good connectivity through transport to school/college/university				
22	There is a wine shop around our locality				
23	The drainage system in our locality is inadequate				
24	There is a slaughter house around our locality				
25	Our locality suffers from water logging during rainy season				
26	We get the foul smell from some garbage dumping/Industrial emission				
27	We get disturbed with the noise of domestic fights in the neighbourhood				
28	During festivals we are disturbed by loud noise from speakers				
29	We have frequent power cuts/ breakdown in supply of electricity				
30	The roads are dumped with garbage in our neighbourhood				
31	We have good Wi-Fi connectivity				
32	We have poor signals for cell-phones				

Assessment Tool 7: Scale for Mutual Perception of Child's Influence on Parent (SMPCIA) (Form A and Form B)

Developed by Meena Hariharan and Sandra Roshni Monteiro (2016).

Purpose:
This scale was developed to assess the quality of the interpersonal relationship shared between the parent and child, focusing especially on the influential power of the child to convince the parent of a predetermined goal for the child. A numerical index could also be calculated based on the responses of the parent and child to achieve a quantitative measurement of the influential factor.

Psychometric Properties:
The content validity ratio was calculated for each of the items. A content validity ratio of higher or equal to 0.54 was found for 17 items. The scale was found to be feasible and well comprehended, and both forms had a good correlation with each other. For Form A, internal consistency or Cronbach's α was found to be 0.73, whereas its test-retest reliability was found to be 0.66 ($p < 0.01$). For Form B, internal consistency or Cronbach's α was found to be 0.71, and its test-retest reliability was found to be 0.61 ($p < 0.01$). For the main study, Cronbach's α was found to be 0.62 for adults and 0.72 for children.

Scoring:
The responses formatted as a 5-point Likert scale labelled 'Almost always', 'Sometimes', 'Rarely', and 'Never' were assigned as 4, 3, 2, and 1. Half the items, i.e., items 4, 5, 6, 8, 10, 12, 13, 18, 19, 20, 21, 23, 26, 29, and 30 were negatively worded; hence the weight assigned to the labels changed direction and goes as 1, 2, 3, 4. The sum of the item scores of each form is the total score of the particular form.

Interpretation:
Higher score indicates a better-perceived relationship between child/adult. The scores were used to derive the mutuality in the perception of the child and the adult to understand the confluence in their perceived relationship.

Context:
This scale can be very helpful in examining the perceived impact of the child on the parent through the lenses of both parties in the dyad. It can be useful in interpreting the quality of the relationship between the parent and child as well as the level of demand gratification by the parent.

Scale for Mutual Perception of Child's Influence on Parent SMPCIP (Form A) – For Parent

Name:

Age: Gender:

Relationship: MOTHER/FATHER

Instructions The following statements aim to explore the relationship you have with your child. Kindly read each statement carefully and put a tick mark in an appropriate column. The blank space in the statement indicates *your child's name*. Each statement has four options to choose from – 'Almost always', 'Sometimes', 'Rarely', 'Never'. Each option is related to the frequency of behaviour. Depending upon how often you do/ do not do something referred to the statement, you must choose only one response. There are no right or wrong responses. Your honest responses are appreciated.

Example: Arvind is able to persuade me to take him to a movie.
In case you are successfully convinced by your child in this context most of the time, you need to choose 'Almost always'. In case you are never convinced by your child, you need to choose 'Never'.

	Statement	Almost always	Sometimes	Rarely	Never
1.	_____ can easily convince me to buy something he/she wants to eat				
2.	_____ can easily persuade me to take him/her to a place he/she wants to go				
3.	Even though I am busy, _____ is able to make me play with him/her				
4.	I always give _____ pocket money when he /she asks for it				
5.	I willingly give up something _____ likes to eat to pass it to him/her				
6.	I change my plans for the day to go out wherever _____ wants to				
7.	Even though I am tired, I agree to help ____ with school work if he/she asks				
8.	I always patiently listen to _______ when he/she has to say something				
9.	I consider ______ as an important person in my life				
10.	I share my worries with _____				
11.	I and ____enjoy sharing news with each other				
12.	_____ can change my bad mood with his/her presence				
13.	I cannot see ____ crying and give in to his/her demands				
14.	When I am unwell, I prefer to have _____ around				
15.	However much ______tries to make me eat, I will not eat something I don't like				
16.	When I am busy, I ask ______ to go away when he/she tries to interfere				
17.	I hardly spend time with _____				
18.	I do not think _____'s views/ opinions are important				
19.	I am not interested in talks related to _____'s school				
20.	I do not have time to help _____ when he /she needs it				
21.	I cannot predict my behaviour as good or bad with ______				
22.	I don't like the company of ____				

	Statement	Almost always	Sometimes	Rarely	Never
23.	I would rather do things alone than with ____				
24.	I think _______ is an ignorant kid				
25.	I maintain a distance from _____				
26.	I do not allow _____ to express his/ her opinion in family decisions				
27.	I hardly interact with ____				
28.	I and ____have frequent fights over TV channels				
29.	I have frequent complaints about _ ______				
30.	I never let _____ know if I am not well				

Scale for Mutual Perception of Child's Influence on Parent SMPCIP (Form B) – For Child

Name:

Age: Gender: Class:

School:

Name of the parent:

Relationship: FATHER/MOTHER

Instructions The following statements aim to find out the relationship you have with your parent. Kindly read each statement carefully and put a tick mark in an appropriate column. The blank space in the statement indicates *your mother* OR *your father*. You must identify only one relationship to respond to these statements. Each statement has four options to choose from – 'Almost always', 'Sometimes', 'Rarely', 'Never'. That means each statement asks you how frequently the situation occurs for you. Depending upon how often you do/ do not do something referred to the question, you must choose your response.

Example: I can persuade my mother to take me for a movie.
In case you are able to successfully convince your mother most of the times, you need to choose 'Almost always'. In case you are never able to convince your mother, you need to choose 'Never'.

	Statement	Almost always	Sometimes	Rarely	Never
1.	I can easily convince my __________ to buy me something I wish to eat				
2.	I can easily persuade my _________ to take me to a place I want to go				

Statement	Almost always	Sometimes	Rarely	Never
3. I can make my __________ to stop her work and play with me				
4. My __________ always gives me pocket money when I ask for it				
5. My __________gives up something he/she likes to eat to pass it to me				
6. I can make my __________change her/his plans to take me where I want to go				
7. Even though my __________is tired, he/she agrees to help me with my school work if I ask				
8. My__________ patiently listens to me when I have to say something				
9. My __________considers me as an important person in his/her life				
10. My __________ shares his/her worries with me				
11. I and my __________enjoy sharing news with each other				
12. I can change the bad mood of my ___ _______ by being with him/her				
13. My __________ cannot see me crying and gives in to my demands at once				
14. When my __________ is unwell, he/ she prefers to have me around				
15. However much I try, my ________ __refuses to eat something he/she does not like				
16. My __________ asks me to go away when I try to interfere when he/she is busy				
17. My __________ hardly spends time with me				
18. My __________does not consider my views/opinions				
19. My __________ never shows interest when I talk about things related to my school				
20. My __________ has no time to help me when I need it				
21. I never know when my __________ is good to me and when s/he is bad to me				

Statement	Almost always	Sometimes	Rarely	Never
22. I don't like the company of my ___________				
23. I would rather do things alone than with my __________				
24. My __________always treats me as a kid who knows nothing				
25. I maintain a distance from my __________				
26. My __________does not allow me to express my opinion in family decisions				
27. I hardly interact with my __________				
28. I and my __________have frequent fights over TV channels				
29. My __________ frequently complains about me				
30. My __________ never lets me know if s/he is not well				

Assessment Tool 8: Social Skill Measurement

Developed by Meera Padhy and Meena Hariharan (2023).

Purpose:
Social skills help an individual to interact and perform effectively in each social context and are associated with educational accomplishment, psychological adaptation, coping abilities, and employment. In lieu of the growing importance of social skills in every aspect of an individual's life, the measurement of social skills is very much important.

Psychometric properties:
The Cronbach's Alpha of the scale is .84.

Scoring and Interpretation:
The scale consists of 23 items under five dimensions. 1. Leadership skill (Items 3, 6, 17, 18, 21, 22) 2. Team integration skill (Items 5, 15) 3. Affiliative skill (Items 1, 2, 4, 12, 20) 4. Interpersonal skill (Items 7, 8, 16, 19, 23) 5. Social engagement skill (Items 9, 10, 11, 13, 14) Social Skill Scale (All 23 Items). The responses of the participants are to be added to get the total score and dimension scores.

Context:
The scale can be used by counsellors, clinicians, and other psychologists working in Developmental Psychology, Educational Psychology, Health Psychology, etc. The database of the study will constitute a strong reference point for future research.

Social Skills

NAME: ______________________________ AGE: _____ GENDER: ___

School/College/ Organisation______________ Government/ Private________

Class__________ Years of Experience_______

Instructions: For each of the following statements, please tick (✓) in only one box that describes you the best. Please read each sentence carefully and answer honestly.

	Question	Never	Sometimes	Frequently	Always
1.	I actively/patiently listen to what people have to say				
2.	When I realise that it is my mistake I try to make amends with the person				
3.	I can lead/manage a team				
4.	I appreciate the efforts of others				
5.	I am comfortable to work in team				
6.	I am good at handling conflicts in a group				
7.	I can make friends easily				
8.	I keep contact with my friends				
9.	I take part in group activities				
10.	I volunteer to take responsibility				
11.	I stand by my decisions				
12.	I maintain eye contact during conversations				
13.	I take responsibility for my actions				
14.	I am open in my expression				
15.	I feel comfortable when I am in a party or large groups				
16.	I communicate easily with others				
17.	I can manage social events easily				
18.	I have a good sense of humour that keeps others in good spirits				
19.	I have long lasting friendships				
20.	I see the positive aspects in people				
21.	I easily resolve disagreements among others				
22.	I am able to inspire individuals				
23.	I can nurture relationships				

Assessment Tool 9: Psycho-social Support Scale (Psychoss-22)

Developed by Meera Padhy, Meena Hariharan, Sandra Roshni Monteiro, Chelli Kavya, and Padiri Ruth Angiel (2022).

Purpose:
A prerogative in every phase of life, social support has been considered to act as a protective factor against stressful life events and mediators of physical and psychological well-being. It provides us with a certain level of comfort, both physical as well as emotional, and ingrains a sense of belonging with a community of people who care, love, and support one another. The scale measures different aspects of the essential variable of psycho-social support, and the applicability of the instrument is vast and significant. The multidimensionality of psycho-social support offers fascinating possibilities for offering intervention. For instance, the diversity of factors measured by the Psychoss-22 may be useful in understanding the specific social support needs of an individual. This enables the mobilisation of interventions for the specific domains of social support. Clinical interventions may also be tailored to address the gap in perceived social support. Further research is also encouraged in this direction that will isolate social support needs and its interaction with other psychosocial characteristics.

Psychometric properties:
The Cronbach's Alpha of the scale is .79.

Scoring and Interpretation:
The scale consists of both positive and negative items. Answers are converted to numbers (strongly disagree = 1, disagree = 2, neutral = 3, agree = 4, strongly agree = 5). Items marked asterisk (*) are reversed in scoring (strongly disagree = 5, disagree = 4, etc.). These are summed to produce the dimension score and psycho-social support score.

Factor 1. Social support network (Items 1, 2, 4)
Factor 2. Family based psychosocial support (Items 5, 6, 7, 9)
Factor 3. Communicative support (Items 13, 15, 17)
Factor 4. Supportful disposition (Items 3, 18, 19, 20, 22)
Factor 5. Psychological support deprivation (Items 8, 11, 16, 21)
Factor 6. Psychosocial support availability (Items 10, 12, 14)
Psycho-social support (all 22 items)

Context:
The scale can be individually administered or in groups, in both clinical and non-clinical settings. The greatest strength of this scale is that it can be administered to a varied group of populations and not limited to a single or specific group. It can be administered either to terminally/chronically ill patients or to adults having relationship issues, marital issues, adolescents having adjustment issues, or any specific psychological conditions like eating disorders or body image issues. It can even be administered to individuals grieving the loss of their dear ones or among individuals who have faced natural disasters.

Psycho-social Support Scale (Psychoss-22)

NAME: ______________________________ **AGE:** _____ **GENDER:** ___

School/College/Organisation_____________ **Government/Private**_________

Class___________ **Years of Experience**_____ **CGPA/Percentage:** _____

Instructions: Listed below are a few statements. Kindly read them carefully and respond appropriately by giving information regarding the support. You need to read each statement and select by putting a tick (✓) on the response from the five options mentioned in the columns. For example, for each of the following statements, please tick (✓) in only one box that describes you the best. Please read each sentence carefully and answer honestly.

1 = Strongly Disagree 2 = Disagree 3 = Neutral 4 = Agree 5 = Strongly Agree

	Statements	Strongly Disagree	Disagree	Neutral	Agree	Strongly Agree
1.	I believe I will remain close to my friends for a long time	1	2	3	4	5
2.	I can go to my friends when I need advice	1	2	3	4	5
3.	I help others without expecting anything in return	1	2	3	4	5
4.	I have long lasting friendships	1	2	3	4	5
5.	My parents/family members support my decisions	1	2	3	4	5
6.	My parents/ family members understands my needs	1	2	3	4	5
7.	I am encouraged by my friends and family to follow my dreams	1	2	3	4	5
*8.	I don't have friends to spend time with	1	2	3	4	5
9.	My parents give me pocket money	1	2	3	4	5
10.	There is someone to accompany me when I need them	1	2	3	4	5
*11.	I feel lonely even in the presence of friends and family	1	2	3	4	5

	Statements	Strongly Disagree	Disagree	Neutral	Agree	Strongly Agree
12.	There are people to listen to me when I need to talk	1	2	3	4	5
13.	My loved ones celebrate my achievements	1	2	3	4	5
14.	When I feel lonely several people come forward to be with me	1	2	3	4	5
15.	I express appreciations to others help.	1	2	3	4	5
*16.	There is no one I feel comfortable to discuss my personal problems	1	2	3	4	5
17.	There are several people whose company I enjoy	1	2	3	4	5
18.	I provide support as long as one needs	1	2	3	4	5
19.	Once I start supporting others I continue giving support	1	2	3	4	5
20.	I provide help to others if someone needs	1	2	3	4	5
*21.	I help people to get something in return	1	2	3	4	5
22.	I help others without any expectations	1	2	3	4	5

***Reverse scoring**

Assessment Tool 10: Adversity Resistance Scale (ARS)

Developed by Meena Hariharan, Suma Lavanya Mutnury, Meera Padhy (2021).

Purpose:
As the title suggests, this scale assesses the resistance of individuals in overcoming adversities within the age group of 20–65 years by using their internal qualities and external resources. This scale helps in gaining an insight into understanding an individual's capability to keep themselves insulated from adversity or restructure the adversity to their advantage.

Psychometric properties:
Validity: Significant positive correlations were found between resistance to adversities and grit (r = .19, $p < .01$), establishing convergent validity.
Reliability: The reliability of the scale was measured using Cronbach's alpha (.95) for the Adversity Resistance Scale test-retest reliability was also established for the scale (r = .67, $p < .01$).

Scoring:
To obtain the total score on this scale, sum the score of each independent item. The total score of this scale may range from 0–250.

Interpretation:
Higher scores indicate higher resistance to adversities and vice-versa.

Context:
This scale can be used on individuals across various settings such as in the field of healthcare, organisations (workplace), educational institutions and in counselling. This test can be administered individually or in a group to understand individuals' resistance to adversities.

Adversity Resistance Scale

Name:

Age:

Gender:

Education:

Occupation:

Instructions: This sheet consists of 25 items that describe yourself. Please read the statements carefully and relate them to yourself. **Some of these statements may describe you while some others don't. Identify those that describe you.** On the left of the list, a column is earmarked for you to tick against those that describe you. After completing this column, read those items you have ticked. How advantageous is it to have them? On the right side of the sheet, you have 10 columns (1–10) where the lower scores indicate lower advantage and the higher scores indicate higher advantage of such resources. Please read each statement carefully. Decide on its advantage on a score between 1 and 10. Circle the appropriate number that matches with your rating. Consider all the qualities describing you.

NB: Please respond only to those items applicable to you.

Is available	Items	Lower advantage									Higher advantage
	1. I could successfully overcome the adversity because of my faith in God	1	2	3	4	5	6	7	8	9	10

Is available	Items	Lower advantage ______						Higher advantage			
	2. My strong faith in my ability helped me in fighting the adversity successfully	1	2	3	4	5	6	7	8	9	10
	3. I could successfully overcome the adversity as I believe that every problem has a solution and I do not rest until solving it	1	2	3	4	5	6	7	8	9	10
	4. I could successfully overcome the adversity because of my ability to draw inspiration from known/successful role models	1	2	3	4	5	6	7	8	9	10
	5. I could successfully overcome the adversity as I could formulate possible multiple ways of getting out of a problem	1	2	3	4	5	6	7	8	9	10
	6. I could successfully overcome the adversity as I have the ability to keep away the discouraging/negative thoughts which pull me down in the face of problems/setbacks	1	2	3	4	5	6	7	8	9	10
	7. I could successfully overcome the adversity as I have the ability to remind myself about my own strengths when I have hurdles in achieving something	1	2	3	4	5	6	7	8	9	10
	8. I could successfully overcome the adversity as I have the ability to never give up in the face of any failure	1	2	3	4	5	6	7	8	9	10

Is available	Items	Lower advantage ______ Higher advantage									
	9. I could successfully overcome the adversity because I have the ability to initiate and sustain changes in my lifestyle in case of health issues where medical interventions alone are not enough	1	2	3	4	5	6	7	8	9	10
	10. I could successfully overcome the adversity as I have the ability to start re-looking at things positively when I am compelled to do things not to my liking	1	2	3	4	5	6	7	8	9	10
	11. I could successfully overcome the adversity as I never give up even when things appear hopeless	1	2	3	4	5	6	7	8	9	10
	12. I could successfully overcome the adversity as I have the ability to accept an irreversible adversity with grace	1	2	3	4	5	6	7	8	9	10
	13. I could successfully overcome the adversity because of the existing social system	1	2	3	4	5	6	7	8	9	10
	14. I could successfully overcome the adversity because of the existing government schemes	1	2	3	4	5	6	7	8	9	10
	15. I would have failed in overcoming the adversity but for the collective help from community/organisation/society	1	2	3	4	5	6	7	8	9	10

Is available	Items	Lower advantage									Higher advantage
	16. I would have failed in handling the adversity had I not been brought up in a disciplined family/ school environment	1	2	3	4	5	6	7	8	9	10
	17. I could successfully overcome the adversity because of my patience	1	2	3	4	5	6	7	8	9	10
	18. I could successfully overcome the adversity because of my objective way of perceiving things	1	2	3	4	5	6	7	8	9	10
	19. I could successfully overcome the adversity because of my ability to channelise my emotions appropriately	1	2	3	4	5	6	7	8	9	10
	20. I could successfully overcome the adversity because of my personal values	1	2	3	4	5	6	7	8	9	10
	21. I could successfully overcome the adversity because of my communication skills	1	2	3	4	5	6	7	8	9	10
	22. I could successfully overcome the adversity because I think innovatively	1	2	3	4	5	6	7	8	9	10
	23. I could successfully overcome the adversity because of my physical health and stamina	1	2	3	4	5	6	7	8	9	10
	24. I could successfully overcome the adversity because of my ability to understand other's feelings and behaviour	1	2	3	4	5	6	7	8	9	10

Is available	Items	Lower advantage _____ Higher advantage									
	25. I have successfully overcome the adversity because I go by perceiving my major goal in life	1	2	3	4	5	6	7	8	9	10

Assessment Tool 11: Healthy Lifestyle Practice Scale for Children (HELIPSCA)

Developed by Meena Hariharan and Teisovinuo Semou.

Purpose:
This scale assesses the health behaviour of the subjects of this study. It has items consisting of dietary behaviour, exercise or physical activity, water intake, quality of rest or sleep, screen time, hygiene, and spiritual practices. A total of nine items (3, 4, 10, 14, 15, 16, 18, 19 and 22) are positively worded. 19 items (1, 2, 5, 6, 7, 8, 9, 11, 12, 13, 17, 20, 21, 23, 24, 25, 26, 27 and 28) are negatively worded.

Psychometric Properties:
The Cronbach's α was found to be 0.70

Scoring:
The responses range in a 4-point Likert scale from Almost always = 4 to Never = 1. Forward scoring for positive items involves 4 = Almost always, 3 = Frequently, 2 = Rarely and 1 = Never. It is scored reversely for negative statements. The higher score denotes healthier lifestyle depicting in an individual's lifestyle choices.

Interpretation:
Higher score indicates higher healthy life practices.

Context:
This scale can be administered on adolescents who need to be assessed on health behaviour.

Scoring:
The responses range in a four-point Likert scale from Almost always = 4 to Never = 1. Forward scoring for positive items involves 4 = Almost always, 3 = Frequently, 2 = Rarely and 1 = Never. It is scored reversely for negative statements. The higher score denotes healthier lifestyle depicting in an individual's lifestyle choices.

Instructions:
We all follow certain practices in our life. This includes certain habits related to eating, sleeping, playing, studying, etc. This scale consists of a few such practices in the life of children like you. Out of these, there are a few we do almost daily (Almost always). Few others though not daily, we tend to do very often (Frequently). Some of the activities we do once in a way (Rarely). There may be some which we don't do at all (Never). Read all

the items carefully. Think of yourself doing that activity, and in case you do it daily, tick in the column ‘Almost always’. Depending upon how often or rarely you do the activities, you have to tick in the column ‘Almost always’, ‘Frequently’, ‘Rarely’, or ‘Never’. For example, If there is a statement such as ‘going to the library’ in the list, you need to see how often you go to the library. If you go to the library every day you must tick in the column ‘Almost always’. In case you don’t go to the library every day but go 3 to 4 times in a week, you should tick the column ‘Frequently’. In case you go to the library once a month or so, you should tick the column ‘Rarely’. On the other hand, if you don’t go to the library at all, you should tick the column ‘Never’.

There are no right or wrong answers to this. Whatever is true in your case is the correct answer for you. What may be correct for you may not be correct for your friend. Therefore, please answer honestly about yourself.

	Statement	Almost always	Frequently	Rarely	Never
1.	Eat chocolates				
2.	Play video games for long hours				
3.	Go out and play in the playground/park/open area				
4.	Do activities such as cycling, skating, swimming, etc.				
5.	Stay awake beyond sleeping time				
6.	Sleep during day time				
7.	Skip a meal (breakfast/lunch/dinner)				
8.	Eat food from outside (such as pizza, burger, momo, noodles, samosa or any deep fried snacks)				
9.	Eat street food (such as pani puri or any snacks sold on the roadside)				
10.	Laugh a lot				
11.	Cry a lot				
12.	Skip brushing my teeth				
13.	Skip bathing				
14.	Eat vegetables				
15.	Eat fruits				
16.	Share personal problems with others				
17.	Get angry				
18.	Listen to music				
19.	Participate in prayers (group prayers in religious places)				
20.	Do not wake up on time in the morning				

	Statement	Almost always	Frequently	Rarely	Never
21.	Drink aerated cold drinks (Pepsi, Coke, lime, etc.)				
22.	Drink adequate water				
23.	Tried certain activities for fun (smoking, chewing tobacco)				
24.	Continue to stay in the place when someone is smoking				
25.	Spent long hours in front of the computer/TV				
26.	Refused to eat things I do not like though they are nutritious				
27.	Over eat				
28.	Skip drinking milk				

Assessment Tool 12: Health Risk Behaviour Scale for Adolescents (HRBS- A)

Developed by Usha Chivukula, Aysha Thasleema, Adarsh Kumar Verma, Meena Hariharan, Meera Padhy (2023).

Purpose:
This scale is developed to assess health risk behaviour among adolescents within an age range of 13 to 19 years.

Psychometric properties:
Reliability: This scale has a total Cronbach's alpha of .85. Cronbach's alpha value for six sub-dimensions viz. high-risk behaviours, risky on-road practices, daily life risky behaviours, self-harming/aggressive/violent behaviours, depressive behaviours, and healthy practices are .88, .88, .80, .69, .60, .56, respectively.

Scoring:
Responses given on a 5-point scale are scored with almost daily = 5, weekly = 4, monthly = 3, less than monthly = 2 and never = 1. Item numbers 1, 2, 17, 18, 19, 35, 36, 39 have to be reverse scored.
High risk behaviours: Item numbers 20, 21, 22, 23, 24, 25, 26, 32, 33
On-road risky practices: Item numbers 34, 35, 36, 37, 38, 39, 40
Daily life risky behaviours: Item numbers 3, 4, 5, 6, 7, 9, 12, 13, 14, 15, 16
Self-harming/ aggressive/ violent behaviours: Item numbers 27, 28, 29, 30, 31
Depressive behaviours: Item numbers 8, 10, 11
Healthy practices: Item numbers 1, 2, 17, 18, 19

Interpretation:
Higher total scores indicate a higher health risk behaviours.

Context:

This scale can be used in both clinical and non-clinical settings to assess adolescents' engagement in health risk behaviours.

Health Risk Behaviour Scale for Adolescents (HRBS-A)

Instructions: Given below are some statements related to your health behaviour. Please read the statements carefully and rate them (using a tick mark ✓) based on how often you carry out the behaviour described in each statement. You can evaluate the statements based on your experiences in the ***last one year***. There are no right or wrong responses. Kindly stay true to yourself while responding.

5 Almost daily
4 Weekly
3 Monthly
2 Less than monthly
1 Never

	Statement	Response				
1.	Engage in physical exercise	*Almost daily*	*Weekly*	*Monthly*	*Less than monthly*	*Never*
2.	Play outdoor games	*Almost daily*	*Weekly*	*Monthly*	*Less than monthly*	*Never*
3.	Spent most of the time sitting or lying down	*Almost daily*	*Weekly*	*Monthly*	*Less than monthly*	*Never*
4.	Use the internet for long hours	*Almost daily*	*Weekly*	*Monthly*	*Less than monthly*	*Never*
5.	Chat with friends on the phone or any electronic gadget for a long time	*Almost daily*	*Weekly*	*Monthly*	*Less than monthly*	*Never*
6.	Binge-watch videos or movies on the electronic screen.	*Almost daily*	*Weekly*	*Monthly*	*Less than monthly*	*Never*
7.	Continuously play video games for several hours	*Almost daily*	*Weekly*	*Monthly*	*Less than monthly*	*Never*
8.	Keep awake till late in the night.	*Almost daily*	*Weekly*	*Monthly*	*Less than monthly*	*Never*
9.	Engage in on-screen activities before going to sleep (e.g., watching movies, playing video games, online chatting)	*Almost daily*	*Weekly*	*Monthly*	*Less than monthly*	*Never*
10.	Bottle up tensions	*Almost daily*	*Weekly*	*Monthly*	*Less than monthly*	*Never*
11.	Worry/brood over things	*Almost daily*	*Weekly*	*Monthly*	*Less than monthly*	*Never*

	Statement	Response				
12.	Eat fast food	*Almost daily*	*Weekly*	*Monthly*	*Less than monthly*	*Never*
13.	Consume sweetened and soft drinks	*Almost daily*	*Weekly*	*Monthly*	*Less than monthly*	*Never*
14.	Eat late at night	*Almost daily*	*Weekly*	*Monthly*	*Less than monthly*	*Never*
15.	Miss a meal	*Almost daily*	*Weekly*	*Monthly*	*Less than monthly*	*Never*
16.	Overeat	*Almost daily*	*Weekly*	*Monthly*	*Less than monthly*	*Never*
17.	Eat fruits	*Almost daily*	*Weekly*	*Monthly*	*Less than monthly*	*Never*
18.	Eat vegetables	*Almost daily*	*Weekly*	*Monthly*	*Less than monthly*	*Never*
19.	Eat protein-rich food (e.g., food items like egg/dairy products/ nuts, beans, lentils/ meat/fish)	*Almost daily*	*Weekly*	*Monthly*	*Less than monthly*	*Never*
20.	Smoke cigarettes	*Almost daily*	*Weekly*	*Monthly*	*Less than monthly*	*Never*
21.	Smoke at least ten cigarettes a day	*Almost daily*	*Weekly*	*Monthly*	*Less than monthly*	*Never*
22.	Consume tobacco products (e.g., Paan, khaini, gutkha, zarda, tobacco leaf, etc.)	*Almost daily*	*Weekly*	*Monthly*	*Less than monthly*	*Never*
23.	Consume alcohol	*Almost daily*	*Weekly*	*Monthly*	*Less than monthly*	*Never*
24.	Take up to or more than 3–4 drinks containing alcohol	*Almost daily*	*Weekly*	*Monthly*	*Less than monthly*	*Never*
25.	Use one or more intoxicants of the following (marijuana, cocaine/crack, heroin, methamphetamine/ crystal meth, hallucinogens, ecstasy/ MDMA)	*Almost daily*	*Weekly*	*Monthly*	*Less than monthly*	*Never*
26.	Use prescription drugs for intoxication	*Almost daily*	*Weekly*	*Monthly*	*Less than monthly*	*Never*
27.	Engage in risky activities that give thrill or rush	*Almost daily*	*Weekly*	*Monthly*	*Less than monthly*	*Never*

	Statement	Response				
28.	Expose to extreme weather conditions (cold/heat/rain) without protection(s)	*Almost daily*	*Weekly*	*Monthly*	*Less than monthly*	*Never*
29.	Have physical fights with others	*Almost daily*	*Weekly*	*Monthly*	*Less than monthly*	*Never*
30.	Have aggressive and abusive clashes with others	*Almost daily*	*Weekly*	*Monthly*	*Less than monthly*	*Never*
31.	Attempt to harm myself physically	*Almost daily*	*Weekly*	*Monthly*	*Less than monthly*	*Never*
32.	Engage in sex without protection	*Almost daily*	*Weekly*	*Monthly*	*Less than monthly*	*Never*
33.	Engage in sex with more than one partner	*Almost daily*	*Weekly*	*Monthly*	*Less than monthly*	*Never*
34.	Tried driving motor vehicles on the road without a licence	*Almost daily*	*Weekly*	*Monthly*	*Less than monthly*	*Never*

Please Note: ***For the following statements (44–49), those who have never driven a two wheeler or four wheeler (whichever is applicable) should tick the column 6 'Not Applicable (NA)'.***

35.	Wear a helmet while riding a two-wheeler	*Almost daily*	*Weekly*	*Monthly*	*Less than monthly*	*Never*	*NA*
36.	Wear a seat belt while driving a car	*Almost daily*	*Weekly*	*Monthly*	*Less than monthly*	*Never*	*NA*
37.	Drove after taking alcohol/drugs	*Almost daily*	*Weekly*	*Monthly*	*Less than monthly*	*Never*	*NA*
38.	Drove while texting, speaking, or browsing on the phone	*Almost daily*	*Weekly*	*Monthly*	*Less than monthly*	*Never*	*NA*
39.	Follow the traffic rules	*Almost daily*	*Weekly*	*Monthly*	*Less than monthly*	*Never*	*NA*
40.	Exceeded speed limits while driving a motor vehicle	*Almost daily*	*Weekly*	*Monthly*	*Less than monthly*	*Never*	*NA*

Assessment Tool 13: HeRBs Gratification Control Inventory

Developed by Usha Chivukula, Adarsh K. Verma, and Aysha Thasleema.

Purpose:
It consists of four subdomains, including alcohol consumption, drug abuse, smoking, and risky sexual practices. This scale aims to assess the ability to delay or completely forego

different health risk behaviours (*HeRBs*) to avoid negative consequences or for a better/more desired reward in the future.

Psychometric Properties:
Reliability coefficient: overall scale ($\alpha = 0.898$), alcohol consumption ($\alpha = 0.907$), drug abuse ($\alpha = 0.931$), and smoking ($\alpha = 0.904$), risky sexual practices ($\alpha = 0.842$); Validity: *Yet to be calculated.*

Scoring:
All the items have a 5-point Likert scale (1 = Strongly Disagree, 2 = Disagree, 3 = Neutral, 4 = Agree, 5 = Strongly Agree) accompanying the not-applicable option (0 = N/A). Several reverse-coded items were inculcated to improve the accuracy of responses. After reverse coding, the total score can be obtained by summing up all the items within the respective subscale.

Interpretation:
Higher score indicates a higher ability to forego gratifying risk behaviours.

Context:
The scale can be used for an assessment in clinical and counselling set up to screen for delaying capacity/cognitive control on encountering the risk behaviour stimuli. The information obtained from this scale can be successfully utilised in designing appropriate interventions.

HeRBs Gratification Control Inventory
Instructions: Read each of the following statements and indicate the extent to which these statements are true of your actual behaviour.
1 = Strongly Disagree, 2 = Disagree, 3 = Neutral, 4 = Agree, 5 = Strongly Agree, N/A = Not Applicable

Alcohol Consumption	1	2	3	4	5	N/A
1 I can control my urge to drink when I am sick						
2 Even when I have no money, I borrow it from others to get a drink						
3 I can restrain myself from taking alcohol if I have to drive afterwards						
Smoking	1	2	3	4	5	N/A
4 Being sick doesn't prevent me from smoking						
5 Even in situations when money is a constraint, I tend to borrow and smoke						
6 Even if my loved ones discourage me from smoking, I cannot resist						

Drug Abuse	1	2	3	4	5	N/A
7 I cannot restrain myself from misusing prescription drugs						
8 I cannot resist taking drugs even if my work is affected						
9 I cannot stop using drugs even when it impacts my interpersonal relationships						
Risky Sexual Practices	1	2	3	4	5	N/A
10 Considering the risks involved, I can control myself from engaging in sexual practices with multiple partners						
11 At times when protected sex is not possible, I can resist sex						
12 Despite the known risks of sexually transmitted diseases (STDs), I cannot resist having unprotected sex						

Assessment Tool 14: Indian Scale of Adolescent Well-being (ISAW)

Developed by Meena Hariharan, C. R. Rao, Meera Padhy and Sai Prasad (2020).

Purpose:
The scale measures the well-being of the adolescent population.

Psychometric Properties:
The scale was found to have sound psychometric properties. The reliability of the scale is 0.65, $p < .001$. The validity is 0.47, $p < .001$.

Context:
Indian scale of adolescent well-being is a diagnostic tool that measures the well-being of Indian adolescents in the age group of 13 to 20 years. The scale can be administered on the adolescents who manifest low well-being and the dimension in which they have a problem is not clear.

Scoring and Interpretation:
The details are given in the manual (given at the end of the scale).

Description:
Well-being refers to a state of equilibrium or homeostasis that individual experiences in the physical, psychological, and social dimensions. This experience is not constant but keeps swinging up and down like a see-saw, where on the one end, there is a resource pool in these dimensions while on the other end are life's challenges targeting these dimensions. The scale is standardised on a sample of 3271 adolescent boys and girls.

It is a 15-item six-point rating scale. The ratings range from 'very much like me' to 'very much unlike me'. The items in statement form are easy to understand, relate and respond to by the target age group. Scoring is done as per the ratings ranging from 1 to 6. The scale evolved after administering the original scale of 117 items measuring 16 dimensions of well-being. The final version of 11 items evolved after putting the data through rough sets, which confirmed that the short version of 11 items is powerful to substitute the 117 items in measuring well-being across 16 dimensions. The application of the Rough set theory evolved weightages for each item. The final score is derived by applying a formula using the weightages.

The scale and its manual are given below to facilitate its use in counselling settings or for research purposes.

Indian Scale of Adolescence Well-being (ISAW)

Name of the student: ______________________________
Gender: Male/Female
Class: ______________________________
School/College: ______________________________

Dear student,
This booklet consists of a number of statements related to you. Please read them carefully. To what extent is each statement is true in your case? In other words how far each one is a description of yourself? Consider each statement honestly in the above way and put a tick mark against each item with the appropriate answer (1, 2, 3, 4, 5, or 6). You have the following options.

6 = Very much like me 5 = Like me 4 = Somewhat like me
3 = Somewhat unlike me 2 = Unlike me 1 = Very much unlike me

For Example:

1	I like to have ice-cream after every meal	1	2	3	4	5	6

The statement is very correct in your case if you are extremely fond of ice-creams. In that case the description is '**Very much like me**'. Hence you have to tick '**6**' against the statement. If you hate ice-creams, then the statement is '**Very much unlike me**'. Hence you have to tick '**1**'. If there are days when you like to have ice-cream with every meal, then the description is '**Somewhat like me**'. Hence you have to tick '**4**'.

Thus, you must answer each statement after an honest assessment. There are no right or wrong answers. Whatever is true in case is right answer for you. Please answer for all statements. After you respond to all the statements we can measure your '**well-being**'.

1	When I face challenging tasks, I do not easily give up	6	5	4	3	2	1
2	While accepting an important assignment, I feel confident and relaxed	6	5	4	3	2	1
3	I don't give importance to spiritual aspects	6	5	4	3	2	1
4	I feel that I live my life the way I want to	6	5	4	3	2	1
5	I worry about past things in my life	6	5	4	3	2	1
6	I have strong, supportive circle of friends	6	5	4	3	2	1
7	I like to make friendship with a stranger	6	5	4	3	2	1

8	I do not find dependable persons around	6	5	4	3	2	1
9	I do my duty even in adverse circumstances	6	5	4	3	2	1
10	I can stop bad things happening in my life	6	5	4	3	2	1
11	I work harder to face challenges	6	5	4	3	2	1
12	My achievements are relatively lower than my efforts	6	5	4	3	2	1
13	My sleeping timings are flexible	6	5	4	3	2	1
14	I prefer to be alone rather than with others	6	5	4	3	2	1
15	I regularly do at least one of the following for exercise (Walk/Yoga/Gym/Swimming/Pranayam/aerobics)	6	5	4	3	2	1

Manual for Indian Scale of Adolescence Well-being (ISAW)

Adolescence Well-being

Well-being during the phase of adolescence is important as this phase lays the foundation for the subsequent growth and development of the person in life. Well-being can be defined as a positive state of adolescents encompassing intra-individual affective, cognitive, and motivational disposition, interpersonal trust, and relationships. It is necessary to understand the well-being of adolescents from the perspective of physical, psychological, and social dimensions. Often, parents and caregivers neither recognise how the adolescents judge and experience nor do they know how to recognise those judgements and experiences. The ISAW is developed to help adolescents (13 to 20 years) to understand their well-being and parents to know about the development of their children. ISAW can be used as a screening, diagnostic, and research tool across a variety of conditions for evaluating adolescents in different settings like home, school, medical setting, and any other specific institution and community. The ISAW is also a useful instrument for intervention and evaluation studies. As a research instrument, this would help in contributing knowledge to policymakers.

Description of ISAW

The ISAW has 15 items or indicators which measure 12 dimensions of well-being: Autonomy, achievement, freedom from anxiety, control, freedom from depression, lifestyle, personal competence, personal morale, spiritual quality, social contacts, social support, and interpersonal trust. Out of the 15 items, nine are positively worded items (1, 2, 4, 6, 7, 9, 10, 11, and 15), and six are negatively worded items (3, 5, 8, 12, 13, and 14). The scale is useful for adolescents of the age group 13 to 20 years. Each of the 15 items is to be rated on a 6-point scale ranging from 'Very much like me' to 'Very much unlike me'. The ISAW consists of three parts. The first part deals with the personal details, whereas the second part contains the instruction. The third part contains the 15 items of the scale, with six options for each item.

Pre-Assessment and Preparation for ISAW

The ISAW may be used as a screening, diagnostic, or research tool. As a screening instrument, ISAW may be administered by educated parents, teachers, counsellors, psychologists, and health professionals. As a diagnostic measure, the ISAW may be administered by a psychology graduate with a training experience in test administration, a trained professional, or any person having potential knowledge in psychological test administration. As a research instrument, the ISAW may be used by the expert for survey, intervention, and evaluation studies for policy. The assessor should be familiar with ISAW before its administration. The ISAW needs to be administered in a calm and comfortable setting where there is less chance of the presence of distractors for the participants. The assessor should be accessible to clarify the doubts, if any, related to the scale of the participants. The assessment of the ISAW can be done both at an individual level as well as a group level depending upon the objective of the assessment. The assessor must establish rapport with participants before starting the assessment. Before responding, the participants should be given instructions in simple language with an assurance of maintaining confidentiality. It may be explained to them that their responses to the items of ISAW will be helpful in knowing how they feel about themselves.

In individual assessment sessions, the assessor must ascertain that the participants have read and understood the instructions of the scale thoroughly. In group assessment, the assessor must read the instructions loudly, emphasising that the instructions are audible and understood thoroughly by the participants. In both individual as well as group assessment sessions, the assessor must give directions to select only one option for each item. The assessor must request the participants to answer each item honestly.

Process of Assessment of ISAW

The ISAW may be assessed individually on an adolescent or a small group of adolescents. A small group of adolescents having 20 participants is preferable in four rows, each containing five participants. During group assessment, the assessor has to ascertain that while responding to the items of the ISAW, the participants do not discuss with each other. Though there is no time limit to administer the scale, yet the assessment of the scale may take approximately 15 to 20 minutes for each participant. Depending on the reading ability and age of the participant, there may be a variation in the duration of the assessment. During the assessment – individual and group – the assessor has to observe the non-verbal behaviour of the adolescent (s), which is essential during the assessment to understand the participant's involvement in the task performance.

Instructions

The test assessor has to provide the following instructions before asking the participant(s) to read the specific instruction mentioned in the ISAW. 'This scale will help you to know about your well-being. Be honest in answering each item. There are no right or wrong answers. Choose the appropriate options for each item that most closely represents your judgement and experiences about life. Read each item carefully and avoid spending excess time on any item.

Post-Assessment Verification

Once the assessment is complete, the assessor must check to verify that all the demographic details are provided and that each item has been attempted. If an item has been attempted twice, the participant is to be asked to choose the most appropriate response. At the end of this verification, the assessor must take a debriefing session.

Table 11.1 ISAW Scoring Key

Nature of Items	*No. of Items*	*Very much like me*	*Like me*	*Somewhat like me*	*Somewhat unlike me*	*Unlike me*	*Very much unlike me*
Positive	1, 2, 4, 6, 7, 9, 10, 11, 15	6	5	4	3	2	1
Negative	3, 5, 8, 12, 13, 14	1	2	3	4	5	6

Scoring Procedure

Step 1. The assessor must enter the participant's raw score for each of the items in the 'Participant's Response' column in the Scoring sheet.

Step 2. In the next step, the assessor must refer to the above Scoring key Table and convert the raw score as per the type of item- whether positive or negative. Considering the above process, the assessor will obtain the converted (X) scores and enter the same in the 'Converted score' column.

Step 3. A weight of 2 is assigned to Items No. 1, 2, 3, 4, 5, 7, 9, 10, 11, and 12 whereas a weight of 1 is assigned to Items No. 6, 8, 13, 14, and 15. These weights (W) are already specified in the Scoring sheet. These weights are to be added ($\Sigma W = 25$).

Step 4. The converted score of each of the items is to be multiplied by its corresponding weight, and the product is known as the transformed score (WX). These transformed scores are to be entered in the 'Transform score' column.

Step 5. The products are to be added and symbolised as ΣWX.

Step 6. The weighted mean is to be calculated by dividing the total of the transformed score by the sum of the weights. The following formula may be followed:

Weighted Mean = $\Sigma WX / \Sigma W$

ΣWX = Sum total of products of weight and raw score (Refer to Step 4)

ΣW = sum of weights (Refer to Step 3)

Step 7. The weighted mean is the level of the well-being of the adolescent and is to be interpreted according to the Norm Table mentioned below the Scoring sheet.

For dimension-wise diagnosis of adolescent well-being, the interpretation of the scores varies. In case of the dimensions having one item (autonomy, achievement, freedom from anxiety, freedom from depression, personal competence, personal moral, spiritual quality, social contacts, and social support), the converted score falling below 2.5 will be considered as low well-being and intervention will be provided for those dimensions. In the case of the dimensions having two items (control, lifestyle, and interpersonal trust), the mean of the converted score will be taken into consideration, and the same 2.5 will be taken as the cut-off point as per one-time dimension.

Level of Well-being____________________________________

Interpretation____

____

____

____

Table 11.2 ISAW Scoring Sheet

Items	*Participant's Raw score*	*Converted score (X)*	*Weight (W)*	*Transformed scores (WX)*
1			2	
2			2	
*3			2	
4			2	
*5			2	
6			1	
7			2	
*8			1	
9			2	
10			2	
11			2	
*12			2	
*13			1	
*14			1	
15			1	
			ΣW = 25	Total of transformed score (ΣWX)=

*Note.** Negative item

Table 11.3 ISAW Norm Table

	Level of Adolescence Well-being	*Well-being Score*
1	Very High Well-being	4.9–6
2	High Well-being	4.43–4.89
3	Average Well-being	3.47–4.42
4	Low Well-being	2.99–3.46
5	Very Low Well-being	1–2.98

Signature of the Administrator

References

American Psychological Association. (2002). Criteria for practice guideline development and evaluation. *American Psychologist, 57,* 1048–1051.

American Psychological Association. (2010). Ethical principles of psychologists and code of conduct (2002, amended June 1, 2010).

Cormier, S., Nurius, P. S., & Osborn, C. J. (2016). *Interviewing and change strategies for helpers,* Cengage Learning.

Donohue, B., Azrin, N. H., Bradshaw, K. M., VanHasselt, V. V., Urgelles, J., & Allen, D. N. (2014). Examination of family behaviour therapy in mothers referred by child protective services for child neglect and drug abuse. *Journal of Clinical and Consulting Psychology, 82,* 706–720.

Gehart, D. R. (2017). *Mastering competencies in family therapy: A practical approach to theory and clinical case documentation.* Cengage Learning.

Hariharan, M., Rao, C. R., Padhy, M., and Sai Prasad P. S. V. S. (2020). Measurement of adolescent well-being: Application of rough set theory. *International Journal of Asia Pacific School Psychology*, *1*(1).

Jacobs, L. (2009). Interview with Lawrence Weed, MD – the father of the problem-oriented medical record looks ahead. *The Permanente Journal*, *13*(3), 84.

Lazarus, C. N., & Lazarus, A. A. (2019). Multimodal therapy. In Norcross, J. C., & Goldfried, M. R. (Eds.), *Handbook of psychotherapy integration.*

Luborsky, L., & Crits-Christoph, P. (1998). *Understanding transference: The core conflictual relationship theme method.* American Psychological Association.

Padhy, M. and Hariharan, M. (2023). Social skill measurement: Standardisation of scale. *Psychological Studies.* https://doi.org/10.1007/s12646-022-00693-4.

Padhy, M., Hariharan, M., Monteiro, S. R., Chelli., and Angiel, P. R. (2022). Psycho-social support scale (PSYCHOSS-22): Development and validation. *Indian Journal of Social Work*, *83*(1).

Weed, L L. (1971). *Medical records, medical education and patient care: The problem oriented record as a basic tool.* Press of Case Western Reserve University.

Index

Note: Page numbers in *italics* denote *figures* and those in **bold** denote **tables.**

For Product Safety Concerns and Information please contact our EU
representative GPSR@taylorandfrancis.com
Taylor & Francis Verlag GmbH, Kaufingerstraße 24, 80331 München, Germany

www.ingramcontent.com/pod-product-compliance
Ingram Content Group UK Ltd.
Pitfield, Milton Keynes, MK11 3LW, UK
UKHW050316071126
477531UK00012B/639
* 9 7 8 1 0 3 2 6 0 4 8 9 3 *